Oracle8

Server

Joe Greene, Advanced Information Systems, Inc., et al.

SAMS

201 West 103rd Street,
Indianapolis, Indiana 46290

Unleashed

Trademarks

EXECUTIVE EDITOR
Rosemarie Graham

ACQUISITIONS EDITOR
Rosemarie Graham

DEVELOPMENT EDITORS
Todd Bumbalough
Marla Reece-Hall

MANAGING EDITOR
Patrick Kanouse

SENIOR EDITOR
Elizabeth A. Bruns

COPY EDITORS
Nancy Albright
Patricia Kinyon
Tonya Maddox
Sean Medlock
San Dee Philips
Linda Siefert

INDEXER
Rebecca Salerno

TECHNICAL EDITOR
Jonathan Gennick

PRODUCTION
Carol Bowers
Ayanna Lacey
Gene Redding

Overview

Contents

About the Authors

Advanced Information Systems, Inc., (AIS) is a professional software development and consulting firm that offers a range of products and services specializing in Oracle and Internet development. The AIS objective is to provide highly technical talent combined with pre-developed software to product rapid results for their clients. This successful approach has lead to their popular Team AIS. Team AIS is a group of proficient Oracle database administrators and programmers who are sent in to solve extremely difficult problems including tuning, migrations, architecture evaluations, auditing, project management, and application design. AIS has a lengthy client list that includes many Fortune 1000 companies.

AIS offers pre-developed code libraries combined with consulting services. The approach enables their clients to receive a well crafted client/server or Internet application while obtaining a skills transfer. The result has been very successful in teaching some of the newer development tools such as Java, CORBA, and Oracle8. AIS can craft a system from the ground up. Clients can benefit from AIS with regard to platform and tools selection. Choosing the proper tools can save enormous headaches later on. AIS can be reached at (800) 327-9725 or online at `http://www.advanis.com`.

Derrick Ashmore is the Senior Vice-President of Development for Delta Vortex Technologies, a Chicago-based consulting firm that develops applications which integrate a wide variety of technologies and platforms. Derek routinely provides consulting services for companies developing or installing Oracle-based applications including: database design, implementation, performance tuning, administration, client/server application development, Internet/intranet development, and project management. Derek has designed, implemented, and managed Oracle-based projects of many different types and sizes including applications with Web-based interfaces, high transaction volume, high availability requirements, and large disk requirements. Derek can be reached at (773) 281-1292 or online at `dashmore@dvt.com`.

James Forgy is a Senior Database Designer and DBA for Advanced Information Systems, Inc. He plays an integral role for AIS as one of a few members of "Team AIS"—a swat team handling rapid turn around projects involving database catastrophes. His knowledge of Oracle and advanced tuning techniques have helped save numerous projects. James can be reached at (212) 786-2100, or by email at `jforgy@advanis.com`.

Virendra Galotra is currently a Sr. Systems Engineering Specialist in Oracle Corporation's Premium Support Group. Prior to this he worked at RDBMS group of World Wide Support for Oracle Corporation at California. During the two years at WWS he provided mission-critical support to DBAs on a wide variety of Platforms like Sun Solaris and HP/UX, Sequent, and Digital UNIX. He has several years of experience as Systems Analyst, DBA, and Consultant. He has presented and published papers in the areas of Intelligent systems using RDBMS tools in the Royal Society of Arts, London, and several international conferences.

Greg Goleash is a Senior Software Engineer and Internet Architect for Advanced Information Systems, Inc. His diverse talents have played a key role in the development of an Internet-based software product called "AIS Web Development Suite." This revolutionary product enables developers to construct Pure Java applications talking to an Oracle database automatically. It accommodates for true database transactions with performance similar to that of client/server applications. Greg can be reached at (212) 786-2100, or by email at ggoleash@advanis.com.

Joe Greene has been working with computers for over 20 years now. He has worked with some of the best, leading-edge technologies for the past 10 years in various computer consulting, planning, and development roles. Much of his work involves databases and system development. He has been working with Oracle databases since version 5. He lives in Pittsburgh with his wife and child. He is the author of *The Oracle DBA Survival Guide* and is a contributing author for *BackOffice Unleashed*, *Oracle 7.3 Developer's Guide*, and *Windows NT Server 4.0 Unleashed*, all from Sams Publishing.

Dan Hotka is a Director of European Operations for Platinum Technology. He has over 20 years in the computer industry and over 14 years experience with Oracle products. He is an acknowledged Oracle expert with Oracle experience dating back to the Oracle V4.0 days. He has co-authored the popular book *Oracle Unleashed* from Sams Publishing and frequently speaks at Oracle conferences and user groups around the world.

Matt Larson is a certified Oracle database administrator specializing in OLTP and data warehouse design. He has written for *Oracle Unleashed, 2nd Edition*. He began working with beta versions of Oracle8 during his tenure at Oracle Corporation. Matt holds a Bachelor of Science in Business Administration with an emphasis on Information Systems from the University of Colorado where he graduated first in his class. He is currently working as a Senior Database Administrator in the J.D. Edwards software development team. Matt can be reached via email at mattlarson@usa.net.

Brett Mark is the Senior Vice President of Development for Advanced Information Systems, Inc. His twenty years of systems experience and leadership provides AIS with a firm foundation of software development techniques and strategies.

With over eight years of experience with Oracle databases, Brett is considered to be a top expert in the industry. He has written several articles for the *Oracle Alliance Journal* on development techniques and system internals. Brett can be reached at (212) 786-2100, or by email at bmark@advanis.com.

Steve O'Hearn is the Webmaster for the Mid-Atlantic Association of Oracle Professionals (MAOP), the nation's largest independent Oracle user's group. He is President of Corbinian Technologies, Inc. (http://www.corbinian.com), a consulting firm in the Washington, DC area specializing in Oracle database design, development, and administration, including Web site development. He has worked with information systems full-time since 1983, working in most of the major third generation languages, as well as Sybase, Informix, and Ingres. He started working with Oracle in 1987, beginning with version 5. He has designed and developed Oracle systems for the U.S. Navy, U.S. Army, Space Station Freedom and other NASA projects, the World Bank, and many other government agencies and corporate customers. Currently, he is developing a Web-enabled data warehouse application for use by several of the Fortune 500. He is also teaching classes on the Oracle RDBMS and Developer/2000. He is a 1983 graduate of George Washington University, and a member of MENSA. Lately, when he's not working, he's playing guitar at his church. Steve would like to thank Terri Robertson, Oracle Corporation, for technical review of the security portion of the Web Applications Server 3.0 chapter. He loves to get email (and respond to it) at soh@corbinian.com.

Ivan Oss started using Basic to write adventure programs at 8 years of age and has been involved in computer technology ever since. His career has ranged from programmer to systems analyst and, most recently, database administrator. He is currently a senior DBA for J.D. Edwards World Source Company in Denver, Colorado, and supports a production ERP software development environment. His special interests include DSS systems, Data Mining, and OLAP. When he's not working you might find him riding his bike, visiting family, or hiking in the Colorado mountains with his wife Deirdre.

Cameron O'Rourke is a technologist in the Government division of Oracle Corporation. Based in Redwood Shores, California, he helps Oracle's government customers understand and plan network computing solutions based on the Web, Java, CORBA, objects, and components. Mr. O'Rourke has been with Oracle for six years and has extensive relational database and application development experience. Prior to Oracle, he spent several years in and around Silicon Valley at firms such as Excelan, Novell, Sybase, and in private consultancy. He has held software development, IT management, marketing, sales, production control, and accounting positions. While he writes Java programs to relax, he strives to make complex technology simple.

Michael Richards is the C.E.O. of Advanced Information Systems, Inc. His vision has lead AIS to become more than just another systems consulting firm.

AIS specializes in Oracle and Web development. This concentration of specialization allows AIS to cultivate and provide top technical talent. It is this talent that has enabled AIS to fill the need for quality Oracle personnel in corporate America. Our dedicated

"Team AIS" provides solutions for critical problems in a kind of SWAT team motif. Mike can be reached at (212) 786-2100, or by email at mrichards@advanis.com.

Paul Singleton is a consultant with Oracle Corporation. Prior to joining Oracle he worked as an independent consultant, and as an Oracle DBA and System Administrator for a number of companies. He lives in Carmel, Indiana, with his wife and three children. Paul can be reached at pws@iquest.net.

Ryan Stephens is an Oracle DBA and President of Perpetual Technologies Incorporated, based in Indianapolis, Indiana. Ryan has worked with Oracle since version 6, when he began his career as a programmer. Today, in addition to his full-time consulting duties as a DBA, Ryan teaches SQL and various other Oracle database classes at Indiana University-Purdue University Indianapolis. Ryan resides in Indianapolis with his wife Tina.

Meghraj Thakkar works as a Sr. Technical Analyst at Oracle Corporation. He has a Masters degree in Computer Science and a Bachelors degree in Electronics Engineering. He has several industry vendor certifications, including Microsoft Certified Systems Engineer (MCSE), Novell Certified ECNE, and Lotus Certified Notes Consultant. He has taught several courses related to Windows NT, including courses taught at the University of California, Irvine. He has presented two papers, titled "MTS on Windows NT" and "Integrating Oracle8 with Windows NT," at the ECO'98 held in New York City, NY, in March 1998.

He has co-authored *Special Edition: Using Oracle8* from Macmillan Computer Publishing. Currently he is co-authoring *Using Oracle8* also from Macmillan Computer Publishing. He has been working with various Oracle products for the past six years.

Edward Whalen is president and CEO of Performance Tuning Corporation (www.perftuning.com), a consulting company specializing in database performance, administration, and backup/recovery solutions. He has had much experience in database system design and tuning for optimal performance. Mr. Whalen has also published other Sams books: *Oracle Performance Tuning and Optimization* and *Sams Teach Yourself Oracle8 in 21 Days*. He is recognized as a leader in Oracle performance tuning and optimization.

Scott Wheeler is currently Vice President of Advanced Technologies at Nortoc, Inc. Scott has over 11 years experience in the computer field. His experience includes areas ranging from main frame to client/server to Internet/intranet technologies. During his career, Scott has worked for Oracle Corporation and has been developing Oracle-based systems since Oracle5. For the past two years his focus has been on providing major corporations with Java and Dynamic HTML-based solutions as front ends to data warehousing, OLTP (Online Transaction Processing), and customer information systems. Scott Wheeler can be reached at dwheeler@nortoc.com.

Acknowledgements and Dedication

We at Advanced Information Systems, Inc., would like to thank Rosemarie Graham, Todd Bumbalough, Jonathan Gennick, and all the editors of Sams Publishing for bringing order to this book out of the chaos that was many times presented to them. Special thanks goes out to the art department for deciphering and transforming the original "art" from our authors. Christa Pylant also needs to be acknowledged for her last-minute editing of our material. We would like to dedicate this book to Dr. Frederick P. Lenz III, who has profoundly influenced the people of AIS with his insights into relational theory, the Internet, and Eastern thinking as it relates to computer science.

Introduction

Servers, Servers, Servers!

Why write a book called *Oracle8 Server Unleashed*? The reason is that Oracle offers so many products along with their core RDBMS that a complete set of the Oracle scriptures would create a book that only a gold medalist could lift.

Since most of us computer types have trouble even lifting a laptop, we offer this specialized book concentrating on the Oracle8 Server. Even within the world of the Oracle8 server, we are faced with a huge plethora of options for the many computer configurations that are popular today.

To be honest, even some of the topics covered here, such as replication, data warehouses, and the Web Application Server, could be books themselves. But it was decided that in the jungle of a production environment, it might come in handy to have this massive "quick reference machete" cutting through to the complete world of the Oracle Server and its components.

This isn't to say that this book is only a quick reference guide; it is more like the embedded knowledge of the top Oracle consultants in the country who were each chosen to tackle particular topics relating to the Oracle8 Server. Unlike reading a manual, this book moves you into the core material quickly, yet also never fails to explain the "big picture."

Understanding the Oracle8 Server and its components is the key to gaining mastery in the Oracle profession. Of course there are tools like Oracle*Forms, Discoverer, and Programmer/2000 which can help one create a great deal of dazzling software. But all of these products revolve around the Oracle8 Server and are designed to fit within the mindset that Oracle used in the implementation of Relational Database Technology. The key to understanding any Oracle product is to understand first the Oracle Server.

Is This Book for Me?

Regardless of your role or interest in Oracle, this book will be very helpful. It is our belief that technical information can be embedded within informative and even (mildly) entertaining material. We have structured this book so that someone who is very technical will not be bored, while at the same time we step back and paint the big picture so that a non-technical manager will also gain a great deal of high-level understanding regarding the Oracle8 Server and the many non-technical concerns that revolve around the technology.

Because we so boldly tackle huge topics such as the Oracle Media Server, Replication, and Distributed Gateways, we cannot claim to be a manual for each of these vast undertakings.

This book is more like a companion. For instance, if one found himself or herself in the predicament of needing to connect and synchronize an Oracle8 Server to an IBM mainframe running DB2, he or she probably couldn't do it with this book alone. Instead, the constant reader would first study this book to gain an understanding of the many issues surrounding this Herculean task, using the expert knowledge and examples as a template when referring to specific documentation regarding the many tasks that they faced. Once the large picture has been grasped, the reader might then dive into specific Oracle manuals in order to extract useful details needed to complete the task.

Using *Oracle8 Server Unleashed* in this way, the reader will save a great deal of time. Instead of getting lost in endless reams of manuals, by first referring to this book, one can focus on the issues and hotpoints surrounding the complex tasks faced in purchasing, installing, and implementing the appropriate Oracle technology.

Grab Your Snowboards

Oracle8 Server Unleashed should be approached as more of a circle than a straight line. One need not read through the book in a linear fashion. Instead, we invite the reader to step into the center of the circle of this informative book and draw towards him or her that aspect of the Oracle Server that is needed.

We refer to the wisdom of a Buddhist monk in the book *Surfing the Himalayas*, written by Dr. Frederick Lenz. The monk explains to a young snowboarder:

> Let us say that we have placed a great deal of information along a straight line. Now, if we are at one end of the straight line, and the piece of information we want to get to is all the way at the other end of the straight line, it will be necessary for us to journey all the way through the information that is between us and the piece of information that we want to access in order to reach it.

> But suppose we took the same data and arranged it along the circumference of a circle—and then let us further suppose that we sat down in the middle of that circle of data. Now, all of that information would be equidistant from us, because it is arranged along the circumference of the circle that we are sitting in the middle of.

From this quote we see the power of *Oracle8 Server Unleashed*. We have arranged information in a circle, so the reader need not sift through endless pages of manuals in order to get to the small piece of information needed. Instead, this book can be read in as many different sequences as there are business needs and professionals who use the Oracle RDBMS.

This type of relational thinking, in which information relates to other pieces of information, yet not in a static order, is the foundation of relational database theory and is also the way in which we have structured this book for you. In the spirit of snowboarding, we wish you good surfing down the many mountains of knowledge you will face. We have designed this book so you can easily jump the deep chasms into which many Oracle acolytes often fall. We dedicate this book to Dr. Frederick Lenz, the young snowboarder who learned this form of relational thinking from an old Buddhist monk many years ago. In the same way, we have gained a great deal of insight and vision from him regarding the world of relational theory and, without which, much of this book would not have been possible.

Put on your bootstraps, and happy snowboarding!

Oracle8 Server

PART

I

CHAPTER 1

Oracle8

by Joe Greene

When Oracle changes the first number in its product designations, it signifies a major change in the functionality of that product. Oracle has produced the 7.*x* family of database management system products for several years now. Each of the incremental revisions (7.0, 7.1, 7.2, and 7.3) has shown a significant increase in the functionality of the product. For example, parallel query processing started with version 7.1 of the product, and version 7.3 started to introduce some products, such as a video server, that are part of Oracle's vision of the universal server.

With that in mind, there must be some significant changes in the Oracle8 product. What is surprising is the fact that these changes have taken the form of additions to the existing Oracle architecture as opposed to a complete revision of that architecture. I was impressed by this fact and also a little relieved. Take some of the object-oriented constructs that were introduced into Oracle8. When I had to learn object-oriented programming, the first challenge was dealing with the fact that everything had a new name (the correct object-oriented term). There are a number of pure object-oriented databases out there that have strong differences from the relational databases with which I was comfortable. An Oracle version 7 database could be upgraded to Oracle8 without any software or database object revisions. My investment in terms of experience is safe. I will list the new features a little later in this chapter.

Of course, in addition to the functional changes, the marketing arm of Oracle has introduced a number of naming and bundling changes. They did not have these details worked out when the product was first released, but have since come out with the new names and bundles. An entire chapter (Chapter 4, "Oracle8 Servers and Options") is devoted to this subject. I have found that even the best techie can become perplexed when it comes time to deal with marketing and sales arrangements.

The Latest Oracle

As I mentioned in the last section, Oracle8 is a significant upgrade to the Oracle database management system. There are some interesting themes to consider when evaluating this new product before directly addressing the technology discussion:

- There was a significant beta test period for this product. Oracle has always performed beta testing, but this time they invited a much wider group of users to test out the product. This testing included some of the smaller shops, and I think that it has helped cover a diverse set of environments and also users who are not just the straight, large data centers.

- This was the first significant release of the Oracle database management system that included Windows NT as a tier one development platform. For those not familiar with this term, the tier one platforms are the eight or ten computer

environments that are the first to receive new ports of the Oracle software. These are generally the most important (sell the most) environments for the Oracle software. They also tend to have the best support, the fewest bugs, and the latest releases. This is an important strategic direction for those places where NT is a significant factor.

- There was a significant amount of preparation and training for business partners and even customers on this new product. This may not seem important to some developers and end users. For those that rely on outside consultants, however, it means that these consultants will not have to learn while doing. Instead, consultants have had advanced preparation and copies of the software so they can be productive when the product is released. The utility of a piece of software is a combination of its inherent functionality and the ability of people to use it; therefore this preparation makes the transition to Oracle8 much easier.

- This was the first release where the Web and network computer environment were a primary emphasis for the system. True, these concepts were around in 7.3 and even earlier versions of the database. However, because Oracle has put much of its time and resources over the last several years into developing Internet-related technology, Oracle8 was optimized to provide support for these environments. This emphasis comes at a time when the core enabling technologies (HTML, Web browsers, and Java) are reaching maturity and practical use in the business world.

- Oracle put significant effort into helping developers build applications for this environment. Microsoft has always worked to get information about its development tools and operating systems into the hands of developers. This has helped Microsoft's operating systems as other companies develop applications that users want and Microsoft has not thought of or had the time to develop. Oracle8 has been promoted to developers, especially Web-application developers, who want to take advantage of the cartridge architecture and other development options.

There are some things about this latest version of Oracle that some people do not like. I agree with Oracle's decisions, but want to mention some of these complaints here:

- Oracle8 is not 100% CORBA compliant. CORBA stands for the Common Object Request Broker Architecture. It is a technology standard that allows applications to use functions and data (objects) from within other applications. A competing standard is the DCOM (Distributed Common Object Model), promoted by Microsoft. I mention this because this may be your first introduction to shared objects if you have ever included a link to a spreadsheet in the middle of your word processing document. The code to read and process the spreadsheet data is not duplicated in the word processing code. Instead, it is accessed from the spreadsheet software. Many purists have objected to the fact that Oracle did not include full CORBA support as part of Oracle8. The CORBA technology was still being finalized as Oracle8 was being developed. It is much easier for a Silicon Valley startup to jump on the bandwagon of potentially unstable technology than it is for a company such as Oracle that is being used as the basis for a large number of business data processing centers. Oracle will incorporate compliance with CORBA in a later revision when both CORBA and Oracle are ready for this new technology.

- Java is not a native procedural language for the database. PL/SQL still reigns as the internal programming language. Again, there are plans to include Java as an internal programming option for the Oracle database management system. However, the Java language still continues to evolve at a somewhat dizzying pace. When Java and Oracle are ready, it will be an option for internal programming. Until then, you still have the option of writing Java applications to access the database (via J/SQL) that are stored external to the database.

The latest release of the Oracle database management system is definitely something worthy of your consideration. While many leading-edge enthusiasts salivate at the object-oriented technologies and possibilities for Web cartridges, the Oracle database managment system still provides support for all of the traditional databases that were developed for Oracle version 7. You can run an application and database developed for Oracle7 without any conversion. When you do move to Oracle8, you will be able to take advantage of many of the "under the hood" improvements for speed and scalability that have been built into Oracle8. When a new customer asks whether they should buy Oracle8 or start with Oracle version 7, I recommend going right to Oracle8 and using whatever features they need and are comfortable with. It is everything Oracle version 7 was, and more.

Major Improvements

First, let me discuss the enhancements to the Oracle technologies that were available in version 7.3 that make Oracle8 even better. Most of these are not directly observable by the average user, developer, or even DBA. However, in most of the actual business uses of Oracle, they are probably far more important than the new features that will be discussed later. The key enhancements to existing technology in Oracle8 include the following:

- *Parallel updates, inserts, and deletes.* Oracle has supported parallel queries since Oracle 7.1. In the past, updates, inserts, and deletes have been serial in nature (one process works to complete the given task). With partitioned tables and indexes, Oracle8 can now assign a number of processes to complete the insert, update, or delete process, thereby speeding up these operations. This can become significant in such tasks as data warehouse loads.

- *Incremental backups.* Previous versions of Oracle have relied on complete backup strategies. You backed up an entire tablespace or database using the cold and warm backup techniques. You performed exports of an entire table or set of tables. This is easy on relatively small databases (a few tens of gigabytes). However, for very large data warehouses, this can become impossible (there is not enough time in a day to complete the backups). The incremental backups allow you to perform multiple levels of backup, capturing only the transactions that have occurred since the last time this level of backup was performed. A level is a reference point starting with 0 (complete backup). Higher numbers indicate that these backups are performed more frequently and usually back up less information than lower numbers.

- *DBLink concentration.* Supporting a large number of users (thousands or tens of thousands) can become quite a challenge for a database server. One solution is to implement multiple tiers of processing. One server, for example, can perform most of the business logic processing while another performs the database retrieval functions. DBLink concentration allows multiple user connections to share one physical (network interface) and operating system connection to link to other databases.

- *Connection pooling.* Connection pooling allows large number of users to connect to a database. As opposed to allocating memory and processes for each individual user connection, the system uses a pool of connections that all users share. Only the active users consume a resource.

- *Improved parallel server.* For reliability, Oracle implemented the parallel server in version 7. Under a parallel server, you have multiple computers accessing a single database on a shared set of disk drives (where the hardware architecture permits such sharing). In Oracle8, this functionality has been improved to reduce downtime during the failover process. Also, the performance has been improved by minimizing the overhead tasks associated with the parallel server.

- *Improved replication.* Replication is used to duplicate a set of tables from one database to another. In Oracle 7, the replication was based on row IDs and used a series of triggers to implement the process. In Oracle8, the replication function has been improved in several ways. First, parallel propagation is now allowed to update a given site with multiple process streams (similar to parallel query) as opposed to a single process. Also, the replication functionality has now been built directly into the server software, as opposed to being a series of triggers, for improved performance. Finally, you can now update a snapshot based on the primary key of the table involved, as opposed to using row IDs, which can change in certain databases that require frequent reorganization.

•*Enhanced support for unstructured data.* One of Oracle's initiatives is to extend Oracle to become a media server. To do this, the large object types have been enhanced in size, breaking the old 2GB limitation. Also, you are now allowed to have more than one large object type per table. Finally, the access and update functionality has been enhanced to be more efficient.

• *Optimizer enhancements.* The optimizer is that section of the Oracle software that determines which algorithm to use when retrieving information from the database. The optimizer has been improved to make better decisions. One enhancement of special note is the improvement of the algorithms used for a star schema commonly found in data warehouses.

In addition to these enhancements, there were a number of new features added to Oracle8:

• *Table partitioning.* This is a big improvement when it comes to very large tables. Here you can divide a table into multiple sections based on some logical index value (divide an Orders table into sections based on month ordered, for example). Each section can be placed on a separate disk drive. One advantage to this arrangement is that Oracle is smart enough to know which sections are needed. When performing a query, it ignores the partitions that are not needed, thereby reducing the amount of data that must be scanned. It can also enhance reliability in that you can operate the database with a given section of a table down due to a failed disk drive or some other reason. You cannot issue queries that require information from the missing section; however, you can issue queries against the other section and add new data to another section.

• *Index partitioning.* Index partitioning is similar to table partitioning described previously. Here you divide an index into multiple partitions (disks) based on the values of that index. It can be very useful for large indexes in splitting disk input/output.

• *Backup and recovery management within the server.* Previous versions of Oracle relied on operating system utilities to perform backups. As databases grow, simple backup strategies are usually not sufficient to keep up with the growing data volume. To implement more sophisticated backup strategies, a knowledge of the database and how it is structured is required. In Oracle8, the database now implements a more sophisticated backup strategy, coordinated through the Enterprise Manager tool. You can use this tool to determine what has been backed up and implement the most efficient recovery.

- *Connection Manager*. To implement some of the features that make better use of system resources when it comes to user and database connections, Oracle has implemented Connection Manager.

- *Security Server*. Some of the problems when you start building a distributed database environment are the maintenance tasks associated with keeping each of the databases current. One of the biggest chores can be adding and deleting users in each of the databases and granting them the appropriate privileges. The Security Server centralizes this administration in a single location that can be maintained through a graphical user interface in Enterprise Manager. All databases now access this central repository for security information, as opposed to having it maintained internally. Chapter 19, "Oracle8 Administrative Requirements," discusses administration of Oracle8 databases in more detail.

- *User-defined data types*. While Oracle provides a wide range of data types, advanced users are thinking up complex data types that are combinations of some of the basic forms of data (an X-ray image with the associated patient information could be considered as a single data entry). Oracle8 allows users to define data types composed of the basic data types that are treated as a single object.

- *Object-oriented extensions*. Oracle8 implements a number of features found in object-oriented programming, including data methods and data types. These data and methods are treated as a grouped entity (object).

- *Data cartridges*. Users have long used Oracle database to write applications. However, many people today want to tightly integrate their software with Oracle. A data cartridge can be configured to handle more complex data types (video, for example) or to provide extended software (image recognition system software). The key here is that data cartridges are tightly connected to the database through an application programming interface (API), as opposed to just connected through client-server data access mechanisms.

The Oracle8 Product Family

Oracle8 is actually a family of products. It includes the software that provides database management services. It also includes a series of tools that allow you to access and update the data in the database (SQL*Plus, Loader, Import, and Export). It also includes a series of administration tools to help keep the database operational and perform routine administrative tasks (Server Manager and Enterprise Manager). Finally, there are a number of optional components (enhanced replication and parallel server among them) you can purchase as additions to the basic Oracle8 server package and that allow you to perform specialized functions. Chapter 4 will go over these options, tools, and components in more detail.

Fitting Oracle8 into an Application Environment

One of the purposes of this book is to provide you with an understanding of Oracle8 so you can integrate it into your application environment. There are a number of different architectures Oracle8 will support. You can use Oracle8 as a traditional host-terminal system where the software is written to run on the server using some character mode interface. You can also implement Oracle8 using a client-server function with a PC providing the front end and the server providing database management functions. You can also implement a Web server or an application server where you have three different computers providing services that are part of your application. This book will discuss the technologies associated with these environments and how to implement them so you can decide which ones best fit your needs.

Summary

This chapter provides a brief introduction to Oracle8. It highlights the new functions that are provided by Oracle8. This should help those already familiar with Oracle7 to focus on those areas that have changed. This chapter also provides a brief overview of the history of the Oracle Server product line and some material on product direction that will be useful when trying to understand why certain features have been added.

Oracle Database Architecture

by Joe Greene

Oracle8 is a rather complicated animal, even if you just consider the database itself and ignore all of the optional components, tools, and applications that are built on the Oracle8 architecture. There are a number of people who are expert Oracle developers or system support types who have never seen the need to understand what is "under the hood" in the Oracle database. This chapter is designed as your first peek into the guts of the Oracle relational database management system so you can understand why the system works the way it does and what you can do to take advantage of its architecture.

For those of you who are truly brave, I invite you to examine Part III of this book ("Oracle8 Components and Objects") for a more detailed discussion of the topics previewed in this chapter. The chapters in this section go into the details that might help you speed up a job here or reduce your memory utilization there to make your application lean and efficient. For those of you who are already comfortable with the architecture of the Oracle version 7 database management system, you can probably skip this chapter. I was impressed at the way the Oracle7 architecture was able to accommodate the significant functional changes listed in Chapter 1, "Oracle8," without a major rewrite. For the rest of you, I present this chapter to discuss what the components of Oracle8 are and how they interact with one another.

Database Architecture

Oracle is primarily designed to work in multiuser, multitasking computer environments. There have been versions of Oracle that work in batch processing environments (for example, IBM mainframes running S) and single-user, single-task environments such as the PC. However, the basic architecture is designed to work well with operating systems such as UNIX, VMS, and so forth. There are a few key concepts about these operating system environments you should know:

- These operating systems run multiple jobs or processes at the same time. The system cycles between the jobs and gives processing time to the processes that are ready to do something. Some operating systems enable you to control the priority of the jobs so that certain jobs get more time than others.

- The memory of these computers is divided into space reserved for the operating system, space reserved for the users, and space that is shared by multiple processes. The shared memory areas are not normally used by applications; however, as you will see, Oracle makes extensive use of shared memory areas.

- The disk drives are shared between multiple users. Some form of security is usually present to control which users or groups of users can access data on particular disk drives.

Instances

One of the first concepts you need to understand about Oracle is the difference between an instance and a database. Think of this as your first Oracle-ism (those little quirks seen when you walk in the world of Oracle). A *database* is an organized collection of data stored in data files. An *instance* is the set of processes and memory areas that provide the capability of accessing this data. You need both to have a useful system.

The complexity and wonder of the Oracle RDBMS (see Figure 2.1) can be divided into three simple parts:

- Background processes
- Shared memory areas
- Disk data storage areas

FIGURE 2.1.

The pieces of the Oracle RDBMS.

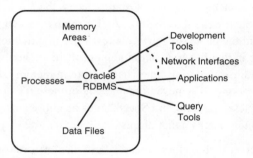

In most PC database environments, such as dBASE and Access, you interact directly with the data files using their DBMS commands. This works well for single-user, PC-based systems, but causes problems for large, multiuser systems such as Oracle. For example, how would the system coordinate two users writing records to a single table and index? Oracle, like most other multiuser database management systems, uses a series of background processes to accomplish the data writing process. Splitting the tasks into multiple processes also reduces the complexity of each of these processes, which is significant, considering how complex the system already is. These processes can be thought of as a series of specialists, each working on a particular task. For example, when a user writes changes to the database, these changes are placed in a memory area. When the memory area is ready to be written to disk, the database writer process transfers the changes from memory to the appropriate records on disk. The only data transmissions across the network are the query/transaction and the results. This reduces the network traffic and speeds application processing.

The exact number and configuration of the Oracle background processes depends on operating parameters, tuning parameters, and the optional packages selected by the database administrator. For example, if you want to keep all the files that log transactions applied to the database, you start an archiving process that copies these log files to tape or another area on disk. If you want to have many input/output database write operations being performed at the same time, you start multiple asynchronous database writer processes (you set up the number as a configuration parameter). If you are starting to get confused about how many processes to start, don't worry. The basic configuration (hard coded into the DBMS software) works well for most situations. Later chapters discuss when to start the additional processes to improve performance or provide additional services (the checkpoint process, for example). For now, it is enough to understand the basic concepts of the background processes.

The final component in the Oracle database architecture is the memory areas. It is based on a very simple principle—memory is much faster to access than disk. When users need to write something, have them write it to memory and then go on about their business. When retrieving rows from the database, retrieve a few extra into memory and hope the next row the user needs is in that batch. A fair amount of the complexity of the Oracle RDBMS lies in the algorithms used to decide what to store in memory. Much of the tuning process involves working to achieve proper sizing of these memory areas. There's a section later in this chapter, "Memory and Speed," plus an entire chapter of this book (Chapter 10, "Oracle Memory Areas") that discuss the memory areas.

The user applications interact with memory areas. These memory areas store data retrieved from disk and data to be written to disk, which is the permanent storage medium. Background processes provide data retrieval and storage functions, linking the memory areas to the disks. There are background processes to perform other system monitoring and maintenance functions. However, if you understand the basic concepts in this paragraph, you're where you should be for now.

Oracle Processes

Now it is time to delve a little more deeply into the major components. The Oracle processes can be divided into four categories:

- Servicing user requests
- Writing data to the data files
- Recording transactions in log files
- Monitoring the functioning of the database

User Processes

The first group of processes are those involved with servicing user requests. Think of them as your liaisons to Oracle. When you need for information, they go after it for you. When you have updates or inserts for the database, they store the transaction in the shared memory areas for later transfer to the data files. There are different types of user processes, but for now it is enough to understand that they are there and that their purpose is serving as your interface to the Oracle database.

Data Writing Processes

The next group of processes write data to the data files. Recall that when you write to the Oracle RDBMS, the data is stored first in a shared memory area. Oracle has one or more database writer processes that take the data from this shared memory area and write it to the data files efficiently. This creates free space in the memory area that can be used for other transactions and queries. There is also an optional checkpoint process that updates all data with a record of the latest transaction that has been applied to the database (using the internal Oracle transaction number). If the checkpoint process is not started, the database writer process takes over this function.

Logging Processes

The third group of processes records transactions in log files. One of the major differences in a commercial-grade, multiuser database is that the capability of recovering from a failure such as the loss of a disk drive is very important. Oracle accomplishes this, in part, by recording each transaction (that is, inserting a record in a particular table) in a separate file from the data files. In the event of the loss of one of the data files, these log files can be applied to a copy of the data file retrieved from a backup to bring the data file up to the point where the failure occurred. More on this topic later, but it is important to understand the concept of these log files and that there are one or more processes devoted to taking transactions stored in the shared memory areas and moving them to these log files.

Monitoring Processes

The final group of processes under this simple classification scheme is those that monitor the functioning of the database. You may already be worried about the complexity of the database as it has been described so far. Perhaps you looked at the next couple of chapters where the topics introduced in this section are discussed in more detail. Fortunately, you do not have to keep track of what is happening and manage the details of the database by yourself. Oracle has implemented a number of processes whose job it is to keep an eye on the database and correct problems when they occur.

Memory and Speed

As mentioned earlier, shared memory is the key to speed in the Oracle RDBMS. It is also one of the most elusive areas to keep track of and therefore it is important to understand. It is elusive because you can run operating system utilities to see which processes are running and you can look at the data files to see when they were updated, what their size is, and so forth. With memory, there is very little in the way of utilities that enable you to look at all of the shared memory components to see whether they are working well. Memory areas are discussed in more detail in Chapter 10, however I wanted to present an introduction here to show how the memory areas fit into the overall Oracle architecture. The following are the various components or areas of memory used by Oracle (see Figure 2.2):

- Software code areas
- System Global Area (SGA)
- Program Global Area (PGA)
- Sort areas

FIGURE 2.2.

A simplified view of the Oracle memory areas.

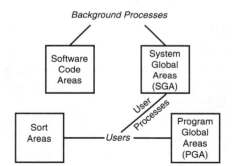

Software Code Areas

The first memory area of interest is the one that stores software code for the Oracle database itself. On some operating systems, this software area can be shared between instances. Note that this is the software that runs the database itself, not the applications that you have written and are running.

System Global Area (SGA)

The System Global Area or SGA is the next memory area of interest. Actually, I like to think of this as the heart of an Oracle database. Your processes send transactions to this memory area and try to get data that has been cached here for speed. There are four components stored in the SGA:

- The database buffer cache contains database records that are waiting to be written to disk or are available for reading.

- The redo log buffer stores a copy of transactions that have been applied to the database and are waiting to be written to the redo logs.

- Shared SQL areas store queries that have been parsed and are ready for execution. In many databases, users execute the same query many times and performance is enhanced when these queries are waiting to be executed in memory. Some of this information is actually stored in the PGA (described in the next section) in Oracle version 6.

- The data dictionary cache stores data about the database itself, its objects (tables, views, and so forth), and users.

Program Global Area (PGA)

In contrast to the SGA, which contains information shared by everyone in the instance, the Program Global Area or PGA stores information that is used by a single user process. When someone creates an Oracle session (Oracle's way of saying that the user connects to a database instance), Oracle creates the PGA. The PGA contains stack space, and in many cases, information about the user session.

Sort Areas

Finally, sort areas can greatly improve the performance of one of the most common database operations—sorting. Very few people want to review data records in the order that they were input (or in Oracle's case, the order that Oracle chooses to store the data). The data for most applications has some form of ordering to it (you sort a list of names alphabetically, sort dates, and so forth). Using the logic that memory access is much faster than disk access, Oracle likes to store a list of values to be sorted in memory and perform the sort there. That is the purpose of the sort area.

Disk Storage

After that glowing discussion about the wonders of memory, it is time to address the somewhat slower, but inexpensive and nonvolatile storage mechanism found in most Oracle instances—the magnetic (hard) disk drive. These little jewels enable us to build those multigigabyte (or in some cases terabyte) store houses of corporate wisdom. This section provides a brief introduction to the types of files that Oracle employs in its battles with information overload. Now, you need to look at the seven types of files used by the Oracle RDBMS (see Figure 2.3):

- Data files
- Online redo log files
- Archive log files
- Initialization files
- Control files
- SGA definition files
- Oracle processing log and error (trace) files

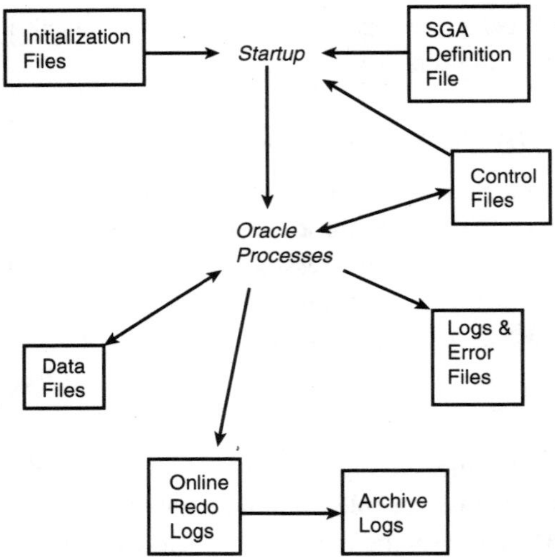

FIGURE 2.3.

The basic types of Oracle data files.

Data Files

The easiest place to start is with the data files. These contain exactly what you would expect to find in a relational database management system—a series of records of data arranged in tables. There are a number of other types of database objects (indexes, views, and so forth) that you will find in these files, but for now, it is enough to understand that this is where you will find your data. One interesting point to note is that Oracle enables you to store software within these database files (in the form of packages and procedures).

Log Files

The next set of files is the online redo log files. The concept of these files is simple—record every transaction made to the database in a file separate from the main data files. These can be used to recover all changes made to the database in the event that a data file is damaged. Oracle uses several of these files so that when it gets done writing to the last file in the series, it begins overwriting to the first online redo log file. An obvious question is, how can you recover from a damaged data file if you overwrite one of your online redo log files?

The answer lies in the archive log files. Their function is simple. When you finish writing to an online redo log file, a background process makes a copy of that redo log file to a separate file that is given a unique sequential number. This file can be placed on a magnetic disk drive or a magnetic tape. Then, if you want to recover a data file that has been destroyed, you get a copy from the archive log tapes that you have been religiously making and apply all transactions in the redo and archive log files that have occurred since that backup was made.

Supporting Files

Now that data storage has been taken care of, it is time to investigate some of the supporting files that Oracle uses. The initialization files are the equivalent of Microsoft DOS's `autoexec.bat` and `config.sys`. There are two files in the Oracle initialization file set, although you could get by with one or even more than two. These files are called `init.ora` and `config.ora`. The exact name of a file for a particular instance has the ID (SID) of your particular Oracle instance in it. For example, if your Oracle instance has an ID of `test`, your files are called `inittest.ora` and `configtest.ora`. With that out of the way, the purpose of these control files is to specify the following startup parameters to Oracle:

- Values for all those tuneable parameters that Oracle uses to improve performance
- Locations of the control files and archive log files
- Locations for some of the log and error files

Control Files

The next set of files that helps Oracle keep track of what is going on is the control files set. These files keep track of where the data files are and also record the number of the latest transaction applied to the database. This latter feature helps Oracle during recovery to know how many transactions need to be applied to come up to date. These files are stored in a binary format that you cannot read using standard operating system text file commands (such as `more` on UNIX or `type` on VMS).

SGA Definition File

Another binary supporting file is the SGA definition file. You will have one of these for each of the Oracle instances that you create. This file tells Oracle some details about creating the SGA on startup. Most of the DBAs that I have worked with are either not aware or are only vaguely aware of these files. This is a good sign for you new DBAs, because it means that you do not need to worry about these files.

Log and Error Files

The final type of Oracle file that you will deal with is the log and error files. Oracle is designed to be a production, business-grade database. Therefore, when problems occur, you need to determine what is wrong quickly and get it fixed. To support this need, Oracle records all major database activities (inserts, updates, and so on.) in a set of log files. In addition, when Oracle's monitoring processes detect a problem, they write as much relevant data about the problem as they can find to a series of error logging files (called *trace files* in Oracle). In this way, the DBA can look at a few files and determine what happened.

An interesting sidelight while on the subject of Oracle files is the task of finding all these files on your system. Many of the DBAs that I have come across do not know where all these files reside. This makes troubleshooting much more difficult. You will learn how to find all these files on your systems later in this book.

Interfacing with the DBMS

The Oracle DBMS software is designed to handle all of the details of storing and retrieving data for your applications. This differs from the old world of flat files where your applications had complete control over the storage and retrieval processes. You now have to learn the interface requirements that Oracle has developed to control your interaction with their data storage application.

You can think of this interaction on two levels. The first level involves the communications mechanisms used to interface your application with the database management system. The second level is after you are communicating with the database, how do you have to format your requests and in what format will the outputs be returned to your application?

Let me first address the communications mechanisms that Oracle supports. Basically, there are three ways to communicate with Oracle as shown in Figure 2.4:

- The first mechanism relies on standard operating system interprocess communications mechanisms. These are the basis for all interaction between applications on the host computer system. This applies when the user application program is running on the same computer as the Oracle DBMS.

- The second mechanism relies on Oracle's communications utilities known as SQL*Net (pre-Oracle8 and still supported by Oracle8) or Net8. This software handles the details of interfacing to the appropriate communications protocols, transmitting the queries/transactions and then interfacing these transmissions to the database management system.

- The final mechanism uses the standard protocols and tools that were originally developed for the World Wide Web (http and html). You have the option of installing a fully functional Web server with your Oracle8 system. This server is capable of receiving transmissions and sending responses to Web browsers connected to both intranets and the Internet. The communication between the Web server and the DBMS uses one of the above communications mechanisms (that is, SQL*Net or ODBC), but the client workstation is only responsible for using the standard Web protocols. This enables you to have a relatively "thin" client workstation with minimal memory, disk storage, and processing capabilities. It also saves a lot of client configuration work.

FIGURE 2.4.
Oracle communications mechanisms.

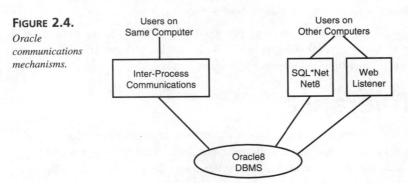

You can call methods within other programs (that is, the Oracle server) when Oracle implements its ORB. You will be able to access data via standard methods (think of them as selects and updates) provided as part of the CORBA standard. You can make these references either on the local computer or to a database on a remote computer. While you can do this with SQL*Net or Net8, the advantage of learning the CORBA APIs is that you can use these same techniques to access data and methods associated with a wide variety of applications. It will also provide a standard interface between Oracle products which should simplify the development team efforts when it comes to porting software.

Multiprocessor Configurations

The architecture shown in the previous section applies equally to both single and multi-processor configurations. However, when you have multiple processors, you are probably not content to see your job running for a long time while a number of CPUs are idle. Oracle has realized that the way to support really large queries is to design their software to use as many CPUs as possible to perform a single operation. Some have even been heard to utter the slogan "parallel everything." Anyway, for those operating systems that support multiple CPUs, Oracle has added a series of processes to take advantage of the additional CPUs:

- *Parallel query processes.* These processes enable you to split the load for a given query between multiple processors. Depending on the query, Oracle may use one processor to scan the index while another retrieves information from the associated table. Oracle might choose to use separate processors to query different tables that are to be joined together. The key is that you have multiple CPUs and possibly multiple disk drives working at the same time on a single query.

- *Parallel load processes.* This enables you to split up a bulk database load into multiple processes, similar to those used for parallel query.

- *Parallel DML statements.* This enables you to do inserts, updates, and deletes on partitioned tables using multiple processors. You can also perform `insert…select` statements using multiple processors for nonpartitioned tables.

Fault Tolerance

Some systems are so critical to the operation of a company or organization that people are willing to spend extra money just to minimize any chance that the systems will be unavailable. As databases and their associated applications take over the processing functions of an organization and implement the basic business processes, up time becomes essential. Realizing this, Oracle has built into its architecture a couple of ways to increase the system's tolerance to failures of CPUs, power supplies, memory, or disk drives.

The first option that came onto the market to increase fault tolerance actually had nothing to do with Oracle itself. Disk drive manufacturers developed technology to mirror disk drives (often referred to as RAID level 0). RAID 0 causes the operating system to make duplicate writes to two disk drives. If one disk drive fails, the operating system can still use the other drive for data storage and retrieval. There are both hardware-based and software-based disk mirroring solutions. One Oracle implementation of mirroring is the capability of mirroring the online redo log files. This provides both performance and security improvements.

The next fault tolerance feature that protects Oracle databases is the parallel server technology that Oracle has built as an optional product for the DBMS. This option applies to computer systems where multiple computers can access a common set of disk drives. The Oracle parallel server coordinates the activity and transactions across the multiple CPUs. It handles the locking that can occur between the CPUs. Finally, it provides a means for other processors to pick up tasks that were being accomplished by a CPU that fails.

A final fault tolerant feature that is new to Oracle8 is the table and index partitioning features. Here you are allowed to store different portions of a given data table (for example, all of the data from June on one disk and all of the data from July on another). The search algorithms have been implemented such that if a disk drive fails, you can still perform queries against the partitioned table as long as you do not need to access data from the failed partition. If the June disk drive fails, you can still run all of your July queries. This can be very useful when you have very large systems where a certain portion of the data is accessed often (and is therefore a candidate for disk mirroring) and the rest of the data is needed infrequently.

Microsoft Windows NT Configurations

Who cares about Microsoft and Windows? Oracle for one. Almost every day, Oracle representatives take swipes at Microsoft, DCOM, SQL*Server, and Visual J++. Many UNIX loyalists will claim that Windows NT is just a fad and that UNIX will eventually rule the day. However, Oracle is not betting on this. Last year, Oracle made Windows NT a tier 1 platform. This means that Windows NT is one of the few operating systems to which new Oracle server products are ported. Recently, that status has been upgraded so that Windows NT is now sharing the title of reference port with Sun Solaris. What this means is that when Oracle develops server products, they are developed on both Solaris and NT at the same time. The Solaris version is then ported to other UNIX variants.

Hopefully by now you are convinced that Oracle is serious about Windows NT. There are several advantages to this version of the Oracle server products that you might want to consider:

- You do not have to relink object modules when you install the software as you would under UNIX. Due to the standards imposed by Intel and Microsoft, you are able to load directly executable software (that is, `.exe` and `.dll` files). This prevents anomalies in various versions of the UNIX operating system from making it long or difficult to complete the Oracle installation.

- Due to the use of the Registry, Oracle is much more aware of the operating system and Oracle environment. This means that it is less dependent on which environmental variables you have set up to determine installation parameters. It may not seem like much, but it can save a lot of time fussing over getting the environment set up correctly for your installation.

- You can install the DBMS software and have a working database in less than 30 minutes.

- Because a graphical user interface is presumed with Windows NT, Oracle can implement a full graphical tool set to control and interact with the database under NT. It does not need to have a character-based tool set to accommodate users who telnet into the server (telnet support is an optional third-party product under NT).

Of course, there are a few disadvantages to Windows NT from an Oracle perspective. I actually split my time fairly evenly between NT and UNIX versions of Oracle, so I feel compelled to list the following disadvantages of the Windows NT version of Oracle when compared with the UNIX varieties:

- Windows NT does not scale up to support as large a number of CPUs. This limits the overall processing capabilities of an NT Oracle database when compared to very large multiprocessor configurations running UNIX (which make up a small percentage of the total number of Oracle databases out there today).

- Windows NT does not support as much disk storage. If your database is on the order of terabytes, you will probably be looking to large UNIX multiprocessors to support this load.

- Windows NT does not support a number of different versions of Oracle installed on the same system. You can have multiple instances on the same NT server if they are running the same version of the DBMS. The NT philosophy for Oracle is that because you can buy a relatively cheap development and test computer, run your tests on a separate computer. I actually prefer this philosophy in that I do not want development and test going on anywhere near my production databases.

Oracle8 Under Windows NT

One of the first things that you would notice under a Windows NT installation of the Oracle DBMS is that you cannot find the familiar processes that are described previously in this chapter. They are functionally still there and operating, it is just that Windows NT is not designed to be a collage of a large number of background processes. Instead, background processes are organized into what Windows NT designers refer to as services.

Each of these services can have a number of threads associated with them representing what would be considered background processes in an operating system such as UNIX. The NT operating system gives designers incentives to group threads together into services by providing enhanced interprocess communications mechanisms within the service. Under Windows NT, you would have the following services:

- Oracle start service for each instance. This service is used to start the main Oracle DBMS service. The two are tied together so that when you start the Oracle start service, the main DBMS service is started without user intervention.

- Oracle service for each instance. This service encompasses the main database processing functions described previously (database writing, log writing, process monitoring, and system monitoring).

- Oracle Net8 or SQL*Net listeners. These services monitor communications via SQL*Net or Net8 and transfer information between the network and the DBMS.

Summary

This chapter has provided an overview of the architecture of the Oracle8 DBMS. This system can be thought of as a collection of background processes, memory areas, and data files. Together, they provide an environment that takes care of the details of data storage freeing the developer to concentrate on the business needs of an application. There are several options and variations to this architecture that accommodate specific computer environments. However, the beauty of these implementations is that the system remains pretty much the same on a conceptual basis.

In Part II, "Installation, Upgrade, and Migration," I will cover the components of the Oracle8 system in much greater detail. This information can be useful when you are trying to push the envelope of performance on your system. Only when you fully understand what is happening can you use the system to your advantage.

Oracle8 Network Computing

by Cameron O'Rourke

In This Chapter

This chapter focuses on how Oracle fits into the emerging world of network computing. First, the industry factors that have led up to network computing are discussed; then you survey some of the enabling technologies. This will be followed by an overview of Oracle's Network Computing Architecture and supporting products, and finally, some words on the Network Computer.

The Emergence of Network Computing

The information industry is maturing, and network computing is the convergence of much that we have learned during the last 30 years of computing. In this section, you explore the impact of new technology and other unique conditions that have brought about network computing.

Convergence

Since departments in large organizations began to purchase minicomputers to supplement the services provided by the glass house, information managers have been in a struggle to balance the needs of the enterprise with the needs of the user. The arrival of the personal computer further added to the conflict by setting new expectations for graphical interfaces, personal control, and ease of use. As shown in Figure 3.1, many information managers feel that the priorities have shifted in ways that are unhealthy for the enterprise.

FIGURE 3.1.

Are we unbalanced?

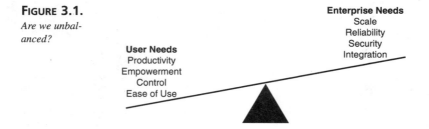

Now we are in the midst of a new convergence of attitudes and technology, as shown in Figure 3.2.

First, there is a unique set of conditions in the information industry. Both users and information managers now have some experience with, and an understanding of, the limitations of existing technology:

- Many businesses have begun to look closely at the total cost of ownership (TCO) of their personal computer purchases. Some are putting off upgrades until a better alternative can be found.

- Some businesses have found that an unintended consequence of having lots of low-cost servers is astronomical management costs. The topic of server consolidation is popular at seminars and in magazine articles. Perhaps coincidentally, mainframe computers are selling better than ever.

- The Web has shown end users how they can get real value by using services provided for them on a network. There may be some alternative to do-it-yourself computing.

Second, there is a wave of emerging technology that is network-centric, object-oriented, and based on standards. For the first time we have industrywide, vendor-neutral standards for data formats, code, middleware, and components. This could be as significant as interchangeable parts were to the industrial revolution, or as the integrated circuit was for the electronics industry.

FIGURE 3.2.

A convergence of circumstances that open the way for network computing.

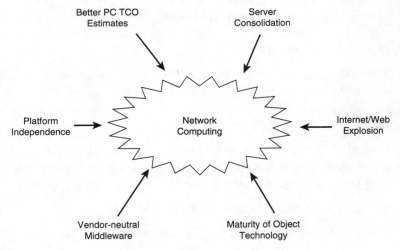

These events signal a major shift that represents a maturing of the information industry, because a new style of computing, called network computing, is emerging.

Network computing represents the best of the last 30 years of computing technology. Some have called it the fourth great wave of computing (see Figure 3.3). Whether this proves true or not, network computing is refreshing, because the industry is addressing the practical needs of the enterprise, rather than simply hyping the latest new technology.

FIGURE 3.3.
Four generations
of computing.

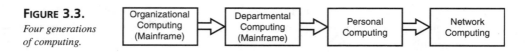

Network computing promises to finally put an end to the struggle between the needs of the enterprise and the needs of the user, and is computing's next big evolutionary step.

The Web Changes Everything

It is amazing to consider the very rapid and wide-scale adoption of the Web. The Web is a great example of the social, cultural, and economic explosion that can take place, given an open standard.

From the Web, users get what they want: information, immediacy, ease-of-use, communications, and collaboration. Enterprises get what they want: a single point of control, low cost, simple administration, easier maintenance, better security, and at least a shot at systems reliability and scalability.

Whole new categories of information and services have been created. Web-enabled office suites now allow easy document publishing. Many businesses are quickly Web-enabling their internal applications. Why? Because everyone has a browser, it is easy to use, and it requires a minimum of hassle.

This underscores a big point: Most people simply need access to information, and they need to communicate. Most people don't need large amounts of personal computational power (except, perhaps, software developers, artists, and scientists); they need better access.

Prior to the Web, the only way for two computers to talk to each other was by prior arrangement. The Web, based on vendor-neutral networking standards, has made it effortless and transparent to fetch data from any location in the world.

Yet the Web is based on relatively simple technology.

Imagine what might happen if program components were as mobile as HTML and as transparent to invoke as Web pages? What if software components could easily collaborate and recombine over the Web to form more complex applications?

This is only the beginning. Vendors of network computing technology are currently integrating new technologies to deploy mission-critical applications to the Web. The future of the Web will be based on plug-and-play mobile components that will enable the next wave of "killer applications."

Pitfalls of PC Computing

Personal computers have many desirable properties, but few would argue that the PC was architected for enterprise computing. The PC was designed for personal productivity; adapting it to become a good network citizen and work in a large organizational environment has been a long and difficult process.

Nevertheless, PCs have become the most common client for client/server architecture, even though they are cumbersome to deal with in large numbers. The number of potential hardware combinations in today's PC is almost unlimited. Plus, all users are essentially free to install and remove both application and operating system software from their PCs. PCs have become like fingerprints: No two are ever the same.

Consequently, 2-tier client/server has had a difficult time becoming the mainframe killer it was predicted to be, because it has run into several limitations of the PC platform. It has become an administrative nightmare and too costly to deploy on a widespread basis. The rapid adoption of the Web as an application platform speaks to this. (I sometimes wonder whether we would find ourselves in this same crisis had X.11 terminals and Motif taken off just a bit faster.)

Even the current state of the art in automated software distribution systems still requires some amount of installation and periodic maintenance at each workstation, a situation that is completely unacceptable to larger organizations with hundreds or thousands of connected users.

Business managers have recently placed much attention on the total cost of ownership (TCO) for desktop computing. The personal computer industry has responded with a raft of initiatives and products designed to try to lower costs by easing the maintenance burden. However, most of these initiatives involve taking some degree of control away from the operator, which has not proven popular with end users, because they don't get anything in return.

But even if users would accept them, managed or locked-down PCs are not enough. In order for users to want to give up control of their personal mainframes, they will have to be provided with a compelling array of services, applications, productivity tools, and personal freedom that is better than what they have today.

To remain competitive, companies must find a way to more quickly build and deploy applications at a lower cost, integrate them with existing systems, and manage them with a smaller staff, handling a much larger base of users with greater security. And, they need to get off the treadmill of constant software upgrades and the continual need for more memory and processor power.

A new architecture for rapidly developing and deploying reliable applications is needed. The computer industry is hard at work on the technologies to make network computing a near-term reality.

Network Centricity and Network Computing

First and foremost, network computing is about standards. Just as plumbers and electricians have developed standard parts, measurements, and construction techniques, so must those who produce computer programs begin to standardize. This is how the information industry, which has become the most important industry in the world, will begin to mature. Object technology and modeling standards, such as the Uniform Modeling Language (UML), will help.

Network computing is about universal access to data. By using standards for data and applications content such as HTML, Java, and XML, it is possible to configure a universal client. This client can be in the form of a variety of hardware devices, including personal computers, graphical terminals, Network Computers, or even mobile personal digital assistants. The client may also function as a terminal to a variety of host types, including UNIX, 3270, and Windows servers.

Network computing is also about universal access to applications. The location at which programs execute should be just as transparent to the end user as the location of a Web page is today. It should be easy to integrate all our business systems so that they can be uniformly accessed from the universal client. Standards for distributed processing and middleware services, such as CORBA, are providing, for the first time, a vendor-neutral way for applications to transparently run anywhere on the network. The choice of server operating system is becoming less relevant as the network becomes a single large computer system (witness the number of new commercial sites that are running versions of Linux and FreeBSD).

Network computing is about network services. The intelligence is in the network rather than all at your desk. High-powered, high-value services are centralized, as are access to massive content and computational power. Personal storage is professionally managed on secure, fast RAID. Powerful, reliable, and secure database servers and enterprise-class applications' platforms guarantee that mission-critical information keeps flowing.

Finally, network computing is about bringing new applications online faster and at lower costs. The buying and selling of companies, acquisitions, mergers, and a high rate of change are the norm. The good news is that standards for component software are rapidly emerging and generating a huge amount of excitement and venture capital in the computer industry. Powerful applications servers will take simple objects such as Enterprise JavaBeans and turn them into reliable, scalable, and robust applications services.

Programmers will not have to constantly reinvent the wheel. And software, or at least common facilities and services, will become plug-and-play, enabling organizations to mix and match best-of-breed components into their information architectures.

The Appeal of Network Computing

For users, network computing promises to relieve the end user from unpleasant tasks such as system configuration, management, backups, installing software, getting everything to work together, and software upgrades. All of this is possible while still providing excellent personal productivity, individuality, and control.

For IT managers, network computing addresses the integration of disparate systems so that a single universal client can access any application or perform any function that is needed. It lowers costs by placing systems management chores in the hands of professional network administrators who can leverage their time and expertise by providing these services for hundreds of users at a time.

For developers, network computing is about rapidly developing and deploying new solutions or new interfaces to existing systems. The technologies lend themselves to rapid prototyping and iterative development. By creating object-oriented components that run on powerful application servers, developers can concentrate on just the functionality needed to solve the business problem at hand, instead of having to constantly reinvent and reimplement infrastructure.

Emerging Technologies

To understand how network computing will achieve all these benefits, you need to know the underlying technology that makes it possible. In this section, you look at briefly the benefits of objects; then you explore Java, CORBA, and Enterprise JavaBeans.

The Benefits of Object Technology

It is assumed that you understand the basics of object technology; however, here is a reminder of some of the benefits that objects bring to a system. All the other technologies covered are object-based, and as such, share in these benefits.

Object technology has been delivering three main benefits to developers and the organizations for which they build applications. Developers of all types, using all sorts of tools on a broad range of projects, have consistently achieved ease of maintenance, ease of extensibility, and reuse:

- **Ease of Maintenance:** Because they are modular, object applications are easier to maintain than procedural applications. There tend to be fewer dependencies between program components. The program logic can be expressed more naturally and in smaller chunks of code. Objects allow for uniform modeling techniques throughout the development life cycle. It's generally easier to isolate problems and test program revisions.

- **Ease of Extensibility:** The property of polymorphism makes object-oriented applications easy to extend. Developers can subclass existing interface definitions to add new object types. Through the use of common design patterns, existing capabilities continue to function. Integration and testing are so much simpler than with procedural applications.

- **Reuse:** Reuse is the most promising benefit of object technology. Developers have been able to reuse small objects, coarsely grained components or business objects, frameworks and templates, and even entire application designs. Objects enable component models that enable developers to implement applications with much less effort.

The bottom line is that object technologies allow larger and more complex systems to be built faster, more flexibly, and more reliably.

Java

Java has many properties that make it an ideal platform for network computing. Let's look at these in detail and do a bit of comparison with C++:

- Java is a fully object-oriented programming language. Java is designed to look like C++, but Java is far simpler to use. Unlike C++, you cannot use Java to write non–object-oriented programs. Features such as automatic garbage collection make it easier and faster to write solid code.

- Java comes with a large set of classes arranged in packages that you can use in your programs. As shown in Figure 3.4, there are classes for creating graphical user interfaces (awt), handling I/O, providing network support (net), accessing a database (sql), and creating reusable components (beans). Java provides a lot of high-level support for networking and distributed objects. It is easy to make your programs network-aware, and the Java Remote Method Invocation (RMI) API enables a Java program to invoke remote Java objects as if they were local.

- Java is an interpreted language. The Java Development Kit (JDK) includes a Java compiler that produces bytecodes for the Java Virtual Machine (JVM) rather than native machine code. To actually run a Java program, you use the Java Runtime Environment (JRE), either standalone or as part of a Web browser such as Netscape.

FIGURE 3.4.

*Components of
the Java platform.*

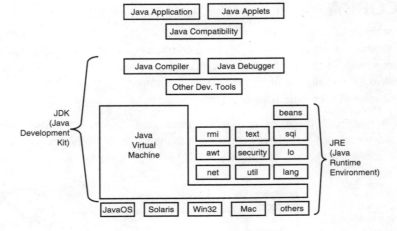

- There are Just-in-Time compilers that boost the runtime performance, and Javasoft's upcoming "Hot-spot" runtime compiler may make interpreted Java as fast as compiled C++.

- The Java bytecodes are architecture-neutral, which allows portability to any system that has a Java runtime. Java also ensures that there are no implementation-dependent aspects of the language specification. This is different from C, where an int type can be 16, 32, or 64 bits, depending on the platform.

- Java is a dynamic language because it has no link phase. Any Java class can be incrementally loaded into a running program and dynamically instantiated at any time. This provides high-performance, incremental loading of programs over a network versus plug-ins and ActiveX. You also can obtain information about a class at runtime using the Reflection API.

- Java is a robust language. It provides built-in support for threads and makes it relatively easy and safe to build high-performance user interfaces and servers. By providing features such as strong-typing, exception handling, and extensive compile-time checking, whole classes of common programming errors are eliminated.

- Java is secure. It assumes the presence of a network. All bytecodes are verified at runtime. Untrusted code is run inside a "sandbox," where it has limited access to the local system resources, such as memory and disk. Java also supports digital signatures based on X.509 certificates.

CORBA

Diversity in hardware and software is a fact of life, and our networked environment is becoming more diverse—not less—as computers evolve. Today, businesses spend a large percentage of their technology budgets trying to integrate different elements of their environment into a total solution. Instead of improving their business processes, the majority of their time is spent on infrastructure.

The problem is that every transaction, messaging, database, or system service had its own proprietary API. Every application that used one of these services had to individually implement the API (see Figure 3.5). This led to a morass of nonintegrated systems.

FIGURE 3.5.

Applications have been hardwired to servers using proprietary APIs.

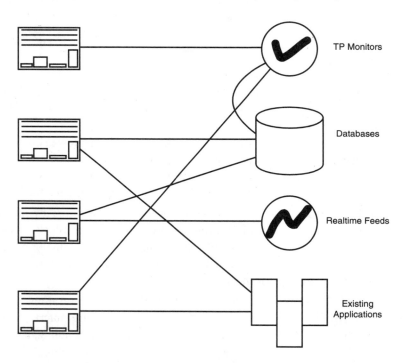

TP Monitors

Databases

Realtime Feeds

Existing Applications

Many good attempts to solve the integration problem have been offered, including remote procedure calls (RPC), message-oriented–middleware (MOM) systems, queuing systems, and TP monitors. However, these products were not able to solve the entire problem, because they were vendor specific, language specific, platform specific, or did not offer enough flexibility.

The Common Object Request Broker Architecture (CORBA) provides an open specification with multivendor support to enable objects and components from various platforms to communicate with one another across networks. CORBA provides platform, vendor, operating system, network, language, and location transparency. It is fully object-oriented and provides for dynamic binding and typing.

The CORBA specification is produced by the Object Management Group (OMG), a consortium of over 1,000 companies, including most of the major vendors of systems and software. The OMG was formed in 1989 as a nonprofit organization to create a component-based software market by accelerating object standards.

An Object Request Broker (ORB) is the heart of the CORBA architecture and provides the transport mechanism between objects. As shown in Figure 3.6, it provides a layer of abstraction that allows all applications access to all services. Client applications are coded to call and use services on the network as if they were local. Applications can also browse a repository of available object implementations and invoke them dynamically.

Client applications and services communicate using Internet Inter-ORB Protocol (IIOP), which runs on top of TCP/IP and is the standard way that CORBA components communicate.

FIGURE 3.6.

A common communications layer allows all applications to access all services.

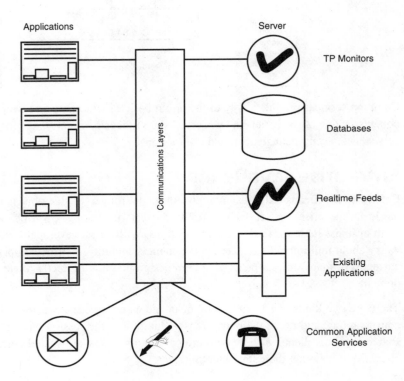

In addition to the ORB and related components, the OMG provides for application objects, common facilities, and common services through its Object Management Architecture (OMA). As shown in Figure 3.7, these higher-level objects and facilities build upon the Object Request Broker foundation and CORBA Services.

FIGURE 3.7.

The Object Management Architecture (OMA).

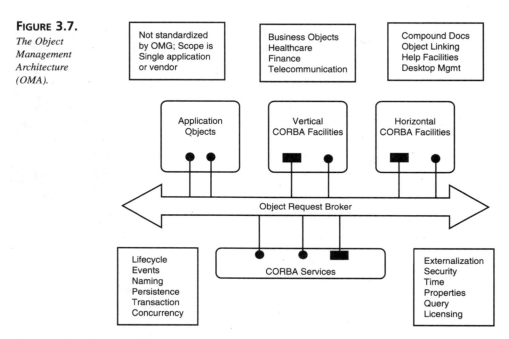

Common services provide a way to factor out basic functionality from application components. A few of the better-known services are lifecycle, security, naming, directory, persistence, event management, and transactions.

Enterprise JavaBeans

Enterprise JavaBeans (EJB) is a component model for server-side objects that is part of the Java Enterprise API set. EJBs simplify the task of creating server objects that implement business logic for thin-client applications. With EJBs, developers don't have to worry about multithreading, state-management, scalability, distributed operations, concurrency, or many other aspects of system design that don't directly relate to the problem domain.

There are two kinds of EJB: a session bean and an entity bean. *Session beans* are conversational and retain their state for the duration of the session only. They are not shared between clients. *Entity beans* are persistent objects, are shared among many clients, and maintain their state indefinitely.

An application server implements an Enterprise JavaBeans container, which provides services to an EJB. As shown in Figure 3.8, those services may include lifecycle support, security, transactions, communications (ORB), resource management, and database access (JDBC).

FIGURE 3.8.
Enterprise JavaBeans architecture.

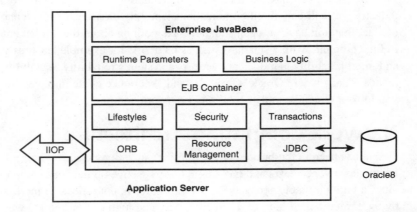

A key benefit of the EJB specification is that existing vendors of network servers can become interoperable and host industry-standard components via the EJB container abstraction. Vendors of transaction monitors, database servers, message queuing systems, security management systems, and other network services can expose their native capabilities simply by implementing an EJB container on top of their existing product.

Enterprise JavaBeans will help build the market for both components and containers, because vendors will compete on functionality rather than by locking out competitors with proprietary APIs. Application servers can differentiate themselves by offering different sets of price points and capabilities in areas such as

- Thread and process management
- Network access
- Transaction management
- Authentication and authorization methods
- Resource pooling
- Concurrency management
- Support for clustered systems
- Support for high availability

3

ORACLE8 NETWORK COMPUTING

An Architecture for Network Computing

The emergence of vendor-neutral enabling technology is a great boon to the computing industry and will benefit all organizations who rely on information technology. However, the fact that you have an open standard says nothing about the implementation quality. Being compliant with a standard such as CORBA, for example, ensures compatibility and interoperability, but does not address a system's reliability, scalability, and performance. That's where Oracle's products and experience come into play. In this section, you look at Oracle's implementation of network computing.

Network Computing Architecture

Oracle has been in the business of helping organizations manage their information assets for the last twenty years and has a unique perspective on network computing. Oracle provides a highly reliable and scalable server platform, but it became increasingly frustrated by the limitations of the PC. The complexity and high cost of the PC was limiting the deployment of client software that could access its servers.

Oracle introduced the concept of network computing in 1996 to address its customers' concerns over administration cost, system reliability, integration, and inexpensive access to data.

Unfortunately, the Network Computer was also introduced at about the same time as network computing, and this has caused quite a large amount of confusion. As you'll see in a later section, the Network Computer is a particular type of client device. It is not a requirement for network computing; rather it is the icing on the network computing cake.

Oracle's Network Computing Architecture is a vision, brand, and product road map for enabling network computing. It does not depend on any particular type of computer or client device. It is based on the vendor-neutral, emerging Internet technologies such as Java, CORBA, and Enterprise JavaBeans that were discussed earlier. It is a way of arranging the technologies in such a way as to be useful for driving product development and helping customers make architecture decisions.

From 2-tier to 3-tier Computing

In the traditional 2-tier client/server model, the client (typically a PC) was responsible for both the user interface, as well as most of the application logic. The 2-tier approach forces a lot of complexity and computations onto the user's desktop and is generally referred to as *fat client*.

NCA is essentially a 3-tier distributed processing architecture defined by open standards and built upon Oracle's server products. The user interface is logically and physically separate from the application logic, which is run on a "middle-tier" application server.

Before you explore each platform, here are a few general attributes of the 3-tier model, shown in Figure 3.9:

- The client can be any device, rather than just a PC. Anything that can, at minimum, render HTML can be a network computing client. The client can even be a mobile device.

- Clients use either HTTP or IIOP (the CORBA standard protocol), rather than a proprietary client/server protocol, depending on whether they require lightweight or session connectivity.

- Application logic is moved to the middle tier. The middle tier can be either a Web server or an application server. The middle tier provides an abstraction layer for data and system services.

- In addition to the RDBMS, existing systems, TP Monitors, messaging systems, and so forth can be incorporated.

FIGURE 3.9.
General NCA architecture.

As NCA is based on component technology; each of the three tiers provides a framework for application-specific components and access to common services and facilities.

As shown in Figure 3.10, application-specific logic is programmed as components, and the runtime infrastructure is supplied by the server platforms. Common services are factored out of each application—they are provided through a common interface for all applications.

Next, we'll discuss each of the three tiers.

Client

The role of the client tier is to render a nice user interface, be responsive, and be easy to learn and easy to use. The ideal client UI would give useful indications and feedback, get updates automatically, save changes when offline, protect the work until it is safe, and be available anywhere.

FIGURE 3.10.
NCA platforms support application components and access to common services.

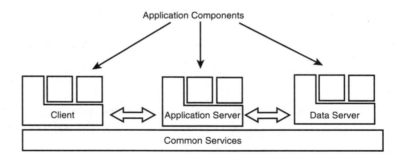

As shown in Figure 3.11, there are various capabilities that may be implemented by any given client device.

FIGURE 3.11.
Capabilities in the client tier.

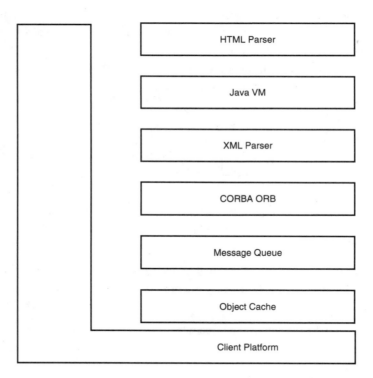

Any device that can render HTML can potentially be a (limited) NCA client. However, to support Oracle's Developer/2000 server or any other 3-tier application, the device will also require the Java Runtime Environment.

Future applications will likely rely on a CORBA ORB for communications and may use XML as a format for data interchange. Today, the Borland/Visigenic ORB is bundled with Netscape Communicator.

For mobile clients, Oracle offers Oracle Lite 3.0, which provides a Java-enabled object database that can be used to cache a user's data. Oracle Lite 3.0 runs in only 350KB of memory and is being ported to several handheld devices. If you can spare another 300KB, Oracle Lite can provide you with a full SQL parser and bidirectional replication with an Oracle8 Enterprise Server.

Oracle also has a 2-tier solution for Java applets that need to connect to the Oracle8 database. The ThinNet8 driver is an implementation of the Java Database Connectivity (JDBC) API that emulates portions of Oracle's Net8 protocol, written entirely in Java. This enables downloaded applets to connect to Oracle8, with no requirement that software be installed on the client.

To improve memory utilization and response time of the server, ThinNet8 applets can connect to the Oracle8 Connection Manager instead of connecting directly to the database. As shown in Figure 3.12, the Oracle8 Connection Manager can multiplex the incoming user connections to the Oracle8 server.

FIGURE 3.12.
Java applets being multiplexed to Oracle8.

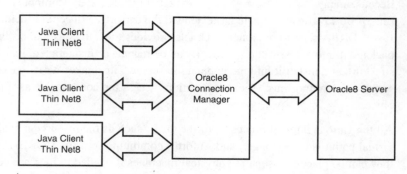

Application Server

The role of the Web/Application Server tier is to run application code and abstract common services. The ideal application server would run application components fast and support lots of users in a safe, secure, and manageable way.

The Oracle Application Server (OAS) is actually two servers in one.

As a Web server, (as shown in the top half of Figure 3.13) it provides all the normal functions, including virtual path management, CGI, and realm-based security. But it goes beyond traditional servers by providing an ORB-based architecture for running Web programs. Any URL that does not request a static page or CGI program is directed to the Web Request Broker (WRB). The WRB manages the startup and shutdown of cartridges that run Web programs written in Java, PL/SQL, C, or Perl. The PL/SQL cartridge is particularly good at dynamically creating Web pages based on data in the database and is very effective for creating simple Web-based applications.

FIGURE 3.13.

Oracle applica-tion server.

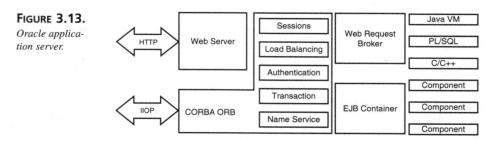

As an application server, (shown in the bottom half of Figure 3.13) OAS provides an industry-standard container for Enterprise JavaBeans and provides access to high-quality implementations of common services such as transactions, naming, security, and so forth.

Because many developers are not yet experts in CORBA and component models such as Enterprise JavaBeans, Oracle has extended the cartridge concept to include support for Java-CORBA server components. Oracle provides tools that take an ordinary Java class, package it into a "cartridge" so that it can be managed (instantiated, load balanced, and so forth), and install it into the application server. This makes it really easy to create new server-side components. Client applications access the components as if they were local objects.

All the various internal processes of the OAS (such as the resource manager, dispatcher, virtual path manager, logger, and so forth) communicate using CORBA. This means that they can be placed on separate physical machines if needed to increase capacity of the server. In this manner it is possible to create "cartridge farms," a machine dedicated to running a particular set of application objects.

Database Server

The role of the Database Server is to provide very fast access to large amounts of data, respond to huge numbers of concurrent requests, never lose anything, keep it secure, and provide powerful development and administrative facilities.

The Oracle8 Server supports access through Oracle's Net8 protocol. It runs the PL/SQL code used by the PL/SQL cartridge and supports data access via SQL.

As of release 8.1, the server also provides a Java Virtual Machine, an EJB execution environment, and a CORBA ORB in the kernel (see Figure 3.14).

FIGURE 3.14.

Services available in the database kernel as of release 8.1.

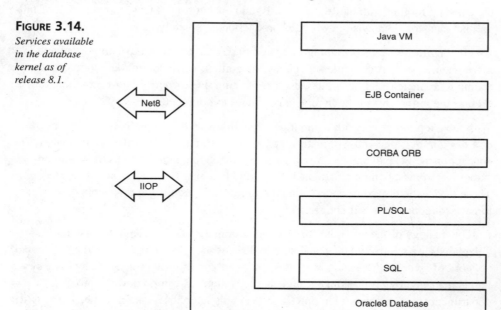

These new services provide many important benefits:

- Stored procedures, triggers, and other application logic can be coded using industry-standard Java in addition to Oracle's PL/SQL. Java classes will be able to call PL/SQL procedures and vice versa.

- The database will directly host EJB components, which will be ideal for Entity beans that maintain persistent state in the database.

- CORBA clients will be able to communicate with the database via IIOP in order to invoke stored procedures or EJB components.

These new Oracle8 capabilities will provide the developer with exciting new architectural options for implementing 2-, 3- and N-tier network computing systems.

The Network Computer

Less than half of our computer operators need personal productivity software in order to carry out their primary work processes. Studies have shown that approximately 40 percent of all installed networked PCs are primarily used as display terminals. The costs of learning, configuring, and maintaining a PC are a nonproductive use of the operator's time and have become a nonproductive cost of doing business for the Enterprise. Beyond the constant fooling with hardware, installs, and backups, the PC is a single point of failure that can stop a knowledge workers' production completely.

And the hardware keeps becoming more complex. PC vendors are packing more and more features such as computer-telephony integration, voice control, and video conferencing to an increasingly overburdened architecture. PC ownership costs continue to rise, even as the initial cost of the hardware continues to plummet.

With the adoption of network computing technology, fewer people will need the power of a desktop machine and will instead opt for smaller, mobile, multifunction devices. The concept of the PC ball and chain will go away as vendors blur the lines between consumer electronics, communications devices, and Personal Digital Assistants (PDAs). These devices will need to be based on a more reliable architecture—people don't want to have to reboot their cell phones.

A good analogy of the potential for Network Computers is the telephone system. Telephones are relatively cheap and simple devices that plug into a vast and complicated network of switches, repeaters, satellites, and who knows what else. The telephone system is managed by professionals, and it is very reliable. I can go down to any local department store, pay about ten dollars for a simple telephone, take it home, and plug it in. It just works. I can call anywhere in the world and use my voice, send data, or send a fax.

A Typical NC

Deployment of Network Computers is one way to reap the benefits of implementing an architecture based on network computing.

A Network Computer typically contains no hard disk, and boots its operating system from a file server via NFS. Once booted, the NC prompts from login information and then displays the user's desktop, as configured by the system administrator.

Typical applications available on the desktop include

- A Java-enabled Web browser
- An email client and news reader
- A contact list, calendar, and task list
- A simple word processor and/or an HTML editor
- Telnet and 3270 emulation
- A file manager for organizing a user's personal files

The NC Reference Specification

The Network Computer Reference Profile was originally released by Oracle, Sun, IBM, Netscape, and Apple in July 1996 and transferred over to an independent standards body, The Open Group, in June 1997 as X/Open Document Number X975.

The specification is hardware-platform–independent, but includes a few minimum requirements, such as a pointing device, input device, sound, and so forth.

The latest version of the specification also includes the following software standards:

- Web support, including HTTP, HTML 4.0, JavaScript, and the following file formats: GIF, JPEG, AU, WAV, and Adobe Portable Document Format (PDF)
- Support for the Java Developer Kit 1.1
- A CORBA ORB with Java bindings
- Support for the Network File System (NFS)
- Network support protocols, including the Simple Network Management Protocol (SNMP) for network management and Dynamic Host Configuration Protocol (DHCP) for automatic network configuration
- VT100 Telnet and TN 3270 for connection to IBM Hosts
- Electronic mail protocols, such as the Simple Mail Transport Protocol (SMTP), Post Office Protocol (POP) version 3, and the Internet Message Access Protocol (IMAP) version 4

Open Issues

The term Network Computer has been coopted by some of the terminal vendors to include devices that act as dumb terminals for 3270, UNIX, or Windows hosts. Although these devices have been selling well as terminal replacements, users are not likely to give up their PCs until we have full-fledged Java-based NCs running compelling distributed application suites.

Unfortunately, the deployment of Java-based NCs has been quite slow as vendors struggle to learn the ins and outs of the new technologies and architectures. Currently, each of the available systems requires a different type of boot server—a situation that the major vendors have promised to resolve.

However, now that Sun is shipping its JavaStation and Lotus has released its eSuite productivity suite written in Java, we can expect other vendors to quickly follow suit.

Summary

In addition to NCA, Oracle is working with the other major players who are behind non-proprietary, network-centric computing, such as IBM, Sun, and Netscape, to create open standards for communications, applications components, and metadata. Creating a standard information infrastructure will make it easy to have a large number of choices in components that can all interoperate—just like buying plumbing fixtures at the local hardware store.

Also, Oracle is committed to providing enterprise class implementations of these emerging technologies. For example, in Oracle 8.1, Oracle intends to provide a relational database server that runs Java within the kernel and provides a container for running Enterprise JavaBeans. It also intends to provide access to all server functionality via CORBA.

The end result of implementing a network computing architecture might be that a company could deploy low cost, easy-to-use, and highly manageable Network Computers.

Oracle8 incorporates many of the features of TP monitors, message-oriented middleware, queuing systems, DataWarehouse engines and now application servers, ORBs and transactions servers. To use Oracle8 only as a repository for data is to waste a powerful resource for your enterprise.

Oracle8 Servers and Options

by Advanced Information Systems, Inc.

IN THIS CHAPTER

CHAPTER 4

So Many Options—So Little Time

It is important to remember that Oracle is just another company selling products. Let's tear away the religious mystique of Oracle as a company coming down from their mountain in Redwood Shores delivering to us the stone tablets of relational databases. Instead, picture Oracle as a large car dealership with colored flags blowing in the wind. On this ever-changing lot, Oracle offers many models and sizes of their relational database for all different types of customers. From the motor scooter to the Mercedes, Oracle has a database just right for you. Their goal, like all companies, is to move merchandise.

This is not to ridicule Oracle, for after all, what does the Oracle database depend on? Well, ultimately, it must exist on some computer hardware. To the degree that computer hardware and architectures vary in the marketplace, likewise Oracle will offer different software configurations, options, and database "models," all tailored to fit the needs of the many customers visiting them with the world's computer hardware strapped to their backs.

To even a greater degree than hardware, Oracle must tailor their products around the needs of the customer. Today, storing a vast amount of data for many users is paramount. Yet maybe in the future, mathematical computation will be more important, or artificially intelligent databases; the Oracle database of the future will look different than Oracle today, because ultimately Oracle's database, like all software, is driven by need.

There are three considerations we must explore to understand the different models we see on the Oracle "lot." These factors are scale, architecture, and utility.

Scale—Bambi Meets Godzilla

The scale or "size" of the hardware, meaning the capacity of the computing power, will help you narrow down which Oracle database you might want to drive off the lot with. For example, if you own a 300MHz Pentium PC and want to use Oracle for a simple small-office operation, you are definitely looking for something different than the customer with the large super-computer running the corporate headquarters.

Architecture—Welcome to the Jungle

The next consideration is architecture. Computer Hardware is simply not measured by the size of the box, the number of boxes you unpack, the power of the CPU, or even the capacity of the hard-drives. Today, computing is characterized by the many complexities regarding how different pieces of hardware are hooked together and how operating systems deal with these complex configurations. Ultimately, this drives what type of Oracle software you are looking for, since Oracle's software must be able to function and prosper as a *guest* installed within these environments.

Utility—Taking Care of Business

The third factor you must consider is utility. How will the database be used? Are you developing software storing a huge amount of data that only a few people will see, or a small amount of data that many people will see? Is the database application only for in-house users, or are you building a Web application? How will Oracle be used in its interface with other software products? These are the questions you need to ask about use and utility which, when answered, determine options and software packages appropriate to purchase with Oracle's database offering.

These three considerations: scale, architecture, and utility, are the basis for understanding Oracle's different offerings and options for its database software. As you review the different options Oracle offers for its Server products, you will be considering these three factors and seeing how they have shaped the different software options for Oracle.

The Oracle8 Server

Every release of a new version of Oracle can be viewed as a response to new computing needs and paradigm shifts within the world of relational databases. The design and business strategy that drove the shape of Oracle8 was also a response to important factors dealing with scale, architecture, and utility. We will discuss the major trends in computing that have shaped the current version of the Oracle database.

The Movement Towards Object-Oriented Paradigms

Oracle8 can be seen as a response to the demand for object relational technology. This simply means that business databases today need to store more sophisticated information in their computers than in the past (see Figure 4.1).

With Oracle8, the customer can store graphics, HTML pages, media objects, and user-defined data types aside from simple dates, characters, and numbers. Although much of this was possible with previous versions of Oracle, with an object relational database, each element is formally defined as a specific class containing objects. In previous versions of Oracle, these complex objects needed to fit into generic data types such as *long* or *raw* variables. With an object relational database, data is specifically defined in the data dictionary of the database.

FIGURE 4.1.

Object relational technology allows for more descriptive, complex data definitions.

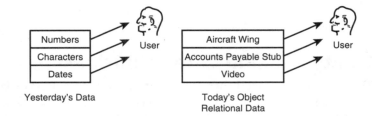

The Growing Complexity of Computer Architecture
==

The Growing Complexity of Computer Architecture

Another phenomena that version 8 of Oracle is responding to is the increasing complexity and sophistication of computer architectures. Today many larger environments are characterized as utilizing *cooperative processing* where operating systems and/or programs run under multiple hardware CPUs.

When either multiple operating systems or applications utilize many hardware CPUs, you enter the advanced architecture of *parallel processing* and/or *clustering*.

The term parallel processing refers to multiple CPUs within a computer or a group of connected computers having the ability to work on the same tasks. Today, these types of architectures are popular and give the computer world a way to replace older *legacy* systems with more powerful machines. In this configuration, multiple CPUs can work on the same problems.

This structure is more like the human mind. How many times have you gone to sleep with a problem on your mind, only to wake up in the morning with a clear solution. All night your brain was taking care of the physical functions of the body, as well as working on your problem. This is an example of parallel processing, just as is the breathing you are doing now as you read this.

In the world of computing, it is no different; it is much easier to work on multiple tasks at once, rather than wait for each task to complete before continuing to the next step of a problem. You can see this readily in the world of SQL, the universal language of relational databases. For instance, the following SQL can be tackled by multiple CPUs faster:

```
Select
sum(sales_price)
from sales
where exists
(
    select
```

```
from
prefered_customer
where prefered_customer.customer_id = sales.customer_id
)
```

This query will give you the sales total for all your preferred customers. It contains a *sub-select*, meaning a second `select` statement within the parenthesis. By assigning multiple CPUs to parse and execute the two `select` statements within the query, the job can be performed faster than a single CPU doing the same work (see Figure 4.2).

FIGURE 4.2.
SQL queries that contain multiple "questions" can be processed simultaneously.

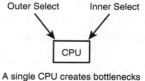

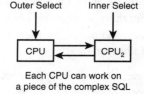

This ability to run parallel queries is vital for any database in today's market, if the database product is to utilize the full capacity of today's multiple CPU architecture.

Aside from parallel queries, a database engine itself, the brain of the database, is better optimized if multiple copies of the database "brain" are each running off of different CPUs. This is a higher-level of parallelism. In Oracle, the "brain" of the database is the *database instance;* by running many database instances on different CPUs, you obviously can yield faster results for the many users of larger systems that are requesting data from the database and demanding the attention of the Oracle RDBMS (see Figure 4.3).

FIGURE 4.3.
Multiple CPUs can handle user requests for data faster.

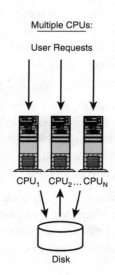

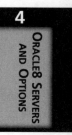

This higher-level form of parallelism introduces you to clustering. In clustering, multiple clones of the operating system are run on more than one machine at a time. In this way, many smaller machines can be clustered together to perform record-breaking results. The operating systems, although separate, can work together to solve problems. One common characteristic of clustering is that these multiple operating systems, when running, share a common portion of disk space. This means that the different copies of the operating system must work together to coordinate things on the disk.

Along with the operating system coordination needed in clustering, a database must exist that can run on all of these separate *nodes* of a cluster just as a standalone database would; but these separate *database instances* need to act as one database, sharing disk space, data, and managing users that are using the database through the many different nodes of the cluster.

Oracle8 has been specifically developed to take advantage of the these complex changes in the world of computer hardware and architecture. The Oracle database has many different options which relate to the types of parallel processing and clustering that the client needs. The degree to which Oracle can utilize this architecture determines how fast the Oracle database will be "rated" on different popular *benchmarks*. Furthermore, for every hardware vendor configuration that Oracle supports, Oracle will have the ability to make sales of software; likewise, for configurations they do not support, they will be unable to sell software. Parallel processing and clustering are life and death issues for Oracle8.

The Proliferation of Internet Business

Obviously the 90s will be remembered for the explosion on the Internet in both personal and business use. Today, millionaires are being made by the selling of wares over the Internet and the World Wide Web. More importantly, with many consumers online, businesses are rushing to find, sell, and support customers who "surf" the Web to buy products and conduct business.

Databases handle the pressing need to interface many users with large amounts of data. As the World Wide Web becomes more popular and useful, more and more users are going to surf to company Web sites to do business. Obviously, handling data and user requests over the Web will necessitate the use of a database, just as does a traditional configuration of data and multiple users (see Figure 4.4).

Oracle8 not only needs to provide the traditional database functions over the Web, but must offer interfaces for third-party or in-house developers to build and customize applications around this new technology. New standards, such as CORBA (Common Object Request Broker Architecture), and new languages, such as Java, are going to be the major Internet building tools of the future. The Oracle8 database must interface with these new standards and allow for easy interface between Web applications and the Oracle8 RDBMS.

FIGURE 4.4.

There is little fundamental difference between a traditional RDBMS and a Web-based RDBMS.

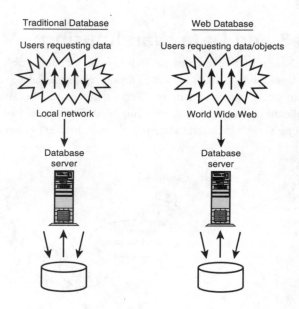

Aside from traditional Internet business, Oracle itself is pushing the new NC (Network Computer) architecture onto the market. With network computers, the intranet becomes the basis for in-house computing. The same standards and technology that exist for the Web application will exist for the intranet, because the network computer is simply a browser requesting information from a server using similar protocols as a computer interfacing over the World Wide Web. This vision of the Network Computer points towards a standard way that all applications are built, be they applications running over the Web or simply in-house applications (see Figure 4.5).

FIGURE 4.5.

With the Network Computer, both Web applications and office intranets can be built using the same standards.

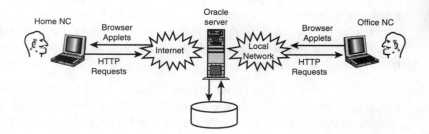

4

ORACLE8 SERVERS AND OPTIONS

One important note, these new forms of applications that run through a user's browser are called *applets*. When you see that name it is simply a computer program or set of programs that need to run on top of browsers and are standardized around browser technology.

Oracle8 and Data Warehousing

As the database world matured in the 1980s, in many companies, data was slowly moved off slower *legacy* systems and moved to newer relational databases. Over time, this led to a problem where corporate data resided in many places, because in many cases, not all legacy applications and databases were migrated. Companies had a difficult time getting the "big picture" with their data scattered all over different computer environments (see Figure 4.6).

FIGURE 4.6.

When data first moved off the mainframe, IS managers were like puppeteers manipulating too many puppets.

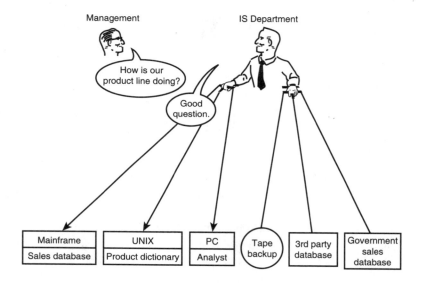

Furthermore, the earlier *open systems* that people moved older applications to were smaller environments than the legacy mainframes. They did not have the storage capacity or the computing architecture to handle huge amounts of data. Today that has changed, so now data is being moved from the mainframe legacy systems to the new UNIX and NT architectures.

This new residence of massive amounts of corporate data has led to the demand for data warehouses. In earlier days, Oracle worked primarily on applications that supported business directly, for instance a sales database and application. Today, Oracle is asked to also store historical data that is collected from day-to-day applications. This is really what a data warehouse is (see Figure 4.7).

FIGURE 4.7.

A data warehouse can store long-term data for the purpose of finding trends.

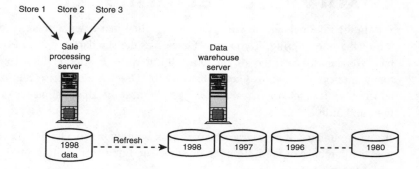

Companies are realizing the value within the piles and piles of their data, which only grows in size. By looking at this data over time, patterns can emerge that give the business person insight into specific parts of their business or overall trends within their industry.

Another new paradigm, that of OLAP (On-Line Analytic Processing) comes to us tightly woven into the new fad of data warehousing. OLAP is a loose standard which dictates strategies and look-and-feel for a tool that gives users and business analysts the ability to look at data as either separate elements or aggregates. With this tool, the mass of data within a data warehouse can make sense to the business analyst.

Oracle offers the Discoverer product, an OLAP tool, with the Oracle8 database. More importantly, within Oracle8 there are low-level methods needed to optimize the sometimes very intensive task of grouping and summarizing huge amounts of data. This enhances Oracle's position as a major player in data warehousing.

Aside from Oracle's Discover product, Oracle8 can handle huge masses of data faster by the use of new methods for storing and retrieving data. Without these new tricks, Oracle's data warehouses would have serious drawbacks and would run too slowly in many cases. When you look at the Enterprise Edition of Oracle8, you will see many of its options tailored toward making access of very large databases more efficient.

4

ORACLE8 SERVERS AND OPTIONS

Oracle8 Enterprise Edition— Luxury and Performance

Within the fictional car-lot where Oracle is selling its software, there is, of course, the top-of-the-line offering. If you view Oracle8 as the standard "Factory Equipped" database you can drive off the lot, the Oracle8 Enterprise Edition is the luxury car, with many comfortable options like leather interior. Oracle's Enterprise Edition is full of added modules and strategies, all designed to meet the changing needs of scale, architecture, and utility.

If you are under-taking a large database task with your new Oracle8 server, I would suggest the purchase of the Enterprise Edition. The Enterprise Edition supports many advanced options your business will need. Many of the trends in computing addressed earlier are handled more thoroughly with this high-end offering by Oracle.

Let's peel back the stickers on the Oracle "lot" and ignore the man riding the elephant to sell you a database. Look instead at the exact differences between Oracle8 and the "luxury" Oracle8 Enterprise Edition. Here are some of the major features of the Oracle8 Enterprise Edition you simply don't get with your standard Oracle8 purchase:

- Enterprise Manager Performance Pack
- Incremental and parallel backups
- Point-in-time tablespaces
- Bit-mapped indexes
- Parallel query
- Parallel DML
- Parallel index scans
- Parallel bit-mapped Star Query joins

Enterprise Manager Performance Pack

This feature, if you chose to drive off the lot with it, is a life-saver. One aspect of Database Administration that drives DBAs crazy is the ability to monitor and tune Oracle. If you printed everything regarding this subject and put it in a pile, you would need oxygen masks to hike to the summit.

With The Enterprise Manager, Oracle simplifies this aspect of database administration using simple GUI tools. With the Performance Pack you have the ability to monitor the many different parameters that affect database performance: disk usage, memory usage, process and lock contention, and SQL performance. All of these hot-points are more easily managed with the Performance Pack. It is true that you can monitor any of these aspects of a database's health without the Enterprise Manager by querying low-level system tables, yet the Performance Pack is simply an easier way to do this.

Aside from this tool, many companies turn to third-party DBA tools. If you have another tool you are comfortable with, don't run out and buy the Enterprise Edition based on this feature alone.

Incremental and Parallel Backups

This is an important feature for a company with a large amount of data, or data that needs to be backed up nightly. With most traditional database backups, when you started the utility to backup the database the procedure would back up large chunks of the data, *regardless of whether or not the data had changed since the last backup*. With an incremental backup, only data changed since the last backup is moved.

The advantage of an incremental backup is that each night, or whenever your backup cycle is, the database only backs up changed data, not all data specified. So for instance, if your users only change 1 percent of the data each night, instead of backing up 1GB of data, you will only need to backup 10MB. This saves space and more importantly time, which is at a premium in many batch cycles that need to run every night, every week, or every month. By only saving data that was changed, you are more efficient in your backups (see Figure 4.8).

FIGURE 4.8.

An incremental backup saves a great deal of space for databases that do not change constantly.

Oracle server

Incremental backup

Traditional backup

Data

Today's changes

4

ORACLE8 SERVERS AND OPTIONS

It is also logical that if you can back up a given set of your database, this task can be done in parallel. That is why Oracle offers the parallel backup with version 8 of its database because it is such a logical area where multiple CPUs can work on the same task together.

This type of backup is critical for large data-warehousing operations. So you see again how *utility*, meaning how databases are used, has driven the evolution to Oracle8.

Point In Time Tablespaces

This allows for a backup to begin at a point in time, the start-point of a backup; any data changed after this is not part of the backup. The great advantage of this method is that tablespaces can remain online for usage when backups are occurring.

Bit-Mapped Indexes

A traditional index sorts data in a column or columns using a *binary tree* to store the ordered sequence of each data value. For instance, if you index on a *unique key*, a traditional *b-tree* (binary tree) index will sort out the values into a *search tree* structure such as is shown in Figure 4.9.

If you assume that a pure binary tree with two branches per node, a huge amount of data can be stored this way so that a search of only a few nodes will find one row out of billions. For instance, if your tree is 32 levels deep in a pure binary tree, you can search 4.4 billion rows with 32 reads.

FIGURE 4.9.

A binary tree 32 levels deep can store a huge amount of index nodes.

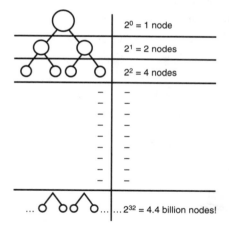

2^0 = 1 node

2^1 = 2 nodes

2^2 = 4 nodes

2^{32} = 4.4 billion nodes!

Of course, real-world indexes are rarely this efficient. Yet without the use of indexes, very little computer business would ever get done.

The problem with these binary indexes is that many times you need to search on a value that is not unique. Consider the simple table `Army`:

Army
Name
Rank
Serial No

For instance, in a military database of the complete army, you have one serial number per soldier. When you search on this column you retrieve only one row. Even if you search by Name, in most cases, you will only receive a few rows. Let's say you wanted to search by rank in this database. You might have 20 ranks for one million people. A binary index like this is "flat" looking and needs to be stored in a huge amount of space without improving the search. Even if you know the rank, you are still sifting through many identical rows of data and a large number of rows will need to be returned.

Rows like Rank are said to have a *low cardinality,* because there is a lower percentage of different values occurring in the data.

Because of the need to search, summarize, and drill-down with many of today's databases, especially in data warehouse OLAP systems where one might want to view trends regarding soldiers based on rank, bit-mapped indexes approach the problem of searching a low cardinality column differently.

All rows are given a numerical value, a set of bits that represent them. With 32 bits you can represent 4.4 billion rows, as you saw earlier. You could store that many rows, using simple 4-bit variables in the C language. Obviously Oracle uses a more complex representation, but the result is that, in small amounts of space, a bit representation of a `row_id` that usually has many *bytes* can save space by a factor greater than 10. At run-time, these bits are converted to `row_ids`. See Figure 4.10.

FIGURE 4.10.

A bit-mapped index saves a great deal of space, yet involves an additional conversion to `row_id`*.*

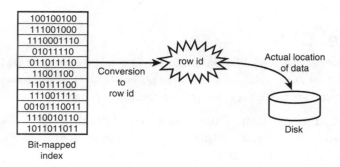

This saves space and file search time for the Oracle database. The only increase in time with bit-mapped indexes is the conversion from bit representation back to `row_ids`.

Creating a bit-mapped index in Oracle8 Enterprise Edition is not a big production; only the will to do so is required and using the new reserved word `bitmap` which appears after the `create` statement in SQL used to create indexes:

```
create bitmap index index_name on table(column);
```

Parallel Query

As mentioned earlier, due to the new hardware architectures that include multiple CPUs, Oracle has felt compelled to offer the ability to split a query over many CPUs to receive a faster result.

Consider a company with employees who are listed in the `employee` table residing in a database. For each sale the company makes, recorded in the `Sale` table, the employee who made the sale is related back to the `employee` table by using the `salesperson_id`:

```
EMPLOYEE              SALE

employee_id      ->      salesperson_id
```

Select all the employees who sold over 100,000 dollars:

```
select employee_id
from employee
where 100000 <
(
    select
    sum(total_sale)
    from
    sale
    where salesperson_id = employee.employee_id
)
```

In this query you can see that if you break up the *inner select* from the *outer select* and allow different CPUs to work on the two different `select` statements, you will gain in response time.

Parallel DML

Like the parallel query, parallel DML refers to parallel processing of DML statements. DML stands for *Data Manipulation Language*. The three DML statements in SQL that are not queries, are the `Update`, `Insert`, and `Delete` statements.

An example of parallel DML would be an update of all salaries for any salesperson who sold over $100,000 of products. Again, you would use the `employee` table and the `sale` table. Give these "smooth talkers" a $1000 raise:

```
update employee
```

```
set salary = salary + 1000
where 100000 <=
(
    select
    sum(total_sale)
    from
    sale
    where salesperson_id = employee.employee_id
)
```

In this query you again can see that having a separate CPU work on the inner `select` statement and another CPU working on the actual update, the parallel option will save you time.

Even with a simpler update, Oracle needs not only to update the column you specify, but if the column is indexed, Oracle will need to update the index, write all this information to the redo logs, and move the old data to the rollback segments. This processing can be more readily accomplished with multiple CPUs (see Figure 4.11).

FIGURE 4.11.
Multiple CPUs can make the tasks of updating an Oracle database easier.

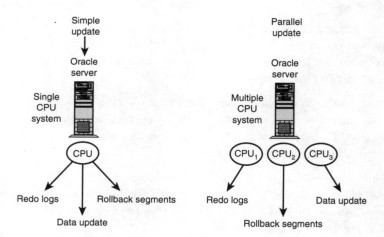

Parallel Index Scans

Oracle8 Enterprise Edition allows multiple CPUs to scan index pages together. An index page is usually a 2KB block that contains the value you are indexing and the `row_id`, meaning the location, of that row on disk. By offering the ability to scan many pages at once with different CPUs, Oracle speeds up the process of browsing the nodes of an index b-tree.

Parallel Bit-Mapped Star Query Joins

A star query is a way of creating a data cube for an OLAP database. Instead of aggregating values at run-time, the data cube keeps these running totals at all times in a cube. Since a relational database deals with tables and not cubes, a *star schema* is simply a tabular representation of a data cube containing aggregate values.

To be able to scan the many combinations and aggregations of this data cube in parallel is another example of how Oracle intends to take the lead in OLAP processing, thus enhancing its position in the world of data warehousing.

Oracle Lite—Tastes Great, Less Calories

Personal Oracle is a strange name for the single-user, PC version of Oracle. The marketing manager who thought this one up must have come from a soft drink company.

In the fictional Oracle car lot, Personal Oracle is the cute little economy car. The car you buy your kid on his or her 16th birthday. Yet to view Personal Oracle in only this way is misleading, for the greatest value this product has is probably not for the small user, but for the largest Oracle shops.

The reason for this is simply that a large Oracle shop is probably doing a great deal of development, testing, and training. With this product, developers can move off the expensive powerful hardware that runs their business applications and work on their own PCs using Personal Oracle.

In traditional environments, large machines were often shared by developers and business end-users. Oracle was often configured with a *production instance* and a *development instance*. The problem with this was that developers tend to be very rough with whatever CPU they are using.

With Personal Oracle, your production machine can remain free from the ravages of developers. Development can occur on PC machines that are less expensive and totally separate from the production environment. This keeps the production machines running faster and free from the junk that development tends to generate.

The beauty of Personal Oracle, as has been the case with Oracle for many years, is the salability of development. A user can write PL/SQL, embedded C, Java, SQL reports, front-end interfaces and have them seamlessly port upwards from the PC to the mainframe or super-computer. This allows the "garage developer" to build a sophisticated Oracle application without the need to bring in a computer on a forklift.

Personal Oracle, allows development and testing to occur on inexpensive PC machines, usually Windows 95 or NT environments. From here, code can be moved "up" to larger machines for testing and finally production.

Personal Oracle makes Oracle an "Enterprise" solution because data can be moved up from this product to larger Oracle8 databases using the Enterprise Edition (see Figure 4.12).

FIGURE 4.12.

By allowing developers to work on PCs, code can be physically moved to insure accountability in the QA process.

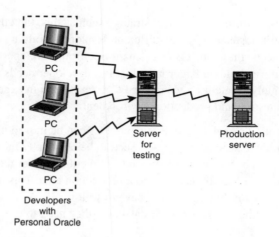

Personal Oracle is also a great way to train developers and testers in using the various aspects of the Oracle product line they need to know. I suspect many of you who are reading this now are programmers, Oracle gurus, and DBAs who all want to learn more about Oracle to enhance your careers.

Well aside from browsing material like this, which, granted, is probably less expensive than a prescription of sleeping pills, all of you Oracle devotees should spend some time with Personal Oracle. If you can write the triggers, procedures, and SQL on Personal Oracle, you can do it on any Oracle platform.

Oracle offers many programs for developers who want to learn more about its products and eventually master them. Personal Oracle can be obtained for a few hundred dollars by joining the Oracle Technology Network, formally known as the Oracle Developer Programme.

Aside from the brave individuals who want to learn Oracle, large companies should consider Personal Oracle as a training tool for both developers and end-users. Why should anyone train people on their most expensive hardware that is used for production or critical development when the same training can be done on a PC?

4

ORACLE8 SERVERS AND OPTIONS

By training users on Personal Oracle, and by allowing developers to work on these separate Oracle environments, a company will also save the development headache of needing DBAs to support development and training. DBAs waste a great deal of time in political struggles with developers, and as being general "den mothers" for chaotic development machines, when they should be concentrating on optimizing business-critical production applications. Oracle Lite can save you a great deal of money in this type of waste.

By employing a multi-platform development strategy such as this, the quality assurance process will also benefit. Instead of having different developers building critical tables and other database objects, these objects can remain free from developer's whims and be built with a single uniform style on larger machine. If a developer needs a table to test with, he or she can simply create it on his or her PC. Later, a design expert can recreate the necessary table in testing and production environment.

Code that may be chaotic on each of the developers PCs can be moved up the hardware chain for testing on a stable schema. Code will need to be physically moved for acceptance. This decreases the chances that at any point in time throughout the development life-cycle, untested code will sneak its way into a production area. This also makes better use of developers' time. With this they do not have to wait for DBAs to work on modifying databases and giving them passwords for databases they need to use in development of their software.

Operating System Wars—UNIX Versus NT

Right now, even if you have mastered the concepts in this chapter and understand the evolution of the Oracle RDBMS, you, like I, are still deep in "no man's land" as the UNIX versus NT operating system war rages on. You may not know it, but shells are exploding all around us that may shape the future landscape of database computing.

Microsoft NT and How It Compares to UNIX

Microsoft's NT, at first, was a way to defeat Novell and the small office networks Novell could offer. Soon it became apparent that the modular design of this operating system could be scaled to much larger hardware. Today companies, such as Unisys, are offering machines that run hundreds of CPUs and store terabytes of data, all clustered around the NT operating system.

The attraction to NT is that it is simpler for most people to use. The look and feel is not like the 70s command-line style of UNIX, but a GUI interface modeled after Windows

95. It also is designed with networking and Web-addressing concepts in place, not as extensions as with UNIX.

The disadvantages NT has versus UNIX are the following:

- NT is owned, controlled, produced, and managed by one company, Microsoft; many companies maintain their own flavors of UNIX. This makes your NT effort very dependent on the whims of Microsoft.

- 64-bit UNIX, for instance, is simply faster when running intensive database operations. With NT, the RDBMS and the System Administrator cannot really manage things at quite as low a level with NT (raw disks for instance). With UNIX, more low-level control is possible, thus allowing for better performance.

- UNIX also comes with powerful GUI interfaces, such as HP's SAM utility. A UNIX server can be managed through these tools with no need to memorize strange commands designed by some people in Bell Labs 30 years ago.

- UNIX allows the purchaser to modify the "kernel," meaning the UNIX operating system itself. NT is a black-box that is much harder to customize.

The advantages NT has over UNIX are the following:

- Many hardware vendors are focusing their hardware for NT now. If you have found the perfect piece of hardware for your server, don't shy away from it just because it is running on NT.

- Because most client machines are Windows 3.1 or Windows 95 workstations, it is obviously easier to hook Microsoft-to-Microsoft client/server configurations together than UNIX-to-Microsoft. This uniformity makes the network connections more seamless since you are dealing with one standard interface. This advantage is small, though, because both OSs use TCP/IP as their network protocol.

- UNIX is more hybrid. By accepting the freedom of many UNIX vendors, you are opening up the chances of small differences between different flavors of UNIX that might in some way either affect software you are writing for more than one UNIX machine, or even software you are purchasing. NT is a marriage to Microsoft, but it does give you uniformity, since there is only one NT.

- The time to train an NT Administrator is less than the time to train the UNIX System Administrator. This is because UNIX gives you much more control over the operating system and, therefore, the low-level architecture of UNIX must be more fully understood than the architecture of NT, which for the most part, is unalterable by the Administrator. This difference, of course, can be minimized by a GUI tool that a hardware vendor provides with their flavor of UNIX.

I hope this sheds no light on the battle between UNIX and NT, because the dawn has not broken on the battlefield. These points are only offered as considerations for you to keep in mind as the war goes on. I am sure this short analysis would get us both shot if we were to venture into one of the warring camps. It is important to focus not on the war but on your application and system needs which will be served by the different OS choices. Ask yourself: How will these different OSs benefit me, given scale, architecture, and utility? Don't be afraid to ask your hardware vendor for testimonials of others who have already purchased their OS in this glorious battle.

Summary

Yes we should de-mystify the purchase of a database…these tools are driven by your needs and by the type of hardware you have purchased. Never plan your IS strategy around a database, find one that will fit into your existing plans.

Remember your constraints are scale, architecture, and utility. If you understand the scale, the size and power needs of your database, if you have a fixed type of architecture, and if know how your database will be most commonly used, you can steer clear of all but the necessary options that Oracle offers with its RDBMS.

Fortunately Oracle has addressed the computing needs that face us as we move into the 21st Century. The trends that were discussed and how Oracle addresses them, show us that Oracle is ready to support systems that we not only need but will need in the coming years.

Installation, Upgrade, and Migration

PART

II

Implementation Planning—PC to Enterprise Server

by Advanced Information Systems, Inc.

IN THIS CHAPTER

CHAPTER 5

Often one of the biggest challenges related to an Oracle database is the installation of the database management system software. Under some operating systems, such as Windows NT, this process is relatively easy. There is a defined standard for binary files and it is merely a process of copying software and updating the Registry. However, under other operating systems it can be a challenge. The Oracle software needs to be linked with object code from the operating system and with itself. This can be a complicated process that requires operating system setups, correct paths, and a bit of effort.

This chapter is devoted to providing some advice on how to plan for an Oracle installation. Its goal is to minimize the headaches associated with the installation process. In my experience, a disciplined approach in which you carefully sketch out your plan and then test it is best. I will go over the various planning steps to consider when you are laying out your new system. Chapter 6, "Installation and Upgrades" will cover the actual installation and upgrade process.

Overview of the Installation Planning Process

One of Oracle's strengths is that it works on platforms ranging from PCs to mainframes. There are a variety of operating systems that are supported. Each of these operating systems has certain standards that it enforces when it comes to installations. By far, one of the easiest Oracle installations is the one for Windows NT (Intel). Here you are guaranteed to have a graphical user interface and a standard operating system API (Win32). You go through a simple wizard interface, answer a few questions, copy some files, update the Registry, and you are off and running.

Not all of the installations of the Oracle database management system have these advantages. For example, while most modern UNIX systems support a graphical user interface (usually X Window/Motif based), most of their installations do not have graphical consoles. The users access the operating system through a character-based interface such as a telnet session. Also, the UNIX operating system is a bit of a collage. It is a collection of a number of programs written by different authors. You have a choice as to what you install and often get to choose where you put it. This makes the task of the Oracle installation script developers quite challenging. They have to deal with operating systems that have more variations. There have been only three versions of the Windows NT operating system that were really serious database platforms. However, most UNIX operating systems are updated frequently. They also contain a number of patches to their core components, some of which are required for Oracle to function properly.

I could go on for quite some time, but I think that you get the key points. Oracle installations can be a bit tricky. The process also varies between the various operating systems that Oracle supports. Finally, the installation process continues to be worked on by Oracle developers. You will follow a slightly different series of steps between various release levels of Oracle.

Starting with Business Needs

Determining the needs of a business is a simple concept. The users and developers tell you what they want and you can implement it. The problems arise when the users describe things in general terms and you are the one left to determine the details. Here are some specific details that you need to have as a DBA before you can construct a sound installation plan:

- The supporting tools that will be used for application development or operation
- The rough size of the database and any logical groupings of tables
- A feel for the daily processing cycle
- The expected data traffic patterns for the various tables
- If you are not acting as system administrator, a feel for the disk drives and tape drives that you will be allocated
- User requirements for data backup, recovery, and reliability

Tools

The first requirement you should be provided with is a list of the tools that are required to support the database itself. Oracle provides a number of options for development. There are the Forms and Reports generators provided by Oracle and third-party vendors. There are also a number of precompilers that are available as part of the Oracle environment (Pro*C, Pro*COBOL, and so forth). These types of products are relatively simple to integrate. They usually involve merely loading them from the distribution media and linking them with the database as part of the installation process.

If you are using a third-party development tool, you should check its requirements for interfacing with the Oracle database. There may be options required or specific version levels of products that you need to install. The vendor may also require table space or dedicated memory processes to be operational and you need to plan for these items. This process is no more difficult than the one that you use for the Oracle-supplied products. You just need to remember to add this during your planning process so that you do not have to come back later and reconfigure your system. As always, make sure that the products will work with one another (especially the operating system and Oracle release).

Sizing

Next on your list of data to collect before planning the instance is a rough estimate for the tables that the users or developers want to create. It is also important to determine whether there are any logical groupings of tables (base data tables, frequently used lookup tables, and so forth). This affects the tablespaces that you design and how you split tables between disk drives to level input/output loads. It also helps you determine the size of supporting tablespaces, such as `temp` and `rbs`.

Traffic Patterns

Another important factor when laying out data is an understanding of the expected data traffic patterns for the tables. You may want to locate tables that have heavy usage on different disk drives. If you have a small number of tables that receive extremely high data traffic, you may want to consider disk striping, multiple database writers, and the parallel query option when laying out your plans.

Daily Processing Cycle

You should also be provided with a feel for the daily processing cycle of the application. This is important when you decide whether to use archive logging. For data warehouses wherein data updates occur in a single large batch at night, it is possible to perform cold backups just after the batch upload and not use archive logging. On heavy transaction processing applications, you need to use archive logging to be able to recover all the transactions made during the day. If all the activity is concentrated during specific periods during the day, you might need to consider options such as parallel query and multiple database writer processes.

Map System Resources

Because your task is to map user requirements to the Oracle software and available system resources, you need to know what those system resources are. If you are also the system administrator for the server, you can map this out for yourself. If you are not, you need to coordinate with the system administrator to determine the following:

- The memory that will be available for Oracle and Oracle user processes. In most database servers, you can use all the system memory except that used by the operating system. However, there are other applications that have memory-resident components, so you should check to see whether you are competing with anything else. This can vary from as little as 16 megabytes to well over a gigabyte.

- The tape drives available and whether any of them can be dedicated to Oracle uses such as archive logging. Some systems have tape drives that are available only to operators and therefore cannot be used by the DBA for routine tasks.

- You need to know which disk drives are available, how large they are, and what options are available to you for RAID storage, disk striping, disk mirroring, and so forth.

Backup, Recovery, and Reliability

Finally, it is important to get confirmation from the users as to what their requirements are for backup, recovery, and reliability. Specifically, if ultrahigh availability is desired and the users are willing to pay for it, you can mirror the disk drives so that if one drive fails, you can still access data from the other drive. Some development installations are cost-conscious and some developers are willing to live without disk mirroring or disk space for archive logging in return for lower system costs. The key from the DBA point of view is to document the requirements, get everyone to buy into them, and then construct a database that meets these requirements.

The Installation Documentation

The basic installation instructions for the Oracle software products are contained in the Installation and Configuration Guide. This document is specific to the operating system and Oracle product release level with which you are working. Never assume that you can follow the same instructions for installing Oracle 8.1 on an IBM RS/6000 that you used to install Oracle8 on an HP H50. This is almost guaranteed to fail. Both Oracle and the operating system are constantly changing.

The exact contents of this manual vary somewhat with each release and with each specific operating system, but the layout is similar to the following:

- Overview of the installation process
- Requirements for loading the various products on the system
- Issues and restrictions related to this specific implementation of the Oracle products
- A section on planning for the installation process
- Preinstallation tasks for the database and other Oracle products
- Installation of the database and products
- Post-installation tasks for the Oracle database and other products
- Overview of the upgrade and migration process
- Upgrade procedures
- Information to supplement the standard product documentation that Oracle ships with all operating systems
- Additional information on upgrading the Oracle tools

The overview section presents a very brief discussion of how to lay out your Oracle database and tools. It presents the standard layout that Oracle recommends for disk files. It also presents some of the issues that you will run across. Finally, it discusses the components of the Oracle server, which may vary as new releases of the product come out, so it is not a waste of time to spend a half hour reading this section.

The requirements section is very important when installing the software for the first time. Sometimes I wish that they shipped this section to you when you are planning your purchase. Unfortunately, you usually get the Installation and Configuration Guide when the software arrives and everyone is breathing down your neck to have the database ready by that afternoon. This section offers a number of tables that you can copy and fill in to determine the amount of disk and memory space required by the products and the number of users that you are expecting. It also has a list of requirements for each of the products that you should validate before you begin the installation process.

The next section is also important. It provides you with the issues and restrictions that are applicable to your particular release of Oracle and your operating system. The available capacity for such parameters as maximum number of extents in a table vary with the operating system that you are using. This is all internals stuff that the Oracle developers have to decide on when they are performing the port of the Oracle software to your operating system. You do not have a vote in the matter; you merely have to note what these restrictions are and live with them. You get to control how you set up your parameters, up to the limits imposed by the developers for your operating system.

Preinstallation activities involve the system administrator who needs to set up accounts, groups, and directories that you can use during the installation. There are several permission grants that only the system administrator can perform because Oracle tries to do things with memory areas and file permissions that are typically restricted to the operating system utilities. This is part of the price that has to be paid to get improved performance. These activities are important and should be added to your plan when you prepare it.

The actual installation chapters deal with the tasks that you will perform on the day of installation. There are separate chapters for the RDBMS products and the development tools, CASE products, and so forth. This makes good sense because you do not have to install the development products on the server in environments such as client/server. Also, you can have installations wherein the development tools may be linked to a database on another server via Net/8. I have always found the RDBMS installation to be more challenging, with the other products usually linking into the environment.

You also have to perform some post-installation tasks on your new software. This includes tasks such as editing the initialization and oratab files (under UNIX) and tuning your new instance as needed for your particular environment. You have to set up your user accounts to access the Oracle software (setting environmental variables and placing the Oracle executable directory in the search path). Finally, there is a script that has to be run by the operating system administrator to set some final permissions and turn control over to the Oracle user.

The next chapters that are interesting to DBAs performing new software installations are those that contain additional information on the use of Oracle with this operating system (you get to skip the chapters on upgrades until later in this book). The restrictions chapter is designed to show limits for parameters that are operating system-specific, such as the number of files. These chapters provide the details of how Oracle is implemented under your specific operating system. Contents normally include such items as performance tuning and disk configuration.

Finally, there are a number of appendixes that are contained in this book that provide more detailed information about the installer software, troubleshooting, and multilingual options. I tend to read these sections only when I run into a problem. However, these sections may be of interest to you, especially if you are not using American English, which is the default that I have always used.

The installation manuals are not fancy, glossy, and bound like most of the Oracle documentation (they are often printed and bound with binding tape), and they go to press well before the software is actually ready for shipping. I have found a number of important changes that are referenced only in the README file. So *always* read the README file after it has been off-loaded from tape. Of course, if you have a CD-ROM drive, you can read the README file before you do the installation—which is even better.

The Installation Manual is essential reading both for planning and performing the installation. I have to warn you that this discussion is based on the installation processes that I have seen using versions of Oracle up through 8.0. There is always the chance that Oracle will completely revise its installation processes and documentation just to put experienced DBAs on a level playing field with beginners. Figure 5.1 depicts the installation process.

The README File

The stated purpose of the README file is to show the differences between the actual release of the Oracle RDBMS and related products (SQL*Plus, Server Manager, Import, Export, SQL*Loader, and PL/SQL) and the documentation. This documentation has been prepared well in advance of the product release to provide time for the printers and editors to review the material. Although the main features of a given release are fixed early in the development cycle (for example, table partitioning in Oracle8), many of the other features wait until fairly late in the product cycle. Many bugs are fixed after the main coding is done on the software. The README file is the only way you know what has been done since the installation manuals were sent to press.

FIGURE 5.1.

Oracle new installation process overview.

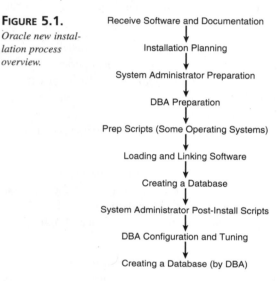

Receive Software and Documentation
↓
Installation Planning
↓
System Administrator Preparation
↓
DBA Preparation
↓
Prep Scripts (Some Operating Systems)
↓
Loading and Linking Software
↓
Creating a Database
↓
System Administrator Post-Install Scripts
↓
DBA Configuration and Tuning
↓
Creating a Database (by DBA)

The README file is also the best reference for the list of bugs fixed in the product and any final restrictions that were placed on this product since the manuals were published. The table of contents for this README file usually looks something like the following:

- A list of documentation available
- Forward- and backward-compatibility notes
- Changes made to the Oracle server
- Upgrading and downgrading notes
- A list of bug fixes and enhancements in this release
- Known server restrictions
- Additional detail on topics that are pertinent to this release and platform

Developing Your Own Installation Plan

In one of my previous careers, I drove submarines. In this environment, life was run by a series of written procedures and checklists. (This was a good idea because you really do not want someone to "wing it" when starting up a nuclear reactor.) There even was a written and posted procedure for flushing a toilet. You may think this to be a bit ridiculous, but submariners are quite sensitive about any system that is connected to the sea, especially when you are down deep in the ocean. Anyway, this part of my life taught me to love checklists and plans.

I do not use lists for such routine functions as adding a user to the Oracle database—I use scripts that I have developed to automate this task. These scripts are written to set up default tablespaces and so forth, for me. However, because installing or upgrading the database is such a significant evolution and is known to have some problems, I am pretty religious about writing lists and plans. Many of the new DBAs that I have worked with (even the ones that were not in submarines) have commented that they like these checklists and plans. You should consider them for the following reasons:

- Physically, they are easier to read from than a bound book that won't lie flat.

- You have to execute steps from several different sections of the book, in just the right order, to complete the evolution. It is easier to sequence these steps first and execute them from a single list.

- The written procedure that you have checked off when you complete steps is useful when discussing any problems that come up with Oracle support.

- If you record start and stop times (along with any notes that you feel are important) on the plan, you can use it for future reference. It comes in handy when you load another system, create another instance, or just estimate the time it will take to complete this task in the future. In some organizations, it may also come in handy when preparing a time sheet.

When I prepare my checklists and plans, I always try to make a list that is "good enough." I have no desire to write a long-winded work that reproduces every word in the Installation and Configuration Guide. I also eliminate steps that are not applicable to this particular installation. They usually relate to steps in the Installation and Configuration Guide that begin with something like, "If you are installing the distributed option,...." Finally, I always include the specifics of the directories that I plan to use, tablespace names, sizes, and so forth. I do not like to trust my memory or have to reference a number of sizing calculations when I am actually in the heat of battle. You have to find a style that you are comfortable with (bullets, numbered steps, little detail, lots of detail). Figure 5.2 shows part of an installation plan.

The Oracle installation procedures and requirements change from release to release and platform to platform. *Please* read the installation instructions that are specific to the version of Oracle you are installing and make up your own checklist. You may want to go into more or less detail, depending on your comfort level with the installation process.

FIGURE 5.2.

Sample installa-tions.

6.   Initial Oracle Instance Configuration Options

 a.   Disk drive configurations:

/usr/oracle	Oracle base application directory
/usr/oracle/product	Oracle home directory
/usr/oracle/product/7013	Install point for this release
/d1/oracle/devel	Development instance directory
/d2/oracle/devel	Development instance directory
/d3/oracle/devel/redo	Storage for online redo logs
/d3/oracle/devel/archive	Storage for archive logs
/d4	Future use
/d5	Future use

7.   Preparation Tasks

 a.   HP admin create dba group.

 b.   HP admin create database administrator logins within dba group.

 c.   HP admin create oracle owner account in dba group.

 d.   HP admin create oracle user logins. Note, some thought needs to go in to how the regular user groups will be arranged. There is no need to worry about users who will access only via client-server. This applies to developers and others who will log in to the server.

 e.   HP admin create files in figure 2-3 on page 2-9.

 f.   HP admin alter the Unix kernel parameters as follows:

SHMMAX	0X4000000	{4 million}
SHMMNI100		
SHMSEG12		
SEMMNS	128	
SHMMNI10		

 g.   Root user create all mount point directories (/d1, /d2, etc).

 h.   Root user create the directories listed in 6a above with owner oracle and mode 755.

 i.   User oracle set ORACLE_BASE environment variable.

 j.   Create the following subdirectories in ORACLE_BASE:
 - product
 - admin
 - data
 - local
 - TAR

 k.   Create version 7013 subdirectory under ORACLE_BASE/product.

 l.   Set ORACLE_HOME environmental variable to ORACLE_BASE/product/7013.

Some Good Reviewers

After going through the Installation Manual and making a wonderful plan of the installa-tion process that you will be using on your new database, get a second opinion. I usually route the checklists that I prepare to several individuals who can provide me with useful comments. The following people may be able to help you in preparing the ultimate plan:

- *The operating system administrator.* Look for comments in the area of disk and memory utilization.

- *The application developers and lead users.* They can provide a good feel for the number of concurrent users, tools that will be used, and so forth.

- *Your management.* It never hurts to have them look at the plan before you imple-ment it. That way they are less critical when problems arise.

- *Other DBAs.* It is helpful to have one or more Oracle DBA in your area to serve as a sounding board, a fresh set of eyes, or the voice of experience.

System Hardware

Hopefully you were given the chance to complete the configuration analysis discussed previously before the final hardware configuration was established for your new database server. However, if the box were purchased long before the Oracle software and documentation arrived, you would not be the first person who had to try to make do with a system that was not optimized for the Oracle database envisioned for it. However, if you do have the option, I would like to present you with a few considerations:

- Oracle runs on a number of platforms; however, the support for some platforms is better than the support for others. If you are trying to implement a mission critical system or large system, you will probably be very interested in having the latest updates to the Oracle database management system. Hence, you may want to stick to a tier-one platform (Sun, HPUX, AIX, Windows NT, and the other platforms Oracle develops and releases its products on first). There are some platforms that are supported (for example, Data General UNIX), but may not have all of the additional products that you desire or that are several revisions behind the others.

- Consider some form of disk mirroring or RAID (redundant array of inexpensive disks). While Oracle provides facilities to recover from a failed disk drive, it is much better for production if you can keep going while the technicians are on their way to fix the problem. Disk prices are relatively low and this is a good use of funds for important production systems.

- Be conservative on your memory estimates (get a little more than you need). Memory is also relatively inexpensive these days and with Oracle, memory is speed. You may find that you need to increase some of the memory areas over your calculations as the database grows in popularity. If you do not want to buy the memory at the start, at least make sure the computer memory can be easily expanded.

Software Module Planning

Another checklist that you will work through as part of your installation planning is building the list of software options that you want to install. Depending on what you purchase, you may be licensed for several of the optional modules that make up the Oracle database. What I wanted to stress here is that you include these modules as part of your plan when determining the disk and memory space required on your system. Some of these modules (that is, those involved with video) can also provide performance stresses on lesser computer systems (disk transfer, network transfer, and CPU), so be sure that you have done your homework to ensure that your system is up to the tasks. How? My favorite method is to ask the salesman for test results or references of similar customers. It is worth the time talking to a few people before you try to implement an impossible solution.

Optimal Flexible Architecture (OFA)

When I installed my first Oracle version 6 database, the documentation told me that I needed places to put my software and data. It did not provide any real, clear guidance as to how to arrange my files in a manner that would promote growth in data and software upgrades. Many people installed their systems only to realize that they had to do a lot of rearranging when it was time to grow. To address this problem, the folks at Oracle's consulting arm got together and came up with the Optimal Flexible Architecture (OFA). Recall that it is a recommended architecture for locating information on disks. Figure 5.3 illustrates the portions of this architecture that are applicable to Oracle installations.

FIGURE 5.3.

Oracle's Optimal Flexible Architecture (OFA).

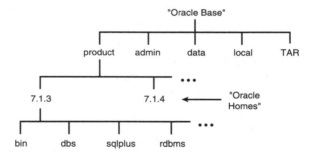

With OFA, you allocate a directory that is referred to as the ORACLE HOME (in UNIX, it is stored as the environmental variable ORACLE_HOME). This directory is placed somewhere in the array of disks that matches your other goals. Some versions of the Oracle installation guides recommend placing it under the user home directories. Later versions, however, place it on an applications disk drive that your system administrator allocates for you.

> **NOTE**
>
> I strongly agree with the idea of using a separate applications disk, because newer releases of the software consume a great deal of disk space and user home data disks are notorious for filling up rapidly. This causes problems when Oracle needs to write an error log file and finds that the disk is full because Charlie insists on keeping 25 versions of all software that he writes.

The other key directory shown in Figure 5.3 is the ORACLE_BASE directory. This directory serves as a gathering point under which you can store multiple versions of the Oracle software. For example, you may be running on version 8.0.1, but want to try out the 8.0.4 software. Having multiple Oracle homes enables you to test the new 8.0.4 software on a test database while keeping the production database running on the 8.0.1 software.

The next issue when you are planning where to put the software is how much space to allocate for this purpose. There is no magic number. As part of the exercise in the next section, you learn how to figure the amount of disk space for the Oracle software based on which products you are loading. Remember, Oracle makes a wide range of software. It is too difficult to make tapes for each customer based on what that customer orders, so Oracle ships in a few different bundles. This usually means that you get far more software on your distribution tape or CD-ROM than you need for your work. Therefore, you must go through and determine the software packages that you will be using and allocate space for them on the software disk, in the database itself (for support tables and so forth) and in memory.

I always plan on having at least two full releases of the Oracle software on my system when I am performing the sizing exercise. Obviously, I do not want to maintain two versions routinely, and I like to have all databases (production and development) using the same version to make things run more smoothly. However, when Oracle ships out a new version of the database, I always like to run a thorough test against a test or development instance before I try it out on the production databases. I also like to test it against each of the test instances, if there is more than one, because different applications can run into different problems with a new release of supporting software, such as the RDBMS. Of course, if you have far more nerve than I do, you can just let this new, untested software fly on your most important, mission-critical production database. One final note: Leave yourself at least a 10 or 20 percent margin for error when sizing the disk space for your software. The software has grown in size since I have worked with it, so this space helps accommodate your next version. You also may find out that you need additional components (for example, SQL*Net) as your applications and user needs change over time.

Administrative Directories

The other structure that I tend to use frequently under the ORACLE_HOME directory is the admin tree. This is where you will find log and trace files that can tell you what is and has been happening to your database. I also like to put create directories under here to store the data definition language (DDL) SQL scripts that I use to create database objects. I like putting them here because these directories are set up so that only DBAs can access them. In locations where the DBA does not control the DDL, I store these scripts with the application software.

Local Directories

Oracle recommends putting a local subtree for locally developed Oracle software, but I have found that most places have their own directories for applications. If they use version control software such as PVCS, a number of directories are used. There will be some kind of scheme to control the level of the software modules (production, test, development, and so forth). This local subtree can be useful if you have the responsibility of controlling software builds in addition to being the DBA. Otherwise, put the local applications somewhere else.

Data and Log Directories

The next requirement is some disk space to store your data, log, and other files. In a really small instance, you can put your data on a single disk in a single directory. Generally, I like to split data files from different databases into different directories, which have names that identify the database. When I restore a test database that has been corrupted, I want to make sure that I am restoring the test data from tape and not the production data. Of course, input/output loading is a function of the disk drive itself, so having multiple directories does not balance this load. Think of it as being a neat housekeeper. The basic concepts for data directories are shown in Figure 5.4.

FIGURE 5.4.
Recommended data directory layouts.

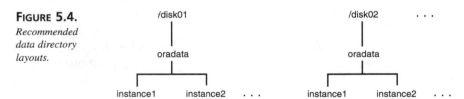

The exact names of the disks and directories vary between different computer systems. On some operating systems, you may have to specify the disk drive by a letter (for example, Novell o:\oracle) or some other designator. However, the general concepts remain the same. You designate an Oracle Home and some data directories. You lay out the data files depending on the number of disk drives that you have and what the input/output load is that you expect to balance based on application needs.

Memory Allocation and Alternatives

A few additional thoughts on memory area planning are in order. The estimates that you obtain from filling out these requirements tables are based on the minimum needs for the tool itself. For example, suppose you come up with an estimate of 7.6MB for SQL*Forms 3.0 Runtime for your estimated 10 users. This means that 7.6MB ensures that SQL*Forms Runtime will function for you. It does not take into account the fact that if you are running a complex decision-support application, your performance will be severely degraded if you do not allocate an additional 10M to sort the large lists of values that the application returns. It also does not take into account the larger log and database buffer space that is needed for intensive transaction processing environments.

Don't worry—there is a chapter coming up on tuning that discusses these subjects (Chapter 24, "Oracle8 Database Tuning"). For now, just realize that the numbers that you come up with for memory do not take these factors into account. I always recommend buying a little extra memory. Buying 2GB of memory for a small system is a waste of money. However, trying to get a large system functional with 32MB is almost impossible. Chances are, if you buy a little extra memory, you applications will grow and new releases of the operating system and Oracle will probably need it soon anyway.

Logical Database Design

In many cases, you will be installing your Oracle database before you have completed the design for your system. The logical database design is a description of the tables, indexes and other database objects that will be needed for a given application. You need to have the logical database design completed before you can begin the physical database design. So what if you do not have the logical database design for your application completed? Basically, you allocate space for the data files that you expect to put in place for the user data and concentrate on the physical database design associated with the core Oracle tablespaces (that is, `system`, `rollback`, and `temp`).

Physical Database Design

Recall that your first task in the installation process was to go through the Installation and Configuration Guide to verify that you have the correct versions of supporting software, operating systems, and so forth. Just after the tables listing the compatibility requirements, you will find a series of tables that enable you to calculate the distribution (Oracle software) space requirements, the database (internal control tables for the particular Oracle tools), and the memory space requirements for the software components that you are loading. This takes the form of a series of tables. Figure 5.5 shows an example table of some selected line items from a typical space requirements table for the UNIX versions of Oracle.

FIGURE 5.5.

A typical space requirements table for Oracle.

SPACE REQUIREMENTS Oracle Server Products

Product	Disk Storage Requirements		Memory Space Requirements			
	Dist (MB)	DB Space (MB)	First User (KB)	Additional Users		
				#Users	KB/User	Total KB
Oracle Server	36.60	12.5	6458		489	
SQL*DBA			2589		283	
SQL*Loader			1778		204	
Export			1654		223	
Import			1590		207	
Parallel Query Option	0.08	N/A				
Toolkit II	43.06	N/A				
Common Libraries & Utilities	22.10	N/A				
Sub Totals						

DBAs usually photocopy these tables so that they can write on them. Several copies can be useful because you may need to fill in different sheets for each instance. Although you have to load only one version of the Oracle software on a given machine, you have to allocate database space in each application that uses a particular tool. I also find that it is easier to come up with estimates of the number of users on an instance-by-instance (application-by-application) basis for large installations. You will find a number of space calculator tables for the basic server products, the networking products, the development tools, and so on. The goal is to fill out each of these tools as best you can (this is tough when you first start out, so err on the high side whenever possible) and then total the individual sheets to come up with an instance-by-instance total for software space, database space, and memory.

RAID and Other Storage Alternatives

On many computer systems, disk drives used to cost in the five-figure range for storage capacities that were much smaller than your average PC hard disk of today. The thought was that these mainframe and midrange disk drives were engineered so well that they provided a high degree of reliability. Then some folks came along with the concept of RAID. This originally stood for redundant array of inexpensive disks and is now often described as redundant array of independent disks. The concept is that you take a number of disk drives and connect them together logically for speed, reliability, or both.

There are two key concepts associated with RAID. The first is mirroring. Here you store the same information on multiple disk drives. The thought behind this is that if you lose one of the disk drives due to a hardware failure, you still have your data online and available from the other disk drive. When you repair the physical problem with the failed disk drive, you copy the contents of the working disk drive to this drive to resynchronize (resilver) their contents. Mirroring is the key to reliability in a RAID system.

The second concept associated with RAID is striping. Here you scatter the contents of a single file sequentially across multiple disk drives. You can then read block 1 from disk 1, block 2 from disk 2 and so forth. Striping provides speed in that you are now working multiple disk drives in parallel to read a single file, thereby eliminating bottlenecks associated with the data transfer speed of a single disk drive.

The next topic that I want to touch on is RAID levels. Mirroring is RAID level 0 and striping is RAID level 1. If you use both mirroring and striping, it is referred to as RAID 0 plus 1. However, there are also RAID levels 2 through 5. These RAID levels are alternatives to mirroring that provide much the same protection. It costs twice as much to make two copies of a given data file on two disk drives. If you work through some storage algorithms, you can find ways to scatter the information across multiple disk drives with check sums that would enable you to reconstruct data that might be lost if a given physical disk drive were to fail. That way, you have to spend some time calculating these check sums, but you save disk space. The most common RAID level other than 0 and 1 that you will run across is RAID level 5. With this technology you can use approximately 75 to 80 percent of the total disk storage space for storing your data as opposed to 50 percent utilization if you were mirroring your data.

There are a couple of other concepts associated with RAID that you should be aware of when planning the installation of your database. Some systems implement RAID at the hardware level. Here disk controllers take care of the functions such as making copies of the data or calculating check sums. Hardware RAID tends to be faster and does not add an extra burden to your CPU. Software RAID, on the other hand, uses operating system software to implement the RAID algorithms.

One final concept that you should be aware of when planning your database system is that of warm recovery. This is usually associated with hardware RAID arrays. What this enables you to do is remove a bad disk from an operating system and replace it with a new disk. The RAID array senses the new disk and automatically resilvers the new disk with the correct content. This can be important on systems were you have to be up a high percentage of the time.

So why did I put all of this hardware stuff in the midst of an Oracle planning chapter? Some Oracle databases are used to support the most critical systems at organizations. If the database is down, the business is down. Oracle internally has a number of features that promote a high degree of availability. However, there are also system options that can be used in conjunction with Oracle options to provide the needed reliability.

Processing Options

Even though it is not really required in the basic Oracle installation procedure, take a little time to plan out the processes that you will be using in your Oracle instances. The installer will create an instance for you that is running the four basic Oracle processes: Process Monitor (PMON), system monitor (SMON), log writer (LGWR), and database writer (DBWR). However, because you have spent so much time planning out your disk and memory usage, take a little time to consider the other processes that you may want to start up as part of the post-installation activities that you will perform.

Recall the introductory discussion of the Oracle processes in Chapter 2, "Oracle Database Architecture." The following are some of the additional processes that you may want to configure via the initialization files and the rationale for using them:

- *Multithreaded server processes.* These processes enable multiple users to use a single set of server processes. These processes eliminate the need for dedicated server processes for users who are not all that active on the system. Consider these on all systems that use SQL*Net and have a relatively large number of users connecting to the system.

- *Multiple database writer processes.* Consider these if you have write operations that go to multiple disk drives and you have a relatively large write volume on operating systems that do not have asynchronous input/output capabilities.

- *Checkpoint process.* Use this process only when your log writer process is having trouble keeping up with the volume of checkpoints.

- *Archiver.* This process is needed if you want to be able to guarantee recovery from the loss of a disk drive (or pair in the case of mirrored disks).

- *Recoverer.* This process comes into play only when you are implementing a distributed database.

- *Net/8 listeners.* If you are planning a client/server installation, you need to start up Net/8 listeners for each of the versions and protocols of Net/8 that you are using.

- *Parallel query processes.* Consider this option when you have databases that execute heavy queries. Typically, this is used in applications such as data warehouses.

Upgrades Versus New Installations

In some respects, upgrades are more challenging than initial installations. On initial installations you often have to learn more than you ever wanted to know about Oracle and your operating system. However, people often are more understanding when you are asked to implement a new technology. Upgrades, on the other hand, are often looked on as just applying a few bug fixes. You also have to deal with people who are using your database for production purposes and who cannot tolerate a lot of down time. They often do not understand the time it takes to unload and relink the Oracle software. They almost certainly will be very upset if the new version of Oracle introduces bugs or causes applications to fail due to changes in functionality within Oracle. This section provides a few considerations for the upgrade process.

Other Factors to Consider

On most production systems, you do not have the luxury of switching back and forth between releases as you explore your new software. Always have a test instance, even if it is small, to test your new RDBMS release against your production applications before you even think about trying it on production.

The new features that are available with the new release are some of the first things that you should be considering. Many of these are internal to the database and of concern only to the DBA. Bug fixes are generally appreciated by all, but you may want to remove some work-arounds that you had made to keep the old release of the software going after you have tested the new release. You also may want to publish the list of new features and bug fixes to your developers. They often do not get their own copies of the Oracle documentation and therefore do not take advantage of the new features that may save them time and also save database resources. I always say that an informed developer is one who is not coming to you with questions all of the time.

You should also be especially sensitive about any features that were available in the previous release, but that are no longer available in the new release. Typically, Oracle works very hard to ensure backward compatibility, but in the release documentation you will find a few features mentioned that are being phased out. You should also publish these to developers and consider removing them from your own software (admin scripts and so forth) before it becomes a crisis.

The next factor to consider is that the new version may increase the amount of memory that you use. Some of this comes about when you take advantage of new features, such as additional background processes. Others creep in when you find that you need to allocate additional space for Oracle tunable parameters to support the new software. For example, I was very surprised at the increased number of cursors that Oracle 7.1 used. We had to increase the init.ora file setting for cursors by a factor of 100 to get our existing applications to work under Oracle 7.1. Who knows what Oracle 8.1 will hold compared with Oracle8? This was not bad in that it did not appreciably increase the amount of shared memory space used, but the principle should be considered. Always check the disk and memory requirements of your new software, along with other tuning suggestions in the installation documentation.

It's always a good idea to clean up the instance before upgrading it. Perhaps it is just the mental attitude of wanting to have the instance "fresh" after the new installation, or perhaps it is the only time that you get to think about such things. Anyway, if you get the chance, clean out old, unwanted tables, indexes, and so forth. Although there is usually not a lot to do in a production instance, most development instances need this routine cleaning. Typically, I send a list of objects to the development manager and ask him to get his people to indicate which objects are still needed and which can be deleted. Some developers try to keep as much as possible, but when disk space is limited, you can use peer pressure to keep their tablespace free of clutter to support new projects.

Finally, even though the software goes through a reasonable test suite at the factory and at beta test sites, you should always plan to run a thorough test of your applications running against the new database software before making it available to users. You may discover that you are using features that are no longer supported and therefore you have to make some changes to your application software. You may find that your application finds a new bug in the Oracle software and you have to develop a work-around or get a patch from Oracle. Finally, your application may exceed the capacity of certain resources (like my cursors problem with Oracle 7.1). In this case, you have to adjust your tuning parameters until you get everything working happily again.

Send out the information to your developers so that they are better prepared for their development efforts. Many of these issues may not be applicable in your case. You may find that you are running only a packaged application such as Oracle Financials, and therefore you do not need to concern yourself with development issues.

The Backout Plan

Perhaps this is another legacy of my submarine days, but I always like to have a plan in place to handle the situation wherein problems come up and I have to abandon my upgrade efforts. Perhaps it is just that I do not want to have to "wing it" when the problems come up and everyone is yelling for a solution, or perhaps I just want to assure my customer or boss that I can handle it if the software is bad or some other problem arises. This is especially important when performing upgrades to production systems.

What are some of the items that should be in this backout plan? Well, the first thing is the criteria that would cause you to have to perform the backout. It's a good idea to get management people to agree to this in advance so that they do not act like armchair quarterbacks the next day and tell you that you should have done it sooner or waited a little longer. State the criteria in terms of time ("If there are still problems at 5 p.m. and there is no immediate solution, begin backout so the system can be operational for nightly batch processing") and other conditions ("There is a bug that Oracle needs to investigate and it indicates it may be several days"). Again, much like the installation plan, send the backout plan to managers (project managers, DBA group managers, and so forth) so that they can look at it and get their shots in before problems occur. Make them understand that if they do not give you comments, you have their approval to proceed according to the plan.

The main part of the backout plan is the steps needed to recover the instance fully so that it can run under the old software. This usually means restoring a complete, cold backup of the data and resetting parameter files, such as oratab, to point to the old version of the software. List all the files that need to be restored. This serves two purposes. First, you do not have to rely on your memory when it is late, you have been struggling for hours with a particularly annoying bug, and you have to restore the old instance to get production going again. Second, it serves as a good checklist for your backup that is performed as part of the upgrade plan. You really want to ensure that you have backed up all the files that your backout plan will require. This may seem simple on small, single-disk computer systems, but when you have files scattered across 135G of disk or more, it can be a challenge. Remember, Oracle is not forgiving if you remember to restore only 95 percent of the files that it needs.

Lining Up Support

As has been mentioned frequently in this chapter and Chapter 6, there can be problems with the installation and upgrade process. They can be worked through, but it takes time and support from other people to make the installation and upgrade process work. Specifically, there are a few resources that you should consider lining up during the planning stage so that you can have them ready when you actually perform the upgrade:

- The system administrator should be available to provide support ranging from tape backup restores to simple things such as resetting directory write permissions. If you also act as the system administrator, you can do this yourself, but be careful to not act too quickly and to think things through. The system administrator accounts have a lot of power and therefore can do a lot of damage (recursive deletes of files when you are in the wrong directory, for example).

- If you and your system administrator are not very familiar with the host operating system, you may consider performing the upgrade during a time when you have access to operating system vendor technical support. This can come in handy when the installer is screaming that it cannot find mk and you do not even know what mk is.

- You should understand what level of service you have with Oracle technical support and perform your upgrade during the period in which you are allowed to call Oracle. Like most vendors, Oracle provides 24-hour support, but it charges you much more than the 8-hour, weekday support contract. A fair percentage of installation problems can be solved quickly by Oracle over the telephone, so schedule yourself accordingly.

- It is helpful to have a developer available to test out applications after you have completed your upgrades. In most of the instances that I have worked on, I knew the data structures and basic processing flow, but I was not a user and therefore was not familiar with navigation between panels.

- Finally, it is helpful to have a shell script programmer available in case you have to perform functions such as manually linking the software. Usually you can do this with support from Oracle over the telephone, but you might need to find someone locally who knows all the tricks you need to do, such as setting up your path and environmental variable to access these development utilities. System administrators are familiar with the general concepts, but they usually do not work with these utilities regularly.

A Sample Plan

Customer XYZ

HP Oracle Installation Analysis

DRAFT 1/24/98

1. Overview

This document seeks to capture the design rationale used when installing and configuring the Oracle Relational Data Base Management System on the HP 9000 series 800 server at customer XYZ.

2. Overall System Conceptual Design

Several applications are being developed or converted to run in a client/server environment. The HP 800 computer will act as the database server in this environment. In addition, several off-the-shelf applications may be purchased and loaded on this computer. Some of these applications may use the client/server model and others may require the users to log in to the HP 800 as a terminal and execute the applications on the HP 800 itself.

3. Oracle Installation Conceptual Design

   Instances will be arranged based on development, test, and production needs.

4. Initial Configuration Recommendation

   Install only a development instance. Ensure that the methodology allows expansion to future instances.

5. Significant Installation Notes

   a. Oracle8.1 requires HP-UX 10.0.

   b. Dependencies:

SQL*Plus	Oracle8 server
	Help tables
SQL*Net TCP	Oracle8 server

   c. Space Requirements

Product	Disk (MB)	DB (MB)	Memory (KB)
Oracle server	35.28	12.5	4,456
PL/SQL	0.08	0	807
SQL*Net TCP	0.73	0	0
SQL*Plus	4.47	3.0	1,617
Pro*C	3.49	0	2,437
Totals	84	12.5	N/A*

   *Not applicable because many of the packages, such as SQL*Plus, may not be in use at all times.

   d. SQL*Plus 3.3 or later is needed for Oracle8.

   e. After loading, but before installing, in `.login` file, set `LDOPTS="-a archive";export LDOPTS`. Then log in and log out.

   f. Purchase includes Oracle RDBMS version 8.0 for HP 98xx/HP-UX 10.0, Model H50 for 32 concurrent users full-use license.

   —SQL*Plus version 3.3
   —SQL*Net version 3.0
   —SQL*Net TCP/IP

   g. The CSI # is   123456 (good through 12/27/99)
      Oracle support # (650) 506-1500
      PO #   99999

6. Initial Oracle Instance Configuration Options

   Disk drive configurations:

/usr/oracle	Oracle base application directory
/usr/oracle/product	Oracle home directory
/usr/oracle/product/801	Install point for this release
/d1/oracle/devel	Development instance directory
/d2/oracle/devel	Development instance directory
/d3/oracle/devel/redo	Storage for online redo logs
/d3/oracle/devel/archive	Storage for archive logs
/d4	Future use
/d5	Future use

7. Preparation Tasks

   a. HP admin create dba group.

   b. HP admin create data base administrator logins within dba group.

   c. HP admin create oracle owner account in dba group.

   d. HP admin create oracle user logins. Note, some thought needs to go in to how the regular user groups will be arranged. There is no need to worry about users who will access only via client/server. This applies to developers and others who will log in to the server.

   e. HP admin create files.

   f. HP admin alter the UNIX kernel parameters as follows:

SHMMAX	0x4000000	{4 million}
SHMMNI	100	
SHMSEG	12	
SEMMNS	128	
SEMMNI	10	

   g. Root user create all mount point directories (/d1, /d2, and so on).

   h. Root user creates the directories listed in 6a with owner Oracle and mode 755.

   i. User oracle set ORACLE_BASE environmental variable.

   j. Create the following subdirectories in ORACLE_BASE:

      —product
      —admin

        —data

        —local

        —TAR

  k. Create version 801 subdirectory under `ORACLE_BASE`/product.

  l. Set `ORACLE_HOME` environmental variable to `ORACLE_BASE`/product/801.

Summary

This chapter has provided some discussion related to the installation of the Oracle database server. I must emphasize that it is not intended as a replacement for the installation manual. You cannot survive without your installation manual, its sizing checklists, and other information. What I hoped to provide are some of the considerations that are either not in the installation manual or that are not emphasized enough. Oracle installations and upgrades are challenging affairs that require careful planning and sufficient time to accomplish. Having a test system on which you can work out the bugs without impacting users is one of the best things that you can do, both for your users and for yourself. I hope that this chapter has not been too gloomy for you. Let me end it by saying that I have not run across a system where I could not complete the installation of the Oracle server. It may take a little bit of time and a few calls to Oracle, but I've always found that it can be done.

Installation and Upgrades

by Virendra Galotra

In This Chapter

CHAPTER 6

Oracle runs on some 100 platforms. Each platform has its own specifics for installation and can be found in the Oracle8 platform-specific installation and user guide. The chapter discusses Sun Solaris as one of the example platforms to illustrate the generic UNIX installation process. Other popular UNIX platforms follow a similar installation procedure with minor changes. Be sure to go through the Oracle documentation for any specifics. The most important part of the process is to carefully go through the README.DOC file, which comes bundled with the software on most of the platforms.

Oracle has made numerous changes to provide an easy-to-use installation process. With Oracle8, it is fairly straightforward to install the server, the client, or any of the supported options. Oracle8 has distributed, replication, and parallel query options integrated in the kernel. They are no longer optional. They do not show up in the server manager banner.

Overview of the Installation Process for Sun Solaris

Installing the server involves making sure the local system satisfies the hardware, software, memory, and disk requirements for the products you want to install. Also, you need to ensure that the UNIX environment is set for the chosen products to be installed. You can make use of the Installer to install the software. After the software is installed, you need to configure the Oracle8 system by creating the database objects, establishing the user environment, and so forth for the installed Oracle products.

Hardware and Software Requirements

Please make sure that your system satisfies the hardware and software requirements as outlined in Table 6.1 and Table 6.2 before you attempt to install the Oracle8 server.

Hardware Requirements

TABLE 6.1. HARDWARE REQUIREMENTS.

Hardware Component	Requirements
Memory	A minimum of 32MB RAM is required, but it is recommended you have 64MB. In the case of special options such as ConText, the preferred minimum is 128MB.
Swap	As a rule of thumb, approximately three times the recommended RAM is required.

Hardware Component	Requirements
Disk Space	If you choose to install the entire Oracle8 server, a minimum of 600MB is required. Requirements will be less if you choose to install a subset.
CD-ROM Device	A CD-ROM device supported by Solaris is required.

NOTE

600MB of disk space does not include the size of your database.

Software Requirements

As part of the Oracle8 installation, you must make sure to determine which operating system (OS) patches are installed and which OS packages are installed. You can use the following commands:

```
$ showrev -p ( for OS patches )
$ pkginfo -i [package_name] ; pkginfo -i would list all installed
➥packages.
```

Table 6.2 lists the OS software requirements for the Oracle8 installation.

OS Software Requirements

TABLE 6.2. SOFTWARE REQUIREMENTS.

OS Software	Requirement
OS	Solaris 2.5.1 or 2.6.
OS Patch	Contact Sun Microsystems for the latest Kernel Patch.
OS Packages	SUNWarc, SUNWbtool, SUNWlibm,SUNWlibms, SUNWsprot, SUNWtool, SUNWhea,SUNWmfrun.
Window Manager	Any Sun-supported window manager.

For any product-specific installation requirements, refer to the Sun Solaris installation guide.

Table 6.1 from Oracle8 Installation Guide for Sun Solaris, *pp. 1-3. Copyright© 1997, Oracle Corporation. All rights reserved.*
Table 6.2 from Oracle8 Installation Guide for Sun Solaris, *pp. 1-4. Copyright© 1997, Oracle Corporation. All rights reserved.*

Software Requirements for Networking Products

The network software must be installed and running prior to installation of the Oracle Net8 products, which is the de facto standard for the Oracle8 server. The adapters require the underlying software and OS libraries for the supported network.

Optimal Flexible Architecture (OFA)

The database and the new installation should comply with the OFA standard by providing a minimum of four mount points: one for the source software and three for the database files. You must enter a value for `ORACLE_BASE`. If you decide to create a non-OFA structure, the Installer enables you to specify the same value for `ORACLE_HOME`.

Installation Preparation and Installation

This section helps you prepare the environment for installing the Oracle8 server. To achieve the objective, you set up the UNIX environment. There are certain tasks that need be done as the root and Oracle user. You also need to perform certain setup tasks for individual Oracle products.

Log in as the root user by using the following steps:

Step 1. To set up the UNIX environment, you need to set Solaris-specific kernel parameters, which include `SHMMAX`, `SHMMIN`, `SHMSEG`, `SEMMNS`, `SEMMNI`, and `SEMMSL` (`SEMMSL` can be set equal to `PROCESSES`, the initialization parameter). The value of `SHMMAX` indicates the maximum allowable size of the shared memory used. You can add these parameters in the `/etc/system` file.

You need to have the adequate shared memory to accommodate the SGA. It requires configuring the UNIX kernel Interprocess Communication Parameters. Use the `ipcs` command to list the current shared memory and shared segments.

The total shared memory equals `SHMMAX` times `SHMSEG`.

The Oracle Installer will automatically create the directories listed in Table 6.3. The access permissions on Oracle directories and files should match those in Table 6.3.

TABLE 6.3. ACCESS PERMISSIONS ON ORACLE DIRECTORIES AND FILES.

Directories/Files	Permissions
`$ORACLE_HOME/network/trace`	777 (for Development database)
	730 (for Production database)
`$ORACLE_HOME/lib`	644 (provides read-only access)
`$ORACLE_HOME/bin`	6751*
`$SQL`, Shell, and other admin scripts	644
`$ORACLE_HOME/rdbms/log`	751
All control, database, log files	640

Step 2. You require at least four mount points, all at the same level of directory structure. Three mount points are consumed by the database (OFA-compliant), and one by the source software.

Step 3. Create a DBA group for the OSDBA role. Members of this group have DBA privileges.

Step 4. Create a UNIX Oracle account, a member of the DBA group. This account owns the Oracle distribution. The Installer should be run under this account.

Step 5. Create the local `bin` directory; in Solaris, it is `/opt/bin`.

Step 6. Create an `oratab` file containing the information about the Oracle instance:

cdrom_mount_point`/orainst/`*oratab.sh* script create/set the permissions of
➥this file in `/var/opt/oracle` directory.

Log into the Oracle account to perform the following steps:

Step 7. Set `umask` to `022`.

Step 8. Choose the appropriate `DISPLAY` by setting the machine name.

Step 9. Set the following variables appropriately in the .profile or .login file of the Oracle account: `ORACLE_TERM`, `ORACLE_BASE`, `ORACLE_HOME`, `ORACLE_SID`, `LD_LIBRARY_PATH`, `PATH`, `SRCHOME`, `TWO_TASK`, and `TMPDIR`.

---

* 6 sets the setuid *bit so the executables are executed as the Oracle user and DBA group, regardless of who executes them.*
Table 6.3 from Oracle8 Installation Guide for Sun Solaris, *p. 4-4. Copyright© 1997, Oracle Corporation. All rights reserved.*

> **NOTE**
>
> ORA_NLS33 can be set optionally if you want to create the database with a character set other than US7ASCII.
>
> The search PATH must include: $ORACLE_HOME/bin, /bin, /opt/bin, /usr/bin, and /usr/ccs/bin in the search order.

After setting the environment variables in the .profile or .login file, update the environment in the current shell session:

```
$ . .profile ( Bourne Shell)
$ source .login ( cshell)
```

To install individual Oracle products, perform the steps as necessary for your installation.

Installing Documentation

Oracle documentation is available in two categories: OS-specific and generic. Both documentations are available in HTML and PDF formats.

You can install OS specific documentation during installation from the source CD-ROM. The generic or product documentation is available on a separate CD-ROM and can be installed in a separate Installer session.

At this point, execute the product-specific steps as necessary for your installation.

Post-Installation Steps for Oracle8 Server

As an example, let's look at the Recovery Manager (RMAN) and Time Series Cartridge post-installation steps.

New Installations—Recovery Manager

Recovery Manager is an automated utility to perform recovery and is installed as part of the Oracle8 server. This is a new feature introduced in Oracle8. It stores information in a separate catalog database. The catalog database should be essentially on a separate machine to provide maximum fault resistance.

> **NOTE**
>
> RMAN can also be used in a restricted mode without a recovery catalog in certain situations.

The following are the steps to create a recovery catalog:

1. Install an Oracle8 server on a different machine and create a database for the recovery catalog. You could create the default database with the Installer.
2. Create a user in the recovery catalog database to be the Recovery Manager user.
3. Log into Recovery Manager user, execute the `catrman.sql` script in the `$ORACLE_HOME/rdbms/admin` directory. Execute the script using `svrmgrl`.

You can look in the installation guide for appropriate postinstallation steps for different products on your platform.

New Installations—Time Series Cartridge

The Installer performs the following steps when the Create Database Objects option is selected.

Install the `UTLREF` package as it is needed by the cartridge:

1. As DBA, execute
   ```
   svrmgr> @ORACLE_HOME/rdbms/admin/utlref.sql
   ```
2. Create the `ORDSYS` account if needed. As DBA, execute
   ```
   svrmgr> create user ORDSYS identified by <password>;
   ```
3. Set the privileges:
   ```
   svrmgr> grant connect, resource, create library to ORDSYS;
   ```
4. Install Time Series Cartridge types and procedures:
   ```
   svrmgr>connect ORDSYS/<password>;
   svrmgr> @ORACLE_HOME/ord/ts/admin/ordinst.sql
   ```

Execute privileges will be granted to `PUBLIC` for all Time Series types and packages.

Migration to Oracle8

In order to migrate a database, as a DBA you need to understand the procedures involved in the process. It needs careful planning, testing the migration process and the migrated test database, preparing and preserving the source database, migrating the source database, and testing and tuning the new production database. Typically, as a DBA you are responsible for ensuring the success of the migration process. The application developer is responsible for ensuring that the application designed for the Oracle7 source database works the same way with the migrated Oracle8 target database. Users should not have access to the migrated database until all applications have been tested properly.

> **CAUTION**
>
> Always back up your version 7 database before you migrate!

There are three methods available for migrating or upgrading a database to Oracle8:

- The migration utility, for migrating from Oracle7, release 7.*x* to Oracle8.
- Export of an Oracle7 (or version 6) source database into an Oracle8 target database. It could be a full or partial export followed by full or partial import.
- Copying data from a source database into an Oracle8 database. It could be either the COPY command or AS clause of the CREATE TABLE command.

The migration utility converts the files and structures in the source database (Oracle7) by changing the file headers and possibly the definitions of the data in the files. It does not affect the data portions of the datafiles; also their format and content remains unchanged. It is good for quick migration of the entire source and not for selective datafiles, which is best handled by Export and Import.

- As typical of Export/Import, these utilities physically copy the data from the source to a new database. However, it requires that the new target Oracle8 database must have already been created before the Import utility can be used to migrate the Export file. The main advantage is that the source database is available throughout the migration process. However, if a consistent snapshot of the database is required, the source database must be up in the Restricted mode during the Export process. Thus the two databases could be running in parallel before the Oracle8 database is released to users.

The Export and Import utilities provide the following benefits over and above the migrate utility:

- Creates an entirely new database, restructured and defragmented
- Allows specified migration of objects or users
- Serves as a backup archive

These advantages do have the regular disadvantages associated with any export/import procedure: Export data is a logical copy of the data. It can allow recovery to the date and time the export was taken. An Export file should not be edited and can be used by Import only. Import imports only full tables and cannot be used to do a conditional load. In terms of time and disk space requirements, Export/Import is very expensive.

Copying Data

You can copy data from one Oracle database to another using database links. The data can be copied using the regular SQL*Plus COPY command or using the INSERT INTO, CREATE TABLE FROM command, CREATE TABLE ... AS. This method offers the same advantage of moving selected objects or even specified rows across the databases. Copying also requires less disk and memory buffer space for migration than export/import.

Develop a Testing Plan

The migration procedure requires planning and testing, involving the path from the source to the new migrated database, irrespective of any of the methods—migration utility, export/import, or copying data. Regardless of what method you choose, as a database administrator, it is your responsibility to establish, test, and validate a migration plan. The testing plan normally includes functional, integration, performance, and volume/load stress testing and pre- and post-migration testing.

Be sure to include timing tests, data dictionary growth, observations and resource usage observations. Collecting this information will help you compare the source and the target database. You can use EXPLAIN PLAN on both source and target to compare the execution paths followed for SQL statements.

Migration Utility

You need to install the migration utility as explained in the following steps.

Stage 1. Install the Oracle8 migration utility.

1. Run orainst from the Oracle8 distribution CD-ROM with ORACLE_HOME and ORA-CLE_SID pointing to your Oracle7 database:

```
$ cd /cdrom/cdrom0/orainst
$ ./orainst /m
( /m is required for motif version)
```

2. Go to the Install Type screen and select Default or Custom Install.

   On the Installation Activity Choice screen, choose appropriately any of the options from Install, Upgrade.

   You must bypass the creation of a new database.

   On the Installation Options screen, select Migrate from Oracle7 to Oracle8.

   You need to enter the following options on the prompts shown below, before running the `mig` utility:

Prompt Screen	*Selection / Enter Value*
Installation Options:	
Home Locator	Enter the Oracle7 `$ORACLE_HOME` location.
Logging and Status	Confirm and/or change the log file location (installer log, sql log, makefile log, and OS log). (You are prompted for this if you select Custom Install.)
Migration	Select Install Migration Utility.
Install Source	Select either Install from CD-ROM or Install from Staging Area. If you select Install from Staging Area, you will get the Source Staging Area to enter the pathname of the source staging area directory. (You are prompted for this if you select Custom Install.)
NLS	Choose the language to be installed.
Software Asset Manager	Choose Migration Utility: Oracle7 to Oracle8 (8.0.3.0.0).

Now choose Install and exit from `orainst`.

Please make sure that the Oracle8 migration utility executable `mig` resides in the Oracle7 `$ORACLE_HOME/bin` directory; `migus.msb`, the new version of the message file, resides in the Oracle7 `$ORACLE_HOME/rdbms/mesg` directory; `migrate.bsq` resides under the Oracle7 `ORACLE_HOME/dbs` directory; and all the NLS files are under the Oracle7 `ORACLE_HOME/migrate/nls/admin/data` directory. During the process of migration, `migrate.bsq` will create a number of objects that are normally created by `sql.bsq`, but it will create them under the migrate schema. Later, during the convert phase, the ownership of `migrate`'s objects will be changed to `sys`.

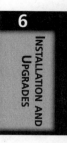

> **NOTE**
>
> If your Oracle7 `sql.bsq` was customized (which it should not be, but might be for very specific reasons), you need to make the same changes to `migrate.bsq` prior to running the migration utility.
>
> You can locate `migrate.bsq` under `$ORACLE_HOME/dbs` (as mentioned previously). You have to search on `sql.bsq` to find the exact script.

Migration Preparation

Stage 2. Prepare the database for migration.

Go through `README.doc` and check for any patches that need to be installed:

1. Check `'PL/SQL Release'` in the `sqlplus` or server manager banner to ensure that the procedural option is installed:

   ```
   drop view dba_histograms;
   drop view v$bh if it exists;
   ```

   Make sure that `TWO_TASK` is not set. (You can use echo `$TWO_TASK` at the `unix` prompt to confirm).

   Also check that you do not have a user/role named `migrate`.

2. If you do not use the default character set US7ASCII, make sure to have the ORA_NLS33 set to `$ORACLE_HOME/migrate/nls/admin/data`.

3. It is better to offline normal or make read-only all tablespaces except `SYSTEM` and those containing rollback segments. If migration fails, only the `SYSTEM` and rollback datafiles need to be restored.

4. Check the status of the datafiles:

   ```
   Select name, status, enabled from v$datafile;
   ```

   It should be either online or offline. Any file with a recover status cannot be opened after migration.

5. Make sure to incorporate a rollback big enough that it does not fail during the operation. Ensure that the `OPTIMAL` parameter of the storage clause is not set for the `SYSTEM` rollback segment.

6. To check that `SYSTEM` rollback is not hitting the `maxextents`:

   ```
   select extents from v$rollstat where usn=0;
   ```

7. Check to ensure that `AUD$` belongs to the `SYSTEM` tablespace if the database auditing is enabled.

8. There should not be any pending or uncommitted transactions. The migration utility does check for it and aborts the execution.

   You can check using `select * from x$kttvs;` to list such tablespace transactions by selecting the `kttvstnm` column. This column corresponds to the `ts#` column of `ts$`.

   You can execute

   `select name from ts$ where ts#=<"kttvstnm">`

   This select lists the tablespaces that have save undo.

   Further, you can issue

   `Alter tablespace tablespace_name online;`

   This eliminates the save undo.

   Make sure to alter the tablespace offline normal again by issuing the command

   `Alter tablespace tablespace_name offline normal;`

9. If you are supporting replication, disable it. If replication is enabled and the logs have not been cleared, migration will fail.

10. Oracle8 has a larger data dictionary. The SYSTEM tablespace should be about two to three times the one needed in Oracle7. Make sure to add a datafile or resize the existing file. Look into the "Common Problems and Troubleshooting" section of this chapter to learn how to verify the space in the SYSTEM tablespace.

Stage 3. Migrate the database.

This is your only chance to take the backup if you have not taken it so far. Shut down normal or immediate the Oracle7 database. So, take a backup now.

Backup of the Existing System

Make a complete backup of the Oracle7 home, that is, the `$ORACLE_HOME/` directory. The safest way to back up is to include the parameter files, control files, datafiles, and online logs. It is also a good idea to include the sql code that was used to create the objects in the Oracle7 database—any sql code that you might want to use to restore the database. If you are backing up after the `mig` utility is executed successfully, back up the convert file.

Now continue with Stage 3.

You can run `mig` from the command line or the Installer. The utility name may vary depending on the operating system. You should run the `mig` via the command line in case the database character set is other than US7ASCII. If `mig` aborts for any reason, shut down the database cleanly and execute the `mig` again. `mig` starts the database, so you must shut it down if you need to restart.

The command line is

```
mig dbname=oracle7db new_dbname=Oracle8dbname V803
spool=\"/tmp/migrate/mig.spool\"
```

Some of the command line options are

CHECK_ONLY	When TRUE, space use calculations are performed without any actual migration (this is mutually exclusive with NO_SPACE_CHECK).
	When FALSE, space usage is checked and migration is performed.
DBNAME	Specifies the name of the database to migrate.
NEW_DBNAME	Specifies a new name for the migrated database.
NLS_NCHAR	Specifies the character set in the Oracle8 database.
PFILE	Specifies the name of the parameter file with complete pathname.
SPOOL	Specifies filename to which to spool output with complete pathname.

> **NOTE**
>
> Pathnames must be enclosed by double quotes masked by a backslash on UNIX. Here is an example:
>
> ```
> mig PFILE=\"/tmp/mig/initSAMS.ora\"
> ```

If you want to use orainst, it is pretty self explanatory, and each prompt is easy to follow.

Essentially, either of the two steps drops all the obsolete views and tables; creates new Oracle8 tables, views, and clusters, updates base tables, and creates a migrate user. They also create a convSID.dbf file in the $ORACLE_HOME/dbs directory, containing a list of tablespaces, datafiles, and redologs. The convSID.dbf file also contains the close scn generated when the database is shut down by the migration utility.

The migration is complete and you need to convert the database after this step. Even at this stage, with some effort you can go back to Oracle7 without a restore. All you have to do is to drop the migrate user and run catalog and catproc scripts and re-create the DUAL table.

Stage 4. Prepare for conversion.

1. Because you finally decide to go ahead to Oracle8, keep pointing the ORACLE_SID to Oracle7 and change the following variables to Oracle8:

   ```
   PATH
   ORACLE_HOME
   ORACLE_PATH
   LD_LIBRARY_PATH
   ```

   Change ORA_NLS33 to point to the Oracle8 ORACLE_HOME/ocommon/nls/admin/data.

2. Install the Oracle8 executables. They are about two to three times larger than the Oracle7 executables. Execute the Installer.

3. You need to take care of the following changes in the initialization file (initSID.ora) for Oracle8:

   ```
   compatible = 8.0.0.0
   control_files = new control file names
   Change:
   snapshot_refresh_interval to job_queue_interval
   snapshot_refresh_process to job_queue_processes
   ```

   These parameters are no longer valid for Oracle8. Including the old parameters, you may not get any error but will not yield the required effect.

   Change db_name as you run mig with new_dbname to change the database name under Oracle8. Some parameters are obsolete in Oracle8. They are init_sql_files, lm_domains, lm_non_fault_tolerant, checkpoint_process, parallel_default_max_scans, parallel_default_scan_size, sequence_cache_hash_buckets, serializable, session_cached_cursors, db_writers, use_async_io, async_read, async_write, and ccf_io_size.

   It would be a good idea to call Oracle Support to confirm any other precautions to be taken at this stage and confirm any other latest changes or bugs that you need to take care of through events or patches. You may need to set an event or so that can be done under the supervision of Support.

4. At this stage, copy files to the Oracle8 ORACLE_HOME. It would be better to install Oracle8 executables into a separate ORACLE_HOME rather than the existing Oracle7 ORACLE_HOME. Further, copy the convSID.dbs file to the Oracle8 $ORACLE_HOME/dbs directory. Never modify this file. Make sure it contains Oracle8SID as a part of its name. If you need to, rename it.

   Ensure that you have the Oracle8 $ORACLE_HOME/dbs directory empty to accommodate the new files that will be generated. Move the password file, if any, to the $ORACLE_HOME/dbs directory.

Stage 5. Convert and open the database.

Perform the following steps to finally convert the Oracle7 database to Oracle8:

```
svrmgrl> Connect internal;
```

```
svrmgrl>Startup nomount
```

> **CAUTION**
>
> Starting the database in any other mode might cause corruption.

```
svrmgrl>Alter database convert;
```

You are now at a point of no return.

It is at this stage that new control files are created and all the headers of the online datafile undergo transformation as per information provided in the convSID.dbf file. If you are not successful in executing this command, or if you want to go back to Oracle7, you need to restore all the files for tablespaces that were online when you initiated this process. Also, you must restore the convert file and delete the control file that might have been partially created.

In order to open the database, execute the regular command with the resetlog option:

```
svrmgrl> Alter database open resetlogs;
```

This causes all the online rollback segments to be converted to the Oracle8 format and automatically generates the new online redologs.

In the final stage, you run the cat8000.sql scripts to create the system data dictionary and catalog views for Oracle8. Before the scripts are executed, it is always a good idea to have a SPOOL file open so that the error log can be created, which is very helpful for debugging any errors that might occur during the execution of these scripts:

```
svrmgrl> SPOOL SAMSLOG
```

```
svrmgrl> @$ORACLE_HOME/rdbms/admin/cat8000.sql
```

This drops the migrate user and creates and alters some objects. Finally, run cat8003.sql and cat8000s.sql. These scripts run catalog.sql and catproc.sql scripts and take the database to the 8.0.3 version.

If you want to install the advanced replication option, run CATREP8.sql also:

```
svrmgrl> SPOOL OFF
```

At this stage, all packages, procedures, functions, triggers, and views need to be recompiled. You cannot just run dbms_utility.compile_schema, because the migration does not track dependencies.

It is a good idea to check for invalid objects and recompile them using the following script, which does take care of the dependencies:

```
/* . . . . . . . . . . . .
Script to recompile the invalid Objects
. . . . . . . . . . . .*/
set heading off
set pagesize 0
set linesize 79
set verify off
set echo off
spool compile_all_objects.tmp

select
    decode( OBJECT_TYPE, 'PACKAGE BODY',
    'alter package ' || OWNER||'.'||OBJECT_NAME || ' compile body;',
    'alter ' || OBJECT_TYPE || ' ' || OWNER||'.'||OBJECT_NAME || '
compile;')
from
    sys.dba_objects a,
    sys.order_object_by_dependency b
where
A.OBJECT_ID = B.OBJECT_ID(+) and
STATUS = 'INVALID' and
OBJECT_TYPE in ( 'PACKAGE BODY', 'PACKAGE', 'FUNCTION', 'PROCEDURE',
'TRIGGER', 'VIEW' )
order by
DLEVEL DESC,
OBJECT_TYPE,
OBJECT_NAME;

spool off;


. . . . . . . . . . . . . . . . . . . . . . .
```

You can execute the this script connected as System. This generates a compile_all_objects.tmp file.

Rename compile_all_objects.tmp to compile.sql, which can be executed to fix the invalid objects getting connected as svrmgrl.

Because this script checks for the dependencies, make sure that this is excuted only once. It should normally fix all the invalid objects in the database. You do not need to compile each user schema separately.

Above steps consolidated from Oracle8 Server Migration Guide, *Copyright© 1997, Oracle Corporation. All rights reserved.*

At this stage, shut down normal or immediate. This flushes all caches, clears buffers, and performs other housekeeping duties, such as alters online your offline files (the file headers will be altered for Oracle8).

If you want to upgrade to 8.0.4, you need to run the scripts accordingly and call Support to get patches for some of the fixes. There are some patches that need to be installed for 8.0.3; a list of these can be requested from Worldwide Support.

Abandoning the Migration

Once you execute the migrate utility, it eliminates the Oracle7 catalog views. Therefore, to return to the Oracle7 database after the utility has been run, you restore the Oracle7 catalog views by rerunning the CATALOG.SQL script. The steps are as follows:

1. Restore the Oracle7 database; start up the Oracle7 database:

   ```
   Svrmgrl> Connect internal;
   svrmgrl> Startup
   ```

2. Drop the user MIGRATE:

   ```
   svrmgrl> drop user migrate cascade;
   ```

3. Rerun the Catalog and Catproc scripts:

   ```
   svrmgrl> @$ORACLE_HOME/rdbms/admin/Catalog.sql
   svrmgrl> @$ORACLE_HOME/rdbms/admin/Catproc.sql
   svrmgrl> catsvrmg.sql
       ( if the server manager is installed)
   svrmgrl> @$ORACLE_HOME/rdbms/admin/CatPARR.sql
       ( if parallel option is installed)
   svrmgrl> @$ORACLE_HOME/rdbms/admin/CatREP.sql
       ( if replication option is installed)
   ```

> **NOTE**
>
> This will leave the data dictionary compatible to Oracle 7.3. You will have to follow the regular downgrade procedure to go to any other 7.*x* version.

Common Problems and Troubleshooting

1. Alter database open resetlogs will ensure only that all the rollbacks are converted to Oracle8 and online redologs are created as per Oracle8 format.

Above steps consolidated from Oracle8 Server Migration Guide, *Copyright© 1997, Oracle Corporation. All rights reserved.*

2. If you have pending or in-doubt transactions, look at the following tables:

```
pending_trans$
pending_session$
pending_sub_session$
```

   and do the usual manual rollback or commit the pending transaction. In some cases, you might have to manually remove these transactions from the tables listed previously. When the pending transactions are taken care of, it paves the way for the successful migration. Some scenarios might warrant a call to Oracle Support.

3. To verify the space availability in the system tablespace, make sure that your iniSID.ora is in the default $ORACLE_HOME/dbs directory; execute the following command:

```
$ mig SPOOL= '"filename"' CHECK_ONLY=TRUE
```

   Otherwise, you can specify the pfile option in the command line:

```
$ mig PFILE='"initSID.ora"' SPOOL= '"filename"' CHECK_ONLY=TRUE
```

4. The sys.dual table gets accidentally dropped during migration. You need to re-create it.

   You need to get connected as user SYS in order to re-create the dual table;

```
/* Creating the sys.dual table */
drop public synonym dual;
create table dual
(dummy varchar2(1)) storage ( initial 1);
insert into dual values('X');
commit;
create public synonym dual for dual;
```

   When it is created, grant the select on the dual table to public:

```
Grant Select on dual to public with grant option;
```

5. It is always a good idea to spool an outfile when you run any scripts. You can debug it very easily going through the spool file.

6. After completing the process, try to do a shutdown immediate or normal only. This will accomplish the required flushing of buffers, caches, and so forth.

7. If you have rowids stored, execute the dbms_rowid package to convert it into Oracle8 format. The file header will be converted when the datafiles are altered online.

   You can refer to the *Server Administrator Guide* for the details on the dbms_rowid package.

8. You may call Oracle Support for some postmigration patches you might need to install.

Summary

The key to successful Oracle8 installation and upgrade lies in adequately preparing the system to fulfill hardware and software requirements. As a DBA, you must make sure that the system satisfies the memory and disk requirements for the products you want to install.

Upgrade needs careful planning, testing the developed plan, and preserving the source database after you have chosen a particular method for moving from an existing server release to a newer release.

There is no facility for migrating directly from version 6 to version 8. You must first migrate from Oracle6 to Oracle7 before moving to Oracle8.

If you migrate between operating systems, the export/import method is the only supported method. The migration utility does not support different operating systems in the source and destination environments.

Migrating from Non-Oracle Databases

by Advanced Information Systems, Inc.

CHAPTER 7

System Migration—The Sum of All Our Fears

If you are considering the migration of data from a non-Oracle to an Oracle database, you may feel that you are on the edge of the precipice, about to fall over. This is a common perception of a very typical scenario for the owners of a new Oracle application. With the standardization of the Relational Database and the tendency to migrate from *legacy* systems, there are many newer Oracle applications using converted data from other databases and/or file systems. Whatever problems you may face, they have probably been solved before, so there is a great deal of opportunity to purchase tools and expertise. Yet it is important not to rely only on general knowledge; the migration of data into Oracle many times depends on specific domain and technical expertise within your company and the willingness of all parties involved to bring about a successful migration.

This chapter will look at the topic of migration from both a higher-level managerial standpoint and the more concrete level of a programmer analyst. We will define, in general terms, the key issues of migrating data from another source into Oracle, and will supply examples from today's most common migration platforms and databases that tend to be evolving into new Oracle applications.

The Realities of System Migration

In most cases, you view the migration from another data store to Oracle as the replacement of one application or database with another; yet it is more of an evolution, because many times the domain expertise of the old application and maybe even portions of the applications code will not change throughout the migration. An example of this might be a migration of a Sybase database to Oracle, where the PowerBuilder front-end does not change; it is just modified to speak to Oracle instead of Sybase (see Figure 7.1).

FIGURE 7.1.

A Sybase to Oracle database migration with only portions of the front-end code changed.

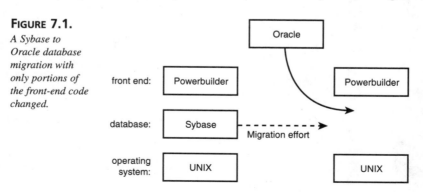

On the other end of the spectrum, there are times where most of the previous system will be put out of existence once the new Oracle system is created to replace it. These systems are called *sunset systems* and have a limited life-span after which the new Oracle system will exclusively survive. Even with these systems, human resources who used the old system and management and technical structures which supported it will need to adapt to the new system (see Figure 7.2). For instance, if you are replacing an IBM Mainframe CICS/VSAM application with an Oracle/Oracle*Forms 4.5 application, you still do not want to lose all of the human domain knowledge from the older system. You also will need to rely on the experts of the older system for help in the migration effort.

FIGURE 7.2.

Even with the complete migration to a totally new physical system, business domain expertise must evolve from one system to another.

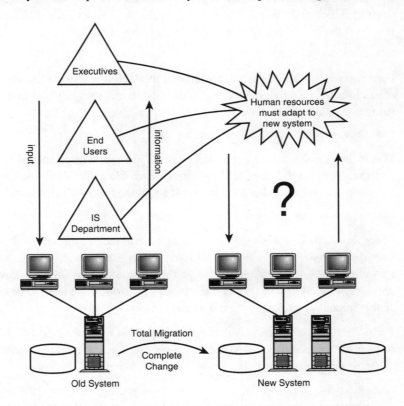

This discussion is to stress that along with technical tools, an organization needs the human experts of both the old and new systems to be willing to go forward with the migration. If there is resistance to any migration effort, whatever technical tools you may possess, the migration will suffer. For example, if a mainframe group is resisting a downsizing effort to an Oracle RDBMS, this will upset the needed communication and knowledge transfer that must exist for the downsizing to succeed.

The Myth of ANSI SQL

For those migration efforts where you are moving from one relational database to another, there is the myth of a standard SQL to be shattered. Although you were told when you bought our first relational database that it was compatible with any SQL database, the odds are that your application is not. This is due to the bells and whistles each vendor adds to its SQL implementation.

When we speak of "bells and whistles," we don't mean far-fetched extensions of SQL but simple operators such as the string concatenation. If you want to combine the two strings "Hello" and "World" together in Oracle, you use a totally different operator than you do with Sybase. For Oracle, the operation would be

```
'Hello ' || 'World'
```

Here you see the concatenation operator || used. Notice also the use of single quotation marks to denote a string in Oracle. On the other hand, using Sybase or SQL Server the string command would be

```
"Hello " + "World"
```

This is the reason why many migration efforts just take a large amount of man hours to perform. Now, maybe you could go through each file and replace every + with a || symbol using an editor or other tool, but what about the following statement:

```
select 1 + interest_rate from econ_table;
```

Using this method, you would be changing all arithmetic expressions of + to || and invalidating your mathematical code! Even in this simple case, you are forced to ponder a more complex operation. And once you're successful, you still have covered only one operator of the SQL language and are faced with strings that need to be changed from double quotation marks to single quotation marks.

The point of this discussion is that even a migration from one ANSI SQL database to another will be complex unless the original system was written in standard SQL. Even in this case, time-consuming changes will need to take place.

In the best-case scenario, even when you are migrating from one database to another and not changing the application code, the most you can hope for is a modular set of database calls within libraries that the application uses (see Figure 7.3). With this isolation, you can change the database libraries to fit another RDBMS without going through all of the application code.

FIGURE 7.3.

If the database calls of an application are isolated, the migration to another database will be more efficient.

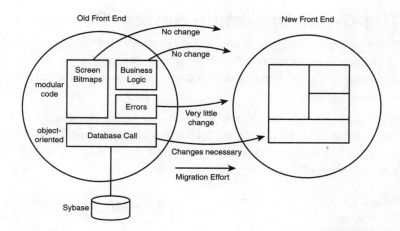

Another problem with vendor SQL is that it is so enticing to use vendor "extensions" to the SQL language. As a developer, there is no reason to refrain from using these tools unless you are informed that the code needs to be as compatible to standard SQL as possible.

This may seem heartless that I would code an Oracle SQL application using big, mean SQL extensions such as the DECODE statement. I might have a module or "method" that requires that I sum on salary for all employees but those in the sales department. In this case, I would use a DECODE statement like the following:

```
Select
dept_code,
sum( DECODE(dept_code, 'SALES', comm + salary, salary) )
from Employee
```

By doing this, I would save time by eliminating the need for if/else logic in my application code. Therefore, by designing applications to be very open and portable, you will sacrifice development time and cost if you look to maximize portability. The lesson learned is: Portable software is something you need to plan.

What you can do if you want to build applications that are more portable is isolate database calls to certain modules of your application. (For the object-oriented fans in the audience, you would just have a class like DATABASE_LIBRARY which contained all the database methods.) Ultimately, though, you probably will face differences in vendor SQL and will need to code those changes.

The Great Operating System Barrier

When you need to migrate across operating system platforms, you are always in for drastic changes in an application. There are some exceptions to this. For instance, if your application is written in a vendor tool that is portable across the different OS environments, a migration is easier.

An example of this would be a SQL*Forms 3.0 application residing on DEC VMS and being ported to UNIX (see Figure 7.4). In this case, you would only need to regenerate the forms and possibly change a few scripts. In these instances, a vendor layer shelters you from the specifics of each OS environment.

FIGURE 7.4.

A software vendor's code should shelter the user from the specifics of each OS environment so as to make migrations easier.

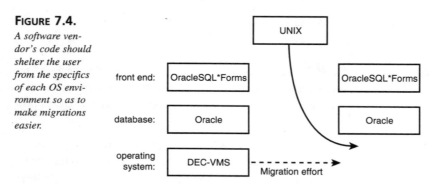

Contrast this with a COBOL/CICS/DB2 application being moved to a Windows NT/Oracle environment. From the front-end to the database, every module would need to change. More importantly, the functionality of the application would be designed differently in a GUI environment than in a character-mode environment. The farther away you move in the philosophies of the two different environments, the more extensive your migration efforts will be.

Oracle Alliance—Design and Migration Services to the Rescue

The Oracle corporation, whose goal it is to make any migration from any other platform to an Oracle RDBMS easier, offers the Design and Migration Services (DMS). It is a department that works closely with the Oracle Alliance.

DMS provides very inexpensive documentation and conversion kit software for most of the major migration combinations. Along with this comes detailed documentation describing the differences between your old environment and the new Oracle environment.

The Conversion Kit software can be run against different portions of your code, and will automatically convert different parts of your old code into new Oracle-compliant code. Of course, as stated earlier, these kits or services cannot replace the human expertise needed to make the port and cannot provide the organizational communication that will be needed.

Along with this, Oracle provides consulting through DMS and works with a variety of vendors to provide more specialized services that require human resources.

Common Migration Scenarios

In most cases, it is important to understand what type of migration you are undertaking. There are a few basic migration pathways most commonly seen in business:

- *A total application migration from one environment to another (DB2 to Oracle).* In this case, you are replacing one software application with another. In most cases, you are also moving to different physical machines and changing operating systems. The application code of the old system will be all replaced with new code. The database(s) (if any) of the old system will be replaced with Oracle.

- *A migration of databases to support the same application (Sybase to Oracle).* Here, you see the application code and front-end remaining the same, yet the database supporting the application changing. In many cases, this is simply a database migration and the application will even remain on the same or similar physical machines and operating systems. Application code changes are minimized to the changes needed to support the new database.

- *A migration of only a subset of one application (VSAM to Oracle).* In this case, only one module of an application, probably part of a very large application, is migrated to a different hardware/operating system and/or database.

- *An application that needs existing data from another system—one-time data transfer (Informix to Oracle).* This is the easiest form of migration. Your new application is simply built and tested, according to new specifications. Once the application is finished, old data is loaded into it. There is no transfer of the application logic from the old system to the new; there is just the need for old data, possibly from more than one source.

You will explore these four common scenarios throughout this chapter by using different technologies as examples. You will learn about many of the common technical issues faced in migration. You will also look at different aspects of the migration mindset that must manage the many resources and tasks that make a migration successful.

Downsizing

Downsizing from a mainframe to a more open environment by using Oracle not only requires you to battle technical issues that span these different types of systems, but to wage battle across time itself as older paradigms give way to newer paradigms.

Assume you are migrating a complete system from a mainframe environment to an Oracle environment, UNIX/Oracle/Oracle*Forms 4.5, for example. This migration is so difficult because so many components need to be moved (see Figure 7.5).

FIGURE 7.5.

A legacy downsizing migration, where all components of the old system need to be replaced.

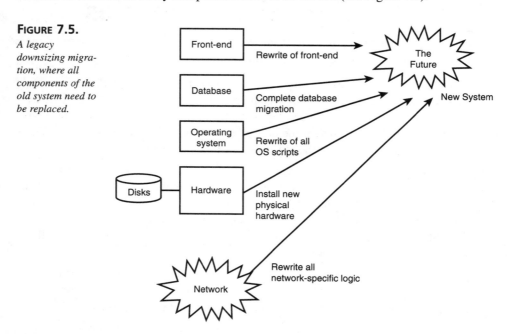

Aside from the many changes that need to be made, there is a radical paradigm shift when moving from a mainframe to a more open system. For one, IMS uses a hierarchical model to store data, whereas Oracle uses a relational model. Secondly, you are moving from character block-mode CICS screens to a GUI front-end interface. In this case, you need to redesign both the database and the front-end.

Not only will you be undertaking a massive redesign effort, but the new design of both the database and front-end will come from a totally different paradigm; therefore, the design process must change. The way that relational databases are designed differ greatly from the way hierarchical databases are designed. The way that GUI front-end systems are designed is also different from the way character-mode systems are designed.

Front-End Considerations

If you decide to minimize changes to the front-end, you might just copy all the screens using Oracle Forms 4.5. But by doing this, you would have a very nonstandard GUI interface. True, you could elect to build character-mode forms in Oracle Forms 4.5, but this choice would be only a partial system migration, because the front-end would be still designed for a system it was no longer using.

Sometimes cost and time considerations can force you to first complete a partial migration. You might decide that character-mode screens are the best choice for now, because users will not have to be retrained for as long as when the new system comes online. This decision is valid, but eventually you might want to redesign your front-end, given new possibilities and GUI standards. Many two-phase migrations are centered around this type of philosophy (see Figure 7.6).

FIGURE 7.6.

Sometimes a system is migrated in stages so as to minimize impact in user retraining.

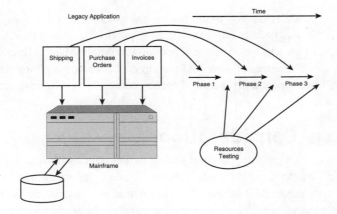

As long as you are conscious of your decision to delay a redesign of the front-end, you are not in peril. If, instead, you think that because you have an old front-end mapped to a new GUI tool you have a valid GUI front-end, you are mistaken. There are many GUI standards make different GUI front-ends easy to learn. If you do not use these features, your system may technically have a GUI front-end, but will force GUI users to spend more time learning the system (see Figure 7.7).

Aside from the future training costs of a nonstandard GUI application, you may suffer in terms of functionality. Assume your front-end is designed to buy and sell stocks; you might realize faster speeds for the end user in task completion and fewer keystrokes if you used modern GUI features. This would translate into a large, value-added gain for the migration project because transaction speed is of paramount importance to any trading system.

FIGURE 7.7.

When you don't design a front-end around its new environment, you confuse users and fail to realize processing gains.

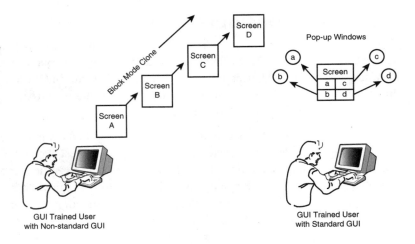

GUI Trained User
with Non-standard GUI

GUI Trained User
with Standard GUI

Like any business decision, you must choose how much money you want to invest in your downsizing. You need to consider all of the previous factors when deciding how much money and time to spend on the front-end migration. Many migration efforts have failed to see the differences of front-end paradigms between mainframe and GUI environments, and have spent a great deal of money ending up with a front-end that belonged to neither world.

Database Considerations

When you cross back into the past and look at earlier database forms, you might at first think how different they are from one another. Say that you are migrating data from an IMS database to an Oracle database. This means that you're crossing the bridge between the hierarchical model and the relational model and are in need of a complex translation between both worlds.

Many times, items in a hierarchical model, or in any earlier form, data is not in *Third Normal Form*. This is the standard form you try to approach when designing a relational database. Data tends to be flatter, containing attributes of many keys. Most times, when you migrate from a mainframe to Oracle's RDBMS, if you chose to normalize, you would end up with more tables on the new target system. This is important to realize when planning to migrate your data; the mapping of data won't necessarily be a one-to-one process (see Figure 7.8).

A mainframe-to-Oracle downsizing effort usually involves a great deal of data. Mainframes pride themselves on the capability to store large amounts of information and handle a large number of users. It is important not to blindly rush into a downsizing effort just to obtain a new technology. Many times, the amount of data you see on a mainframe will involve more complex disk strategies, such as the purchase of RAID technology. From the database perspective, this amount of data might require more advanced Oracle strategies, such as clustering and/or parallel processing, to handle all the requests the mainframe did (see Figure 7.9).

7

MIGRATING FROM NON-ORACLE DATABASES

FIGURE 7.8.
Most mainframe downsizing efforts to Oracle involve a complex mapping of data.

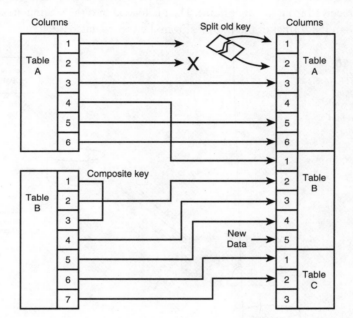

FIGURE 7.9.
In many cases, downsizing large mainframe applications require you to employ advanced technology to realize the same performance on a "smaller," open system.

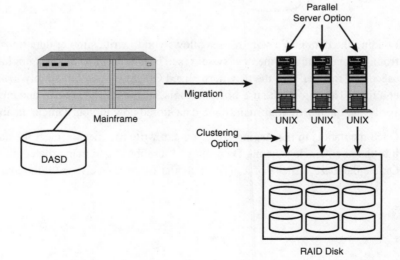

The actual volume of data that needs to be moved from the mainframe to the newer system needs to be taken into consideration and estimated. If you have enough space, you can set up a "staging area" for the new data (see Figure 7.10).

Normally, a staging area consists of a set of Oracle tables that are designed around the flat files received from the mainframe. Data is loaded into the staging area as it is received—in the format of the flat files from the source database.

FIGURE 7.10.

If you have the space, a staging area allows you to load data into Oracle as you receive it.

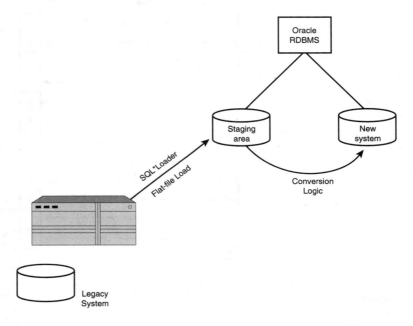

Loading the data into a staging area allows you to write simpler data transfer routines from the mainframe to the new system (see Figure 7.11). Data does not have to be massaged and mapped into the new normalized Oracle format, but simply loaded one flat file at a time. This allows the use of faster tools, such as SQL*Loader, and enables you to verify the quality of your mainframe data stored now in your Oracle database.

Once the data is in the staging area, you can write routines to select the data and move it into the new Oracle schema. Data can be "scrubbed" and manipulated directly from an Oracle database, instead of a mysterious flat file you receive from the mainframe.

FIGURE 7.11.

Coding data translation to read from an Oracle staging area gives a wider range of tools and greater ability to check for mistakes.

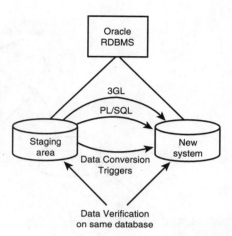

The only problem with a staging area is that you need to duplicate at least a portion of the data twice in your Oracle database. If you have a 1-terabyte mainframe application, a full staging area for the mainframe data and an area for the new Oracle database would take up 2TB!

Of course, you can plan out your staging area in steps if you have limited space, or you can decide not to use a staging area and therefore spend more time developing routines to convert data from flat files directly into the new normalized format. It is a trade-off between disk space versus the cost and time to write a more complex single-step conversion from the mainframe to Oracle.

If you decide to perform a one-time data conversion from a mainframe to an Oracle system, first download the flat files and transfer them to the newer system. After this is done, you would use a structured language such as C++ or Java to read data in from a file and perform the complex mapping and data conversion routines. Data can then be loaded into new files mapped to your normalized target tables, or be inserted directly into the database through the language's SQL interface.

Without a staging area, you don't have the luxury of trapping data and number conversion errors in your intermediate tables (see Figure 7.12). You also are not able to use a simpler and faster tool such as SQL*Loader, needing, instead, to encapsulate all of your logic in one set of programs that load data.

FIGURE 7.12.

Without a staging area, all of the logic and error-handling need to be coded into load routines that perform the complex translation.

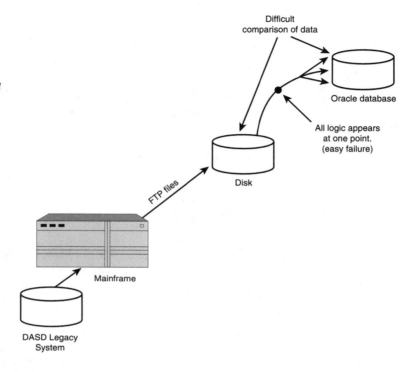

Remember that if you choose to write your own one-step load, record logs and error logs will have to be manually created to handle data exceptions.

Management Considerations

The management of the migration process in a downsizing effort becomes an art in itself. Many companies totally split the functionality of those who manage the older mainframes and those who work with newer, open systems. This philosophy, from the start, increases the chances of a power struggle.

Often the legacy system group resents that their tasks are being taken away and given to people who use a newer technology. You must assure your employees that they are not obsolete just because they use older technology. It is desirable in this market to retrain computer talent, considering the great shortage. If you can help move the legacy team into new positions in your company, you reduce the chance they will hold back the migration.

The group receiving the data and managing the new Oracle system must also be flexible. Data often will not come in an ideal format for Oracle, but Oracle probably has the built-in SQL or PL/SQL to make the conversion easier. There is no need to force the mainframe group to massage all of the data using tools like COBOL. With a well-thought-out plan, many of these tasks are quicker to do in Oracle than on the mainframe. This is why it is ideal to have at least a partial staging area. Other tasks, like sorting data and removing packed-decimal data, still need to be performed by the mainframe group.

As manager of a downsizing effort, it's also good to migrate your system in logical pieces rather than all at once. You can solve many technical issues and improve your project plan once you have completed even a partial transfer of data from the mainframe to Oracle. This will allow you to improve and refine your migration process.

Using Oracle's Data Conversion Tool—DCT

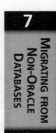

Oracle offers a product called the DCT. More than being an super-advanced piece of software, it is encapsulated knowledge from Oracle's experiences with migration. What you are really purchasing with DCT is automated experience in the migration process.

What the Conversion Tool Is and What It Is Not

Oracle's Data Conversion Tool, the DCT, is not a magical box that will allow you to move any application from any environment to Oracle. It is, instead, a methodology centered around a series of conversion tools. The major tools within the DCT are the following:

- Schema Reference
- Flat File Layout
- DDL Generator
- SQL Loader Generator
- Conversion Mapper
- Object Deployer
- Conversion Generator
- Impact Analyzer

The DCT is run from a new, open-system environment such as UNIX or Windows NT, and has an easy-to-use graphical front-end. From the database the DCT uses, you can create a central repository for the schemas used in both the old and new systems.

Data mapping is defined between your older system and the Oracle system you are migrating to when using this tool. The DCT will also generate simple SQL*Loader scripts and COBOL data-mapping information as a template for the conversion.

The methodology of the DCT is to create a staging area for data. First, data is moved from the mainframe to this staging area by using extract files created by the DCT. After this is done, data is moved into an Oracle database that supports the staging area. PL/SQL then translates data from the staging area into the new schema that exists in the DCT repository (see Figure 7.13).

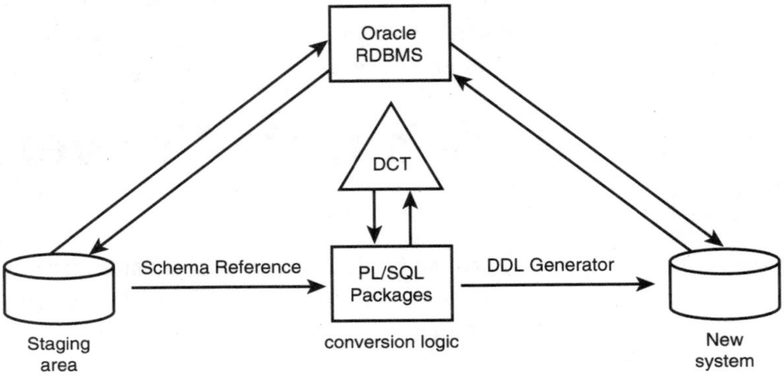

FIGURE 7.13.

The DCT uses a migration methodology to create the key elements needed in a migration effort, and a way to keep track of these elements.

Even with this tool, much of the coding still needs to be performed manually by a programming analyst. That is why the DCT creates many shells of PL/SQL procedures, all within a conversion PL/SQL package. These statements need to be modified and filled in with logic because they involve specific mapping rules unique to your migration effort.

What the DCT gives you above all else is a way to manage and keep track of all the data schema details in a large migration effort. It also provides standard templates and a step-by-step methodology for the migration of data from a non-Oracle database to an Oracle database.

A Step-by-Step Tour of a Data Migration Using the DCT

Follow the step-by-step methodology of the DCT to better understand its components. Along with learning about what automation the DCT offers, you will understand the methodology that Oracle is selling with the tool. This methodology is a very clear and straightforward way to migrate a database to Oracle.

Step One: Identify and Load Schema Data

In this step, DCT basically is used by data analysts to plan how data is going to be moved into the new Oracle database from the existing system(s). Obviously, this process will, to a great degree, drive how the new Oracle database is designed.

When using DCT, you can opt to purchase SQL*Net and/or a Transparent Gateway. You can directly link the new database to the older systems with these expensive tools, and DCT can perform an almost automatic mapping. When you choose this path, you cause the old system's data to appear to Oracle as an Oracle database, so many of the steps to download and massage data can be avoided. What you are really doing in this case is moving data from a virtual Oracle database to an actual Oracle database (see Figure 7.14).

FIGURE 7.14.

*If you chose to use DCT in conjunction with SQL*Net and/or a Transparent Gateway, DCT can automatically determine the older system's schema.*

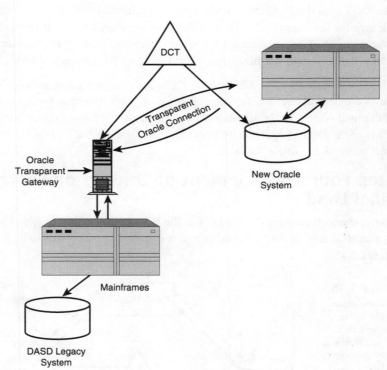

Step Two: Identify and Load Legacy Extract Files

If you are not so fortunate as to have transparent gateways between your old system and the new Oracle RDBMS, you need to extract data from the old system into a flat file by using either the other database vendor tools or a language such as COBOL.

DCT will automatically use a COBOL file layout to generate schema elements. Other languages can also be used and added to the DCT to automate the data definition process. A user can also manually enter flat-file layouts using the Flat File Layout (FFL) screen.

Step Three: Design, Create, and Load the Oracle Staging Area

The staging area's purpose is to create a data schema that will allow quick mapping from the source database or the flat files to the destination database. This will create a straight-forward load into Oracle by mapping data and tables one-to-one. By using this method, you can use Oracle's SQL*Loader tool.

The DCT uses the Flat File Layout, which is defined by the FFL tool, to create the staging area for the migration automatically. After the copy of the old source data exists in Oracle, the DCT will use the SQL Loader Generator (LDRG) to generate SQL*Loader scripts that will load flat files from the old system into the staging area.

Along with tables for the staging area, DCT can also create conversion views. These views are helpful because they show data in the staging area as the data will appear later in the final target Oracle database. At this point, you are using the conversion mapper (CM) of the DCT to specifically map columns from the DCT to their converted counter-parts in the final Oracle database.

Step Four: Development of Conversion Package and Final Load

The conversion package for the DCT is the bridge between the staging area and the old system. It is able to keep track of complex mappings between the two systems (see Figure 7.15).

FIGURE 7.15.

The conversion model represents the logic that will map data from an older (source) database into the Oracle (destina- tion) database.

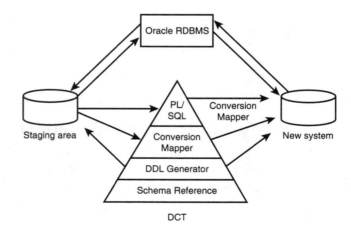

In the development process, the DCT will generate a PL/SQL package that will be the heart of the conversion process. This PL/SQL package consists of the following components:

- *Global object definitions and specifications*. This defines the calling parameters of the conversion package and the global variables that will be used.

- *Main procedure*. This procedure will contain the main cursor loop. You use a cursor because the DCT is looping through every row in the source table that exists in the staging area and changing that row for either insert, update, or delete in the new target database.

- *Group procedures*. These procedures provide the actual brute-force mapping that might need to be done between data elements. For instance, if your source system has a date format of 251295 (DDMMYY) and you want the format 25-DEC-1995 (DD-MON-YYYY) for your new system, you need to perform SQL operators like TO_DATE and TO_CHAR on the old data to convert it into the new data.

  There are four types of group procedures:

    Main

    Update

    Insert

    Delete

- *Initialization code for package*. This is usually not used because the package is normally executed by a human operator in a tool like SQL*Plus.

By packaging the logic that will move data from the Oracle staging area to the target Oracle database, you have more ability to structure and keep track of data movement.

The order in which group procedures are executed can be specified with the DCT's PL/SQL template. This is extremely useful if you want to update records that already exist in the Oracle database and insert only records that exist in the older source database. This scenario is common with a new system that has been run in parallel with the older system and already contains most of the data (see Figure 7.16).

Regardless of the magic that the DCT can perform in organizing the conversion tasks, the "conversion developer" (the person writing the conversion routines) needs to be able to use the SELECT, INSERT, UPDATE, CREATE VIEW, and CREATE PROCEDURE functions within SQL and Oracle's PL/SQL. The final PL/SQL that will be placed in the DCT procedure shells can be very complex and will probably utilize many SQL extensions to convert the data. It is important to assign technical people to this aspect of Oracle's migration methodology.

FIGURE 7.16.

By specifying the order of your data conversion, you can use PL/SQL to insert new records into Oracle and update older records.

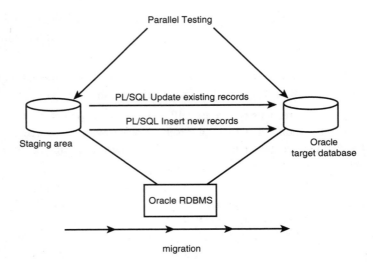

Step Five: Verification and Maintenance

After the data has been migrated, you need to verify the data through extensive testing. In most cases, not everything will be perfect on the first pass, and you will need to reload data. Oracle's DCT helps you keep track of the process by logging the migration of data for every column. DCT uses the Schema Reference to track these changes. The Schema Reference stores the following information regarding each field that is being mapped:

- Field—Description of field
- Table\View—Name of table or view
- Owner—Owner of table or view
- Database—Database name on which a field resides
- Host—Hostname
- Last Update—Date of last modification or data update
- Create Date—Date of Table/View creation
- Status—Is the Table/View available?
- Column_Name—The Oracle column name for the field
- Data Type—The Oracle datatype of the field

With this structure, your migration effort does not become a nightmare, as many do, because you can keep track of all the mappings from the old system to Oracle and of the changes to this translation process.

Aside from accurate record-keeping, the DCT offers more glamorous options like the Impact Analyzer which can point to cascade effects that may occur when you change a simple data element or mapping in the migration. This is useful because, in most migrations, the mapping and design process can be invalidated by an inadvertent change to one field, especially if that field is a foreign key for many tables (see Figure 7.17).

FIGURE 7.17.

Changing one field of source data can invalidate much of a migration unless it is anticipated.

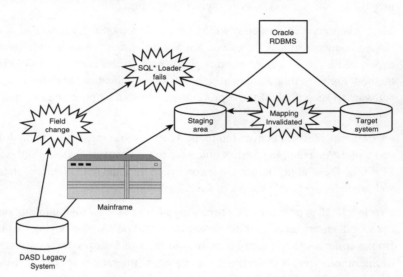

Migrating a Front-End Using DCT and Oracle*Forms 4.5

The DCT offering by Oracle also can fit in with automatic form generation using Oracle's Oracle*Forms 4.5. The catch is that these forms cannot be generated from your original forms written with tools, such as CICS. But Oracle*Forms can generate simple block-mode or GUI forms based on table and column definitions.

For most complex systems, this is not useful, because forms can contain a great deal of flow-of-control logic for the users and also may communicate with many different tables, given the functions performed on the form. In most cases, this forces you to redesign or, at least, redeploy the existing forms on the new front-end.

Oracle's form generation utility is useful for less complex systems and for the generation of maintenance screens that map to either one table alone or one table driving a multi-row display of another table. Sometimes these quick forms that are easy to generate can help greatly in the testing and the verification of the new Oracle system in parallel with the old system, so they should not be discounted.

Oracle DCT—Is It Worth It?

Guess what, the answer to the question is "Yes." The reason might not be the one Oracle would want you to believe. The DCT alone is not a cure-all and requires the participation of many database and programming experts. What the DCT does give you, which is invaluable, is a methodology for system migration.

Many glamorous corporations will simply sell methodology tools and documentation for huge amounts of money. What you are buying in these cases is a philosophy from an expert and a way to implement that philosophy. In this case, you would be looking for methodologies to migrate/downsize a software application. Step-by-step procedures, and software to keep track of those procedures, can also be purchased from a methodology vendor.

Other companies sell conversion tools. They have no interest in methodology but only sell a tool. An example of this would be a tool to convert Sybase ISQL to Oracle PL/SQL. These companies are not concerned with the overall approach to migration, but sell products to complete a set of specific tasks.

Oracle's DCT is of great value because you are buying a methodology on downsizing by the world's most successful database company. You are also buying this methodology from a company that directly benefits—in sales of their product—whenever a downsizing or migration effort is undertaken; Oracle wants migrations to their platform to succeed. Along with this methodology, you are purchasing a set of tools that, although requiring programming expertise, help enforce and facilitate the methodology down to the coding level. With Oracle's DCT, you get the best of both worlds: a methodology tool and a conversion tool.

Summary

As stressed in this chapter, a successful migration is more of a managerial effort than a technical effort. Once you have a solid conversion plan in place, a way to track progress, and the support of human resources from both the source system and the target system, you have fought half the battle.

In general, migrations are very difficult because you have to translate a different mind-set into a new one. Even if you're moving across relational platforms, ways of doing things in one database environment and powerful shortcuts have influenced the development process and will need to be examined in the migration. Sometimes, rewriting a huge amount of code that no one understands is more costly than simply building a new system.

Even though the front-end will be the only direct evidence the user has of a migration, the most important and time-consuming task for most systems migrations is the translation of data. The farther apart the source and the target system are in database philosophies, the more difficult this translation will be.

Even though it wasn't mentioned in this chapter, migration efforts often hinge upon how well you can tune and configure the new instance(s) of the Oracle database on which the source data will reside. Mapping data is only the beginning of the migration process; once the data is there, you must unlock those features of Oracle that will enable the new target system to perform as well or better than the old system, and thus justify the cost of the migration effort itself.

Coexisting with Non-Oracle Databases

by Advanced Information Systems, Inc.

IN THIS CHAPTER

Sleeping with the Enemy

Although any database vendor will tell you that his database should be running 100 percent of your systems, this isn't usually the case. In the first place, converting all a company's systems to one database at once will put too much strain on the existing resources. Secondly, it might not be logical to move all the systems to one database. Different applications demand different types of database software. This is why in most large or medium corporate operations, you need to connect disparate database software.

Because of this phenomenon, you might be in a situation where you purchased an Oracle RDBMS, and you have a number of separate systems that need to be interfaced to Oracle, systems that have major differences in their environment from yours. Here are some of the differences:

- Different operating systems
- Different hardware vendor
- Different RDBMS vendor
- Different paradigms

A project team and an RDBMS software application might need to contend with these four areas when dealing with outside systems.

Different Operating Systems

This is a more difficult obstacle if these two systems do not talk to each other for any other reason. In this case, linking a system with a different OS than your Oracle database means that your project needs to establish the links from the lowest networking level to the level of screen interfaces. Different operating systems can have many subtle differences.

Picture a fictitious airline that purchased Oracle as its Web server. Soon customers are ordering flights over the Web and querying flight information. This information processing has been traditionally performed on a huge mainframe, but now this new Oracle database needs to connect to a different mainframe. Say that the database is running UNIX. This is a classic example of two very different operating systems that many times need to talk to each other.

The situation can be compounded with three operating systems that need to communicate database application logic. If this fictitious airline purchased a huge Windows NT cluster for a data warehouse, you would need to send data directly to Windows NT from both the UNIX and MVS operating systems as shown in Figure 8.1.

FIGURE 8.1.
A corporate environment usually has many generations of different hardware and operating systems.

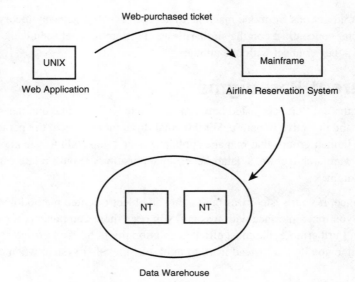

Connecting three databases over different operating systems is not inherently more difficult, but managing the underlying connection between the OSs and any data translation is.

Different Hardware Vendors

The complexity of a database gateway over different hardware systems isn't drastic if you run the same operating system. If you run the same operating system and the same database, the differences are minor. If you are running different RDBMS products by different vendors, the complexities increase.

Looking at the Microsoft NT operating system, differences in hardware evaporate when the Windows NT services are in place because Windows NT is the product of one vendor. UNIX, however, differs more between hardware vendors; therefore, linking a SUN SPARC to an HP-9000 does involve the consideration of minor operating system differences or kernel configuration differences.

Different RDBMS Vendors

Even when you solve any lower-level adjustments that you must make to realize communication between two databases on two separate machines, you still might be running two different RDBMSs. For instance, if you run Oracle on one Windows NT machine and SQL Server on another Windows NT machine, you need a translation process when

8

COEXISTING WITH
NON-ORACLE
DATABASES

sending transactions from one machine to another. Most of gateway theory as related to this chapter concentrates on the similarities and differences between databases and common ways they connect with one another.

Different Paradigms

The first three differences listed between an Oracle RDBMS and another system were physical and objective in nature. Yet this final difference refers to the paradigms of the different human groups that manage applications and must talk to one another. The way that hardware architecture, a database, or an application are built relate very closely to this paradigm.

For instance, if your system was built using an object-oriented methodology, yet the system that you must interface with was not, you need more components for a successful interface. Furthermore, the most efficient solution might not be to force another system to think like you do but instead learn to think like the other system when communicating with it.

You see this paradigm split most commonly between mainframe systems and more *open* systems. Both systems have been successful doing certain tasks but need to talk to each other. In this case, if you use Oracle, you are probably on the "open" side wondering how you are going to communicate with a mainframe. Suddenly, your "open" system doesn't appear very open when it needs to interface with a legacy mainframe.

If the paradigm of the people who manage the mainframe is similar to yours, in that they might also use another relational database such as DB2, you can communicate and build bridges rather quickly. If they come from a completely different paradigm of VSAM files or IMS, it will be harder to map their data to yours because both data sets are structured from different paradigms.

It is important for an Oracle project to have flexible methods for propagating data to other systems that add value to the Oracle system. Many times, your Oracle system will have to conform to the data structure of the system to which you need to interface. This will probably involve many table joins and other complex SQL to "flatten" and denormalize your data for a mainframe dataset.

Your system interface will need to communicate to a legacy system from which it is very different. But this foreign system also needs to talk to your system. Both systems need to understand the other's protocol to communicate through a network. At a higher level, both databases on these two systems need to talk to each other and understand a part of the other's language.

Instead of building this interface from scratch, you can purchase products that connect networks, isolating you from the problems of protocol differences. The Oracle network offering that isolates you from different protocols is SQL*Net. Likewise, you do not need to build the database interface; you can purchase one. This interface between two different databases is a *gateway*.

The Gateway to Everywhere

When you enter the world of gateways, you soon realize from all the vendors selling them that your database can talk to just about anything from a mainframe to a mountain goat. Therefore, you must determine which gateway you need and which gateway will be most cost-effective given your budget and resources.

What Kind of Gateway Do You Need?

Gateways can be broken up into three major areas:

- **Transparent Gateways**—These are the top-of-the-line gateways where the interface is so perfect that your Oracle systems believe that they are talking to other Oracle instances, when they are communicating with different databases on different platforms: The gateway "tricks" the Oracle instance to think that another remote foreign database is actually an Oracle database, as in Figure 8.2.

FIGURE 8.2.

Oracle's Transparent Gateway appears as an Oracle database to the other Oracle databases it is linked to.

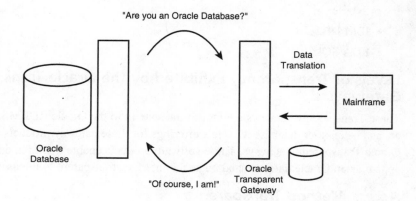

- **Procedural Gateways**—At this level, the Oracle database does not believe that it is talking to another Oracle database, but instead the database can communicate to a set of libraries written in either C or PL/SQL. These libraries provide a set of calls that need to be used explicitly when linking any portion of one database's activity to another.

- **Passive Gateways**—Most of these gateways are homegrown and involve moving data through a series of steps, first moving data to another machine, and then at a point in time having the other system read in the data. The gateway is passive because there is no direct communication between database systems. Data is simply being sent from one database to the other by an independent set of processes.

Now consider how these three forms coexist with your Oracle databases and other "foreign" databases. As you can probably guess, as you move from Passive Gateways up again to Transparent Gateways, the cost of them becomes greater as functionality and ease-of-use increase. You incur a greater cost for a more sophisticated gateway, so unless that sophistication adds value, the most profitable solution might be a less expensive gateway.

Transparent Gateways

As defined in the previous section, a Transparent Gateway "tricks" the Oracle instance into thinking that an Oracle machine exits remotely when, in fact, it is a completely different database offering. Here are some of the major databases where you can purchase this type of interface to Oracle:

- Microsoft SQL Server (offered free sometimes)
- Informix
- Ingres
- Sybase
- IBM DB2
- EDA SQL

Levels of Transparency Exhibited by the Oracle Transparent Gateways

These Transparent Gateways are indeed transparent to the Oracle RDBMS, and they can act as just another database. Oracle's offerings for these gateway products are called the Oracle Transparent Gateways. These software products enable a foreign database to appear as an Oracle database and make the interface transparent to the users.

Access Method Transparency

This means that just as Oracle access is SQL-based, a user can use SQL on the gateway to retrieve data from a non-Oracle database using SQL just as if it were an Oracle database. The only catch with this is performance. Regardless of the gateway's speed, if data on the remote machine is not indexed or sorted, the same SQL runs on the remote machine, and the local Oracle machine might vary a great deal in the time that it takes to retrieve the data.

Location Transparency

This simply is an extension of Access Method Transparency in that not even the physical location of the data needs to be known by the user. Oracle's gateway will map a request to the different physical machines and databases on which the data resides.

One note here: To realize Location Transparency, an administrator needs to set up SQL*Net on both machines and create the proper database links, grants, and synonyms.

Network Transparency

This really should be called SQL*Net Transparency. You still need Oracle's standard network layer running over all your different networks to shelter each database from network differences and to provide a common protocol. SQL*Net is the portion of the gateway that handles network communication. When SQL*Net is working, there is network transparency between databases.

Operating System Transparency

This means that for database functions, users do not have to be concerned with which operating system the two different databases reside on.

Benefits of Oracle's Transparent Gateways

As mentioned earlier, the Oracle Transparent Gateway is a top-line solution. It makes coexistence between an Oracle database and a non-Oracle database easier to manage. The potential buyer of these expensive systems should first ponder the benefits of this solution to determine whether the extra cost spent will add enough value to make the gateway profitable.

Full SQL Support

Advanced Oracle extensions to ANSI SQL such as the Outer-Join operator or the Decode function might be used to access a remote database that does not even use SQL.

Full PL/SQL Support and Trigger Support

This is an important feature, in that you can now code referential integrity triggers that can create streams of business logic between two remote machines, and enforce table uniformity between two databases.

For instance, as in Figure 8.3, you can have an Order/Entry system residing on Oracle. Whenever an order is shipped, a trigger can fire out to the remote table on the other database and subtract from the inventory or the warehouse from which the goods will be shipped.

FIGURE 8.3.

With Oracle's Transparent Gateway, developers can use common tools such as PL/SQL to communicate to totally non-Oracle systems. The gateway handles the translation.

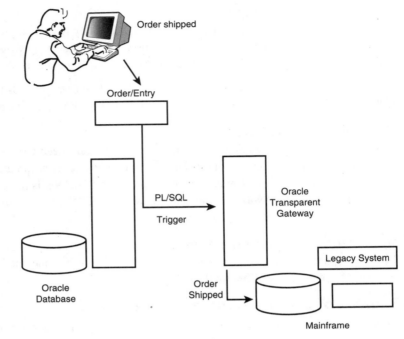

Distributed Transactions Use Two-Phase Commit

This refers to a change in data that must take place on two or more machines, as seen in Figure 8.4. Data is committed in the usual way on the first machine and then sent across the network and the gateway to the next machine. Not until the remote commits are all complete is the transaction considered final. This is useful for tables on two different databases that need to be replicated and/or need to always be synchronized.

In the previous example, if you never wanted a sale to be shipped until you were sure that you subtracted it from the inventory, you would use the two-phase commit in the following way.

Cost-Based Distributed Joins

If you use cost-based optimization and have run the proper SQL to populate Oracle's internal tables, Oracle can choose a join across a distributed network in an efficient way.

FIGURE 8.4.

A simple request to ship an order results in a two-phase commit that will not be successful unless the mainframe database confirms that inventory exists for the shipment.

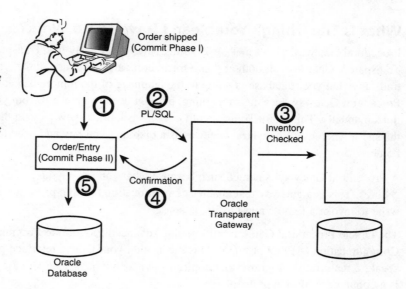

Transparent Schema Mapping

This refers of the gateway's capability to view a foreign database's tables and columns in the same way that Oracle tables and columns are defined. This includes mapping of dates, characters, and LONG data. This transparency can provide a seamless mapping between an Oracle character string and a DB2 character string residing on MVS. To do this, you need to account for vendor differences in data storage between DB2 and Oracle and convert to the ASCII character set from the mainframe EBCDC character set.

Transparent Views of Data Dictionaries

According to Codd's original writings on Relational Theory, a relational data dictionary appearing as tables to the user is a vital aspect of a relational database. Oracle's gateway provides this illusion, so a remote non-Oracle schema, at least in part, appears to the user as an Oracle data dictionary.

Procedural Gateways

Procedural Gateways can be as powerful as Transparent Gateways; the only catch is that the logic linking Oracle to a non-Oracle database has to be explicitly coded. These are ideal gateways if you have, or are willing to purchase, the in-house talent to use these "procedures" to create a gateway.

What Is This Thing? You Mean I Have to Do Work?

Procedural Gateways don't make everything better right away like Transparent Gateways. Transparent Gateways sit both at your Oracle computer's site and at the remote site and translate what your database is doing to the language of the remote database. A Procedural Gateway does the same thing, but you need to invoke it from your applications manually. Think of a Transparent Gateway as a brand-new bicycle that you pick off the shelf, whereas a Procedural Gateway is a bike that you buy and need to assemble at home.

A Procedural Gateway is named such because what you are buying is a gateway for procedures. This is a gateway that enables communication through procedures that you must write to invoke a remote non-Oracle database.

The Oracle Procedural Gateway utilizes the Advanced Program to Program Communication (APPC) protocol. This means that your Oracle interface programs can speak to mainframe programs that don't use Oracle but have access to the APPC, which is a popular mainframe protocol.

With the APPC Oracle Procedural Gateway, you can communicate with the following Mainframe tools:

- CICS/MVS
- IMS/TM
- CA-IDMS
- CICS/VSE
- CICS/400
- REXX (for the REXX fans in the audience)

This means that within your CICS code, you can call these procedures to communicate with a remote non-MVS Oracle database. With the APPC, you can also communicate with the following databases and file systems:

- DB2
- IMS
- CA-IDMS
- ADABAS
- VSAM

Oracle uses the X/Open Common Programming Interface for Communication. This makes the Oracle gateway very flexible because this is a common mainframe communications standard.

A Day in the Life of a Procedural Gateway

When using a Procedural Gateway, refer to the Web-based frequent-flier database (Figure 8.5). Reward your airline patron with a free flight. Assume that you cannot book flights over the Web. After you determine that your traveler has the necessary miles, call a PL/SQL procedure to book the flight on the mainframe. At this point, the procedure flies through SQL*Net to the Oracle Procedural Gateway waiting for you on the ancient mainframe. The gateway builds an APPC transaction and routes it through the SNA (mainframe) network. The response is returned via SQL*Net again to your application. This means that someone on the Web can cash in on free miles and book a flight on a mainframe. Here is how the whole "procedure" looks.

FIGURE 8.5.

With a Procedural Gateway, all you need to do is build the logic; the gateway takes care of all networking and request translations needed by the non-Oracle database and hardware environment.

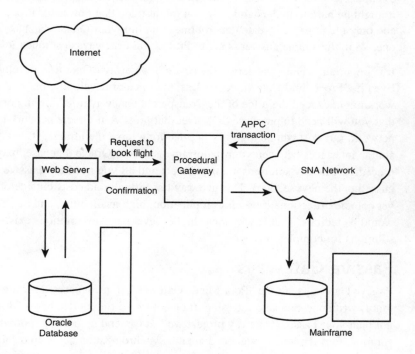

IBM's MQSeries

If you use IBM's MQSeries messaging products, Oracle also has a Procedural Gateway that links a mainframe or newer IBM product using this protocol for databases on another system. Oracle's procedure library supplies you with PL/SQL when you buy this gateway, so your development staff does not need to learn a new set of APIs.

With these procedure calls, you can employ logic affecting a remote mainframe through PL/SQL, database triggers, Oracle Developer/2000, and third-party tools. This tool even enables you to build distributed databases or, at least, distributed tables because the MQSeries messaging supports two-phase commits. You can have your frequent-flier database share a table called REWARDS that exists on the mainframe and on your Oracle instance. With the MQSeries gateway and the two-phase commit, you can ensure that these tables remain in sync.

Why Purchase a Procedural Gateway?

Because you understand that Transparent Gateways ensure that your non-Oracle databases appear as Oracle databases, thus leaving you with an integrated database environment, it might be hard to understand why you might trade that power for Procedural Gateways and only the *ability* to create data routines that link your Oracle database to a remote one. Well, the simple answer is price. Procedural Gateways cost much less.

It is important when considering the cost of a gateway to factor in development time. Even if a Procedural Gateway costs less, the price of developing the routines to make it work might exceed the price of the Transparent Gateway. It is also important to realize that you will need to purchase SQL*Net that links your Oracle network to the remote network; this cost can be high if you price for a large mainframe. If you need only a few simple interfaces between your mainframe and your Oracle database, maybe both the preceding gateway solutions are not correct and all you need is a Passive Gateway (discussed in the next section). This gateway has virtually no costs outside of development; yet complex functionality such as replication, high availability, and distributed data would be tedious. That is why these higher-level gateway solutions exist—they give us solutions for complex problems.

Passive Gateways

Passive Gateways are the "Poor Man's Gateway." In most cases, they are simple programs written in-house to refresh portions of two different databases. However, if you do not plan your Passive Gateway project well, it can end up costing more than any other solution. Furthermore, if you need greater synchronization between databases, a Passive Gateway might just be a "redesign of the wheel" that can be avoided using one of Oracle's gateway options. It is important to use these simple gateways only when the task is not too complex.

The Zen Gateway——Does It Really Exist?

I have termed a Passive Gateway as one where data is moved across one database to another remote database manually. This data movement can be termed as "passive" because it does not occur within the structure of transactions but is only moved when a user-defined process is started. It is also passive because from the point of view of each database and each process, the gateway itself does not exist. The Passive Gateway comes into existence only for a brief moment in time.

A monthly data refresh between two separate computer systems is an example of a Passive Gateway. Data is simply transferred as a series of files by a user-defined set of programs. These programs move data first out of one computer's database into an operating system file and then move it into another computer's file system and database. Both databases consider these programs no different from any other database-related process that moves data from the database to a flat file.

The advantage of the Passive Gateway is that it is usually less expensive. To unload data from one database, transfer it, and then load it into another database is much simpler than the low-level translations of SQL*Net and Oracle's Transparent Gateways. You can perform this operation with standard tools that do not cost extra—no need to purchase SQL*Net with this method.

The disadvantage with Passive Gateways is that they are so simple and fit such a specified need that they usually need to be custom built. Yet if development costs are managed for a simple Passive Gateway, the cost of Oracle's SQL*Net product and of Oracle's Open Gateway products will be greater. The hours spent simply configuring SQL*Net and an Open Gateway can be higher than the development of a simple Passive Gateway.

It is important to decide which kind of gateway you need. If you want to keep replicated databases running at two sites, probably designing your own data-transfer and logging routines will be too complicated. Yet if you need data from one machine periodically sent to another, consider a Passive Gateway.

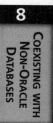

8

COEXISTING WITH
NON-ORACLE
DATABASES

Building a Passive Gateway, Mainframe to Oracle Example

Look at your fictitious airline business (Figure 8.6). Assume that there is only a frequent-flier Oracle database that is running over the Web; it cannot book flights. The database to reserve and purchase flights exists separately on a mainframe.

The frequent-flier application is running on a UNIX server that is running the Oracle8 database and the Web server. The main database of airline purchases exists on a mainframe running DB2. The only reason that these applications need to talk to each other is because flight data must be moved monthly from the mainframe database and used to update the Oracle/UNIX frequent-flier database.

FIGURE 8.6.

With a transaction such as a monthly refresh that does not need to occur for each transaction, many times a Passive Gateway can handle this simpler relation.

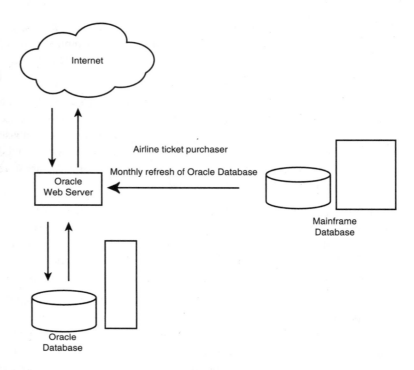

Because data is moving from the mainframe to the UNIX environment, you first must extract the information from DB2 and convert it to a flat file. The query might be something such as this:

```
EXEC SQL
Select
Customer_name, sum(miles_traveled)
From flight_activity
Where month = :current_month
Group By Customer_name

END EXEC
```

This query can be written with SQL embedded in COBOL that writes to a file (dataset) on the mainframe with the results of the query as in Figure 8.7. You can also use DB2's SPUFI tool instead to execute this query and spool data to a dataset.

You would create a JCL script that would run once a month to execute this COBOL job, on the night of the last day of the month. The results of the job would sit in a dataset called monthact.

That same evening on the Oracle UNIX box, there would be a `cron job` command that might run every 15 minutes to ping the network and see if the MVS dataset existed and was available. After the data finished loading, a UNIX command from the Oracle box would pull the dataset through FTP with the `Get` command and move the information to a file on the UNIX file system.

FIGURE 8.7.
With a Passive Gateway for a periodic refresh, you see many different user-created programs working together yet not communicating with one another.

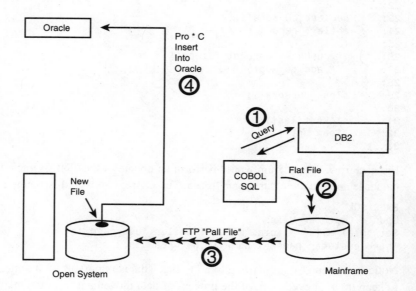

After this UNIX *cron job* finished and the UNIX file existed with the month of new flight activity, the *cron script* would call a PRO*C program. This program would read in the rows of the data that were extracted from the DB2 Select statement:

Our data:

```
 1: Ernie Salesnutt     34000
 2: Bill Gateway        12000
 3: Garuda Deli         10000
 4: GetMainframeData.pc - Program Shell:
 5: EXEC SQL BEGIN DECLARE SECTION;
 6: VARCHAR    customer_name[48];
 7: int        miles;
 8: EXEC SQL END DECLARE SECTION;
 9:
10: EXEC SQL INCLUDE SQLCA;
11:
12: EXEC SQL WHENEVER SQLERROR GOTO err;
13:
14: FILE *fp_data, *fp_log;
15:
```

```
16: main()
17: {
18:     init();
19:
20:     open_file_from_mainframe(fp_data, "monthact.dat");
21:     open_log(fp_log,  "monthact.log");
22:
23:     declare_cursors();
24:     while ( read_a_row() == 0)
25:     {
26:         update_frequent_fliers();
27:         add_to_log();
28:     }
29:     close_cursors();
30:
31:     close_files();
32:     clean_up();
33: }
```

For each row, the program would perform an update of the UNIX Oracle frequent-flier database and the table Customer_Miles. The C program would issue the following SQL:

```
EXEC SQL
Update Customer_Miles
Set total_miles = total_miles + :miles_just_read_in
Where customer_name = :name_I_just_read_in;
```

Notice that you also are writing to a log file. This is important for a homespun gateway, to keep track of every step of the process of data movement from the mainframe to the Oracle instance.

In a more realistic case, of course, you would just use the frequent-flier number of the customer and not a nonunique name. But using the name illustrates that you are updating a customer's miles based on new travel for the month. Leave it here for teaching purposes only.

Instead of a direct update from a file, you can simply load the DB2 file directly into an intermediate Oracle table called monthly_upload. Use a SQL*Loader script (Oracle Loader) to accomplish this. After this is tested, you can write a trigger to automatically update the customer_miles table whenever data is inserted into the monthly_upload table. This table is your record of the previous month's transfer. If late transactions need to be loaded later, they can be loaded without affecting your Passive Gateway. This would be the trigger used to update your customer_miles table:

```
1: Create or replace trigger customer_miles_ins
2: Before insert
3: on MYDATABASE.Monthly_load
4: For each row
```

```
 5: Begin
 6:     Update customer_miles
 7:     Set total_miles = total_miles + :new.miles_loaded
 8:     Where customer_name = :new.customer_name;
 9:
10: EXCEPTION
11:     WHEN others THEN
12: Raise application_error(-20000,'update of ' ¦¦:new.customer_name¦¦'
➡for ' ¦¦:new.miles_loaded¦¦' failed.');
13:
14: End;
15: /
```

In a production system, your error-handling would probably be more exact. Yet with
these simple SQL scripts on the mainframe and the UNIX machine, you can create a
Passive Gateway that both databases are unaware of, yet is vital in keeping both systems
synchronized.

Of course, we are using the network software to convert the character sets; furthermore,
we are planning our DB2 COBOL download so that problems such as "packed decimal"
numbers won't need to be translated on the Oracle end of the process. We can even eliminate the network and have a *very* Passive Gateway where each month a tape would be
physically mailed to the Oracle site and read from tape by a PRO*C process (see
Figure 8.8).

8

COEXISTING WITH
NON-ORACLE
DATABASES

FIGURE 8.8.

*Mainframe data
transferred into
the Oracle
RDBMS via
overnight mail
due to unaccept-
able transfer rates
from the main-
frame.*

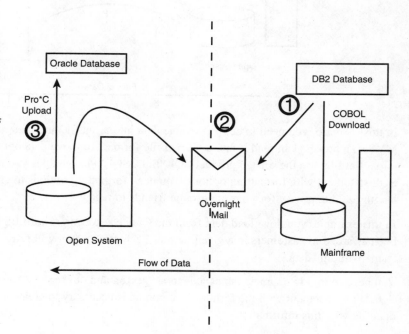

Building a Passive Gateway, Oracle to Mainframe Example

In today's computing world, a gateway from an Oracle application on an *Open System* back to a mainframe is more common. Many times, corporations have slowly moved applications off of mainframes in their *downsizing efforts,* yet need these new Oracle applications to communicate back to the mainframe and the other applications that have not been downsized.

Again assume we have a frequent-flier database over the Web, but we need to send reward flights for our best customers into the accounting system every month end. Our accounting system is running on an ancient system using VSAM files and is remote from us on a distant mainframe. In this case, the data needs to move from the Oracle RDBMS to the mainframe (Figure 8.9).

FIGURE 8.9.
SQL*Plus extract of data for an FTP cooperative processing upload back into a mainframe.

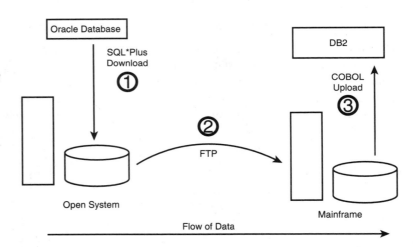

In this scenario, you need to convert Oracle data into a flat file and then move this file to MVS so a process can read it into a VSAM file format. To move data out of Oracle and into a flat file, use the trusted product SQL*Plus. SQL*Plus enables you to spool any SQL statement with formatting options. You need formatting options to create a fixed-length file that is easy for your mainframe friends to read.

In this example, you download data from the Oracle server on reward flights that have been awarded to customers in a given month. Each month, you will refresh the mainframe with this data:

You need to join two Oracle tables, `Customer_Miles` and `Customer_Flight`. Here's the SQL*Plus statement with the formatting commands necessary to create a fixed-length data file with this information.

```
 1: set pagesize 0
 2: set linesize 80
 3:
 4: set term off
 5: set feed off
 6: set echo off
 7: set show off
 8: set veri off
 9: set head off
10:
11: col customer_id      format9999999999
12: col reward_miles      format 999,990.00
13: col depart_date      format a10
14: col return_date      format a10
15: col flight_no         format 99999
16:
17:
18: spool outputfile
19:
20: Select
21: cm.customer_id,
22: cm.reward_miles,
23: to_char(cf.depart_date, 'mm/dd/yyyy'),
24: to_char(cf.return_date, 'mm/dd/yyyy'),
25: cf.flight_no
26: from
27: Customer_Miles cm,
28: Customer_Flight cf
29: where cm.customer_id = cf.customer_id
30: and    to_char(cf.depart_date,'MM/YYYY') = '&1'
31: /
32:
33: spool off
34:
35: exit
36: /
```

This SQL will be executed by a *cron file* at the end of each month. The constant `'&&1'` accepts the first parameter that, in this case, will be the two-digit month code and the year. When the script fires for December 1999, this six-digit code will be 121999. No year 2K problem here!

After this script creates the output file outputfile, the cron job fires again and calls an FTP process using the put command to move the output file to the mainframe.

At this point, the spool file can be loaded into a VSAM file and the mainframe accounting package can access the new data.

One important note here: We performed a join in our SQL because we are operating under the relational paradigm of normalized data. In most cases, nonrelational data appears "flatter" and might necessitate many joins of our tables. This is a common phenomenon when moving data from a relational database to an older mainframe database that is nonrelational.

By writing a few simple programs, we have bypassed the need to use expensive networking and gateway products. We can add more complexity, such as error and status logs, that would be passed along with the data between our "open" Oracle system and the legacy mainframe with which we want to coexist.

Coexistence and Replication

The purest form of database coexistence is a distributed database. A distributed database appears as one database to users and developers, yet is a series of separate databases at the physical level. To accomplish this task, we need to replicate data on these different databases so that at the higher levels data appears uniform regardless of which system we query or modify.

Replicating What Is Different

We have talked in this book about replication between two separate Oracle databases. Now we must tackle the task of replication among databases that might be totally foreign to Oracle in every way. The ideal form, where a large network of connected databases act as one database, replicating one another's data, is a *distributed database.*

A distributed database is singular in that although data physically exists at many sites, it is still one database at the highest level that is simply distributed physically, as in Figure 8.10.

Oracle solves the mystery of the distributed database in a twofold way. Oracle first offers a Transparent Gateway to the foreign machines, so they all appear to be Oracle databases. This also involves the purchase of SQL*Net to make different network protocols appear the same. After these tasks are accomplished, proceed with replication in the same way as if the databases were all Oracle databases.

If instead you only need consistency, at day's end, you don't need to constantly refresh transactions but can *defer* them for propagation to other nodes of your distributed database. To do this, you need to store logs of your transactions and then at a given time use the log information to refresh remote nodes. This type of replication is *Asynchronous.*

FIGURE 8.10.

A distributed database appears to users as one database.

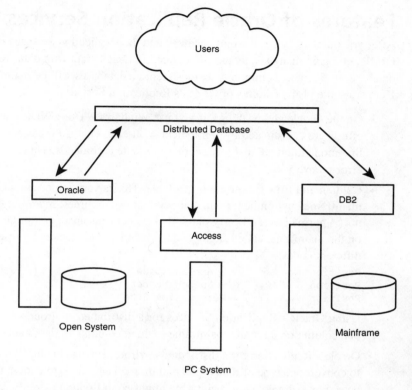

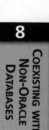

Obviously, Asynchronous replication is less sophisticated in that each transaction does not need to be propagated to other nodes of the distributed database but instead to a log file. Because of this, a two-phase commit will not need to exist for a transaction to complete. This makes for a faster transaction rate.

With Asynchronous replication, we do have the added worry of our transaction logs. Even though they fill up only with rowids, timestamps, and other logging information, after many transactions, log files can become large. Therefore, Asynchronous replication can take up more space. But today, with speed more valuable than space, this is not a major concern. A megabyte of storage can be purchased for a rupee.

One catch with Oracle's replication, even if you have a Transparent Gateway, is that you need the IBM Data Propagator to move data from the mainframe database back to Oracle, either synchronously or asynchronously. This is vital in configurations where a mainframe is still the central computer of an operation with new Oracle departmental servers existing to perform local processing.

Features of Oracle Replication Services

After you purchase a Transparent Gateway and the Replication Services software from Oracle, you gain many advantages in replicating Oracle data with data from a remote database. In the most common case, these remote databases will be mainframe databases. Here are some of the features of Oracle's Replication Services:

- On the Oracle end of things, if you use Windows NT or UNIX, your replication efforts are coordinated by a graphical front-end. This is far easier to use than a line-mode interface that forces you to execute commands. This includes automatic error-recovery.

- Column and Row subsetting is available. This is very important when interfacing a mainframe environment to an open system. Many times, mainframe columns are not as normalized and carry old-style keys. For instance, you might have a column on the mainframe called flight_code, which is 17 characters representing three different codes:

```
Position 1 - 2        Airline Code
Position 3 - 10        Coupon Number
Position 11 - 17     Reservation Code
```

Using Oracle's Replication Services for a distributed environment lets you map this one column on a remote mainframe to three columns in the Oracle database.

- Oracle's Replication for a distributed environment also enables you to write code to convert one type of data in the mainframe and map it to data in the Oracle database. For example, your mainframe might be in London using European dates, yet your Oracle Server in New York needs to read in these dates and convert them. You can code functions that perform complex translations on columns.

Summary

Most people don't need Transparent Gateways between systems; instead they will build a Passive Gateway between systems. It is a minority of Oracle shops that need a Transparent Gateway to turn their many Oracle and non-Oracle databases into one large distributed database.

One reason for this is price. If the Transparent Gateway were free, believe me, the majority of Oracle shops would use it; but a Transparent Gateway is instead more expensive. The Transparent Gateway is a high-end item that is very profitable for Oracle to maintain even if only a small portion of Oracle shops purchase it.

Another reason why the Passive Gateway is more popular is simply that the movement to downsize from the mainframe to an open system is more popular than the movement to hook up existing open systems to mainframes. In most downsizing, we don't strive to create one virtual distributed database with a mainframe; we instead seek to move applications off of the mainframe and eventually pull the plug on the old steel itself.

The issue of downsizing does fuel the need for coexistence between Oracle and mainframes when we realize that downsizing a system in phases leaves us with dependencies between parts of an IS Operation that have been migrated to an open system and those parts that await migration and still run on the mainframe. When these interdependencies exist, there is a need to share data between Oracle and a legacy system that, in turn, implies some sort of explicit (Transparent, Procedural) or implicit gateway (Passive) to bridge the two systems.

It's not wise to plan a brand-new distributed database with anything but one database software product running on separate nodes that all run the same operating system. Altering databases and/or operating systems simply slows down the distributed database. This slowdown occurs at all phases from design and planning to actual transaction processing. When we consider mixing mainframes and open systems, this slowdown can be due to an added layer of physical, software, and planning complexity needed to link the two systems.

In reality, most downsizings are planned to minimize dependency between open systems and mainframe components of an IS effort. The planning is such because a greater dependency between systems implies higher software costs. In effect, passive low-maintenance gateways are more popular than Transparent Gateways, replication, and distributed architecture and will remain so until the price of these glamorous and admittedly complex products goes down.

If Oracle gave away its gateway and replication products for free (or almost free), they would lose a great deal of revenue in the short term but would encourage more mainframe dependence with the Oracle database and open systems. It remains to be seen whether Oracle will take this strategic path in the future.

8

COEXISTING WITH NON-ORACLE DATABASES

Oracle8 Components and Objects

IN THIS PART

Oracle Processes

by Joe Greene

This chapter covers the processes associated with an Oracle database instance. Chapter 2, "Oracle Database Architecture," introduced the three main components in the Oracle architecture (files, processes, and memory areas). This chapter covers processes in more detail. Its goal is to help you sufficiently understand this component of the Oracle architecture to be prepared for the tuning and administration discussions in future chapters.

Map of the Oracle Processes

Since it may have been a while since you read Chapter 2, let me present a brief map that will guide you through the discussion of the Oracle processes. I use the term process to describe any one of the operating system programs (threads, jobs, and so on, depending on your operating system's terminology) that are executed to complete functions within the Oracle database management system.

For purposes of my discussion, I will group these Oracle processes into two categories—main and optional. The main processes are those associated with the minimal functions of the Oracle database. The optional processes are those you would start to improve performance, or those that have several alternatives from which you can choose (dedicated server processes or the multi-threaded server, for an example). The key here is that if any of the main processes are not present on a system (when you issue the ps command under UNIX, for example), your database is not operational. If an optional process is not present, it indicates that you chose not to start that optional process or that no one needs it at the current moment (as in the case of dedicated server processes that are only started when a user is connected to the database instance).

The Main Oracle Processes

The following are the main processes associated with an Oracle instance. If any one of them dies, the others will detect this problem and shut themselves down and the database instance. The four main processes are

- System Monitor (SMON)
- Process Monitor (PMON)
- Database Writer (DBWR)
- Log Writer (LGWR)

Figure 9.1 shows where these processes fit in the Oracle architecture. These are the key processes that service the data files and memory areas associated with an Oracle database instance. If your database had no connectivity to users to the outside world, you could still execute functions within the database using these processes (stored procedures running on a routine basis). Of course, such a database would be of little use to the world.

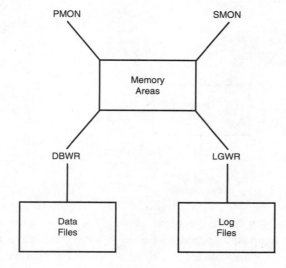

These four main processes, combined with the memory areas, are what Oracle refers to as an Oracle instance. These four main processes can be connected to a number of different databases if needed. When these processes are started they derive parameters from one or more initialization files. You can use different initialization files to start the same database. This allows you to adjust performance characteristics for special functions such as bulk data loads.

To keep track of the various processes, Oracle uses the system identifier (SID), which is the key to connecting to a given instance. When the Oracle processes are started, they contain the SID as part of the process name for ease of identification. This parameter is also used by local connections, SQL*Net and Net8, to route a given request or transaction from a user to the appropriate database instance.

System Monitor

The first) main Oracle process I want to discuss is the system monitor (SMON). The System Monitor's assignment is to clean up after the Oracle instance itself. SMON is the janitor for the Oracle background processes and data files. The System Monitor is activated under three circumstances (see Figure 9.2). First, it checks at startup to see whether the instance needs to be recovered. If the instance was not shut down cleanly (shutdown normal), there may be transactions that were in process that need to be rolled back, temporary segments (places where Oracle stores data in the data files that are not permanently committed) for such things as sorts that were being used that need to be cleared out, and so forth.

FIGURE 9.2.

The Oracle) System Monitor (SMON).

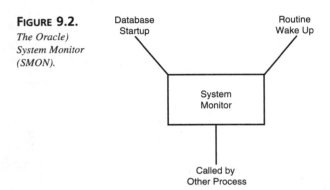

Second, the System Monitor is also designed to wake up routinely to see whether the Oracle instance needs some cleanup. SMON checks to see whether there are any temporary segments that are no longer needed and could be cleaned up. This is important to ensure that the maximum amount of temporary space is available for new requests. SMON also has the task of searching for ways to group together the free extents in the data files. If you ask for a 1M extent for a table, Oracle searches for a 1M contiguous extent (all the blocks are located next to one another for speed of access). You could find yourself in a situation where you have several megabytes of free space within a data file, but they are scattered in a large number of small chunks. SMON will try to move things around so you have larger free chunks of disk. However, its capabilities are limited, so you may occasionally have to compress extents within a tablespace.

One specialty function that System Monitor performs in parallel server environments is recovering an instance on a failed CPU or instance. This is actually quite a tricky operation in that you want to recover as much as possible about what activities, jobs, and so on were running on the CPU or instance at the time of failure. A number of features have been built-in to track the activity of a given parallel server instance) in the common database files and allow this recovery to take place.

The third case where System Monitor is activated is when it is called by other processes. For example, if the Database Writer detects the need for temporary segments, it can ask the System Monitor to see what it can do to free up some. This is an important feature to note with Oracle.

Process Monitor

The Process Monitor (PMON) devotes its time to cleaning up after processes. It wakes up routinely (determined by operating system) and can also be called by other processes when they detect the need for its services. The following are some examples of tasks that PMON may have to perform when a user process dies:

- Removes the process ID

> **NOTE**
>
> You might wonder whether this number is then made available again? This is operating system dependent. On UNIX, the ID is not reused, on others it is. Process ID is not an internal Oracle consideration, it is a table in the kernel of the operating system that controls processing functions.

- Removes the appropriate rows from the active transaction table
- Releases any locks the process may have
- Removes items in cache the process was using

In the Net/8 multithreaded server environment, PMON is responsible for restarting any dispatcher or server processes that have died. The multithreaded server has a minimum and a maximum number of processes that can be active (see Chapter 24, "Oracle8 Database Tuning," for information about tuning parameters). Here PMON intervenes only if the number of multithreaded server processes is less than the minimum level for this instance.

Cleaning up unnecessary processes is a very important function on systems where you have a large number of connections. Each connection on a typical UNIX system consumes several megabytes of memory and a fair amount of processor time. This may not seem significant on large, multiprocessor systems with several hundred megabytes of memory. However, if you accumulate several dozen or hundred unnecessary or open-ended processes (a data warehouse user who turns off his PC in the middle of a poorly formed query that takes many hours to complete, for example), you could easily consume a large number of processors and hundreds of megabytes of RAM if PMON were not there to detect the condition and kill those processes.

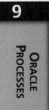

9

ORACLE
PROCESSES

Database Writer

The Database Writer (DBWR) process is responsible for transferring data that has been modified in the buffer cache memory area to the appropriate disk data files. It ensures that there are always free buffers waiting in memory when a user process wants to write a modified record to the database buffer cache. To review our buffer cache theory from a few chapters back, whenever a user adds or modifies a record from a table, the modified record is written to the buffer cache. Oracle uses the term "dirty" to specify that the buffer in memory needs to be transferred to disk before it can be overwritten. You have only a fixed number of buffers in memory (determined by the size of the database buffer cache you establish in your initialization file). Every time you dirty a buffer it reduces the number of free buffers (available for writing). If the total number of free buffers becomes too low, there will be none available for user processes to place the data obtained on queries (remember, you read multiple records one-at-a-time and store the ones you do not immediately need in the buffer cache). This is where DBWR gets called into action.

The Database Writer writes records to database files that have not been used for the longest period of time. The user interface processes (dedicated server processes) also comply with this procedure in that they write to non-dirty buffers that have not been used recently. Many records can be used and updated frequently. The database writer avoids writing records to disk that are likely to be needed soon (as determined by their frequent usage in the past). A classic example of relatively inactive records is order data on an order-entry system. Typically, an order is entered and not accessed again until someone is ready to ship that product. These types of records are quickly removed from the buffer cache to make room for other orders. A type of record that typically stays longer in the buffer cache is a frequently used lookup table of legal values. For example, these values may be scanned every time an order is entered into the system to validate that it is correct.

> **TIP**
>
> Does the lookup table stay in the buffer cache permanently just because it is used frequently? For example, if you have a frequently used lookup table containing the list of 50 state codes, it will be one of the last things that Oracle clears from the buffers. Oracle will clear it though, if it needs the space. The DBA has the option to manually "pin" a table in memory, in which case it stays there no matter what.

So far, you have learned what the Database Writer does. You also have seen how DBWR determines which records to write to disk from the buffer cache. The next piece in this puzzle is to determine when the Database Writer does its writing. There are four conditions under which DBWR is called into action:

- A user process writes a new dirty buffer into the database buffer cache. The user process is smart enough to detect that the number of dirty buffers has exceeded a limit the DBA has set for dirty buffers (one-half of DB_BLOCK_WRITE_BATCH, which Oracle calculates based on your database buffer size). Being a good citizen in the Oracle background process world, the user process politely informs DBWR that it is time to wake up and do some writing.

- A user process is looking for a free buffer to write to and cannot find it. It does not scan every possible buffer in the buffer cache because this takes too much time. Instead, it searches a number of buffers specified by a parameter set by you, the DBA (DB_BLOCK_MAX_SCAN_CNT, which is calculated by Oracle based on your database buffer size). When it has looked at this many buffers and has not found a free one, the user process concludes that it is time for some writing (there are a lot of dirty buffers out there). It then signals DBWR to begin writing.

- The Database Writer wakes itself up routinely to see whether there is any work for it (dirty database buffers). This period is set to three seconds.

- Finally, the Log Writer or the checkpoint process needs to have those records that show the latest change number applied to the database written to each of the data files when a checkpoint occurs. Because this function is especially important for database recovery purposes, these processes get special attention and signal the Database Writer to write these records when they are ready.

How much does the Database Writer transfer to disk when it is called into action? The checkpoint records are directed for immediate write when the Database Writer is awakened for a checkpoint. For the other situations, the number of records written depends on how DBWR was awakened and certain Oracle configuration parameters.

If the Database Writer is awakened by user processes that detect that the number of dirty buffers is too high or cannot find a free buffer, DBWR goes to the list of dirty buffers and writes a batch of records. There may be times when there are not enough buffers available on the list of dirty buffers that Oracle maintains (there is a time delay between dirtying the buffer and this list being updated). If DBWR cannot find enough data on the dirty list to fill up its transfer quota, it scans the list of buffers, starting at the least recently used end, to find dirty buffers to write to disk. The Database Writer is a very service-oriented process.

If DBWR is awakened on a user process timeout waiting for a non-dirty buffer, it uses a slightly different approach to writing data buffers. It goes through the list of buffers, starting at the least recently used end, and selects dirty buffers to write to disk. It searches twice as many buffers as was specified by the DB_BLOCK_WRITE_BATCH parameter on each awakening (remember, many of these buffers will not be dirty and therefore not need writing). Any dirty buffers it finds are written to disk. Each time DBWR wakes up it searches a new set of buffers on the least recently used list of buffers. Eventually, if the database has a relatively light data entry rate, all the dirty buffers in memory will be written to disk. This is the case in most of the systems I have worked with and would probably apply to all but the busiest transaction processing systems.

Certain operating systems (UNIX, for one) enable you to activate multiple database writer processes to share the load. The number of DBWR processes you use is controlled by the DB_WRITERS parameter in the init.ora file. Oracle recommends having at least one Database Writer process for each disk drive in your system. You would not implement 135 DBWR processes for the one large information warehouse I worked on that had 135 mirrored disk drives (2GB each). I would recommend having enough DBWR processes for the expected number of disk drives that would be written to at a given time. Start with a value you consider reasonable and then increase its value and see whether your performance improves.

Now is as good a time as any to bring out one of the fundamental design concepts used by Oracle to improve performance in its processes—parallelization. Oracle enables you to assign multiple database writers to do the work when it becomes too much for one to handle. You need to understand your computer's architecture before you jump at the chance to improve performance by adding additional processes. Parallelization techniques are useful for systems with a number of disk drives (parallel Database Writers) and computer processors (as in the parallel query option). Certain computers, such as most of the HP and IBM UNIX servers, are based around a single processor architecture. They would not benefit from the multiple query processors as much as a large multiprocessor-based computer such as the Sequent and Pyramid families. Also, computers with all their Oracle data stored on one or two disk drives would not benefit from a large number of DBWR processes. Just ensure that you understand what you are trying to do when you add parallel processes and that it will work with your computer architecture.

Log Writer

Recall from Chapter 2 that Oracle writes every committed transaction in two places to promote its capability of recovering in case a data file is completely destroyed. The first location, the data file itself, was written to by the Database Writer process covered in the previous section. This section deals with writing the other record of a transaction from the redo log buffer to the redo log files. This function is performed by the Log Writer background process (LGWR).

The general concept of the Log Writer is simple. Every transaction made to the database is recorded in the Log Buffer. This buffer operates on a first-in, first-out basis. There are multiple redo logs in the system and the Log Writer writes to them in a cyclical manner. A slight complication to consider is the fact that users can enter transactions on the system and wait for a while until they commit them. Until the user (or the software package) issues a commit statement, these records are not official and can be backed out without any changes to the data files. Normally, commits occur frequently and you do not have a large number of uncommitted transactions hanging around. Sometimes you do have a lot of uncommitted transactions. LGWR is designed to deal with this situation and makes special exceptions for handling commit statements received. Therefore, the processing rules for the Log Writer process are the following:

- LGWR wakes up and performs a write when a commit statement is received from a user process.
- LGWR wakes up and writes redo log buffers every three seconds. The processes that read the logs on a recovery are smart enough not to record changes in the data files until that commit statement is received for that particular transaction.
- LGWR writes redo log buffers when the redo log buffer becomes one-third full.
- Finally, when the Database Writer process writes records in the database buffer to disk, LGWR ensures that the corresponding redo log buffers are written to the redo logs.

Of course there are some fine points to this process. For example, if there are a lot of commits occurring in your database, Oracle may choose to transfer groups of commit records to the log files for efficiency. Recall also that you can actually have several identical members in a group of redo log files. That way, if one of the members of the group is not available (say the disk is busy with other input/output operations), the writes can occur to an available member of that group. Finally, under normal circumstances where there is not a separate checkpoint process, the Log Writer is responsible for writing records to the database buffer that records the latest system change number (SCN) applied to the database in the headers of all data files. DBWR then transfers these records from the database buffer to the disk files.

9

ORACLE
PROCESSES

Optional Processes

In addition to the main processes described previously, Oracle8 gives you several processing options you may want to implement. Many of these are designed to meet special needs that do not apply to all databases. The following sections describe these processes.

Archiver

The Archiver (ARCH) is a conceptually simple process. When the Log Writer finishes filling up one of the online redo log files, it signals ARCH to copy it to the next archive log file in the sequence. ARCH sends the copy of the online redo log file to either a new file on a disk drive or to a tape you have designated. Of course. it can do its job only if there is room available on the tape or the file system on which you tell it to write the archive log file. The Archiver process is started by the Log Writer only when the database is operated in ARCHIVELOG mode (that is, the DBA issues an ALTER SYSTEM ARCHIVE LOG START command, or you start your instance with LOG_ARCHIVE_START = true in the initialization file).

Recoverer

Another process that is present only when you use an optional database mode is the Recoverer (RECO). This process provides service when you have chosen to implement a distributed database (discussed in Chapter 4, "Oracle8 Servers and Options"). The purpose RECO is to deal with problems that occur during distributed transactions. There are special rules that have to be applied when you are trying to deal with replicated data tables or other remote tables. Many problems can occur when wide area networks are used. The basic transaction writing processes are trained to yell immediately if there is a problem writing to the local disk drives. Oracle has designed RECO to be a lot more tolerant of such problems. It waits until connection is reestablished with the remote database and then goes over the transactions it's not sure were recorded in the remote system. It resolves whether there were any updates made from other remote systems (you can link many different computers with different Oracle instances via the distributed option).

Lock Writer

The next specialist process is the Lock Writer (LCK). This process is present only when the parallel server option is being used. In this situation, you cannot use the single instance locking mechanisms provided by the Oracle memory areas of your instance. Instead, these special Lock Writer processes (you can have up to 10) talk to one another and ensure that records are properly locked for shared databases. Again, the logic for splitting out this function is that you do not want to weigh down your existing background processes with the burden of negotiating between instances. This is a much slower process because the messaging is not occurring through the fast shared memory area mechanisms of a single instance.

Dedicated Server Processes

These processes serve as the interface between a user process that is sending requests to the database and the memory areas and disks of the Oracle instance. They provide all the intelligence as to who to talk to for what service and where to find things. They have been used in Oracle since its beginning to provide this connectivity. The key to remember is that all users get a Dedicated Server process when they connect to the Oracle instance and it needs to remain available until they disconnect from the instance.

Net8 Processes

An architecture that has become popular in recent years is the client/server architecture. Figure 9.3 illustrates the basics of this architecture. Here a job runs on the client workstation that is responsible for display functions and perhaps some calculation. The server is still responsible for some of the processing, which includes functions such as database management and some of the calculation.

FIGURE 9.3.
Net8 Connectivity.

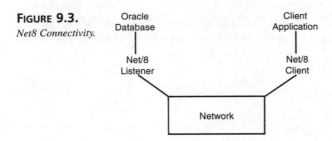

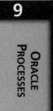

The key process associated with the client/server architecture from the point of view of this discussion is the listener. This process monitors a defined communications channel (a specific port such as 1521 set up under TCP/IP that is reserved for SQL*Net and Net8) waiting for a request from a client. It then routes this request to an appropriate server user process for processing. When the server user process completes it processing, the results are routed through the listener to the appropriate client computer.

Parallel Query Processes

Parallel query processes are available in Oracle8. When you look at the tasks involved with complex queries, you find that there are a lot of steps that have to be performed. These tasks can be performed by a single operating system process. However, because most operating systems assign these tasks to a single CPU, you are limited in the total number of steps that can be executed per second and this helps to fix the total response time for the query. If you can take this big query and divide it into a series of tasks (either by dividing a large table into sections for different processes, or one to do a query on the index and another to search the main table for the records that match the index search), you can assign multiple CPUs to perform the work and therefore get the job done more quickly. This is the purpose of the parallel query processes in Oracle. The DBA spawns a number of them when you operate the database in parallel query mode. They wait until a user process issues a query that can benefit from their services. When this happens, they jump in and start performing parts of the query as determined by a special set of logic used to divide the work.

Web Server Processes

An architecture that is conceptually similar to the client/server architecture presented earlier in this section is the Web Server architecture. This technology was developed to deliver images and texts over the Internet. It has since been expanded to include other forms of multimedia content and even distributed programming (Java applets or Active/X controls, for example). From a process point of view, this architecture is relatively simple (see Figure 9.4).

FIGURE 9.4.
Web Server Process.

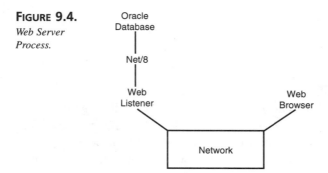

Here the Web Listener process functions similar to the SQL*Net listener. It connects user workstations to the appropriate server processes for further processing. Of course, the Web Listener also has other duties such as retrieving Web pages (HTML) and other media content directly from disk files. However, the key is that this process functions primarily as an information router as opposed to a process that performs a lot of computation. If there are computations to be performed on the server, it will either send those tasks to another existing process (those associated with an Oracle database) or spawn a new process to perform the work.

There are several options for connecting to the Oracle database via a Web Server process. You can use the Oracle Web or Web Applications Server that has a higher degree of native Oracle database connectivity built into it. You also have the option of using a third-party Web server such as those provided by Netscape or Microsoft. In this case, you usually have to write small applications that take raw requests from the user and turn them into a format that can be processed by a database. This takes the form of ODBC or JDBC drivers which are discussed in more detail in Chapter 3, "Oracle8 Network Computing."

Summary

This chapter has covered the Oracle database processes and how they function together to make the Oracle database management system work. The discussion was divided into sections covering the main Oracle processes needed to make any Oracle server work, and the optional processes you may choose to implement based on local needs. As with many other topics in this book, there are a number of implementation options that you face. With the information in this chapter, you should be able to recognize what is running on your operating system and know how to implement options to improve performance.

9

ORACLE PROCESSES

Oracle Memory Areas

by Joe Greene

IN THIS CHAPTER

For Oracle, and most other multi-user database management systems, physical memory means speed. Data stored in physical memory can be accessed much faster than that stored on even the fastest magnetic or optical disk drives. This chapter presents a discussion on memory at the level of detail needed by Oracle database. While most developers do not need this level of detail, it can come in handy when developers are trying to get that extra ounce of performance out of their applications. This chapter focuses on the topics that have practical uses, such as the following:

- In what memory areas does Oracle store various types of information?
- What is the impact of inadequate space for the various memory areas?
- How are the values of the storage parameters for the various memory areas set?

Uses of Memory Within Oracle8

A good starting place is the overview picture of the Oracle memory areas that was presented in Chapter 2, "Oracle Database Architecture." Refer to Figure 2.3 in Chapter 2.

Before getting into the details of what each of the memory areas contain, it is useful to step back and consider what you need to put in memory to make a database management system work efficiently. This depends somewhat on the DBMS designer's preferences and style, but generally speaking, a multi-user DBMS that wants to use memory to achieve speed would want to put the following into memory:

- *Rows of tables that have been added or changed.* These are written to memory first so the user process can go on without waiting for the disk to receive the data.
- *Rows that are "close" to the row with which the user is currently working.* In most applications, it is likely that the next row the user will want will be close to the current row. Because most operating systems read entire blocks (512 bytes or more) from disk drives, if you save these extra retrieved rows in memory, you can get lucky and have the next row needed waiting in higher-speed memory.
- *Space for the application programs that are running.* Computers execute instructions stored in memory. If you want your general ledger application to work, you need to have memory space available for it. This same concept applies to storing code for the various Oracle background processes.
- *Administrative space to keep track of who is logged in, what needs to be done, and so forth.*
- *Information being passed between Oracle database processes and end-user processes.* This information enables the many operating system processes involved with applications using the Oracle database to coordinate their activities.

Virtual Memory

One of the considerations you will run across is the use of real and virtual memory. For those who are not used to these terms, real memory consists of the random access memory (RAM) chips of the computer. This is the memory that gives all the speed benefits I have been discussing in this chapter. Most multi-user computer systems, and even Microsoft Windows and the Macintosh operating system, provide what is known as virtual memory. Virtual memory is a section of a disk drive that is allocated to storing the overflow of the real memory area. This enables you to have more processes running than would be possible if you were limited to storing these processes in real memory. It works especially well when you have a number of processes that run infrequently, and therefore there is not much of a performance impact when they need to be swapped out to disk. The swapping out process transfers the program and data as they reside in memory to a special area on one or more of the disk drives, thereby freeing up real memory to be used by other processes. In Oracle's case however, you really want all of Oracle's memory areas to be stored in real memory, because speed is the whole purpose of this architecture.

System Global Area

Oracle divides its memory areas into several sections. The System Global Area (SGA) holds all the common database storage areas (transactions being buffered, data dictionary information, and so on). The Program Global Area (PGA) stores data related to your individual process. User spaces are related to the software being run by the Oracle background processes and user processes. Finally, sort areas are used for sorting data associated with a user's query. This is a nice, clean division of function and, if you can understand these basic concepts, you are well on the way to understanding enough of how Oracle works to be an effective DBA.

Sharing Memory

An important concept to understand as a DBA is the control of how memory regions are set up for sharing. Most memory areas (such as the one allocated to your shell when you log on to UNIX or the one for Microsoft Windows) are not sharable. You have sole access to that memory and that is the way it should be. Shared memory is the exception to the rule. It usually takes some special permissions from the system administrator to share a memory area. The exact method for setting this up varies from operating system to operating system. The RDBMS software provided by Oracle is normally set up so that when it creates a new database instance, it has the permissions (typically through the user ID that owns it) necessary to set up the memory areas as sharable without you having to take any overt actions.

> **NOTE**
>
> What if you get a message indicating the SGA is not available? You may have lost your operating system permission to create shared memory areas if the following are true:
>
> - You see the Oracle instance running properly.
> - Only the user who started the Oracle instance (`oracle`) can access Oracle successfully.
>
> Check with the system administrator regarding shared memory permissions.

You may be curious about how you can control all these wonderful memory areas to set them up properly for your particular application environment. The answer lies in the combination of initialization files (discussed in detail in Chapter 12, "Oracle Database Objects") and the default parameters that Oracle has established for its products on your operating system. Let's start with the default settings. Oracle takes into consideration the average configuration of a particular type of computer and comes up with a set of default values for those parameters that determine the size of the SGA, PGA, and sort areas. Obviously, the configuration for the Microsoft Windows version of Oracle is set up to be much smaller than that of a large VAX computer. The settings of these parameters can be overridden by values entered in the initialization files. Chapter 12 presents how to make entries in the initialization file to change the values of these parameters. Chapter 25, "Oracle8 Application Tuning," shows you how to analyze your instances to determine how to adjust (or tune) these parameters. However, the basic concept is simple. If you use the initial settings for database block buffers (200) and you get a lot of contention for these items (as determined by your tuning run), you would edit the following line to double the value of the buffer:

```
db_block_buffers =  400
```

System Global Area (SGA)

The SGA can be thought of as the heart of Oracle itself (see Figure 10.1). It holds changes that you make to your database until a process is ready to write the data to disk. It stores things that can help speed up your access to data. Without the SGA, you do not have an Oracle database. Anything that is this important deserves some attention from the DBA. In this section, you explore what the SGA does. Although the SGA usually works just as well whether you understand it or not, this knowledge can come in handy some day when a performance problem arises and the cause is not obvious.

FIGURE 10.1.
The System Global Area (SGA).

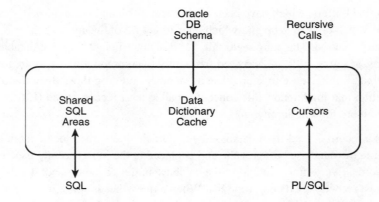

As with most of the topics in this book, it is easiest to break the SGA into its components and discuss each of them individually. The only time you have to be concerned with how the pieces fit together is when you calculate the total amount of memory space required for the SGA. Sizing is discussed later in this section. For now, the pieces of the SGA are the following:

- Database (block) buffer cache
- Redo log buffer
- Shared pool
- Interprocess communications area
- Queues for the multi-threaded server (when used)

Database Buffer Cache

The database buffer cache stores records from various tables within the Oracle database (actually, because reads and writes are in blocks, it stores the entire database block that contains the records you are working with). These blocks contain either rows that have been read from the data files or records that need to be written to the data files. In effect, the database buffer cache is a way-station for data that sits between users and the data files. As with most hotels, there is a limited capacity for accommodating these guests. Therefore, it is important for the DBA to understand how Oracle determines how long an individual block gets to stay.

The easiest decision involved in determining how long a block of records needs to stay in cache involves new or modified records that are waiting to be written to disk. They stay in the database buffer cache until they get written by the database writer process. It would not work if Oracle got to throw out data blocks when it felt too full. For the

10

ORACLE MEMORY AREAS

remaining buffers, which have been read in from disk and not modified, Oracle has to decide which ones to keep and which ones to get rid of. Many systems use a "first-in, first-out" method. This may seem fair, but it is not efficient for most database circumstances. Many records are accessed frequently (a common look-up table, for example), so it makes more sense to keep those in memory and drop those that are not used. The algorithm that implements this concept is called least recently used (LRU for those of you who are fond of acronyms).

When a record is read from database by an Oracle query, the block containing its data is stored in the database buffer cache and is placed at the most recently used end of the list of records. Every time a record in the database buffer cache is used, it gets promoted to the most recently used end of the list. When a query needs space to store data that has to be pulled off the disk drives and all of the buffers in the database cache are full, it overwrites buffers that are at the least recently used end (top) of the list that are not dirty (have been changed since being recalled from disk). If records that are overwritten are needed again, they are called in from disk.

This process works well and saves you time by storing data in memory to avoid slow data transfers from disk. Let me challenge you with an opportunity to save even more time and show your database that you know more than it does. Unless you have an extremely large amount of real memory, you have to limit your database buffer cache to some reasonable value. The LRU algorithm therefore looks at data from a short-term (maybe several minutes) point of view. You, however, know your applications and users very well and understand the "big picture." You know that there are several relatively small tables that are used frequently (perhaps they are used to look up values to make calls against your big data tables). The LRU algorithm may call these rows into the database cache at the beginning of one of these queries, but they are eventually pushed out as you move in row after row of data from that large main table. When the next user issues a query, you have to start this process over again. However, Oracle7.1 and later gives you the option of caching a table in memory. This has the effect of bringing the entire table into memory and keeping it near the most recently used end of the database buffer cache. You have to be careful, because too many cached tables can fill up the buffer cache making that slow disk access a necessity for every row read. However, used with good judgment, this can be a useful tool to speed up databases that are suited to benefit from it. An example of how to do this would be:

```
SELECT /*+ CACHE(jgreene.lookups) */
       parameter
       FROM jgreene.lookups;
```

The next area of the SGA to explore is the redo log buffer. As discussed in Chapter 2, updates to the Oracle data files are recorded in the data files and also separately in the redo log files. This record of the transaction enables Oracle to recover data in the event of the complete loss of a disk drive. The redo log transactions are stored in memory to optimize their write performance. Because most operating systems read and write blocks that are several kilobytes in size, it is more efficient to queue up an entire block of data and then write it.

Because the redo log buffer is designed for writing as opposed to reading, it uses the first-in, first-out approach to storage. Redo log entries are added in the order they are received and the log writer process of Oracle comes along and takes one or more blocks of these records and writes them to the online redo log files. The redo log buffer then serves as the way-station for redo log entries, sitting between the Oracle process that creates the database update transaction and the redo log files on disk.

Shared Pool

The third of the five areas within the SGA is the shared pool. You have seen the benefits of storing data that has recently been read from disk or needs to be written to disk (data and log files) in memory. The developers of Oracle looked at the services performed by a database and came up with a number of other things that should be stored in memory areas to improve overall performance. The shared pool contains three of these performance improving memory areas (see Figure 10.2):

- Shared SQL areas
- The data dictionary cache
- Cursors

FIGURE 10.2.
The shared pool memory areas.

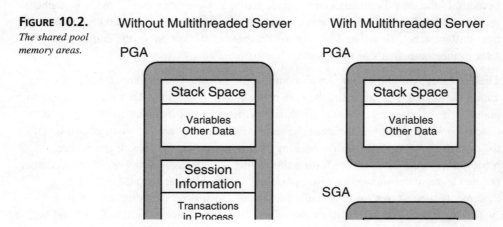

The first of these shared pool area stores what Oracle calls shared SQL. The structured query language (SQL) is a standard way of interacting with the database that is common to Oracle, IBM's DB2, Informix, and a high percentage of the multi-user databases on the market today. An example of an SQL statement would be the following, which pulls back all the rows and columns from the fictitious `big_payroll` table.

```
select * from big_payroll
```

Oracle performs a fair bit of work to service this request. For example, Oracle needs to figure out what are the columns in the `big_payroll` table, whether there is an index that can be used to speed the query, whether the user has access privileges to this data, and many other bits of information to get the data for the user. In many databases, there are a series of queries that are frequently used (an order entry system may routinely pull up a list of valid product codes, for example). The shared SQL area stores the analyzed (or parsed) query for any user to access without having to re-parse the query. Queries are stored in this area, which is also referred to as the library cache, using a modified form of the LRU algorithm.

The second part of the shared pool area is the data dictionary cache. In all queries and transactions with the database, the database management system needs to determine where the data is. This includes such details as what the object (table) names are, what tablespaces they are located in, where their records are within the data file, and what their columns are. In addition, database security requires Oracle to verify that the user has the appropriate access permissions for that database object. All this dictionary data information is stored within various system tables in the database. Such frequently used information is a wonderful candidate for caching. The data dictionary cache stores this for rapid access by the RDBMS.

Sometimes the data dictionary cache is referred to as the row cache. To me, row cache would be what I would call the area that stores rows of data from the database (the database buffer cache). However, I am not the designer of the system or the names used to refer to the components of the system.

The final area within the shared pool contains the cursors. Cursors are actually stored within the shared SQL area, but they are conceptually different so let's look at them separately. The previous `select` statement causes the results of its query to be displayed onscreen. What if you want to store the results in a memory area so you can manipulate the data in some way? Basically speaking, that is what a cursor does. It stores data retrieved from the database for further processing. Oracle creates its own internal cursors (known as recursive cursors) when it performs statements such as CREATE TABLE. Statements such as this cause a number of updates to various data dictionary tables (which are a series of SQL statements, referred to as recursive calls, that Oracle takes care of behind the scenes). Both of these forms of cursors take up space in the shared SQL area and should be considered when you are sizing the shared pool. You should also note that part of the storage required to support cursors is in the PGA (discussed in the next section).

With the shared pool covered, it is time to move on to the fourth area within the SGA. This area does not have a fancy name. It is used to store messages transmitted between various processes associated with the operation of the Oracle database. Many features, such as locks applied to objects by a process, are conveyed using this area. The good news is that there are no special tuning parameters and intervention required by the DBA for these message areas. As long as there is sufficient size in the shared pool, you're set.

The final component that can take up space within the SGA is space for the multi-threaded server queues. One of the difficulties in writing a book that discusses a tightly integrated system such as Oracle is that sometimes you have to introduce a topic before its time. Basically, the multi-threaded server is a feature of Oracle that enables users to share the memory areas and processes used to connect user applications to the Oracle database. The logic is, why waste memory duplicating these relatively common areas for perhaps hundreds of users? For purposes of this chapter, all you need to know is that if you are using the multi-threaded server option, these memory areas are stored in the SGA and affect its size.

As DBA, you may be the only one aware that there is such a thing as the SGA; therefore, you will be the one to manage it. Many business book writers argue that you cannot manage anything you cannot monitor, so the first task is to monitor the SGA. My favorite way is to issue the following command in Server Manager:

```
show sga
```

This command produces a result similar to what is shown in the following example. Those of you familiar with large Oracle databases on such machines as Sequent, Sun, and VAX may wonder why the numbers are so small. This printout comes from Personal Oracle. This command works the same on the large boxes (although most of them have much larger memory areas than I could afford for my PC):

```
SQLDBA> show sga
Total System Global Area      4767460 bytes
Fixed Size                      36432 bytes
Variable Size                 3846292 bytes
Database Buffers               819200 bytes
Redo Buffers                    65536 bytes
```

The final issue to discuss regarding the SGA is how to control it. In Chapter 25, you learn how to tune Oracle instances. For now, know that there are variables within Oracle you can set using initialization files. These control the space allocated to the redo log buffer, database buffer, and other areas within the SGA discussed in this chapter. You

10

ORACLE MEMORY
AREAS

will not be ready to alter these parameters until you learn how to determine *when* you need to adjust them in Chapter 25.

Program Global Area (PGA)

The System Global Area provides memory for those things all users need to share. There are several things users need to keep to themselves, and that is the purpose of the Program Global Area. All users are allocated PGAs when they connect to the Oracle database. The size of this memory area is fixed by the operating system and remains constant as long as the users are connected to Oracle.

For Personal Oracle users and those that have a small number of users, this is a workable arrangement. However, many of the larger transaction processing systems may have dozens or hundreds of users connected to the database at a given time. When you map out the large amounts of memory required for the SGA on such large databases and then add in space for each of the user processes and the operating system itself, there is not much space available for a large number of PGAs.

That is where the multithreaded server comes into play. In most situations, there may be a large number of users logged on the database computer at a given time, but a much smaller number are actively executing queries or updates. Most of the users are either reading the outputs of the system, typing at rates that seem slow to the computer, or just thinking. Oracle's multithreaded server is designed to allocate a specific number of spaces for the information involved with a particular transaction. This information includes the private SQL areas and other such items that relate to a particular question or update. The users still retain space, known as stack space, dedicated to their individual sessions, to hold variables and other data associated with their work. The data stored in the PGA, with and without the multithreaded server, is show in Figure 10.3.

A few final notes about the PGA seem appropriate at this point:

- The PGA is owned by a single-user process and only that user can read from or write to it.
- If you do not use the multithreaded server and there is not enough memory available on your computer, you will receive an error message from Oracle to that effect.
- If you are running a client/server configuration, the PGA for a user will be allocated on the machine that acts as the database server.
- Some literature refers to the PGA as the Process Global Area rather than the Program Global Area. Either way, it works the same.

FIGURE 10.3.
The contents of the Program Global Area (PGA).

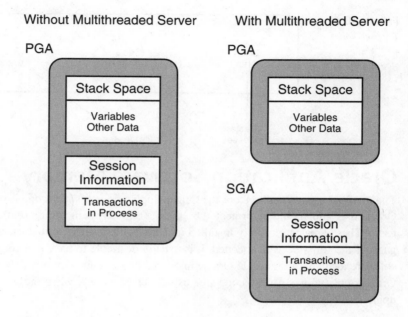

- The size of the PGA varies between versions of Oracle that run on different operating systems. Three parameters affect the size of the PGA in a given instance: the number of open database links, the number of database files, the number of enabled roles and the number of log files.

This is enough for most DBAs to understand about the PGA. DBAs typically do not have to do much with the PGA unless they are running short on memory in their computer system. Because the parameters mentioned are controlled by application needs, the DBA usually has to acquire additional memory or use the multithreaded server option to solve problems with PGA memory limitations.

User Work Spaces

So far you have explored the memory areas Oracle uses internally to perform database services for the user. Where are the actual applications that are designed to perform specific processing tasks? Every application needs memory areas in which to run—work spaces. There are many important bits of data stored in this area (see Figure 10.4):

- Software code areas for Oracle processes
- Software code areas for user processes
- Sort areas

10

ORACLE MEMORY AREAS

FIGURE 10.4.

The user work spaces.

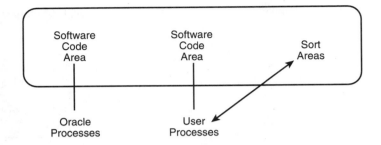

Oracle Application Software Memory

The memory space used to store the Oracle application software code is owned by the Oracle user and should be protected by the operating system from modification by other users. These areas are usually installed in a shareable fashion so that users can access parts of the software when needed. It is usually desirable to have one copy of the Oracle software available to multiple Oracle instances on the same computer. The size of the Oracle application software code area usually changes only when the software is upgraded.

The next software area to discuss is the memory space used by regular user processes. Most of the Oracle tools and utilities the DBA will work with are shareable. However, most custom applications require separate work areas for each user. Each of these user areas is relatively small when compared with the SGA, for example; however, the DBA and system administrator may need to keep an eye on these processes when there are a large number of users on the system. Unlike the SGA, it is not an extreme performance problem if inactive user processes are swapped out to disk.

The final user memory area to consider is the sort area. One of the most common clauses in a SQL select statement is the order by clause. Very few people want to have to search a long list of output in the order that Oracle chooses to return it. Therefore, most applications perform a fair amount of sorting. The speed of memory is especially noticeable when performing sorts. It can easily take five to ten times longer (or more) for a sorted query if it will not fit in memory. However, especially in large data warehouse Oracle instances, you may have to sort data that will not fit within the physical memory of the system; therefore, you have to live with disk-based sorts.

The sort area size varies depending on application needs. Its maximum size is controlled by the SORT_AREA_SIZE parameter set either in the initialization file or the Oracle default for your operating system. Once the sort is completed, the size of the sort area is reduced to the value specified by the SORT_AREA_RETAINED_SIZE parameter. If the entire set of data to be sorted does not fit within the sort area, the data is sorted in chunks that do fit into memory and then the chunks are merged together.

Summary

This chapter has covered the composition of the various memory areas used by the Oracle DBMS. The goal of these memory areas is to store information likely to be needed in a format that can be accessed quickly by applications. It also serves as a store where key control information related to the database and user processes are stored. The sizing of these memory areas is one of the key factors that can be controlled to improve performance in database tuning.

10

ORACLE MEMORY AREAS

Oracle Files

by Joe Greene

IN THIS CHAPTER

Next on the list of Oracle components are the data files associated with the database. Memory areas store data only while the computer is operational. For permanent storage of information, you need to use media such as magnetic disks. Also, while memory prices have declined, the cost of disk media is still much less than that of physical computer memory. Therefore, Oracle has been designed to balance the need for speed using physical memory and the need for storage cost efficiency using files on disk drives. This chapter discusses the various files associated with an Oracle database, their contents, and how they are used.

Oracle Files and Their Purposes

For a typical PC software product installation, you place a few dozen files in one directory or a series of subdirectories under one main directory. You know where everything that you need is and the world is wonderful. This chapter deals with the files of the Oracle database world. Here there are hundreds, perhaps thousands, of files that are scattered over a number of directories. This chapter shows the overall picture of where the files are stored and then highlights those files that the DBA usually uses.

It is not as bad as it may seem. There are an enormous number of files out there in the Oracle system. Each of the Oracle add-on packages (Oracle Forms, SQL*Net, Net8, and so forth) add many more files to that collection. However, from a DBA point of view, you can divide the many files into the following categories:

- *Oracle software.* These are the files that are purchased and installed to make the system work. These files make up the vast majority of the hundreds or thousands of Oracle files on your system. The good news is that, typically, you need to concern yourself with these files only at installation time. If they do not load and link correctly, your only recourse is to call Oracle support and have them help you get things working (unless you feel like rewriting major portions of Oracle in your spare time).

- *Data files.* When you first create an instance, you have only a few data files. In fact, you can have a single data file under earlier versions of Oracle (6 and below). In Oracle8, you get at least four data files by default. If you have very large databases that span many disk drives, you may have dozens of data files. These are a relatively easy resource to manage because there are database views to enable you to locate the files quickly. You typically perform size maintenance on your data files more often than on any other type of Oracle file.

- *Redo log files.* You have only a handful (normally about four) of redo log files on your system. There are views to help you locate these files from within the database. These files typically need maintenance only when you are changing their size or moving them for enhancing performance.

- *Archive log files.* These will be your biggest concern when operating a database in archivelog mode (which is explained in more detail later). If these files fill up their destination device, it stops all updates and inserts to the database from happening and perhaps crashes the instance. It is definitely enlightened self-interest to know where your archive logs are and to monitor their size and clean them up routinely.

- *Control files.* If you are lucky, you may never bother with your control files after you create an Oracle instance. These files are used to help Oracle start up by providing configuration information and status. You alter their contents when you modify the database configuration, but Oracle takes care of this behind the scenes.

- *Initialization files.* These files store the information that is needed to start the system. They contain the locations for the control files and all the tuning parameters that you set to adjust the performance of your instance. You will typically bother with these files only when you get into tuning the Oracle database.

- *Log and trace files.* Many books do not emphasize these files. I was a pretty experienced DBA before I found the log file used for SQL*Net (which had grown to 1.4MB because no one knew that it was there to clean out). However, these little jewels are your keys to troubleshooting major problems such as a crash of the instance. The major Oracle processes are designed to leave a last message on the system when they encounter problems and are crashing. The system actually has processes that monitor the activity of other processes and record messages when they detect that something is wrong.

- *Audit files.* Oracle enables you to audit certain events that occur in the database (see Chapter 19, "Oracle8 Administrative Requirements"). You can store the record of activities either in the database or in a file that you specify in your initialization file.

From a DBA perspective, I have just narrowed that list of hundreds or thousands of files associated with Oracle down to a list of a few dozen. When you consider that once you understand one control file or log file, you understand them all, this makes it much more manageable. The key is getting a handle on where things are and what they do for you. Then when a problem arises, you know where to go for help.

Data Files

Data files perform perhaps the most important function in an Oracle system—storing data in a retrievable format. These files cannot be read directly from operating system utilities such as More in UNIX or Notepad under Microsoft Windows. You access their contents via SQL queries, which brings up an important point: You have little control over where things are stored within a given tablespace or data file. Instead, when working with SQL commands, you specify logical structures such as tablespaces and tables. The physical structures are Oracle's responsibility. Then you, as the DBA, map the two together (see Figure 11.1).

FIGURE 11.1.

Physical versus logical data structures.

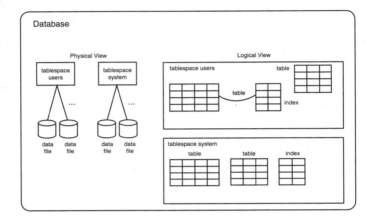

Remember that each data file is associated with only one tablespace. A tablespace has one or more data files. The DBA has to make a tradeoff when determining the number of data files associated with a given tablespace. One large tablespace with all the data tables is easier to administer, and you do not have a table running out of space in one tablespace when there is a large amount of space in other tablespaces that it cannot use. However, because you cannot control the placement of a table or index within data files in a tablespace, you are unable to split the input/output load between disks. There also are situations where you would rather a user be stopped by filling up a tablespace before taking up all the space available to the system. An example of this is where you allocate space between various projects sharing a single database. It takes system resources to keep track of the large number of data files, so you usually want to keep the number of files down to a reasonable value.

Let's explore what these data files look like internally, at a conceptual level. Stored within every Oracle data file is a record of the latest change number (SCN in Oracle terms) that has been applied to the system. In this manner, when you restore a backup data file from tape, Oracle can determine which changes need to be applied to the file to bring it up to date. Another point to remember about data files is that they are preallocated by the operating system to the full size that you specify in the creation command. If you allocate a file for a tablespace to 100MB, the data file takes up 100MB even though it

contains no tables or data. This preallocation concept applies to the database objects, such as tables that you create within the tablespace, and their data files. If you create a table with an initial extent of 10MB, there will be a 10MB section of the tablespace reserved for that table even though it does not contain any rows of data.

The following summarizes other facts that you should know about your data files:

- There are two general types of data files—*raw* and *cooked*. (Don't you just love these computer terms?) The normal operating system files that you work with are considered to be cooked because they use the file system utilities provided by your operating system. In some older operating systems, especially older UNIX implementations, the overhead associated with the operating system file management utilities slowed Oracle down unnecessarily, so Oracle enhanced its software to talk directly to the disk drives. These were referred to as raw disks. With most modern operating system implementations, the speed difference between raw and cooked disk drives is small and there are cases wherein the cooked disk drives can provide better performance.

- One of the primary benefits of having a number of tablespaces is to balance the input/output load across several disk drives or disk controllers. Generally speaking, you want to split tables and their indexes into separate tablespaces located on separate disks to maximize performance (at least in larger Oracle instances). You also want to separate the rollback and temporary segments (see Chapter 10, "Oracle Memory Areas") from the table and index data files to prevent input/output to these tablespaces from competing with each other.

- Because every write transaction to a data file is mirrored with a transaction to a redo log file, you usually want to locate your data files on separate disk drives from those of your redo log files.

- Finally, Oracle provides an interesting feature—the read-only tablespace. Tablespaces designated read-only are assumed to be up-to-date without having to check their latest update number (the SCN). This finally enables you to place tablespaces on such devices as CD-ROMs (to which you could not write to record SCN updates). It also can save time for tablespaces that contain reference data that you do not update. If one of these data files is lost, you copy the data file from the backup tape and bring it directly on line. Oracle understands that it does not have to try to apply redo and archive log transactions to bring the file up-to-date.

This information should start you on the way to understanding Oracle data files. Later chapters discuss the objects that you place within a data file and maintenance of the tablespaces and data file. For now, be sure that you understand what these data files are and their relationship with tablespaces. The following is the SQL query that enables you to determine the location of your data files:

```
SQL> select * from sys.dba_data_files;

FILE_NAME
-------------------------------------------------------------------
    FILE_ID TABLESPACE_NAME          BYTES    BLOCKS STATUS
---------- --------------------- ---------- --------- ---------
C:\ORAWIN\DBS\wdbrbs.ora
         3 ROLLBACK_DATA           3145728      1536 AVAILABLE

C:\ORAWIN\DBS\wdbtemp.ora
         4 TEMPORARY_DATA          2097152      1024 AVAILABLE

C:\ORAWIN\DBS\wdbuser.ora
         2 USER_DATA               3145728      1536 AVAILABLE

C:\ORAWIN\DBS\wdbsys.ora
         1 SYSTEM                 10485760      5120 AVAILABLE

SQL>
```

You might be wondering what else you can do with data files. Actually, there is very little to do with data files after you create them. This is a good thing in that you focus your maintenance efforts on the database objects as opposed to file structures and other technical details that are managed by the Oracle DBMS software. However, the following actions might be of interest to you in some rare circumstances:

- Taking a specific data file offline or online (`alter database datafile 'filename' online` or `alter database datafile 'filename' offline`).
- Renaming or moving a datafile (`alter database rename file 'filename_old' to 'filename_new'`). Note that this makes a copy of the data file but does not delete the old data file, which you have to do manually.

Log Files

Redo log files are often referred to as the online redo log files to distinguish them from the archive log files (covered in the next section). You can control the number and size of the redo log files for your system. Basically, having a small number of redo log files that are larger can be beneficial on log switches when you are archiving the log files. This spreads out the times when the redo logs are copied to archive logs. This is important when input/output transfer rates to the disks on which the archive log files are being created is limited. (You have to complete the copy operation before the online redo log can be overwritten.)

You have a fixed number of online redo log files that are used in a cyclical manner (see Figure 11.2). When you finish writing to the first file, further transactions are written to the second file. This process continues until you finish writing to the last file in the sequence, at which time you begin to write to the first file again. You have to be careful when you are operating in archive log mode, because you cannot overwrite the contents of an online redo log file until that file has been completely copied to an archive log file. This is important. If Oracle cannot write a redo log file to an archive log file because, for example, the file system for the archive log files is full or offline, Oracle cannot accept transactions. It sticks, giving error messages to users who try to perform updates, deletes, or insertions. Worse still, it sometimes gets so confused in this mode that it is very difficult to get things moving again.

FIGURE 11.2.
Online redo log file recycling.

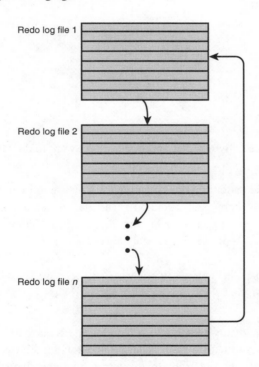

Redo log file 1

Redo log file 2

Redo log file *n*

CAUTION

Carefully monitor the file system where the archive log files are being written to prevent locking up Oracle's capability of accepting transactions.

This setup, where one redo log file at a time records every transaction made to the system, can turn into an input/output bottleneck. You have the option of creating groups of redo log files. If one of the members of the group is on a disk that is busy, the transaction is written to an available redo log file in that group and the busy log file is synched-up at a later time. You can have several members of each of several groups of log files.

As with most of the topics in this book, there is more information to cover than space available. The following is an example of the command you use to determine what redo log files are associated with in your instance:

```
SQL> select * from v$logfile;

    GROUP# STATUS
- - - - - - - - - - - - - - - -
MEMBER
- - - - - - - - - - - - - - - - - - - - - - - - - - - - - - - - - - - - - - - - - - - - - - - - - - - - - - - - - - - - - - - -
        2
C:\ORAWIN\DBS\wdblog2.ora

        1
C:\ORAWIN\DBS\wdblog1.ora

SQL>
```

Here are a few maintenance activities that you rarely might want to do with online redo logs:

- You might want to add additional redo log files. If you use individual log files as opposed to groups, the command would be `alter database add logfile 'filename' size ###K`. If you are using log file groups, the command would be `alter database add logfile group # ('filename1','filename2',…) size ###K`.

- You might want to delete existing redo log files. The command here would be `alter database drop logfile 'filename'` or `alter database drop logfile group #`.

- You might want to manually switch which redo log file is currently being written to so that you can perform some maintenance. Oracle will not let you do any maintenance on a log file or log file group that is currently in use. Therefore, to switch log file or log file groups, you would use the command `alter system switch logfile`.

From the previous section, you should understand that archive log files are merely sequential copies of the online redo log files. Their contents is a series of transactions that have been applied to your database. What else do you need to know about archive log files? Two key points: the options that are available for storing archive log files and how to set up the database to use archive log files.

Archive log files have two basic storage options. The first option is to use space on one of your disk drives. The other option is to write these log files directly to magnetic tape. There are pros and cons to either approach:

- Writing archive logs to tape saves the much more expensive disk storage space for other purposes.

- Archive logs written to tape have to be recovered from the slower tape medium in the event you need to do a recovery.

- Writing archive logs to tape requires a dedicated tape drive, which is not available on all systems.

Getting Oracle to start writing archive logs is a somewhat more difficult subject. When you create a data file within a tablespace, Oracle writes to it automatically when users place data into that tablespace. Oracle automatically writes to the redo logs that are created when you create your instance. However, the DBA has to go through a somewhat redundant and extremely sensitive process to get Oracle to write archive logs:

1. Go into the initialization files and set the `LOG_ARCHIVE_START` parameter to `True`. Don't be fooled; this parameter doesn't really start archive logging as you would expect. It sort of gives Oracle permission to start archive logging if all the other parameters are set up and only takes effect when you restart your Oracle instance.

2. Tell it the format for the name of your archive log files. The exact syntax can be found in the SQL Language Reference, but you often can accept the default format.

3. Tell Oracle where to stick the files and how to name what you are about to start archiving. This entails specifying a directory path and the first few characters of the archive log files themselves (it is not just a directory path). An example might be to have a series of archive log files that begins with the text string `alog` located in the `/disk57/oracle/logs` directory. Set the `LOG_ARCHIVE_DEST` parameter to the following:

   ```
   LOG_ARCHIVE_DEST = /disk57/oracle/logs/alog
   ```

   The second part of the archive filename is a variable string of characters that typically include sequential numbers. This format is specified by the `LOG_ARCHIVE_FORMAT` parameter. There are a number of options for this parameter, but the default usually works well and looks something like:

   ```
   LOG_ARCHIVE_FORMAT = '%s.arc'
   ```

4. Shut down (normally) your Oracle instance, perform a complete backup (for safety's sake, please don't skip this step), and bring up the instance with the database not open (that is, just give SQL*DBA the startup mount exclusive command). When the database has been started, enter the following command:

   ```
   alter database archivelog;
   ```

5. You can now open up the database. Be sure to verify that archive log files are actually being created. This is a very sensitive procedure and it is ripe with opportunities to make little mistakes in syntax that will cause you problems. You can verify that log files are being written by manually forcing a redo log file switch with this command:

```
alter system switch logfile
```

You may have guessed by now that archive log files have bedeviled me on several occasions. I usually wind up grousing when Oracle rejects my LOG_ARCHIVE_DEST parameter for some little syntax error. It is a tedious procedure. Once you have archive logging operational, you always have to be concerned with running out of space for archive log files and locking up Oracle's capability of writing transactions to the database. However, you have the comfort of knowing that you can recover all data committed up to the point of failure of a disk drive.

Control Files

After that rather invigorating discussion of the archive log files, it is time to cool off a bit and discuss a relatively easy topic—the control files. If you are lucky, the only time that you have to bother with control files is when you create an Oracle instance. This is because control files are used by Oracle internally. You cannot manually edit them, you cannot control their size, and you can move them if you have to. Otherwise, the only time you will notice them is if one is missing. (Oracle will give you an error message indicating which control file is missing or damaged.) When this happens, you copy one of the other control files (they are identical to one another) into the location of the missing control file and restart the system.

Control files are a road map of the database as it is physically laid out on your computer system. They store such tidbits as the name of the database, the data files and redo log names, and a record of when they were created. You can add control files and delete existing ones if you want. One rule to remember when locating control files is that you always want at least one control file available so that you can re-create the others. You can re-create the control files manually in, but you do not want to have to try this. Therefore, spread your control files out over several disk drives whenever possible so that you always have one to start your instance.

Initialization and Configuration Files

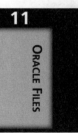

Oracle determines the physical configuration of an instance by accessing the control files. However, there are a number of configuration parameters related to tuning that you do not want to reset manually each time you start an instance. To make this easier, Oracle provides a series of initialization files that are similar to the `autoexec.bat` and `config.sys` of Microsoft DOS. On multiuser Oracle systems, there are two primary initialization files that are used:

- `init.ora`. This is the main file. The actual filename contains the Oracle instance's SID (system ID), so that an instance named `blue` would have an initialization file called `initblue.ora`.

- `config.ora`. Typically, `config.ora` files contain the locations for the control, archive, and dump files. They also contain the database name and the database block size parameters. Oracle intended these files to contain values that have parameters that are the same between instances; `init.ora` files contain parameters that are tuned and vary between instances. As with `init.ora` files, the `config.ora` files contain the SID in their name (for example, `configblue.ora`). The `config.ora` file is called by placing a line in the `init.ora` file that says to use a second initialization file (`ifile = filename`).

The initialization files are simple text files that you can edit with standard operating system editors, such as the wonderful `vi` editor in UNIX or Notepad under Microsoft Windows. The format is simple; you set a variable equal to a value. I have two gripes about the setup of these files. First, I hate to have to keep two files edited when one can do the job (personal preference). Second, the data is so scattered in these files with so many options commented out that it is difficult to see what you are setting and you have no history of what you were using in the past. Therefore, I like to redo my initialization file to contain the following sections (a sample `init.ora` file for UNIX systems is contained on the disk):

- A header that contains the name of the file, its purpose, and a history of all parameter changes (so that if a parameter change does not work out, you know where to set it).

- A grouping of all parameters that affect the size of the SGA. I do not keep commented-out parameters, only live ones.

- A grouping of all parameters that affect this size of the PGA.

- A grouping of all parameters that deal with logging.

- A grouping of the parameters associated with national language support (NLS), which is Oracle's tool to support databases that use multiple languages for the data and such things as date formats.

- A grouping of all parameters associated with the multithreaded server, if that option is used.

- A general category that contains the other miscellaneous parameters, such as whether multiple database writer processes are used.

- Finally, in certain cases Oracle will suggest you add some undocumented parameter to your system to make it run better. This is often the case when you are working with a large data warehouse. I like to keep these parameters in a separate section so that I know where they originated.

Before moving on to the next section on log and trace files, you need a few more notes. In multiuser Oracle systems, you can find the `init.ora` files in the `dbs` subdirectory under the `ORACLE_HOME` directory (the directory under which you locate all your Oracle software and administrative files. If this does not contain the actual file, it will contain at least a link that points to the `init.ora` file. The `config.ora` files are located in the `pfile` subdirectory under the `ORACLE_BASE/admin/`*instance_name* directory. In Personal Oracle, there is only an `init.ora` file, located under the `/orawin/rdbms` directory. This is probably enough to get you started in the world of Oracle initialization files. If you have a test Oracle instance available to you, try altering the configuration files and tuning parameters in this instance before you work on the instance that your company is depending on for its daily operations. If you do not have this luxury, be careful, make a copy of the original initialization files with another name (for example, `initblue.ora.1jan98`), and then try adjusting one parameter at a time until you build up your confidence.

Here is a list of the common parameters that you will find in your initialization files for Oracle databases. The other parameters are used in special circumstances, but these are the ones that you will see in almost every initialization file:

- `db_name`   This is the internal name of the database. I usually make it the same as the name of the SID, just to keep things simple, but there are no restrictions on this. It does get coded into the control files, so you have to use the right name once the database is created.

- `db_files`   This lists the maximum number of database files permitted.

11

- `control_files`   This parameter lists the control files that are out there. These control files need to be identical to one another and all must be available at startup. If one control file is missing due to a damaged disk drive, you can remove it from this list of control files and start the database with the remaining control files.

- `compatible`   This sets up the internal configuration of Oracle's data dictionary to be compliant with a certain release of the Oracle DBMS software. You could, for example, set compatibility to 7.2 while running Oracle8 software (there is no guarantee that this compatibility will function exactly as it would if you had the 7.2 software installed, but there is a good chance that it will). This enables you to have database applications that were written for older versions of the software running under newer versions of the software without being updated internally.

- `db_file_multiblock_read_count`   This determines the number of data blocks that are written at a time.

- `db_block_buffers`   This determines the number of blocks in the SGA that are allocated to database block buffers.

- `shared_pool_size`   This determines the amount of shared memory that is allocated to the shared pool.

- `log_checkpoint_interval`   This determines the period in seconds between log checkpoints.

- `processes`   This determines the maximum number of processes that can be associated with the Oracle instance.

- `log_buffer`   This determines the number of blocks allocated to the redo log buffers in the SGA.

- `audit_trail`   This parameter is either TRUE or FALSE, depending on whether you want to enable auditing.

- `max_dump_file_size`   This limits the size of a dump file when there is a problem detected within Oracle. It prevents you from overflowing the disk space that you have allocated for dumps.

- `log_archive_start`   This determines whether the archive log process is started.

- `background_dump_dest`   This specifies the file location for the alert log and dump files associated with the Oracle database processes.

- `user_dump_dest`   This determines the file location for dump files associated with problems with end user processes.

- `db_block_size`   This determines the size of a block in this Oracle database (both on disk and in memory).

- `rollback_segments`   This specifies which rollback segments are to be brought online at database startup.

Log and Trace Files

Recall that Oracle really wants to help you out when a problem occurs. Therefore, it takes a few CPU cycles in its utilities to write out a record of important events that occur to a set of log files. The log file that records major events in the RDBMS itself is the alert log file. As always, the exact name and location of this file is a little more complicated than just alert_log. The actual file contains the name of the instance with which the events are associated. For our near-famous blue Oracle instance, the alert log file would be called alert_blue.log. The next logical question is what exactly gets placed in the alert log:

- Major DBA activities, such as starting or stopping the instance or issuing commands that create, modify, or drop the database, its tablespaces, or rollback segments
- Internal Oracle errors
- Messages related to multithreaded server problems
- Errors related to automatic refreshes of a snapshot

The trace files are produced by the Oracle background processes when they sense that they have a major problem or when one of the processes detects that another background process is in trouble or missing. The content of the message varies depending on how much information the process writing the message can sense. It usually contains the date and time of the problem, with which background processes the problems occurred, numbered Oracle error messages that you can use to discuss the problem with Oracle, and some explanatory text. If you have a problem with Oracle, save these messages until after you have determined the exact cause of the problem and have a fix for it. Some versions of Oracle write trace files every time you start. This does not indicate errors; it's just logging a successful start.

One common Oracle feature that does not store its logging information in the alert log file is the SQL*Net or Net8 process. Instead, you will find a log file under the appropriate SQL*Net directory related to the protocol you are using for your system (TCP/IP, for example). This makes some sense in that alert logs are tied to a specific instance, but a single SQL*Net process can service multiple instances.

Now that you are enthusiastic about the wealth of information that is available to you in the log and trace files, you probably can't wait to learn where to find them. The answer is that the location where these log files are kept is a parameter specified in your initialization files (specifically the config.ora for the instance in question). That parameter is called BACKGROUND_DUMP_DEST (the destination for the dump files of the Oracle background processes, which is typically ORACLE_BASE/admin/instance_name/bdump).

One final topic to consider is cleaning up after yourself. The log files just keep growing and growing as more events are recorded. The trace files sit out there until you do something with them, eating up more and more disk space. Therefore, it is a good idea to implement housekeeping procedures wherein you regularly clear out the log, core, and trace files. My favorite option is to set up a script that automatically copies the alert and SQL*Net log files to files that have the date that they created as part of their name (for example, alert_blue.log.013095). Then purge all the trace and log files in the appropriate directories that are over 30 days old. The system stays clean and you never have to scan through a 1MB log file to look for data on a problem that you encounter.

Automatic Resizing of Files

One feature in Oracle8 that became available with Oracle 7.3 is the automatic resizing of data files option. One of the biggest problems for database administrators in the past was running out of space for a new extent within a tablespace. You had to be constantly vigilant to ensure that you had both enough space and large enough blocks of contiguous space to accommodate table and index growth. The difficulty was that you could never tell when a particular table or index was going to need another extent.

This was a serious problem in that applications would crash and data entered could be lost when you ran out of space. For data warehouses, this problem usually occurred when data was being loaded in the middle of the night causing the DBA to be awakened to fix the problem. Believe me, this was a serious problem for married DBAs whose spouses did not like to be awakened every week with phone calls. It also meant that the database might not be available on time for users in the morning while the problems were being corrected.

The solution to this was to specify in the SQL syntax that it would be okay for the tablespace to add more space to a given data file. This space would be consumed on the same disk drive. Of course, you would still want some control over this resizing, so the SQL syntax has to take this into account. The following is an example of how you would specify the `autoexend` option (which is not the default):

```
Alter database
datafile '/u03/oradata/devel01.ora'
autoexend on
next 50M
maxsize 500M;
```

Distribution of Data for Tuning

What I want to do here is point you to Chapter 24, "Oracle8 Database Tuning," which discusses database tuning. Some of you may just be reading this chapter preparing to lay out your data files without thinking of the impact on tuning. True, if you just have a 20MB database in mind, you can do almost whatever you want when it comes to file layout. However, if you are talking about storing and reading through gigabytes worth of information, you probably want to spend some time scattering the data and software intelligently between the disk drives to improve performance. This is often the cheapest way to improve the performance of an Oracle system.

Standard File Locations

Before going into detail on the various types of files associated with the Oracle system, let's step back and provide an overview of how these files are arranged on the disk drives of your system. If you had Oracle6, it was hard to predict precisely where files were going to be stored. Most installations did not have sound guidance and used whatever the DBA at the time preferred. Starting with Oracle7, Oracle issued guidance as to how to lay out your files in what they refer to as the Optimal Flexible Architecture (OFA). You may wish to do things slightly different than the OFA would. Note, too, that the configuration of the Personal Oracle7 product that runs under Microsoft Windows is slightly different from those of the other products.

The Optimal Flexible Architecture was designed by the Oracle consulting staff for installations that it performed for customers. Oracle liked it so much it presents it in its Installation and Configuration Guide as a recommendation. This architecture is also the default for its Oracle installer scripts on most computer systems. Figure 11.3 shows the configuration of Oracle7 for UNIX. This figure also shows the general concepts of the OFA, although the names of the directories may vary on other operating systems.

The starting point for this architecture is known as the Oracle base. There are three key directories under Oracle base. Admin stores log files and other information for the DBA. Data is designed to store data files. Product stores the Oracle application software and the configuration files for the Oracle home instances. The other two directories are less frequently used, at least in my experience: TAR is designed to hold tape downloads, and Local is designed for items you create and may want to store with the Oracle software.

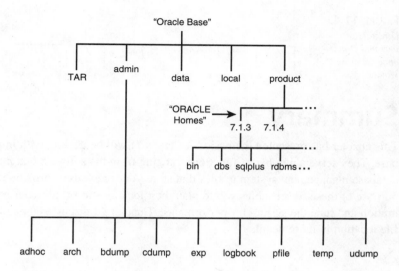

FIGURE 11.3.
The Optimal Flexible Architecture (OFA) for UNIX.

This architecture has a place for everything that you will find in a typical Oracle database. As with most standards, once you learn where things are placed in it, you can find those same things in any other Oracle databases. The large number of directories helps in that each lower-level directory has a specific focus and limited number of files that you have to sort through (from a few files to a few dozen if you keep things cleaned out properly). There is a single directory that contains all the executable files that you will typically need. This makes it easy to set your path so that you can access the Oracle applications. Finally, this architecture is designed to easily accommodate having multiple versions of the RDBMS software on the system at the same time. This is especially useful when converting over instances. You can bring up the new release of the RDBMS on your test database to see how it works while maintaining production on the existing release.

Very large installations usually alter the storage of data files to maximize performance at some point. Configuration alternatives are explored more thoroughly in the installation planning discussions in Chapter 5. For now, just try to get a good feel for the types of data files that you have. Each type of file will be discussed to provide you with an understanding of what it can do for you.

In almost all PC-based installations, creating a number of directories that can be split across multiple disk drives is not worth the effort. Most PCs have a single disk drive, and most DOS/Windows users are used to having software products installed at a single directory hierarchy located off the root directory. Part of the balancing act a product has to do when porting between platforms is maintaining the same command structure and interfaces yet adapting to the customers of the host environment. In Oracle's case, they have implemented the directory structure shown in Figure 11.4.

FIGURE 11.4.
*Directory of
Personal Oracle
under Microsoft
Windows 95.*

Summary

This chapter has presented the basic files that you will be dealing with in an Oracle database. They serve a number of functions, ranging from the software that makes up the database management system to files that store your precious information. Knowing the purpose of these files enables you to plan their locations to fit into your hardware configuration and tune the system for performance. Chapter 24 discusses the tuning aspect of file location in more detail.

Oracle Database Objects

by Joe Greene

In This Chapter

The word *object* is rather heavily used in the computer industry these days. Development tool vendors argue over whose product is more object-oriented. Almost everyone claims some form of object-oriented capabilities (with Oracle8, that list now includes Oracle). However, the term object has been used for some time in the Oracle database world to describe those entities that exist within the database files. These are the logical entities with which users interact. For developers, understanding these database objects is all that they may need to know about Oracle databases other than their user ID and password. This list of database objects includes:

- Tables
- Indexes
- Views
- Synonyms
- Sequences
- Partitions
- Clusters
- Stored procedures and packages
- User-defined data types (new to Oracle8)
- Tablespaces
- Constraints

This chapter explains these objects so you can better understand the tools that are at your disposal during the database design process. Some of the topics, such as extent sizing and grouping tables into tablespaces, may seem to be a bit philosophical at this point. However, knowledge of these features is useful when you are trying to extract the best performance out of a given database system.

Oracle8 Database Objects

In the introduction to this chapter, I listed the database objects that I planned to discuss. In this section, I will go over how these objects fit together to form a database. I will then go into more detail on these objects in the remaining sections of this chapter. The purpose of the basic Oracle8 database objects are as follows:

- *Tables*. Tables are the basic unit of data storage within an Oracle database. They are typically the entity that you issue your query against and make your data changes to. It is possible to conceive of a database without any user data tables, but such a database is highly unlikely.

Oracle Database Objects
CHAPTER 12

219

12

ORACLE
DATABASE
OBJECTS

- *Indexes*. Some database tables can get quite large. While it would be possible to scan these large tables every time that you wanted to extract a single row of data, it would not be very efficient. Therefore, if there is a common selection criterion used to select a row (for example, employee ID in a table about staff members), you would probably want to build an index to track which row or rows in the table are associated with a given value for this selection criterion. This enables Oracle to retrieve a single row from the large table after scanning the much smaller index, thereby saving processing time.

- *Views*. Sometimes, you may want to give a user access to only some of the data in a table. Other times, you may need to join together several tables to produce the data that users want to access. These goals can be accomplished through the use of a view. A view can be thought of as an SQL select statement that selects part of one table or joins multiple tables together but can be accessed as though it were a simple table.

- *Synonyms*. There are instances when you may want to use an alternate name for a database table or view. Perhaps you use a very formal scheme for naming tables that makes sense to developers but is a little bit cumbersome to end users. Perhaps you have a number of different table and view owners and you do not want to have your users type in fully qualified table names (for example, owner.table_name). In these and some other circumstances, you may want to use a synonym to give the table or view an alternative name to make typing the SQL statements a little easier.

- *Sequences*. There are many cases in database programming where you want to be able to guarantee that something (a row in a table) has a unique attribute value. To implement this rather common need, Oracle8 supports sequences (a unique series of numbers) that can used in your tables. This is often used to generate primary keys.

- *Tablespaces*. When databases grow larger, it becomes advantageous to group tables and indexes together to spread data between disk drives for performance reasons. The mechanism to accomplish this task is the tablespace. Tables and indexes are created in a given tablespace. Tablespaces have data files (located on one or more disk drives) associated with them to enable you to control what information is placed on which disk drive.

- *Partitions*. A new feature to Oracle8 is the partition. Take the situation where you want to scan January's transactions in a table that contains 10 years' worth of data. You would waste a lot of time scanning records that do not meet your criteria. Oracle8 enables you to group data within a table into partitions that can then be placed on explicit disk drives. Oracle's query engine is smart enough to ignore partitions that do not meet the selection criteria, thereby saving time. A reliability feature is that if a given partition is unavailable due to a disk drive failure, you can still access data in the other partitions associated with that table.

- *Clusters.* Clusters are an older construct within Oracle used primarily in the data dictionary of Oracle itself. What this construct enables you to do is group data in different objects together for efficient access. For example, if you have a lookup table that always leads to a main data table, you could cluster them together for rapid access. However, as Oracle's storage algorithms have improved, it is rare when you have to use a cluster.

- *Stored procedures and packages.* The Oracle8 database enables you to store and execute software within the database itself. This software processing mechanism lets you automatically execute certain algorithms (whenever a table is updated) or on demand (the user or program makes an explicit call to that procedure).

- *User-defined data types (new to Oracle8).* Real-world objects (here using the business definition of an object) have multiple bits of information that are applicable to them. For example, an employee may have an employee ID, a series of addresses, and perhaps even a photograph. Oracle8 enables you to group these dissimilar or repeating datatypes together logically so that you can access them.

- *Constraints.* A primary concern of a production database is not just to store data, but to store good, valid data. This can be quite a challenge when there are a number of programmers working on an application or users who have ad hoc access to the database. Oracle provides constraints to help control what can be put into a given column in a given table to enhance the accuracy of the information.

Tables

The basic unit of information storage within an Oracle database is a table. A table contains rows of data which represent instances of a given entity (for example, addresses for employees). The table also has columns which represent attributes associated with the rows (for example, the city and state for a given address). Oracle has expanded its column capabilities over the years to progress from simple number and character data storage to more complex data types such as video, audio, or image data.

You might be interested in knowing how Oracle chooses which bytes on the disk to use to store the file and how it delimits the various columns and other such detailed storage data, but it's not necessary. When you insert a row into a table, Oracle finds the correct spot within the extents that you have allocated for that table and stores the data in a manner that you can retrieve it. Oracle keeps track of the exact location of the bits and bytes. The only internal storage feature that you might use is the row ID. This unique number specifies a given row in a given table. That way, if you have multiple rows in a table that have the exact same values and you want to get rid of one of them, you can use the row ID to do it.

Here is a sample command used to create a table called `golf_scores`:

```
create table golf_scores
(course         char(20),
date_played    date,
partner        char(20),
front_nine     number(3),
back_nine      number(3),
total          number(3))
initrans 1
maxtrans 100
tablespace user_data
storage (
initial 10K
next 10K
pctincrease 0
minextents 1
maxextents 100);
```

The most straightforward approach to analyzing this command (and tables in general) is to break down the command into its components:

- `create table golf_scores` tells Oracle what to do (create table). Every table needs a name, which is any valid combination of characters and underlines (spaces are not allowed) that is 30 characters or fewer. I like table names that tell me what is in the table versus the old mainframe code and number systems. By the way, Oracle has certain reserved words, such as `order`, which you cannot use as the table name (although `order` could be part of a larger name).

- The next six lines (contained within parentheses) list the names of the columns for this table. Associated with each column is a datatype (for example, `char` for character) and size. (The various types of data and sizing are discussed later in this section.)

- `initrans` and `maxtrans` are similar to the `initial` and `next` extent parameters, except they allocate space to record transactions that are in progress to the table. This space is allocated in the header of the table and is in chunks of 23 bytes each. This space is not recovered when the transaction is completed. The maximum value for these is no more than 255 and may be less on some operating systems. If you run out of transaction space for a table, new transactions have to wait until transaction space is freed up by existing transactions completing. If you do not specify values for these parameters, default values that apply to your instance are used.

- `tablespace user_data` is where you tell Oracle to put your table—in this example, a tablespace called `user_data`. If you do not specify this parameter, the default tablespace for your user ID will be used.

- `storage()` contains five parameters within the parentheses that are the storage parameters for this table. If you do not specify any of these values, the default value for that parameter in this tablespace is used.

- `initial` and `next` are the initial extent and next extent parameters described under tablespaces.

- `pctincrease` is the percentage of increase in size applied to each of the next extents. Take an example where the initial `extent` size was 1KB, the `next` is 2KB, and `pctincrease` is 50%. The third extent would be 3K (1.5 times 2KB). The fourth extent would be 4.5KB and so on.

- `minextents` and `maxextents` are the minimum and maximum number of extents that you have for this table.

Each column in a table has a column name, a datatype, and some sizing parameters. The rules for column names are the same as the rules for table names, and it's a good idea to use column names that are meaningful. Character data has a size to it that specifies the maximum length of the character string. Numbers have precision and scale. *Precision* refers to the total number of digits, not including the exponent when this number is expressed in exponential notation. The *scale* specifies the number of digits to the right of the decimal place. A number with a precision of 5 and a scale of 2 will range between –999.99 and +999.99 and is considered to be datatype `number(5,2)`. Table 12.1 lists datatypes supported by Oracle (older versions may not support the `long raw` or `varchar2` datatypes):

TABLE 12.1. ORACLE DATATYPES.

Datatype	Meaning	Fixed/Variable Length
`char(size)`	Character	Fixed length (trailing spaces added)
`varchar2(size)`	Character	Variable length (uses what is needed)
`number(prec,scale)`	Number	Variable length (uses what is needed)
`date`	Date and time	Seven bytes per column (year 2000 compliant)
`long`	Character	Variable length up to 64KB in Oracle6 or 2GB per row in Oracle7
`raw(size)`	Free-form	Variable length up to 2,000 bytes per row
`long raw`	Free-form	Variable length up to 64KB in Oracle6 or 2GB per row in Oracle7

Data Type	Meaning	Fixed/Variable Length
rowid	Binary	Six bytes per row that can be represented as a number in queries

Access to the tables in most cases is with the Structured Query Language (SQL). Unlike flat-file systems or simpler data management tools, you do not have direct access to the raw data storage formats. This language has a number of statements that you need to learn to work with Oracle tables properly. It is important to understand that when you issue the select command to retrieve a row from a table, you actually get one or more blocks of rows back from the data files. In many cases, if you want multiple rows from a table, they are located relatively close to one another (in that they were stored at about the same time). By retrieving a block of data into memory, Oracle avoids accessing the disk separately for each row.

Of course, you do not want every user in your instance creating tables all the time. Therefore, Oracle enables the DBA to control who can create or modify these objects via the privileges mechanism. Chapter 11, "Oracle Files," discusses privileges in some detail, but for now, understand that there are two basic privileges related to table creation and modification:

- CREATE TABLE
- ALTER TABLE

One final topic before we leave this section: It is useful to be able to determine what tables are out there and how they are set up. Once again, there is a DBA view that provides the information that the DBA needs to manage tables. Figure 12.1 shows a screen with a sample of a query to the DBA view that verifies the table created earlier in this section is set up the way you intended. Note that the where clause is used to narrow the range of information that you want to see.

Indexes

The where clause is a commonly used construct in database programming. Very few users want to see all the data in a table displayed for them on every query. Instead, most queries are designed to return a series of rows or perhaps even a single row that matches the users' criteria. Without indexes, Oracle would have to read all of the rows in the table and then filter out the ones that are not of interest. However, with indexes, you scan the small index to see which rows are of interest and then only retrieve those rows from the table. For smaller tables, it is not a big deal to read in all the rows and check them off one by one to see whether they match the selection criteria input by the users.

However, for large tables (I once saw a table that was 17GB), this is extremely slow and places a large load on the system for every query. To help solve this problem, indexes were created.

FIGURE 12.1.

A query against the DBA_TABLES view.

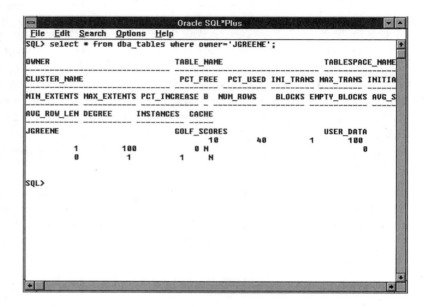

An *index* is a sorted list of data from one or more columns in the table that are commonly used as selection criteria. Thus, rather than searching through a large number of long personnel records to find the record of an individual, you can sort through a relatively short index containing just the last name and first name (see Figure 12.2). When Oracle finds the name that matches your search values, it retrieves just the block of rows that contains the data you need. Because the data is already presorted, Oracle does not have to read every record in the index. Instead, it uses a more efficient search routine (modified B-TREE whose search pattern resembles the branches of a tree) to reduce the number of index records that it needs to analyze.

Because indexes are extracted lists of values for tables, Oracle needs a place to store them. Therefore, indexes have storage clauses similar to tables. Here is a sample command that creates an index on the date_played field of the golf_scores table in the previous section:

```
create index golf_scores_dates
on golf_scores (date_played)
tablespace user_data
storage
(initial 2K
```

```
next 2K
minextents 1
maxextents 100
pctincrease 0);
```

FIGURE 12.2.
Indexed searches.

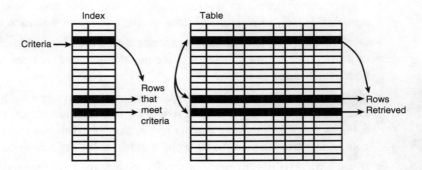

How do you get your queries to use these wonderful indexes that you have created? The answer is that Oracle automatically uses indexes if you issue a query that can use the index (that is, the values in your where clause are among the fields of the index). That makes life a whole lot easier for developers. Even better, indexes are maintained automatically by Oracle. When you add, delete, or modify rows in a table that has one or more indexes, the indexes are automatically updated to reflect the changes. This brings up an important design consideration. It takes Oracle time to update an index. If you have a table that has a large number of indexes, it takes longer to add data to this table. Therefore, tables in which the key to performance is the capability of adding data (for example, an order entry on a system that is heavily loaded during the day) benefit from fewer indexes. Conversely, systems that are used primarily for queries (such as decision support systems) benefit from having as many indexes as are useful based on the types of user queries.

It is sometimes difficult to answer the question as to what indexes are useful in a table. Obviously, indexing every column in the table is probably not a good idea. Even though an index search is more efficient than a table scan, it does take some time. When you add the time of searching a large index to the time it takes to retrieve the rows you need from the table, you usually wind up taking longer than if you just scan the table. It also may not be justifiable to build and maintain indexes that support the selection criteria of infrequently used queries. In this case, it costs more time on the updates than it saves on these infrequent queries. Being trained as a scientist with a love for experimentation, I always try constructing an index that I am curious about and then see its effect on the performance of my queries and update routines. Based on this data, I decide on whether it was worth keeping.

The following are a few more notes about indexes:

- Tables are not affected by the presence or lack of indexes. You can drop and re-create indexes at will without affecting any of the data in a table.

- It is sometimes beneficial in systems where you perform large batch updates to drop the indexes, perform the updates, and then re-create the indexes.

- One rule of performance tuning is to locate the indexes for a table on a separate disk from the table itself. This splits the input/output load for queries that access both the table and an index.

- You have the option of creating unique indexes. If you create a unique index, it gives an error if you try to insert a row in the table that has values in the index columns that match those of another row in the table. This is a good way to enforce a primary key on the table and build an index in a single step.

- If you have privileges to create or modify a table, you have the privileges you need to create or modify indexes associated with that table.

Indexes are very useful tools to improve the performance of queries. However, like all tools, you need to consider their design carefully to ensure that you get the performance gains that you desire. Figure 12.3 shows a screen with the query that you would issue to view the indexes associated with a particular user in the database.

FIGURE 12.3.

Determining the indexes owned by a user.

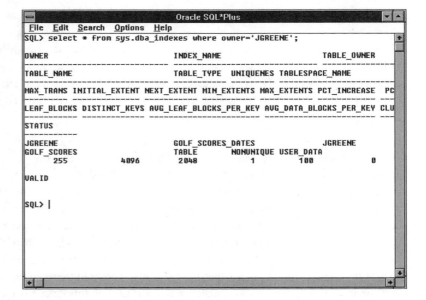

The following example shows the columns in the indexes associated with a given table name:

```
SQL> select index_owner,index_name,column_name
  2  from dba_ind_columns
  3  where table_name='WORLD_CITIES';

INDEX_OWNER                      INDEX_NAME                       COLUMN_NAME
-------------------------------  -------------------------------  ------------
JGREENE                          SYS_C004325                      LOCATION_ID
```

Views

Next on your list of database objects to study is views. You have already seen a number of views in the examples where we queried the database for a list of tables, tablespaces, and indexes. The actual data retrieved is stored in one or more internally controlled Oracle tables, and I would have to do some research to figure out what they are. I honestly don't care. I have these nice little views that I issue simple queries against to get my answers.

A *view* is merely a selection of one or more rows from one or more tables. The data is not duplicated. The view is merely a structure that references the data that is actually stored in the tables. You could think of it as a stored SQL query (with join and filtering logic) from which you can select data as if it were a table. Therefore, they do not require storage parameters and do not reside in tablespaces. Views can be used to achieve a number of objectives for designers:

- Your users do not want to write complex queries that join two or more tables together. Therefore, you build the logic joining the two tables into the view and let the users access the data as if it were a single table.

- You may have tables where certain users are permitted to access data only from certain columns. You can create views that contain the columns that they are allowed to access and give those users access to only the view and not the base table.

- You have tables where the column names may not make sense to certain users. You can create a view that renames these columns to names that make sense.

- You may want to deal with simpler structures than tables. For example, your table may have hundreds of columns of data. It may be easier to create a view and then have the users worry about only the simpler view.

One of the best features about views is that you access them the same way you access tables. You do not have to learn any separate language constructs. You cannot create indexes on views. To create a view, you need the CREATE VIEW privilege assigned to your Oracle user ID. You cannot alter a view. Instead you just drop it and re-create it. You can do this in a single command by using the CREATE OR REPLACE VIEW format of the CRE- ATE VIEW command. The advantage of the CREATE OR REPLACE VIEW format is that you do not lose the privilege grants that may have been granted on the view. This is not a problem, because dropping or creating views has no effect on the data in the tables asso- ciated with that view.

Views are convenient database objects that do not store any data themselves. Instead, views reference data located in one or more tables in the instance. They have many uses, including making queries more convenient for the users and providing additional security for the database.

Synonyms

A *synonym* is merely a way of assigning an alias with which users can reference a table or view. This makes it easier to access tables that you do not own. When you own a table, you use its name in your SQL queries. When you want to access a table owned by another user, you need to specify both the owner of the table and the table name (in the `owner.table_name` format). When you reference tables located in a different database using SQL*Net, the format can be rather complicated. Synonyms simplify this access because you can create a simple synonym that contains the details of a complex refer- ence string (see Figure 12.4).

FIGURE 12.4.

Synonyms.

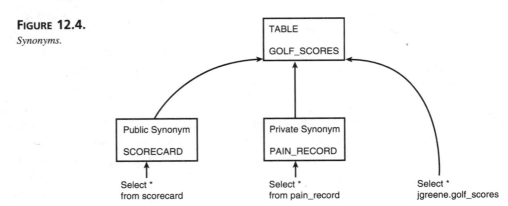

There are two types of synonyms—private and public. *Private synonyms* are those that you create for your own personal use. *Public synonyms* are those that you create that any user in the database can use. Obviously, from a DBA point of view, you usually want to restrict the number of users who can create public synonyms. You usually want to be even more restrictive with the number of users who can drop public synonyms. There are three primary system privilege sets with which the DBA is concerned related to synonyms:

- `CREATE SYNONYM` (which also allows you to drop private synonyms)
- `CREATE PUBLIC SYNONYM`
- `DROP PUBLIC SYNONYM`

Finally, it is interesting to consider what you get when you issue a query that goes against an object name that states the following: You own a table with that name, you have a private synonym with that name, and there is also a public synonym with that name. I had to try this out once to figure out what Oracle would do. After I got the results of this experiment, it made sense to me. So, here is the order in which Oracle accesses objects that have the same name in the database:

- If you own a table with a particular name, you always access your table on a query to that object name.
- If you do not own a table with that name, but have a private synonym with that name, you access the object associated with that private synonym.
- Finally, if you have neither a table nor a private synonym with the object name you are searching for, you access the object specified by the public synonym.

Stored Procedures and Packages

As mentioned earlier in this chapter, *stored procedures* are a way of storing software within the Oracle database. Basically, anything that you can develop in a PL/SQL script can be saved as an Oracle stored procedure. A collection of stored procedures can be saved as a package in the database. Stored procedures can present several interesting advantages for Oracle developers:

- Oracle security mechanisms, such as roles and grants, can be used to protect both the data and the software. This also provides one place of control for security administration.
- When you execute a stored procedure, you execute it as if you were the person who created it and not with the privileges that you would normally have. This fits well with certain environments, which need to implement security features in the

software, such as audit trails and special validity checking. The DBA can grant write access only to the user who creates the stored procedures. Users who are authorized to perform write operations are not given that permission in their Oracle accounts. Instead, they are given access to the stored procedures that must be executed (and hence the software security features enforced) to perform the write operations. If they try issuing SQL commands to write to these tables from SQL*Plus, they are denied access.

- Another advantage of stored procedures is that Oracle stores both the source code and a parsed version of the software. This saves Oracle the time of having to parse the statements each time as it would for SQL queries received from external software applications.

There are two problems with stored procedures. First, all stored procedures are stored in the system tablespace, usually thought of as sacred ground for use only by the DBA. However, the Oracle developers do not agree. Therefore, you have to let non-DBA software be placed in your most special tablespace. The other problem is that the software has to be written in PL/SQL. PL/SQL gets the job done; however, it is difficult to debug and does not support normal input/output operations. Stored procedures are very useful if you are willing to live with these two annoyances.

Stored procedures require special system privileges for creation (as you would expect with something that can be this powerful and that has to be placed in the system tablespace). Without getting into the details that are of concern to software developers, you need to grant CREATE PACKAGE, CREATE PROCEDURE, DROP PACKAGE, and/or DROP PROCEDURE to users who will be developing stored procedures in your system. Chapter 17 will cover stored software in greater detail.

Clusters

Recall that a *cluster* is a group of tables that you want to store together because they contain a number of common columns and are often joined together in queries. I have never used clusters. They were common in Oracle6, but the basic data storage algorithm for Oracle8 is a lot smarter that in Oracle6, and it will arrange tables in an efficient manner without creating clusters. One nice feature about clusters is that users have no idea whether the tables that they are accessing are in a cluster. Only the developers and DBAs know which tables are in clusters.

The basic Oracle references provide a good description of the details of setting up clusters. They also go into more detail about when you might use them. However, for purposes of this book, it is enough for you to know what they are. If you have performance problems with queries that always join together a few tables that have common columns, you may consider experimenting with clusters. Otherwise, you may never see a cluster. (Although many of the Oracle internal tables are supposed to use clusters, you may never deal with these tables directly because that is what you purchased the RDBMS software to do for you.)

Sequences

The next database object to consider is the sequence. As discussed in the introduction, *sequences* are tools used to generate a unique sequential number that you can use in your data tables. It is an excellent way to generate a guaranteed unique number to use as an internal key to link two tables in an application. One of the best features of sequences is that they guarantee that you will get a unique value when you access the sequence. If, for example, you create your own sequence table and write applications that read the next available value, increment it by one, and then update the sequence table with this new value, there is always a chance that someone else can access the same record that you did before your update statement is issued (you could get around this if you played fancy games with locks, but why bother when sequences are available?). If this is a primary key to a table, you will have a corrupted primary key. One final note: You cannot roll back your incrementing of a sequence value. If you decide not to insert the row with that sequence value into your table, you do not recover the sequence number.

There are three parameters associated with a sequence—start value, max value, and increment (which is usually 1). The following shows the syntax used for creating a sequence:

```
SQL> create sequence location_id
  2  increment by 1
  3  start with 1
  4    maxvalue 999999999
  5    cycle;

Sequence created.
```

Sequences are easy to access. For example, if you create a sequence called `staff_id` to track a unique, internal key for each staff member entered into a personnel database, you can enter a new record of data and generate a unique key with a simple SQL statement such as the following:

```
insert into personnel
values(staff_id.nextval,
'Jones',
'Sandra',
'123-4567');
```

The maintenance issues associated with sequences are associated with the sequence not reaching its maximum value or the sequence not being updated during certain data loads into its associated data tables. By default, indexes are created with the cycle option, which means that they will recycle. This can cause problems if the sequence is feeding a column with a unique constraint or index. Therefore, you have to ensure that the sequence and column are large enough to hold a large array of unique values for the sequence. The other common problem with sequences is when someone writes software that makes up its own ID numbers as opposed to using the sequence. When a user tries to use the sequence, he will be given a value that has already been inserted into the associated data table. Therefore, if you use programs that do not use sequences, you have to update the sequences after this program is run to ensure that the sequence is up-to-date.

As a final note on sequences, there are a series of Oracle system privileges that are needed to create or work with sequences. These privileges are CREATE SEQUENCE and DROP SEQUENCE. This should be enough to get you started and enable you to understand what sequences are. There is additional background material in the basic Oracle documentation set if you want to try to get fancy with sequences.

Tablespaces

The fundamental unit of storage within a database is the *tablespace*. The tablespaces contain the various other types of objects to store user data. They also contain the series of tables, views, and so forth that Oracle uses to store information related to the operation of the database. The tablespace is the fundamental unit of storage for a second reason: It is the link to the physical storage world. A tablespace has one or more data files associated with it. You cannot control which data file Oracle uses to store a row that you are adding to the table, but you can control the tablespace, which at least narrows the list of data files that you will be accessing. Many of you may be uncomfortable with this lack of control. There are two points to be made in favor of this setup. First, you are already busy enough managing the database, so the burden of controlling physical storage is something you should welcome passing off to it. Second, you can always control which disk receives the data by creating tablespaces that have only one data file (if you really have to be certain on which disk a table is located).

It will be useful now to go over a command that enables you to see what tablespaces you have on your system. This illustrates an important general concept when dealing with Oracle. To find out what you want to know, you usually issue a Structured Query Language (SQL) query. Some prefer to use Oracle's SQL*Plus product and others prefer SQL*DBA or Oracle Server Manager. However, either way you are accessing a view created for the database administrator that searches the internal Oracle tables to find the information that you need. I keep a list at my desk of the DBA views for those times when I am going after a view I rarely use. These are your windows into what is happening with your database. Oracle provides a GUI-based tool (Enterprise Manager) that executes these queries and then displays the results in the form of charts and numbers. For those of you who do not have access to Enterprise Manager, you can always get the data executing the basic queries.

One of the first things you will notice if you query the `all_tablespaces` view within Oracle8 is the series of columns that deal with `extents` or `pct_increase`. These are the default *storage parameters* for the tablespace. Every object that takes up space in the database (for example, tables and indexes) uses preallocated chunks of space known as *extents*. Oracle could have been designed to put rows of data into a big tablespace in the order in which they were received; however, with larger systems, you would have to scan a large amount of disk space to find all the rows associated with a particular table. Recall that Oracle chose to group the rows of a table into areas on the disks known as extents. This helps because Oracle reads extra rows into the SGA buffer cache (which makes sense because most operating systems read entire blocks of data from disk at a time).

Oracle could have stopped with the idea of having everything in a single extent for a database object; however, that would force developers to size each table accurately at the beginning of the project. You also would have to preallocate a large amount of space at creation for tables that may grow slowly over time. The compromise position that Oracle adopted was to make extents even multiples of the operating system block size and enable each table to occupy a reasonable number of extents. The maximum number of extents that a given object can occupy varies by operating system, but can usually go to over 100 extents.

Now that you have the concepts of storage under your belt, you are ready to understand the default storage parameters in `all_tablespaces`. These are only defaults; you can override them for database objects that you create (as is shown in the sections that follow). If you do not specify the default storage parameters when you create the tablespace, you will get the default values associated with the database. If you do not specify default parameters for your database, you inherit a set of defaults that Oracle provides that are tailored to your operating system. The following are the basic storage parameters for a tablespace:

- `initial_extent` enables you to specify the size of this first extent. You have to allocate at least one extent when you create database objects. Note that you cannot create an extent larger than the largest contiguous extent that is available in a single data file. You may have a lot of space available, but if it is scattered between disk files and is interrupted with other extents, you will be limited to a small extent size for new objects.

- `next_extent` specifies the size of the second extent that you allocate. All further extents are sized according to the value for this extent increased successively by the percent increase factor discussed later.

- `min_extents` is the minimum number of extents you specify. You do not have to create just one extent when you create an object. I almost always create one extent, but you can specify any number of extents in this field, limited only by the `max_extents` parameter. The only scenario that I could come up with for allocating more than one extent is if you had a very large table which you knew was going to have to be split between multiple data files on multiple disks (for example, you have three 2GB disk drives and a table that needed three 1.5GB extents). You might want to allocate the large extents before allocating any other extents in the database or loading any data.

- `max_extents` is the maximum number of extents that this object can occupy. As stated in the earlier discussions, if you have a large number of extents, it may take some time for the disks to locate all the extents that you may need in a query and send back the data. Generally speaking, the fewer extents that there are for an object, the more rapid the response time will be.

- `pct_increase` is a parameter that I always set to zero, but some people use it. This factor represents a percentage increase to apply to each successive extent allocated. For example, consider a table where the `next_extent` size is `1000` bytes and the `pct_increase` is `10`. Your second extent would be 1,000 bytes, your third extent would be 1,100 bytes, your fourth extent would be 1,210 bytes, and so on. I do not like to use it because I like to keep the number of extents down to a reasonable value for performance and know exactly what the size of the next extent to be allocated is without having to go to a calculator. For example, the 20th extent allocated in this example would consume over 5,500 bytes. Imagine what the 500th extent would be.

Another feature in `all_tablespaces` is the status column. You do not have to have all tablespaces online at the same time. If you do not want data altered for a given application that has its own tablespace, you can take the whole tablespace offline. The users will be told that they cannot gain access to any objects in that tablespace while it is offline. This comes into play later when you learn about recovery. If a single data file is damaged, you can bring the rest of your Oracle instance up and recover that single tablespace.

Partitions

Partitions are designed to allow you to take a large table or index and split it into multiple pieces based on one of the attributes associated with that table (for example, a date). The partitions are stored in separate tablespaces. While you could store different tables or indexes in separate tablespaces in earlier versions of Oracle, Oracle8 extends this concept to enable you to divide a given table into multiple tablespaces. This provides you with the following advantages:

- Increased performance as you level the load between disk drives for a search of a given table. You can even search different partitions in parallel.

- You can alter the storage parameters for different partitions. For example, old data, which is unlikely to be changed, can use minimal `pctfree` and maximum `pctused` parameters.

- If you lose a tablespace due to a disk drive failure, you can still access data in the other partitions that are not associated with the failed disk drive.

- You can back up and recover partitions individually. Here you can stop backups for old, static data and instead back up only the data that is changing frequently.

The following example shows how to create a partitioned table:

```
Create table addresses (employee_id          number(10),
                        Street               varchar2(25),
                        City                 varchar2(25),
                        State                varchar2(2),
                        Zip_code             varchar2(5),
                        Effective_date       date)
        Partition by range (zip_code)
            (partition values less than (30000) tablespace add1,
             partition values less than (60000) tablespace add2,
             partition values less than (99999) tablespace add3);
```

If you are not dealing with large tables or indexes, you may want to consider partitioning for the reliability factor. You might also want to consider partitioning if you have a moderate size table that is the limiting factor for performance because it is accessed all of the time (and it is too big to cache in memory). Otherwise, you can stick to simple, nonpartitioned tables.

Object Datatypes

Object-oriented extensions are discussed in more detail in Chapter 15, "Object-Oriented Extensions in Oracle8." However, I wanted to provide an introduction to this new feature of Oracle8 in this chapter so that you get the complete picture of the data storage tools that are available to you. You have the option of nesting tables within objects to handle cases where there are multiple values of a given attribute associated with a single instance of an object. To create a user-defined object datatype, you would issue a command similar to:

```
Create type address as object
    (street      varchar2(25),
    city         varchar2(25),
    state        varchar2(2));
```

To make use of this object (that is, create a table that contains that datatype), you would issue a command similar to the following:

```
Create table people
    (employee_id     number(10),
    location         address);
```

To access a value within the object (here, the `people` table to which you have assigned an alias of `employee`), you would issue a command similar to:

```
Select employee.location.street from people employee;
```

If this notation seems confusing to you, you have probably not yet been exposed to object-oriented design philosophy and programming tools. Remember, Oracle8 is a fully functional relational database management system. If you find these object-oriented extensions confusing and you do not see a need for them, you can stick to the traditional tables, views, and standard Oracle datatypes.

Constraints

Constraints help the database designer ensure that only "good" data will be placed into the various tables by developers and end users. The following are the constraint types that you will run across in Oracle8:

- `null`. This indicates that the only valid value for the column on which this constraint is applied is null (nothing can be inserted into this column).
- `not null`. This indicates that a value must be specified for this column.
- `default`. This specifies a default value for a given column. If the `insert` statement does not supply a value for this column, the default value is automatically used by Oracle.
- `unique`. This specifies that no two rows will have the same value for that column (except if the column is null, in which case there can be duplicates).

Oracle Database Objects

CHAPTER 12

237

12

ORACLE
DATABASE
OBJECTS

- `PRIMARY KEY`. This specifies that a unique, non-null index will be created for this column or columns. Each row will have a different value which can be used as an absolute reference to that row.

- `FOREIGN KEY`. This specifies that the value for this column (or columns) must either be null or match a corresponding column (or set of columns) in a table specified as part of the foreign key. This is a good way to implement a list of valid values that is stored in a table in the database and therefore is relatively easy to update as business needs change.

- List of values. This specifies that the column contains a value that is in a fixed list specified at the time the table is created. This is acceptable for things that, by their very nature, have only a limited set of values (for example, yes/no, true/false). You can check that the value meets certain logical criteria related to one or more columns in the table. I would recommend using a foreign key and valid values table if there is any chance that the list of acceptable values for a column will change.

There are two places that a constraint can be applied. The first is on an individual column. This constraint applies to the column individually. The second constraint is at the table level and enables you to work with one or more columns. The following examples show a unique constraint applied at the column and table levels:

```
SQL> create table locations
  2  (location_id number(5),
  3  location_name varchar2(30) constraint c_location_name unique,
  4  location_state varchar2(2),
  5  active_flag varchar2(1) check (active_flag in ('Y','N')));

Table created.
SQL> create table locations2
  2  (location_id number(5),
  3  location_name varchar2(30),
  4  location_state varchar2(2),
  5  active_flag varchar2(1),
  6  constraint c_location_name2 unique(location_name),
  7  check (active_flag in ('Y','N')));

Table created.
```

Summary

This chapter provided an introduction to the database objects associated with Oracle. These objects store the information and provide resources (sequences) which enable you to build applications based on Oracle8. All Oracle developers do not need some of these resources (for example, user-defined object datatypes). However, you can think of these resources as a tool kit from which you can choose the tools you need to get a particular job done.

Oracle System and Object Privileges

by Joe Greene

In the days when card decks stored all data, it was easy to control access—you simply locked up the card decks. Since that era, however, computer people have struggled to balance the need to let people have access to the data needed to be productive against the need to protect certain sensitive data items. The Oracle RDBMS provides some pretty sophisticated control mechanisms to enable you to provide just the right amount of access to your database. However, getting that scheme set up requires a fair amount of work by someone. In most installations, there is not a separate security administrator (or at least there is not a security administrator who gets into the actual technical work of granting this access to that person). Therefore, this assignment usually falls on the database administrator.

This chapter is designed to provide an introduction to the first set of security mechanisms that Oracle provides to control access to data. The system privileges are designed to control overall database access permissions. Examples of these are permissions to create and delete tables. Next, you explore the Oracle object privileges with which you grant a particular user the permission to read data from a particular table on the system. Finally, Chapter 14, "Roles and Grants," ties the concepts of the two types of privilege in with the idea of roles and the actual commands that can be used to set up access for a particular user. Taken together, these three chapters enable you to control access to your Oracle database effectively.

This chapter begins with an introduction to some of the concepts and purposes behind Oracle access privileges. Then you review the first type of Oracle access privileges— those related to the system as a whole. An entire section is devoted to the powerful (and therefore dangerous) group of system privileges that I refer to as the "any" privileges. Finally, several examples of combinations of privileges that I have run across in my travels are presented. This will be a starting point for you when you start working out the privileges that you will give to your various users.

Before we jump right into system privileges, let's go over the reason Oracle has implemented this set of privileges. The quick and simple answer is that customers wanted it and Oracle wanted to sell its database product. There was a balancing act involved with making it simple to get small, nonsecure organizations working quickly and still provide detailed control for those that need it.

This chapter presents what the privileges are and which privileges are applicable to which objects. Some are obvious. You can execute a procedure but not a table. Some are not so obvious. You may wonder why you can't just alter a view to which you want to add one column. This chapter reviews both of these points from the point of view of the DBA.

Overview of Oracle Security

If everyone did exactly what they were told, never made any mistakes, and could be absolutely trusted, there would not be a need for security systems in database management systems. Now back to the real world. Certain people lack the knowledge or need to create and drop database objects such as tables and indexes. Additionally, most business organizations limit who can read or update certain types of information based on confidentiality laws, financial responsibility considerations, or management preferences.

In the era where computers were not accessible by mere mortals, the locked data center, combined with controlled batch jobs for update and report output, provided adequate security. Then information systems were made available throughout the organization to increase productivity. Although the vast majority of users violated no access rules or performed no accidental deletions, there were a few painful problems that received a lot of management attention. This caused businesses to tighten their security picture.

This was difficult in the flat-file era because the operating systems at first either allowed access or didn't. Eventually, the operating systems became smart enough to distinguish between read and write privileges, so this at least controlled those who could not perform updates. When developers received a requirement to limit access to a certain portion of the data, they could always move that data to a new file and limit the operating system write access to that file.

The trend toward database management systems created a need for the database to control access to various tables internally. This came from the fact that businesses usually did not want to have a separate operating system file for each table in the database. Therefore, control mechanisms were created to limit various types of access to the tables. In addition, because the majority of database users had no need to create database objects, certain restrictions were developed to prevent such activities.

This brings us to the era of Oracle6. In this world, there are three classes of users. The *connect users* are allowed to access the system (read and write as controlled by grants to the individual objects), but they cannot create any new database objects. The *resource users* are allowed to read and write data as controlled by individual object grants, and they can also create new tables, indexes, and so forth. Finally, the DBAs have the keys to the kingdom and can access any of the objects on the system, create new objects, and also perform all the administrative functions that are needed to keep the database operational.

This was a functional system; however, it had some severe limitations for larger databases and information systems. One of the classic large-system problems was that the operators needed to have DBA privileges to perform functions such as database startup and shutdown. This was uncomfortable because even though these were trusted individuals, they usually lacked the training to have all the power of the DBA account. With only three categories, you also had no way of qualifying various types of developers or limiting their capability of creating certain types of database objects.

The Oracle7 and Oracle8 privilege scheme was enhanced to enable a much greater degree of control over the privileges assigned to individuals. It broke up the three types of system privilege in Oracle6 (connect, resource, and DBA) into 78 specific privileges. If, for example, your organization allows operators to perform database startups, shutdowns, and backups, you have the fine control to grant just these privileges to the operators. Figure 13.1 illustrates this concept. Operators do not have the DBA's privilege of deleting any data table in the system, for example.

FIGURE 13.1.

Comparison of Oracle6, 7, and 8 system privileges.

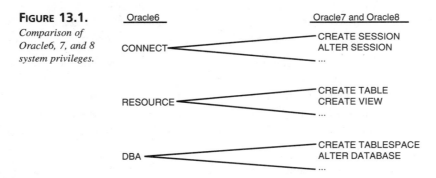

With this fine level of control came the burden of administering all these privileges over a large number of users. That is where the Oracle7 and Oracle8 concept of roles comes into play. The example given in the previous section showed the set of privileges required by computer operators. In most organizations, the DBA grants privileges based upon an individual's function within that organization (computer operator, developer on the sales data warehouse project, manager of general ledger accounting, and so forth). Therefore, it is useful to be able to say that all people who have a certain job function have a common set of privileges. You assign a certain set of privileges to the role and then assign individuals to that role.

The next concept that ties in with system privileges is where the security is going to be implemented. In many traditional mainframe systems, the security was built into the applications. This enabled each organization to implement very specific data access rules for each application. However, this scheme required a lot of testing and maintenance of the security mechanisms that were put into place. Oracle's concept has been that you buy most of the security mechanisms as part of the RDBMS product. You may have to do some administration, as is the case of creating roles and granting access to the users, but this is much less complex than writing and testing the basic security software. Only in a few specific cases that I have run across (mostly in areas that involve money, such as banks) is there a need to add locally-developed software to enhance the basic security mechanisms.

This becomes especially important as greater access is provided to the database, especially through client/server mechanisms. It is the classic tradeoff. You need to protect your data, but the data is useless if people cannot access it. The moment you provide general-purpose access tools to your users, such as SQL*Plus or Excel with a link to the Oracle database, you have given the users the means to bypass your application security (see Figure 13.2). The users can connect to the database with whatever privileges you assign them. They can then access or update data using tools that are designed to allow them to do whatever they want. Therefore, it is important to develop a sound security scheme for databases that provide this type of access. Some solutions to this problem will be found in Chapter 14, after the discussion of the security mechanisms is complete.

FIGURE 13.2.

Database versus application security.

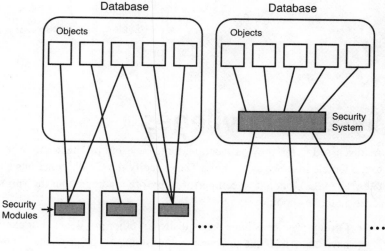

It is important to understand that the *access privileges* comprise only half of the Oracle database security picture. These privileges control what you can do to the database as a whole. The other set of privileges, the *object privileges*, provide a fine level of control as to what a user can do with an individual database object (tables, views, and so forth). Not all objects are directly controllable. Indexes, for example, are used automatically whenever users have permission to access their associated tables. Figure 13.3 illustrates the relationship between these two types of Oracle privileges. You need the correct system privileges to create the objects within the Oracle database and tablespaces. You also need privileges to manipulate the structure of existing database objects. Finally, to access the objects for read, write, or execution, you need to have the correct object privileges given to you by the object owner.

FIGURE 13.3.

Oracle system and object privileges.

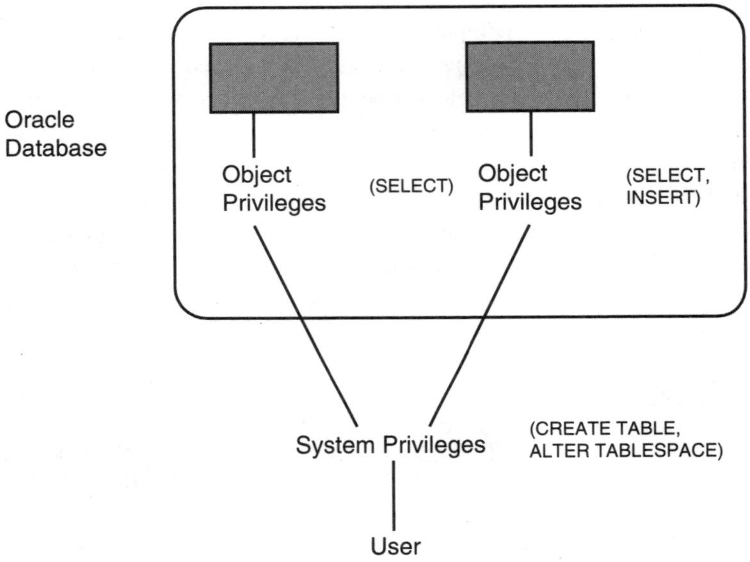

System Privileges

As discussed in the previous section, Oracle system privileges control a user's access to the Oracle instance as a whole. They specify the Oracle functions (for example, CREATE TABLE) that a user can perform. Before reading about the various system privileges, note these points:

- Certain privileges have prerequisites of other privileges. For example, you must have CREATE TABLE to have the CREATE SNAPSHOT privilege.

- Read the descriptions of the privileges. There are a few privileges (such as GRANT ANY PRIVILEGE) that are not exactly what you would expect by just reading their titles.

- The key to being able to grant an Oracle system privilege in Oracle6 is having the DBA privilege.

- The key to being able to grant an Oracle system privilege in Oracle7 is having the GRANT ANY PRIVILEGE privilege assigned to your account.

- There are additional mechanisms to provide finer levels of control that are available to the DBA. For example, if you want to allow users to create tables, but only in a certain tablespace, you can give them the CREATE TABLE privilege and then give them a space quota only on the desired tablespace.

First, let's review the privilege sets that are available under Oracle6. Oracle6 users fall into three categories:

- CONNECT. These users can access Oracle data as permitted by the object privileges that are assigned to them. They cannot create database objects or perform any administrative functions.

- RESOURCE. These users can access Oracle data as permitted by their object privileges and also create database objects such as tables and views. They cannot perform any database administrative functions.

- DBA. These users can access data, create objects, and perform Oracle administrative functions. They have full access to all data in the database and can delete any database objects. There are very few restrictions placed on users with the DBA privilege, so be extremely careful when using these accounts.

Now on to the more sophisticated privilege scheme in Oracle7 and Oracle8. Rather than present system privileges as a laundry list, one after the other, these privileges are grouped into functional categories (see Figure 13.4).

- *The User Privileges.* These privileges relate to users who will access the system, but not create any objects. These are similar to the CONNECT users under Oracle6.

- *The Developer Privileges.* These privileges relate to the creation of database objects. These are similar to the RESOURCE users under Oracle6.

- *The "Any" Privileges.* These are an especially powerful set of privileges within Oracle. Normally, I would give these only to DBAs and extremely senior developers working in dedicated development instances. These are similar to regular privileges except that they apply not only to objects that you own, but objects that other users (including SYS and SYSTEM) own.

- *The Database Maintenance Privileges.* These privileges relate to the care and feeding of the database. They are typically assigned only to DBAs and other computer support staff.

- *The Monitoring Privileges.* These privileges relate to keeping an eye on the Oracle database. They are typically assigned to DBAs, but can also be used by separate security administrators to monitor system security.

13

ORACLE SYSTEM AND OBJECT PRIVILEGES

Figure 13.4.
System privilege categories.

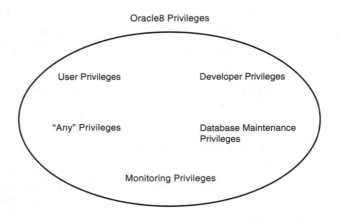

Oracle8 Privileges

User Privileges · Developer Privileges · "Any" Privileges · Database Maintenance Privileges · Monitoring Privileges

Object Privileges

Every object in the database has a set of access privileges associated with it. Some are implied by the type of object. Public synonyms, for example, are universally accessible by their very definition. However, most objects have some form of protection that the owners and database administrators need to keep track of as part of the overall security schema. That is what this chapter is all about.

The first subject to master is the list of privileges provided by Oracle:

- ALTER allows the user to modify the internal structure of the object. For example, it allows the user to add columns to a table. It does not allow the user to modify the contents of the data itself (see UPDATE, INSERT, and DELETE). Note that you cannot drop columns from a database object; you can only add or modify them.

- DELETE allows the user to remove one or more rows of data from the object.

- EXECUTE allows the user to execute a stored package, procedure, or function.

- INDEX allows the user to have access to the data in a table to create an index associated with the table. Note that the select privilege is not enough for a user to create an index on the table.

- INSERT allows the user to add rows of data to the object.

- REFERENCES allows the user to create or alter another table that references this table as a foreign key. It does not allow the user who granted this privilege to alter this table in any way. Instead, it grants that user permission to create a new table, which has a rule that the contents of one or more of its columns has to match a corresponding column in the table on which the REFERENCES privilege is being granted (or else be null).

- SELECT allows the user to read rows from the object using the SQL select statement. This is probably the most common privilege.

- UPDATE allows the user to modify the contents of existing rows in the table by using the update command.

The owner of the object has the full set of privileges available on that object when the object is created. These privileges can be given up via the revoke statement, but usually the owner can do anything that is necessary.

Figure 13.5 shows how the object privileges apply to the various objects within the database. There is some overlap between system and object privileges. Some objects within the database require system privileges for creation and others require object privileges. The objects use object privileges to restrict access to the appropriate users (see Table 13.1).

FIGURE 13.5.

Mapping object privileges to objects.

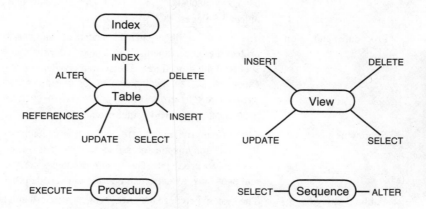

TABLE 13.1. PROTECTION MECHANISMS FOR DATABASE OBJECTS.

Object	Protections
Database	System privilege ALTER DATABASE.
Tablespace	System privileges CREATE TABLESPACE, ALTER TABLESPACE, MANAGE TABLESPACE, DROP TABLESPACE.
Tables	System privileges CREATE TABLE, CREATE ANY TABLE, ALTER, ALTER ANY TABLE, and DROP ANY TABLE protect the table itself. Object privileges DELETE, INDEX, INSERT, REFERENCES, SELECT, and UPDATE protect the data within the table. System privileges SELECT ANY TABLE, INSERT ANY TABLE, UPDATE ANY TABLE, and DELETE ANY TABLE can be used to override the object privileges.

continues

TABLE 13.1. CONTINUED

Object	Protections
Indexes	The system privilege CREATE INDEX gives the user the privilege to create indexes. The object privilege INDEX is required to access the data in a table to build the index. The system privileges CREATE ANY INDEX, ALTER ANY INDEX, and DROP ANY INDEX can override the object privileges.
Views	The system privileges CREATE VIEW, CREATE ANY VIEW, and DROP ANY VIEW protect the object itself. Object privileges DELETE, INSERT, SELECT, and UPDATE protect the data within the view.
Sequences	The system privilege CREATE SEQUENCE protects the object itself. The object privileges ALTER and SELECT protect the data in the sequence. The system privileges CREATE ANY SEQUENCE, ALTER ANY SEQUENCE, DROP ANY SEQUENCE, and SELECT ANY SEQUENCE can override the object privileges.
Procedures and so on	The system privileges CREATE PROCEDURE and CREATE TRIGGER protect the objects themselves. The object privilege EXECUTE protects access to the procedures. The system privileges CREATE ANY PROCEDURE, ALTER ANY PROCEDURE, DROP ANY PROCEDURE, CREATE ANY TRIGGER, ALTER ANY TRIGGER, DROP ANY TRIGGER and EXECUTE ANY PROCEDURE can override other privileges.
Synonyms	The system privilege CREATE SYNONYM protects the object itself. Private synonyms are accessible only by their owners and do not have object privileges. The system privileges CREATE ANY SYNONYM and DROP ANY SYNONYM can be used to override other privileges.
Public Synonyms	The system privileges CREATE PUBLIC SYNONYM and DROP PUBLIC SYNONYM protect the object itself. All public synonyms are accessible by all users and therefore there are no object privileges associated with public synonyms.
Objects	The system privileges CREATE TYPE, DROP TYPE, CREATE ANY TYPE, DROP ANY TYPE, CREATE LIBRARY, DROP LIBRARY, CREATE ANY LIBRARY, and DROP ANY LIBRARY protect these objects.

Figure 13.6 illustrates the protection of the objects themselves, and Figure 13.7 shows the protection of the data within the object.

FIGURE 13.6.
Protection of the objects themselves.

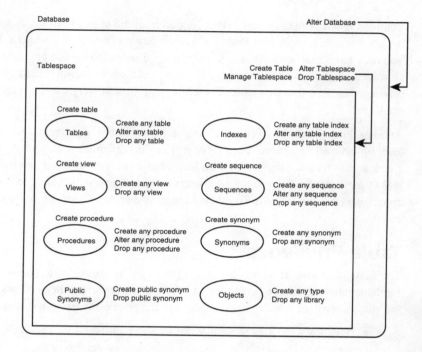

FIGURE 13.7.
Protection of the data within the object.

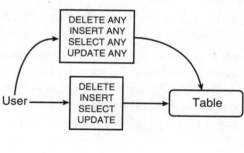

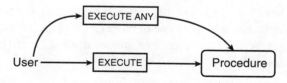

13

ORACLE SYSTEM
AND OBJECT
PRIVILEGES

You may feel a little challenged right now with all the things to think about while devising a scheme to protect your data. Let's add a few more considerations to the challenge. You may have a table to which you have granted access to no one other than yourself. However, any user who has the SELECT ANY TABLE or, worse yet, DELETE ANY TABLE privilege has access to that table. Therefore, you must be very careful with these "any" privileges.

Another thing to consider is Oracle's capability of restricting access down to the column level on tables. I have never used it for fear of the performance impacts of having to check access on a column-by-column basis, but it is a tool that you can use when it makes sense. Basically, you can give users an object access (SELECT) on only certain columns within the table. It would be a tough system to administer, but it could be necessary.

Table Privileges

The first group to start with is the object privileges associated with tables. These are the fundamental data storage constructs and the type of object privilege grants that make up the vast majority of most systems. These are the privileges that you can grant on tables:

- ALTER allows the user to change the structure of the table. This includes adding columns and changing the storage parameters associated with the table.

- DELETE allows the user to delete rows of data from the table. It does not allow the user to delete the table itself.

- INDEX allows the user to access the data in the table to create an index. This can be important in that Oracle automatically maintains indexes on its tables (updates the index when values in the table change). If a large number of users are creating indexes on tables, your data entry performance will suffer. One interesting feature of this privilege is that it cannot be granted to a role. It can be granted only to individual users.

- INSERT allows the user to add new rows of data to the table.

- REFERENCES allows the user to use the table as a foreign key in another table. This links the data in the two tables via one or more columns in each table. This is the other table object privilege that cannot be granted to a role. It can be granted only to individual users.

- SELECT allows the user to read information from the table. This is the most common privilege granted to the user community. It may be the only privilege granted to users in data warehouses.

- UPDATE allows the user to change the contents of existing rows of data in the table. It does not allow new rows to be created or existing rows to be deleted.

View Privileges

The next objects that have privileges associated with them are the views. Note that users have access to data from a table through a view even though they do not have access to the base table. This technique can be used to limit the amount of information that certain users can work with, thereby eliminating the need to use column-level access privileges. When a view is used to join together columns from multiple tables, the creator needs the appropriate access to all the tables included in the view to create the view. Note that you cannot alter the structure of a view. Because it does not contain any data itself, the designers of Oracle felt that it was easier to drop and re-create a view than to allow modification of the view. Therefore, Oracle enables you to issue a command to CREATE or REPLACE VIEW (which enables you to keep any privileges or grants that you may have made before re-creating the view). The following are the object privileges associated with views:

- DELETE allows the user to remove rows of data using the view. This can be very tricky because you may not want to delete the rows of data from both tables when you have the two joined together. Try to avoid allowing users to delete data using a view.

- INSERT allows the user to add rows of data using the view. Again, this can be somewhat tricky because there may be mandatory fields in the base table that are not included in the view (for example, primary keys). INSERT does not work for views that contain data from multiple tables.

- SELECT allows the user to read data using the view. This is the "safe" view privilege because all the user looks at is the data.

- UPDATE allows the user to modify existing data using the view. Allowing the user to modify such things as primary keys should be avoided in views. UPDATE does not work for most views that contain data from multiple tables.

13

ORACLE SYSTEM
AND OBJECT
PRIVILEGES

Sequence Privileges

Another database object that has its own set of object privileges is the sequence. These are relatively simple objects (a list of numbers). There are only two object privileges associated with sequences:

- ALTER allows the user to modify the structure of the sequence.
- SELECT allows the user to read the next value from the sequence.

Procedure Privileges

The final database object with object privileges is the procedure. This group includes packages (PL/SQL routines) and functions (which are similar to procedures, but have slightly different calling parameters). It does not include triggers, which are bits of software that are automatically tied to tables. The procedure has only one object privilege applicable to it—EXECUTE. This allows a user to run the software contained within the procedure.

Column Privileges

A final note on the column privileges capability of Oracle: As mentioned earlier, I have never used them because of the overhead associated with having to check column privileges in addition to table privileges in a query. I usually use views for this function, but there are applications wherein column privileges are the only practical answer. The good news is that column privileges are relatively simple to grant and revoke. You use all the privileges that your are familiar with for tables (for example, SELECT) and merely put the names of the applicable columns in parentheses after the table name.

User Privileges

The first set of privileges belongs to common users of the database (see Table 13.2). Even though these users share this common and relatively simple function (read and write to existing objects), Oracle provides a few variations in access privileges that allow organizations to tighten up security to the maximum extent possible (for example, by removing the ALTER SESSION privilege).

TABLE 13.2. THE USER PRIVILEGES.

Privilege	Description
CREATE SESSION	Allows the user to connect to the Oracle database. Without it, a user has no access to Oracle.
ALTER SESSION	Allows the user to issue the alter session command, which permits such actions as setting National Language Support parameters, controlling database links, and using the trace facilities.
FORCE TRANSACTION	Allows the user to commit or roll back a distributed database transaction in the local database. Not a commonly used feature.

Developer Privileges

The user privileges are simple and straightforward. The next set of privileges relates to developers who may be working with the system (see Table 13.3). These privileges can be a little trickier in that you may not want to give out all the developer privileges in your instance (there are some rather powerful ones).

TABLE 13.3. THE DEVELOPER PRIVILEGES.

Privilege	Description
CREATE CLUSTER	Creates clusters of tables that the developer owns. The developers can also drop clusters that they own.
CREATE PROCEDURE	Creates stored procedures, packages, and functions owned by the developer. The developers can also drop any of these objects that they own.
CREATE DATABASE LINK	Defines a database link. This feature is similar to a synonym because it is a named pointer to the other database. A key difference is that you store the Oracle ID and password for the remote system as part of the link, thereby establishing access privileges in the remote system. The developers can also drop any database links that they create.
CREATE PUBLIC SYNONYM	Creates an alternative name for referencing a database object such as a table or view. Any user in the instance can use this name to make a call for that object. Object privileges are still needed for that user to have access to an object. In certain situations, you may want to give this privilege only to DBAs or certain senior developers.
DROP PUBLIC SYNONYM	Deletes an alternative name for referencing a database object that is available to all users in that instance. In certain situations, you may want to give this privilege only to DBAs or certain senior developers.
CREATE SEQUENCE	Creates a sequence owned by the developer. The developers can also drop any sequences that they create.
CREATE SNAPSHOT	Creates a local copy of a table located on another Oracle instance. The developers can also drop any snapshots that they own.
CREATE SYNONYM	Creates a private synonym (for the developer's use only). The developers can also drop any private synonyms that they own.

continues

13

**ORACLE SYSTEM
AND OBJECT
PRIVILEGES**

TABLE 13.3. CONTINUED

Privilege	Description
CREATE TABLE	Creates a table. The developers can also create indexes on and drop tables that they own.
CREATE TRIGGER	Creates a trigger (command executed when a specified event occurs) owned by the developer. The developers can also drop triggers that they own.
CREATE VIEW	Creates a view owned by the developer. The developers can also drop views that they own.
UNLIMITED TABLESPACE	Allows the developers to create objects that consume as much space in any tablespace as is available. This overrides any quotas assigned in that tablespace. You could consider this to be very much like an "any" privilege.
CREATE TYPE	Creates a new object type.
DROP TYPE	Drops the object type.
CREATE LIBRARY	Creates a new object library.
DROP LIBRARY	Drops the object library.

These are the privileges that are normally considered for developers. You may find cause to grant some of the "any" privileges described in the next section or even certain database maintenance privileges to certain developers. However, this is the common list that you should consider and a good place to start.

DBA Privileges

One of the candidates for the most powerful but dangerous features in the Oracle system is what I call the "any" privileges (see Table 13.4). If you grant CREATE TABLE to developers, they have the power to destroy (via the SQL drop table command) tables that they have created. However, if they had the DROP ANY TABLE privilege, they can destroy any table in the system. This is a serious privilege. DBAs need to think of this every time they execute destructive commands because, by default, they have most of these "any" privileges assigned to them. In many cases, this is needed. What happens when a developer leaves the company and has a lot of personal tables that are no longer needed? The DBA can delete these tables and drop the user from the system. However, be aware that if you drop a table, especially one referenced by a public synonym, you may not get the table you anticipated, and your DROP ANY TABLE privilege allows you to do it. Enough said. Please be careful when you use your "any" privileges.

CAUTION

DBA accounts have most of the "any" privileges by default. This enables you to do almost anything in the system. Be extremely careful that your syntax and purpose are correct before issuing a command that takes advantage of your "any" privileges.

TABLE 13.4. THE "ANY" PRIVILEGES.

Privilege	Description
ANALYZE ANY	Allows the user to collect optimizer statistics, validate the structure, or identify migrated and chained rows in any table or cluster in the database.
AUDIT ANY	Allows the user to perform object auditing on any object in the database.
CREATE ANY CLUSTER	Allows the user to create a cluster and assign ownership to any user in the database.
ALTER ANY CLUSTER	Allows the user to alter clusters owned by any user in the database.
DROP ANY CLUSTER	Allows the user to drop clusters owned by any user in the database.
CREATE ANY INDEX	Allows the user to create an index on any table in the database and assign ownership to any user in the database.
ALTER ANY INDEX	Allows the user to alter any index owned by any user in the database.
DROP ANY INDEX	Allows the user to drop any index owned by any user in the database.
GRANT ANY PRIVILEGE	Allows the user to grant any system privilege to any user in the database. This is the prime requirement for DBAs being able to grant system privileges. Note, this does not allow the users to grant object privileges. Only the object owners can grant object privileges.
CREATE ANY PROCEDURE	Allows a user to create a procedure, package, or function and assign ownership to any user in the database. Has the prerequisites of ALTER ANY TABLE, BACKUP ANY TABLE, DROP ANY TABLE, LOCK ANY TABLE, COMMENT ANY TABLE, SELECT ANY TABLE, INSERT ANY TABLE, UPDATE ANY TABLE, DELETE ANY TABLE or GRANT ANY

continues

TABLE 13.4. CONTINUED

Privilege	Description
	TABLE, depending on what the function actually does. Note that CREATE ANY PROCEDURE is good enough to create a procedure that accesses database objects (for example, tables) that are open for public access. The prerequisites come into play when you try to access (select or update) a database object and you do not have an explicit access grant for your user ID.
ALTER ANY PROCEDURE	Allows the user to modify any procedure, package, or function owned by any user in the database.
DROP ANY PROCEDURE	Allows the user to drop any procedure, package, or function owned by any user in the database.
EXECUTE ANY PROCEDURE	Allows the user to execute any procedure, package, or function owned by any user in the database. This overrides the object privileges assigned to the procedure, package, or function by the owner.
ALTER ANY ROLE	Allows the user to modify any role created in the database.
DROP ANY ROLE	Allows the user to drop any role in the database.
GRANT ANY ROLE	Allows the user to assign a role to another user in the database.
CREATE ANY SEQUENCE	Allows the user to create a sequence and assign ownership to any user in the database.
ALTER ANY SEQUENCE	Allows the user to modify any sequence owned by any user in the database.
DROP ANY SEQUENCE	Allows the user to drop any sequence owned by any user in the database.
SELECT ANY SEQUENCE	Allows the user to select values from any sequence owned by any user in the database.
CREATE ANY SNAPSHOT	Allows the user to create a local copy of a table in another instance and assign ownership to any user in the database. The user must have CREATE ANY TABLE privileges.
ALTER ANY SNAPSHOT	Allows the user to compile any snapshot owned by any user in the database.
DROP ANY SNAPSHOT	Allows the user to drop any snapshot owned by any user in the database.
CREATE ANY SYNONYM	Allows the user to create a private synonym and assign ownership to any user in the database.
DROP ANY SYNONYM	Allows the user to drop any private synonym owned by any user in the database.

Privilege	Description
CREATE ANY TABLE	Allows the user to create a table and assign ownership to any user in the database. Note that the assigned owner's privileges and quotas will be used to see whether the table can be created.
ALTER ANY TABLE	Allows the user to modify the structure of any table owned by any user in the database.
BACKUP ANY TABLE	Allows the user to use the Export utility to back up tables owned by any other user in the database. This is needed by DBAs or operators who use the Export utility for database backups.
DROP ANY TABLE	Allows the user to drop any table owned by any user in the database.
LOCK ANY TABLE	Allows the user to issue locks to any table (or rows within the table) owned by any user in the database.
COMMENT ANY TABLE	Allows the user to enter comments on any table owned by any user in the database.
SELECT ANY TABLE	Allows the user to retrieve data from any table owned by any user in the database.
INSERT ANY TABLE	Allows the user to add new rows to any table owned by any user in the database.
UPDATE ANY TABLE	Allows the user to update rows in any table owned by any user in the database.
DELETE ANY TABLE	Allows the user to delete rows from any table owned by any user in the database. This privilege is needed to truncate tables owned by other users.
FORCE ANY TRANSACTION	Allows the user to commit or roll back distributed database transactions related to any user in the database.
CREATE ANY TRIGGER	Allows the user to create a trigger and assign ownership to any user in the database.
ALTER ANY TRIGGER	Allows the user to modify (enable, disable, or recompile) any trigger owned by any user in the database.
DROP ANY TRIGGER	Allows the user to drop any trigger owned by any user in the database.
CREATE ANY VIEW	Allows the user to create a view and assign ownership to any user in the database. The creator must also have ALTER ANY TABLE, BACKUP ANY TABLE, DROP ANY TABLE, LOCK ANY TABLE, COMMENT ANY TABLE, SELECT ANY TABLE, INSERT ANY TABLE, UPDATE ANY TABLE, or DELETE ANY TABLE, depending on the exact view that

continues

13

ORACLE SYSTEM
AND OBJECT
PRIVILEGES

TABLE 13.4. CONTINUED

Privilege	Description
	the user is trying to create. These prerequisites come into play only when you are trying to access a database table for which you do not have a specific access granted to your user ID. If you have specific access grants to your user ID or the table is available to PUBLIC, you do not need the prerequisite privileges described.
DROP ANY VIEW	Allows the user to drop any view owned by any user in the database.
CREATE ANY TYPE	Create a user type owned by any user in the database.
DROP ANY TYPE	Drop a user type owned by any user in the database.
CREATE ANY LIBRARY	Create a library owned by any user in the database.
DROP ANY LIBRARY	Drop a library owned by any user in the database.

Privileges such as CREATE ANY VIEW and CREATE ANY PROCEDURE include a series of privileges that I qualify as being needed, depending on what the user is trying to do. If the user to whom you are trying to assign the object does not have another object with the same name as the object that you are trying to create, you do not need any of these special privileges. However, if you are trying to create a table with the same name as one that the user already has, you need to have DROP ANY TABLE to get rid of the existing table so that you can replace it with the new one.

As mentioned earlier, the "any" privileges are something that I use every day. Many of them are not particularly harmful. SELECT ANY TABLE may pull in a lot of data, but nothing is destroyed if you make a typing mistake. Many of them I have never used (ALTER ANY TRIGGER, for example). Let's go over some guidelines that I use when working with these "any" privileges using my DBA account:

- When deleting database objects, always use the fully qualified name and do not rely on synonyms. It takes only a few extra characters to specify *owner.table_name*.

- Use dummy accounts (accounts that are not associated with an end user) to create the objects that you want controlled in the database. You can do it using your DBA account with its CREATE ANY TABLE privilege, but remember, you need to access this dummy account to perform the object privilege grants anyway. An advantage to coding your object creation scripts with the *owner.table_name* format is that if you are logged into the wrong account when you execute them, it tells you about your mistake. Yes, I have occasionally built a few dozen tables only to realize that I was distracted and put them in the wrong schema.

- If your data is particularly sensitive to mistakes and you have other functions to perform such as development, consider making a less-privileged account for yourself. Utilize your personal DBA account only when needed and that will minimize the chance that your "any" privileges will do something that you do not want. Also avoid using the SYS and SYSTEM accounts whenever possible because they own too many sensitive objects that you might overwrite.

The Database Maintenance Privileges

Next on the list of system privileges are those that you use to maintain the database itself. These are some of the traditional DBA privileges that you use to create the database, add tablespaces, and so forth (see Table 13.5).

TABLE 13.5. THE DATABASE MAINTENANCE PRIVILEGES.

Privilege	Description
ALTER DATABASE	Allows the alter database command to be issued. Some of the functions of this command include mounting and opening the database, managing log files and control files, and changing the archivelog status.
CREATE PROFILE	Allows the user to create profiles that set limits on the usage of certain Oracle resources by users assigned that profile.
ALTER PROFILE	Allows the user to modify profiles.
DROP PROFILE	Allows the user to drop profiles.
ALTER RESOURCE COST	Allows the user to change the cost assigned to various resources when these costs are tracked by the database.
CREATE PUBLIC DATABASE LINK	Allows the user to create a link to another Oracle instance that is accessible by all users in the system.
DROP PUBLIC DATABASE LINK	Allows the user to drop a public database link.
CREATE ROLE	Allows the user to create a role.
CREATE ROLLBACK SEGMENT	Allows the user to create rollback segments within a tablespace.
ALTER ROLLBACK SEGMENT	Allows the user to modify the structure of existing rollback segments.
DROP ROLLBACK SEGMENT	Allows the user to drop a rollback segment.

continues

13

ORACLE SYSTEM
AND OBJECT
PRIVILEGES

TABLE 13.5. CONTINUED

Privilege	Description
ALTER SYSTEM	Allows the user to issue the ALTER SYSTEM command. This command is used to switch log files, check data files, set certain system parameters, kill user connections to the Oracle instance, and other similar functions.
CREATE TABLESPACE	Allows the user to create a new tablespace. Note that the Oracle user ID needs to have operating system permission and that directory. There also must be sufficient disk space available.
ALTER TABLESPACE	Allows the user to modify the configuration of existing tablespaces. This includes adding data files to the tablespace.
MANAGE TABLESPACE	Allows the user to perform warm backups of the tablespace and switch the tablespace offline and online.
BECOME USER	Switch to become another user in the database. Used for full database imports and exports only. It does not work from the SQL*Plus prompt.
ALTER USER	Change the configuration of any Oracle user account (including changing passwords).
DROP USER	Remove a user from the system.

Monitoring Privileges

Finally, there is a privilege used to control access to the auditing utilities that Oracle uses (see Table 13.6). (Actually, there are two, but the AUDIT ANY privilege, which enables you to audit access to database objects of any users, is covered under the "any" privileges.)

TABLE 13.6. THE MONITORING PRIVILEGE.

Privilege	Description
AUDIT SYSTEM	Allows the user to issue audit commands related to the usage of certain SQL statements, especially those related to system privileges.

Default Privileges

The next logical question after this discussion of privileges would be "Which privileges do I get by default?" When a user is created, it has no privileges to do anything within Oracle. You have to grant that user the CREATE SESSION privilege (or a role that contains CREATE SESSION) before the user can even connect to the Oracle database. This is just as applicable to client/server connections as it is to local connections.

The same logic applies to database object access. When a user is created, it has no access to any of the objects in the database other than those that have had PUBLIC access grants provided for them. There are a number of common database objects (for example, the USER_ views) that do have this PUBLIC access grant provided. However, if you have tables built for a local application, you have to grant access to those tables either to PUBLIC, the new user or to a role assigned to that new user.

Connecting Internally

One special case for database access is connecting internally. Under UNIX operating systems, you are allowed to connect internally if you belong to the correct operating system group (usually DBA by default). Under Windows NT, you have to supply a special password created for internal connections at database creation time. When you connect internally, you have DBA level access to the database. This allows you to perform startups and shutdowns in addition to other database and object maintenance tasks.

Dummy Object Owners

The previous sections present the list of privileges associated with the various types of database objects. The next couple of sections tie all these concepts of system and object privileges together. You'll see several examples that represent environments that I have come across in my travels. These may not match your individual needs exactly, but you should be able to take these concepts and adapt them slightly.

The first concept is that of the dummy user. We all have users who just do not seem to be able to grasp the concepts of computers, but I would not call them dummies. We in the computer industry are not known for our understanding of their business functions, and let's hope that they are not calling us dummies when they write accounting books. A dummy user is an Oracle user ID that is not associated with a person. It exists strictly to own objects within the database. There are several advantages to this scheme:

- The password to this account can be restricted to DBAs or senior developers. This enables you to control precisely who can perform major modifications to these critical database objects, especially the more serious functions such as DROP TABLE.

- You or some senior developers need access to this account to perform the object privilege grants on the database objects.

- Because it is not often possible (due to inadequate space to copy large tables) to transfer database objects when the original owners leave the project and their accounts need to be deleted, these dummy owners are always with the project.

- No developers can accidentally delete a key production table when they type an incorrect table name or forget that they are working in the production instance versus the test instance. The dummy account is restricted to key individuals and used only for object creation and deletion purposes. Some of you will not allow any developers at all into the production instance with anything other than connect privileges; but for others of us this is a real concern.

A Typical Privilege Scheme

This section sketches out some typical privilege schemes that are a combination of what I have seen in several instances during my travels. Consider whether any of them could be used as a starting place for your instance. For this discussion, you explore four privilege schemes:

- An order entry system
- A data warehouse system
- A data warehouse development instance
- A laboratory or research environment

The first environment is an order entry system (see Figure 13.8). In these systems, you typically have a group that enters orders into the system. This data is stored and forwarded to groups involved with accounting/billing functions and shipping. Most of the order entry staff is permitted to enter new orders, but supervisor permission is required to change prices and other functions. Finally, there are often groups, such as buyers, who monitor what is selling and what is in stock to ensure that the correct products are being built and acquired.

FIGURE 13.8.

A sample order entry environment.

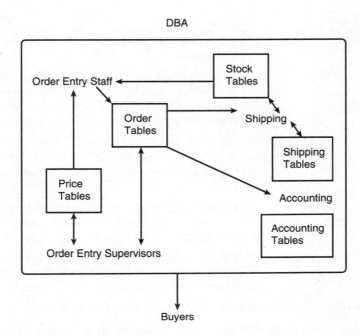

The exact details of how this works will vary between companies, but let's divide the users into six roles:

- DBA. This is a book on database administration, I would not forget to include us.
- order_entry. Staff involved with taking the orders and entering the data into the system.
- order_supervisor. Supervisors in the order entry process who are allowed to update certain data fields that the order_entry staff is not permitted to modify.
- accounting. These people perform credit checks, billing, and so forth, and update the tables associated with accounting data.
- shipping. These people put the components of the order together and ship it out. They also update the shipping data tables.
- buyers. These people are allowed to monitor the flow of goods and orders, but not to change anything. They are strictly observers in this process.

Now let's divide the many user data tables in the instance into five categories—order, shipping, stock, accounting, and pricing. Let's also assume that there is a dummy user account called "oe" (for order entry) that owns all the user data tables. Based on the scenario described, and giving some leeway to fill in the blanks because this is a fictitious company, I would propose the following schedule of privileges:

Group	Privileges
DBA	Default Oracle8 DBA privileges. This gives DBAs full access to the database.
order_entry	CREATE SESSION, INSERT on the order tables. SELECT on the shipping tables (provide order status to customers). SELECT on stock tables (see if the item is in stock). No access to accounting tables. SELECT on pricing tables (to quote prices).
order_supervisor	CREATE SESSION, SELECT, INSERT, UPDATE, DELETE on order tables. SELECT on shipping tables. SELECT on stock tables. SELECT on accounting tables. SELECT, UPDATE on pricing tables.
accounting	CREATE SESSION, SELECT on order tables. No access to shipping or stock tables. SELECT, INSERT, UPDATE, DELETE on accounting tables. SELECT on pricing tables
shipping	CREATE SESSION, SELECT on orders and accepting tables (see credit check was okay). SELECT, INSERT and UPDATE on stock and shipping tables. No access to pricing tables
buyers	CREATE SESSION, SELECT on all the tables.

Notice in this example that all the users in the system are covered and I did not have to give out the DROP ANY TABLE or DELETE ANY TABLE privileges. These nasty and powerful privileges are usually used only by DBAs and, in some cases, senior developers. You can have a fully functional instance with everyone limited to what they need to get their jobs done.

An environment that contrasts sharply with that of the order entry system is the data warehouse. The data warehouse concept states that you make a copy of data stored in an operational system, such as an order entry system, and store it in a separate database instance. You often summarize the data and store the summary information in new tables that promote rapid answers to common questions.

Consider the situation where the buyers in the order entry system start to work very hard to analyze their product mix, distribution of purchases throughout the year, and other factors so that they always know exactly what is selling at the time. The system administrators and order entry staff notice that the order entry system is slowing down significantly when these buyers run their analyses. The solution chosen is to purchase a new computer with Oracle and transfer the data from order entry to this new Oracle instance nightly for buyer analysis.

Now management throws in a slight wrinkle into this system. They decree that all purchases will be categorized according to the four product groups sold by this company.

They do not want buyers to be able to access data that does not fall into their category. The decision is made to split all orders coming down from the order entry system into four sets of tables, each set representing a product group (for simplicity, no order will cross two product groups). All the objects are owned by the dummy user known as "warehouse." All the nightly data update jobs are run using this user ID. Therefore, all that is needed is to create four roles. Each role will have CREATE SESSION and SELECT privileges on the tables that correspond to a particular product group. It's a simple and effective setup. No one but the DBAs and the dummy user can update anything.

Development instances present a series of challenges that are not found in production instances. In production, it is easy to restrict users to all but the most basic privileges. Application developers need to have enough power to get their work done, but not enough power to do any real damage. For the next example, let's choose the Oracle instance used to develop the data warehouse discussed in the previous section. This company is wise enough to use a separate instance for development and testing (I recommend it whenever possible). In this instance, I would recommend the following roles and privilege sets:

- The default DBA role (of course).
- Each of the four roles used in production. You should also create dummy users who each have one of these roles. This enables you to test your applications with the same security scheme that is used in production. It would not be valid to test an application as the table owner and expect it to work the same for a different user account.
- A developer role. Assign the following privileges to this role:

CREATE SESSION

ALTER SESSION

CREATE TABLE

ALTER TABLE

CREATE VIEW

CREATE PROCEDURE

CREATE SYNONYM (not CREATE PUBLIC SYNONYM)

CREATE SEQUENCE

CREATE TRIGGER (perhaps, if they are used)

Again, this is a rather simple scheme. It avoids using the nasty "any" privileges and still should enable the developers to get their jobs done. I would like to emphasize the importance of testing new software with accounts that will have the same security scheme as

13

ORACLE SYSTEM
AND OBJECT
PRIVILEGES

the end users. As mentioned earlier, I once received an application that was tested with operating system accounts that, in effect, had system administrator privileges and Oracle accounts that had full DBA privileges. Surprisingly, nothing worked when the application was transferred to the real world where users were just users, not DBAs. Trust me, testing using only developer or object owner Oracle IDs is inviting the opportunity for you to shoot yourself in the foot.

Finally, on the other end of the spectrum from most of the systems listed previously is the laboratory or research system. In this case, every group wants to be able to create and freely manipulate its own data. I always suggest setting up roles for each project team so that they can share data with one another freely (that is, grant to the role as opposed to giving grants to all the members of that group individually). I suggest giving each of these roles the same privilege sets that were given to the developers in the test data warehouse system. Of course, there may be lab environments (for example, pharmaceutical testing) that need to exercise stringent controls over lab data. However, this example covers a number of installations wherein the database is a general-purpose tool to store data as opposed to a repository of controlled corporate business application data.

Summary

This chapter took on the rather ambitious task of covering the privileges associated with an Oracle8 database. These privileges are the key to security for the database. The Oracle8 system allows you a fine level of control over access to both the database internal functionality and to data stored in the database. In the next chapter I discuss how roles can be used to simplify the process of granting access to the database and its data.

Roles and Grants

by Joe Greene

IN THIS CHAPTER

The last several chapters may have been tough for the more action-oriented types. You had to learn *what* you have control over before you could see *how* you control it. This chapter is designed to address these how-to topics. Again, it is impossible to guess what roles and privilege sets are best for your individual situation. Therefore, this chapter discusses the commands and concepts needed to build a privilege scheme and then shows several examples. You can then use these examples to build your own privilege schemes.

The first goal is to present the concept of roles in Oracle, which greatly simplify security maintenance. Next, security administration without roles, available in Oracle7 and Oracle8, is explored. Then several typical privilege schemes that I have run across in my consulting travels are presented. The chapter winds up with one of my favorite topics— the use of scripts to capture privilege grants for future use.

> **NOTE**
>
> Oracle7 and 8 simplify security administration with roles, if you choose to use them. Oracle6 makes you grant privileges to each individual user.

By the end of this chapter you should be comfortable with what it takes to assign and revoke Oracle privileges to users. You should also be able to build up a security scheme for new applications as they arrive. Of course, if you purchase some off-the-shelf applications, such as Oracle Financials, the privilege scheme may be highly determined by the vendor. However, you will know the questions to ask about their security schemes so you can assign the correct privileges to your users.

Managing Grants and Roles

Access to Oracle starts with a series of privilege grants made by the database administrators and object owners. You will probably want to plan this scheme out in advance to ensure that both users have enough access to the data, and that sensitive data and privileges are properly protected. Once you have mapped your basic access needs, it is time to consider roles. A role is a group of users that share a common privilege set.

Grants

There are no rights, only privileges. Before you can do something in Oracle, you need to have the appropriate person grant you the privilege to do it. In Oracle, DBAs typically control system privileges, and object owners control access to the objects they own.

DBAs and object owners assign privileges using the SQL `grant` command. The format of this command is rather simple:

```
grant privilege to user/role;
```

The words `grant` and `to` are the easy parts. The *user* or *role* is fairly easy. You insert the name of the role or user. If you want to grant the same set of privileges to multiple users or roles, you separate these names with commas. The only remaining part of this command is the `privilege` itself. There are two forms of this command. For system privileges, you merely list one or more system privileges in this part of the command. If you wish to grant multiple privileges in a single command, you separate the privileges by commas. The privileges are exactly as you saw them in Chapter 11. For privileges that contain multiple words, you separate the words with spaces. (Oracle is smart enough to figure out what you mean.) For example, to grant the system privileges `create table` and `create view` to `bsmith` and `jsmith`, you type the following:

```
grant create table,create view to bsmith,jsmith;
```

For object privileges, you need to specify both the privilege being granted and the object on which the privilege is being granted. If you wish to grant more than one privilege in a single statement, you separate the list of privileges by commas. You separate the list of privileges from the object on which these privileges are granted by the word on. As with system privileges, you can grant the privileges to one or more users, separated by commas. For example, to `grant` `select` and `delete` privileges on the famous `golf_scores` table to `bsmith` and `jsmith`, you type the following:

```
grant select,delete on golf_scores to bsmith,jsmith;
```

Because user needs can change over time, another important capability is taking granted privileges away from the users. Perhaps the users have changed jobs, or you have been told to tighten up security in your database. Whatever the reason, the command to remove specific privileges from a given user is the following:

```
revoke privilege from user/role;
```

Here is an example of this command that `revokes` the `select` privilege granted to `bsmith` on the `golf_scores` table:

```
revoke select on golf_scores from bsmith;
```

So far, you have learned the commands needed to give and take permissions away from users on both the system as a whole and individual database objects. When a user is having access problems or when you are performing routine security audits, it is necessary to be able to determine what privileges are currently granted in the database. To do this, there are two DBA views (`dba_sys_privs` and `dba_tab_privs`) that can be queried

14

ROLES AND
GRANTS

to find this information. Views are discussed in a later chapter, but for now, think of these DBA views as objects that you can query to find out information. The first provides insight into the system privileges that have been granted to users. The second shows the table access that has been granted. The following are examples of queries to the dba_sys_privs and the dba_tab_privs views. Note that you can use where clauses to focus in on the particular tables or users you want:

```
SQL> select * from dba_sys_privs;


GRANTEE                        PRIVILEGE                                    ADM
----------------------------   ----------------------------------------    ---
CONNECT                        ALTER SESSION                                NO
CONNECT                        CREATE CLUSTER                               NO
CONNECT                        CREATE DATABASE LINK                         NO
CONNECT                        CREATE SEQUENCE                              NO
CONNECT                        CREATE SESSION                               NO
CONNECT                        CREATE SYNONYM                               NO
CONNECT                        CREATE TABLE                                 NO
CONNECT                        CREATE VIEW                                  NO
DBA                            ALTER ANY CLUSTER                            YES
DBA                            ALTER ANY INDEX                              YES
DBA                            ALTER ANY PROCEDURE                          YES
DBA                            ALTER ANY ROLE                               YES
DBA                            ALTER ANY SEQUENCE                           YES
DBA                            ALTER ANY SNAPSHOT                           YES
DBA                            ALTER ANY TABLE                              YES
DBA                            ALTER ANY TRIGGER                            YES
DBA                            ALTER DATABASE                               YES
DBA                            ALTER PROFILE                                YES
DBA                            ALTER RESOURCE COST                          YES
DBA                            ALTER ROLLBACK SEGMENT                       YES
DBA                            ALTER SESSION                                YES

SQL> select * from dba_tab_privs
  2  where owner='JGREENE';

GRANTEE                        OWNER                        TABLE_NAME
----------------------------   --------------------------   --------------
GRANTOR                        PRIVILEGE                                    GRA
----------------------------   ----------------------------------------    ---
BSMITH                         JGREENE                      GOLF_SCORES
JGREENE                        DELETE                                       NO

JSMITH                         JGREENE                      GOLF_SCORES
JGREENE                        DELETE                                       NO
```

```
JSMITH                    JGREENE                    GOLF_SCORES
JGREENE                   SELECT                              NO

SQL>
```

You may have noticed the `ADM/GRANTABLE` columns in the output of these views. This column reflects whether this user has administrative privileges to grant this privilege to other users. For example, if you grant `select` on the `golf_scores` table to `bsmith` with the `admin` option, `bsmith` can grant `select` on `golf_scores` to other users. `bsmith` can't grant delete on `golf_scores` to other users unless `bsmith` has the `grant` option associated with the `delete` privilege on this table. Here is the format for granting the `admin` option to a user:

```
grant privilege to user/role with admin option;
```

Limiting creation privileges is a start to controlling the contents of your database. You may also wish to limit certain creation privileges granted to users. For example, you won't want one developer to consume every byte of space in every tablespace in your instance. A tool that you can use to limit this access is the tablespace quota. For now, just understand that you can limit the amount of space consumed by the user and also specify which tablespaces the user can use for entering data. For example, the following grants a limit of 10M in the user's tablespace to user jsmith (once quotas are implemented, Oracle assumes that you have a quota of zero on all tablespaces for which users have not explicitly been granted a quota, unless that user has the unlimited tablespace system privilege):

```
alter user jsmith quota 10M on users;
```

Finally, you may wish to grant certain privileges to every user in the database. Perhaps you live in a very open environment where everyone should be enabled to view all data tables. Perhaps you do not wish to have to remember to `grant create session` (which is needed to even connect to your Oracle instance) to every user ID in the system. Anyway, you can grant privileges to everyone by putting the word `public` in as the grantee:

```
grant create session to public;
```

Roles

This section is of no use to Oracle6 DBAs (sorry!). Roles make the database administrator's security job much easier, but you have to have Oracle7 or 8 to get this benefit. Let's hope that the remaining version 6 DBAs can convert their applications to version 8 soon so that they can take advantage of this and other new features.

14

ROLES AND GRANTS

Roles are an incredibly simple and powerful concept for the DBA. When databases were small and accessed by a limited number of individuals, it was acceptable to grant a specific access to each table a user required. However, as databases grew and the number of users grew with them, this became a nightmare of maintenance. Operating systems have used the concepts of groups for years to give file access to individuals based on their job descriptions. In fact, many business organizations determine what access individuals have to a particular data set by their job descriptions (payroll clerk, accounts receivable manager, and so forth) The Oracle role accommodates this real-world privilege scheme by allowing the DBA to assign privileges to users based on a series of roles the DBA can define to the database.

The concept of roles is relatively straight forward. The real trick for the DBA is to map out a scheme of roles that enables users to get their jobs done and is maintainable. This topic is covered later in this chapter. The first step in the process is to create the roles you need with this SQL command:

```
create role role-name;
```

For a role to be useful, it needs privileges to be granted to it and the role granted to users. After the user is created, you grant privileges to the role using the grant command discussed in the last section. You then grant access to users to the role by using that same grant command (where the role name is the privilege.) For those of you familiar with object-oriented concepts, the users inherit the privileges of the role when they are assigned to the role. This is a dynamic relationship. If you assign users to roles and later change the privileges assigned to the roles, the users acquire those new privileges when they next connect to Oracle. The following shows the format of a role grant:

```
Grant role to user;
```

Perhaps a concrete example would be beneficial here. Let's create a role called developer for software developers. In this world, the developers are allowed to create and modify packages, views, and tables. They need the ability to connect to the system, but do not need any other special privileges. Let's also add a user with ID bsmith to the system and this group. The following example shows a sample SQL*Plus session the DBA would run to set up this plan:

```
SQL> create user bsmith identified by brad;

User created.

SQL> create role developer;

Role created
```

```
SQL> grant create procedure,create table,create view,create session to
➥developer;

Grant succeeded.

SQL> grant developer to bsmith;

Grant succeeded.

SQL>
```

With the basics of roles out of the way, there are a few other topics a DBA should understand to get the most out of roles. The first is the concept of default roles. When you grant a role, it is a default role, one users have active whenever they connect to the Oracle instance. You can establish certain user's roles as default roles. The nondefault roles require an overt act on the part of the user to obtain his or her privileges. To establish a specific list of default roles, you issue this command:

```
alter user userID default role list-of-roles;
```

Here is an example:

```
alter user bsmith default role manager,developer;
```

If users want to access roles other than their default roles, they have to issue a command of the format

```
set role list-of-roles;
```

This is a somewhat tricky command. When you provide the list of roles, it does not add to the roles you already have in place. Instead, it becomes the list of roles that are enabled. Any roles that are not in this list become disabled, including default roles. The user can still access privileges from this role by issuing another `set role` command.

If you think of a role as a bucket for privileges, it is important to understand what that bucket can contain. First, it can contain most object privileges. It can also contain system privileges. Finally, it can contain other roles. I normally do not recommend having a hierarchy of roles. It may make it easier to grant the role privileges by building this hierarchy, but you can lose track of the individual privileges granted and accidentally grant an inappropriate privilege to a certain user. However, there are DBAs who are quite comfortable with using a role hierarchy, first building fundamental roles and then building higher-level roles that are made up of the fundamental roles. In the end, you have to choose whichever method works best for you.

It is sometimes useful to apply passwords to various roles. Users will not be challenged for this password if this is one of their default roles. However, if you set it up so that this is not a default role, they will be challenged for a password when they attempt to access that role. This is a way to implement some password security for special functions even when using automatic login accounts (`OPS$`), which are explained later when you explore user administration. The following is an example of a role that is created with a password:

```
create role developer identified by birdseye;
```

If you can create something, you can also remove what you have created. Perhaps there have been major changes to the application and a role is being split into several roles, each with privileges in different areas of the application. You want to create the new roles and then drop the old role that had all the privileges. The command to perform this is the `drop role` command:

```
SQL> drop role developer;

Role dropped.

SQL>
```

Remember that you can still grant privileges to individual users when you are using roles. For example, if there is a common privilege set for all finance department managers with the exception of Susan, who can also define the list of valid budget categories, you can assign all the basic privileges to the `finance_manager` role and assign all finance department managers including Susan to this role. You can then perform separate grants to Susan to perform her special job functions. I always prefer to keep things simple, but if you have a special need, remember that this capability is available.

Grants Without Roles

For those of you who have Oracle6 or just do not want to use roles, there is the old-fashioned way of granting every privilege to each individual user. You have to grant the appropriate system privileges to each user. You also have to grant the appropriate object privileges to each user. If you have an average user with five system privileges and five access privileges on 10 tables, you would have a total of 55 privileges to grant per user. A system with just 20 users would have 1100 individual grants. Such a system would include grants such as the following:

```
grant select,insert on golf_scores to jsmith;
grant select,insert on golf_scores to bsmith;
grant select on golf_courses to jsmith;
grant select on golf_courses to bsmith;
```

and so on. There are a few things you can do to make this easier. First, build scripts for each type of user that enable you to input a user name and the script, and then performs all the grants appropriate to that type of user. This can be thought of as implementing roles through scripts. Another way to make things easier is to grant as many privileges as possible to `public`. You do not want to compromise security, but if it is a privilege that everyone has, save yourself some time.

Use of Scripts to Capture Privilege Sets

After a few weeks on the job, most database administrators come to the conclusion that change is eternal. Developers find glitches in their software and need to make changes, new applications are constantly being installed, and every now and then you run into a problem where data is lost and you need to restore it. One of my favorite concepts in Oracle7 and 8, and especially in Oracle6, is storing all the grant commands used to set up the instance in a script file on disk. These scripts come in handy when you have to drop and re-create tables, or when you want to compare actual privilege grants to those you originally created. It also is easier to copy an existing grant line and make modifications to it than to type the new command from scratch at the SQL prompt.

It is relatively simple to create these scripts. You can use whatever text editor you prefer on your system to create a file that contains one or more lines just as you would type them at the SQL prompt, terminated by semicolons (;). The last line in this SQL script file should contain a backslash (\). The back-slash is automatically inserted when you use the edit command within SQL*Plus. Here is an example of such a file:

```
grant create session to golfer;
grant create session to golf_pro;
grant select,insert on golf_scores to golfer;
grant select,insert,update,delete on golf_scores to golf_pro;
```

To execute a multiple-line SQL script file such as this, you use either the `start` command or the at sign (@). The following is an example of executing the previous SQL script:

```
SQL @\odbasg\grants.sql

Grant succeeded.

Grant succeeded.

Grant succeeded.
```

14

ROLES AND GRANTS

```
Grant succeeded.

SQL>
```

Enterprise Manager Role and Grant Management

Enterprise Manager (covered in more detail in Chapter 21) makes role and grant management much easier than it was in olden days. You use the standard tree view to access a list of either users (who have a property page that contains their roles) or roles (which has a property page for users). You also have a property page to assign object privileges to roles or users. Refer to Chapter 21, "Administration Using Enterprise Manager," for a more detailed discussion of this process.

Command Line Role and Grant Management

For those of you who have not set up Enterprise Manager or who use dumb terminals (or PCs emulating dumb terminals), you can still perform all of the privilege management functions using Server Manager or SQL*Plus. The basic process is to connect to the database using an account with the correct privileges (remember only the object owner can grant access to its objects). Once connected, you issue the grant commands described earlier or run a script that contains all of the grants needed.

A Typical Privilege Scheme

There probably is no such thing as a single typical privilege scheme. Instead, let's look at several examples. The details do not matter as much as understanding the differences between the examples and the concepts behind them. If you capture this knowledge, you can create the privilege scheme that works for your environment. The keys to implementing this scheme are a sound knowledge of the Oracle privileges and an understanding of your user and application needs. Chapter 13, "Oracle System and Object Privileges," should serve as a foundation for Oracle privilege knowledge. The understanding of your user and application needs is left to the student as an exercise.

Let's examine three typical privilege schemes I have run across in my adventures in consulting. The first scheme is a typical online transaction processing system where different people can enter different bits of data. The second scheme is the data warehouse, where almost everyone accesses data and only a handful of accounts can actually write data. The last scheme is a sample security scheme for a development Oracle instance, where there are some developers who are trusted with more power than others.

The first is a fictitious accounting general ledger system. You research your user needs (or have the developers do this for you before you allow them to transition the application to production), and determine that the following rules apply to this system:

- You have clerks who can enter transactions. They are not allowed to modify any data or control the lists of valid accounts or legal values. If they make a mistake, they have to make a correcting entry.

- You have supervisors who can enter transactions and modify the lists of valid accounts and legal values. Not even supervisors can modify the data in the general ledger itself.

- Data is downloaded nightly from electronic data interfaces with other vendors and customers. This data needs to be entered automatically by nightly batch processing routines. Again, this processing adds new records, it does not allow existing data to be updated or deleted.

Many of you may work in similar environments. Perhaps you are wondering why a few obvious considerations for security have not been mentioned. Perhaps you have some personal opinions as to how these things should be set up based on problems you have run across in the past. These are valid points to consider. Businesses are not homogenous. Every organization adapts its business processes to its particular business area, corporate culture, region, and country. A good application adapts to the business needs. These security rules are the part of the application that ensures that data is properly accessed and should be thought of in that light.

Based on the rules previously described, I would create the following roles in this database:

- DBA
- gen_led (an object owner account not associated with a person)
- clerk
- supervisor
- EDI

14

ROLES AND GRANTS

Once the roles are established, it is time to grant system and object privileges to these roles. For simplicity, let's group all the application tables into two groups—transactions and valid values. I have found that for transaction processing systems, as opposed to data warehouses and development environments, the main goal of security is to control who can do what with various types of data (insert, update, select, and delete). Of course, this would all have to be reviewed with users because they usually do not tell you all of the rules in your initial discussions. However, from the data I have presented, I would construct a role scheme as follows (see Figure 14.1).

- DBA—The standard privileges granted to the default DBA role in Oracle.
- gen_led—An object owner account. Only the DBA or project manager has access to this account to add new tables, modify existing tables, and provide grants to these database objects. These are the privileges for this account:
    - CREATE SESSION (an easy one to forget, but is needed)
    - CREATE TABLE
    - CREATE PROCEDURE
    - CREATE PUBLIC SYNONYM
    - DROP PUBLIC SYNONYM
    - CREATE SEQUENCE
    - CREATE SYNONYM
    - CREATE TABLE
    - CREATE TRIGGER
    - CREATE VIEW
    - unlimited tablespace (possibly, if used by the DBA)
- clerk—The first line of users of the system. Their job is defined to enter data. For control reasons, you do not overwrite existing data (update or delete). Instead, you make a correcting entry that shows an audit trail. They are not permitted to modify the valid values tables, only the transaction tables. The following is a good scheme for the clerk role (or users if you have version 6):
    - SELECT, INSERT on transaction tables
    - SELECT on valid values tables
    - CREATE SESSION
- supervisor—The supervisors in the accounting general ledger group are the highest level of users who interact with this system. In many locations they are allowed to modify transaction data; however, in this instance, they cannot because having a

detailed audit trail of all entries made (even bad ones) is important for financial control. The supervisors are allowed to modify the valid value data (including adding new rows, modifying existing rows, and deleting rows).

- `CREATE SESSION`
- `SELECT, INSERT` on transaction tables
- `SELECT, INSERT, UPDATE, DELETE` on valid values tables

- EDI—This is a fictitious account used to record nightly data downloads from and prepare data uploads to other companies. Notice that even though these uploads and downloads are done through batch scripts run at night, the `CREATE SESSION` privilege is still needed to connect to the Oracle instance. Note that the following scheme is almost identical to the clerk role. A separate role is used for this radically different function to deal better with changes in privileges that may come up in the future (for example, users allowed to modify certain tables). This may be a consideration when you plan out your security scheme.

- `CREATE SESSION`
- `SELECT, INSERT` on transaction tables
- `SELECT` on valid values tables

FIGURE 14.1.

Sample transaction processing system privilege scheme.

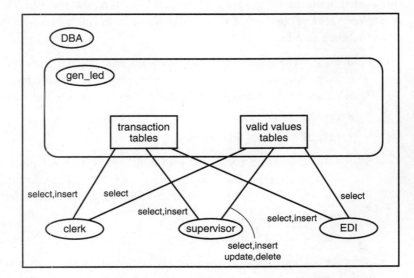

The first example provided the methodology for developing a security scheme for a new application. I tend to do very few tasks from scratch. Instead, I like to get out reference books and look at scripts that I have created before to use as examples in my current task. For those of you who think in a similar manner, the next example is a security scheme for a very common Oracle application today—the data warehouse. In the typical data warehouse scenario, you have an online or batch transaction processing system (often on a mainframe computer) that serves as the source of data for the warehouse. At some routine interval you receive data from the transaction processing system. I have usually seen nightly downloads, but you could do it hourly, weekly, or whatever interval fits your business needs.

The key difference in a data warehouse is that most of the security rules related to who can update, delete, or insert are not applicable to the user accounts. There are controlled download routines that are run using special Oracle accounts used only for download, or the privileges required by the download scripts are granted to the system operators. The only restrictions for the users concern what data they are allowed to read.

For this example, let's consider a system that stores information related to orders downloaded from a transaction processing system. The orders themselves are stored in tables not directly accessed by the users. Instead, scripts are run that extract and summarize key data elements into tables designed to answer the questions of production, sales, and shipping. The common users in each of these groups are not allowed to access the data in the other areas. Certain corporate planners are permitted to access data in all systems to provide overall performance and planning reports. Assuming that the rules I have presented here are correct and complete, I would propose the following privilege scheme for this data warehouse (see Figure 14.2):

- Production—These users are concerned with assessing the impact of orders on what the company is producing. They divert resources, acquire raw materials, and so on, based on the orders that are placed. They require the following privileges:
  - CREATE SESSION
  - SELECT on production tables

- Sales—These users are concerned with fulfilling sales quotas, profit margins, pricing, and similar things. They use the data to plan where to market the products and the price at which to market the products. They require the following privileges:
  - CREATE SESSION
  - SELECT on the sales tables

- Shipping—These users are concerned with planning what items will be shipped to what locations. They arrange trucks and so forth for the products. They require the following privileges:
  - CREATE SESSION
  - SELECT on the shipping tables

- Planner—These users are concerned with coordinating the overall process and, perhaps, providing reports to management. They require the following privileges:
  - CREATE SESSION
  - SELECT on the production tables
  - SELECT on the sales tables
  - SELECT on the shipping tables
- DBA—These are the standard privileges granted via the Oracle6 DBA grant or the Oracle7 DBA role.
- data_owner—This is a dummy user ID that owns all the application data tables. This user (and role) requires the following privileges:
  - CREATE SESSION
  - CREATE TABLE
  - CREATE PROCEDURE
  - CREATE PUBLIC SYNONYM
  - DROP PUBLIC SYNONYM
  - CREATE SEQUENCE
  - CREATE SYNONYM
  - CREATE TABLE
  - CREATE TRIGGER
  - CREATE VIEW
  - unlimited tablespace (possibly, if used by the DBA)
- Operator—In this particular company, the nightly update scripts are run by the operators using their own Oracle user IDs. Therefore, these accounts require the following privileges:
  - CREATE SESSION
  - SELECT, INSERT, UPDATE, DELETE on the order tables
  - SELECT, INSERT, UPDATE, DELETE on the production tables
  - SELECT, INSERT, UPDATE, DELETE on the shipping tables
  - SELECT, INSERT, UPDATE, DELETE on the sales tables
  - ALTER DATABASE (startup and shutdown)
  - ALTER SYSTEM (kill user processes when needed)

14

ROLES AND
GRANTS

FIGURE **14.2.**

Sample data warehouse privilege scheme.

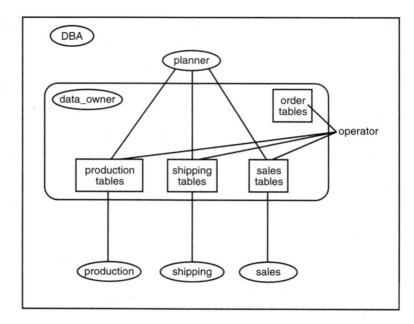

The final configuration is a sample security scheme for a development instance. This is a different environment from either of the two considered previously. Here, data security is not as important as having access to the system privileges required to get the job done. Many development systems go too far in the direction of granting unlimited privileges. Although it may sound good to have people not restricted from being productive, you eventually have to implement the controls you will use in production so that your testing reflects how the system will perform.

Balancing acts like this are always a challenge. The way I usually like to set up a development instance is to have two classes of developer. The first class contains people who develop software but are not trained or involved with the development of database objects. Perhaps they are good with the front-end tools, but are not sure what the word normalized means. The second class of developer develops new table structures, views, and perhaps even stored procedures. By having two separate sets of roles for these developers, you do not give too many privileges to developers who are not ready for them.

As part of the balancing act, you also create the same object owner account that you will have in production. When the developers have settled on the format of a particular set of tables, they transfer the object creation scripts to someone (developer or DBA, depending on how your organization functions) to be run from the object owner account. All the fine points, such as the creation of public synonyms and the grants of privileges to roles, are added to these scripts.

Finally, it is important to create dummy Oracle user IDs that have roles and privileges similar to those of the actual users of the application. You prove nothing if you do all your testing from the object owner account, which has full access to all the objects that it owns. The developer accounts presented in Figure 14.3 have some additional privileges, such as select any, that speed the development process; they are also not valid for testing. You could grant all these roles to the developers and trust that they would set their roles accordingly before testing. However, I do not trust schemes where there is a lot of setup work that needs to be done before conducting tests, and therefore I create these accounts that simulate real-world users. The test cases developed then specifically state that they need to be run as a certain user.

FIGURE 14.3.

Sample development instance privilege scheme.

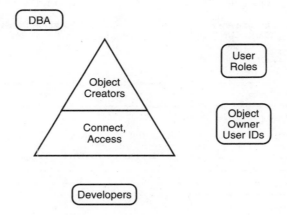

This section has provided you with three samples to consider when you develop your own security scheme. It is important to remember that the security scheme should be tightly tied to the business rules and needs. Therefore, your own individual schemes may be different from those presented in this section. I have tried several means to help develop my security schemes. My current favorite is illustrated in Figure 14.4. It has the advantage of including the common roles and grants I would use, while fitting on a single sheet of paper. Feel free to modify it into something that fits your own style.

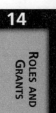

FIGURE 14.4.

Sample role security checklist.

Oracle Role Security Privilege Checklist

Application: _____

Date: _____   Prepared by: _____

Role Name: _____

System Privileges:

___ Create Session	___ Alter Session
___ Create Cluster	___ Create Procedure
___ Create Database Link	___ Create Public Synonym
___ Drop Public Synonym	___ Create Sequence
___ Create Snapshot	___ Create Synonym
___ Create Table	___ Create Trigger
___ Create View	___ Unlimited Tablespace
___ Execute Any Procedure	___ Select Any Sequence
___ Backup Any Table	___ Lock Any Table
___ Select Any Table	___ Insert Any Table
___ Update Any Table	___ Delete Any Table

Object Privileges:

Object	S I U D E	Object	S I U D E

Summary

This chapter has covered the Oracle role and grant scheme used in Oracle8. It is the key to Oracle database security and therefore cannot be treated lightly. Users start without any privileges (not even the privilege to connect to the database). You then have to add privileges to users to allow them to perform their jobs. These privilege grants can take the form of Enterprise Manager property page modifications, commands issued at the command line, or scripts containing the grant commands that are executed.

CHAPTER 15

Object-Oriented Extensions in Oracle8

by Matt Larson

IN THIS CHAPTER

Introduction

The object-oriented design model has been in place for over twenty years. The basic concept is to treat everything as an object. This is similar to how we perceive things. For example, an automobile is seen as one object. We do not see the automobile as a collection of small parts. We see it as a single object that is made of many parts. We also store objects in a completed form. This means that we prefer to keep an object put together during its useful lifetime. Imagine how complicated it would be to go to work in the morning if the car needed to be put together before it could be driven. The relational database management systems act in this fashion. It stores items at the lowest atomic level. When an object is needed in a relational database, it must pull all of the parts from various tables inside the database and put them together. When the object is no longer used, it is thrown away. If the object is ever needed again, it must be fully rebuilt.

The Basic Elements of an Object

An object is typically made of attributes and methods. Attributes will hold the data of the object. They may be null or may hold a certain type of value. Attributes can also be changed to reflect a modification in the overall object. Methods are procedures that perform actions against the attributes. The methods are the same across all objects of the same type. Figure 15.1 shows an example of a product object.

FIGURE 15.1.

The basic elements of an object.

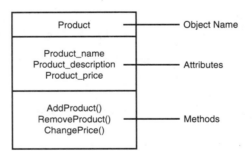

Many types will have attributes but no methods. This will often be the case when an application is converted from a relational database to an object-oriented database. The application must still handle all of the procedures against the data. The database is used solely as a storage mechanism.

The attributes can consist of standard datatypes such as the following:

- `number`
- `varchar2`
- `char`
- `date`
- `long`
- `long raw`

Attributes can also consist of other user-defined datatypes.

- `first_name`
- `address`
- `sales_order`

The following code is an example of a type without attributes:

```
CREATE OR REPLACE TYPE student_type
AS OBJECT(
first_name varchar2(200),  --standard database datatype
last_name varchar2(200),  --standard database datatype
major major_type  --user-defined datatype, the creation of this type was
➥not shown.
);
```

Methods

In object-oriented databases, activity performance against an object can be done through methods. This gives the designer more flexibility and control. In these cases, the data should not be accessed directly; it should only be used through methods. Consider the automobile. The person driving the car uses several methods to control the car. One method could be called StartCar(). The StartCar() method is a simple interface to the complex function of starting a car. The person executing this function is not required to understand the complexity. In fact, the internal procedures of StartCar() are implemented differently on many cars.

Programmers can use methods to provide a simple application program interface (API). Other programmers, who use the methods, also prefer to have the data and processes hidden. This frees other programmers from the details of the function. They only need to learn the interface to fully utilize the method. Methods can actually be implemented at two levels.

- Database level
- Application level

Currently, most methods are implemented at the application level. These methods are only usable within one application. This allows a certain amount of database independence. An application using standard SQL can easily switch database vendors. However, two applications must duplicate a method to perform the same function. This redundancy can lead to problems when changes need to be made. Implementing methods at the database level allows reuse of those methods. It also allows better control over the data.

Creating a type with methods is a two-step process. First, the type specification must be created. The specification lists all attributes of the type as well as the declaration of the methods. Second, the type body is created which specifies the code of the methods.

Listing 15.1 illustrates several method concepts:

LISTING 15.1. CREATING A TYPE WITH METHODS.

```
-- This is the specification for the type, it is similar to the way
packages are specified.
CREATE OR REPLACE TYPE product_type
AS OBJECT(
-- All attributes for the type are declared in the specification.
product_name varchar2(200),
product_description varchar2(4000),
product_price number,
product_price_date date,
-- Functions and procedures are declared here.  The code is stored in the
body of the type.
-- If methods are not used, then the body is not necessary
MEMBER PROCEDURE AddProduct (p_product_name varchar2,
➥p_product_description varchar2, p_product_price number,
➥p_product_price_date date),
MEMBER FUNCTION DaysSincePriceChange
RETURN NUMBER
);
/
CREATE TABLE product_table OF product_type;

CREATE OR REPLACE TYPE BODY product_type AS
 MEMBER PROCEDURE AddProduct
 (p_product_name varchar2, p_product_description varchar2, p_product_price
➥number, p_product_price_date date) AS
-- This is the body of the AddProduct procedure.
 BEGIN
    insert into product_table values (p_product_name,
p_product_description,p_product_price, p_product_price_date);
 END AddProduct;
MEMBER FUNCTION DaysSincePriceChange
RETURN NUMBER IS
BEGIN
    RETURN sysdate-SELF.product_price_date;
```

```
END DaysSincePriceChange;
END;

/
```

The `AddProduct()` method is a fairly simple piece of code that adds a product. It performs an insert into the product table. The designer may later decide to change the code of the `AddProduct()` function. First, the code is rewritten in the body of the type. If the specifications of the type do not change, the designer can issue a CREATE or REPLACE statement. In Listing 15.2, the designer has added a line of code into the `AddProduct()` method.

LISTING 15.2. ADDING CODE TO THE `AddProduct()` METHOD.

```
-- First, we create the audit table
CREATE TABLE product_audit_table (
product_name varchar2(200),
product_description varchar2(4000));

-- Next, we add a line in the AddProduct() function that inserts data
into the audit table
CREATE OR REPLACE TYPE  BODY product_type AS
 MEMBER PROCEDURE AddProduct
 (p_product_name varchar2, p_product_description varchar2, p_product_price
➥number, p_product_price_date date) AS
BEGIN
   insert into product_audit_table values (p_product_name, sysdate); --
➥This will insert an entry into the audit table for each product that is
added insert into product_table values (p_product_name,
p_product_description, p_product_price, p_product_price_date);
 END AddProduct;
MEMBER FUNCTION DaysSincePriceChange
RETURN NUMBER IS
BEGIN
   RETURN sysdate-SELF.product_price_date;
END DaysSincePriceChange;
END;

/
```

However, the designer may need to make a change in the specification of the type. If a table or type has been created that is based on the product type, the table or type is a dependant of that type. Any type that has dependants cannot be dropped or changed. Thus, the product type specification cannot be changed without dropping the dependants. Needless to say, this makes it difficult for a designer to change the specification. In Listing 15.3, the designer has decided to delete the parameter `product_description` from the `AddProduct` procedure.

15

OBJECT-ORIENTED EXTENSIONS IN ORACLE8

LISTING 15.3. DELETING product_description FROM AddProduct.

```
-- The analyst attempts to change the type specification.
SQL > CREATE OR REPLACE TYPE product_type
AS OBJECT(
product_name varchar2(200),
product_description varchar2(4000),
product_price number,
product_price_date date,
-- The p_product_description has been removed from this procedure
MEMBER PROCEDURE AddProduct (p_product_name varchar2, p_product_price
➥number),
MEMBER FUNCTION DaysSincePriceChange
RETURN NUMBER
);
/
CREATE OR REPLACE TYPE product_type
*
ERROR at line 1:
ORA-02303: cannot drop or replace a type with type or table dependents
-- An error is returned notifying the user of a dependency. Since, the
product_table table is a dependent, it must be dropped. This is usually
not a viable option. Standard types such as first_name, last_name and
address may have hundreds of dependent tables and types. In order to
change one of these types, the dependant tables would need to be dropped,
recreated, and reloaded with data. In addition, the permissions would need
to be re-granted and objects that are dependent on these tables would need
to be re-compiled.
SQL> DROP TABLE product_table;
SQL> CREATE OR REPLACE TYPE product_type
AS OBJECT(
product_name varchar2(200),
product_description varchar2(4000),
product_price number,
product_price_date date,
-- The p_product_description parameter has been removed from this
➥procedure
MEMBER PROCEDURE AddProduct (p_product_name varchar2, p_product_price
➥number),
MEMBER FUNCTION DaysSincePriceChange
RETURN NUMBER
);
/
Type created.
-- After the dependent table was dropped, the replacement of TYPE product
➥is successful.
SQL>
```

Due to these dependencies, the designers should ensure that changes will not need to be made in the TYPE specification. This requires an extra look at each method before releasing the type for general use. The designer should ensure that the specification will be sufficient for long-term use. One way to prevent changes to the specification is to specify methods that may be used in the future. The benefits of a flexible type will far exceed the overhead of unneeded methods in memory and system tables.

Object Ordering

Since objects are composed of several pieces of information, the database must determine how to order the objects. Oracle internal datatypes have predefined rules of ordering. For example, the varchar datatype has a rule to list values that start with an A before values that start with a B. Objects, however, are ordered according to rules that are specified by the creator of the type. If a query requests the objects from a table in descending order, the database must have a way of ordering the objects. Figure 15.2 illustrates this dilemma.

Figure 15.2.
Object ordering.

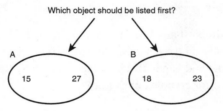

Which object should be listed first?

A   B

15   27   18   23

Some possibilities:
1) The object with the higher value on the right (Object A)
2) The object with the higher value on the left (Object B)
3) The object with the greater product of the two values (Object B (18*23=414) > Object A (15*27=405))
4) The object with the larger sum (Object A (15+27=42) > Object B (18+23=41))

There are two comparison methods that can perform the ordering function: map methods and order methods.

Map Methods

Map methods return a single value from the object. They return an internal datatype that Oracle can order according to internal rules. For example, a map method may return a Number datatype. Oracle will execute this map method against each object requested in the query. Each object returns a number that Oracle will store in a temporary structure. Once all the relevant objects have return a number as a map value, Oracle orders the numbers by the normal number ordering rules (1 comes before 2, 2 before 3, and so on).

Each object is then returned to the user in order of the map values. The value returned by the map method often uniquely identifies each row. This type of map value is the equivalent of a primary key in a relational database. The following is an example of a typical map method. It sorts the objects based on the value of the customer id.

```
CREATE OR REPLACE TYPE customer_type
AS OBJECT(
customer_id number,
first_name first_name_type,
last_name last_name_type,
address address_type,
MAP MEMBER FUNCTION CustomerMapFunction RETURN NUMBER
);
/

CREATE OR REPLACE TYPE BODY customer_type AS
MAP MEMBER FUNCTION CustomerMapFunction RETURN NUMBER IS
    BEGIN
        RETURN customer_id;
    END;
END;

/
```

Map methods are the simplest and fastest comparison method. They are easy to understand and execute quickly on the database. Map methods are preferred over order methods. However, a map method is not always robust enough to handle object ordering. Order methods are used for complex object ordering.

Order Methods

Order methods are used for specialized ordering. They can perform almost any type of calculation to determine the ordering of objects. The order method looks at two objects at a time. Values from each object are used to determine a return value. The order method is much slower than a map method because the database must compare each object to all the other objects. Listing 15.4 ranks employees by salary. It looks at the salary of each employee and compares it to the salary of all other employees. If the difference between the two salaries is less than $10,000, the function considers both employees to be equal.

LISTING 15.4. USING AN ORDER METHOD TO COMPARE EMPLOYEE SALARIES.

```
CREATE OR REPLACE TYPE employee_type
AS OBJECT(
employee_id number,
first_name first_name_type,
last_name last_name_type,
```

```
address address_type,
date_of_hire date,
rank number,
salary number,
ORDER MEMBER FUNCTION EmployeeOrderFunction(my_input IN employee_type)
➥RETURN NUMBER
);
/

CREATE OR REPLACE TYPE BODY employee_type AS
ORDER MEMBER FUNCTION EmployeeOrderFunction (my_input IN employee_type)
RETURN NUMBER IS
    BEGIN
        IF (ABS(salary - my_input.salary)) < 10000   THEN
            RETURN 0;
        ELSE
            RETURN salary - my_input.salary;
        END IF;
    END;
END;
/
```

The new object ordering methods do not replace the old ways of ordering. Oracle still has the ability to sort on the attributes of an object. Attribute ordering is still the most common type of ordering in applications. Object ordering, however, allows the designer to imply ordering to the user. The user may choose to order based on an attribute (or attributes) or may use the object-ordering methods. The object-ordering methods are invoked with the ORDER BY VALUE() clause. Listing 15.5 orders the employee table by using the order method. The table name must have an alias for the VALUE parameter.

LISTING 15.5. ORDERING THE Employee TABLE BY USING THE ORDER METHOD.

```
CREATE TABLE employee OF employee_type;
INSERT INTO employee VALUES (101,
first_name_type('Marti'),last_name_type('Hester'), address_type('101 Oak
St.','Denver','CO','USA','Mail Drop 32','Moving in six
➥months'),to_date('01-86','MM-YY'),1,20000);
INSERT INTO employee VALUES (102,
first_name_type('George'),last_name_type('Smith'), address_type('3 Lincoln
St.','New York','NY','USA',null,null),to_date('01-94','MM-YY'),1,40000);
SELECT * FROM employee e ORDER BY VALUE;
SQL> SELECT * FROM employee e ORDER BY VALUE;

EMPLOYEE_ID
FIRST_NAME(FIRST_NAME)
LAST_NAME(LAST_NAME)
ADDRESS(STREET, CITY, STATE, COUNTRY_CODE, MISC_MAIL_INFO,
MISC_NON_MAIL_INFO)
```

continues

15

OBJECT-ORIENTED
EXTENSIONS IN
ORACLE8

LISTING 15.5. CONTINUED

```
DATE_OF_H       RANK      SALARY


        101
FIRST_NAME_TYPE('Marti')
LAST_NAME_TYPE('Hester')
ADDRESS_TYPE('101 Oak St.', 'Denver', 'CO', 'USA', 'Mail Drop 32', 'Moving
➥in six months')
01-JAN-86           1       20000


        102
FIRST_NAME_TYPE('George')
LAST_NAME_TYPE('Smith')
ADDRESS_TYPE('3 Lincoln St.', 'New York', 'NY', 'USA', NULL, NULL)
01-JAN-94      1       40000
```

Type Versus Instantiation of a Type

It is important to understand the difference between a type and the instantiation of a type. The CREATE TYPE and CREATE TYPE BODY statements do not create objects in the database. Instead, they create a blueprint for future objects. A type is similar to the standard datatypes.

- number
- varchar2
- char
- date
- long
- long raw
- and others...

The following example will clarify. Consider a university that uses Oracle8. Figure 15.3 shows the types that are used as building blocks for the course and professor types.

FIGURE 15.3.
Course and Professor types based on other building block types.

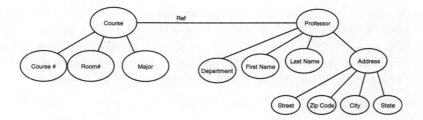

In order to create the book and author types, the building block types must first be created. The designer must start at the lowest level of types and work up (see Listing 15.6).

LISTING 15.6. BUILDING-BLOCK TYPES.

```
-- This is the lowest level sub-type in this diagram.
-- It must be created before the types above it.
CREATE OR REPLACE TYPE address_type
AS OBJECT(
street varchar2(200),
city varchar2(200),
state char(2),
zip varchar2(20)
);
/

CREATE OR REPLACE TYPE professor_type
AS OBJECT(
department varchar2(20),
first_name varchar2(200),
last_name varchar2(200),
address address_type   --The address type is used from above.
);
/

CREATE OR REPLACE TYPE course_type
AS OBJECT(
course_number number,
description varchar(255),
number_of_credits number,
professor REF professor_type   --The professor type is used
);
/


CREATE TABLE professor_table OF professor_type;


CREATE TABLE course_table OF course_type
(professor with rowid scope is professor_table);
```

Notice that none of the subtypes were ever used directly in a CREATE TABLE statement. Only course_type and professor_type were used to create physical objects. However, the tables are fully dependent on all the building-block types. Although the creation of type can be complicated, the creation of the tables becomes amazingly simple. The details of the underlying type are hidden from the person creating the table.

This listing also shows an example of REFs.

REFs

The specification of course_type shows a REF to the professor_type. REFs are used to describe a relationship (or reference) between two distinct objects. The professor_type is not a building-block type of the course_type. Think in terms of real-world objects. A course has a course number, a course description, and a number of credits. Each of these items belongs to an individual course. A course number will only belong to one course. The professor is not a part of the single course. The professor is a separate object that is referenced by the course. In fact, a professor may teach several courses. The REF column stores an object ID for the object that is referenced. It will only refer to a single object, not a group of objects. One may also notice that the CREATE TABLE statement of the course_table uses the SCOPE FOR phrase. This is similar to the REFERENCES phrase in relational designs. It limits the possible objects that can be referenced. In this case, only an object from the professor table can be referenced in the course_table.professor attribute.

The REF attribute stores the OID of the object to be referenced. It is also worth noting that a scoped REF uses less space than an unscoped REF. A scoped REF uses 16 bytes, whereas an unscoped REF uses almost 200 percent more space (46 bytes). Since most REF columns will be created for a specific object, it is common to use scoped REFs.

For faster access, the ROWID may also be included in the REF column. The ROWID takes up additional space, but it retrieves the referenced object much faster. The WITH ROWID clause can be used with both scoped and unscoped REFs.

Nested Tables and VARRAYs

Oracle has provided a new mechanism of storing sets of data inside of a row. In a relational database, data sets associated with a row are stored in separate tables. This type of relationship is called a one-to-many relationship. The data set is related to the row through a primary key/foreign key relationship. For example, a musical CD-ROM will store a set of songs. A relational database would contain a parent record which holds information relating to the entire CD-ROM, as well as several child records in a separate table that contains data on each individual song (see Figure 15.5).

FIGURE 15.4.

A one-to-many relationship in a relational database.

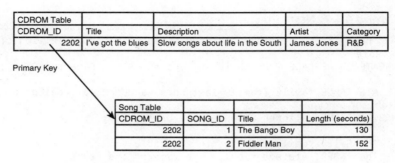

This method is inefficient. An expensive join must be performed every time the two sets of data are used together. Storing the child records inside the parent record is a better solution. This allows a faster retrieval of data as well as being a model that better resembles real-world objects. New object types in Oracle8 may be created with nested tables and VARRAYs.

Nested Tables

A nested table is a table that is embedded inside of a record in a table. Figure 15.6 shows the conceptual storage of a nested table, as well as how the data is actually stored in the database. A storage table is created for each column in a table that holds nested tables. A table with three nested table columns will have three storage tables associated with it. The nested tables for each row are stored in this storage table outside the main table. Storage tables cannot be accessed directly. They must only be accessed through the parent table.

FIGURE 15.5.

Nested table storage.

Conceptual Storage of a nested table

Title	Description	Artist	Category	Song		
I've got the blues	slow songs about life in the South	James Jones	R&B	SONG_ID	Title	Length (seconds)
				1	The Bango Boy	130
				2	Fiddler Man	152

Actual Storage of a nested table

CDROM_ID	Title	Description	Artist	Category	Song		
2202	I've got the blues	slow songs about life in the South	James Jones	R&B	SONG_ID	Title	Length (seconds)
2203	Happy Cowboy	upbeat country dance songs	Jimmy Ray	Country	1	The Bango Boy	130
					2	Fiddler Man	152
					1	Cows and Horses	142
					2	The Dusty Trail	128

A nested table can be used through the creation of a type. Once the type has been created, it may be used in a CREATE TABLE statement. Listing 15.7 shows some of the SQL that can be performed involving nested tables.

15

OBJECT-ORIENTED EXTENSIONS IN ORACLE8

LISTING 15.7. NESTED TABLES.

```
-- The AS TABLE OF clause is used to specify the definition of a nested
➥table
CREATE OR REPLACE TYPE children_type AS TABLE OF varchar2(30);

CREATE TABLE family (family_last_name varchar2(40), children
➥children_type)
NESTED TABLE children STORE AS children_table;

-- The Smith family is added to the table
-- The INSERT statement calls the type of the nested table
INSERT INTO family VALUES ('Smith', children_type
➥('Sally','Billy','Joey'));

-- Susy is born and is added to the family record
UPDATE family SET children = children_type('Sally','Billy','Joey','Susy');

-- The Smith family is deleted from the table
DELETE FROM family WHERE family_last_name = 'Smith';
```

The CREATE TABLE clause contains the NESTED TABLE clause. This clause specifies the
name of the storage table that will be used to contain the rows for the nested tables.
Again, this table cannot be accessed directly. The data must be accessed through the parent table.

VARRAYS

A VARRAY is similar to a nested table in the way it associates a set of child records with
the parent record. Unlike the nested table, a VARRAY stores the child data in the same
blocks as the table. VARRAYs also have a set limit on the number of values that can be
stored. A maximum is set at the creation of the type. First, a type is created that will hold
the VARRAY. Next, a table is defined that uses the type to create a VARRAY column. In
Listing 15.8, a VARRAY type is created that specifies a maximum of 100 rows of var-
char2(30) records. In this particular case, a maximum of 100 children can be in a single
family. The name of each child can use a maximum of 30 characters. This listing also
shows how to add, change, and delete a VARRAY. Notice that the SQL for inserts, updates,
and deletes is similar (in this case identical) to the SQL for nested tables.

LISTING 15.8. USING VARRAYS.

```
CREATE OR REPLACE TYPE children_type AS VARRAY(100) OF varchar2(30);
CREATE TABLE family (family_last_name varchar2(40), children
children_type);
-- The Smith family is added to the table
INSERT INTO family VALUES ('Smith', children_type
```

```
➥('Sally','Billy','Joey'));
-- Susy is born and is added to the family record
UPDATE family SET children = children_type('Sally','Billy','Joey','Susy');
-- The Smith family is deleted from the table
DELETE FROM family WHERE family_last_name = 'Smith';
```

CAUTION

Nested tables and VARRAYs should not be used for all relationships. If other applications will directly access the data, it may be best to stick with separate objects.

Using Base Types

Base types are created for use inside other types. They are well-planned types that will make future development easier. Some examples of base types include the following:

- First Name
- Last Name
- Age
- Marital Status
- Social Security Number
- Zip code
- Address
- Phone number
- Customer id
- Sales id

If a designer wanted to create a customer table, he or she would look at the list of base types and use those that are appropriate. For example, a designer creating a customer table would create it with the following CREATE TABLE statement:

```
CREATE TABLE customer(
cust_first_name first_name_type,
cust_last_name last_name_type,
cust_address address_type.
cust_hair_color varchar(15)
);
```

The designer has used three user-defined base types that were specified in the database. This ensures that a well-thought-out standard has been used inside the application. If the designer had decided to create new definitions for these columns, it is likely that they would not have been able to interact easily with other applications. Listing 15.9 shows table definitions created for two different applications.

LISTING 15.9. TABLE DEFINITIONS FOR DIFFERENT APPLICATIONS.

```
CREATE TABLE customer (
cust_first_name varchar(20),
cust_last_name varchar(20),
cust_street varchar(20),
cust_city varchar(20),
cust_state char(2),
cust_zip number(5),
cust_hair_color varchar(15)
);

CREATE TABLE employee (
emp_first_name varchar(25),
emp_last_name varchar(25),
emp_street varchar(255),
emp_city varchar(30),
emp_state varchar(15),
emp_country varchar(30),
emp_other_addr_info varchar(255)
);
```

Notice that the columns to hold `first_name` and `last_name` are different sizes. In most cases, the designer will simply guess at the correct size. These guesses may be appropriate for each specific application, but make it difficult to merge this data at another time. The designers also chose different datatypes to hold address information. One decided that the `state` field will hold the two-character abbreviation for each state; the other decided to put the full state name in the field. Finally, one added a field to hold the country information as well as a miscellaneous field for other address data. Both might have designed a better application if base object types had been designed for them. The base types might be defined as follows.

```
CREATE TYPE first_name_base_type AS OBJECT(
first_name varchar2(50)
);

CREATE TYPE last_name_base_type AS OBJECT(
last_name varchar2(50)
);

CREATE TYPE address_base_type AS OBJECT(
```

```
street varchar2(100),
city varchar2(100),
state char(2),
country varchar2(100),
misc_mail_info varchar2(2000),
misc_non_mail_info varchar2(2000)
);
```

The first two types consist of only one standard datatype. The `address_base_type` contains several standard datatypes. Hopefully, it holds all the information that the company would like to record about addresses. The `misc_mail_info` column is information that will be printed on mailings sent to this address such as "Attn: Robin McRae, 10th floor, office 35." The `misc_non_mail_info` will not be put on mailing labels, but will show up on a clerk's screen. An example is "Mr. Smith has told us that he will be moving in the next six months. Ask him for his new address when he calls back!"

Generally, implementing base types will promote better application development. Data will be formatted in objects that can easily migrate from one application to the next.

Object Views

The Oracle8 database is an object-relational database management system (ORDBMS). An ORDBMS allows the designer to use object-oriented techniques, relational techniques, or a combination of both. The designer has the flexibility to use each technology where it is best fitted. An ORDBMS also allows a slow migration from a relational to object-oriented design. One of the reasons Oracle has provided object views is to help this conversion process.

Object views make relational tables appear to be objects.

There are four steps to creating a object view.

1. Determine the query the view will represent.
2. Determine the datatypes the query will return.
3. Create a type that has the same structures as the query.
4. Create the view based on the type.

First, the user determines the columns from each table that should be included in the view. In this case, the view should display the first and last names from the patient table in a hospital database.

Next, the user determines the datatypes of those fields.

```
SQL> describe patient
patient_id number,
first_name varchar2(30),
last_name varchar2(40),
and many other columns...
```

Then the user creates a type that contains datatypes for each column to be returned in the view.

```
SQL> CREATE TYPE patient_name_type AS OBJECT (
patient_id number,      --This field is needed although the user did not ask
➡for it in the view.
--Notice that the field names may be different from the field names in the
➡table,
--however the data types are the same
f_name varchar2(30),
l_name varchar2(40)
);
```

Finally, the user creates the view.

```
SQL> CREATE VIEW patient_names OF patient_name_type
WITH OBJECT OID (patient_id) AS
SELECT patient_id, first_name, last_name FROM patient;
```

The `employee id` field is used to uniquely identify the rows returned from the relational table. This field will be used instead of a true Object Identifier because the objects are not stored in the database as objects. They are dynamically created from the relational tables when they are needed.

Once the view has been created, the data can be treated as normal objects.

INSTEAD OF Triggers

The `INSTEAD OF INSERT` trigger may be used to manipulate inserts, updates, or deletes against the view. The `INSERT` trigger is especially helpful when a view is based on several tables. The `INSTEAD OF` triggers act in a similar way to normal triggers. In the next code example, two triggers are created on the `employee_names` view.

The first trigger will insert directly into the employee table. It will also discard the value for the employee id that is in the `INSERT` statement. Instead, it will insert the next value from a sequence which has been defined to generate employee id numbers.

The second trigger will generate a user-defined error statement that scolds the user on an attempt to delete employees through this view. Although the permissions on the view often handle this type of activity, it is nice to be able to generate an error that is more descriptive than the usual "ORA-01031: insufficient privileges."

```
CREATE OR REPLACE TRIGGER employee_names_trigger
INSTEAD OF INSERT ON employee_names
BEGIN
INSERT INTO employee VALUES
(employee_sequence.NEXTVAL, :NEW.f_name, :NEW.l_name, NULL, NULL, NULL,
NULL);
END;

CREATE OR REPLACE TRIGGER employee_names_trigger_delete
INSTEAD OF DELETE ON employee_names
BEGIN
RAISE_APPLICATION_ERROR(-20000, 'You may not delete employees through this
view!');
END;
```

> **NOTE**
>
> INSTEAD OF triggers are not limited to object views. They can be placed on normal views as well.

Large Objects

The previous sections have shown how object-oriented program design is beneficial for use with standard datatypes such as char, varchar, number, and date. However, many companies are looking toward object-oriented databases for the use of complex datatypes. Complex datatypes include pictures, video, spatial objects, and custom applications. Custom applications probably have the greatest potential in object-oriented databases.

For example, consider an architectural company that designs houses. The firm uses a specialized architectural design software package. This software will save blueprints into special files called .arc files. With current database technology, the .arc files can be stored in a LONG RAW datatype. Other columns in that table can hold descriptive columns about the .arc file. Unfortunately, these descriptive columns are not very beneficial to the architectural firm. It takes extra work to populate these columns, and they are limited in their ability. Figure 15.7 shows an example of files stored inside a relational database.

15

OBJECT-ORIENTED EXTENSIONS IN ORACLE8

FIGURE 15.6.

Storing files in a relational data-base.

File_name	#_of_windows	window vendor	cost_of_windows	type_of_roof	file
smith_house.arc	4	Pella	$40	flat	0000101010001111101010101000111100011101

With object-oriented technology, the .arc files will be stored in new Oracle8 BLOB columns and accessed through object-oriented methods. These methods will probably be designed by the developer of the architectural software. The developer will focus on creating methods that can manipulate groups of .arc files as well as individual files. This functionality will allow the architectural firm to perform functions on a set of blueprints that cannot be performed if each blueprint is stored as a separate file on an operating system disk. One method may give the ability to query the architectural blueprints. An architect could ask the following questions:

- How many windows were installed by our company in the last month?
- How many houses have at least a three-car garage?

These questions cannot be answered if individual files are spread out on workstations. The analyst can also make changes to the set of blueprints. If the architectural firm receives a good deal on windows from a certain company, the analyst can execute a method that will change all the blueprint designs to use the new window where appropriate.

Another example is using the Oracle8 database to hold Microsoft Office documents. If all corporate office documents were stored in a central database, several functions could be performed.

- Search Word documents for a reference to a particular product in the footer
- Replace the company logo in all documents (Word, Excel, and PowerPoint)
- Change the mileage reimbursement rate in Excel spreadsheet documents

Most of these files need to be stored in a large datatype. Oracle8 has four new datatypes for storage of large objects:

- BLOB
- CLOB
- NCLOB
- BFILE

They can hold up to 4GB of data. This size limit is sufficient for most objects. Some objects, such as a full-length movie, will not fit in 4GB of space. These objects must be split into several rows to fit into these new datatypes. These datatypes are greatly enhanced from the previous large datatypes (LONG and LONG RAW). These old datatypes (which are still supported) are limited in usability. Oracle corporation has lifted many of these restrictions with the new datatypes. Table 15.1 lists the four datatypes and their capabilities.

BLOB

BLOB stands for binary large object. This datatype holds raw binary data that the database does not understand without the use of data methods. The data methods interpret the binary data and make it usable within the database. The binary data will not be converted with other character set conversions. Any character sets of the objects in the BLOB can be converted with methods. BLOB data participates fully in transactions. This means that changes to BLOB data may be rolled back or committed along with the other types of data.

CLOB

CLOB stands for character large object. It stores up to 4GB of single-character data. A CLOB is used to store large text items such as documents and Web pages. Like the BLOB, the CLOB fully participates in transactions.

NCLOB

NCLOB stands for national character large object. It is similar to a CLOB except that it has the ability to store fixed-width, multi-byte character data that corresponds to a national character set.

BFILE

The BFILE is used to give Oracle8 access to files stored outside the database. The database stores a pointer to the BFILE inside the table. BFILEs can reside on operating system devices such as disks and CD-ROMs. Due to the fact that BFILE resides outside the database, Oracle8 does not support transaction consistency with BFILEs. This is irrelevant, however, because BFILEs are also read only. Oracle8 uses directories as a layer between the operation system and the BFILE object. An Oracle8 directory is created with the CREATE DIRECTORY statement.

```
CREATE DIRECTORY company_logos AS '/u01/company_pictures/logos';
```

The extra layer between the BFILE and the operating system allows flexibility. If the logos are moved to another directory, the DBA will simply issue this command.

```
CREATE OR REPLACE DIRECTORY company_logos AS
'/u02/pictures/company_logos';
```

No tables will need to be updated to reflect the change in directories.

> **CAUTION**
>
> Do not grant the CREATE ANY DIRECTORY to anyone outside of the DBA group. This privilege allows the user to point to any directory on the operating system that the Oracle user has permission to access. Operating system security can be violated by granting this privilege.

TABLE 15.1. LOB DATATYPES IN ORACLE8.

LOB	Extended Name	Type of Access	Storage Capacity	Storage Location	Support Transactions	Character Type Data Conversions
BLOB	Binary Large Object	Read/Write	up to 4GB	inside the database	Yes	No, binary
CLOB	Character Large Object	Read/Write	up to 4GB	inside the database	Yes	Yes, single-byte character data
NCLOB	National Character Large Object	Read/Write	up to 4GB	inside the database	Yes	Yes, fixed-length multi-byte National Character data
BFILE	Binary File	Read-Only	up to 4GB	outside the database (stored in the file systems)	No	No, text or binary

Creating Tables with LOBs

Creating a table with a LOB (the generic name for this group of datatypes) is quite simple. The following example shows the creation of a résumé table.

```
CREATE TABLE resume_table (
first_name    varchar(20),
last_name    varchar(20),
resume        CLOB
);
```

Unlike the LONG and LONG RAW datatypes, multiple LOBs may exist in each table.

```
CREATE TABLE candidate (
first_name    varchar(20),
last_name    varchar(20),
picture      BLOB,
```

```
resume     CLOB,
acceptance_letter    BFILE
);
```

It is beneficial to use the storage options of the LOBs. In Listing 15.10, there is a picture (BLOB) and a résumé (CLOB). Each has a separate STORE AS clause. The STORE AS clause has several parameters, as listed in Table 15.2.

TABLE 15.2. PARAMETERS FOR THE STORE AS CLAUSE.

TABLESPACE	Specifies the tablespace that will hold the LOB data; it will often be different from the tablespace that holds the table data.
ENABLE/DISABLE STORAGE IN ROW	If ENABLE is chosen (default), all LOBs that are smaller than 4000 bytes (minus overhead) will be stored inside the table. All larger LOBs will be stored outside the table. If DISABLE is chosen, all LOBs will be stored outside of the table.
CACHE/NOCACHE	Specifies if the data should be cached in memory. This is used for LOBs that will be accessed frequently.
LOGGING/NOLOGGING	Specifies if the data should be written to the redo logs. If CACHE is chosen, LOGGING is assumed.
CHUNK	Specifies the number of blocks that will be used at one time. Db_block_size * CHUNK cannot be greater than 32K. In other words, tables in an 8K block size database could have a maximum CHUNK size of 4.
PCTVERSION	Specifies the percentage of space that can be used by earlier version of LOBs.
INDEX	Specifies the storage parameters of the LOB index. This index is different from normal indexes—it cannot be dropped, rebuilt, or renamed.

The following CREATE TABLE statement uses the STORE AS clause.

LISTING 15.10. CREATE TABLE STATEMENT.

```
CREATE TABLE candidate (
first_name varchar(20),
last_name varchar(20),
picture BLOB,
pesume CLOB,
acceptance_letter BFILE
)
```

15

OBJECT-ORIENTED
EXTENSIONS IN
ORACLE8

continues

LISTING 15.10. CONTINUED

```
--Options specific to the Picture BLOB
LOB (picture)
STORE AS (TABLESPACE picture_blob
STORAGE (initial 500K next 500k)
ENABLE STORAGE IN ROW
CACHE
LOGGING
CHUNK 4
PCTVERSION 15
INDEX (TABLESPACE picture_indexes))

--Options specific to the Resume CLOB
LOB (resume)
STORE AS (TABLESPACE resume_clob
STORAGE (initial 50K next 50K)
ENABLE STORAGE IN ROW
NOCACHE
NOLOGGING
CHUNK 2
PCTVERSION 5
INDEX (TABLESPACE resume_indexes)
);
```

Figure 15.7 shows the how the candidate table data is stored. The picture and résumé
LOBs are stored inside the database; the acceptance letter BFILE is stored in operating
system files.

FIGURE 15.7.

*The candidate
table.*

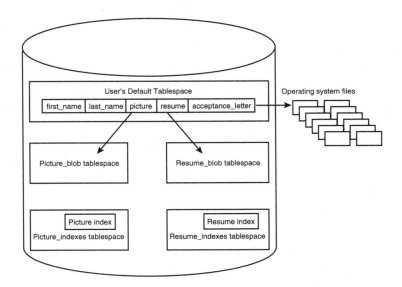

Summary

The object-oriented features of Oracle8 have added to the versatility and complexity of the Oracle database. Used properly, objects can improve application speed and enhance the productivity of application development. Objects are designed to model the real world and will continue to make strides in the database arena.

Replication

by Advanced Information Systems, Inc.

IN THIS CHAPTER

CHAPTER 16

Replication: "Why Ask Why?"

Replication sounds like something out of a science fiction book, regarding space aliens and DNA. At first glance, it might not appear to be relevant to your business; it is hardly an intuitive term. If we were to deduce what Oracle's replication might be, it would probably be the replication of databases because that is Oracle's business. We would be correct.

Replication means to make a copy of one thing from another. In the world of databases, it means to make a copy of one database or subset thereof from separate databases. You might at this point storm out of the room, asking yourself why in the world you might want to replicate your database when you can hardly manage it as it is now!

Good question! Let's take the road of science fiction to answer it and hopefully entertain. Let's beam onboard *Star Trek*'s Enterprise, a starship in the federation of planets.

On our starship we have a computer. Probably one that talks because we want good TV ratings. Now assume that as captain you discover a new planet, a new species, a new spin-off series! Now assume you enter all this new information in your ship's database.

A month later, many light years away, I come flying by in my ship, also a member of the federation. I encounter this new race of beings that you discovered. I check my database and find out that they love Jolt Cola—a fact that you found out on your initial mission.

Now how did the data get from your computer into mine? That would be my first question. Assume that we are too far out into space to log into a central computer; our shipboard computer is all we have; and instead we somehow need to update each other's database periodically. Well, what we need is replication, plain and simple.

In business, many times for larger companies, databases are functioning in different parts of the world or simply performing different tasks. Maybe we are an international corporation and we do business in New York, London, and Hong Kong. We have three huge databases logging the sales of *Star Trek* trinkets in each of the three cities and a massive WAN (wide area network) linking the databases as in Figure 16.1.

In this situation, clerks in New York, London, and Hong Kong are entering thousands of orders a day for the alien dolls that like Jolt Cola. Each database is being pressed to the limit! On each node of our *distributed database*, we have executives who need to see not only sales for their region but total sales. How do we show them that? Well, we use replication techniques just like our friends from the future do.

FIGURE 16.1.
Our Star Trek *sales data center architecture.*

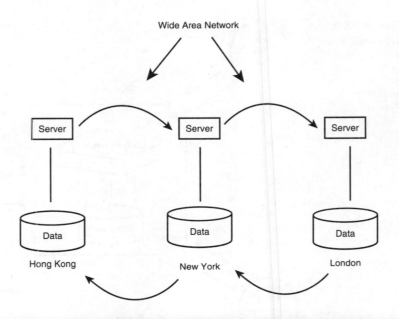

If you have this ability, replication is of no value.

In this second scenario, Figure 16.2, we might have a fast enough database server and network and/or light enough sales volume so we can structure our London, New York, and Hong Kong business in the following way.

Here we have a server that can handle all the requests and a network that can enable the amount of data we receive to pass through efficiently. Now say we also have the ultimate fail-over system for our dream server. If your business can do something like this, please do not consider implementing replication just to be one of the beautiful people.

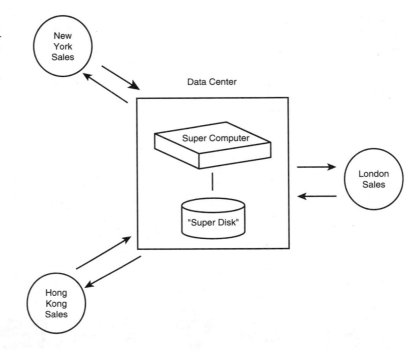

FIGURE 16.2.

A powerful server and network that is fully recoverable negates the need for replication.

Replication and the Data Warehouse

Here is an interesting caveat to my premise: Even with an efficient database server and fast enough network, we still might need replication. Imagine that we do have the dream database and the dream network—New York, London, and Hong Kong are all running effortlessly off our amazing central database.

Suppose this *Star Trek* thing has been going on since the 1960s. After a while, our perfectly-running database is going to fill up with a great deal of data. If we enter a modest 300 gigabytes per year of sales data, after 30 years we have 9 terabytes. Our year 2000 problem is going to be that our computer is going to choke itself to death and die if we don't do something about our older data.

Furthermore, our *Star Trek* trinket company has hired a bunch of fancy business consultants, who are running long-term trend studies on our sales database! When these people log in to find out if our Jolt Cola alien action figures are losing popularity, suddenly the database slows down and sales people all over the world have trouble entering data. Our perfect system is slowly dying of data overload and being choked to death by business consultants who took one too many statistics courses in college (see Figure 16.3).

FIGURE 16.3.

At some point, you need to know how to say "when" in the storage of historical data and statistical data.

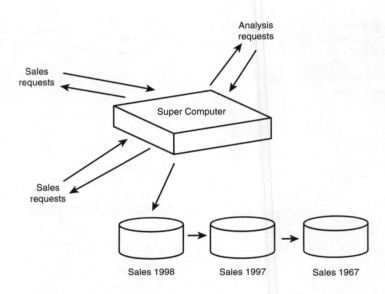

If I were to enter the stage as your consultant, after I handed you my modest bill, I would suggest that you separate the old sales data into a *data warehouse*. A data warehouse is a large repository of data that is generally not changed day-to-day. It is a place where our business analysts can analyze as much historical data as they can get their hands on.

We might decide to keep only the last three years online because we do have returns and other common events with this newer sales data, yet move the last 28 years to a data warehouse. Our architecture now looks something like Figure 16.4.

As you can see, our OLTP (Online Transaction Processing) sales database is much smaller and faster, and it is also separate from the grueling business studies being done on the historical data.

At this point though, the business analyst—pocket-protector and all—might protest that the more recent data must be visible from the data warehouse because he is running a time-series analysis.

What we need is a way to query the new sales data in our data warehouse; we need some sort of "snapshot" of current data to go along with our historical data. Luck is on our side because Oracle has the exact thing we are looking for, and it is called a *snapshot*—how convenient.

Because the business expert only wants to view our sales data, and, of course, not change it, we decide to implement a read-only snapshot.

A snapshot is defined as a copy of a complete table(s) or a subset of a table(s) that reflects a recent state of that table that is defined periodically by the user.

FIGURE 16.4.

By moving analytic and historical data off an OLTP sales server, we improve performance.

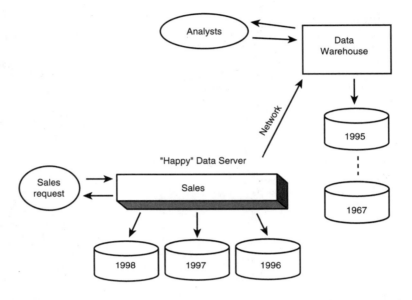

Now we have all the data the business analyst needs because we have placed a snapshot of our recent sales database on our data warehouse server (see Figure 16.5).

FIGURE 16.5.

By using a snapshot, we can incorporate current data into a data warehouse.

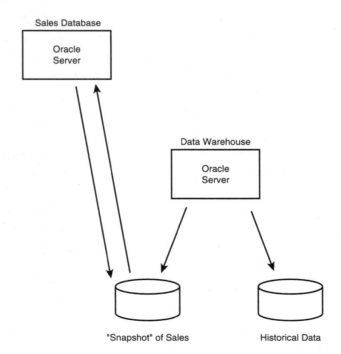

This type of snapshot is a *transaction consistent snapshot* in that it is being refreshed in a given period by actual sales data and therefore remains consistent with the reality of our sales transactions. The period of refresh might be hourly, daily, or even weekly, depending on our needs. When this period occurs, data is physically moved to our snapshot and we are said to be in a *snapshot refresh*. Obviously, this refresh takes time and resources so, in many cases, it is accomplished at night or when the system is being lightly used (see Figure 16.6).

FIGURE 16.6.

A nightly refresh of a snapshot does not disrupt analysts or sales activity.

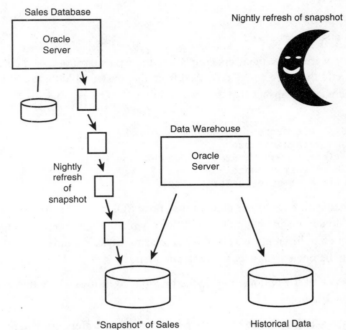

Nightly refresh of snapshot

Sales Database

Oracle Server

Nightly refresh of snapshot

Data Warehouse

Oracle Server

"Snapshot" of Sales

Historical Data

Read-Only Replications and Snapshots

Let's create our snapshot for this fictitious sales company. In this case, we are doing it strictly because users of the data warehouse want to see current sales data. In this case, we have *primary site* replication because we are replicating a central sales database for another separate database, a data warehouse. Our sales database is the *master database* that owns the *master table*; we will call it `Sales`.

Here's a simple `Sales` table that is logging the thousands of sales we receive each day:

Sales
Transaction_id
customer_id
product_id
location
quantity_sold
unit_price
purchase_timestamp

In our data warehouse, the users simply want a table snapshot called current_sales that looks exactly the same and is refreshed from the master table, Sales, in our OLTP database. To create a snapshot like this, we simply use SQL as in the creation of any other object:

```
Create Snapshot current_sales
Tablespace data_warehouse
Storage (Initial 900m Next 100m Pctincrease 0)
Refresh Fast Next sysdate + 7
As Select * From sales@sales.nj.com;
```

As seen here, we refer to our table in the above SQL as `sales.nj.com`. This implies that we have already installed Oracle's SQL*Net, which needs to be present when we refer to any object on a different instance of Oracle using SQL. We have also created a database link using the `create database link` command.

Look at some of the options used in the previous SQL to see how they relate to replication principles:

Tablespace—This refers to the tablespace in our data warehouse where we want the snapshot; the original data already exists, so we are just telling Oracle where to place the copy of the original data. In this case, we used a tablespace name called `data_warehouse` for simplicity.

Storage—Because a snapshot is an actual copy of data, meaning that data is replicated to a second physical location, storage parameters informing Oracle of the size needed for this copy must exist. In our example, we posited 300 megabytes per year, so our three-year sales table snapshot takes 900 megabytes.

Refresh—This clause refers to what strategy Oracle will use. There are three basic types of refresh strategies:

1. **Fast**—This form updates only the snapshot with data that has changed. Oracle uses a *snapshot log* to keep track of this.

2. **Complete**—In this form, Oracle re-executes the query. In this case, `select *`
   `from sales` represents a total refresh of all table data.

3. **Force**—This option instructs Oracle to try a fast replication and if not possible a
   complete replication.

Next—This clause tells Oracle when to next perform a refresh of the snapshot. So if I
execute this `create snapshot` statement on a Saturday, every Saturday afterward this
snapshot will be refreshed because I specified `sysdate + 7` and in Julian date arithmetic,
the number 7 refers to 7 days.

> **NOTE**
>
> For automatic refresh to function, the DBA or system administrator must refer
> to his operating system-specific startup file for local instances and start an addi-
> tional snapshot refresh process that will run in memory as does the Oracle8 ker-
> nel processes. Many times this file is called dbstart.

AS—Notice here at the end we preface our *select statement* clause with an AS. This is
similar to creating a view, and because a snapshot is a view of a sort, this makes perfect
sense. In our simple case, we are creating a complete snapshot of the table with the simple *select statement* in the example.

Note that because of the power of a snapshot, we might decide to create a more sophisticated snapshot. We might only want sales data that is three months old because of the
many returns. But further assume that Hong Kong has a new no-return policy, so now
our data warehouse analysts need all sales data in Hong Kong, yet only sales data three
months old from New York and London. In this case, our AS condition becomes more
sophisticated:

```
AS select * from sales
where (location != 'HONG KONG'
and purchase_timestamp < add_months(sysdate, -3))
or
(location = 'HONG KONG');
```

This lends a great power to Oracle replication because we can create snapshots of *subsets*
of an original table or tables. Our analysts can just as easily do an analysis of customer
profiles in the data warehouse by creating a snapshot that joins a second customer table:

```
AS select
sales.purchase_timestamp,
sales.quantity_sold, sales.unit_price,
customer.age,
```

```
customer.gender,
customer.zip_code
from
sales,
customer
where sales.customer_id = customer.customer_id
```

With this query, the business analysts can track specific traits relating to the sale of these *Star Trek* trinkets. If, for instance, it's found that people in their 60s purchased the largest amount, commercial time can be bought for reruns of the *Golden Girls*; whereas, if only young men liked the *Star Trek* trinkets, advertising money might better be spent during a football game.

Snapshot Logs

As mentioned before, Oracle uses *snapshot logs* in the *fast* option when refreshing a snapshot. Snapshot logs help in a situation where only a small percent of the rows of a table are changed per refresh; we really don't want to recopy all the rows to our snapshot from the master table. The way Oracle does its housekeeping to keep track of only changed rows is accomplished by the use of snapshot logs.

Whenever you have an update, insert, or delete of the master table, the snapshot log records the activity. This obviously takes time and might slow down an OLTP application. In cases where the penalty is too great, consider nightly or weekend *complete*-style snapshots.

Here is the syntax to create a snapshot log:

```
Create Snapshot Log On sales
tablespace sales_tablespace
storage (initial 1m next 1m pctincrease 0);
```

Our snapshot log size here is an initial amount of 1 megabyte, each row that is changed in our sales table (or any table for that matter) takes up approximately 25 bytes in the log. This means that our log will not fill up its initial extent until 1,000,000/25 (*extent size/25)* rows have been changed in the sales table. This figures out to 40,000 rows.

Obviously, the log size should reflect the time period in which you do your snapshot refresh. If you refresh only once a month, you need a bigger log than if you perform a nightly log refresh.

Aside from the `Create Snapshot` command, Oracle provides a package called `DBMS_REFRESH` that is a library of PL/SQL calls that a DBA can use to manually refresh a snapshot.

One important note: Oracle locks the master table in Exclusive mode when a refresh occurs. This means that users can only query the data during this time period. If someone performs a snapshot refresh during business hours, no new sales can be entered throughout our corporate empire! Sales clerks across the seven seas would receive strange Oracle locking errors or timeouts as they tried to process customers.

Remote Databases

Many times the database that you are accessing is totally outside of a local cluster of hardware. In these cases, you will use a *network protocol* such as TCP/IP to communicate with these remote sites. Atop the *network protocol* is an Oracle protocol called SQL*Net. Atop SQL*Net, the *database protocol* between two remote databases is facilitated through a *database link*. A *database link* is a short Oracle type of URL, which can point to remote parts of an SQL*Net network.

In the previous example, the actual physical order/entry was in New Jersey; then our sales data warehouse in New York City needs to be refreshed with SQL that included the database link to the New Jersey node in the network. Here would be the snapshot create statement's AS portion that brings us data from New Jersey.

```
AS Select * From sales@sales.nj.com;
```

This networking interface to replication is vital to make replication possible between any two Oracle databases, regardless of physical location. The database link is the object we refer back to again and again throughout remote replication. It is important to understand database links and to properly create and manage them.

Complex Replication—Distributed Databases

When we talk about complex replication, we enter the world of distributed databases. This is a favorite topic among academia because it extends relational algebra to include multiple databases. In simpler terms, a distributed database can be defined as many databases appearing as a single database to the user.

Replication and the World of Virtual Databases

In our original example of the business database, each location had a separate OLTP sales database. Refer back to Figure 16.2 to view this. Read-only replication that we just discussed was offered only for a data warehouse viewing one central OLTP database.

In the case where we instead have multiple active databases that need to see each other's data as data is being updated, deleted, or inserted, we need to use *multi-master replication*. In the sales database example we had three equally important databases in London, New York, and Hong Kong—hence the term *multi-master*. All these databases perform OLTP server functions for the regions of the world they are assigned to.

In a more complex scenario, assume that order clerks at all three locations need to coordinate billing, inventory, and shipping. What is required are three separate Oracle servers, each sharing current information from each other on sales data. Although each database is separate, a *virtual database* must exist that shows table data from all three as if it were one database, as in Figure 16.7.

FIGURE 16.7.

User sees all data as if it were one database.

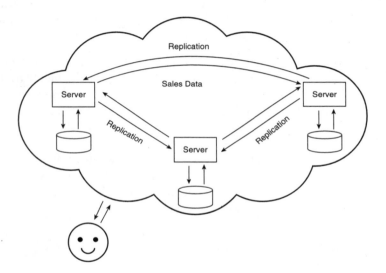

This is a scenario called *replicated environment,* where we merge information from one physical database to another. In a replicated environment, three types of users need to be a part of the management of our system:

1. **Replication Administrators**—Users under this umbrella are responsible for setting up replication among databases and implementing it.
2. **Symmetric Replication Agents (propagators and receivers)**—There are certain replication activities that need to be run as SYS, Oracle's super-user account within a given database.
3. **End Users**—Users that will be using the replicated information to either query and/or change it.

Let's set up replication at our three *Star Trek* trinket sale sites and assign the DBAs the privileges needed to replicate the sales database. To do this, we use the package

DBMS_REPCAT_ADMIN and the procedure within that package, GRANT_ADMIN_REPSCHEMA. Here is the following call; notice that this procedure takes in the Oracle username as a parameter:

```
dbms_repcat_admin.grant_admin_repschema('SALES');
```

Here we assume that the SALES user owns the sales data.

Creating a Replicated Environment "Replication God"

If we wanted to create a new user called rep_god that can replicate any schema at the current site, we first create the user:

```
Create User rep_god Identified By <password>
```

We would then call the same package as before but a different procedure to give this new user full replication power, thus making the user a *global replication administrator:*

```
dbms_repcat_admin.grant_admin_any_schema('REP_GOD');
```

At this point, we have created a replication administrator with the username 'REP_GOD'. But before we plunge ahead and set up replication, we must set up database links for the two offices in Hong Kong and London; thus we need N - 1 database links for a replication of N nodes.

At each of the two physically remote sites, we create a *surrogate replication administrator.* This is a user at the remote site that initiates all the low-level replication processing for the SYS account that is necessary. We now create a user called surrogate_hong_kong for our Hong Kong office:

```
Create User surrogate_hong_kong Identified by <password>
```

Now we grant this user surrogate status within our replication sub-system:

```
DBMS_REPCAT_AUTH.GRANT_SURROGATE_REPCAT('surrogate_hong_kong');
```

Back at the central node in New York, we create a database link for each surrogate:

```
create database link new_york.sales.com CONNECT to surrogate
IDENTIFIED BY <password> USING hongkong.sales_com;
```

At this point, we will replicate our schema. For this example, the schema is simply the owner of the sales data that we are replicating: SALES. We need to register the SALES database as a candidate for replication; to do this we call on the DBMS_REPCAT package again:

```
DBMS.REPCAT.CREATE_MASTER_REPGROUP('SALES','new_york.sales.com',
'comment', 'asynchronous'));
```

After we have made possible the replication of all database objects owned by SALES, we now specify which objects we intend to replicate. In this case, we need to replicate the central sale table. Here's the following PL/SQL package call needed with example parameters followed by comments defining them:

```
DBMS_REPCATE.CREATE_MASTER_REPOBJECT(
'SALES',
/* Owner of object to be replicated */
'SALES',
/* Object name replicated */
'TABLE',
/* Type of Object */
'TRUE',
/* Use Existing Object */
' ',
/* DDL Text if object does not already exist at master site */
'HI THERE',
/* Comment */
FALSE,
/*  Retry, yes or no? */

TRUE,
/* copy rows, yes or no? */
'SALES',
/* Object Gropu */
);
```

At a low level, Oracle replication consists of a series of PL/SQL packages, procedures, and triggers that are either PL/SQL or new internal triggers that are simply C language functions. These objects are generated as you define your replication. With Oracle8, we can use a front-end tool that executes many of these calls automatically. The example of the Sales table being replicated in Figure 16.8 shows that some sort of trigger needs to fire and propagate our replication when a user changes a row in the table.

FIGURE 16.8.

Just as with standard development, replication uses triggers to propagate changes with one table across a set of other tables; the difference is that the replication triggers fire across a distributed database network to tables residing on remote nodes.

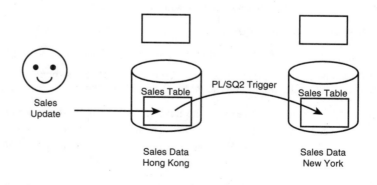

The actual command that initiates the creation of the proper trigger can be accessed as a PL/SQL package call. Now create these low-level objects for our Sales table using this call:

```
DBMS_REPCAT.GENERATE_REPLICATION_SUPPORT('SALES','SALES','TABLE, NULL,
NULL, TRUE, 'SALES', TRUE);
```

This procedure is given in the general form: The last variable, a Boolean, is set to TRUE to indicate that we are in a distributed environment.

Now say that our corporation opens a West Coast operation in San Francisco (see Figure 16.9). We now want to integrate a new sales database application to our existing replication schema and create a four-node replicated network.

FIGURE 16.9.

Oracle replication enables us to enter new nodes after we have an operating replicated environment.

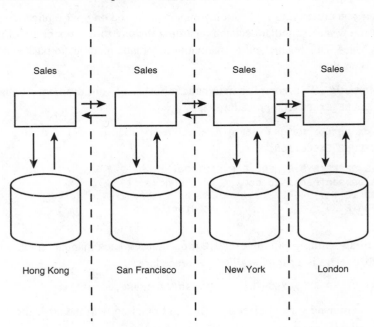

To do this, we must first create a replication user on the local site and a proper database link for the site. Then we call the following procedure from our central node:

```
DBMS_REPCAT.ADD_MASTER_DATABASE(
'SALES',                            /* Schema */
'sales@sales.sanfrancisco.com',     /* database link */
TRUE,                               /* Use existing objects*/
TRUE,                               /* copy row */
'Hi there',                         /* Comment */
);
```

Managing Your Replication and the Mystery of the Two-Phase Commit

After you create your replication components based on your replication strategy, you must now make another decision regarding the day-to-day operation of the replicated databases. This regards either manual or automatic methods to push synchronized data between sites.

Automatic—To accomplish automatic refreshes of your different databases, use the SCHEDULE_EXECUTION procedure.

An example of this is to set up a refresh every hour. Do this by calling SCHEDULE_EXECUTION:

```
DBMS_DEFER_SYS.SCHEDULE_EXECUTION(
'sales.sanfrancisco.com',  /* the node */
SYSDATE + 1/24,            /* the interval */
SYSDATE                    /* start date */
);
```

Manual—Simply call the EXECUTE procedure for each manual replication task that is needed. Here is a sample call to this procedure:

```
DBMS_DEFER_SYS.EXECUTE('sales.sanfrancisco.com');
```

This command synchronizes sales in San Francisco with the other three nodes, whenever it is called.

NOTE

If you use the Replication Manager, you do not need to memorize any of these replication calls, but instead can use a GUI interface to execute them.

The place where Oracle stores transaction information as users enter sales at each of the four sites is a *deferred transaction queue*. With this queue, we accomplish the magical task of the two-phase commit.

The two-phase commit is a trendy name, but replication is more similar to a "commit and flush" because after your data is committed to your database, the transaction is not final until the remote site successfully accepts the transaction. At this point, the deferred transaction queue is flushed, as in Figure 16.10.

FIGURE 16.10.
The deferred transaction queue makes sure that our transaction is not complete until we receive confirmation from the remote site(s).

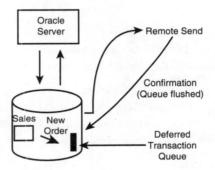

This is why a two-phase commit is called as it is; for a transaction to be final in a two-phase commit, aside from the initial single database commit, a second validation must occur with remote sites before the transaction can be completed. Thus we have a two-phase validation.

The difference between these two phases is that the first commit is part of ANSI SQL. It can be defined explicitly in relational algebra; the second phase of a commit is more vendor dependent and flexible regarding what constitutes validation of data transfer to remote sites.

Oracle has actually implemented a new "distributed transaction protocol" that is actually just a more efficient form of the traditional two-phase commit.

Conflict Resolution

Just as with people performing different tasks at remote locations for the same company, computers need to be explicitly taught the procedures for coordinating their tasks over a network. When two computers produce conflicting results, a *virtual policy* must be in place to first find and then resolve mistakes that might arise when work performed at two locations is not consistent with local or corporatewide business rules.

Types of Conflicts

Because we are creating one *virtual database* out of N number of database schemas, this virtual database must obey all the relational rules of conduct for us to consider the replication valid. For instance, we cannot have two users on separate sites both inserting the same unique primary key.

Because this second part of the two-phase commit is more nebulous, we must make sure that our replicated system adheres to the strict standards that keep a relational database from turning into sets of chaotic data.

In an example where two separate nodes of our *distributed database* change the same data, we have a potential for disaster. In Oracle's replication, any change by any node on a table causes Oracle to store the old and new values for the row.

To identify rows across a *distributed database*, Oracle cannot use a *rowid* that is only a physical identifier of a row, unique only for a given node of the distributed database. Across nodes, rowid is not unique. Oracle instead needs to use the actual primary key definition of the table to perform uniqueness operations.

With the information of a table's primary key and with the old and new values of a data change, Oracle can automatically detect three types of conflicts:

1. **Uniqueness Conflicts**—An example of this might be that two sales sites sell a new corporate customer a bunch of *Star Trek* trinkets on the same day. Both applications, for example, in New York and San Francisco insert a new row for this customer in the customer table. If the same unique identifier is used, such as Tax ID, there now exists two duplicate rows in the virtual *distributed database*. This error must be resolved.

2. **Update Conflicts**—In this case, we have two of the separate database servers performing changes on a row before they are reconciled with one another.

   An example in our *Star Trek* trinket factory in Figure 16.11 would be if an order in Hong Kong reduced a shipping inventory in San Francisco while an order in San Francisco also reduced the same inventory. Say the combined order was for 150 units and yet we only had 140 units in our warehouse.

   The Hong Kong site issues the following SQL:

   ```
   update inventory set amt = amt - 100
   where trinket_type = 'KLINGON DOLL'
   ```

   Because of an unrelated order in San Francisco the inventory is lowered again and this second transaction is allowed to go through even though we now possess only 40 units after the preceding sale:

   ```
   update inventory set amt = amt - 50
   where trinket_type = 'KLINGON DOLL'
   ```

In the second case, the computer still thinks that inventory is at 140, not at 40, where it should be set after the first order.

Oracle would compare the following values.

FIGURE 16.11.

We try to order 50 units for San Francisco. If we don't yet "see" the Hong Kong transaction, we will pledge to ship 50 units when we have only 40 units.

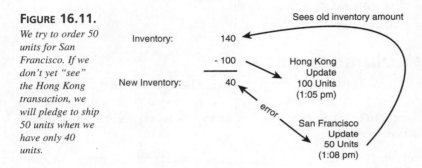

Oracle solves this by using procedures at the receiving site to detect these forms of update conflicts.

3. **Delete Conflicts**—A delete conflict occurs if a row is deleted at one site but the values of this row's remote replicated relatives are different. This occurs if someone cancels (deletes) an order at one site—for example, in New York—and later another person updates that row in Hong Kong not knowing it was deleted.

Managing Update Conflicts

To manage an update conflict, we first assign sub-sets of our column definitions that are being replicated into *column groups*. These are simply logical groups of column definitions that enable you to specify exact rules for the resolution of a conflict.

With numeric data, many times we just allow the changes to be aggregated without any further logic. With character data, we might need a timestamp. We cannot sum characters logically. For instance if special instructions were left with both the San Francisco office and the Hong Kong office for a particular order, we might just decide to take the instruction with the most current timestamp.

Here are some resolution strategies that you can set for Oracle to use after you create column groups to define your replicated data:

1. Apply the data with the latest timestamp.
2. Apply all data additively.
3. Apply the maximum value if the column is being increased.
4. Apply the data with the earliest timestamp.

5. Apply the minimum value.

6. Apply the maximum value.

7. Apply the value from the highest priority site.

8. Apply the value assigned the highest priority.

9. Apply the average value.

Creating Column Groups

When we consider a conflict strategy, we should always look toward the most current release of Oracle's Server and Replication facility. The method to create a strategy is based again with calls to PL/SQL packages, thus the system is very flexible and Oracle might have added new options.

When we have a strategy in mind for the replication of a certain set of columns, we can define that column group. Let's define a column group for UNIT_PRICE and QUANTITY_SOLD. To do this, we call a procedure:

```
DBMS_REPCAT.MAKE_COLUMN_GROUP('SALES', 'SALES', 'MYGROUP',
'unit_price,quantity_sold');
```

This column group is now called MYGROUP as specified for the third parameter. If later we want to add another column, this is not difficult: just another call to a PL/SQL procedure. In this next example, we are adding a column called cash_back; it obviously must exist in our Sales table.

```
DBMS_REPCAT.ADD_GROUPED_COLUMN('SALES','SALES', 'MYGROUP', 'cash_back');
```

We can also remove a name from a column group by using the following command to remove the column unit_price from the group:

```
DBMS_REPCAT.DROP_GROUPED_COLUMN('SALES','SALES','MYGROUP', 'unit_price');
```

To drop this complete column group that we have created, we call another package:

```
DBMS_REPCAT.DROP_COLUMN_GROUP('SALES','SALES','MYGROUP');
```

Defining a Conflict Resolution Method for a Column Group

Above we defined the three major conflicts of replication; Oracle has created three procedures to handle the three scenarios of update, uniqueness, and delete conflicts. The three procedures in the DBMS_REPCAT package to define conflict resolution routines are respectively named ADD_UPDATE_RESOLUTION, ADD_UNIQUE_RESOLUTION, and

ADD_DELETE_RESOLUTION. They also exist as internal triggers with version 8 that give the user more security against unwanted changes to them.

For instance, say that we want to make sure that the latest prices and unit sales figures are entered into the system, we would use our column_group 'MYGROUP' in the following PL/SQL replication call:

```
DBMBS_REPCAT.ADD_UPDATE_RESOLUTION
(
    'SALES ', /* Table Owner */
    'SALES', /* Table Name */
    'MYGROUP', /* Column Group */
    1, /* Sequence */
LATEST_TIMESTAMP, /* Update Method */
    'purchase_timestamp', /* parameter column name*/
NULL, /* priority group */
NULL, /* function name */
'the latest purchase timestamp will decide the conflict' /* comment */
);
```

In this case, we are instructing Oracle's replication mechanism to resolve all update conflicts for the mentioned Column Group using the greatest timestamp on the column purchase_timestamp.

There are many other types of conflict resolution and the use of priority levels for a column_group. We will not go into all these variations. The basic principle of setting up these different conflict resolution strategies through calls to the package DBMS_REPCAT remains the same or through Oracle's replication manager remains the same.

One major benefit of Oracle's strategy in using PL/SQL as the foundation of replication is that this enables the user to create customized conflict resolution logic. Logic such as this can be in the form of a user-defined PL/SQL function that returns a Boolean value, TRUE or FALSE. Here a more complex strategy can be defined using the PL/SQL language. This might be useful because the default resolution strategies might not be adequate for your replicated environment.

Survivability

One of the attractions of replication is survivability. This refers to the capability of the *distributed database* to remain online with current data from even a site that has gone down.

For instance, if California fell into the sea and our fourth sales site, San Francisco, suddenly disappeared into the surf, we would still have all the data that had been refreshed from that site on any other master site. The only data that would be missing would be data that had been logged in San Francisco yet not transferred. Transactions that needed to send data from other sites to San Francisco could either be "rolled back" from the second phase of our two-phase commit, or these transactions could instead be accepted manually using the packaged PL/SQL or the Replication Manager.

Survivability can be easily obtained using Oracle's Parallel Server. Never move into replication for this feature alone, unless your two database sites are physically separate. If you plan to create a *highly available* system, the Parallel Server is a better choice. If one node goes down on the parallel server, the server will fail-over without any lost transactions.

The drawback to the Parallel Server is that this configuration is characterized by many CPU's and/or operating system instances sharing the same disks. If your disks crash, you can have all the survivalist procedures in place yet you will not have access to your data or your database. In a replicated system, the hardware is totally physically separated, connected only by a network, so a hard-disk crash on one system will still not bring the system down and might only affect a few transactions.

Figure 16.12 shows the differences in architecture between survivability in a replicated environment and survivability in a parallel environment.

FIGURE 16.12.
Because data and hardware are physically separated in remote replication, if one location fails, the system will survive.

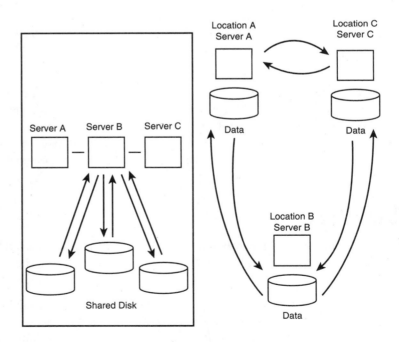

If you do decide to use replication as a survivability tool, here are a few tips to remember when setting up your replication strategy:

- The replicated sites must keep up with the master site or sites. If, for instance, our New York office does 10 times the volume and we can only refresh the other sites at night, a crash in the day will make inaccessible all the orders in New York for that day.

- If a failure does occur, it is important not to panic because transactions at both ends of the replicated network, meaning transactions at the failed site and at the site that is still running, might appear to be lost because they either have failed in the second phase of the two-phase commit or they were lost at the primary site. They are not lost if we chose to ignore the second phase of our commit.

- A strategy must be in place that database administrators can follow for the recovery of sites that have gone down. When the failed site returns, simply pushing across all the old transactions can cause conflicts because much of this shared data has changed or has been duplicated in the time after the fail-over.

- Consider using a read-only fail-over site if you need survivability. In this case, bringing that site back online will not cause conflicts. And furthermore, the refresh rate for that site can be faster because the demands on it are lighter.

- Consider a third-party tool for survivability instead of replication. Many vendors offer these tools along with their hardware. These tools mimic a parallel server. They are usually referred to as *high availability* options that can be purchased for specific hardware/OS configurations.

The Advantages of Oracle8 and the Replication Manager

It might seem that Oracle's replication strategy would be tedious for the DBA who needed to run an endless array of PL/SQL packages with many different parameters. Oracle has mercifully hidden this from the casual user with the Replication Manager. This product is a series of GUI screens that allow for intuitive drag-and-drop manipulation of a replication scheme.

The Replication Manager issues the preceding PL/SQL and new C routines to perform the same tasks, but instead hides this mess from the casual user that instead uses intuitive GUI tools to configure a replicated environment, as in Figure 16.13.

Figure 16.13.

The Replication Manager in version 8 of Oracle shelters the user from SQL, C, and PL/SQL tasks.

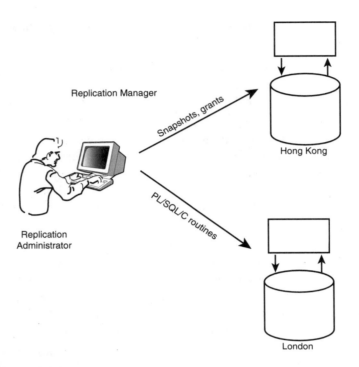

The Replication Manager has a Setup Wizard that enables you to create the replication links and needed privileges to configure a replicated environment. Along with this is the Snapshot Wizard, which enables users to point-and-click while creating snapshot groups, snapshot logs, and snapshots.

One important feature this product offers is a validate procedure that validates an existing configuration. This is valuable because with manual validation and use of PL/SQL, a user at another replicated node can invalidate a portion of the replication strategy without us being aware of it. This forces someone concerned with the overall replication state to create a set of validation routines.

The Snapshot Wizard can also handle *primary key snapshots* that enable you to reorganize a master table without blocking other sites in performing a fast refresh. It also saves time because we might need to propagate only new values in the primary key.

The new *deferred constraints* feature speeds up replication refresh by not checking referential integrity on the remote site until the end of a refresh. This speeds up the process but might result in a large listing of errors at the end of a forced or automatic refresh.

Another advantage that comes with using Oracle8 replication is the use of *fine grain quiesce,* which in Oracle-speak means that you can manage different replication groups down to the column level. For instance, if you have an engineering and an accounting group both looking at your Product table, with this level of replication control, you can define further columns or tables for replication to your engineering group and not your accounting group. This can be useful if your engineering group needs technical documents and specifications that go with each product; whereas your sales group only needs the product code and the description. In this case, whenever you have a sale, we wouldn't need to move down all the information we had on the product sold.

Oracle was forced to move to internal triggers in Oracle8 simply because traditional PL/SQL code is not as fast. Oracle needed to improve performance so now they offer C modules that are compiled directly into the Oracle kernel.

I was puzzled when Oracle introduced replication without these changes to the Oracle kernel. By simply using PL/SQL, you are creating a flexible, yet flimsy, layer for your replication logic. The internal C libraries are always faster than PL/SQL, which is, at best, interpreted code as shown in Figure 16.14.

FIGURE 16.14.

PL/SQL needs to be interpreted before CPU execution; C executables do not.

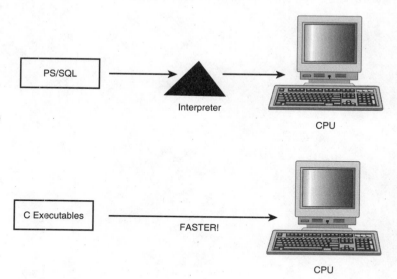

Oracle is now using a new distributed transaction protocol that ensures that no transaction is ever applied twice, which is what a two-phase commit is defined as. This protocol reduces network traffic and has the same user transparency as the two-phase commit. Oracle actually claims that this protocol eliminates the two-phase commit. I think I will stay out of that war!

Summary

On our long voyage through the universe of replication, we have seen the strategy of Oracle's replication offering. It appears Oracle has made the correct move by rewriting much of the replication logic in the form of C modules that link to the kernel. This strategy adds speed but doesn't throw away the detail to which a replication DBA can configure a replicated site. Flexibility was the power of the PL/SQL packages that we learned.

It is important to remember that replication takes place between physically separate machines. Two instances of Oracle can perform perfect replication if they are on the same cluster by using the Oracle Parallel Server and not replication. There are also tools that give highly available database server functionality to a system that can be purchased from a third-party along with a hardware server. Don't consider replication until these other alternatives are ruled out. Replication is a whole layer of complexity that affects every database that is being replicated; it is not a trivial task that is performed by a black-box. In most cases, replication demands a great deal of design and planning before it is implemented and a vigilance to maintain the replicated databases after implementation. Beware before you enter its many hallowed halls!

Query and Transaction Processing

by Edward Whalen

Transaction Processing

Transaction processing is the heart of any RDBMS. In fact, without transaction processing there would be no reason to have an RDBMS. According to the ANSI/ISO SQL standard, a transaction is one or more SQL statements executed by a single user that either succeed or fail as a whole. The transaction starts with the execution of the first SQL statement and ends when they are explicitly committed or rolled back. In many cases, the commit or rollback statement is specifically executed; in others, the application such as SQL*Plus does the commit on behalf of the user automatically.

It is important that a transaction be thought of as a single logical unit of work. A transaction must either succeed or fail as a whole. A transaction that only partially works will probably leave your database in an unknown state. For example, a bank transaction that transfers money from one account to another may use SQL statements that withdraw money from one account, and then add that money to another account. If only the first part of that transaction worked, your money could be completely lost.

In a typical transaction, the following steps are executed:

A. Application Connection (Optional)

1. The application processes the user input and creates a connection to the server through Net8.

2. The server picks up the connection request and creates a server process on behalf of the user or passes the request to a shared server process via the dispatcher.

> **NOTE**
>
> The application-connection process occurs only when the application is signing on. The application does not have to connect each time a statement is processed.

B. Transaction Processing

1. The user executes an SQL statement or statements and commits the transaction. For example, the user changes the value of a row in a table.

2. The server process takes this SQL statement and checks the shared pool to see whether there is a shared SQL area that has this identical SQL statement. If it finds an identical shared SQL area, the server process checks to see whether the user has access privileges to the data and uses the shared SQL area to process the request. If a shared SQL area is not found, a new shared SQL area is allocated, the statement is parsed, and it is finally executed.

3. The server process retrieves the data from the SGA (if present) or retrieves it from the data file into the SGA.

4. The server process modifies the data in the SGA. Remember that the server processes can only read from the data files.

5. The LGWR process writes out the redo information. Not until this redo information has been written to the log is the statement considered committed. At some later time, the DBWR process writes the modified blocks to permanent storage.

6. If the transaction is successful, a completion code is returned across the network to the client process. If a failure occurs, an error message is returned.

7. Return to phase B, "Transaction Processing," and submit more transactions until you are finished and want to exit the application.

The Application Processing phase is repeated indefinitely until the user is finished with this particular application and exits the application.

NOTE

A transaction is not considered committed until the write to the redo log file has been completed. This write may be triggered by the COMMIT statement or may have already been done based on changes to the database. This arrangement ensures that a committed transaction is recoverable in the event of a system failure. When a transaction has been committed and the redo entry has been written, the transaction is considered finished.

C. Application Termination

1. The application logs off the RDBMS. This event signals Oracle that all the associated resources can be deallocated.

2. The Oracle PMON process makes sure that the server process has been terminated.

3. All resources are released. Any memory resources the application has allocated are released.

NOTE

The application-disconnect process occurs only when the application or user is signing off. The application does not have to connect each time a statement is processed.

While this process is occurring, the Oracle background processes are doing their jobs keeping the system running smoothly. Keep in mind that while your application is being processed, hundreds of other users may be doing similar tasks. It is Oracle's job to keep the system in a consistent state, managing contention and locking and performing at the necessary rate.

Even though your application may have modified some data in the database, that data may not yet be written to the data files. It may be some time later that the DBWR process writes those changes out to permanent storage.

With this overview of how the application is processed, you are ready to focus on what happens in step 2 of phase B: how the SQL statement is parsed and the execution plan is formed.

SQL Statement Processing

By understanding how Oracle processes SQL statements, you can have a better understanding of how to optimize these statements. The following sections look at the SQL statement parsing process and how an execution plan is formed. For each SQL statement that is executed, several steps occur:

1. A cursor is created.
2. The statement is parsed, if it is not already in the shared pool.
3. Any query in the statement is processed.
4. Variables are bound.
5. The statement is executed. If possible, the statement is parallelized.
6. Rows to be returned are fetched.

Cursor Creation

Each time an SQL statement is executed, a cursor is automatically created on behalf of the statement. If you want, you can declare the cursor manually. Remember that a *cursor* is a handle to a specific private SQL area. You can think of a cursor as a pointer to, or the name of, a particular area of memory associated with an SQL statement.

Statement Parsing

Once the cursor is created, a determination is made about whether the SQL statement is already present in the shared SQL area in the shared pool. If the SQL statement has already been parsed and is in the shared pool, there is no further need for parsing and the execution of the SQL statement continues. By using stored procedures or carefully crafting SQL statements to be identical, there is a good chance that those statements will be in the shared SQL area already parsed.

Query and Transaction Processing
CHAPTER 17

341

17

QUERY AND
TRANSACTION
PROCESSING

For an SQL statement to take advantage of SQL or PL/SQL statements that may have already been parsed, the following criteria must be met:

- The text of the SQL statement must be identical to the SQL statement that has already been parsed. This includes whitespaces and case.
- Reference to schema objects in the SQL statements must resolve to the same object.
- Bind variables must match the same name and datatype.
- The SQL statements must be optimized using the same approach; in the case of the cost-based approach, the same optimization goal must be used.

You may think that these conditions make it difficult to take advantage of the shared SQL areas. In fact, users sharing the same application code meet these criteria quite easily. It is to the advantage of the application developer to use the same SQL statements to access the same data, ensuring that SQL statements within the application can also take advantage of the shared SQL areas.

> **TIP**
>
> Using stored procedures whenever possible guarantees that the same shared PL/SQL area is used. Another advantage is that stored procedures are stored in a parsed form, eliminating runtime parsing altogether.
>
> Standardizing naming conventions for bind variables and spacing conventions for SQL and PL/SQL statements also increases the likelihood of reusing shared SQL statements.
>
> The V$LIBRARYCACHE table contains statistics on how well you are using the library cache. The important columns to view in this table are PINS and RELOADS. The PINS column contains the number of times the item in the library cache was executed. The RELOADS column contains the number of times the library cache missed and the library object was reloaded. A few number of reloads relative to the number of executions indicates a high cache-hit rate for shared SQL statements.

If the already parsed SQL statement is not in the shared pool, the following steps are executed to parse the SQL statement:

1. *The statement is validated.* The SQL statement must be verified as a valid statement.
2. *The data is validated.* The data dictionary lookups are performed to verify that the table and column definitions are correct.

3. *Locks are allocated.* Parse locks must be acquired to make sure that object definitions don't change during the execution of the parsing.

4. *Privileges are verified.* Oracle validates that the user has permission to use the schema objects being accessed.

5. *The execution plan is determined.* The optimal execution plan is determined based on several factors, including optimization plans, hints, and database analysis.

6. *The statement is loaded into the shared SQL area.* Once the execution plan has been determined, the statement is loaded into the shared SQL area.

7. *The distributed statement is routed.* If the statement is used as a distributed transaction, all or part of the statement is routed to the other nodes involved in this statement.

As you can see from the number of steps that must be executed, it is important to try to keep the SQL statements in the shared pool to avoid the parsing phase of the execution process.

Query Processing

Queries are handled differently than other SQL statements because queries return data as the result of the statement. Other SQL statements need only return a return code that indicated success or failure. In addition to the other steps that must be executed, queries may require the following additional functions:

- *Read consistency.* Because you may be executing several statements that take considerable time, it is important that the data remain consistent through the lifetime of the query.

- *Use of temporary segments.* Because queries may perform additional functions such as joins, order bys, sorts, and so on, it may be necessary to use temporary segments.

The following functions also may be executed outside of the RDBMS:

- *Describe the results (optional).* This phase is necessary if the characteristics of the query's results are not known (for example, with an interactive query, the datatypes of the results must be determined before the results can be returned).

- *Output definition (optional).* If the output location, size, and variable datatypes are defined, it may be necessary for Oracle to perform data conversions.

The preceding functions are necessary only for queries, in addition to the other SQL statement processing.

Bind Variables

Variables, when used, must be defined before the statement can be processed. The application program must specify to Oracle the address of the variable before Oracle can *bind* that variable. Because the binding is done by reference, you do not have to rebind a variable before re-executing the statement; simply changing its value is sufficient.

You must supply the datatype and length of each variable you bind to Oracle unless these datatypes or lengths are implied or defaulted.

Statement Execution

Once the statement has been parsed and the variables have been defined, the statement is executed. In array processing, the execution step may happen many times. Any necessary locks are applied before the execution of the statement.

Parallelization

If the Oracle Parallel Query option is used and the statement being executed is parallelizable, the following steps take place:

1. The query coordinator determines which operations can be performed in parallel.
2. The query coordinator determines how many query servers to enlist.
3. The query coordinator enlists query servers that perform the query.
4. The query coordinator reassembles the resulting data and passes it back to the user.

The degree of parallelism is determined by using the following order of precedence:

1. *Query hints.* User-defined hints included in the SQL statement have the highest precedence.
2. *Table definition.* The default degree of parallelism defined for the table is second in the order of precedence.
3. *Initialization parameters.* Finally, the Oracle initialization parameters are used to determine parallelism.

The processes that execute the query are taken from the set of query servers available in the query server pool. This number is specified by the Oracle initialization parameter PARALLEL_MAX_SERVERS.

Fetch Rows to Be Returned

If the statement is a query, the final step in the processing of the SQL statement involves fetching the returned data in a loop until all the requested data has been returned to the user process.

REVIEW OF SQL STATEMENT PROCESSING

By understanding the process that takes place when an SQL statement is executed, you can see the value in avoiding some of these steps.

Taking advantage of SQL statements that have already been parsed is one way to limit the amount of overhead associated with the processing of the statement.

This chapter begins to look at ways to produce a well-tuned application. The key to having an optimized application is at the heart of the application: the SQL statements themselves. Optimizing your SQL statements and reducing unnecessary overhead will result in an optimized application.

An optimized application together with the tuned and optimized RDBMS server will provide a well-balanced, highly tuned system. Because users are mainly interested in response times, having both a well-tuned application and an optimized server is essential. To get an optimized application, you must start with an optimized SQL statement.

So, what *is* a well-tuned, optimized SQL statement? Here's a list of some of the characteristics of a well-tuned SQL statement:

- *Makes efficient use of RDBMS features.* The well-tuned SQL statement uses indexes or hashing as available. If possible, the application should also take advantage of features such as array processing and discrete transactions.

- *Uses PL/SQL to improve performance.* PL/SQL allows blocks of statements to be sent to the Oracle server at one time. If you don't use PL/SQL, you must send each statement individually.

- *Uses stored procedures.* By using stored procedures, you reduce the amount of data that must be sent across the network and increase the chance that the statement may already be parsed in the shared SQL area.

- *Uses packages.* Packages increase performance because the entire package is loaded when the package is called for the first time.

- *Uses cached sequences to generate primary key values.* This improves the performance of key generation and makes it unnecessary to generate the key in the application.

- *Makes efficient use of space.* The SQL statement uses the VARCHAR2 datatype instead of CHAR, when possible, to avoid unnecessary blank padding.

- *Uses hints where necessary.* A well-tuned SQL statement uses hints where appropriate to allow the programmer's understanding of the SQL statement and the database design to override Oracle's choice of optimization method.

These attributes, in conjunction with your own specific attributes, make a well-tuned SQL statement in your configuration. The properly tuned SQL statement avoids unnecessary functions and executes with the minimum amount of resources necessary to perform its function.

Using the Oracle Optimizer

During the execution of SQL statements, Oracle chooses a plan by which these statements are executed. The execution plan is determined by the Oracle optimizer by using the optimization approach specified in the initialization parameters. The optimization approach can be overridden by the use of hints.

The effectiveness of the execution plan depends mainly on the optimization method chosen. This optimization method can consist of either a rule-based or cost-based approach. Which approach you take depends on both your application and your data.

How the Optimizer Works

To understand how the optimizer optimizes your SQL statements, it is useful to first look at how the optimizer works. When an SQL statement is parsed and passed off to the optimizer, the following occurs:

1. The SQL statement is analyzed and evaluated. In this first stage, the SQL statement is checked by the optimizer.

2. The SQL statement is modified by the optimizer. If the statement is complex, the optimizer may change the statement to be more effectively processed, if necessary.

3. View merging is performed. If the statement is accessing a view, the Oracle optimizer sometimes merges the query in the statement with a query in the view before optimization.

4. The choice of optimization method is made. The optimizer chooses between a cost-based or rule-based approach, based on the amount of analysis data available for the object and also on any hints. If there is analysis data available, the cost-based approach is used; if not, the rules-based approach is used.

5. The access path is chosen. The optimizer chooses one or more access paths to each table referenced in the SQL statement.

6. The join order is chosen. If more than one join is done in the SQL statement, Oracle chooses the most appropriate order in which the joins will occur.

7. The join operations are chosen. The optimizer chooses the most appropriate operations to use to perform the joins.

As you can see, the process through which the optimizer chooses the most optimal execution plan for the SQL statement is quite complex. But it is in this fashion that the best execution plan is usually chosen. At the basic level, the optimizer breaks the statements into their constituent components and determines their individual costs.

Optimizer Initialization Parameters

There are a number of Oracle initialization parameters that can be set to modify the behavior of the optimizer. These parameters can be used to configure the optimizer mode and the amount of time spent in the optimizer, and to set other optimizer defaults.

The optimization modes (cost-based or rule-based) can be chosen using either of the following methods:

- The OPTIMIZER_MODE initialization parameter
- The OPTIMIZER_MODE parameter of the ALTER SESSION command

When specifying the optimization method with either the initialization file or the ALTER SESSION command, you can specify the following options:

Option	Description
CHOOSE	This option allows the Oracle optimizer to choose an optimization mode based on the availability of statistics on a particular table, cluster, or index. If statistics are available for any of the tables accessed in the SQL statement, the cost-based approach is used with the goal of best throughput. If none of the tables has statistics available, the rule-based approach is used; the rule-based approach is also the default if no optimization approach is specified.
RULE	This option causes the Oracle optimizer to always use the rule-based optimization approach, regardless of any statistics that may have been gathered for the tables being accessed.
ALL_ROWS	This option causes the optimizer to used the cost-based approach on all SQL statements, even if there are no statistics available for the tables being accessed. This approach has the goal of best throughput, with the least amount of system resources being used.
FIRST_ROWS	This option causes the optimizer to use the cost-based approach on all SQL statements, even if no statistics are available for the tables being accessed. This approach has the goal of best response time.

> **NOTE**
>
> If the cost-based optimization approach is used and no internal statistics are available for a table that is being accessed, other information such as the number of data blocks in the table is used to estimate the cost of various operations.

Other optimizer parameters that can be set include the following:

Option	Description
OPTIMIZER_FEATURES_ENABLED	This parameter can be set to 8.0.0, 8.0.3, and 8.0.4. The effect of setting this parameter is to, in turn, set other initialization parameters. If set to 8.0.4, the following parameters are set to TRUE: PUSH_JOIN_PRED ICATE, FAST_FULL_SCAN_ENABLED, COMPLEX_VIEW_MERGING, and B_TREE_BITMAP_PLANS. If this parameter is set to 8.0.0 or 8.0.3, those other parameters are set to FALSE. They can, of course, be set independently. Note: This feature is new in Oracle8.0.4.
OPTIMIZER_PERCENT_PARALLEL	This parameter specifies the amount of parallelism that is used in the optimizer's cost function. By default, this parameter is 0, which favors serialized transactions or index scans. Setting this parameter to 100 will allow the optimizer to take into account each table's degree of parallelism, thus favoring table scans.
OPTIMIZER_SEARCH_LIMIT	Specifies the maximum number of tables in the FROM clause for which all possible join permutations are considered. By setting this low, the optimizer will spend less time considering different possibilities. In cases where there are a large number of tables in the FROM clause, the optimizer time can be significant.

By configuring the optimizer for your particular needs, you will achieve better results.

Optimization Methods

In general, the cost-based approach is the recommended approach. In most cases, the cost-based approach determines an execution plan that is as good or better than the rule-based approach. If you have manually tuned your SQL Statements, however, you may get better performance with rule-based optimization than with cost-based.

The rule-based approach can be useful if you are moving a highly tuned application from an older version of Oracle that has been using the rule-based approach. This and a lack of statistics may cause rule-based optimization to be more efficient than the cost-based approach. However, as you gather statistics on your database, you may want to migrate to cost-based optimization.

The following sections examine both approaches. Hints can also be very useful in optimizing the execution of your SQL statements.

Rule-Based Approach

The rule-based approach to Oracle optimization is the simpler of the two methods. In the rule-based approach, the execution plan is derived by examining the available paths and comparing them against a table of the rank of these paths. The table of costs is shown in Table 17.1.

TABLE 17.1. COST OF ACCESS PATHS FOR RULE-BASED OPTIMIZATION.

Rank	Access Path
1	Single row by ROWID
2	Single row by cluster join
3	Single row by hash cluster key with unique or primary key
4	Single row by unique or primary key
5	Cluster join
6	Hash cluster key
7	Indexed cluster key
8	Composite key
9	Single-column indexes
10	Bounded range search on indexed columns
11	Unbounded ranch search on indexed columns
12	Sort-merge join
13	MAX or MIN of indexed column
14	ORDER BY on indexed columns
15	Full table scan

Because the rule-based approach is based simply on the SQL statements themselves, it is unnecessary to have any statistics about the database tables. The rule-based approach follows these steps to determine the execution plan:

1. Determine the possible execution plans.
2. Rank the different plans according to Table 17.1.
3. Choose the approach with the lowest ranking.

In this way, the rule-based optimization approach is very efficient and works well. However, if statistics are available for your tables, clusters, or indexes, the cost-based approach can be very efficient.

Cost-Based Approach

The cost-based approach to optimization uses information about the structure and contents of your database to choose the most efficient execution plan. During the normal operation of the RDBMS, or by executing the ANALYZE command, statistics are gathered on the data distribution and storage characteristics or your database tables, clusters, and indexes. The cost-based optimizer uses this information to determine the most optimal execution plan.

This approach is done in three steps:

1. The optimizer generates a set of possible execution plans, just as the rule-based optimization approach does.
2. The cost of each plan is determined based on statistics gathered about the database. This cost is based on CPU time, I/O, and memory necessary to execute the plan.
3. The optimizer compares the costs and chooses the execution plan with the smallest cost based on your specifications.

> **NOTE**
>
> The number of tables in the FROM clause the optimizer uses to determine the best join permutation can be set by the initialization parameter OPTIMIZER_SEARCH_LIMIT as described next.

The default goal of the cost-based optimizer is to generate an execution plan that gives the best throughput. You can specify other optimization goals, including the following:

Optimization Goal	Description
Minimal Resources	This goal causes the optimizer to choose the execution plan that uses the least amount of system resources. This is done by selecting ALL_ROWS.
Best Response Time	This goal causes the optimizer to choose the execution plan that has the best response time. This is done by selecting FIRST_ROWS.

By choosing the optimization approach that best suits your particular installation and application, the performance of your SQL statements can be tuned to specifically meet your needs.

Using the ANALYZE Command

You can use the ANALYZE command to gather statistics about your system that can be used for the cost-based optimizer. This command can be used not only for statistics gathering but for other purposes as well. The ANALYZE command can be used to do the following:

Function	Description
Gather statistics	The ANALYZE command can be used to gather statistics about tables, clusters, and indexes to be used to assist the cost-based optimizer in choosing the best execution plan for your system.
Check data integrity	The ANALYZE command can be used to validate the integrity of the structure of a table, index, or cluster.
Chained-row statistics	The ANALYZE command can be used to gather statistics about the number of chained rows in a table or cluster.

The statistics gathered by the ANALYZE command can better help the optimizer make the correct choice in determining an execution plan.

How to Run the ANALYZE Command

How you run the ANALYZE command is determined by the type of statistics or analysis you want to perform. The ANALYZE command can be used in several different modes. The mode you choose depends on the data you want to gather as well as on the configuration of your system.

Using ANALYZE to Gather Statistics

You can use the ANALYZE command to gather statistics in one of two modes. The first mode scans the entire table, cluster, or index and calculates statistics exactly, based on your data. Although this is the most accurate method, it requires enough temporary space to hold and sort all the rows of the table or cluster (no space is required for an index). Computing the statistics also uses a great deal of system resources.

The second mode of the ANALYZE command estimates statistics. This method performs a sampling of the table, cluster, or index in order to estimate statistics. In this method, the entire table or cluster is not scanned; a portion of the data is used to determine the statistics. The amount of data used can be specified when you invoke the ANALYZE command.

Using ANALYZE to Compute Exact Statistics

To use the ANALYZE command to compute exact statistics, invoke ANALYZE with one of the following syntaxes.

For Tables:

```
ANALYZE TABLE table_name
    COMPUTE STATISTICS;
```

For Table Partitions:

```
ANALYZE TABLE table_name PARTITION ( partition_name )
    COMPUTE STATISTICS;
```

For Clusters:

```
ANALYZE CLUSTER cluster_name
    COMPUTE STATISTICS;
```

For Indexes:

```
ANALYZE INDEX index_name
    COMPUTE STATISTICS;
```

For Index Partitions:

```
ANALYZE INDEX index_name PARTITION ( partition_name )
    COMPUTE STATISTICS;
```

Using ANALYZE with the COMPUTE STATISTICS option scans the entire table, cluster, or index and computes exact statistics. When you compute the exact statistics, the resultant data is more accurate than that achieved by estimating the statistics; however, you use more system resources to get this information. When you compute statistics for tables and clusters, you must have enough temporary space to load and sort the entire table or cluster. You do not need this temporary space for indexes.

Using ANALYZE to Estimate Statistics

When you use the ANALYZE command to estimate statistics, Oracle does much less work and uses much less temporary space. To run the ANALYZE command to estimate statistics, use one of the following syntaxes.

For Tables:

```
ANALYZE TABLE table_name
    ESTIMATE STATISTICS;
```

For Table Partitions:

```
ANALYZE TABLE table_name PARTITION ( partition_name )
    ESTIMATE STATISTICS;
```

For Clusters:

```
ANALYZE CLUSTER cluster_name
    ESTIMATE STATISTICS;
```

For Indexes:

```
ANALYZE INDEX index_name
    ESTIMATE STATISTICS;
```

For Index Partitions:

```
ANALYZE INDEX index_name PARTITION ( partition_name )
    ESTIMATE STATISTICS;
```

When you use ANALYZE with the ESTIMATE STATISTICS option, Oracle scans a portion of the table, cluster, or index and computes estimated statistics. You can specify the amount of data scanned and used for statistics by including one or both of these additional parameters:

```
SAMPLE xxxx ROWS;
SAMPLE yy PERCENT;
```

Place the SAMPLE xxxx ROWS parameter at the end of the ANALYZE command, as follows:

```
ANALYZE TABLE table_name
    ESTIMATE STATISTICS
    SAMPLE 10000 ROWS;
```

Place the SAMPLE yy PERCENT parameter at the end of the ANALYZE command, as follows:

```
ANALYZE TABLE table_name
    ESTIMATE STATISTICS
    SAMPLE 40 PERCENT;
```

Although estimating statistics does not give you as accurate a representation as computing statistics does, the lesser amount of resources consumed usually makes estimating statistics a better choice. By making the percentage of data scanned as large as possible for your system, you can increase the effectiveness of the statistics you gather.

> **TIP**
>
> When analyzing both tables or indexes and their partitions, analyze the object first, and then the object's partitions.

Using ANALYZE to Check Structural Integrity

In addition to gather statistics, you can use the ANALYZE command to validate the structure of a table, cluster, or index. You should run this command only if you feel there is some problem with the structure of these objects. These problems can occur as the result of a hardware or software problem where data corruption may have occurred. Any problems can be found immediately by analyzing the structure of the schema objects, thus avoiding a system crash.

When you analyze the integrity of the structure of tables, clusters, or indexes, the command returns any structural problems. If there are problems with structure of these objects, you should drop the object, re-create it, and reload the data.

Using ANALYZE to Determine Chained Rows

You can also use the ANALYZE command to determine the extent and existence of chained or migrated rows in your table or cluster. The existence of chained or migrated rows can cause severe performance degradation and should be corrected.

17

QUERY AND
TRANSACTION
PROCESSING

SUMMARY OF THE ANALYZE COMMAND

As you have seen, the ANALYZE command can be quite useful for gathering statistics as well as for analyzing the structural integrity of tables, clusters, and indexes. The ANALYZE command can also be used to determine the existence and extent of chained and migrated rows. By using the ANALYZE command to gather statistics, the effectiveness of the cost-based optimizer can be increased; therefore, performance itself can be increased.

Data Dictionary Statistics

When you use the ANALYZE command to create statistics for the cost-based optimizer to use, these statistics are inserted into some internal Oracle performance tables. These tables can be queried through several views. Although these views provide essentially the same information, depending on the particular view you choose, the scope of the information changes slightly. The following views are prefixed with the characters:

View	Description
USER_	This view contains information about the objects owned by the user.
ALL_	This view contains information about the objects accessible by the user. These are objects owned by the user as well as objects with PUBLIC access.
DBA_	This view contains information on all objects in the system.

These views provide information about different parts of the system, such as tables, clusters, indexes, and columns. Following is a brief list of the views available that contain performance information:

- Table views: USER_TABLES, USER_PART_TABLES, ALL_TABLES, ALL_PART_TABLES, DBA_TABLES, DBA_PART_TABLES
- Cluster views: USER_CLUSTERS, ALL_CLUSTERS, DBA_CLUSTERS
- Index views: USER_INDEXES, USER_PART_INDEXES, ALL_INDEXES, ALL_PART_INDEXES, DBA_INDEXES, DBA_PART_INDEXES
- Column views: USER_TAB_COL_STATISTICS, USER_PART_COL_STATISTICS, ALL_TAB_COL_STATISTICS, ALL_PART_COL_STATISTICS, DBA_TAB_COL_STATISTICS, DBA_PART_COL_STATISTICS

The information contained in the internal tables referenced by these views is used by the optimizer to make decisions about which execution plan to take. The decision about which execution plan to take is also based on information about the size of the object and the data contained in the object. Some of the information contained in these tables is presented in Tables 17.2 through 17.7. Note: This is only a sample of the data in those tables;

TABLE 17.2. DATA FOR TABLES IN USER_TABLES, ALL_TABLES, DBA_TABLES.

Column	Description of Contents
AVG_SPACE	The average amount of free space in the table
AVG_ROW_LEN	The average length of a row
BLOCKS	The number of blocks in the table
CHAIN_CNT	The number of chained rows
EMPTY_BLOCKS	The number of blocks that have never been used
NUM_ROWS	The number of rows in the table

TABLE 17.3. DATA FOR TABLES IN USER_PART_TABLES, ALL__PART_TABLES, DBA_PART_TABLES.

Column	Description of Contents
OWNER	The owner of the object
TABLE_NAME	The name of the table
PARTITIONING_TYPE	The partitioning algorithm (RANGE)
PARTITIONING_COUNT	The number of partitions in the table

TABLE 17.4. DATA FOR CLUSTERS IN USER_CLUSTERS, ALL_CLUSTERS, DBA_CLUSTERS.

Column	Description of Contents
AVG_BLOCKS_PER_KEY	The average number of blocks that have rows that use the same key
CLUSTER_TYPE	The type of cluster: whether it is an index cluster or a hash cluster
HASHKEYS	The number of hash keys if it is a hash cluster

TABLE 17.5. DATA FOR INDEXES IN USER_INDEXES, ALL_INDEXES, DBA_INDEXES.

Column	Description of Contents
AVG_LEAF_BLOCKS_PER_KEY	The average number of leaf blocks per key
AVG_DATA_BLOCKS_PER_KEY	The average number of data blocks per key
BLEVEL	The level of the B-Tree
CLUSTERING_FACTOR	The amount of order or disorder in the table the index is referencing
DISTINCT_KEYS	The number of distinct keys in the index
LEAF_BLOCKS	The number of leaf blocks (lowest level index blocks) in the index
UNIQUENESS	States whether the index is UNIQUE or NONUNIQUE

TABLE 17.6. DATA FOR INDEXES IN USER_PART_INDEXES, ALL_PART_INDEXES, DBA_PART_INDEXES.

Column	Description of Contents
OWNER	The owner of the object
TABLE_NAME	The name of the table
PARTITIONING_TYPE	The partitioning algorithm (RANGE)

TABLE 17.7. COLUMN DATA IN USER_TAB_COL_STATISTICS, ALL_TAB_COL_STATISTICS, DBA_TAB_COL_STATISTICS.

Column	Description of Contents
DENSITY	The density of the column (rows per data block)
HIGH_VALUE	The highest value in this column of the table
LOW_VALUE	The second-lowest value in this column of the table
NUM_DISTINCT	The number of distinct values in this column of the table

TABLE 17.8. COLUMN DATA IN USER_PART_COL_STATISTICS, ALL_PART_COL_STATISTICS, DBA_PART_COL_STATISTICS.

Column	Description of Contents
TABLE_NAME	The name of the table
PARTITION_NAME	The table partition name
DENSITY	The density of the column (rows per data block)
HIGH_VALUE	The highest value in this column of the table
LOW_VALUE	The second-lowest value in this column of the table
NUM_DISTINCT	The number of distinct values in this column of the table

With this information, the optimizer can more precisely determine the optimal execution path based on data about your specific system. When you run the ANALYZE command with the ESTIMATE STATISTICS option, many of these values are estimates rather than actual computed results.

Analyzing SQL Statements

Badly tuned SQL statements tend to access the database in a very inefficient way, causing unnecessary amounts of data to be scanned and transferred across the network. Badly tuned statements can cause a well-tuned server to expend large amounts of unnecessary processing power and I/O resources.

You can identify badly tuned SQL statements with the Oracle EXPLAIN PLAN command and SQL*Trace facility. Some of the attributes of a badly tuned SQL statement are the following:

- *Indexes are not used.* If a query is not properly formed, you may bypass an index that could be used to reduce I/O and CPU processing.
- *Hashing is bypassed.* If a hashed cluster is improperly accessed, performance could be severely degraded.
- *Unnecessary table scans are performed.* If the SQL statement is improperly formed, you may be doing unnecessary table scans.
- *Range partitions are not used.* If the SQL statement does not contain the partitioning key column in the WHERE clause, range partitioning will be bypassed.
- *Unnecessary amounts of data are returned.* This is an unnecessary burden not only on the network but on the application as well.

These attributes should alert you to the fact that the SQL statements are not optimally tuned for the task being done. If your SQL statement exhibits any of these characteristics, you should make some correction to the statement.

In addition to looking at the SQL statement itself, you should also look at the effect of the SQL statements. In many cases, some detail that is unimportant by itself can become a problem when the application and SQL statements are run by hundreds or thousands of users at the same time. The effect of this can be a bottleneck on a specific table or even a specific row. Here is a list of some things to look for when analyzing the effect of the SQL statements:

- *Is the SQL statement updating a specific row?* If you update a specific row as a counter, it may cause a bottleneck.
- *Where is the majority of the table activity?* Is a specific table being heavily accessed? This could indicate an I/O bottleneck.
- *Is there significant* INSERT *activity?* Is it all to one table? This may indicate a contention problem on a certain table.
- *How much activity is there?* Can the system handle it? You may find that the SQL statements overload your particular system.

These are just a few of the things to consider when looking at the effects of the application on the system. I have seen cases in which an application, fully tested in the lab, moves into production and fails because it was tested with only one or two users. It is important to take into account the effect of hundreds or thousands of users simultaneously accessing the application.

Analyzing the SQL statements can be done with the Oracle tools SQL Trace and EXPLAIN PLAN. These are independent tools, but SQL Trace can be run in such a manner as to automatically run EXPLAIN PLAN.

Using EXPLAIN PLAN and SQL Trace

Probably the best way to determine whether your SQL statements are properly optimized is by using the Oracle SQL Trace facility and the EXPLAIN PLAN command. You can use the SQL Trace facility and the Oracle program TKPROF, which is used to translate trace files, to trace production SQL statements and gather statistics about those statements.

You use SQL Trace to gather information into a trace file; the Oracle program TKPROF formats the trace information into useful, understandable data.

The EXPLAIN PLAN command is used to display the execution plan chosen by the Oracle optimizer. After using EXPLAIN PLAN, you can rewrite your SQL statements to take better advantage of such things as indexes and hash keys. By analyzing the output, you may be able to provide hints that the Oracle optimizer can use to take better advantage of your knowledge of your data. By using hints, you may be able to take better advantage of features such as the Oracle Parallel Query option.

SQL Trace

The SQL Trace facility and the Oracle program TKPROF are designed to give performance information about individual SQL statements. You can use this information to determine the characteristics of those statements.

You can enable SQL Trace for a session or for an entire instance. Of course, because this facility gathers an abundance of information about SQL statement functionality and performance, SQL Trace has an effect on the performance of the system. If you use SQL Trace on a single session, the effect is fairly minimal, but if you use SQL Trace on an entire instance, you will see a substantial effect on the performance of the system. Avoid running SQL Trace on an entire instance for this reason.

SQL Trace Initialization

Before you run SQL Trace, you must make sure that certain Oracle initialization parameters are set:

Parameter	Description
TIMED_STATISTICS	Setting TIMED_STATISTICS=TRUE enables SQL Trace and some of the dynamic performance tables to collect timed statistics such as CPU and elapsed times. Enabling timed statistics incurs significant overhead, because most Oracle operations are now being timed, and should be avoided except when necessary.
MAX_DUMP_FILE_SIZE	Specifies the maximum size of trace file dumps in OS blocks. Set this fairly low to avoid filling up the file system with trace files. If the SQL Trace output files are being truncated, increase this value.
USER_DUMP_DEST	This parameter specifies the destination for the trace file. The default destination is the same as for system dumps on your OS.

You can turn SQL Trace on and off on a per-session basis by using the ALTER SESSION command or on an entire instance by setting the Oracle initialization parameter SQL_TRACE to TRUE. By setting SQL Trace on a session, you can see the resources of a particular task. By setting SQL Trace on for the entire instance, you can view information on all tasks.

SQL Trace Functionality

Once SQL Trace is enabled, it gathers the following information:

- *Parse, execute, and fetch counts.* These counts can give you vital information about the efficiency of the SQL statements.

- *CPU and elapsed times*. This information can tell you which statements take the most time to execute.
- *Physical and logical reads*. This information can help you determine the effectiveness of the database buffer pool.
- *Number of rows processed*. This information can be used as an indication that more rows are being processed than you expected, thus indicating a problem.
- *Library cache misses*. This information can show you the effectiveness of the shared SQL area and how well you are reusing already parsed SQL statements.

SQL Trace puts this information into a trace file in an unreadable form. You then use the Oracle program TKPROF to format the trace information into useful, understandable data.

Interpreting SQL Trace

This section looks at some of the statistics available from SQL Trace and how to interpret them. For each SQL statement executed, SQL Trace provides the following information:

Parameter	Description
count	Number of times the OCI procedure was executed. (The OCI interface is the standard set of calls used to access the Oracle database.)
cpu	CPU time in seconds executing. This value is the amount of time Oracle uses to process the statement.
elapsed	Elapsed time in seconds executing. This value is equivalent to the user's response time.
disk	Number of physical reads of buffers from disk. This value tells you how many reads actually missed the buffer cache and had to go to physical disk.
query	Number of buffers gotten for consistent read. This value represents the number of buffers retrieved in consistent mode. Consistent mode guarantees consistent reads throughout the transaction; it is used for most queries.
current	Number of buffers gotten in current mode (usually for update). In current mode, the data blocks gotten reflect the value at that instant in time.
rows	Number of rows processed by the fetch or execute call. This value gives you an idea of how many instructions have been executed.

By looking at each of these parameters, you can get an idea of how your SQL statements are being processed and which statements are taking the most time. By analyzing which statements are taking the longest, you may be able to find some inefficiencies you can correct.

Using EXPLAIN PLAN

The EXPLAIN PLAN command shows you the execution plan the Oracle optimizer has chosen for your SQL statements. With this information, you can determine whether the Oracle optimizer has chosen the correct execution plan based on your knowledge of the data and the application. You can also use EXPLAIN PLAN to determine whether any additional optimization should be done to your database (for example, the addition of an index or the use of a cluster).

The EXPLAIN PLAN command is used to display the execution plan chosen by the Oracle optimizer for SELECT, UPDATE, INSERT, and DELETE statements. After using EXPLAIN PLAN, you can rewrite your SQL statements and see whether the new SQL statement is better optimized than the original statement. By analyzing the output, you may be able to provide hints the Oracle optimizer can use to better take advantage of the data. By using hints, you can take better advantage of features such as the Oracle Parallel Query option.

EXPLAIN PLAN Initialization

When you run SQL statements with the EXPLAIN PLAN command, the output of EXPLAIN PLAN is put into a table with the default name plan_table. You must create this table before you can run EXPLAIN PLAN. The table can be created in one of two ways:

- Use the UTLXPLAN.SQL script provided by Oracle.
- Create the plan_table table by hand.

The plan_table table is defined as follows:

```
SQL> describe plan_table
 Name                            Null?    Type
 ------------------------------- -------- ----
 STATEMENT_ID                             VARCHAR2(30)
 TIMESTAMP                                DATE
 REMARKS                                  VARCHAR2(80)
 OPERATION                                VARCHAR2(30)
 OPTIONS                                  VARCHAR2(30)
 OBJECT_NODE                              VARCHAR2(128)
 OBJECT_OWNER                             VARCHAR2(30)
 OBJECT_NAME                              VARCHAR2(30)
 OBJECT_INSTANCE                          NUMBER(38)
 OBJECT_TYPE                              VARCHAR2(30)
 OPTIMIZER                                VARCHAR2(255)
```

```
SEARCH_COLUMNS                         NUMBER
ID                                     NUMBER(38)
PARENT_ID                              NUMBER(38)
POSITION                               NUMBER(38)
COST                                   NUMBER(38)
CARDINALITY                            NUMBER(38)
BYTES                                  NUMBER(38)
OTHER_TAG                              VARCHAR2(255)
PARTITION_START                        VARCHAR2(255)
PARTITION_STOP                         VARCHAR2(255)
PARTITION_ID                           NUMBER(38)
OTHER                                  LONG

SQL>
```

You do not have to name the table `plan_table`. You can direct EXPLAIN PLAN to use a table of another name if you want.

Invoking EXPLAIN PLAN

Invoke the EXPLAIN PLAN command with the following Oracle command sequence:

```
EXPLAIN PLAN
    SET STATEMENT_ID = 'myplan'
    INTO plan_table
    FOR
        SQL Statement;
```

STATEMENT_ID should reflect the statement's function so you can recognize it at a later time. The plan_table parameter is the name of the table you created as described in the preceding section. If the INTO clause is omitted, the command defaults to the name plan_table.

Here is an example of a completed command:

```
SQL> EXPLAIN PLAN
  2   SET statement_id = 'myplan'
  3   FOR
  4   SELECT *
  5   FROM perftable, perftable2, perftable3
  6   WHERE perftable.id1 = perftable2.id1
  7   AND perftable.id2 > 5000
  8   AND perftable3.id1 > 100 AND perftable3.id1 < 400
  9   ORDER BY perftable.id1;

Explained.
```

The results of the EXPLAIN PLAN are written into the table `plan_table`. The following section explains how to retrieve the information in that table.

Extracting EXPLAIN PLAN Results

The output of EXPLAIN PLAN is written to the table specified in the EXPLAIN PLAN command (by default, to the table named plan_table). You must extract this information in order to look at the results of EXPLAIN PLAN. The results can be displayed with a query such as this:

```
SELECT SUBSTR(LPAD(' ',2*(LEVEL-1))||operation,1,30)
||' '||SUBSTR(options,1,15)
||' '||SUBSTR(object_name,1,15)
||' '||SUBSTR(DECODE(id, 0, 'Cost = '||position),1,12)
"Statement Execution Plan",
SUBSTR(optimizer, 1, 10) "Optimizer"
FROM
    plan_table
START WITH
    id = 0 AND statement_id = 'myplan'
CONNECT BY PRIOR
    id = parent_id
AND
    statement_id = 'myplan';
```

This query results in the following output:

```
Statement Execution Plan
Optimizer
-------------------------------------------------------------- --------
SELECT STATEMENT    Cost = 25012                                CHOOSE
  MERGE JOIN
    SORT JOIN
      MERGE JOIN CARTESIAN
        TABLE ACCESS FULL PERFTABLE
        SORT JOIN
          TABLE ACCESS FULL PERFTABLE3
ANALYZED
    SORT JOIN
      TABLE ACCESS FULL PERFTABLE2

9 rows selected.
```

If the optimizer had chosen a cost-based approach, the cost of the query would have been reflected in the first line of the optimization plan. Any features such as parallel query are also reflected here.

With this information, you can tell whether your SQL statements take advantage of indexes, clusters, or hash clusters. If you use EXPLAIN PLAN, you can see precisely how your SQL statement is being executed and what effect any changes you make to the SQL statements have on the execution plan. Changing your SQL statements to take advantage of an index or a cluster, for example, will show an immediate improvement. EXPLAIN

PLAN output is ideal for pointing out your execution plan and may indicate that where you thought that you were taking advantage of an index, you actually were not.

Designing New SQL Statements

Although this part of the chapter is directed at tuning SQL statements associated with new applications, it may be appropriate for you to make these changes to existing applications if you have the flexibility to do so. The reason these guidelines are separate is because many of them involve not only tuning the SQL statements and application, but changing the database schema as well.

In the design stage, it is important to plan the application and the database design together. By properly designing the application to take advantage of the design and features of the database, you can take optimal advantage of both of them. At the same time, the database should be designed to function properly with the application that uses it. The design of the database should reflect the purpose of the application. The following sections look at some of the optimizations that are possible.

Using Indexes

One of the most powerful performance enhancing features available in an RDBMS is the index. The index can greatly reduce the number of I/Os necessary to retrieve the requested data and thus greatly improve performance. It is necessary, however, to coordinate the use of the index between the database designer and the application designer. By not carefully coordinating, the two indexes may be bypassed when a small change in SQL coding may be able to take advantage of the index. Remember that the more indexes on a table, the more overhead is incurred during updates, inserts, and deletes. It is important to index selectively.

What Tables Should Be Indexed?

Use the following guidelines to decide which tables to index:

- Index tables when queries select only a small number of rows. Queries that select a large number of rows defeat the purpose of the index. Index the table when queries access less than 5 percent of the rows in the table.

- Don't index tables that are frequently updated. Updates, inserts, and deletes on indexed tables incur extra overhead. Base your decision about whether or not to index a table on the number of updates, inserts, and deletes relative to the total number of queries to the table. If the table is frequently accessed as well as updated, you may or may not choose to index it.

- Index tables that don't have duplicate values on the columns usually selected in WHERE clauses. Tables for which the selection is based on TRUE/FALSE values are not good candidates for an index.

- Index tables that are queried with relatively simple WHERE clauses. Complex WHERE clauses may not be able to take advantage of indexes. This may be solved by creating a complex index, by simplifying the SQL statement, or by using a hint.

Once you decide to use an index, you must then decide on which columns to put the index. You may index one or more columns, depending on the table.

What Columns Should Be Indexed?

Use the following guidelines to decide which columns to index:

- Choose columns frequently specified in WHERE clauses. Frequently accessed columns can most benefit from indexes.

- Don't index columns that do not have many unique values. Columns in which a good percentage of rows are duplicates cannot take advantage of indexing.

- Columns that have mostly unique values are excellent candidates for indexing. Oracle automatically indexes columns that are unique or that are primary keys defined with constraints. These columns are most effectively optimized by indexes.

- Index columns that are foreign keys of referential integrity constraints in cases where large numbers of concurrent INSERT, UPDATE, and DELETE statements access both the parent and child tables. Such an index allows the child table to be updated without having to lock the parent table.

- Columns that are commonly used to join tables are good candidates for indexing.

- Frequently modified columns probably should not be index columns because of the overhead involved in updating the index.

> **NOTE**
>
> Remember that some penalty is associated with performing INSERT, UPDATE, and DELETE statements on columns that are indexed. If you have a lot of those statements, an index may hurt more than help. Use SQL Trace on the SQL statements that access tables both with and without an index. Compare the results.

Composite Indexes

Composite indexes may be more effective than individual indexes in situations such as the following:

- When two columns are not unique individually but are unique together, composite indexes may work very well. For example, columns A and B have few unique values, but rows with a particular A AND B are mostly unique. Look for WHERE clauses with AND operators.
- If all values of a SELECT statement are in a composite index, the table is not queried; the result is returned from the index.
- If several different queries select the same rows by using different WHERE clauses based on different columns, consider creating a composite index with *all* those columns used in the WHERE statements.

If carefully designed, composite indexes can be quite useful. As with single-column indexes, they are most effective if applications are written with the indexes in mind.

Once you create the index, periodically use SQL Trace to determine whether your queries are taking advantage of the index. It may be worth the effort to try the query with and without indexes and compare the results to see whether the index is worth the space it is using.

How to Avoid an Index

If you have an application that can take advantage of an index, but contains a few SQL statements that result in poor performance when they use an index, you can tell the optimizer to bypass the index. There are several ways this can be done:

- Write the SQL statement to avoid using a SELECT statement on an indexed column. By not selecting the column or set of columns that are indexed, you avoid the index.
- Use hints. When you use hints in your SQL statements, you can tell the optimizer not to use the index for this particular SQL statement.

In this manner, you can design your database to effectively use indexes and have the flexibility to avoid the index when it is not optimal to do so.

Clusters

Oracle clusters allow tables that are frequently accessed together (as with join operations), to be stored together. These clusters can be defined to be index clusters or hash clusters. With index clusters, the key value that the cluster is arranged around is indexed with hash clusters, the key value is hashed.

Clusters can be advantageous in certain situations and disadvantageous in others. You must be careful in determining whether a cluster can help performance in your configuration. Typically, clusters are advantageous if the clustered, related data is used primarily in joins because the data to be used in the join is retrieved together in one I/O operation.

If you have two tables with related data that are frequently accessed together, having a cluster can improve performance by preloading the related data into the SGA. Because you frequently use the data together, having that data already in the SGA greatly reduces access time.

If you do not typically use the information together, you will find no performance benefit from using a cluster. There is even a slight disadvantage because the SGA space is taken up by the additional table information.

Another disadvantage of clusters is a reduction in the performance of INSERT statements. This happens because of the additional complexity of the use of space and because there are multiple tables in the same block. The clustered table also spans more blocks than the individual table would, causing more data to be scanned.

Hash Clusters

A *hash cluster* is similar to a cluster but uses a hash function rather than an index to reference the cluster key. A hash cluster stores the data based on the result of a *hash function* (a numeric function that determines the data block in the cluster based on the value of the cluster key).

To find the data block in an index cluster, there must first be one or more I/Os to the cluster index to find the correct data block. In a hash cluster, the cluster key itself tells Oracle where the data block is. This arrangement can reduce to one the number of I/Os required to retrieve the row.

In contrast to the index cluster, which stores related data together based on the row's cluster key value, the hash cluster stores related rows together based on their hash values.

The decision to use hash clusters is an important one. Hash clusters can be beneficial because, when they are effectively used, the requested data can be retrieved in just one I/O. Unfortunately, if a hash cluster is used on a table that is not a good candidate for hashing, performance can be severely degraded.

Although hash clusters can be used in a similar fashion to index clusters, you do not have to cluster the tables to use a hash cluster. In fact, in many cases, it is useful to create a single table as a hash cluster. By using hashing, you can retrieve your data with a single I/O rather than the multiple I/Os required to retrieve the same data using a B^*-Tree index.

Because hashing uses the value of the data to calculate the data block the desired data is in, hashing is best used on tables that have unique values for the cluster key and that are queried primarily by equality queries on the cluster key. In the case of equality queries, the data is usually retrieved in one read operation. The cluster key need not be a single column; if the typical query uses an equality on a set of columns, use these columns to create a composite key.

A good candidate for hashing has the following properties:

- *Unique cluster keys*. Hashing performs best when the value of the cluster key is fairly unique. Because the data is laid out based on the key value, a column with a lot of duplicates is not a good candidate for the hash key.

- *Equality queries*. The majority of queries are equality queries on the cluster key. This type of query reaps the greatest benefit from the hash cluster.

- *Static size*. Hashing is optimal when the table or tables are fairly static in size. If the table stays within its initial storage allocation, you do not see any performance degradation from using a hash cluster; but if the table grows out of its initial allocation, performance can degrade. In this case, overflow blocks are required.

- *Constant cluster key*. Hashing can also degrade performance when the value of the cluster key changes. Because the location of the block in which the data resides is based on the cluster key value, a change in that value can cause the row to migrate to maintain the cluster.

- *No table scans*. Hashing can degrade the performance of table scans because the scan must read blocks that may not have much data in them. Because the table is originally created by laying out the data in the cluster based on the value of the cluster key, there may be some blocks that have few rows.

Do not use a hash cluster on a table if the application frequently modifies the cluster key or the table is constantly being modified. Because the cluster key is based on a calculation, you can incur significant overhead by constantly recalculating the key.

Anytime you have a somewhat static table with a unique column value or set of column values, consider creating a hash cluster.

Range Partitioning

A *range partition* allows you to divide the data in tables into separate pieces or *ranges* based on the value of data in a column or number of columns. By partitioning data in cases where table scans are common, such as data warehouses, you may be able to reduce the amount of data that is scanned.

You will be able to take advantage of these ranges by carefully coordinating the application and the database's partitions. If the column that is specified in the range partition is used in the WHERE clause of a query, the optimizer will be able to convert a table scan into a range scan, where only certain partitions are scanned. This can reduce the amount of data being read dramatically. Any reduction in I/O is always a performance winner.

Packages, Procedures, and Functions

Another way to improve performance of your SQL statements is by using packages, procedures, and functions. Packages can help improve performance by storing together procedures and functions that are often used together. By storing these elements together, you can reduce the I/O required to bring them into memory from disk. Because these elements are often used together, they can also be loaded from disk together.

By using stored procedures, you benefit in several ways. Stored procedures allow you to reduce the amount of data sent across the network. The stored procedure requires fewer instructions to be sent to the server; in many cases, less data must be sent back to the client from the server.

A second benefit of a stored procedure is the increased chance that the SQL statement can be used by other processes. Because the SQL statement is defined and used by many processes, chances are good that the SQL statement will already be parsed in the shared SQL area and available to other users.

Using Hints

The Oracle optimizer is very efficient and works quite well to produce the best execution plan for your SQL statements based on the information with which it has to work. The optimizer does not, however, have the amount of information about your database and your data that you do. This is why Oracle allows you to use hints to tell the optimizer what kind of operations will be more efficient based on knowledge you have about your database and your data.

By using hints, you can tell the optimizer such things as these:

- The best optimization approach for a particular SQL statement
- The goal of the cost-based approach for an SQL statement
- The access path for a statement
- When table scans are more efficient than the use of indexes
- The join order for a statement
- A join operation in a join statement
- The degree of parallelism in a parallel query statement

By using hints, you can use specific information you know about your data and database to further enhance the performance on certain SQL statements. With hints, you can enhance specific operations that might otherwise be inefficient. Here are some examples of conditions in which hints may significantly improve performance:

- *Indexed columns with a large number of duplicate values.* Telling the optimizer to bypass the index when the value is one you know has a large number of duplicates is more efficient than letting the optimizer use the index.
- *Table access that performs a large table scan.* By specifying a larger number of parallel query servers, you can improve performance.
- *Table access that performs a small table scan.* If you know that the amount of data to be scanned is small, you may want to disable the parallel query option for this particular operation.

These are just a few of the exceptional conditions in which the default optimization may not be efficient. The information you know about your data and application can be used to make more efficient optimization choices.

Because you know more about your data and your application than the Oracle optimizer does, you can make significant improvements to the execution plan of the SQL statements. The Oracle optimizer is very efficient and works quite well to produce the best execution plan for your SQL statements based on the information with which it has to work; however, anything you can do to give the optimizer additional information about the execution process will help performance

Summary

When SQL statements are executed, the Oracle optimizer determines the execution plan based on the available data. The Oracle optimizer uses the optimization approach specified in the initialization parameters to determine the execution plan, as you have seen in this chapter.

The effectiveness of the execution plan depends on the optimization method chosen and the availability of good statistics for your database. When using the cost-based optimization approach, the effectiveness of the optimization can be enhanced by including more and better database performance statistics. This chapter described the various optimization approaches, methods of displaying the execution plan, and how to improve SQL performance. By taking advantage of features in Oracle such as the Parallel Query Option, indexes, and range partitioning, you can greatly enhance your performance.
Implementing these features will work only if your SQL statements are coordinated with the features in order to take advantage of them.

Supplied PL/SQL Packages

by Ivan Oss

IN THIS CHAPTER

Introduction to Supplied Packages

Any Oracle application developer or DBA knows how useful PL/SQL is for combining DML statements with the features of a procedural language. PL/SQL is a powerful language for building transactional applications, but how do you perform operations like scheduling jobs or writing files to the operating system or creating objects? The answer is, of course, the packages provided with PL/SQL. These packages allow you to perform a variety of useful tasks that extend the functionality of the language. Among others, these tasks include:

- Writing and reading from files.
- Manipulating LOB data.
- Issuing DDL and dynamic SQL statements.
- Communicating between processes.
- Scheduling jobs.

These packages extend the basic features of PL/SQL and make it a powerful language for developing database applications. There are also packages designed to address other areas of functionality, such as remote procedure calls and user-defined locking. The packages covered here are among the most useful and commonly applied. Application developers and DBAs should familiarize themselves with these packages in order to get the most out of their Oracle databases.

In PL/SQL 8.0, some new packages are introduced that address issues such as more robust job queuing and the reading and writing of LOBs. These packages will be discussed in detail, along with some of the more important standard packages of earlier PL/SQL releases.

I have grouped the packages by the tasks they perform. Hopefully this format will make them easy to find when you know what you need to accomplish, but don't know which package to use. This chapter provides quick references for packages' syntax and a basic conceptual overview of their use.

Creating the Packages

The supplied packages are stored in two files: the package headers and the package bodies. The package bodies are in a wrapped format that is unreadable, but the package headers are a useful source of information because they contain programmer comments and parameter requirements. The location of these files depends on the operating system. On UNIX systems, they are in $ORACLE_HOME/rdbms/admin and are created by running `catproc.sql` as SYS from that same directory. The user of the packages must have EXECUTE permission or be connected as SYS. There are public synonyms for the packages, so it's not necessary to prefix their names with SYS when calling them.

Package Summaries

The following is a syntactical summary of packages that address the major areas of functionality. They are arranged by their function, and there are brief examples of their use.

Reading From and Writing To Files

Applications developed for in PL/SQL usually retrieve and store data in the database itself, and interaction with the operating system is limited to the database's physical storage activities. One might think there is no way to access the database by any other means than SQL statements, but there are other ways. Imagine writing a sentence like "Initiate backup sequence" to a file on the operating system and having the database respond by running all the necessary steps for a hot backup. Such a task would be easy if you were using the UTL_FILE package. The database engine becomes a freeform writer and reader of data generated by all manner of processes through this simple interface.

UTL_FILE

This package allows you to write to and read from files on the operating system. You might want to write to the operating system when logging events or creating reports. You could also use it as a debugging tool. UTL_FILE's counterpart TEXT_IO is used for client-side I/O.

To use UTL_FILE, the operating system user that the Oracle RDBMS is running under must have the appropriate rights at the operating system level because this is the user that performs all reads and writes. Also, the directory being written to must be registered in the init.ora file. Several directories can be registered:

```
UTL_FILE_DIR = /u01/app/oracle/logs
UTL_FILE_DIR = /u01/app/oracle/admin/prod/bdump
UTL_FILE_DIR = *
```

> **NOTE**
>
> TEXT_IO enforces no database-level security. All of the following procedures apply to TEXT_IO as well.

```
FUNCTION FOPEN(
    location IN VARCHAR2,
    filename IN VARCHAR2,
    open_mode IN VARCHAR2)
RETURN FILE_TYPE;
```

location	The directory path where the file either exists or is to be created. This value must be quoted (for example, '/u01/app/oracle').
filename	The name of the file. If open_mode is 'w', an existing file of the same name will be overwritten.
open_mode	The mode to open the file in: 'r' opens the file for reading text. 'w' creates the file and keeps it open for writing. 'a' creates or opens the file for appending text.
return value	The file handle used to identify the file in later procedure calls.

Exceptions:

```
UTL_FILE.INVALID_PATH
UTL_FILE.INVALID_MODE
UTL_FILE.INVALID_OPERATION
UTL_FILE.INTERNAL_ERROR
```

> **NOTE**
>
> UTL_FILE.INTERNAL_ERROR may be raised for any UTL_FILE procedure or function.

FOPEN is the first operation that must be performed when reading from or writing to a file. A file that is opened in write mode cannot be read from, and vice-versa. The file must first be closed and then reopened in the new mode.

```
PROCEDURE FCLOSE(
    file_handle IN FILE_TYPE);
```

file_handle	File handle returned from FOPEN.

Exceptions:

```
UTL_FILE.WITE_ERROR
UTL_FILE.INVALID_FILEHANDLE
```

> **CAUTION**
>
> All files that are opened should also be closed to ensure that pending changes are written from the buffer into the file.

```
PROCEDURE FCLOSE_ALL;
```

Exceptions:

```
UTL_FILE.WRITE_ERROR
```

This procedure applies all pending changes and closes all opened files. It requires no parameters and has no return value. FCLOSE_ALL is usually used for cleanup.

```
FUNCTION IS_OPEN(
     file_handle IN FILE_TYPE)
RETURN BOOLEAN;
```

This function returns a TRUE if the file is open and a FALSE if it is not. No exceptions can be raised except possibly UTL_FILE.INTERNAL_ERROR.

```
PROCEDURE PUT(file_handle IN FILE_TYPE,
        buffer IN VARCHAR2);
```

file_handle	File handle returned by FOPEN.
buffer	String to be written to file.

Exceptions:

```
UTL_FILE.INVALID_FILEHANDLE
UTL_FILE.INVALID_OPERATION
UTL_FILE.WRITE_ERROR
```

A string can be written to a file opened in the 'w' or 'a' mode using this procedure. It appends the string to an existing line and will not create a new line character. Use NEW_LINE or PUT_LINE to create a line terminator.

```
PROCEDURE NEW_LINE(
     file_handle IN FILE_TYPE,
     lines IN NATURAL := 1);
```

file_handle	File handle returned by FOPEN.
lines	Number of line terminators to create. Default is 1.

Exceptions:

```
UTL_FILE.INVALID_FILEHANDLE
UTL_FILE.INVALID_OPERATION
```

This procedure inserts the number of line terminators specified by *lines*. The operating system determines the type of termination character to use.

```
PROCEDURE PUT_LINE(
     file_handle IN FILE_TYPE,
     buffer IN VARCHAR2);
```

This procedure is identical to PUT, except that it appends a single-line terminator after the specified input string.

```
PROCEDURE PUTF(
    file_handle IN FILE_TYPE,
    format IN VARCHAR2,
    arg1 IN VARCHAR2 default NULL,
    arg2 IN VARCHAR2 default NULL,
    arg3 IN VARCHAR2 default NULL,
    arg4 IN VARCHAR2 default NULL,
    arg5 IN VARCHAR2 default NULL);
```

file_handle	File handle returned by FOPEN.
format	String and special characters /n and %s.
arg1—5	Substitutions for %s in the format value.

Exceptions:

```
UTL_FILE.WRITE_ERROR
UTL_FILE.INVALID_OPERATION
```

This procedure allows a formatted string to be inserted into the file in the same manner as the C function *printf()*. Up to five substitutions using %s can be performed. Substitution strings are provided at the end of the *format* string as *arg1* through 5. A substitution string without a corresponding argument is replaced with a NULL. /n is interpreted as a new line character.

```
PROCEDURE FFLUSH(
    file_handle IN FILE_TYPE);
```

Exceptions:

```
UTL_FILE.INVALID_HANDLE
UTL_FILE.INVALID_OPERATION
UTL_FILE.WRITE_ERROR
```

Use FFLUSH to flush the output buffer and write it to the file. Normally, all writes are buffered until the buffer reaches max capacity. Only FCLOSE, FCLOSE_ALL, or FFLUSH will flush this buffer if it is not full.

```
PROCEDURE GET_LINE(
    file_handle IN FILE_TYPE,
    buffer OUT VARCHAR2);
```

Exceptions:

```
UTL_FILE.INVALID_FILEHANDLE
UTL_FILE.INVALID_OPERATION
UTL_FILE.NO_DATA_FOUND
UTL_FILE.READ_ERROR
UTL_FILE.VALUE_ERROR
```

This procedure returns the next line from a file in *buffer*. If the line is empty, NULL is returned. If the line does not fit in *buffer*, VALUE_ERROR is raised. After the end of the file is reached, NO_DATA_FOUND is raised.

Here is a simple example of how UTL_FILE works:

```
-- Lets mess around a bit with UTL file.
DECLARE

Directory VARCHAR2(50);
Filename  VARCHAR2(30);
Message   VARCHAR2(255);
Garbage   VARCHAR2(255);
ReturnedLine VARCHAR2(255);
Counter NUMBER;

-- You must declare a variable of the following type to hold the file
identifier
-- returned by UTL_FILE.FOPEN

FileHandle UTL_FILE.FILE_TYPE;

BEGIN
    Directory := '/u01/app/oracle/logs' ;
    Filename := 'test.log' ;
    Message := 'Maybe this will do it.' ;
    Garbage :=
'lfkdsafldgjfhfdkldsakfjlkjsalkdaosskfwlamffkmewkfmwlmfmfkewmkefmwkm';

    FileHandle := UTL_FILE.FOPEN(Directory, Filename, 'w');

    UTL_FILE.PUT(FileHandle, 'This thing actually seems to work!!');
    UTL_FILE.PUT(FileHandle, ' I wonder if I can break it.');
    UTL_FILE.NEW_LINE(FileHandle, 2);
    UTL_FILE.PUT_LINE(FileHandle, Message);
    UTL_FILE.PUTF(FileHandle, 'Still not broken eh?  Well take this! %s!
And this! %s!\n\n', Garbage, Garbage);

    -- Remember to close the file

    UTL_FILE.FCLOSE(FileHandle);

        -- We've written to a file, now let's see if we can get stuff back
out of it.
    -- First we have to open it in read mode.

    FileHandle := UTL_FILE.FOPEN(Directory, Filename, 'r');

    -- Then we read the first line.

    UTL_FILE.GET_LINE(FileHandle, ReturnedLine);
```

```
-- Close the file and open it again in append mode.

    UTL_FILE.FCLOSE(FileHandle);
FileHandle := UTL_FILE.FOPEN(Directory, Filename, 'a');

-- Write the line we got back to the file 10 times - for proof it
worked.

Counter := 0;
    WHILE Counter < 10 LOOP
    UTL_FILE.PUT_LINE(FileHandle, ReturnedLine);
        Counter := Counter + 1;
END LOOP;
UTL_FILE.FCLOSE(FileHandle);

EXCEPTION

    WHEN UTL_FILE.INVALID_PATH THEN
        RAISE_APPLICATION_ERROR(-20100, 'Invalid Path');

    WHEN UTL_FILE.INVALID_MODE THEN
        RAISE_APPLICATION_ERROR(-20101, 'Invalid Mode');

    WHEN UTL_FILE.INVALID_FILEHANDLE THEN
        RAISE_APPLICATION_ERROR(-20102, 'Invalid Filehandle');

    WHEN UTL_FILE.INVALID_OPERATION THEN
        RAISE_APPLICATION_ERROR(-20103, 'Invalid Operation');

    WHEN OTHERS THEN
        UTL_FILE.FCLOSE(FileHandle);
        RAISE;
END;
/
```

The following is the contents of the file the preceding code would generate:

```
This thing actually seems to work!!  I wonder if I can break it.

Maybe this will do it.
Still not broken eh?  Well take this!
lfkdsafldgjfhfdkldsakfjlkjsalkdaosskfwlamffkmewkfmwlmfmfkewmkefmwkm! And
this! lfkdsafldgjfhfdkldsakfjlkjsalkdaosskfwlamffkmewkfmwlmfmfkewmkefmwkm!

This thing actually seems to work!!  I wonder if I can break it.
This thing actually seems to work!!  I wonder if I can break it.
This thing actually seems to work!!  I wonder if I can break it.
This thing actually seems to work!!  I wonder if I can break it.
This thing actually seems to work!!  I wonder if I can break it.
This thing actually seems to work!!  I wonder if I can break it.
This thing actually seems to work!!  I wonder if I can break it.
```

```
This thing actually seems to work!!  I wonder if I can break it.
This thing actually seems to work!!  I wonder if I can break it.
This thing actually seems to work!!  I wonder if I can break it.
```

Working with LOB Data

Large objects, or LOBs, are designed to hold up to four gigabytes of RAW, binary data. In Oracle 7, the LONG RAW data type could only be accessed serially through PL/SQL or the Oracle Call Interface (OCI). This presented a unique challenge when it came to searching for a specific bit of information within such an object, because Oracle did not provide any piecewise operations for reading, writing, or copying LOB data. Parsing LOB data was left to applications outside Oracle. Oracle8 changes all that by providing new internal and external LOB data types along with OCI and PL/SQL support for piecewise reading, writing, and comparison of LOB data.

DBMS_LOB

PL/SQL 8.0 introduces DBMS_LOB, which is used to manipulate "large object" data—namely, Oracle8's new BLOB, CLOB, NCLOB, and BFILE data types. Similar data types such as LONG, RAW, and LONG RAW were only serially accessible in earlier releases of PL/SQL, but with DBMS_LOB these new data types can be accessed piecewise for reading, writing, and comparison operations.

Because BFILE data is stored outside the database as a file, writes are not supported except through the operating system. There are several procedures that apply to BFILE data only. These are

```
FILEEXISTS
FILEGETNAME
FILEOPEN
FILEISOPEN
FILECLOSE
FILECLOSEALL
```

Other LOB data is accessed through the following procedures:

```
LOADFROMFILE
GETLENGTH
READ
SUBSTR
COMPARE
INSTR
COPY
WRITE
APPEND
TRIM
ERASE
```

In order to access data using DBMS_LOB, a "locator" must be retrieved for the LOB in question. This locator must be stored in a variable whose data type matches the LOB it references. The locator is then passed to DBMS_LOB, where it is used like a pointer is used in a C program. In the case of a BFILE, this locator must be retrieved using the BFILENAME function. We will refer to locators for BFILEs as "file locators," and the rest will be called "LOB locators."

> **NOTE**
>
> There are two things you must do before you can access a BFILE.
>
> First, create a directory alias in the database for an existing path using the CREATE DIRECTORY command.
>
> Then retrieve the file locator for the BFILE calling the BFILENAME function and passing in the directory alias and a filename. The alias must be uppercase, and the file must already exist on the operating system.

```
PROCEDURE APPEND(
     dest_lob IN OUT BLOB,
     src_lob IN BLOB);
```

This procedure appends the *src_lob* to the *dest_lob* and is overloaded to accept BLOB, CLOB, and NCLOB data.

```
PROCEDURE APPEND(
     dest_lob IN OUT CLOB CHARACTER SET ANY_CS,
     src_lob IN CLOB CHARACTER SET dest_lob%CHARSET);
```

The 'ANY_CS' in the syntax of DBMS_LOB routines for CLOBs allows them to accept a CLOB or NCLOB variables as inputs. The %CHARSET returns the character set of its argument to ensure that the source and destination objects are of the same character set.

```
FUNCTION COMPARE(
     lob_1 IN BLOB, CLOB, NCLOB or BFILE
     lob_2 IN BLOB, CLOB, NCLOB or BFILE
     amount IN INTEGER DEFAULT 4294967295,
     offset_1 IN INTEGER DEFAULT 1,
     offset_2 IN INTEGER DEFAULT 1)
RETURN INTEGER;
```

lob_1	The locator variable of the LOB to be compared to lob_2.
lob_2	The locator variable of the LOB that lob_1 will be compared to.
amount	For CLOB and NCLOB, the maximum number of characters, and for BLOB and BFILE, the maximum number of bytes to be compared.

offset_1	Offset in characters or bytes of the first character or byte to begin comparing.
offset_2	Offset in characters or bytes of the last character or byte to compare.

You can use this function to compare the two entire LOBs or two same-length pieces. The LOBs must be of the same type. It returns a 0 for a non-match and a 1 for a match.

```
PROCEDURE COPY(
    dest_lob IN OUT BLOB, CLOB or NCLOB,
    src_lob IN BLOB, CLOB or NCLOB,
    amount IN INTEGER DEFAULT 1,
    dest_offset IN INTEGER DEFAULT 1,
    src_offset IN INTEGER DEFAULT 1);
```

dest_lob	Locator of the LOB to copy to.
src_lob	Locator of the LOB to copy from.
amount	Number of characters or bytes to copy from the source LOB. If the amount exceeds the data in the LOB, only the remainder of the LOB is copied.
dest_offset	Offset in characters or bytes of the position to begin writing the copied data. If the offset is past the end of the destination LOB, the difference is padded with spaces.
src_offset	Offset in characters or bytes of the first character or byte to copy.

This procedure is used to copy LOB data to another like-type LOB. The data occupying the destination LOB is overwritten from the point of the offset specified. If the *dest_offset* value is greater than the length of the LOB being copied to, the difference is padded with 0 byte spaces. This procedure is not valid for BFILE-type data.

```
PROCEDURE ERASE(
    lob_loc IN OUT BLOB, CLOB or NCLOB,
    amount IN OUT INTEGER,
    offset IN INTEGER DEFAULT 1);
```

lob_loc	The locator of the LOB to erase from.
amount	The number of characters or bytes to erase.
offset	The character or byte after which to begin erasing.

This procedure erases data in a BLOB, CLOB, or NCLOB and leaves spaces in its stead.

```
FUNCTION GETLENGTH(
    lob_loc IN BLOB, CLOB, NCLOB)
RETURN INTEGER;

FUNCTION GETLENGTH(
    file_loc IN BFILE)
RETURN INTEGER;
```

This function returns the length of the LOB specified with *lob_loc* or file_loc (in bytes for BLOB or BFILE, and in characters for CLOB and NCLOB types):

```
FUNCTION INSTR(
     lob_loc IN BLOB,
     pattern IN RAW,
     offset IN INTEGER DEFAULT 1,
     nth IN INTEGER DEFAULT 1);

FUNCTION INSTR(
     lob_loc IN CLOB CHARACTER SET ANY_CS,
     pattern IN VARCHAR2 CHARACTER SET lob_loc%CHARSET,
     offset IN INTEGER DEFAULT 1,
     nth IN INTEGER DEFAULT 1)
RETURN INTEGER;

FUNCTION INSTR(
     file_loc IN BFILE,
     pattern IN RAW,
     offset IN INTEGER DEFAULT 1,
     nth IN INTEGER DEFAULT 1)
RETURN INTEGER;
```

lob_loc or *file_loc*	LOB locator.
pattern	String of bytes or characters to search for.
offset	Number of bytes or characters after which to search for the given pattern.
nth	Indicates the number of pattern matches that must exist before the return value is TRUE.

The INSTR function looks for the nth occurrence of the given pattern in the specified LOB and returns the offset position of the occurrence, or a 0 if the specified occurrence is not found.

```
FUNCTION SUBSTR(
     lob_loc IN BLOB, CLOB, NCLOB or BFILE,
     amount IN INTEGER DEFAULT 32767,
     offset IN INTEGER DEFAULT 1)
RETURN RAW or VARCHAR2;
```

lob_loc	Locator for LOB to read from.
amount	Number of characters or bytes to read.
offset	Offset in bytes or characters before reading should begin.

This function reads a portion of the specified LOB, beginning at the offset and ending after the number of bytes or characters specified is reached. It returns the portion of the LOB as a RAW in the case of a BLOB or BFILE, and VARCHAR2 in the case of a CLOB or NCLOB.

```
PROCEDURE READ(
     lob_loc IN BLOB, CLOB, NCLOB or BFILE,
     amount IN OUT BINARY_INTEGER,
     offset IN INTEGER,
     buffer OUT RAW);
```

lob_loc	Locator of LOB to read from.
amount	Number of characters or bytes to read.
offset	Offset in bytes or characters to begin reading from.
buffer	Variable to hold returned data.

Much like SUBSTR, this procedure retrieves a portion of a LOB. There are a few differences, though. One is that the number of characters or bytes actually read is returned in a binary integer.

```
PROCEDURE TRIM(
     lob_loc IN CLOB or BLOB,
     newlen IN INTEGER);
```

You can use this procedure to shorten a CLOB or BLOB to the specified *newlen*. If the length specified exceeds the length of the LOB to be trimmed, an ORA-22926 is returned. Unlike ERASE, removed data is not padded with spaces.

```
PROCEDURE WRITE(
     lob_loc IN BLOB, CLOB or NCLOB,
     amount IN BINARY_INTEGER,
     offset IN INTEGER,
     buffer IN RAW);
```

lob_loc	Locator of LOB to write data into.
amount	Number of characters or bytes to write from the buffer.
offset	Offset in characters or bytes to begin writing buffer data.
buffer	Data to be written.

This procedure allows you to copy RAW data into a LOB. Like COPY, the new data overwrites the existing data. If the offset is past the end of the destination LOB, the difference is padded with 0 byte spaces.

The following routines are applicable to BFILEs only.

```
FUNCTION FILEEXISTS(
     file_loc IN BFILE)
RETURN INTEGER;
```

Use this function to confirm the existence of the BFILE as specified by the file locator passed in *file_loc*. This function returns a 1 if the file exists, and a 0 if it does not. A NULL is returned if an operating system error occurs or there are insufficient privileges to the file system.

18

SUPPLIED PL/SQL PACKAGES

```
PROCEDURE FILEGETNAME(
    file_loc IN BFILE,
    dir_alias OUT VARCHAR2,
    filename OUT VARCHAR2);
```

file_loc	Locator of the BFILE.
dir_alias	Name of the DIRECTORY object.
filename	Returned name of the BFILE.

This procedure retrieves the name of the file identified by the file locator passed in *file_loc*. The *dir_alias* is the name of the DIRECTORY object created with the CREATE DIRECTORY statement. This is a new type of object in Oracle8, designed to hold the operating system path of files such as those associated with BFILE data.

```
FUNCTION FILEISOPEN(
    file_loc IN BFILE)
RETURN INTEGER;
```

This function can be used to determine if the file identified by the file locator passed in *file_loc* is open or not. A 1 is returned if the file is opened with the given file locator, and a 0 is passed if it is not. Only the status of the passed locator is checked, so the file could still be opened by way of another file locator even if a 0 is returned.

```
PROCEDURE FILEOPEN(
    file_loc IN OUT BFILE,
    open_mode IN BINARY_INTEGER DEFAULT FILE_READONLY);
```

FILEOPEN opens the specified BFILE in read-only mode. Oracle does not support writing of BFILEs, but the presence of the *open_mode* parameter suggests that it will in the future.

```
PROCEDURE LOADFROMFILE(
    dest_lob or dest_file IN OUT BLOB, CLOB, NCLOB or BFILE,
    src_lob IN BFILE,
    amount IN INTEGER,
    dest_offset IN INTEGER DEFAULT 1,
    src_offset IN INTEGER DEFAULT 1);
```

dest_lob	Locator for BLOB, CLOB, or NCLOB to be written to.
src_lob	Locator of BFILE to get data from.
amount	Number of bytes to copy into the dest_lob.
dest_offset	Offset in bytes or characters to start writing to the destination LOB.
src_offset	Offset in bytes to start reading data from the source BFILE.

Use this procedure to copy data from a BFILE into another LOB. If the *dest_offset* exceeds the length of the destination LOB, the difference is padded with spaces. If the *dest_offset* is less than the total length of the destination LOB, the existing data is overwritten by the new data. No check is performed to verify that character sets match when loading CLOB or NCLOB data.

```
PROCEDURE FILECLOSE(
     file_loc IN OUT BFILE);
```

This procedure closes the file specified with *file_loc*.

```
PROCEDURE FILECLOSEALL;
```

This procedure closes all files currently open by the current session.

The following is a brief example of how DBMS_LOB works. The first listing creates the objects needed for the demo.

```
DROP TABLE lobs;
CREATE TABLE lobs (
    id NUMBER PRIMARY KEY,
    clobs CLOB,
    blobs BLOB,
    bfiles BFILE
    );
```

```
REM We have already created a file here called test.log during the
UTL_FILE demo.
REM We'll use the same file as a BFILE in the DBMS_LOB demo.

DROP DIRECTORY bfile_dir;
CREATE DIRECTORY bfile_dir AS '/u01/app/oracle/logs';
```

Once the objects are successfully created, the following demonstration code will work.

```
-- Here's some things you can do with LOB data.



SET SERVEROUTPUT ON

DECLARE

    ClobLocator CLOB;
    BlobLocator BLOB;
    BfileLocator BFILE;

    ClobBuffer VARCHAR2(255);
    BlobBuffer RAW(32767);
    BfileBuffer RAW(32767);

    Offset NUMBER;
```

```
BEGIN

    -- First we need to populate some LOBs

    INSERT INTO lobs (id, clobs)
        VALUES (1, 'A doo doo doo, a daa daa daa.  That's all I want to
say to you.');

    INSERT INTO lobs (id, blobs)
        VALUES (2, HEXTORAW('04CC13FF65AB'));

    -- What we're really doing below is linking the temp.logs file to row
3 using
    -- the BFILENAME function.  The contents of the file will appear when
this column
    -- is queried.

    INSERT INTO lobs (id, bfiles)
        VALUES (3, BFILENAME('BFILE_DIR', 'test.log'));

    -- Now lets do some stuff with DBMS_LOB!
    -- First well get locators for the LOB data we created.

    -- Notice I've selected the CLOB and BLOB using the FOR UPDATE clause
    -- in order to lock the rows.  This is necessary if you plan to do any
       updates.

    SELECT clobs INTO ClobLocator FROM lobs WHERE id = 1 FOR UPDATE;
    SELECT blobs INTO BlobLocator FROM lobs WHERE id = 2 FOR UPDATE;
    SELECT bfiles INTO BfileLocator FROM lobs WHERE id = 3;

    -- Find out how long it is and have a look at it.

    Offset := 1 + DBMS_LOB.GETLENGTH(ClobLocator);
    DBMS_LOB.READ(ClobLocator, Offset, 1, ClobBuffer);
        DBMS_OUTPUT.PUT_LINE(ClobBuffer);

    -- Now lets write some stuff to the end of the CLOB and read it again.

    DBMS_LOB.WRITE(ClobLocator, 34, Offset + 1, ' Sting is quite a
lyricist -- no?');
        Offset := DBMS_LOB.GETLENGTH(ClobLocator);
    DBMS_LOB.READ(ClobLocator, Offset, 1, ClobBuffer);
    DBMS_OUTPUT.PUT_LINE(ClobBuffer);

    -- Lets get something out of the BFILE.
        -- Unfortunately we can't look at what we got because it's RAW
data.

    DBMS_LOB.FILEOPEN(BfileLocator);
```

```
        Offset := 1 + DBMS_LOB.GETLENGTH(BfileLocator);
        DBMS_LOB.READ(BfileLocator, Offset, 1, BfileBuffer);
        DBMS_LOB.FILECLOSE(BfileLocator);

        -- We could go on forever, but just one more.
        -- We'll get a string from the CLOB.

        Offset := DBMS_LOB.INSTR(ClobLocator, 'no', 1, 1);
        ClobBuffer := DBMS_LOB.SUBSTR(ClobLocator, 2, Offset);
        DBMS_OUTPUT.PUT_LINE(ClobBuffer);

EXCEPTION

    WHEN DBMS_LOB.ACCESS_ERROR THEN
        RAISE_APPLICATION_ERROR(-20100, 'Maximum Lob Size Exceeded');

    WHEN DBMS_LOB.INVALID_DIRECTORY THEN
        RAISE_APPLICATION_ERROR(-20101, 'Directory is Invalid');

    WHEN DBMS_LOB.NOEXIST_DIRECTORY THEN
        RAISE_APPLICATION_ERROR(-20103, 'Directory Does Not Exist');

    WHEN DBMS_LOB.NOPRIV_DIRECTORY THEN
        RAISE_APPLICATION_ERROR(-20104, 'Insufficient Directory
Privileges');

    WHEN DBMS_LOB.OPERATION_FAILED THEN
        RAISE_APPLICATION_ERROR(-20105, 'Operation on File Failed');

    WHEN DBMS_LOB.UNOPENED_FILE THEN
        RAISE_APPLICATION_ERROR(-20106, 'File Not Open');

    WHEN OTHERS THEN
    RAISE;
END;
/
```

Issuing Dynamic SQL and Data Definition Language Statements

Normally, a PL/SQL block can only contain static DML statements. You cannot issue DDL or dynamic SQL without using the DBMS_SQL package. The reason for this is that PL/SQL blocks are compiled into a format called *p-code* before they are executed. This process checks object definitions and binds values to all variables. Although this early binding increases the code's efficiency, it makes it impossible to use dynamic or DDL statements because the object definitions and bind variables of such statements cannot be resolved until runtime.

In order to overcome this limitation, PL/SQL 2.1 introduced the DBMS_SQL package. This package gives the programmer control over the execution phase of SQL statements so that all object definition checks and binding can be done at runtime.

DBMS_SQL

The steps to execute a SQL statement using DBMS_SQL are as follows:

1. Store the SQL in a string.
2. Open a cursor using OPEN_CURSOR.
3. Use PARSE to parse the block out of the string.
4. Bind any variables using BIND_VARIABLE.
5. For anything other than a query, use EXECUTE and/or VARIABLE_VALUE to execute the statement and CLOSE_CURSOR to close the cursor.
6. For queries, use DEFINE_COLUMN to set up variables for the output.
7. Use EXECUTE to execute the query and FETCH_ROWS, COLUMN_VALUE, and VARIABLE_VALUE to retrieve the data.
8. Use CLOSE_CURSOR.

```
FUNCTION OPEN_CURSOR
RETURN INTEGER;
```

Use OPEN_CURSOR to open a new cursor in which to execute the SQL statement and retrieve a cursor ID number for future references to it. Typically we think of cursors as storage for the results of a query, but DBMS_SQL requires a cursor to store SQL statements you plan to issue whether they are meant to return data or not. When you parse a statement it overwrites the contents of the cursor, so you can use the same cursor to execute as many statements as you like. When you are finished, you must close all cursors using CLOSE_CURSOR.

```
PROCEDURE PARSE(
    c IN INTEGER,
    statement IN VARCHAR2,
    language_flag IN INTEGER);
```

c	Cursor ID returned by OPEN_CURSOR.
statement	SQL statement to parse—usually passed in a variable. No semicolon unless it's an anonymous PS/SQL block.
language_flag	V6, V7, or NATIVE. The database will behave as if it is version 6 or 7, or as installed based on language_flag.

The PARSE procedure is used to send the SQL statement to the database for parsing. The maximum length of the statement—*size_t*—is operating system-dependent. For large SQL statements, use the PARSE procedure.

> **NOTE**
>
> Parsing happens immediately when the SQL statement is issued, and cannot be deferred until execution time as it can when using the Oracle Call Interface (OCI). Deferred parsing is useful for reducing network traffic between the application and the Oracle server, because only one call is necessary to perform both parsing and execution of statements. With immediate parsing, two calls are needed—one to parse and one to execute. Support for deferred parsing will eventually be included in DBMS_SQL, so applications should not rely on this immediate parsing behavior.

```
PROCEDURE PARSE(
    c IN INTEGER,
    statement IN VARCHAR2S,
    lb IN INTEGER,
    ub IN INTEGER,
    lfflg IN BOOLEAN,
    language_flag IN INTEGER);
```

c	Cursor ID returned by OPEN_CURSOR.
statement	PL/SQL table of statements to parse. See the VARCHAR2S type description. No semicolon, unless it's an anonymous PL/SQL block.
lb	Lower bound that specifies the first row of the statement from the PL/SQL table.
ub	Upper bound for elements in the statement.
lfflg	Line feed flag. TRUE means insert a line feed after each element of the statement. FALSE means the statement will be concatenated into one long line.
language_flag	V6, V7, or NATIVE. The database will behave as if it is version 6 or 7, or as installed based on language_flag.

This procedure accepts a PL/SQL table of type VARCHAR2S and concatenates its contents into a string before parsing. You can use this to pass statements or blocks that will not fit into a single VARCHAR2. The definition of VARCHAR2S is as follows:

```
TYPE VARCHAR2S
    IS TABLE OF VARCHAR2(256)
INDEX BY BINARY_INTEGER;
```

```
PROCEDURE BIND_VARIABLE(
     c IN INTEGER,
     name IN VARCHAR2,
     value IN <datatype>
     out_value_size IN INTEGER);
```

<datatype> can be any one of the following types:

```
NUMBER
DATE
MLSLABEL
VARCHAR2 CHARACTER SET ANY_CS
BLOB
CLOB CHARACTER SET ANY_CS
BFILE
```

In order to bind CHAR, RAW, and ROWID data, use the following procedures:

```
BIND_VARIABLE_CHAR
BIND_VARIABLE_RAW
BIND_VARIABLE_ROWID
```

These procedures take the same variables as BIND_VARIABLE, except that BIND_VARIABLE_ROWID does not support *out_value_size*.

c	Cursor ID.
name	Name of the bind variable (also known as a substitution variable) used in the SQL statement.
value	Data of the appropriate type to bind to the variable.
out_value_size	This parameter is optional. It can be used for CHAR, VARCHAR2, and RAW binds to specify the maximum size for an OUT value. When an anonymous PL/SQL block is being executed, the bind variable is not protected from outside writes or erroneous values, so this provides a safeguard.

The BIND_VARIABLE procedure is used to assign values to bind variables in the SQL statement. Precede the name of bind variables with a colon. Each variable will be replaced with the value specified for it as many times as it occurs.

```
PROCEDURE DEFINE_COLUMN(
     c IN INTEGER,
     position IN INTEGER
     column IN <datatype>
     column_size in INTEGER);
```

<datatype> can be any one of the following types:

```
NUMBER
DATE
MLSLABEL
BLOB
CLOB CHARACTER SET ANY_CS
BFILE
```

c	Cursor identifier.
position	Column position in returned data. 1 for the first, 2 for the second, and so on.
column	Variable of the intended type and size to hold the column value.
column_size	Expected size of the data. If omitted, the size of the column will be used.

Use this procedure to specify the datatype and length for each column returned when selecting data. DEFINE_COLUMN is overloaded to accommodate the preceding datatypes. The column size value is not used for the NUMBER, DATE, and MLSLABEL datatypes.

For the CHAR, RAW, and ROWID columns, use DEFINE_COLUMN_CHAR, DEFINE_COLUMN_RAW, and DEFINE_COLUMN_ROWID.

```
FUNCTION EXECUTE(
    c IN INTEGER)
RETURN INTEGER;
```

This function returns the number of rows processed for DML statements. For any other type of statement, the return value is undefined and should be discarded, but a variable must be assigned for it. The execution step of the process actually performs the specified SQL statement in the database.

```
FUNCTION FETCH_ROWS(
    c IN INTEGER)
RETURN INTEGER;
```

The name of this function is a bit of a misnomer because FETCH_ROWS is used to return query results to a local buffer one row at a time. These row values can then be retrieved into variables using the COLUMN_VALUE procedure. This cycle can be repeated until FETCH_ROWS returns a 0 to indicate it has fetched all the rows.

```
PROCEDURE COLUMN_VALUE(
    c IN INTEGER,
    position IN INTEGER,
    value OUT <datatype>
    column_error OUT NUMBER
    actual_length OUT INTEGER);
```

18

SUPPLIED PL/SQL
PACKAGES

where datatype is one of the following:

```
NUMBER
VARCHAR2
INTEGER
DATE
MLSLABEL
```

c	Cursor ID.
position	Relative position of the column from left to right, starting with 1.
value	Variable used to hold the return value.
column_error	Optional variable to hold any error code that is generated. Helps isolate the column the errors are associated with. Errors are returned as negative numbers.
actual_length	Optional variable to original column length before it was stored into the specified variable.

The COLUMN_VALUE procedure is used to store a column value from a row returned by FETCH_ROWS into a variable. Once a row is stored into variables, the variable values can be processed or stored in a table before the next row is fetched and stored. Usually the variables specified in DEFINE_COLUMN are used. A COLUMN_VALUE call should be made for each column specified with DEFINE_COLUMN.

For data types other than these, use the following procedures. The IN and OUT parameters are the same:

```
COLUMN_VALUE_CHAR
COLUMN_VALUE_RAW
COLUMN_VALUE_ROWID
```

Here's a very simple example of a dynamic SQL statement being issued through DBMS_SQL:

```
-- This demonstrates dynamic SQL in the most simple select I could come up
with.

SET SERVEROUTPUT ON

DECLARE
    SQLStatement    VARCHAR2(255);
    FileName      dba_data_files.file_name%TYPE;
    TablespaceName      dba_tablespaces.tablespace_name%TYPE;
    CursorID    INTEGER;
    Rows      INTEGER;
BEGIN

    -- Let's pretend the value below came from somewhere outside this
block.

    TablespaceName := 'SYSTEM';
```

```
    CursorID := DBMS_SQL.OPEN_CURSOR;

    -- Normally the statement below wouldn't run because the value for
    -- :p1 is unknown.

    SQLStatement := 'SELECT file_name FROM dba_data_files WHERE
tablespace_name = :p1';

    -- Send it to the server to parse.

    DBMS_SQL.PARSE(CursorID, SQLStatement, DBMS_SQL.V7);

    -- Bind the TablespaceName variable to the :p1 place holder.

DBMS_SQL.BIND_VARIABLE(CursorID, ':p1', TablespaceName);

    -- Set up a buffer column to hold the retrieved data.
    -- Remember the column_size parameter is required.

    DBMS_SQL.DEFINE_COLUMN(CursorID, 1, FileName, 60);

    -- Run that puppy.

    Rows := DBMS_SQL.EXECUTE(CursorID);

    -- Now we need to get the data into our local buffer and extract it
    -- into variables.

    LOOP

        -- Get the data and exit if there's nothing left to get.

        IF DBMS_SQL.FETCH_ROWS(CursorID) = 0 THEN
            EXIT;
        END IF;

        -- Extract the value into our variable.

        DBMS_SQL.COLUMN_VALUE(CursorID, 1, FileName);

        -- Print it to the screen for proof that it worked.

        DBMS_OUTPUT.PUT_LINE(FileName);

    END LOOP;

    DBMS_SQL.CLOSE_CURSOR(CursorID);

EXCEPTION
    WHEN OTHERS THEN
    RAISE;
END;
/
```

18

SUPPLIED PL/SQL
PACKAGES

Communicating Between Processes

Oracle provides a number of ways to communicate between PL/SQL processes. The packages range in sophistication and flexibility from the simple DBMS_PIPE to the rather daunting DBMS_AQ. The package you pick will depend on your need for scheduling, security, and dependability, as well as simplicity of use.

DBMS_ALERT

This package allows one-way communication from one session to another. The alert is sent upon commit, so it is a synchronous signal. If the transaction is rolled back, the alert signal is canceled.

```
PROCEDURE SIGNAL(
    name IN VARCHAR2,
    message IN VARCHAR2);
```

An alert *name* identifies an alert uniquely. Therefore, a particular alert can only be sent by one session at a time. The dbms_alert_info table in the data dictionary records the state of each alert as signaled or not signaled. The SIGNAL procedure is used to set this value to signaled so it will be sent upon commit. If two sessions signal the same alert, the first blocks the second from sending until the first issues a commit and its alert is sent. Then the second alert is sent. The *message* part of an alert can be up to 1,800 bytes. All sessions registered for a given alert will receive it when it is sent.

```
PROCEDURE REGISTER(
    name IN VARCHAR2);
```

This is the first necessary step to receive an alert message. A session can register for any number of alerts.

```
PROCEDURE WAITONE(
    name IN VARCHAR2,
    message OUT VARCHAR2,
    status OUT INTEGER,
    timeout IN NUMBER default MAXWAIT);
```

name	Name of alert to wait for.
message	Buffer to record message from signaled alert.
status	0 = received, 1 = timed out.
timeout	Timeout in seconds. The default is 1,000 days.

This procedure causes the session to sleep until the specified alert is received or the timeout is reached. If the session issues more than one WAITONE, the next is not reached until the first is resolved.

```
PROCEDURE WAITANY(
    name OUT VARCHAR2,
    message OUT VARCHAR2,
    status OUT INTEGER,
    timeout IN NUMBER default MAXWAIT);
```

Identical to WAITONE except that any registered alert is waited for. Only the most recent alert signaled will be received.

```
PROCEDURE REMOVE(
    name IN VARCHAR2);
```

Unregisters the named alert.

```
PROCEDURE SET_DEFAULTS(
    polling_interval IN NUMBER);
```

The polling interval is used to specify the length of time to wait between checking for alerts. SET_DEFAULTS uses a default of five seconds. Normally Oracle is event-driven and there is no need for a polling loop, but two sets of circumstances make them necessary.

When using the WAITANY procedure, it is possible for one session to issue a blocking signal and not commit for more than one second. WAITANY would miss alerts issued in the meantime without a polling interval. In this case, polling is automatically performed, starting with a 1-second interval and increasing exponentially to 30 seconds. SET_DEFAULTS cannot modify this behavior.

When running in shared mode, a polling loop is needed to check for alerts signaled from other instances. The default is one second and can be set with SET_DEFAULTS.

Here's some example code for DBMS_ALERT. The first listing sends a message and the second receives it:

```
-- Here we demonstrate DBMS_ALERT.SIGNAL.
DECLARE
    Message     VARCHAR2(255);
    AlertName   VARCHAR2(30);
BEGIN

    Message := 'This is a test. This is only a test. If this was a real
emergency this message would be in capital letters and have a lot more
punctuation.';

    AlertName := 'TestAlert1';

    DBMS_ALERT.SIGNAL(AlertName, Message);

    -- You must commit in order for the message to be sent.

    COMMIT;
```

```
END;
/
```

Now that we've sent an alert, let's set up a receiver:

```
SET SERVEROUTPUT ON


DECLARE

    MessageBuffer       VARCHAR(255);
    AlertName       VARCHAR(30);
    AlertStatus     INTEGER;
BEGIN

    AlertName := 'TestAlert1';

    -- Step one is to notify the server that you're interested in the
    -- alert.

    DBMS_ALERT.REGISTER(AlertName);

    -- Step two is to wait as long as you're willing for it to be sent.

    DBMS_ALERT.WAITONE(AlertName, MessageBuffer, AlertStatus, 10);

    -- If you don't get one, let us know.

    IF AlertStatus = 1 THEN
        DBMS_OUTPUT.PUT_LINE('Timed out waiting for the alert.');
    END IF;

    -- If you do get one, print it.

    DBMS_OUTPUT.PUT_LINE(MessageBuffer);

END;
/
```

DBMS_PIPE

This package provides a way to send messages asynchronously between two sessions. Unlike alerts, messages sent with DBMS_PIPE are not transaction dependent. Oracle allows you to create pipes within the database that can hold a maximum of 8,192 bytes of information at any given time. Pipes can be public or private, and access to them can be restricted. Unlike alerts, messages sent via pipes are not readable by multiple sessions because the receiving session removes the message from the pipe.

The basic steps to send and receive data with `DBMS_PIPE` are as follows. A pipe is created. A data set consisting of various datatypes is packed into a message and sent to the pipe. From this point the receiving session detects the presence of the message, retrieves it from the pipe, determines the datatype of each item, and unpacks it into a variable of the proper type.

```
PROCEDURE PACK_MESSAGE(
    item IN VARCHAR2);
PROCEDURE PACK_MESSAGE(
    item IN NUMBER);
PROCEDURE PACK_MESSAGE(
    item IN DATE);
PROCEDURE PACK_MESSAGE(
    item IN RAW);
PROCEDURE PACK_MESSAGE(
    item IN ROWID);
```

This procedure is overloaded to handle the listed datatypes. The total size limit of a message is 4,096 bytes. Of this, three bytes are used per item to specify the type, length, and size, and one byte is used to terminate the message.

```
FUNCTION CREATE_PIPE(
    pipename IN VARCHAR2,
    maxpipesize IN INTEGER default 8192,
    private IN BOOLEAN default TRUE)
RETURN INTEGER;
```

Like `SEND_MESSAGE`, this function creates a pipe, but it also allows the pipe to be designated as private. Private pipes are only available to their creator or SYSDBA. Normally, there is no reason to use this function to create a public pipe because `SEND_MESSAGE` creates one automatically. The function returns a `0` for success. If there is a like-named pipe with a different owner, or a public pipe with the same name, `ORA-23322` is returned.

```
FUNCTION UNIQUE_SESSION_NAME
RETURN VARCHAR2;
```

This function returns a string that uniquely identifies the session it is issued from. This string can be used to name a pipe and then be packed into a message that is sent through an existing pipe whose name is known to the receiving session. The receiver unpacks the message and gets the name of the uniquely identified pipe that the sender has prepared, and replies with a message through this uniquely identified pipe. This method allows sessions to set up a private communication on a pipe whose name is known only to them. There is no chance of an outside session getting messages before the intended session can.

```
FUNCTION SEND_MESSAGE(
    pipename IN VARCHAR2,
    timeout IN INTEGER default MAXWAIT,
    maxpipesize IN INTEGER default 8192)
RETURN INTEGER;
```

`pipename`	Name of pipe—30-character limit.
`timeout`	Number of seconds before message send fails. The MAXWAIT default is 86,400,000 seconds.
`maxpipesize`	Maximum bytes the pipe can hold. Default is 8,192.

This function returns a 0 for success, 1 if it times out, or 3 if an internal error interrupts the message.

```
FUNCTION RECEIVE_MESSAGE(
    pipename IN VARCHAR2,
    timeout IN INTEGER default MAXWAIT)
RETURN INTEGER;
```

The parameters provided to RECEIVE_MESSAGE are identical to those provided for SEND_MESSAGE. This function returns a 0 for success, 1 if it timed out, 2 if the message is too large for the buffer, or 3 if there is an internal error that interrupts the call.

```
FUNCTION NEXT_ITEM_TYPE
RETURN INTEGER;

0 = no more items in message
6 = NUMBER
9 = VARCHAR2
11 = ROWID
12 = DATE
23 = RAW
```

This function is used to determine the datatype of the next item in the message. Unless the message follows a known format, this function is a necessary step before unpacking the next item for storage in the variable provided with *item*.

```
UNPACK_MESSAGE(
    item OUT VARCHAR2);
UNPACK_MESSAGE(
    item OUT NUMBER);
UNPACK_MESSAGE(
    item OUT DATE);
UNPACK_MESSAGE(
    item OUT RAW);
UNPACK_MESSAGE(
    item OUT ROWID);
```

The *item* value is the variable in which to store the next value of the message. The data type of the next item is determined either by using the NEXT_ITEM_TYPE function or by prior knowledge of the message format.

```
FUNCTION REMOVE_PIPE(
     pipename IN VARCHAR)
RETURN INTEGER;
```

This function returns a 0 if the pipe is removed or did not exist in the first place, and raises ORA-23322 if the user does not have privileges for the pipe.

```
PROCEDURE PURGE(
     pipename IN VARCHAR2);
```

This procedure flushes the pipe and starts aging it out of the shared pool using the LRU (least recently used) algorithm.

This example code of DBMS_PIPE is in two parts. The first sends a message and waits for a reply. The second receives the message and replies. It's interesting to play with the order of events and see how it affects the sending and receiving of messages.

```
-- Here's a demo of DBMS_PIPE. First we send a message
-- and wait for a reply on a pipe we specified in our
-- message. This is basically a handshake operation you
-- might use to establish a secure line of communication
-- between two sessions.
SET SERVEROUTPUT ON


DECLARE

    OpenPipeName        VARCHAR2(30);
    SecretPipeName        VARCHAR2(30);

    SendStatus        INTEGER;
    ReceiveStatus        INTEGER;

    ReturnedPassword    VARCHAR2(30);
    ReturnedUser        VARCHAR2(30);
    ReturnedMessage        VARCHAR2(255);
BEGIN

    -- Now we get a unique name to send as our
    -- secure pipe. In order to use a pipe you must
    -- know its name, so this isn't likely to be used
    -- by anybody other than the intended sessions.

    SecretPipeName := DBMS_PIPE.UNIQUE_SESSION_NAME;

    -- Name the regular pipe for sending.
```

```
    OpenPipeName := 'OpenPipe';

    -- Pack the secret pipe name into the message.

    DBMS_PIPE.PACK_MESSAGE(SecretPipeName);

    -- Send the secret pipe name out to the regular pipe.

    SendStatus := DBMS_PIPE.SEND_MESSAGE(OpenPipeName);

    IF SendStatus != 0 THEN
        DBMS_OUTPUT.PUT_LINE('Sender Could not send message!');
    END IF;

    -- Now we just wait for a reply on the secret pipe.
    -- If there's a session out there that knows what to
    -- do with the message we sent we can be pretty sure
    -- it's no imposter.

    ReceiveStatus := DBMS_PIPE.RECEIVE_MESSAGE(SecretPipeName, 30);
    IF ReceiveStatus = 0 THEN

        DBMS_PIPE.UNPACK_MESSAGE(ReturnedPassword);
        DBMS_PIPE.UNPACK_MESSAGE(ReturnedUser);
        DBMS_PIPE.UNPACK_MESSAGE(ReturnedMessage);

        -- Do they know the password?

        IF ReturnedPassword = 'Dilbert' THEN
            DBMS_OUTPUT.PUT_LINE('Sender has received the following
reply:');
            DBMS_OUTPUT.PUT_LINE(ReturnedUser);
            DBMS_OUTPUT.PUT_LINE(ReturnedMessage);
        ELSE

        -- If not, ignore them.

            DBMS_OUTPUT.PUT_LINE('Sender received an incorrect
password.');
        END IF;
    ELSEIF ReceiveStatus > 0 THEN

        DBMS_OUTPUT.PUT_LINE('There's nobody out there.');
        DBMS_PIPE.PURGE(OpenPipeName);

    END IF;

END;
/
```

Now that a message is in the pipe, we need a process to receive it.

```
-- All this does is wait for a message on the regular pipe and then
-- sends a reply on the secret pipe specified in the message received.

SET SERVEROUTPUT ON

DECLARE

    OpenPipeName            VARCHAR2(30);
    SecretPipeName           VARCHAR2(30);

    SendStatus           INTEGER;
    ReceiveStatus            INTEGER;

BEGIN

    OpenPipeName := 'OpenPipe';

    -- Wait for a message on this pipe for 30 seconds.

    ReceiveStatus := DBMS_PIPE.RECEIVE_MESSAGE('OpenPipe', 30);

    IF ReceiveStatus = 1 THEN
        DBMS_OUTPUT.PUT_LINE('No message was received.');

    ELSIF ReceiveStatus = 0 THEN

        -- Load the message into our variable.

        DBMS_PIPE.UNPACK_MESSAGE(SecretPipeName);

        -- Create a message to send back.

        DBMS_PIPE.PACK_MESSAGE('Dilbert');
        DBMS_PIPE.PACK_MESSAGE(user);
        DBMS_PIPE.PACK_MESSAGE('Message received -- awaiting your order');

        -- Use the secret pipe name we received to respond.

        SendStatus := DBMS_PIPE.SEND_MESSAGE(SecretPipeName);

        IF SendStatus != 0 THEN
            DBMS_OUTPUT.PUT_LINE('Could not respond to message!');
        END IF;
    END IF;
END;
/
```

Advanced Queuing

Oracle8 introduces advanced queuing, which is a more sophisticated and powerful approach to interprocess communication than DBMS_ALERT or DBMS_PIPE. Advanced queuing can be synchronous or asynchronous, and because all queuing is done in tables, all messages are protected from data loss and are fully recoverable. Messages are also object types, which allows them to contain several attributes in a single unit.

A queue is used to store messages in a queue table. There are two types of queues—user queues and exception queues. An *enqueue* operation is used to insert a record into a queue. A *dequeue* operation is used to remove a record. Records are moved to an exception queue if they expire or cannot be dequeued. Queue users are called *agents*. An agent is a producer or consumer of messages in queues.

A time manager process can be run in the database that allows the use of timeouts and delays in queuing and dequeuing processes.

Two packages are used for advanced queuing. DBMS_AQ is used for enqueue and dequeue processes, and DBMS_AQADM is used for administrative functions, such as creating and dropping queue tables.

DBMS_AQADM

Administrators must be granted AQ_ADMINISTRATOR_ROLE and rights to the object types used for queues, queue tables, and subscribers. To grant use of these object types, DBMS_AQADM.GRANT_TYPE_ACCESS must be run by SYS for each user.

Several data dictionary views are provided for keeping track of queues. These are AQ$QUEUE_TABLE_NAME, DBA_QUEUE_TABLES, USER_QUEUE_TABLES, DBA_QUEUES, and USER_QUEUES.

```
PROCEDURE CREATE_QUEUE_TABLE(
     queue_table IN VARCHAR2,
     queue_payload_type IN VARCHAR2,
     storage_clause IN VARCHAR2 default NULL,
     sort_list IN VARCHAR2 default NULL,
     multiple_consumers IN BOOLEAN default FALSE,
     message_grouping IN BINARY_INTEGER default NONE,
     comment IN VARCHAR2 default NULL,
     auto_commit IN BOOLEAN default TRUE);
```

queue_table	Name to queue table being created.
queue_payload_type	Specifies data type of messages. Can be RAW or an object type.
storage_clause	Table storage parameters for CREATE TABLE statement. See "SQL Reference Guide" for details.

sort_list	Specifies columns to be used for sorting messages. Valid columns are priority and enq_time. The default is to sort by enq_time.
multiple_consumers	TRUE means multiple consumers can exist for each message.
message_grouping	TRANSACTIONAL means all messages queued during the same transaction will be dequeued together. NONE means each message is treated separately.
comment	Gets recorded in the data dictionary.
auto_commit	TRUE means the queue table is created regardless of the current transaction status. FALSE means the queue table is not created until the current transaction commits.

This procedure creates a table to hold queues, a default exception queue, a read-only view of the queue table, and an index for queues set up for multiple consumers. If you named the queue table monitor_qt, these objects would be named aq$_monitor_qt_e, aq$_monitor_qt, and aq$_monitor_qt_i, respectively.

```
PROCEDURE CREATE_QUEUE(
    queue_name IN VARCHAR2,
    queue_table IN VARCHAR2,
    queue_type IN BINARY_INTEGER default NORMAL_QUEUE,
    max_retries IN NUMBER default 0,
    retry_delay IN NUMBER default 0,
    retention_time IN NUMBER default 0,
    dependency_tracking IN BOOLEAN default FALSE,
    comment IN VARCHAR2 default NULL,
    auto_commit IN BOOLEAN default TRUE);
```

queue_name	Name of queue to be created.
queue_table	Queue table to create queue in.
queue_type	NORMAL_QUEUE or EXCEPTION_QUEUE.
max_retries	Maximum number of times an agent can dequeue a message with REMOVE and then roll back. When max_retries is reached, the message is moved to the exception queue.
retry_delay	Time to wait between retries. Cannot be set for queues with multiple consumers.
retention_time	Seconds to keep a message after it is dequeued. Valid values are 0 to INFINITE.
dependency_tracking	For future use. TRUE produces an error.
comment	Stored in queue catalog.
auto_commit	TRUE means the queue is created independently of any transactions, and FALSE means the current transaction must commit before the queue becomes persistent.

18

SUPPLIED PL/SQL PACKAGES

This creates a queue in which to store messages. Before it can be used, START_QUEUE must be run on it.

```
PROCEDURE START_QUEUE(
     queue_name IN VARCHAR2,
     enqueue IN BOOLEAN default TRUE,
     dequeue IN BOOLEAN default TRUE);
```

queue_name	Name of queue to start.
enqueue	TRUE allows enqueuing of messages.
dequeue	TRUE allows dequeuing of messages.

This procedure must be used to enable a queue. Messages in an exception queue can only be dequeued, so the enqueue option does not apply to them.

```
PROCEDURE STOP_QUEUE(
     queue_name IN VARCHAR2,
     enqueue IN BOOLEAN default TRUE,
     dequeue IN BOOLEAN default TRUE,
     wait IN BOOLEAN default TRUE);
```

queue_name	Name of queue to be stopped.
enqueue	TRUE disables enqueuing.
dequeue	TRUE disables dequeuing.
wait	TRUE blocks new processes on the queue while it waits for all pending processes to commit before it stops the queue.

```
PROCEDURE DROP_QUEUE(
     queue_name IN VARCHAR2,
     auto_commit IN BOOLEAN DEFAULT TRUE);
```

This procedure removes the specified queue from the queue table. If auto_commit is TRUE, the drop occurs immediately. If it's FALSE, the drop does not occur until the transaction commits.

```
PROCEDURE DROP_QUEUE_TABLE(
     queue_table IN VARCHAR2,
     force IN BOOLEAN default FALSE,
     auto_commit IN BOOLEAN default TRUE);
```

queue_table	Name of queue table to drop.
force	TRUE means all queues in the table are stopped and dropped. FALSE returns an error if any queues are in the table.
auto_commit	TRUE means the queue table is dropped regardless of the current transaction status. FALSE means the queue table is not dropped until the current transaction commits.

```
PROCEDURE ALTER_QUEUE(
    queue_name IN VARCHAR2,
    max_retries IN NUMBER default NULL,
    retry_delay IN NUMBER default NULL,
    retention_time IN NUMBER default NULL,
    auto_commit IN BOOLEAN default TRUE);
```

This procedure allows changes to be made to `max_retries`, `retry_delay`, and `retention_time` for the specified queue. The changes go into effect immediately if `auto_commit` is set to `TRUE`, and when the transaction commits if it's set to `FALSE`. See `CREATE_QUEUE` for more information on these alterable parameters.

```
PROCEDURE ADD_SUBSCRIBER(
    queue_name IN VARCHAR2,
    subscriber IN SYS.AQ$_AGENT);
```

This is used to add a subscriber to queues that are enabled for multiple consumers. The new subscriber becomes the default subscriber.

```
PROCEDURE REMOVE_SUBSCRIBER(
    queue_name IN VARCHAR2,
    subscriber IN SYS.AQ$_AGENT);
```

Removes the specified subscriber from the queue along with all references to the subscriber in messages in the queue.

```
FUNCTION QUEUE_SUBSCRIBERS(
    queue_name IN VARCHAR2)
    RETURN AQ$_SUBSCRIBER_LIST_T;
```

This function is used to retrieve a PL/SQL table of the subscribers for a queue.

```
PROCEDURE GRANT_TYPE_ACCESS(
    user_name IN VARCHAR2);
```

This grants privileges to the object types created for use with advanced queuing to the specified user. To perform the administrative procedures `CREATE_QUEUE_TABLE`, `CREATE_QUEUE`, `ADD_SUBSCRIBER`, and `REMOVE_SUBSCRIBER`, users must have access to these types.

```
PROCEDURE START_TIME_MANAGER;
```

```
PROCEDURE STOP_TIME_MANAGER;
```

These procedures start and stop activities performed by the time manager process. The Time Manager is started at database startup by setting `AQ_TM_PROCESS=1` in the `init.ora`.

DBMS_AQ

Users must be granted `AQ_USER_ROLE` in order to use the `ENQUEUE` and `DEQUEUE` procedures. Rights also must be granted for use of the object types used for queues, queue tables, and subscribers. To grant use of these object types,

18

SUPPLIED PL/SQL
PACKAGES

`DBMS_AQADM.GRANT_TYPE_ACCESS` must be run by SYS for each user.

Several types are implemented for use with `DBMS_AQ`. They are either PL/SQL records or index-by tables. They are as follows:

```
TYPE SYS.AQ$_AGENT IS RECORD(
     name VARCHAR2(30),
     address VARCHAR(30),
     protocol NUMBER);
```

This PL/SQL record identifies a receiving or producing agent for a queue. Oracle 8.0.3 does not make use of `address` and `protocol`. These fields are for future enhancements.

```
TYPE AQ$_RECIPIENT_LIST_T IS TABLE OF SYS.AQ$_AGENT
     INDEX BY BINARY_INTEGER;
```

The `AQ$_RECIPIENT_LIST_T` type is an index-by table of `SYS.AQ$_AGENT` and is used to store a list of receiving agents in a message.

```
TYPE MESSAGE_PROPERTIES_T IS RECORD(
     priority BINARY INTEGER default 1,
     delay BINARY_INTEGER default NO_DELAY,
     expiration BINARY_INTEGER default NEVER,
     correlation VARCHAR(128) default NULL,
     attempts BINARY_INTEGER,
     recipient_list AQ$_RECIPIENT_LIST_T,
     exception_queue VARCHAR2(51) default NULL,
     enqueue_time DATE,
     state BINARY_INTEGER);
```

`priority`	Set enqueuing priority. Lower numbers are higher priority. Any integer, including negatives, is permissible.
`delay`	Delay, in seconds, before enqueing or dequeing.
`expiration`	Time before message is moved to the exception queue if it is not dequeued.
`correlation`	Groups of messages can be referenced using this identifier.
`attempts`	Used in dequeuing to specify how many attempts to dequeue should be made.
`recipient_list`	Contains a list of agents to receive a message. Used for enqueuing.
`exception_queue`	Specifies the exception queue to use in case of expiration or failure to dequeue. The default exception queue for the queue table is used if this is not set.
`enqueue_time`	Set automatically at enqueue and returned by `DEQUEUE`.
`state`	Returned by `DEQUEUE`. Set and updated automatically. Possible values are `WAITING`, `READY`, `PROCESSED`, and `EXPIRED`.

This type is used in ENQUEUE and DEQUEUE and specifies the options for a given message.

```
TYPE ENQUEUE_OPTIONS_T IS RECORD(
    visibility BINARY_INTEGER default ON_COMMIT,
    relative_msgid RAW(16) default NULL,
    sequence_deviation BINARY_INTEGER default NULL);
```

visibility	ON_COMMIT for synchronous and IMMEDIATE for asynchronous.
relative_msgid	Identifies a message for sequence_deviation.
sequence_deviation	BEFORE inserts the message just before the message specified by relative_msgid. TOP puts the message at the top of the queue. NULL lets the priority determine queue position.

Used to set options for enqueuing.

```
TYPE DEQUEUE_OPTIONS_T IS RECORD(
    consumer_name VARCHAR2(30) default NULL,
    dequeue_mode BINARY_INTEGER default REMOVE,
    navigation BINARY_INTEGER default NEXT_MESSAGE,
    visibility BINARY_INTEGER default ON_COMMIT,
    wait BINARY_INTEGER default FOREVER,
    msgid RAW(16) default NULL,
    correlation VARCHAR2(30) default NULL);
```

consumer_name	Consumer for whom messages may be dequeued.
dequeue_mode	BROWSE returns the message without removing it or locking it. LOCKED reads the message and locks it from writing. REMOVE reads it and deletes or moves it.
navigation	NEXT_MESSAGE returns the next message according to the consumer_name, msgid, and correlation settings. NEXT_TRANSACTION gets the first message of the next message group. (Messages can be grouped by transaction. See CREATE_QUEUE_TABLE.) FIRST_MESSAGE gets the first message fitting the specified criterion.
visibility	ON_COMMIT or IMMEDIATE.
wait	Length of time to wait for a message fitting the criterion. FOREVER, NO_WAIT, or the number of seconds to wait are all valid.
msgid	Message to be dequeued.
correlation	Used to specify a group label for the message.

Here are the procedures for DBMS_AQ:

```
PROCEDURE ENQUEUE(
    queue_name IN VARCHAR2,
    enqueue_options IN ENQUEUE_OPTIONS_T,
```

18

SUPPLIED PL/SQL
PACKAGES

```
message_properties IN  MESSAGE_PROPERTIES_T,
payload IN message_type,
msgid OUT RAW);
```

queue_name	Queue to put the message in.
enqueue_options	Enqueue options.
message_properties	Message properties.
payload	RAW or object type data. The queue must be created to hold data of the type passed here.
msgid Returned	ID for message. Can be used to dequeue the message later.

This procedure is used to insert a message into the queue specified by queue_name:

```
PROCEDURE DEQUEUE(
    queue_name IN VARCHAR2,
    dequeue_options IN DEQUEUE_OPTIONS_T,
    message_properties OUT MESSAGE_PROPERTIES_T,
    payload OUT message_type,
    msgid OUT RAW);
```

queue_name	Name of queue to search for messages.
dequeue_options	Options available for dequeuing.
message_properties	Properties of the message retrieved.
payload	Message data.
msgid	Message ID set by ENQUEUE.

This procedure is used to retrieve messages using the search criterion given in the consumer_name, msgid, and correlation fields of the dequeue_options record.

Upon retrieval, the message is either deleted or removed from the queue.

DBMS_OUTPUT

The DBMS_OUTPUT package is used mostly to communicate between processes running in the same session or for debugging. It allows you to create a buffer in your session and then write or read from that buffer. The buffer is stored in the SGA area, and its contents are not available until the PL/SQL unit for which it was created returns.

> **TIP**
>
> You can print to the screen in your SQL*Plus or Server Manager session by issu-
> ing the SET SERVEROUTPUT ON command. This command implicitly creates a buffer
> using DBMS_OUTPUT.ENABLE, and then prints anything in it with
> DBMS_OUTPUT.GET_LINES when the session ends. Just use DBMS_OUTPUT.PUT_LINE and
> pass in what you want to print at the end of the session.

```
PROCEDURE ENABLE(
    buffer_size IN INTEGER DEFAULT 2000);
```

Before you can actually store anything in the buffer, you need to create it using the
ENABLE procedure. There is no name associated with the buffer, and it can only be
accessed by routines running in the session where it is created. The ENABLE procedure
can be called many times, but only one buffer can exist. The buffer size defaults to 2,000
bytes, which is the minimum, and can be as large as 1,000,000 bytes. If you call ENABLE
more than once, the buffer size is set to the largest of the values provided. This procedure
does not need to be called if you are using the SERVEROUTPUT ON option.

```
PROCEDURE DISABLE;
```

Once you are finished with the data in a buffer, you can purge it and close it using
DISABLE. The buffer can be reused only after it is enabled again. If you're using the
SERVEROUTPUT ON option, you don't need to run this procedure.

```
PROCEDURE PUT_LINE(
    item IN NUMBER, VARCHAR2 or DATE)
```

This procedure is used to put a line, followed by a new line marker, into the buffer. It is
overloaded to accept NUMBER, VARCHAR2, and DATE data, but it converts them using the
TO_CHAR procedure before storing them, so you should format your dates before passing
them to the buffer.

```
PROCEDURE PUT(
    item IN NUMBER, VARCHAR2 or DATE)
```

PUT adds data to the current line but does not append a new line marker. This allows you
to create a line with several PUT calls and then append your own new line marker manually. The new line marker is necessary for retrieval of the line using GET or GET_LINE.

```
PROCEDURE GET_LINE(
    line OUT VARCHAR2,
    status OUT INTEGER);
```

To retrieve a single line from the buffer, use GET_LINE. Along with the line itself, a status
of 0 is returned for success and 1 if there are no more lines in the buffer.

18

**SUPPLIED PL/SQL
PACKAGES**

> **NOTE**
>
> GET_LINE and GET_LINES will not retrieve any lines that are not ended with a new line marker.

```
PROCEDUR GET_LINES(
    lines OUT   CHARARR,
    numlines IN OUT   INTEGER);
```

This procedure acts like GET_LINE, except that it retrieves the specified number of lines into an array and does not return a status. When the DBMS_OUTPUT package is created, it creates CHARARR as a table of VARCHAR(255). This type is used to store the retrieved lines from the buffer. Using GET_LINES rather than GET_LINE can minimize your calls to the server. Like GET_LINE, this procedure will not return any line that does not end with a new line marker.

> **NOTE**
>
> All lines that are not retrieved before the next call to PUT_LINES, NEW_LINE, or PUT are discarded.

```
NEW_LINE;
```

This procedure puts a newline marker at the end of the current line in the buffer. A new-line character is necessary to make the information retrievable, so you should use this after creating a line with PUT statements.

Scheduling Jobs

Dialing in on the weekends to run jobs is no fun and completely unnecessary. Even if you're on an operating system that does not adequately support job scheduling, you can let the database take care of itself by using the DBMS_JOB package. Spend the weekend skiing instead.

DBMS_JOB

This package allows you to schedule PL/SQL processes to be run from a job queue. A job is put into the job queue with parameters to specify when it is to run and how often. Information on jobs is kept in the data dictionary views dba_jobs, user_jobs, and dba_jobs_running.

Background processes called SNP processes are used to execute jobs in the job queue. One process is required for each simultaneously executed job. In Oracle 7 only 10 processes could be created, but in Oracle8 there can be 36. These processes are named SNP0 through SNP9 and SNPA through SNPZ. There are three init.ora parameters that control the behavior of these processes. They are as follows:

JOB_QUEUE_PROCESSES	Creates 0–36 SNP processes at instance startup.
JOB_QUEUE_INTERVAL	Seconds to sleep before checking for a new job, from 1 to 3,600.
JOB_QUEUE_KEEP_CONNECTIONS	TRUE means connections made to remote databases are kept open until the SNP process is stopped. FALSE means remote connections are closed as soon as all the jobs are run.

```
PROCEDURE SUBMIT(
    job OUT BINARY_INTEGER,
    what IN VARCHAR2,
    next_date IN DATE default SYSDATE,
    interval IN VARCHAR2 default NULL,
    no_parse IN BOOLEAN default FALSE);
```

job	Unique identifier assigned to the job. This number does not change as long as the job exists.
what	PL/SQL code—usually a stored procedure call.
next_date	Date to run the job next.
interval	Calculation used to determine next runtime. For example, 'SYSDATE + 1/12' would run the job every two hours starting from next_date.
no_parse	TRUE defers parsing of PL/SQL until it executes the first time. FALSE parses the code when it is submitted.

This process submits a job to the job queue. Once a job is submitted, it can be directly by using the DBMS_JOB.RUN procedure. The current environment settings, like NLS parameters, are recorded when the job is submitted. These settings are called the "job execution environment," and they persist for that job until a session with a different set of environment settings makes a change to it.

```
PROCEDURE RUN(
    job IN BINARY_INTEGER);
```

Used to directly run jobs as specified by the job number they are assigned when they are submitted. Jobs cannot be run before they are submitted to the job queue.

18

SUPPLIED PL/SQL
PACKAGES

When a job is submitted the current environment is recorded with it, and it is always run with those same environment settings.

```
PROCEDURE BROKEN(
     job IN BINARY_INTEGER,
     broken IN BOOLEAN,
     next_date IN DATE default SYSDATE);
```

job	Job number of job to change.
broken	TRUE sets the job's status to broken and it will no longer be run. FALSE resets the broken status for the job so it will be run again.
next_date	Date to run the job again.

This procedure is used to manually flag a job as broken or not broken. Jobs that fail are automatically run again at intervals, starting with one minute and doubling until the job has failed 16 times. After 16 failures, the job is marked as broken and no further attempts are made to run it. Broken jobs can be run directly using DBMS_JOB.RUN.

```
PROCEDURE REMOVE(
     job IN BINARY_INTEGER);
```

This procedure removes a job from the job queue.

> **NOTE**
>
> CHANGE, WHAT, NEXT_DATE, and INTERVAL all cause the prevailing environment settings to be associated with the job, just as they are when the job is first submitted.

```
PROCEDURE CHANGE(
     job IN BINARY_INTEGER,
     what IN VARCHAR2,
     next_date IN DATE,
     interval IN VARCHAR2);
```

This procedure is used to change multiple aspects of a job. The following procedures allow you to change the individual job attributes they refer to:

```
PROCEDURE WHAT(
     job IN BINARY_INTEGER,
     what IN VARCHAR2);
```

```
PROCEDURE NEXT_DATE(
     job IN BINARY_INTEGER,
     next_date IN DATE);

PROCEDURE INTERVAL(
     job IN BINARY_INTEGER,
     interval IN VARCHAR2);
```

Summary

I hope the information in this chapter is enough to get you started in the use of these packages and has given you some idea of their overall capabilities.

Although they can seem cumbersome to work with, once you get into using the packages supplied with Oracle8, you will begin to see some of the possibilities for building useful applications in PL/SQL. There really is no need to reach beyond PL/SQL for scheduling, communications, logging, DDL, or Dynamic SQL.

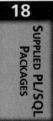

18

SUPPLIED PL/SQL
PACKAGES

Oracle8
Administration

PART
IV

IN THIS PART

Oracle8 Administrative Requirements

by Dan Hotka

IN THIS CHAPTER

Overview of Oracle8 Administration

Oracle8 comprises many complex interrelated processes, files, and memory structures (see Figure 19.1). Connecting to Oracle8 is controlled by SQL*Net and Net8, each controlled by a different set of files. The data files must be backed up periodically, based on business needs. The memory structures greatly affect how well Oracle8 performs on a given hardware platform. Tuning and troubleshooting can be ongoing chores. Data replication needs, Web server access, and partitioning add additional administrative needs to an already complex environment.

FIGURE 19.1.
Oracle processes and files.

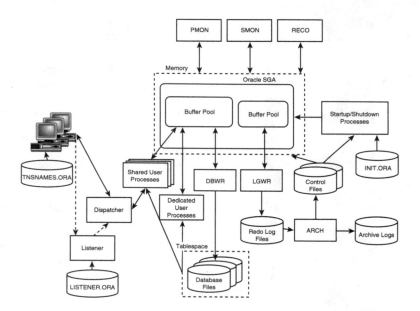

It is the job of the database administrator (DBA) to adequately handle each of these issues. Tasks such as installing the Oracle database software, setting up the SQL*Net and/or Net8 environment, and establishing the default memory usage parameters are handled once or on an infrequent basis. Strategies for database backup are established based on data recovery needs, and likewise, are adjusted rather infrequently. Adding and deleting user access privileges can be a daily task as can addressing connectivity and security issues. The various types of tuning require various types and times of attention: some happen at installation time, some during the application testing phase; some are proactive (monitoring for excessive resource utilization processes) and some reactive (end users, slow response times).

Oracle8 supplies many tools to aid the DBA in these tasks. Server Manager is a single management tool that allows the database to be started and shut down, controls the backup and recovery process, maintains user connectivity and resource access permissions, creates and maintains the tablespaces, and can monitor for various situations in the database such as locking, resource contention, and memory usage. Oracle Enterprise Manager is a series of graphical tools available for the Windows NT environment that provide the same services as Server Manager, but can also set up and monitor the SQL*Net and/or Net8 environments, monitor fragmentation, reorganize individual objects, schedule maintenance or routine tasks, and do almost-real-time monitoring. Oracle Enterprise Manager also contains a graphical interface to Recovery Manager, Oracle8's new backup and recovery tool. Important tools for the Oracle environment since the Oracle V4 days, Export and Import allow for data and objects to be moved between Oracle servers and can play an important incremental backup role. SQL*Loader loads data from flat-file structures into the Oracle environment. Oracle8 provides some significant performance enhancements to this tool, primarily in the areas of table partitioning and parallel processing of the data loading process.

Backup and Recovery Concepts

Any computing environment is subject to a variety of hardware or software failures/problems that can cause a loss of stored data. Many circumstances can affect electronic data processing. Natural disasters, power outages, and machine failures are hard to predict. Other considerations that need to be taken into account are accidental and intentional corruption or destruction of data.

Each application has specific data requirement needs. These needs must be assessed accurately for the business needs of the applications. The frequency of performing backups depends on the application and business needs as well. For example, a database that is loaded from flat files every evening may not require that any backups be performed at all, whereas OLTP applications may not have any acceptable data loss or downtime at all. This application might lend itself well for Oracle's standby database recovery option, utilizing frequent checkpoints and small `archive` log modes (for quick recovery and minimal data loss).

Many hardware issues, such as power outages and disk failure, can be averted entirely with available technology. Accidental data corruption is difficult to predict but, depending on backup/recovery strategies in place, can be nothing more than a temporary inconvenience. The possibility of intentional data corruption is a security issue requiring

19

ORACLE8 ADMINISTRATIVE REQUIREMENTS

provisions for restoring or recovering data. Oracle8 has a variety of options available for all of these scenarios including Oracle's Export and Import utilities, Oracle cold and hot backups, standby database, and Recovery Manager.

Oracle Export can be used to get individual data objects, functions, packages, user definitions, and permissions, entire tablespaces, and even the entire database into operating system files. Import can then import what was exported, to either the same Oracle instance or another Oracle instance. Export and Import tend to be rather slow, sometimes limited by operating system file limits, and are not well suited for very large databases (VLDB).

Cold backups are done when the Oracle RDBMS is in a down state and all of the physical files and initialization files are backed up. This method may be supplemented with Oracle's Export and Import utilities to do incremental backups of changed objects, or better yet, to supplement Oracle's Log Archive (see Chapter 23, "Backup and Recovery"). If archive mode is being utilized, all prior archive log files become irrelevant after a successful backup of all physical files is complete. This method is an "all or nothing" approach to recovery. If ARCHIVELOG mode is not utilized, and no other method is used to capture changes in the database, all changes are lost from the last cold backup.

Hot backups are done at the tablespace level, with the database up and available for reads and writes. Oracle must be set for Log Archive Mode (see Chapter 23 for implementation options of ARCHIVELOG mode). Hot backups utilize the archive log files to store all writes while the physical tablespace files are being backed up. During recovery, all noncorrupted tablespaces are online and available. Oracle will prompt an operator for the needed archive logs to restore the tablespace.

> **NOTE**
>
> Most 24×7 data availability shops use this Hot backup method.

A *standby database* is a duplicate database environment, on duplicate equipment (with some exceptions), identical levels of operating systems, and identical levels of Oracle software. This standby database is in a constant state of recovery; as archive log files are closed on the primary database, they are transferred and applied to this standby database. This method incurs absolutely no overhead on the primary database and the only disadvantage is that the standby database is only as current as the last log file applied. This method is very quick to implement into the primary database so the amount of application downtime is minimal. These archive log files are easy to size and tune. Chapter 24, "Oracle8 Database Tuning," has details on these and other tuning tips.

> **TIP**
>
> Size the archive log files appropriately for the amount of acceptable data loss.

Recovery Manager is a new Oracle8 tool that greatly aids in the backup and recovery process. It works with the Oracle8 kernel and can be accessed via a utility, Oracle Enterprise Manger V1.4, or with an embedded library call. Recovery Manager has a repository so backup file groups can be viewed. The repository is recommended but is not mandatory. Recovery Manager also stores information in the Control File(s). It utilizes third-party storage devices. Recovery Manager can back up the entire database, individual tablespaces, individual data files, or just the changed data blocks.

> **NOTE**
>
> Recovery Manager does not back up externally stored LOBs, SQL*Net configuration files, or INIT.ORA parameter files.

Security and Access Concepts

Access to the Oracle environment is handled in one of two ways: direct access from the computer that contains the database or over SQL*Net or Net8. SQL*Net is the level of software that hides the computing network from the application, allowing connectivity from end users and other databases. Net8 is the next release of the SQL*Net environment. SQL*Net on the server-side uses a listener process and a dispatcher service to assist in the management of user connections and the associated background Oracle processes. These dispatchers can load balance connections among multiple dispatchers. Net8 provides Oracle8 networking environments with enhanced distributed application support, connection pooling, better authentication services, and improved names services. Connection Manager is a new Oracle8 application that works with the multithreaded server option. It can act as a firewall, a multiprotocol interchange, and a concentrator (multiplexing data into a common physical transport). Connection Manager works with both SQL*Net and Net8 environments.

Once one has access to the Oracle environment, security is necessary to ensure that those who were given permission to connect have the correct privileges to access the various application data objects. In addition to the currently available object permissions, Oracle8 has some new password features. These include password history, account locking, password expiration and aging, rule-based verification, and additional user profile settings.

Overview of Oracle8 Permissions and Profiles

Oracle8 supports all the same permissions, roles, and profiles as were available with previous versions of Oracle. Users are established via the CREATE USER command. The permission CONNECT (or CREATE SESSION) must be granted for the user to have access to the database. There are still the same GRANT privilege commands, allowing query and DML access to the data objects, and executing permissions to packages and functions. Roles are groups of privileges given a name that, in itself, becomes another privilege. Profiles are a way of limiting resources to a user or group of users. Enhanced in Oracle8, profiles allow for a certain number of attempts of login, password encryption rules, password aging, and password history. The full list of available permissions is available in the *Oracle Server SQL Reference Manual*.

Overview of SQL*Net, Net8, and Connection Manager

SQL*Net handles all the networking and connectivity issues for the Oracle environment. Oracle has always had a background process started on the server for each connecting process on the server or by a networked user (see Figure 19.2). There has also always been a listener process (it used to be called ORASRV) that ran on each server, monitoring SQL*Net traffic for Oracle databases on that particular server. This listener process used to start the background process (a resource-intensive process), establish connectivity between the connecting process and the background process, and then go back to a wait state until the next new connection was requested. Oracle7 introduced the concept of a multithreaded server (MTS), where a dispatcher (or several dispatchers) was established to take over the SQL*Net traffic once communications from a connected process were established. Multithreaded servers' primary purpose is to allow for the sharing of these background processes. Depending on the application, a dispatcher can allow ten users to share a single background process. With the dispatcher assigning background server processes to connecting processes, it is now possible to monitor and prestart several of the background processes ahead of time to eliminate the overhead and end-user wait time typically associated with connecting to the Oracle database. The dispatcher will assign incoming connections to the background processes in its control. If all of the background processes are in use, the dispatcher will start another background process on the connection's behalf, just as it used to do. This architecture is what Oracle refers to as the multithreaded server. There can be as many dispatchers as needed to handle the SQL*Net traffic. Memory management and machine resources are more efficient because the prestarted background processes are not being constantly terminated and started as connections to the database are established and disconnected. There is at least one listener (with its own dispatcher or set of dispatchers and prestarted background processes) per network protocol (TCP/IP, Dec NET, SPX/IPX, and so on). The listener will load-balance the SQL*Net traffic among the assigned dispatchers (see Figure 19.2).

FIGURE 19.2.

*A typical SQL*Net environment.*

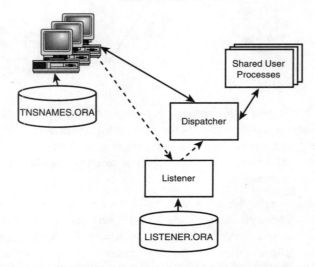

Net8 builds on where SQL*Net leaves off. The Connection Manager process acts as a concentrator for the MTS environment only (see Figure 19.3). This concentrator feature can handle traffic from multiple separate connections by combining the various connections (regardless of network protocol) into one physical link to the dispatchers. SQL*Net has a separate process called a MultiProtocol Interchange that will convert the SQL*Net traffic from one network protocol to another, kind of like a bridge. Connection Manager eliminates the need for this separate function. Connection Manager can also act as a firewall, allowing only authorized connections, and the connections can be based on source, host name, and the Oracle database desired.

Net8 has also enhanced the listener process. The listener has been enhanced to load-balance among participating servers. It supports the traditional two-tier configuration (client/server) and also supports the N-tier configuration, a disconnected environment using a distributed message queue process.

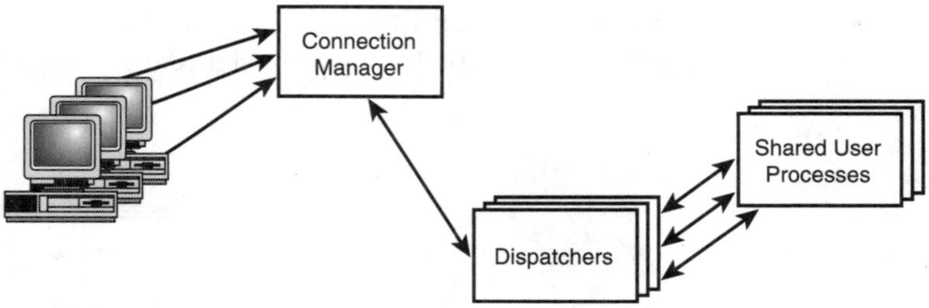

FIGURE 19.3.
Net8 and
Connection
Manager.

Security and authentication have been significantly improved via the Oracle Security Server. Security Server can do single sign-on, can handle the concept of a global user (with global rules), and supports multiple authentication methods. Security Server comes with a tool kit (a set of APIs) to extend this level of security to applications such as email and electronic commerce.

Net8 also has improved the Name Services. SQL*Net has a Names Server to resolve names to locations. This method of naming makes it very easy to move Oracle servers and databases with no impact on the end-user community. The Net8 Name Services has the ability to cache names at the client for much faster resolution, and the various listeners and connection managers register as available with Name Services.

Tablespace Maintenance Concepts

Tablespaces are used to contain all Oracle objects (tables, indexes, clusters, packages, procedures, functions, and so on). The Oracle tablespace is a logical storage area. Physical disk files (RAID, or even UNIX raw partitions) are added to the tablespace level. Tablespace size is limited only by the amount of available disk space. There are a couple of important tablespaces, namely SYSTEM where the Oracle data dictionary resides, and TEMPORARY which is typically used for sorts, merge/joins, and so on. DBAs and developers have a great deal of control over how the space within the tablespace is allocated and shared. Performance can be greatly enhanced using various tablespaces to control object locations on physical disk devices.

A new feature of Oracle8 is that of partitioning. Partitioning enhances Oracle's support for very large databases as partitioning breaks tables and indexes into smaller, easier-to-manage pieces, storing these pieces at the tablespace level. Partitioned tables/indexes are nothing more than a logical collection of tablespaces (see Figure 19.4).

Partitioning greatly enhances database performance. This performance can be monitored and adjusted in a variety of manors. Read/write activity can be load-balanced among disk drives/disk arrays. The Oracle optimizer recognizes partitions and can select only from partitions that contain the data being selected. The Oracle Parallel Server can divide work based on the number of partitions.

Availability is higher, backups are easier, and recovery is shorter. High availability is the single goal of most computer systems. Recovery and time to recover are always an issue. Downtime for maintenance or backups is not possible with some applications. Machine failures are inevitable. Partitions can be backed up online, individually, and only the ones that have changes. This makes the backup/recovery process much quicker. If recovery is needed, the other partitions not affected are still available and online.

FIGURE 19.4.

Oracle tablespace layout example.

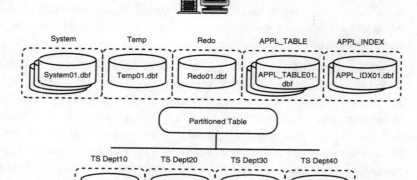

Administration and tuning is much easier. Oracle8 partitioning has many features that make the partitions easy to create, move, split, and so on. One can even swap in an existing non-partitioned table structure and data to an existing table partition. Tuning is enhanced with the additional indexing features available.

Oracle8 supports the read-only tablespace. Read-only tablespaces are more efficient than the traditional full access tablespace: No updates can occur so the read consistency and recovery mechanisms need not apply to this tablespace. This feature is also useful for tablespaces targeted for CD-ROM devices.

19

ORACLE8
ADMINISTRATIVE
REQUIREMENTS

> **TIP**
>
> Prior to running the READ ONLY command, run the SQL statement select count(*) from ... against each table in the read-only tablespace. This will reset the check block level transaction status remaining from any recent updates and eliminate this bit of overhead from any future access to the data.

Importance of Organization

The Oracle tablespace implementation lends itself well to a variety of application needs. The tablespace can be used as a point of user/object organization; its flexibility lends itself well for SQL tuning through object distribution, it can be backed up and restored while still available to applications, and if damaged, it can remain unavailable while other tablespaces remain available.

The Oracle data dictionary resides in the SYSTEM tablespace. Because Oracle relies heavily on the data dictionary for every operation, it cannot be taken offline, or made unavailable for any reason. The ROLLBACK tablespace is typically used by the rollback segments (these segments ensure read consistency and recovery from uncommitted transactions) that dynamically grow and shrink based on usage and the demands of various applications. The TEMPORARY tablespace is where Oracle8 will do its sorting and merge/join operations (more than one table in the SQL statement from clause). No permanent objects can be created here. Additional TEMPORARY tablespaces can be added to the instance with the CREATE TABLESPACE <tablespace name> TEMPORARY command. This default activity can be altered with the DEFAULT TEMPORARY TABLESPACE assignment in the CREATE USER or ALTER USER SQL commands. It is important that any user-defined object (tables, indexes, clusters, and so on) *not* be created in any of these three tablespaces for obvious reasons. Similarly, the DEFAULT TABLESPACE is set by the CREATE USER or ALTER USER SQL commands to point at a tablespace for the user to store objects. Both the TABLESPACE and the TEMPORARY TABLESPACE defaults can be overridden by syntax in the CREATE SQL statement.

Tablespaces can be used to organize and separate various applications sharing an Oracle instance. Their names (and underlying data file names) can make the environment self-documenting. Additional tablespaces are easy to create with the CREATE TABLESPACE SQL statement. The user must have DBA authority or the CREATE TABLESPACE privilege. This statement creates the tablespace and adds the initial file or files. Default storage parameters can be entered at this time as well. These defaults are applied only when the storage parameters are *not* defined at the object creation time.

Tuning Through Distribution

It is desirable in any computing environment to distribute the disk I/O as evenly as possible among the available disk drives and controllers. There were (and still are today) many scenarios for striping or partitioning large tables and indexes across many disk drives. The advent of RAID technology made this process very easy from a hardware point of view. Oracle8 supports partitioning which makes the distribution of specific data much easier to implement and administrate. It is equally important to have the previously mentioned SYSTEM, ROLLBACK, and TEMPORARY tablespaces on separate devices, preferably even separate disk controllers. If the application has a high number of INSERTs and UPDATEs, the online redo logs should be on yet another separate disk drive. Each of these tablespaces will incur large volumes of I/O, depending of course on the application. It will noticeably enhance performance to have the files associated with these three tablespaces separated from each other and separated from the other tablespaces.

In the Oracle tablespace layout example (see Figure 19.4), please note that I have intentionally created APPL_TABLE and APPL_INDEX tablespaces. This will logically allow me to create the tables and indexes in separate storage areas. I would create the underlying files assigned to these tablespaces on separate disk devices, preferably with these disk devices on separate disk controllers.

> **TIP**
>
> Treat RAID partitions as separate disk drives. It would defeat the purpose of distributing the I/O if both data and related index tablespaces used the same RAID partitions.

Take this I/O distribution one step further. Review the FROM and WHERE clauses of SELECT statements that access medium or large objects. Make sure the largest of the tables are on separate devices from the smaller tables. Always keep the indexes on separate drives from the tables. Always put the parent table, child tables, and the primary/foreign key indexes all on separate drives if possible. Referential integrity makes this selection distribution easy as the parent and child tables are easy to identify and should reside on separate physical devices.

Sizing Defaults

Oracle manages its space inside the tablespace in units called *extents*. An extent can be one or more contiguous Oracle blocks. Extents are preallocated space (contiguous Oracle blocks) assigned to individual data-oriented objects. The Oracle block size is defined at

CREATE DATABASE time. Extent sizes are given in sizes of bytes and Oracle does the calculation converting the extent size to Oracle blocks, rounding up to the next multiple of block size.

The tablespace has a default storage clause (see Listing 19.1). This default is used only when a storage clause is *not* specified on objects being created in that tablespace. The storage parameter can be altered; however, any change in storage parameters will have no effect on already existing object storage usage.

LISTING 19.1. STORAGE CLAUSE EXAMPLE.

```
Create tablespace EXAMPLE
     datafile '/ora8/v8.0.3/dbs/Example01.dbs' size 100K
     default storage (
                initial 25K next 10K
                minextents 1 maxextents 100
                pctincrease 0);
```

In Listing 19.1, the tablespace EXAMPLE will be created with one file, Example01.dbs, with a size of 100KB. When the CREATE TABLE SQL statement is entered without a storage clause, the default tablespace storage clause will be used. In this example, if no storage clause is given, the table's initial extent will be 25KB (rounded up to the next even Oracle block size), with each additional extent needed of 10KB. MINEXTENTS is the original number of extents to be allocated, and MAXEXTENTS will be all the extents that will be allocated to this object. If this MAXEXTENTS is reached, the error ORA-01631 max # extents (100) in table xxxxx displays. Pctincrease is a value that will increase the next extent size by this factor over the size of the previously created extent.

Fragmentation and Design Considerations

Tablespace fragmentation can occur in a number of circumstances. Most fragmentation has definite performance implications. Some types of fragmentation are actually good, such as striping. For example, data striping is good when many users are selecting/inserting/updating rows all over a rather large table. Striping allows the associated locking and disk I/O to be distributed across several disk devices. Other types of fragmentation are not good. Extent interleaving, row chaining, and row migration all have performance implications. Tablespace fragmentation doesn't necessarily affect performance, but a significant amount of disk space can be wasted.

Extent interleaving occurs when two or more data objects in the same tablespace are all dynamically growing in such a way that the objects assigned extents are in between extents from other data objects. Oracle performs best with a minimal number of extents, and also when the extents are next to each other. The fewer extents, the fewer trips

Oracle has to make to the data dictionary to find out where the next extent to retrieve is. Having extents sprinkled all over the tablespace also causes excessive disk head movement, a time-consuming task for a computer. Objects that are involved in this interleaving should be exported, dropped, and re-created. The best results would be to reorganize the entire tablespace.

> **NOTE**
>
> Extent interleaving is easily fixed, but, if not done correctly, can cause tablespace fragmentation.

Row chaining is caused when a row being inserted is larger than the Oracle block size. Oracle will *chain*, or link by block number, an additional block (or blocks) to hold the remaining data from the row. This chained block cannot be indexed and cannot be referenced without first referencing the original block. This greatly slows the data access as Oracle has to wait for an additional I/O to retrieve the chained block. If there is significant chaining, performance can be seriously affected. The only way to correct chaining is to export the object and its data and either re-create the database with a larger Oracle block size or import the object and its data into an Oracle database that already has a larger block size assigned.

Row migration is caused by an update where the row will no longer fit in its current block. Oracle will relocate the updated row to a different block where it will completely fit, leaving a ROWID pointer in the original block that references the new data location in another block. Like row chaining, there is no reference to this new location except by accessing the original location first. Once again, Oracle will have to wait while an additional disk I/O is performed to retrieve the new row. It can also be a time-consuming process for Oracle to locate a new block with enough free space to hold the new row. Row migration can be easy to fix, especially if there are not a lot of indexes or references to/from other objects. Exporting the table's data, dropping the table, and importing the data back into the table will correct row migration.

Tablespace fragmentation involves the nonused disk space between objects. This type of fragmentation is caused by deletes and by extents being returned to the free list. It is not a performance issue as much as a space utilization issue. Oracle7 introduced *coalescing*, a process that will make two or more adjoining empty Oracle blocks into a single larger block of available space. The only way to fully utilize these empty spaces is to reorganize the entire tablespace. The following is a syntax example:

```
alter tablespace EXAMPLE coalesce;
```

19

ORACLE8 ADMINISTRATIVE REQUIREMENTS

NOTE

I have noticed the Oracle RDBMS doing a better job of tablespace free space management with each new release of the software.

Most fragmentation is a result of poor database design.

Extent interleaving can be completely eliminated by simply putting tables with static or very little growth together in a tablespace and putting each dynamically growing object in a tablespace by itself. This increases tablespace maintenance but eliminates this type of fragmentation.

Row chaining is a result of the database administrator not being fully aware of the data requirements. The only way to eliminate row chaining is to export the entire database, re-create it with a bigger database block size, and import the entire database.

TIP

If this is an issue in your shop, try to wait until the next upgrade of the Oracle software or the application being relocated to a different machine. Set up the new environment with a database block size large enough to hold an entire row.

TIP

If row chaining is caused by long raw data types, stored binary data, and so on, take advantage of externally storing these objects outside the Oracle8 environment.

Row migration can be limited by making adjustments to the PCTFREE parameters in the storage clause. PCTFREE is the amount of space left in each Oracle block after insertions for the purpose of accommodating future updates. Altering the PCTFREE clause will not have any effect on any existing migrated rows. The table will have to be reorganized to get rid of the existing migrated rows.

Tablespace fragmentation is difficult to avoid as it is caused by row deletions. The best advice I can offer is to put objects with this kind of activity in tablespaces by themselves.

Schema Maintenance Concepts

A schema, or a collection of logical structures, is owned by a user and has the same name as the user. Basically, anything that can be owned by a user, such as tables, triggers, indexes, sequences, basically any database objects are part of that user's schema. Objects that are not part of a schema are tablespaces, roles, profiles, and rollback segments.

Object Maintenance

There are a variety of maintenance tasks that affect objects. The prior section discussed object fragmentation. There are also permissions to be maintained so users have the correct access to the objects. Indexes may need to be added or rebuilt for performance reasons. A whole series of various check and referential constraints need to be added and maintained. Columns may need to be added as well as column attributes changed. The SQL command ALTER TABLE is useful until the requirement is to add a new column into the middle of an existing object. To do this with Server Manager or SQL*Plus, one will have to spool the data out of the table or rename the existing object, create a script of the existing object, alter the script with the new column, drop the existing object (if not renamed), create the new object, repopulate the table with the data, and make sure all referential integrity, permissions, indexes, and any other reference to the object are re-established. Chapter 22, "Oracle8 Tools," will discuss some third-party tools that can assist the administrator with time-consuming tasks such as these.

If the desired task is to successfully create a series of tables, views, and grants, dropping all objects involved if any of the creates are not successful, the CREATE SCHEMA command might be useful. If any of the steps fail, the entire operation is rolled back.

Referential Integrity

Referential integrity is a relationship between a parent table and a child table through the use of unique primary keys and foreign keys. Oracle8 (and Oracle7) supports the Referential Integrity Constraint that enforces this relationship, thus elevating the developers from the time-consuming task of programming such a feature.

19

ORACLE8
ADMINISTRATIVE
REQUIREMENTS

NOTE

The child table must be in the same database as the parent table.

TIP

The option ON DELETE CASCADE (part of the CREATE CONSTRAINT syntax) might be helpful when deleting rows from the parent table, automating the referential integrity delete process.

Loading/Unloading Tables

Oracle has always supplied Export and Import routines to perform the movement of data in and out of Oracle tables. Oracle also supplies SQL*Loader, a fully configurable data loader tool. SQL*Plus can be used to format data, but was not really designed as a data extract tool. There are third-party unload tools that fill the gap on the unloading of data from the Oracle environment. These tools are discussed further in Chapter 22.

Export can easily export the entire database, an entire user schema, or individual tables. The biggest difficulty with Export/Import is that it is proprietary to the Oracle environment. That is, Import cannot be used to populate any Oracle table except from a file created by Export. These routines handle most export/import situations within the Oracle environment.

NOTE

Oracle documentation recommends manually disabling referential integrity constraints and then importing the parent/child tables (or self referencing tables) as conflicts may occur because of the order of the rows being loaded. See the Oracle8 Server Utilities, Chapter 2, "Oracle Database Architecture," the section titled "Disabling Referential Constraints," for more details.

Export has a direct path unload option that can access data directly from the Oracle data files and not use SELECT statements and the associated buffering overhead of the Oracle RDBMS. Export still can create only one file of output which, depending on operating systems, may hit a file size limit when exporting larger objects. Export and Import can handle all the new partitioning features, loading all partitions or single partitions, as desired. Import can also rename a schema owner. Both tools are accessed via command line. Both tools have a series of parameters that control the work to be done. Both tools have three modes of operations: an interactive mode, a command line mode with all options specified on the command line, and a command line mode with all options specified in a parameter file.

Oracle's Export has been improved with Oracle8 in that it has a direct path access option to the data where it does not incur the overhead of the Oracle buffering in accessing the data to be exported. It goes directly to the underlying files and accesses the data directly.

The command line (see Listing 19.2) has the instructions to start Export, export the user Scott's schema, and compress multiple table extents into one initial extent upon import.

LISTING 19.2. EXPORT COMMAND LINE EXAMPLE AND OUTPUT.

```
Unix->exp scott/tiger file=example.exp owner=scott grants=Y rows=Y
➥compress=y

Export: Release 8.0.3.0.0 - Production on Tue Feb 3 9:01:15 1998
(c) Copyright 1997 Oracle Corporation.  All rights reserved.

Connected to: Oracle8 Server Release 8.0.3.0.0 - Production
PL/SQL Release 8.0.3.0.0 - Production
Export done in US7ASCII character set
. exporting object type definitions for user SCOTT

About to export SCOTT's objects ...
. exporting database links
. exporting sequence numbers
. exporting cluster definitions
. about to export SCOTT's tables via Conventional Path ...
. . exporting table                         BONUS          0 rows
➥exported
. . exporting table                          DEPT          4 rows
➥exported
. . exporting table                           EMP         14 rows
➥exported
. . exporting table                      SALGRADE          5 rows
➥exported
. exporting synonyms
. exporting views
. exporting stored procedures
. exporting referential integrity constraints
. exporting triggers
. exporting posttables actions
. exporting snapshots
. exporting snapshot logs
. exporting job queues
. exporting refresh groups and children
Export terminated successfully without warnings.
```

19

ORACLE8
ADMINISTRATIVE
REQUIREMENTS

Listing 19.3 imports the file exported by Export. I told it to ignore any errors due to the object's existence.

Listing 19.3. Import command line example and output.

```
Unix-> imp scott/tiger  file=example.exp ignore=Y


Import: Release 8.0.3.0.0 - Production on Tue Feb 3 9:31:21 1998

(c) Copyright 1997 Oracle Corporation.  All rights reserved.

Connected to: Oracle8 Server Release 8.0.3.0.0 - Production
PL/SQL Release 8.0.3.0.0 - Production
Export file created by EXPORT:V08.00.03 via conventional path
. importing SCOTT's objects
. . importing table                         BONUS          0 rows
➥imported
. . importing table                        "DEPT"          4 rows
➥imported
. . importing table                        "EMP"          14 rows
➥imported
. . importing table                    "SALGRADE"          5 rows
➥imported

Import terminated successfully without warnings.
```

Oracle also comes with SQL*Loader, a table, or multiple table load facility. This tool is capable of reading a variety of formatted files from a variety of sources (disk files, tape, even named pipes), and with some logic, can populate multiple tables from one pass of the data file being loaded. SQL*Loader has a direct path load option, that is, a feature that allows SQL*Loader to ignore the Oracle kernel and directly load the data into Oracle blocks in the underlying files assigned to the tablespace.

> **Note**
>
> This is an unprotected write where there is no read consistency, undo ability, or archive logs of the event.

SQL*Loader can also save rejected records to a disk file.

Listing 19.4, shows the SQL*Loader command line syntax and the associated control file that will load a single table with data from file EXAMPLE.DAT, and it contains some constant values that will populate the table as well.

LISTING 19.4. SQL*LOADER COMMAND LINE AND CONTROL FILE EXAMPLE.

```
Unix->sqlldr USERID=hotka/dan CONTROL=EXAMPLE.ctl, LOG=EXAMPLE.log,
BAD=EXAMPLE.bad


Unix->cat EXAMPLE.ctl
    load data
    infile 'EXAMPLE.DAT'
    append
    into table APPL_PROGRAM_TABLE
      (PROGRAM_NAME position(1:8) char,
    PROGRAM_SUFFIX constant 'COB',
    PROGRAM_SIZE position(15:22) integer external,
    PROGRAM_PATH constant 'C:\COBOL',
    ASSIGNED_ANALYST constant 'HOTKA')
```

Sizing Defaults

Oracle manages its space inside the tablespace in units called extents. An extent can be one or more contiguous Oracle blocks. Extents are preallocated units of disk space assigned individually to data-oriented objects. The Oracle block size is defined at CREATE DATABASE time. Extent sizes are given in sizes of bytes and Oracle does the calculation converting the extent size to Oracle blocks, rounding up to the next multiple of block size.

The tablespace has a default storage clause. This default is used only when a storage clause is *not* specified on objects being created in that tablespace. The storage parameter can be altered; however, any change in storage parameters will have no effect on already existing object storage usage.

In Listing 19.5, I will create the famous EMP table. Its initial extent will be 25KB (rounded up to the next even Oracle block size), with each additional extent needed of 10KB each. MINEXTENTS is the original number of extents to be allocated, and MAXEXTENTS will be all the extents that will be allocated to this object. If this MAXEXTENTS is reached, the error ORA-01631 max # extents (100) in table xxxxx displays. Pctincrease is a value that will increase the next extent size by this factor over the size of the previously created extent. Data blocks are inserted until the percent of the block is within PCTFREE of being full. Inserts will not be allowed again in the data blocks until the percentage of free space reaches PCTUSED. Free space in blocks is accomplished through deletes or updates that make fields smaller.

LISTING 19.5. Create table SYNTAX EXAMPLE.

```
Create table EMP (
    EMPNO               NUMBER(4) NOT NULL,
    ENAME               VARCHAR2(10),
    JOB                 VARCHAR2(9),
    MGR                 NUMBER(4),
    HIREDATE            DATE,
    SAL                 NUMBER(7,2),
    COMM                NUMBER(7,2),
    DEPTNO              NUMBER(2) NOT NULL)
    storage (
                        initial 25K next 10K
                        pctfree 20 pctused 80
                        minextents 1 maxextents 100
                        pctincrease 0);
```

> **NOTE**
>
> Make sure to take into account NULL fields that will eventually contain data when arriving at a percentage for PCTFREE.

Estimating the Size of Objects

The next two sections will discuss in detail how to arrive at a fairly accurate estimate of the amount of space in bytes required to hold certain objects.

Table Sizing

The following calculations will help estimate the number of blocks and the total size in bytes required by table structures. The total size of the object as a result of these calculations is for initial sizing only.

Sizing the table object involves a series of calculations. Some of the data required will come from the table column specifications, some of the data will come from V$ tables, and the others will be from intermediate calculations. Table 19.1 is the Table Size Worksheet that can be used to aid in the collection of necessary information.

TABLE 19.1. TABLE SIZE WORKSHEET.

Calculation Variable	Value
Extimated Number of Rows	
COLUMN SIZES (calculated and totaled)	
DB_BLOCK_SIZE (from v$parameter)	
PCTFREE (from object storage clause, dba_tables, or use 10 if not defined)	
INITRANS (from object storage clause, dba_tables, or use 1 if not defined)	
KCBH (from v$type_size)	
KDBH (from v$type_size)	
KDBIT (from v$type_size)	
KDBT (from v$type_size)	
KTBBH (from v$type_size)	
SB2 (from v$type_size)	
UB1 (from v$type_size)	
UB2 (from v$type_size)	
UB4 (from v$type_size)	
ROWSIZE (from calculation)	
TOTAL ROWSIZE (from calculation)	
HEADER SIZE (from calculation)	
AVAILABLE DATA SPACE (from calculation)	
ROWS PER BLOCK (from calculation)	
BLOCKS REQUIRED (from calculation)	
SIZE in bytes of TABLE (from calculation)	

19

ORACLE8 ADMINISTRATIVE REQUIREMENTS

Calculating the average column size for each column in the table can be done via a query or by a manual calculation. Run the following query once for each column in the table: select avg(vsize(<*COLUMN NAME*>)) from <*TABLE NAME*>;. Record the sum of the returned values in the COLUMN SIZE area of the Table Size Worksheet (Table 19.1). A manual way to arrive at this total is to sum up the result of the following calculation: individual column size = column size + (1 unless the column size > 250, and then use 3). NUMBER field sizes are half the column size but not greater than 21. DATE fields take 7 positions. ROWID takes 10 positions. Use an average size for VARCHAR2 fields. Multiply any NULL fields by a percentage of the time they are expected to be NULL. All other fields use their referenced size value.

The next step is to populate the DB_BLOCK_SIZE, KCBH, KTBBH, KDBH, KTBIT, KDBT, SB2, UB1, and UB4 values. The following two queries will access this information from the Oracle V$ tables:

```
Select VALUE from V$PARAMETER where NAME = 'db_block_size';
```

```
select TYPE,TYPE_SIZE from V$TYPE_SIZE where TYPE in (' KCBH', 'KTBBH',
'KDBH', 'KTBIT', 'KDBT', 'SB2', 'UB1','UB4');
```

Calculate

HEADER SIZE = (DB_BLOCK_SIZE-KTBBH—KCBH—UB4—(INITRANS -1))×(KTBIT—KDBH)

and record the result in the HEADER SIZE area of Table 19.1.

Calculate

AVAILABLE DATA SPACE = round(HEADER SIZE×(1—PCTFREE/100))—KDBT

and record the result in the AVAILABLE DATA SPACE area of Table 19.1.

Calculate

ROWSIZE = (UB1×3) + 10 + COLUMN SIZES

and record the result in the ROWSIZE area of Table 19.1.

Calculate

TOTAL ROWSIZE = (the lesser of ((UB1×3) + UB4 + SB2) or ROWSIZE) + SB2

and record the result in the TOTAL ROWSIZE area of Table 19.1.

> **NOTE**
>
> If TOTAL ROWSIZE is greater than DB_BLOCK_SIZE, each row of this object will chain. I recommend increasing the database block size.

Calculate

ROWS PER BLOCK = round(AVAILABLE DATA SPACE / TOTAL ROW SIZE)

and record your result in ROWS PER BLOCK area of Table 19.1.

Calculate

```
BLOCKS REQUIRED = Estimated Number of Rows / ROWS PER BLOCK
```

and record the result in the BLOCKS REQUIRED area of Table 19.1.

The last calculation is SIZE in bytes of TABLE = BLOCKS REQUIRED×DB_BLOCK_SIZE. Record this number in the last line of Table 19.1.

> **TIP**
>
> Make the initial extent size large enough to hold this table.

Index Sizing

The following calculations will help estimate the number of blocks and the total size in bytes required by index structures. The total size of the object as a result of these calculations is for initial sizing only.

Sizing the index object involves a series of calculations. Some of the data required will come from the index column specifications, some of the data will come from the V$PARAMETER, and the others will be from intermediate calculations. Table 19.2 below is the Index Size Worksheet that can be used to aid in the collection of necessary information.

TABLE 19.2. INDEX SIZE WORKSHEET.

Calculation Variable	Value
Extimated Number of Rows	
DB_BLOCK_SIZE (from v$parameter)	
PCTFREE (from object storage clause, dba_indexes, or use 10 if not defined)	
INITRANS (from object storage clause, dba_indexes, or use 2 if not defined)	
KEYS<127 (from calculation)	
KEYS>127 (from calculation)	
KEY SIZE (from calculation)	
ENTRY SIZE (from calculation)	
HEADER SIZE (from calculation)	

continues

19

ORACLE8
ADMINISTRATIVE
REQUIREMENTS

TABLE 19.2. CONTINUED

Calculation Variable	Value
AVAILABLE INDEX SPACE (from calculation)	_____
BLOCKS REQUIRED (from calculation)	_____
SIZE in bytes of INDEX (from calculation)	_____

The first step is to populate the DB_BLOCK_SIZE value. The following query will access this information from the Oracle V$PARAMETER table:

```
Select VALUE from V$PARAMETER where NAME = 'db_block_size';
```

You need to calculate the KEY SIZE. This is similar to the table column calculation except you need to perform the calculation only on the indexed fields. You are going to need to know the average column length for each column in this index. This can easily be found by running the following query once for each column in the table being indexed:

```
select avg(vsize(<COLUMN NAME>)) from <TABLE NAME>;
```

Record the sum of the returned values in the KEY SIZE area of the Table Size Worksheet (Table 19.2). A manual way to arrive at this total is to sum up the result of the following calculation: individual column size = column size + (1 unless the column size > 250, and then use 3). NUMBER field sizes are half the column size but not greater than 21. DATE fields take 7 positions. Use an average size for VARCHAR2 fields. Multiply any NOT NULL field by a percentage of the time it is expected to be NULL. All other fields use their referenced size value.

Calculate

HEADER SIZE = 113 + (24×INITRANS)

and record this number in the HEADER SIZE area of Table 19.2.

Calculate

AVAILABLE DATA SPACE = (DB_BLOCK_SIZE–HEADER SIZE)–((DB_BLOCK_SIZE–HEADER SIZE)×(PCTFREE/100))

and record this number in AVAILABLE DATA SPACE area of Table 19.2.

Calculate

KEYS<127 = (1×number of indexed columns with a length < 127 bytes)

and record this number in the KEYS<127 area of Table 19.2.

Calculate

KEYS>127 = (2×number of indexed columns with a length > 126 bytes)

and record this number in the KEYS>127 area of Table 19.2.

Calculate

ENTRY SIZE = 12 + KEYS<127 + KEYS>127 + KEY SIZE

and record this number in the ENTRY SIZE area of Table 19.2.

Calculate

BLOCKS REQUIRED = (Estimated Number of Rows / (round(AVAILABLE DATA SPACE / ENTRY SIZE)))×1.05

and record this number in the BLOCKS REQUIRED area of Table 19.2.

Calculate

SIZE in bytes of INDEX = BLOCKS REQUIRED×DB_BLOCK_SIZE

and record this number in the SIZE in bytes of INDEX area of Table 19.2.

> **TIP**
>
> Make the initial extent size large enough to hold this index.

Tuning Concepts

There are two basic modes and reasons for tuning: proactive and reactive. Proactive tuning involves capacity planning, including planning for the growth of objects, adequate application and data access response times, and financial benefits. Financial benefits can be achieved if the response times can be made adequate without having to purchase additional hardware. Reactive tuning simply addresses slow response times.

Who Is Responsible for Tuning Tasks?

Several roles have responsibility for various tuning functions. All of these roles may be handled by a single person in smaller shops or by teams of people in larger shops. The system administrator needs to work closely with the database administrator to make sure the system environment is set correctly. The database administrator will handle the init.ora tuning parameters, monitoring, and I/O distribution. The DBA will work closely with the data administrator (or systems analyst) to determine object location needs. The DBA will monitor for resource intensive SQL statements, but the developer will tune and implement the offending SQL statements.

Four Levels of Tuning

Operating system tuning on Oracle's behalf consists of shared memory and semaphore setting adjustments. Research the availability of UNIX raw partitions and RAID drives on your particular hardware platform for the Oracle database files.

Oracle system tuning consists of making sure that the Oracle resources have minimal contention, are not being swapped by the operating system, and have good disk and memory hit ratios. Most of these features are controlled by Oracle's initialization parameters stored in the `init<SID>.ora` file. Contention on rollback segments is caused by several factors: frequent hot backups, frequent checkpoints, and/or redo logs not large enough. The Oracle software should be on separate drives from the UNIX operating system, application software, and other UNIX processes. The Oracle software should be separated from the tablespace data files, and the SYSTEM, TEMPORARY, and ROLLBACK tablespace data files should be on separate drives as well. If the application has a high number of INSERTs and UPDATEs, the online redo logs should be located on their own disk drive as well.

Database design has a great deal to do with how applications will perform. It is important to locate related objects on different disk drives, preferably on different disk controllers as well. The physical location of objects involved with referential integrity and the associated indexes will have a direct effect on performance. The better the I/O distribution on the available disk drives, the better overall performance will be. Dynamic allocation, which occurs when data objects add extents, is a very expensive and time-consuming process for Oracle. Make sure INITIAL EXTENT and NEXT EXTENT are all set accurately to limit the amount of extent-adding to objects. Row chaining and row migrations are also expensive processes for Oracle, both during INSERTs and during a QUERY. Make sure PCTFREE and PCTUSED are set accurately to avoid wasting space in the blocks but to allow adequate space for UPDATEs.

SQL code, particularly poorly performing SQL code, needs to be identified and tuned. There are various monitoring tools available, discussed in detail in Chapter 22, that can identify resource-intensive and/or long-running SQL statements. Tuning these will have the biggest impact on application performance. There are various EXPLAIN and TRACE tools available from Oracle and the third-party vendors. EXPLAIN plans are rather easy to interpret and are discussed at length in Chapter 24.

> **TIP**
>
> Each level of tuning is dependent on the previous level of tuning. The best performance will be achieved only if all four levels are tuned properly.

Chapter 24 is a comprehensive chapter on tuning, covering all of the issues discussed here.

Miscellaneous Tasks

Monitoring and troubleshooting really go hand-in-hand. Problems are generally easier to correct before they become problems. Many of the tasks that would fall into the troubleshooting area, such as certain messages in the `alert.log` file, can be monitored and, sometimes, fixed programmatically.

Monitoring

Monitoring can be done on a continual basis or on an "as needed" basis. The more servers there are to administrate, the greater the need for constant, background-based monitoring. The more servers there are to administrate, the more global the monitoring becomes. Overworked administrators want to know only about impending disasters such as tablespaces about to fill or objects about to reach their MAXEXTENTS, and about the status of certain processes. Many items that can cause database downtime can be monitored and corrected proactively.

There are three main reasons to monitor a UNIX and/or a database server. The first is to be proactive rather than reactive with error resolution. Downtime can be minimized if administrators know, for example, that certain dynamic objects are about to reach their MAXEXTENTS. This can easily be monitored and corrected without the end user even being aware that there was *almost* an application-stopping problem. A reactive approach to this example would be the end user getting the MAXEXTENTS error, calling the help desk or administrator, and waiting.

The second reason is the ability to tune both the server and database environments using real-time information. Disk I/O usage, memory usage, swapping, and dozens of other related processes can be monitored and adjustments made accordingly. Resource-intensive SQL, locking situations, and never-ending tasks can all be monitored and tuned accordingly.

The final reason to monitor is for capacity planning, monitoring the growth of objects and machine utilization, times of day of heavy traffic, and so on. There are sometimes contractual response time commitments, license agreements on the number of concurrent users, and the like. Monitoring can ensure compliance with various vendor and departmental agreements.

Troubleshooting

Many problems can be resolved before they become problems with a little proactive work (and monitoring) by the DBA. Troubleshooting could encompass an entire book; it is beyond the scope of this chapter to do anything more than give some general guidelines.

UNIX Shared Memory and/or Semaphore issues

The first thing to check when getting most any kind of ORA-7xxx errors is to consult the *Oracle Installation Guide* that accompanies the Oracle distribution software. This document lists the recommended settings for SHMMAX (max size of a shared memory segment), SHMMHI (max number of shared memory segments), SEMMNI (minimum number of semaphores on the system), SEMMNS (max number of semaphores on the system), and SHMSEG (max number of segments per process). Make sure these values are set to the recommendations. If Oracle is unable to allocate a semaphore, increase the SEMMNI and SEMMNS values. If Oracle is unable to attain shared memory, try increasing the SHMSEG value.

If Oracle aborts abnormally, it may leave semaphores and locks on shared memory behind, creating problems with trying to restart the Oracle processes.

> **NOTE**
>
> Use the UNIX command `ipcs -s` to identify semaphores, using `ipcrm -s <id>` to remove any Oracle semaphores.

> **NOTE**
>
> Use `ipcs -m` to identify and `ipcrm -m <id>` to clean up any Oracle locks on shared memory.

The following query (Listing 19.6) can be used to monitor both growth and the number of extents as well as the maximum number of extents assigned. A DBA should watch for tables that are getting close to their maximum number of extents. A DBA should monitor the number of extents and check for extent interleaving among various tables in the same tablespace (see Chapter 24 for more details on tablespace fragmentation).

LISTING 19.6. SEGMENT GROWTH AND EXTENT ASSIGNMENT QUERY.

```
SELECT   tablespace_name,
         segment_name,
         extents "EXTENTS",
         max_extents "MAX EXTENTS",
         bytes "SIZE",
         owner "OWNER"
  FROM   dba_segments
WHERE    owner not in ('SYS','SYSTEM','SCOTT','NET_CONF')
  and    extents > 1
ORDER BY tablespace_name,owner,segment_name;
```

If Oracle is having problems starting or stopping, or if there are abnormalities with any of the Oracle processes, the "alert.log" in the Oracle dump dest (see `init.ora` file or query `v$parameters` for location of dump dest) can help identify the processes and any associated Oracle error that was issued. There is some other information in this file as well, including all of the parameters used to start the Oracle instance, and, upon shutdown, the license high water mark, the current log, and the order in which things were shut down.

Sometimes UNIX processes that create large files can hit a `Ulimit` violation and have the process aborted. `Ulimit` is a global file system limit from the early days of UNIX. Its intent was to stop runaway user processes or prevent single users from creating files that exceeded their business need.

19

ORACLE8 ADMINISTRATIVE REQUIREMENTS

> **TIP**
>
> I always set `Ulimit` to a size larger than the largest single disk drive or RAID disk array.

Test any SQL*Net or Net8 changes with SQL*Plus. Test the new TNSNAMES, Server Names, and so on, by using the following syntax: `sqlplus valid_user/valid_password@<new TNSNAMES>`. Problems are easier to debug from the server-side before adding the network and processes outside the server to the mix of things that can cause problems.

> **Tip**
>
> Indexes can be created with a NOSORT option if the index key data is already sorted.

> **Tip**
>
> Indexes can be rebuilt with the REBUILD command much more quickly than dropping and recreating the index.

I would not allow objects to have more than 120 extents. Oracle8 has lifted this restriction, however, at the expense of chaining additional blocks onto the object block header. I would review object growth of objects with more than 50 extents. These objects could benefit from reorganization and larger extent sizes.

Summary

This chapter introduces the reader to the many administrative needs of the Oracle8 server. You learn about backup and recovery needs, security, and access needs. Tablespace maintenance is covered, including an in-depth discussion on various types of tablespace fragmentation issues. Schema maintenance includes how to appropriately size objects. This chapter also contains a good overview of the tuning process that is discussed in detail in Chapter 24. This chapter concludes with a variety of miscellaneous tasks including details on troubleshooting.

Routine Maintenance and Scheduling Tasks

by Ryan K. Stephens

IN THIS CHAPTER

There are many tiers of responsibility associated with the tasks of an Oracle database administrator. Technology surpasses itself each year, especially in the world of Oracle and relational database systems. New tools are constantly made available to the DBA to aid in overall job effectiveness. However, no tool can altogether replace a knowledgeable DBA who can not only install, implement, and configure a database, but can monitor the database and its users, combine database concepts with business rules, and make the best decisions for the maintenance of the database to keep it in tune with itself and other systems belonging to the enterprise.

One of the most robust tools for this purpose is Oracle Enterprise Manager by Oracle Corporation. This tool was designed to assist a database administrator, as would a right-hand man who oversees database activity and offers recommendations to the database administrator to improve database performance. Many of the features in Enterprise Manager can be customized according to each database, helping the DBA to monitor and manage multiple databases with ease. Manual intervention still has its place for many tasks, but the automation of most database systems has drastically increased with client/server technology.

This chapter discusses the tasks common to a DBA with respect to routine maintenance and scheduling for an existing Oracle database. Just like an automobile, a database must be monitored for deficiencies. Some individuals stay on top of vehicle maintenance and tune-ups more than others. Consequently, some vehicles are more reliable and perform much better than others. The same concept holds true with a database. If the DBA does not closely monitor the database and maintain it regularly, its performance will gradually begin to falter until it's no longer acceptable to the end user, resulting in the inability to support an enterprise's application(s).

Just as important as monitoring and regular maintenance is auditing. Auditing is another way of monitoring the database, in that the DBA can easily measure events that occur in it. After you have set up processes to audit the database's activity and monitor its elements, you can use job queues to schedule jobs at the database level. In other words, much of the monitoring and auditing process can be automated. This chapter mainly focuses on issues involved in regular database maintenance, database auditing, and the scheduling of jobs at the database level.

Examples will be shown specifically on auditing and scheduling jobs. Also included are a number of common monitoring scripts that can be used in the management of almost any Oracle database.

User, System, and Batch Processing

Before discussing the intricacies of database monitoring and maintenance, we must discuss the types of processing that occur in the database, including:

- User processing
- System processing
- Batch processing

We will also discuss some data dictionary views that may be used to retrieve pertinent processing information. These views are used to monitor processing and provide measurements that allow the DBA to derive intelligent conclusions.

User Processing

User processing is the primary justification for any database. Therefore, the end user must always be taken into consideration when you're scheduling database activities. When we refer to user processing, we are basically talking about the user's ability to access the required data to perform his or her job effectively and in a timely manner.

Within user processing, there are two main levels:

- Query processing
- Transactional processing

Query Processing

Query processing is of great importance, particularly in a data warehouse or decision support environment. Users must be able to extract the desired data in a timely manner, and without having to contend for system resources in the process. Care should be taken that any major processes that will tax the system aren't scheduled to run during peak hours of query processing (or transactional processing, for that matter). During periods of intense query processing, the DBA should monitor the database to ensure that enough resources have been allocated, such as memory for shared SQL and sort operations. Also, the temporary tablespace should be adequate to handle the overflow of data used by sort operations that cannot be accommodated within allocated memory.

Transactional Processing

Transactional processing is the activity engaged in by end users in the population and manipulation of data in the database for a particular application. Most of these transactional commands involve the INSERT, UPDATE, and DELETE statements, although they're often transparent to the user. Anymore, users need have very little, if any, knowledge of the underlying database system to manipulate the data within it. It is the DBA's responsibility to periodically monitor the database during peak transactional activity, searching for bottlenecks and resource contention. One of the primary concerns with transactional activity is the management of the rollback segments. The database should be able to handle all concurrent transactions effectively. If the database is not monitored during transactional activity and adjusted appropriately, company productivity will inevitably suffer.

Later in this chapter, we'll further discuss the process of monitoring user sessions. To monitor user sessions at the database level, the V$SESSION data dictionary view may be queried. User sessions can sometimes be monitored at the operating system level, to a limited degree. Many other avenues of approach can be taken regarding individual user sessions, space availability, and rollback segment contention.

System Processing

Inherent in every Oracle database is a considerable amount of system processing that takes place behind the scenes. Every database has a significant amount of overhead, much of which is composed of the background processes. Here are some of the most common background processes:

ARCH	Archive processes
CHPT	Checkpoint processes
DBWR	Database Writer processes
LCK*n*	Lock processes for parallel servers
LGWR	Log writer processes
PMON	Process Monitor processes
RECO	Recovery processes for distributed databases
SMON	System Monitor processes
SNP*n*	Job queue scheduling processes
Snnn	Server processes
Dnnn	Dispatcher processes

On a UNIX system, Oracle processes are typically named in the following format:

`ora_process_SID`

where *process* is the name of the Oracle process (such as pmon), and *SID* is the name of the system identifier for the associated database instance.

Monitoring Processes

Oracle processes can be monitored at both the operating system level and the database level. On a UNIX platform, you can list the Oracle processes with the following command, or a similar one:

```
aim% ps -ef |grep pti1 |grep -v grep
```

```
oracle    2377  0.0  2.5 1152 1552 ?  S   Mar 24  0:27 ora_p000_pti1
oracle   10301  0.0  0.0 1172    0 ?  IW  Apr  2  0:01 oraclepti1
oracle    2314  0.0  2.9 1152 1816 ?  S   Mar 24  0:25 ora_ckpt_pti1
oracle    2338  0.0  2.6 1168 1636 ?  S   Mar 24  0:25 ora_db08_pti1
oracle    2318  0.0  0.0 1176    0 ?  IW  Mar 24  0:53 ora_reco_pti1
oracle    2308  0.0  2.9 1152 1772 ?  S   Mar 24  3:06 ora_pmon_pti1
oracle    2336  0.0  2.8 1168 1736 ?  S   Mar 24  0:27 ora_db07_pti1
oracle    2324  0.0  2.4 1168 1464 ?  S   Mar 24  0:33 ora_db03_pti1
oracle    2322  0.0  3.2 1168 1968 ?  S   Mar 24  0:33 ora_db02_pti1
oracle    2329  0.0  3.2 1168 1980 ?  S   Mar 24  0:30 ora_db04_pti1
oracle    2334  0.0  3.0 1168 1856 ?  S   Mar 24  0:29 ora_db06_pti1
oracle    2332  0.0  3.0 1168 1872 ?  S   Mar 24  0:32 ora_db05_pti1
oracle    2379  0.0  2.5 1152 1552 ?  S   Mar 24  0:26 ora_p001_pti1
oracle    2320  0.0  3.3 1168 2024 ?  S   Mar 24  0:41 ora_db01_pti1
oracle    2346  0.0  0.4 1316  256 ?  S   Mar 24  5:45 ora_d001_pti1
oracle    2310  0.0  5.9 1156 3644 ?  S   Mar 24 62:24 ora_dbwr_pti1
oracle    2344  0.0  0.0 1316    0 ?  IW  Mar 24  5:59 ora_d000_pti1
oracle    2340  0.0  0.3 1748  200 ?  I   Mar 24 11:54 ora_s000_pti1
oracle    2342  0.0  0.0 1752    0 ?  IW  Mar 24  6:15 ora_s001_pti1
oracle   10289  0.0  0.0 1172    0 ?  IW  Apr  2  0:00 oraclepti1
oracle    2312  0.0  2.1 1152 1308 ?  S   Mar 24  1:11 ora_lgwr_pti1
oracle    2316  0.0  0.0 1168    0 ?  IW  Mar 24 16:27 ora_smon_pti1
```

Notice how the background processes are named. Also notice the process named `ora-clepti1`. This process represents a current user session in the database instance `pti1`. All processes are owned by `oracle`. In this case, that's the UNIX account identified as the Oracle software owner—and also the account that was used to start up the database instance. Oracle background processes run automatically and require very little manual intervention, if any. However, it does not hurt to monitor these processes for any abnormalities at the operating system level. On Windows NT, look under Services in the Control Panel to view the Oracle processes that are running on the server.

Oracle automatically monitors major database events, such as startup and shutdown, and records information pertaining to these events in a running log file residing at the operating system level. This log file is called the database alert log, and is named `alert_dbname.log`. The database alert log file is an excellent resource for database troubleshooting and should be monitored on a regular basis.

20

In UNIX, you can list the last 20 lines of this running log file as follows:

```
aim% tail -20 alert_pti1.log
starting up 2 shared server(s) ...
starting up 2 dispatcher(s) for network protocol 'tcp'...
Sat Apr  4 13:28:10 1998
alter database  mount exclusive
Sat Apr  4 13:28:11 1998
Successful mount of redo thread 1.
Sat Apr  4 13:28:11 1998
Completed: alter database  mount exclusive
Sat Apr  4 13:28:11 1998
alter database open
Sat Apr  4 13:28:13 1998
Thread 1 opened at log sequence 6
  Current log# 3 seq# 6 mem# 0: /mnt1/oradata/pti1/log30.dbf
  Current log# 3 seq# 6 mem# 1: /mnt2/oradata/pti1/log32.dbf
Successful open of redo thread 1.
Sat Apr  4 13:28:13 1998
SMON: enabling cache recovery
SMON: enabling tx recovery
Sat Apr  4 13:28:20 1998
Completed: alter database open
```

The `tail -f` option will keep a list of the contents of the alert log file open, showing new entries as they are written by Oracle. The location of the alert log file is designated by the `BACKGROUND_DUMP_DEST` parameter in the initialization parameter file.

Another key process to an Oracle database is the `LISTENER` process, which listens for new database connections from a remote client. If the `LISTENER` process is down, remote users cannot connect to the database. The simplest way to check the availability of `LISTENER` is by issuing the following command at the UNIX prompt:

> `lsnrctl status` (for the SQL*Net `LISTENER`)
>
> or
>
> `lsnrctl80 status` (for the Net8 `LISTENER`)

Monitoring Oracle processes from within the database has the potential of yielding a great deal of information, in addition to that from the operating system level. This is accomplished using the data dictionary views:

V$DISPATCHER	Information on dispatcher processes
V$SHARED_SERVER	Information on shared server processes
V$SESSION	Information on user sessions
V$SESS_IO	I/O statistics for user sessions
V$LATCH	Statistics for latches
V$SYSSTAT	General system statistics

Initializing Processes

Oracle database background processes are initialized upon database instance startup. When the database instance is started up, the initialization parameter file is read. Thus, there are many parameters that may be set and readjusted in the parameter file that allow the DBA to control the processes that are used by a database instance. These processes are initialized through parameters such as the following:

```
PROCESSES
MTS_SERVERS
MTS_MAX_SERVERS
PARALLEL_MAX_SERVERS
MTS_DISPATCHERS
MTS_LISTENER_ADDRESS
MTS_SERVICE
MTS_MAX_DISPATCHERS
CHECKPOINT_PROCESS
LOG_ARCHIVE_START
JOB_QUEUE_PROCESSES
```

Scheduling Batch Processes

Batch processing is typically as integral to Oracle processing as both user and system processing, particularly in environments such as online analytical processing (OLAP) systems. Batch processes are used to load data in batch, normally extracting data from one or more foreign databases or file systems and porting it into an Oracle OLAP database system. Batch processes are typically resource-intensive, and although they're necessary to run, they should be scheduled around user processing. Usually, batch processes are scheduled to run during off-peak hours when very few or no users require access to the database. Batch processes should be monitored by the DBA, who should measure the required resources.

Auditing

One of the most prevailing fears of any taxpayer is being audited by the IRS. Theoretically, if you play by the rules you have nothing to worry about. Of course, filing a return can turn into a complex task for some people, and there will sometimes be errors as numbers are continuously juggled. In cases like this, the IRS may step in and offer "corrective action," which may unfortunately involve penalties whether or not the error was intentional.

Auditing in an Oracle database works very similarly. Think of the database users as the taxpayers and the DBA as the IRS. The DBA has the option of enabling auditing in the database, and can choose to audit all database actions or just specific options.

Once activated, auditing may be left on all the time or turned on and used periodically— sort of a spot check, like that of the IRS. If malicious activity is suspected, the DBA may decide to turn on auditing. Upon acquiring evidence, action may be taken to reprimand the offending user. The IRS does not audit every individual, because it costs too much. Likewise, auditing in a database has costs as well.

When auditing is turned on, Oracle creates an audit trail, which is simply a table in the data dictionary. Later, we will discuss the data dictionary views that must be created, which are associated with the audit trail, its management, and the costs involved. For every audited action that occurs in the database, Oracle must make an entry in the audit trail. Because this will be discussed in more detail later in this chapter, you should note that there are costs incurred with auditing.

Typical reasons for database auditing include

- Pinpointing misuse of user IDs/passwords
- Pinpointing malicious activity
- Measuring employees' workload
- Monitoring database changes on specific objects
- Monitoring activities executed by privileged accounts

The following sections discuss auditing in further detail, beginning with the types of auditing. The various auditing options are also discussed, leading into enabling and disabling auditing. Finally, we discuss the overall management of the audit trail and show some examples.

Enabling and Disabling Auditing

Auditing must first be enabled before database actions can be audited and written to the audit trail. The database initialization parameter used to enable auditing is the `AUDIT_TRAIL` parameter. The options available with this parameter are as follows:

TRUE	Auditing is enabled (available for backward-compatibility with previous releases of Oracle).
FALSE	Auditing is disabled (available for backward-compatibility with previous releases of Oracle).
DB	Generates audit records in the database audit trail table.

| OS | Generates audit records in the designated operating system audit trail. |
| NONE | Auditing is disabled. |

The DB option is typically used with Oracle8 to record audit trail information in the audit trail table, which resides in the data dictionary. In order for this parameter to take effect, the database instance must be shut down and restarted.

The Operating System Audit Trail

By default, Oracle audits database instance startup, shutdown, and any connections made to the database with administrative privileges, such as with SYSOPER and SYSDBA. Audit records of this nature are typically written to the operating system audit trail because the database is often unavailable when these actions occur. Setting the AUDIT_TRAIL parameter to OS will cause all audit records to be written to the operating system audit trail file.

The default location for the operating system audit trail is the same directory as the database alert log and background process trace file, which is designated by the database parameter BACKGROUND_DUMP_DEST. The use and location of the operating system audit trail is operating system-specific.

The Database Audit Trail

The database audit trail is composed of a single table that is stored in the data dictionary with the other system tables. The owner of the database audit trail is the user SYS. In addition to the audit trail table, there are a number of views that should be created when auditing is activated. These views contain categories of audit information and are much more user-friendly than a single table. The following sections describe the components of the database audit trail, and provide direction for creating the audit trail views and removing them.

SYS.AUD$: The Audit Trail Table

The name of the audit trail table in the database is SYS.AUD$. A large number of columns compose this table, which contains all recorded database audit information. The following example shows a simple select from this table:

```
SQL> select sessionid, userid,
  2  to_char(timestamp#,'mm/dd/yy hh;mi;ss')
  3  from sys.aud$
  4  /
```

```
SESSIONID USERID                             TO_CHAR(TIMESTAMP
--------- ----------------------------- ----------------
       84 RYAN                              04/04/98 05:24:05
```

When auditing is activated, Oracle generates an audit record for each audited event, with the following default information:

- The username associated with the audited event.
- The action code of the audited event.
- The applicable object(s) audited.
- The date and timestamp of the audited event.

Creating and Deleting the Audit Trail Views

The audit trail views of SYS.AUD$ are created by simply running a script provided by Oracle Corporation. The following SQL script is used:

CATAUDIT.SQL

Regardless of the operating system platform on the host server, this script is stored under ORACLE_HOME or the directory in which the Oracle software was installed. On a UNIX system, the location of this script is $ORACLE_HOME/rdbms/admin. On a Windows NT platform, the location is C:\ORANT\RDBSM80\ADMIN.

To remove the audit trail data dictionary views, run the following script, which resides locally with the previous script:

CATNOAUD.SQL

> **NOTE**
>
> These scripts for creating and dropping the data dictionary views for auditing must be run while you're connected to the database as the SYS user account.

The Audit Trail Data Dictionary Views

The following views are accessible only by the DBA or privileged user:

```
SYS.DBA_STMT_AUDIT_OPTS
SYS.DBA_OBJ_AUDIT_OPTS
SYS.DBA_AUDIT_TRAIL
```

```
SYS.DBA_AUDIT_SESSION

SYS.DBA_AUDIT_STATEMENT

SYS.DBA_AUDIT_OBJECT

SYS.DBA_AUDIT_EXISTS
```

The following views are accessible by every Oracle user:

```
SYS.STMT_AUDIT_OPTION_MAP

SYS.AUDIT_ACTIONS

SYS.ALL_DEF_AUDIT_OPTS

SYS.USER_OBJ_AUDIT_OPTS

SYS.USER_AUDIT_TRAIL

SYS.USER_AUDIT_SESSION

SYS.USER_AUDIT_STATEMENT

SYS.USER_AUDIT_OBJECT

SYS.USER_TAB_AUDIT_OPS
```

If a non-DBA attempts to access the DBA_ views, the following results are received:

```
SQL> desc dba_audit_session
ERROR:
ORA-04043: object SYS.DBA_AUDIT_SESSION does not exist


SQL> desc user_audit_session
 Name                             Null?     Type
 -------------------------------- --------- ----
 OS_USERNAME                                VARCHAR2(255)
 USERNAME                                   VARCHAR2(30)
 USERHOST                                   VARCHAR2(128)
 TERMINAL                                   VARCHAR2(255)
 TIMESTAMP                        NOT NULL  DATE
 ACTION_NAME                                VARCHAR2(27)
 LOGOFF_TIME                                DATE
 LOGOFF_LREAD                               NUMBER
 LOGOFF_PREAD                               NUMBER
 LOGOFF_LWRITE                              NUMBER
 LOGOFF_DLOCK                               VARCHAR2(40)
 SESSIONID                        NOT NULL  NUMBER
 RETURNCODE                       NOT NULL  NUMBER
 SESSION_LABEL                              RAW MLSLABEL
```

The AUDIT Command

Once auditing has been enabled, the SQL command AUDIT is used to activate certain audit options, which will be discussed in the following sections. To turn off audit options that have been previously specified, use the NOAUDIT command. These commands are typically submitted at the command prompt, such as in SQL*Plus or Server Manager. The syntax for the AUDIT and NOAUDIT commands is shown in the following appropriate sections, which also discuss the different audit options.

Types of Auditing

There are various types of auditing that may integrated into an Oracle database. Audit information can be taken from general login information or from specific changes that occur within specific database objects. All actions can be audited, and the task of auditing can be (and should be) tailored specifically to the needs of the database system to ensure proper use of the system and discourage unauthorized database activity through auditing, and do so in a cost-effective manner.

The types of auditing discussed are

- Session auditing
- Statement auditing
- Privilege auditing
- Object auditing

> **NOTE**
>
> As mentioned earlier, Oracle automatically audits database instance startup, shutdown, and any connections made to the database with administrative privileges.

Audit Options

The following sections outline the various auditing options available. The first three (session, statement, and privilege auditing) are auditing options that reside on the database system level. The fourth, object auditing, resides on the schema or object level. As will be explained, certain privileges are required for the different types of auditing.

Session Audits

Session auditing is the process of auditing user sessions. This auditing option is technically part of SQL statement auditing, and mainly involves recording the success/failure of each individual who connects or attempts to connect to the database. By default, both successful and unsuccessful login attempts will generate an audit record. If you prefer, you can specify that only successful login attempts will generate audit records.

Here's the syntax to audit user logins:

```
AUDIT SESSION
[BY username [,username] ]
[BY SESSION ¦ ACCESS ]
[WHENEVER [NOT] SUCCESSFUL];
```

To activate login auditing:

```
SQL> audit session;
```

Audit succeeded.

To audit unsuccessful SYSTEM login attempts:

```
SQL> audit session
  2  by system
  3  whenever not successful;
```

Audit succeeded.

To disable the previous option:

```
SQL> noaudit session
  2  by system
  3  whenever not successful;
```

Noaudit succeeded.

To audit all database events:

```
SQL> audit all;
```

Audit succeeded.

To disable the previous option:

```
SQL> noaudit all;
```

Noaudit succeeded.

Statement Audits

Statement audits are those that record particular statements issued in the database. This section shows how to audit for certain SQL statements.

Here's the syntax of the AUDIT command for SQL statement, privilege-based, and session auditing:

```
AUDIT statement ¦ privilege [,statement ¦ privilege]
[BY username [,username] ]
[BY SESSION ¦ ACCESS ]
[WHENEVER [NOT] SUCCESSFUL];
```

To audit table commands, such as CREATE TABLE, DROP TABLE, and TRUNCATE TABLE:

```
SQL> audit table
  2  by ryan;

Audit succeeded.
```

To audit SELECTs, INSERTs, and DELETEs of tables:

```
SQL> audit select table, insert table, delete table;

Audit succeeded.
```

Syntax of the NOAUDIT command for SQL statement, privilege-based, and session auditing:

```
NOAUDIT statement ¦ privilege [,statement ¦ privilege]
[BY username [,username] ]
[WHENEVER [NOT] SUCCESSFUL];
```

Example:

```
SQL> noaudit select table, insert table, delete table;

Noaudit succeeded.
```

Privilege Audits

Privilege audits are those in which records are generated in the audit trail according to SQL statements that are issued based on privileges granted to a user. The syntax is the same as that for statement auditing.

To audit statements executed using the SELECT ANY TABLE system privilege:

```
SQL> audit select any table;

Audit succeeded.
```

To audit ALTER USER statements:

```
SQL> audit alter user;

Audit succeeded.
```

To audit unsuccessful DELETEs executed by ryan and test for each attempt based on the DELETE ANY TABLE system privilege:

```
SQL> audit delete any table
by ryan, test
by access
whenever not successful;

Audit succeeded.
```

> **NOTE**
>
> To audit sessions, statements, and privileges, you must either be a DBA or have been granted the AUDIT SYSTEM system privilege.

Object Audits

Object-level audits are those in which audit records are generated for actions that occur against database objects.

Object audit options:

Option:	Applies to:
ALL	All objects (applies to AUDIT and NOAUDIT)
ALTER	Tables, sequences, snapshots
AUDIT	Tables, views, sequences, packages, snapshots, directories
COMMENT	Tables, views, snapshots
DELETE	Tables, views, snapshots
EXECUTE	Stored programs, library
GRANT	Tables, views, sequences, stored procedures, Snapshots, libraries, directories
INDEX	Tables, snapshots
INSERT	Tables, views, snapshots

20

ROUTINE
MAINTENANCE
AND SCHEDULING

Option:	Applies to:
LOCK	Tables, views, snapshots
RENAME	Tables, views, stored programs, snapshots
SELECT	Tables, views, sequences, snapshots
UPDATE	Tables, views, snapshots

Here's the syntax of the AUDIT command for object-level auditing:

```
AUDIT option [,option]
ON [schema.]object_name
[BY SESSION ¦ ACCESS]
[WHENEVER [NOT] SUCCESSFUL];
```

To audit data manipulation commands on returns_tbl:

```
SQL> audit insert, update, delete on returns_tbl;

Audit succeeded.
```

To audit all actions performed against the projects table by access:

```
SQL> audit all on projects by access;

Audit succeeded.
```

To audit all deletes on the employees table by access:

```
SQL> audit delete on employees by access;

Audit succeeded.
```

Here's the syntax of the NOAUDIT command for object-level auditing:

```
NOAUDIT option [,option]
ON [schema.]object_name
[WHENEVER [NOT] SUCCESSFUL];
```

To deactivate all auditing options on the projects table:

```
SQL> noaudit all on projects;

Noaudit succeeded.
```

> **NOTE**
>
> To audit objects, you must either be a DBA, own the objects being audited, or have been granted the AUDIT ANY system privilege.

Managing the Audit Trail

So you have decided to turn on auditing. Thousands of audited events later, you may begin to wonder at what point you should take a look at the audit trail table. First of all, remember that the audit trail table, SYS.AUD$, resides in the data dictionary, consequently stored in the SYSTEM tablespace. As you should know, the SYSTEM tablespace should be isolated from other tablespaces and protected at all times.

Normally, the SYSTEM tablespace is relatively small compared to application-related tablespaces in the database, typically somewhere between 50MB and 100MB. If auditing is turned on, you may want to think about adding a datafile to the SYSTEM tablespace to accommodate any additional space that may be required for auditing, depending on the current usage of the SYSTEM tablespace. However, in most cases, adding additional space for auditing should not be necessary if the process is properly managed.

> **NOTE**
>
> The SYS.AUD$ table cannot be moved from the SYSTEM tablespace. However, storage parameters can be modified to control the growth of this table in the SYSTEM tablespace. You might choose to set the NEXT extent to a low number, such as 10KB or 20KB, and specify a smaller number for MAXEXTENTS to provide the table with a growth cap. Eventually, when the table reaches the value for MAXEXTENTS and cannot extend further, an error will be returned and you will be forced to archive the table and purge its contents. This is a good safeguard to ensure that the SYSTEM tablespace is not affected by a growing audit trail.

How much space is required for auditing? There is no way to answer this question without knowing the level of auditing that will take place, the frequency of audited events, and the length of time audit records will be maintained (or the maximum size allowed for the audit trail table). Eventually, you will probably have to archive the contents of SYS.AUD$ to another table or file, and then purge the SYS.AUD$ table. This is one of the very few times the DBA should ever manually manipulate one of the tables in the data dictionary.

At some point, guidelines for auditing must be set, such as the following:

- The specific events that will be audited.
- The maximum amount of audit data allowed before archiving must occur.
- The expected availability of archived audit information.
- The users that will have the privilege of auditing.

> **NOTE**
>
> Auditing should be narrowed down as much as possible to avoid unnecessary database overhead.

Auditing the Audit Trail

You may even want to audit access against the audit trail itself. Doing so falls into the category of object auditing. For example:

```
SQL> audit select, insert, update, delete
on SYS.AUD$
by access;

Audit succeeded.
```

Purging the Audit Trail

The DBA can purge the audit trail table by deleting all records in the table or by truncating the table:

```
SQL> delete from sys.aud$;

43 rows deleted.
```

or

```
SQL> truncate table sys.aud$;

Table truncated.
```

Archiving the Audit Trail

Before purging data from the audit trail table, it is probably a good idea to archive the data first. It is usually better to be safe than sorry when dealing with any type of data.

The easiest way to archive the audit trail before purging it is to create a table based on the contents of SYS.AUD$, as in the following example. After a successful copy has been made, the original table can be purged:

```
SQL> create table audit_copy as
  2  select * from sys.aud$;

Table created.

SQL> delete from sys.aud$;

45 rows deleted.
```

After a copy of SYS.AUD$ has been made, you can append data to the table from future clean-up routines by inserting the contents of SYS.AUD$ into your copy table:

```
SQL> insert into audit_copy
  2  select * from sys.aud$;

43 rows created.

SQL> delete from sys.aud$;

45 rows deleted.
```

There are several methods for backing up the audit trail before it is purged. One method to consider is the EXPORT utility. After an EXPORT dump file has been generated, it can be stored with other files in an archive directory at the operating system level. These files can also be compressed to conserve disk space. Dump files can easily be imported back into the database whenever the data is needed.

Sample Audit Queries

Here's a sample query from the session auditing data dictionary view:

```
SQL> select substr(os_username,1,10) osuser,
  2         substr(username,1,10) username,
  3         to_char(timestamp,'mm/dd/yy hh;mi;ss') "TIME STAMP",
  4         action_name action,
  5         decode(returncode,'0','Succeeded','Failed') result
  6  from sys.dba_audit_session;
```

OSUSER	USERNAME	TIME STAMP	ACTION	RESULT
rkstephe	RYAN	04/04/98 05:24:05	LOGOFF	Succeeded
rkstephe	RYAN	04/05/98 02:17:39	LOGOFF	Succeeded
rkstephe	SYSTEM	04/05/98 04:30:26	LOGOFF	Succeeded
rkstephe	RYAN	04/05/98 04:30:43	LOGON	Succeeded
rkstephe	SYSTEM	04/05/98 04:33:50	LOGON	Failed

To activate the audit option for actions against tables:

```
SQL> audit table;

Audit succeeded.
```

To connect as a user with no privileges other than CREATE SESSION:

```
SQL> connect test/test          (user was created with no privileges)
Connected.
```

To attempt to create a table as test:

```
SQL> create table test_table
  2  (ident number,
  3    name  varchar2(30));
create table test_table
*
ERROR at line 1:
ORA-01950: no privileges on tablespace 'SYSTEM'
```

This was an unsuccessful attempt at issuing the CREATE TABLE statement, which is a "table" auditing option.

Now, we connect as a user with the DBA role. As this user, additional privileges will be granted to test, which will allow table creation:

```
SQL> connect ryan/ryan          Connected.
SQL> grant connect, resource to test;

Grant succeeded.
```

After connecting as test once again, the CREATE TABLE statement is reissued:

```
SQL> connect test/test
Connected.

SQL> create table names
  2  (id      number,
  3    name  varchar2(30));

Table created.
```

Now, the connection back to the account with the DBA role has been reestablished. The object audit view will be queried in hope to find our table commands.

```
SQL> connect ryan/ryan
Connected.
```

Statement auditing:

```
SQL> select username, substr(owner,1,10) owner, substr(obj_name,1,10)
    obj_name,
  2        timestamp, returncode
  3  from dba_audit_object;
```

USERNAME	OWNER	OBJ_NAME	TIMESTAMP	RETURNCODE
TEST	TEST	TEST_TABLE	04-APR-98	1950
TEST	TEST	NAMES	04-APR-98	0

Notice that for unsuccessful commands, the error message code is place in the RETURN-CODE column.

> **NOTE**
>
> Many individuals also choose to audit the database through the use of triggers. For example, you may have a transactional history table that is populated every time a user performs a transaction. The trigger is created on the target table being changed, and then it writes changed data and other information, such as the username and a timestamp, to the history table.

Common Monitoring Scripts

All databases have flaws—in their structure, at the application level, and definitely in the accuracy of user activities. Yes, most database users are human and do make mistakes. Databases are designed by humans and there will inevitably be deficiencies. Databases are implemented, problems arise, and the management wants results—now! We also ought to throw the growth factor into the equation. Database objects grow with increased data, and often the user community grows as well. This is where database monitoring comes into play.

Database monitoring is knowing what is happening in your database at all times, acting in a proactive manner, and making intelligent decisions that may get you promoted—or at least allow you to keep your job.

20

ROUTINE
MAINTENANCE
AND SCHEDULING

Types of Monitoring

The following three types of monitoring encompass the responsibilities of a DBA:

- System monitoring
- Application monitoring
- Session (user) monitoring

What to Monitor

Some common things to monitor from a DBA perspective:

- Rollback segment contention
- Space allocation/usage
- User sessions
- Segment fragmentation
- Fragmented free space
- Temporary segments
- Memory usage
- Summarized space statistics
- Overall database activity
- Oracle processes
- Archived redo log files
- Table and row locks

Sample Monitoring Scripts

The following sample scripts can be used to help monitor your Oracle database. You may have to make a few modifications according to your preferences, but these should steer you in the right direction by providing a handle on the sometimes tedious monitoring process.

Monitoring the size of the audit trail:

```
set echo off
set feedback off
col dt hea 'TIMESTAMP' for a20
spool mon_aud
select to_char(sysdate,'yyyy mm/dd hh;mi;ss') dt,
       substr(segment_name,1,10) "TABLE NAME",
       extents,
```

```
        max_extents "MAX EXT",
        bytes
from dba_segments
where segment_name = 'AUD$'
/
spool off


SQL> @mon_aud

TIMESTAMP             TABLE NAME      EXTENTS    MAX EXT      BYTES
-------------------  -----------    ----------  ----------  ----------
1998 04/05 09:18:07  AUD$                    1         121       10240
```

A sample tablespace utilization report:

```
set echo off
create view v_alloc as
select tablespace_name ts,
       sum(bytes) alloc
from dba_data_files
group by tablespace_name
/
create view v_used as
select tablespace_name ts,
       sum(bytes) used
from dba_segments
group by tablespace_name
/
create view v_free as
select tablespace_name ts,
       sum(bytes) free
from sys.dba_free_space
group by tablespace_name
/
col ts hea 'TABLESPACE' for a18
col alloc for 9,999,999,999
col used for 9,999,999,999
col free for 9,999,999,999
tti 'TABLESPACE UTILIZATION REPORT'
compute sum of alloc on report
compute sum of used on report
compute sum of free on report
compute avg of "PCT USED" on report
break on report
spool space
select a.ts,
       a.alloc,
       u.used,
       f.free,
       round(u.used/a.alloc * 100) "PCT USED"
```

20

ROUTINE
MAINTENANCE
AND SCHEDULING

```
from v_alloc a,
     v_used u,
     v_free f
where u.ts = a.ts
  and f.ts = a.ts
order by 5 desc
/
spool off
rem
drop view v_alloc;
drop view v_used;
drop view v_free;
```

> **NOTE**
>
> This script needs to be run as SYS, unless you have been explicitly granted select access on the applicable data dictionary views. Even if you have been granted the DBA role, the script will not necessarily work. Oracle does not allow objects to be created from other objects based on privileges granted from a role.

```
SQL> @space
```

```
Sun Apr 05                                                    page    1
                     TABLESPACE UTILIZATION REPORT

TABLESPACE                ALLOC           USED           FREE   PCT USED
--------------  --------------- --------------- --------------- ----------
SYSTEM               10,485,760       8,792,064       1,691,648         84
ROLLBACK_DATA        10,485,760       8,140,800       2,342,912         78
TEMPORARY_DATA        2,097,152         958,464       1,136,640         46
USER_DATA             8,388,608         624,640       7,761,920          7
                --------------- --------------- --------------- ----------
avg                                                                  53.75
sum                  31,457,280      18,515,968      12,933,120
```

A script to monitor Oracle user sessions:

```
set echo off
set pause off
set feedback on
set pagesize 23
set linesize 80
set newpage 0
tti off
clear col
```

```
col "Session" for a8
spool session.lst
prompt
prompt #######################
prompt # Oracle User Sessions #
prompt #######################
prompt
select substr(osuser,1,11) "OS Username",
       process "OS PID",
       substr(username,1,10) "Oracle ID",
       sid¦¦'',''¦¦serial# "Session",
       decode(command,'1','CREATE TABLE','2','INSERT','3','SELECT',
                      '4','CREATE CLUSTER','5','ALTER CLUSTER',
'6','UPDATE', '7','DELETE','8','DROP',
                          '9','CREATE INDEX','10','DROP INDEX',
                            '11','ALTER INDEX','12','DROP TABLE','15',
               'ALTER TABLE', '17','GRANT','18','REVOKE',
'19','CREATE SYNONYM','20', 'DROP SYNONYM',
                     '21','CREATE VIEW','22','DROP VIEW','26',
                     'LOCK TABLE','27','NO OPERATION',
'28','RENAME','29','COMMENT', '30','AUDIT',
                     '31','NOAUDIT','32','CREATE EXTERNAL DATABASE',
                     '33','DROP EXTERNAL DATABASE',
               '34','CREATE DATABASE','35', 'ALTER DATABASE',
                     '36','CREATE ROLLBACK SEGMENT',
                     '37','ALTER ROLLBACK SEGMENT',
               '38','DROP ROLLBACK SEGMENT',
               '39', 'CREATE TABLESPACE',
                     '40','ALTER TABLESPACE','41', 'DROP TABLESPACE',
                     '42','ALTER SESSION','43','ALTER USER',
                     '44','COMMIT','45','ROLLBACK',
               '46','SAVEPOINT',null) "Command", status
from v$session
where username is not null
/
prompt
prompt #######
prompt # END #
prompt #######
spool off
```

A script to monitor segment fragmentation:

```
set echo off
set verify off
clear col
clear break
accept owner prompt 'Enter schema owner: '
col segment_name hea 'SEGMENT¦NAME' for a20
col segment_type hea 'SEGMENT¦TYPE' for a10
col extents hea 'EXT' for 999
```

```
col bytes for 9,999,999,999
col max_extents hea 'MAX¦EXT'
col pct_mac hea 'PCT OF¦MAX EXT'
tti 'SEGMENT FRAGMENTATION REPORT'
spool ext
select segment_name,
       segment_type,
       bytes,
       extents,
       max_extents,
       round(extents/max_extents * 100) pct_max
from dba_segments
where owner = '&owner'
  and rownum < 16
order by 6 desc
/
spool off
clear col
clear break
```

```
SQL> @ext
Enter schema owner: RYAN
```

Sun Apr 05   page   1
                  SEGMENT FRAGMENTATION REPORT

SEGMENT NAME	SEGMENT TYPE	BYTES	EXT	MAX EXT	PCT_MAX
EMP_TBL	TABLE	460,800	9	10	90
CUSTOMERS	TABLE	10,240	1	121	1
INVOICES	TABLE	10,240	1	121	1
ACCT_PAY	TABLE	10,240	1	121	1
EMPLOYEES	TABLE	10,240	1	121	1
HISTORY	TABLE	10,240	1	121	1
PRODUCTS	TABLE	10,240	1	121	1
UNDERPAY_TABLE	TABLE	10,240	1	121	1
PAY_STATUS_TABLE	TABLE	10,240	1	121	1
PAYMENT_TABLE	TABLE	10,240	1	121	1
PRODUCT	TABLE	10,240	1	121	1
PROJECTS	TABLE	10,240	1	121	1
VENDORS	TABLE	10,240	1	121	1
ACCT_REC	TABLE	10,240	1	121	1
ORDERS	TABLE	10,240	1	121	1

This report is designed to display the percentage of extents used by a segment according to the MAXEXTENTS parameter that was set upon table creation. For example, EMP_TBL has used 9 out of its 10 allocated extents. You probably want to think about rebuilding this table or increasing the MAXEXTENTS. The good thing about the MAXEXTENTS parameter is that the DBA has a better idea of how the database is growing. This may cause more work up front, but will save headaches in the long run.

Monitoring with Oracle Tools

There are countless scripts that may be created to perform regular database monitoring. In addition to scripts that the DBA can create and customize, Oracle provides utilities and tools that automate the overall tasks of database monitoring. Some of these utilities include

- utlbstat.sql
- utlestat.sql
- utllockt.sql
- catblock.sql
- Oracle Enterprise Manager (see Chapter 21, "Administration Using Enterprise Manager")
- Oracle client software tools

The UTLBSTAT.SQL and UTLESTAT.SQL Utilities

The UTLBSTAT and UTLESTAT utilities are used to gather overall database statistics, which are used mainly to tune the performance of a database. These scripts are provided by Oracle Corporation as part of the software, and are typically stored under $ORACLE_HOME/rdbms/admin.

UTLBSTAT.SQL is run first, to begin the process of gathering statistics. This script must be run while you're connected to a DBA account. Before running this script, be sure to modify the TABLESPACE clause for the tables being created by the script. Those tables are used to store performance statistics from the database as of the time UTLBSTAT.SQL is run.

Upon execution of UTLBSTAT.SQL, the following dynamic performance views are queried to initially populate the statistic tables created:

```
V$SYSTEM_EVENT
V$ROLLSTAT
V$ROWCACHE
V$SYSSTAT
V$LIBRARYCACHE
V$LATCH
```

After a predetermined amount of time (normally after the end of a large process), the UTLESTAT.SQL script is run to end the process of gathering statistics, generating an output file called report.txt. The output of this script offers recommendations for adjusting database parameters to improve performance. These scripts are typically run from Server Manager.

UTLLOCKT.SQL and CATBLOCK.SQL

The UTLLOCKT.SQL script displays locks in the database and sessions that are waiting for locks to be released. Before you run UTLLOCKT.SQL, CATBLOCK.SQL must first be run (typically from SQL*Plus or Server Manager). CATBLOCK.SQL builds the "lock views" used by UTLLOCKT.SQL.

> **NOTE**
>
> In addition to the tools that are provided by Oracle Corporation, many third-party products have been made available to the DBA that are tailored specifically to an Oracle database. A couple of these tools are Patrol by BMC Software and SQLTrace by Platinum Technology. Be sure to check all of your options to optimize the task of monitoring database activity.

Scheduling Jobs

In this chapter, we have covered routine tasks that need to be performed by the DBA. Although all these monitoring and auditing tasks can be accomplished manually, the fact that Oracle provides a way to automate them should be taken into consideration. Similar to the way a crontab job is scheduled on a UNIX system, Oracle has the capability of scheduling jobs in the database. These jobs can include practically any designated task, such as monitoring scripts, auditing, creating general maintenance scripts, and gathering database statistics. Oracle jobs are based on PL/SQL, typically some stored procedure in the database. The concepts from the previous scripts in this chapter may be used to set up Oracle jobs. This section discusses job scheduling in the Oracle environment.

Managing Job Queues

Database jobs are scheduled in what is called a *job queue*, which designates which jobs have been scheduled, where to find the jobs, when to execute them, how often to execute them, and so on. Although these queues are directly managed by Oracle, Oracle provides the user with methods for communicating with these queues in such a way that jobs can be scheduled, modified, and removed from the queues.

Oracle job queues can be compared to those on a UNIX operating system. When a crontab job is set up, the jobs to be executed are placed in a queue. As the user setting up the job, you supply the time to execute it, the frequency, and the name (which is often a shell script or an SQL script file). Crontab jobs are executed according to the specified frequency until the job is removed from the queue. Oracle job queues work in a similar fashion.

There are two levels of job queue management:

- The initialization of SNP processes.
- The scheduling of jobs in the queue.

The first task is accomplished by the DBA. SNP processes must first be initialized before jobs can be scheduled within the database. The second task is accomplished by any user with the appropriate privileges. Many users other than the DBA need to schedule jobs to automate everyday tasks.

How Are Queued Jobs Executed?

Job queues are executed by SNP background processes, which are initialized when the applicable database instance is started. The following section describes the initialization parameters involved in defining the characteristics of these SNP background processes. These processes check for jobs that need to be executed in the database and execute those jobs. The more simultaneous jobs being executed, the more SNP background processes that may need to be initialized.

> **NOTE**
>
> The maximum number of SNP background processes allowed by Oracle is 36. When a background process fails, the database instance as a whole is not affected. Oracle simply restarts failed SNP background processes.

Database Parameters

A database may have multiple job queues. These job queues are driven by SNP background processes, which are initialized by the DBA through the following parameters in the database initialization parameter file:

JOB_QUEUE_PROCESSES	Identifies the number of SNP background processes to be used by the database instance.
JOB_QUEUE_INTERVAL	Identifies the wake-up interval (in seconds) for SNP background processes, at which time the processes check for jobs to be executed.

These parameters do not take effect until the database is shut down and restarted.

The DBMS_JOB Package

As an Oracle user, you can schedule jobs in the job queue as long as you have permission to execute the procedures within the DBMS_JOB package, provided by Oracle Corporation. The DBA must create the DBMS_JOB package by running the dbmsjob.sql script, which is located under ORACLE_HOME/rdbms/admin. This location is operating system-dependent. For example:

UNIX	$ORACLE_HOME/rdbms/admin
NT	C:\ORANT\RDBMS80\ADMIN

The procedures that are stored in the DBMS_JOB package include:

Procedure:	Used to:
DBMS_JOB.SUBMIT	Submit a job
DBMS_JOB.REMOVE	Remove a job
DBMS_JOB.CHANGE	Alter a job
DBMS_JOB.WHAT	Alter a job's description
DBMS_JOB.NEXT_DATE	Alter the next time executed
DBMS_JOB.INTERVAL	Alter the execution interval
DBMS_JOB.BROKEN	Designate a job as broken
DBMS_JOB.RUN	Force a job to run

Each of these jobs has input and output parameters. As the person executing the procedure, you must supply a value for all input parameters, unless the parameter has a default. For instance, to force a job to run, you must supply the job number. The values for the output variables are supplied by Oracle. Later in this section, you will see examples of executing some of these procedures using the input/output parameters.

Job Attributes

All jobs that are placed in the job queue have certain attributes, including:

- Job owner
- Job number
- Job definition
- Job execution interval

Submitting and Manipulating Jobs

Submitting new jobs and manipulating current jobs in the job queues is quite a simple task with the array of procedures supplied in the DBMS_JOB package. Possible job queue actions include submitting a job to the job queue, removing a job from the job queue, changing a specific job's attributes, designating a job as broken, and forcing a job to run. The following sections show examples of running the various procedures associated with managing jobs in an Oracle database.

> **NOTE**
>
> In order to submit, modify, and remove jobs from the job queues, you must either be a DBA or have been granted the EXECUTE privilege on the applicable procedures in the DBMS_JOB package.

Submitting Jobs

Jobs are submitted to a queue using the SUBMIT procedure of the DBMS_JOB package. First, a token procedure is created. The job is submitted, with four parameters passed into the procedure. The parameters are

job	OUT	(Job number, determined by Oracle)
what	IN	(Job to execute)
next_date	IN	(Next date to run job)
interval	IN	(Interval between job executions)
no_parse	IN	(True or false. Tells whether or not to parse a job the first time it is executed)

```
SQL> create or replace procedure chk_extents as
  2    cursor c_extents is
  3      select segment_name, bytes, extents, max_extents
  4      from sys.dba_segments
```

```
 5        where extents > 10;
 6     rec c_extents%ROWTYPE;
 7   begin
 8     open c_extents;
 9     loop
10       fetch c_extents into rec;
11       exit when c_extents%NOTFOUND;
12       insert into extent_stats
13       values (rec.segment_name,rec.bytes,rec.extents,rec.max_extents,
         sysdate);
14       commit;
15     end loop;
16     close c_extents;
17   end;
/

Procedure created.
```

This procedure checks segments with more than 10 extents and inserts records for each segment meeting this criteria into the extent_stats table. This procedure (job) can be scheduled to run periodically. You can query the extent_stats table to measure the growth and frequency of database objects.

```
SQL> execute chk_extents

PL/SQL procedure successfully completed.
```

Although Oracle generates the job number, you need to know it to modify or remove the job. We have initialized a variable from the SQL> prompt called jobnum. Notice the way the job queue request is submitted:

```
SQL>variable jobnum number;

SQL> begin
  2     dbms_job.submit(:jobnum,'ryan.chk_extents;',sysdate, 'sysdate +
       1/2');
  3   end;
  4   /


PL/SQL procedure successfully completed.
```

The SQL*Plus command EXECUTE may also be used to execute procedures, such as follows:

```
SQL> execute dbms_job.submit(:jobnum,'ryan.chk_extents;',sysdate, 'sysdate
+ 1/2')
SQL> print jobnum

    JOBNUM
  ---------
          1
```

The PRINT command was used to print the value of jobnum. The job number can also be derived from the SYS.DBA_JOBS and SYS.USER_JOBS data dictionary views. Also notice that the name of the procedure to run is in single quotations, as is the execution interval (the next date value is not in quotes). This job is scheduled to execute twice a day.

If you haven't already considered it, it would be an excellent idea to schedule a job that will periodically archive the contents of the audit trail, and then purge the audit trail table.

```
SQL> create table aud_archive as
  2  select * from sys.aud$;

Table created.
```

An example PL/SQL routine (run as user SYS):

```
SQL> create or replace procedure p_aud_archive as
  2  begin
  3    insert into aud_archive
  4    select * from aud$;
  5    commit;
  6    delete from aud$;
  7    commit;
  8* end;
```

Once this procedure has been created, schedule it to run periodically using the DBMS_JOB.SUBMIT procedure, as shown previously.

Removing Jobs

Jobs can be removed from the job queue as easily as they are scheduled. The REMOVE procedure is used to remove a job currently in a queue:

```
SQL> begin
  2    dbms_job.remove(1);
  3  end;
  4  /

PL/SQL procedure successfully completed.
```

Altering Queued Jobs

The CHANGE, WHAT, NEXT_DATE, INTERVAL, and BROKEN procedures are used to alter the state of a job. Following are a couple of examples.

To designate the job as a broken job:

```
SQL> begin
  2     dbms_job.broken(1, TRUE);
  3  end;
  4  /

PL/SQL procedure successfully completed.
```

> **NOTE**
>
> A broken job cannot be run unless it is unmarked "broken" using the BROKEN procedure or forced to run using the RUN procedure.

To change the interval of job execution from twice a day to once every two days:

```
SQL> begin
  2     dbms_job.interval(1,'sysdate + 2');
  3  end;
  4  /

PL/SQL procedure successfully completed.
```

Forcing Jobs to Run

Sometimes when a job is already queued, you may want to execute it before the next execution time. You can force a job to run using the RUN procedure:

```
SQL> begin
  2     dbms_job.run(1);
  3  end;
  4  /

PL/SQL procedure successfully completed.
```

Job Queue Information in the Data Dictionary

As with anything else in Oracle, job queue information can be found in the data dictionary. Three views are used specifically to query job information:

`SYS.DBA_JOBS`	All queued jobs, accessible by the DBA
`SYS.USER_JOBS`	Each user's queued jobs
`SYS.DBA_JOBS_RUNNING`	All jobs currently running, accessible by the DBA

Here's a look at one of the views:

```
SQL> desc user_jobs
 Name                                    Null?    Type
 --------------------------------------- -------- ----
 JOB                                     NOT NULL NUMBER
 LOG_USER                                NOT NULL VARCHAR2(30)
 PRIV_USER                               NOT NULL VARCHAR2(30)
 SCHEMA_USER                             NOT NULL VARCHAR2(30)
 LAST_DATE                                        DATE
 LAST_SEC                                         VARCHAR2(8)
 THIS_DATE                                        DATE
 THIS_SEC                                         VARCHAR2(8)
 NEXT_DATE                               NOT NULL DATE
 NEXT_SEC                                         VARCHAR2(8)
 TOTAL_TIME                                       NUMBER
 BROKEN                                           VARCHAR2(1)
 INTERVAL                                NOT NULL VARCHAR2(200)
 FAILURES                                         NUMBER
 WHAT                                             VARCHAR2(4000)
 CURRENT_SESSION_LABEL                            MLSLABEL
 CLEARANCE_HI                                     MLSLABEL
 CLEARANCE_LO                                     MLSLABEL
 NLS_ENV                                          VARCHAR2(4000)
 MISC_ENV                                         RAW(32)


SQL> select job, broken, log_user, schema_user, last_date
  2  from user_jobs;

      JOB B LOG_USER                         SCHEMA_USER                    LAST_DATE
 --------- - -------------------------------- ------------------------------ ---------
        1 Y RYAN                             RYAN                           04-APR-98
```

Summary

A vast amount of territory has been covered in this chapter. There are so many responsibilities in the administration of an Oracle database that it would be difficult to list them all. However, all these responsibilities revolve around the common goals of protecting the data, providing desirable functionality, and optimizing performance as much as possible. These goals can be met through regular maintenance and scheduling of tasks.

Monitoring user and system processes is one of the first steps to a successful database management program. You should be aware of the various background processes that are running, as well as any other processes that run against the Oracle database. Initialization parameters are used to adjust the behavior of many of these background processes. Also understand that each type of process has its place in Oracle, whether it's system, user, or batch. The goal of the DBA is to ensure that all processes can live happily together in the same instance.

Database maintenance involves the regular monitoring of the database. In order to perform good maintenance you must be proactive, studying the activities that occur in the database, such as space utilization, database growth, user functionality, and so on. Understanding the database is imperative to providing a better Oracle environment for the end user. Understanding is derived from study, and study is enabled through manual monitoring and database auditing.

Auditing provides the DBA with the opportunity to monitor specific activities in the database. Without the option of auditing, the DBA could be blind to what is happening in the database. Auditing yields knowledge if used properly. If you decide to activate auditing, be specific as to the tasks you decide to audit. An audit trail filled with a high percentage of unneeded information is a useless resource. You must be able to refer to the audit trail for resolutions, speculations, and even forecasting. Also keep in mind that auditing has its costs, so be frugal with your resources. Audit what you need, and most importantly, learn how to manage your audit trail.

We displayed a few common database monitoring scripts, but these are only a drop in the bucket. Much more can and should be implemented as part of the DBA's everyday schedule. After monitoring scripts are in place, the scripts can be automated along with many other database-related tasks. Oracle provides the database user a means of scheduling jobs by placing them in a job queue. The scheduling of periodic tasks allows database users (especially the DBA) the opportunity to organize database activities effectively and often allows for the automation of many of our otherwise mundane tasks.

Administration Using Enterprise Manager

by Paul W. Singleton

Introduction to Oracle Enterprise Manager

Oracle Enterprise Manager (OEM) is a robust collection of integrated tools that enables you to administer all the Oracle databases and servers in your organization from a central location. You can use Enterprise Manager to monitor databases, schedule jobs, diagnose performance problems, distribute software, and access the many tools provided for database administration tasks.

Enterprise Manager provides an easy-to-use graphical user interface, including drag-and-drop capability and a navigator that is consistent with Windows 95 Explorer standards. The console is divided into the Navigator, Job, Map, and Event systems. See Figure 21.1 for an example of an Enterprise Manager console.

FIGURE 21.1.

The OEM console.

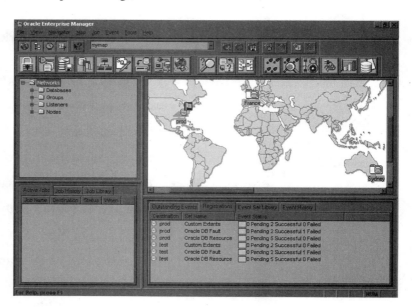

If you are familiar only with an early release of Enterprise Manager, you will find the more recent releases easier to use, configure, and maintain. Enterprise Manager is easy enough for inexperienced DBAs, but includes powerful tools that can save an experienced DBA much time. New learning tools have been incorporated into both the base product and the add-on packs, such as the capability of seeing the SQL that OEM is generating or of learning why a particular decision was made during a tuning session.

This chapter focuses primarily on the base Enterprise Manager product, but it discusses briefly a few of the products included in the add-on packs. The Performance Pack, which was an option with earlier releases, has been replaced by three new add-on packs. These packs are collections of separately licensed products that extend the capabilities of the base product. Performance Pack customers can upgrade to the new Diagnostics Pack and Tuning Pack. The Tuning Pack includes Oracle Expert, the Tablespace Manager, and a new SQL Analyze tool that helps you tune your SQL. The Diagnostics Pack includes Performance Manager, TopSessions, Lock Manager, and a new Capacity Planner.

Installing Oracle Enterprise Manager

There are two components that must be installed in order to make full use of Enterprise Manager's capabilities. On the workstation you must install the Enterprise Manager software, of course. The default installation installs the Net8 client software. If you perform a custom installation, make sure you install Net8, because OEM 1.4 and higher does not work with SQL*Net 2.*x*.

The OEM console uses the Simple Network Management Protocol (SNMP) to pass communications between the console and each of the nodes in your organization. On the console, a product called the Daemon Manager controls this communication, and on the server, the Oracle Intelligent Agent controls it. The Intelligent Agent is an SNMP subagent used to monitor events, schedule jobs, discover new services, and communicate with the OEM Console. You must install and configure an Intelligent Agent on every database server you intend to monitor or on which you wish to schedule jobs. You can use some of the other DBA tools, such as Schema Manager or the TopSessions Monitor, to manage a database even if you don't have an Intelligent Agent running on that database's server.

Enterprise Manager and the Intelligent Agent are both installed with the Oracle Installer program. The 32-bit Windows-based Installer version 3.3.0.1-and-later can support multiple Oracle homes on the same machine. This enables you to install two versions of the same product on the same system, just as you have been able to do on UNIX and other server platforms. The first Oracle home installed on a system is used as the default. All Oracle products prior to 8.0.4 must be installed in this default Oracle home.

Make sure you read the documentation, especially all the README files included with the Installer and OEM. There are some problems and restrictions regarding various releases of the Installer that might be documented for the release you are about to install. For example, you should not install OEM 1.5 into an 8.0.3 Oracle home or in an Oracle home using 8.0.3 Required Support Files.

One other thing to keep in mind is that you might not be licensed to use all the products shipped on the Enterprise Manager CD. In some releases, the Performance Pack, which has been replaced by the Oracle Tuning Pack and the Oracle Diagnostic Pack, was included on every OEM CD-ROM even though it required a separate license to use the product. If you're not sure which products you are licensed to install, your sales representative should be more than happy to point out all the products still available for you to purchase.

Configuring Enterprise Manager

So you're asking, "Now that I've installed everything, how do I get it to work?" Well, that's the fun part. Actually, many people who have configured Enterprise Manager in the past might disagree. If you're careful and you know about a few pitfalls, you can begin using Enterprise Manager in just a few minutes.

There are several steps involved in this configuration:

1. Build the Repository.
2. Configure the Intelligent Agent(s).
3. Discover Services.
4. Set User Preferences.

Building the Repository

The Enterprise Manager Repository is simply a collection of tables used to store information about an organization's database environment and tasks that the DBA wants to perform. If you monitor your databases for an event, schedule a job, or group several databases into a group—all this is stored in the Repository.

There are a few things to keep in mind as you plan for your Repository. First, you should build a Repository for each administrator, unless all your administrators will be sharing one central console. Second, you should not create multiple repositories owned by the same Oracle user ID, even though they are stored in separate databases. If you don't follow these rules, the messages passing between the console and the Intelligent Agents could, and most likely will, be misrouted.

You can create the Repository in any database to which the console will have access. First, create a tablespace to hold the Repository data. Next, create a Repository owner with DBA privileges and make the user's default tablespace the one you just created. Listing 21.1 shows a tablespace and user being created for this purpose using SQL Worksheet.

LISTING 21.1. CREATING THE REPOSITORY TABLESPACE AND OWNER.

```
SQLWKS> create tablespace oem_data
    2> datafile 'C:\ORANT\DATABASE\oemdata.ora' size 30M
    3> default storage (initial 48K next 256K)
    4>
Statement processed.
SQLWKS> create user oemown identified by oemown
    2> default tablespace oem_data
    3> temporary tablespace temp
    4> quota unlimited on oem_data
    5>
Statement processed.
SQLWKS> grant dba to oemown
    2>
Statement processed.
```

After you create the tablespace and Repository owner ID, building the Repository is a simple matter. In fact, there are several ways you can build your Repository. Probably the easiest is to let Enterprise Manager step you through the process the first time you sign on.

Select the Enterprise Manager icon from the Oracle Enterprise Manager program group. Enter the ID, password, and connect string for the Repository owner when the sign-on screen appears. Because the Repository tables do not exist yet, Enterprise Manager asks whether you would like to build a new Repository. Click the OK button and OEM will display the steps it is following as it builds the Repository.

If you have any problems with the automatic build of the Repository described previously, you can use the Repository Manager, also located in the Oracle Enterprise Manager program group. The Repository Manager enables you to create, drop, or validate the Repository for any OEM component.

For those of you who love the command line, you can still manually build the Repository from a DOS prompt. See the appendixes in the *Oracle Enterprise Manager Configuration Guide* for a description of the vobsh utility.

Configuring the Intelligent Agent

If you are configuring an Intelligent Agent to run on a UNIX server, it is much easier than it used to be as long as the server's SQL*Net (or Net8) configuration files are present and are formatted correctly. In earlier releases you had to run some scripts to create a database user ID for the Agent in each of your databases. You then had to edit an snmp.ora file and key in the appropriate information for each of the databases and listeners you intended to monitor.

21

ADMINISTRATION
USING ENTERPRISE
MANAGER

> **TIP**
>
> If you are having trouble getting the service discovery feature of the Intelligent Agent to work, try generating a new set of SQL*NET configuration files (*.ora) using Oracle Network Manager. This produces some nicely formatted files, and the Agent sometimes has better luck using these files to create its own configuration files.

The more recent releases of Oracle and the Intelligent Agent have simplified this process. The Agent user ID, `dbsnmp`, is created in the database when you run the scripts to build your catalog. After the Intelligent Agent is installed, start the Agent by typing `lsnrctl dbsnmp_start`. On some platforms, you will receive a message that an SNMP master agent could not be found. You can ignore this message and just press the Enter key.

The first time the Intelligent Agent is started, it will check for the existence of its configuration files, and because they are not there yet, the Agent will gather the information it needs to create them. First, the Agent will read `/etc/oratab` to obtain the names of the SIDs and the Oracle home for each SID. Next, it will read the `listener.ora` file to see which listeners are servicing the various SIDs. If a `GLOBAL_DBNAME` parameter exists in `listener.ora`, the Agent assumes Oracle Names is being used to resolve service names, and the global name is used in the Agent's configuration files. If there is no `GLOBAL_DBNAME` entry, `tnsnames.ora` is read to determine the service name of each SID. If no entry exists in `tnsnames.ora`, the Agent uses `<sid>_<hostname>` for the service name.

After it has collected this information, the Agent creates its configuration files, `snmp_ro.ora`, `snmp_rw.ora`, and `services.ora` in `$ORACLE_HOME/network/admin`. As you might have guessed, the `ro` and `rw` stand for read-only and read/write. You can add additional parameters to the `snmp_rw.ora` file, if you want to specify a new password for the `dbsnmp` database ID, for example. You should never edit `snmp_ro.ora`. As you add new services, the Agent will take care of updating this file each time you start and stop the Agent. See the "Sample Net8 Configuration Files" section at the end of this chapter for working examples of *.ora files.

> **TIP**
>
> Some documentation might lead you to believe that OEM versions 1.4 and higher will work with the Intelligent Agent delivered with the 7.3.2 release of Oracle. This is not true. If you have servers running 7.3.2 or earlier, save yourself a tremendous amount of time by installing a 7.3.3 or newer Agent in order to use OEM 1.4 or OEM 1.5.

Administration Using Enterprise Manager
CHAPTER 21

489

21

ADMINISTRATION
USING ENTERPRISE
MANAGER

When you install the Intelligent Agent on Windows NT, a service called OracleAgent (or OracleAgent80) is created. To start the Intelligent Agent, open the Control Panel folder and select the Services icon. Scroll down until you find OracleAgent, highlight it, and press the Start button. When the Agent is started for the first time, it will use the Windows NT Registry, your `listener.ora` file, and the `tnsnames.ora` file to create the configuration files `snmp_ro.ora`, `snmp_rw.ora`, and `services.ora`. You can also start, stop, and obtain the status of the Agent from a DOS prompt by typing `net start oracleagent` and `net stop oracleagent`, respectively. Simply typing `net start` enables you to see whether the Agent is already running.

> **WARNING**
>
> If you are automating the startup and shutdown of the Intelligent Agent on a UNIX platform, be careful. Under some circumstances, the Agent might not shut down properly, and the `dbsnmp` process that is left can use large amounts of your system's CPU. It is a good idea to follow up the `lsnrctl dbsnmp_stop` command in your script with a series of commands to list processes, `grep` for `dbsnmp`, and kill any remaining `dbsnmp` processes.

Discovering New Services

The last step you must perform before you can fully utilize Enterprise Manager is to discover new services on the servers you'd like to monitor. Service Discovery defines the services in the Repository and adds them to your `tnsnames.ora` file so you can monitor the databases and listeners, schedule jobs, and perform administrative tasks from the OEM console.

Select the Enterprise Manager icon from the Oracle Enterprise Manager program group. On the sign-on screen, enter the ID and password for the Repository owner and the connect string for the Repository database.

When the OEM console appears, select the Service Discovery option from the Navigator menu. The Discover New Services Wizard will ask whether you would like to proceed with service discovery. Click on the Next button to leave the introduction window and proceed with service discovery.

On the next screen, enter the name of each node on which you have configured an Intelligent Agent, pressing the Add button after each entry.

On the Discovery Interval screen, shown in Figure 21.2, it is best to take the default and allow the wizard to update your `tnsnames.ora` file. If you want to automatically discover new services throughout the day, enter the interval at which you would like this discovery to take place.

FIGURE 21.2.

*The Discovery
Interval window.*

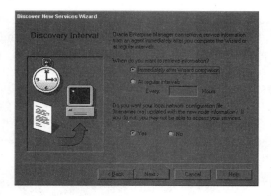

One final window will appear before the discovery begins. This window simply summarizes your choices and shows you any previously discovered nodes that will be refreshed.

If a node is accessible and the server's Intelligent Agent is contacted, you should receive a status of Discovered in the Service Discovery Status window.

You can now use the Navigator to see the databases and listeners you've discovered. If you double-click on one of the databases, you will be warned that no preferences are set for that database, and a sign-on screen will appear.

Setting Preferences

Before you can schedule jobs, you need to set user preferences for that database. This will also enable you to connect to the database from the Navigator window without entering a user ID and password.

The Job Scheduling system and the Navigator will use the username and password defined in user preferences to run an operating system job or connect to a database. You can open the User Preferences window by selecting Preferences from the File menu. On the User Preferences window, select each service and provide the username and password you would like to use for each service (see Figure 21.3). Notice to the left of the User Preferences window that the services discovered in the previous section are now accessible through the Navigator system.

FIGURE 21.3.
*Setting the pre-
ferred credentials.*

Managing Events

An event in Enterprise Manager is anything that might occur on the database server or in the database, which Enterprise Manager is capable of monitoring. Events are grouped into *event sets* or a collection of related events. You tell Enterprise Manager to monitor for an event set by *registering* the event set for a specific node or database. You also define which administrator or operator should be notified if an event within the set occurs and the method of that notification: email, pager, or a message to the OEM Console.

Keep in mind that each Repository is assigned to a specific administrator. If an administrator is monitoring a database for one event and a second administrator is monitoring the same database for a second event, each administrator will receive notification of only his or her own events, not the events of the other administrator. The Intelligent Agent routes the messages according to the owner of the Repository in which the event is registered. This is why you should not create multiple repositories owned by the same user ID.

Creating and Modifying Event Sets

Enterprise Manager is delivered with a number of predefined event sets. These sets are found in the Event Set Library in the Event Management System on the OEM Console (see Figure 21.4). When you create your own event sets, they will also be found in the Event Set Library.

FIGURE 21.4.
The Event Set Library.

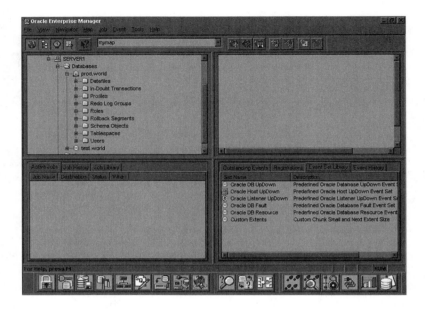

To view or edit one of these event sets, double-click on the event set name and a Quick Edit window will appear. To see which events make up this event set, select the Events tab (see Figure 21.5). The events on the left half of the window are included in the event set, and the right half contains the names of the other events available to be included in the event set.

FIGURE 21.5.
Viewing or editing events in an event set.

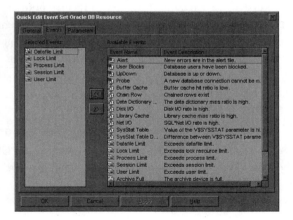

You can add or remove events from an event set by highlighting the event name and pressing the left or right arrow button in the center of the window.

Administration Using Enterprise Manager

CHAPTER 21

493

21

ADMINISTRATION
USING ENTERPRISE
MANAGER

The events that you see on this page are supplied by Oracle and are written as Tool Command Language (Tcl) scripts with Oracle extensions for database access. If you are interested in writing your own Tcl scripts for events, refer to the *Oracle Enterprise Manager Application Developer's Guide.*

To create your own event set, either choose Event from the console window or select the Create Event button on the toolbar. The Create Event Set property sheet will appear. On the General page, enter the name of the new event set, select the service type, and enter a description.

Click on the Events tab and select the available events you would like to include in this event set. Press the left arrow button to include the events. Here, I have included the Chunk Small and Maximum Extents events.

On the Properties page, determine at what interval you would like to check for the events in the event set (see Figure 21.6). Notice that I selected the Chunk Small and Maximum Extents events on the Events property sheet. If you would like to change the thresholds at which a warning or an alert will occur, double-click on the parameter name and modify the value.

FIGURE 21.6.
Setting thresholds and frequency.

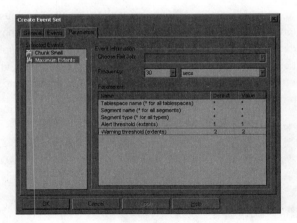

Click the OK button to save your event set, or if you'd like to save this event set and immediately create another, click the Apply button. You should now see your event listed with the predefined events.

Registering an Event Set

Enterprise Manager will not monitor for the events in an event set until that event set is registered. Either click on the Register Event Set button on the toolbar, or select Event from the menu bar and choose Register Event Set from the drop-down list.

When the Register Event Set property sheet appears, select the Service Type for the event set you would like to register. The event sets for this service type will then be available in the Set Name drop-down list. After you've selected the event set, highlight the destinations you would like to monitor and click the left-arrow button in the center of the page to select the destination (see Figure 21.7).

FIGURE 21.7.

Choose a destination for event registration.

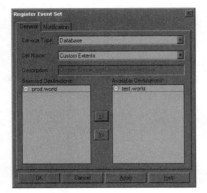

Click on the Notification tab. For each destination selected on the previous page, you can choose who will be notified for this event set and the manner in which they will be notified. If the Notify Operator on Duty box is checked, the event will be displayed on the console if it occurs (see Figure 21.8). If you have configured email or paging services, you can choose which operators and administrators should be notified and the notification method for each of them.

FIGURE 21.8.

Choose notification options.

When you click OK or Apply, a Destination Validation window will appear. Enterprise Manager uses a facility called the Communication Daemon to communicate with the Intelligent Agent on that node. The Intelligent Agent makes certain the destinations for the event set registration are valid and confirms this to the Communication Daemon.

Administration Using Enterprise Manager

CHAPTER 21

495

21

ADMINISTRATION
USING ENTERPRISE
MANAGER

After the destinations are validated, the console window will reappear and the new destinations will be listed under the Registrations tab of the Event Management System. As the Intelligent Agent registers each event in the event set, the number of pending registrations should drop until all the events have been successfully registered.

As you can see in Figure 21.9, I have registered three event sets for destinations test and three for prod. Notice the failed counter for the Oracle DB Fault event set. The Agent will still monitor for the other events in the set, even if one of the events failed to register. If you double-click on a line that has a failure such as this one, the Modify Registration property sheet will appear. On the Status page, you can see which event failed to register and why.

FIGURE 21.9.

Failed event registration.

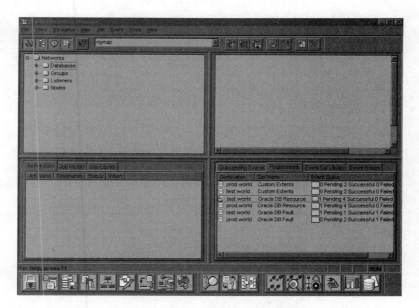

In Figure 21.10, you see that the User Blocks event failed. This is because the `sys.dba_locks` view does not exist. Please note that the other events in the set were registered, and you will be notified if any of these events occur.

In order to correct this, close the Modify Registration window and highlight the line with the failure on the Event Management System screen. Select Event from the OEM menu bar at the top of the screen and choose Remove Registration. In a few moments the registration will be removed and the line will disappear from the Event Management System window. Now you can run the `catblock.sql` script found in the `admin` subdirectory under Oracle `home`. This creates the missing view, and the next time you register the Oracle DB Fault event set, all three events in that set will be registered successfully.

Figure 21.10.
*Checking the sta-
tus of the failed
event.*

Event Notification

When a registered event occurs, a message will appear on the console under the
Outstanding Events tab of the Event Management System. If the warning threshold was
reached, a yellow flag will appear in front of the event name. If the message indicates an
alert, a red flag will appear.

Double-click on the outstanding event and the Acknowledge Event window will open. A
detailed event message will appear under the General tab. You might have to place the
cursor on this message and use the right arrow key on your keyboard to see the entire
message. As you can see in Figure 21.11, there isn't enough free space to allocate another extent for an object in the system tablespace.

Figure 21.11.
*Event acknowl-
edgment window.*

Fortunately, you can add a datafile without even leaving the OEM Console. If you use
the Navigator to find the system tablespace and then click the right mouse button on the
`Datafiles` folder, you have the option to add a datafile. Provide the required information
in the Create Datafile window, click OK, and the datafile will be added. The next time
the status of the Chunk Small event is checked, according to the interval set when the
event was registered, the event will be cleared and the flag will turn to green.

Administration Using Enterprise Manager

CHAPTER 21

497

21

ADMINISTRATION
USING ENTERPRISE
MANAGER

You can then go back to the Acknowledge Event window by double-clicking the cleared event, and click on the Move to History button. The event will remain under the History tab of the Event Management System until you clear the history from the Event option on the OEM menu bar.

> **TIP**
>
> In some circumstances, a flag might stay red or yellow for an extended period of time, even though an event has been cleared. This usually happens if your databases are unavailable for a period of time due to backups, or something else has happened that affects the Agent's communication with the database. You don't have to wait for the event to clear. Simply acknowledge the "outstanding" event, and the notification will be moved to Event History.

Managing Jobs

The Job Scheduling system, located in the bottom-left corner of the console, is used to create and schedule SQL and DBA scripts, DBA tasks such as startup and shutdown, and operating system commands and scripts. After you have defined a job, you can execute it immediately, save it for later execution, or schedule it to run at an interval of your choice. You can also schedule fixit jobs to help automate event handling.

Preparing to Run Jobs

Before you can submit a job on a node, regardless of the destination type, you must set the preferred credentials for that node. If you intend to run a database job, for example, you must set the credentials for the node and the database. Remember that preferred credentials are set by choosing the Preferences option from the OEM Console's File menu.

If the node is a Windows NT server, make sure the user you define in the OEM preferences is an NT administrator ID, and that the user has been granted the Log on as Batch Job privilege.

Remember that an Intelligent Agent must be configured and running on the server. See the section "Configuring the Intelligent Agent," earlier in this chapter.

When scheduling jobs on a UNIX server, root.sh must have already been run on the server. Verify this by checking the permissions on the dbsnmp command in $ORACLE_HOME/bin. The permissions on the executable should be rwsr-xr-x, and the owner should be root. If this is not the case, sign on as root, run root.sh, and then proceed.

Before scheduling database startup and shutdown jobs, you must configure the database to be managed remotely. See the section "Managing Database Instances," later in this chapter.

Creating a Job

To create a job, select Job from the OEM Console menu and choose the Create option. The Create Job window will appear. As you can see in Figure 21.12, I've given the job a name and description, chosen a destination type, and selected SERVER1.

FIGURE 21.12.

Creating a new job.

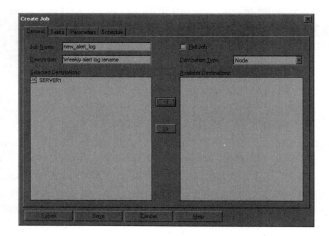

Click on the Tasks tab and select the task you would like to perform. The tasks listed on this page are predefined job tasks provided by Oracle. You can create your own job task in Tcl and submit it through the Run Tcl task on this page. See the *Oracle Enterprise Manager Application Developer's Guide* for instructions on writing job tasks in Tcl.

After you have selected the task, click on the Parameters tab. This page will vary depending on the task that you've selected. In Figure 21.13, because I selected the Run OS Command task, I'm prompted for a command and any arguments required for that command. In this example, I'm renaming one of my alert logs so that the log doesn't grow too large.

The last step in creating a job is to submit it or save it. A submitted job is scheduled for execution, either immediately or in the future. A saved job is added to the Job Library.

To submit a job, first select the Schedule tab on the Create Job window and set the execution preferences. You can run the job immediately, schedule it to run once at some time in the future, or schedule it to run repeatedly at an interval of your choice (see Figure 21.14).

FIGURE 21.13.
Entering job parameters.

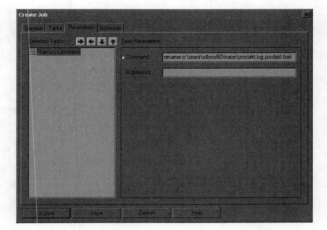

FIGURE 21.14.
Scheduling a job.

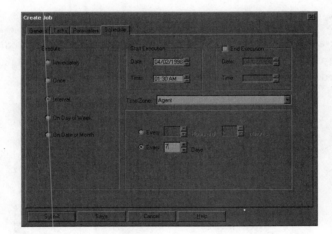

When you finish entering the scheduling information, press the Submit button. The job will appear on the Active Jobs page of the Job system on the console. After the job has been executed, the status and output from the job will be placed in the Job History.

Double-click on an item in the Job History window in order to see its details: the pages that comprise the Job History window when the job ran, what it did, and the parameter settings. The progress page shown in Figure 21.15 shows the status of the job I just scheduled. If the job had failed, or if it had produced any output, the Show Output button would be available. You would find any errors on the Output window.

FIGURE 21.15.

Viewing job details.

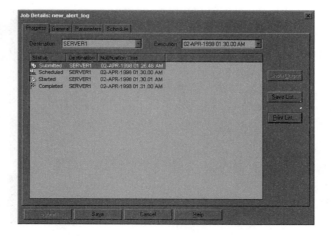

Creating a Fixit Job

A fixit job is used to respond to the occurrence of an event. To create a fixit job, follow all the steps described in the section prior to this one, but on the General page of the Create Job window, select the Fixit Job check box (see Figure 21.16).

FIGURE 21.16.

Creating a fixit job.

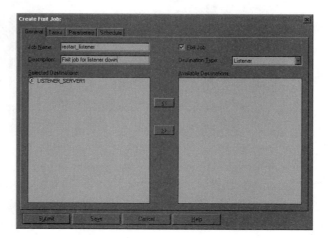

After you've created the fixit job, you can apply the job to an event set in the Event Set Library. In Figure 21.17, I've selected the Listener UpDown event set by double-clicking on that line in the library. On the Parameters page you can choose a fixit job. As you can see, the fixit job just created is now available in the drop-down list.

For more information on editing event sets, see the section "Creating and Modifying Event Sets," earlier in this chapter.

Administration Using Enterprise Manager
CHAPTER 21

501

21

ADMINISTRATION
USING ENTERPRISE
MANAGER

FIGURE 21.17.
Choosing a fixit job for an event set.

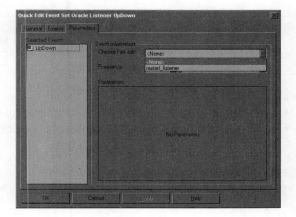

Managing Database Instances

Oracle Instance Manager enables you to perform administrative actions on remote databases, including startup and shutdown. It helps you manage user sessions and enables you to save multiple configurations for your database startup. If your organization is running a handful of UNIX systems for its database servers, remote startup and shutdown might not seem that important. If you are trying to manage a large number of remote database servers running on Novell, Windows NT, VMS, and various other platforms, a single tool that enables you to start and stop any database is very convenient.

Preparing for Remote Administration

Before you can start up and shut down your instances remotely, you must create a password file for each instance and change an `init.ora` parameter. Create the password file from the command line with the `orapwd` command:

```
> orapwd file=<filenm> password=<passwd> entries=<users>
```

The filename should typically be in the same directory as your `init.ora` files, under `$ORACLE_HOME/dbs`. The filename is typically `orapw<sid>`. Some platforms give you the capability of setting environment variables stating the name and location of the password file. The `entries` parameter specifies the number of distinct DBAs and Sysopers who will use this file.

After creating your password file, you must set the `init.ora` parameter `remote_login_password_file = EXCLUSIVE`. Exclusive password files must be created for each instance being managed remotely. When you connect to the database and grant `SYSDBA` or `SYSOPER` to users, they will be added to the password file. You'll also need to run `catdbsyn` for any user who will be using Instance Manager.

Finally, before you can start a database remotely, you need a local copy of the server's init.ora file residing on the workstation or in a stored configuration file.

Log in to Instance Manager as a user who has been granted SYSDBA or SYSOPER. Make sure you select SYSDBA or SYSOPER in the Connect As field.

After you are connected, select Initialization Parameters on the left side of the Instance Manager window. The parameters will appear on the right side of the screen, separated into four pages by category. Select the Save button to save this configuration (see Figure 21.18).

The stored configuration is kept in the workstation's registry. If you move to another workstation and try to start the database, the stored configuration will not exist on the second workstation.

FIGURE 21.18.

Saving initialization parameters.

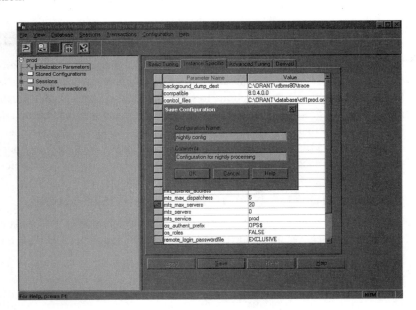

Shutting Down an Instance

Display the database status page by clicking on the name of the database that you'd like to shut down. There are two ways to begin the shutdown process. You could select the Database menu from the Instance Manager menu bar and then choose Shutdown. You could also click the radio button marked Shutdown and then select Apply on the database status page.

On the Shutdown Options window, select the type of shutdown you would like to perform and click OK (see Figure 21.19). You should soon receive confirmation that the instance was shut down.

FIGURE 21.19.
Selecting an immediate shutdown.

Starting an Instance

You begin an instance startup just as you did the shutdown, either from the Database menu or from the status page. Select the radio button that indicates the type of startup you'd like to perform. The Instance Started button performs a `startup nomount`. The Database Mounted button performs a `startup mount`. The Database Open button performs a normal `startup`.

Click on the Apply button to begin the instance startup. You will be prompted for the name of the stored configuration or the name of a local parameter file (see Figure 21.20). Click OK and you should soon be notified that the instance has been started.

FIGURE 21.20.
Select Apply to begin a complete startup.

Editing Stored Configurations

You can modify any of your stored configurations. Simply select the stored configuration name on the left side of the Instance Manager window. The parameters for that configuration will appear in the right side of the window.

Click on the parameter you would like to change, make your modification, and select Apply. Select Save to save the change in the stored configuration. To delete a parameter, click on the right mouse button, select Delete, and then save the configuration.

Managing Schema Objects

Schema objects of all types can be created, modified, and dropped through the use of Oracle Schema Manager. Schema Manager includes most of the schema objects used to support the object-relational model, queuing, and other Oracle8 Server concepts. Some of the newer schema objects in Schema Manager are object types, varrays, nested table types, and queue tables. This section will concentrate primarily on the schema objects introduced in Oracle8, but begins with the creation of a simple table.

Creating Tables

The navigator on the main Schema Manager screen shows all the schema objects supported by this tool. You can create a new schema object by highlighting the object type and clicking the green + icon on the toolbar. You can also right-click on a schema object type and then select the Create option.

When you choose to create a new table, you are given the option of using the Table Wizard or creating the table manually. The next example is from a manual table creation.

The General page on the Create Table window enables you to enter the name and tablespace for the table, as well as the name, datatype, length, and other details for each column in the table (see Figure 21.21). If you scroll to the right, you should have a red X in the Nulls? field for each required column. A green check mark in that field indicates that nulls are allowed.

On the Constraints page, you can add any additional constraints, such as a primary key, to the table.

FIGURE 21.21.

Creating a table.

The Storage page gives you the option of explicitly entering your storage parameters or allowing Schema Manager to calculate the parameters based on characteristics provided by you. The example in Figure 21.22 shows the Auto Calculation feature. Notice the Show SQL button was selected, so you can see the SQL that will be executed to create the table, including the storage clause. When you click on the Create button, the table and its associated constraints will be created.

FIGURE 21.22.

Automatically cal-culating storage parameters.

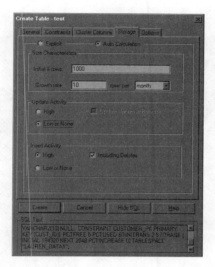

> **TIP**
>
> Grant SELECT privileges on sys.v_$parameter and sys.v_$type_size to the schema owner if you intend to use the Auto Calculation feature to calculate your storage parameters and would like to examine the SQL before executing it. Without these privileges, you will see the message Table or view does not exist in the SQL text box when you attempt to display the SQL.

Creating Object Types

A relational database is based on entities and the relationships between those entities. Manipulation of the data in a relational database must comply with any constraints defined within the database, but there is no information contained within the structure of the database to define what functions or operations will be performed with the data.

Oracle8 is an object-relational database management system (ORDBMS). The object-relational model enables you to define *object types*. An object type defines the entity and the operations that will be applied to the data. These operations are called *methods*.

Object types can build upon one another, so an object type might be made up in whole or in part of other object types. Finally, the object types are used to define the objects stored in an *object table*.

Figure 21.23 shows the creation of an object type called person. The attributes are added one at a time by clicking on the Add button. In the example, three attributes have already been added, and a fourth, home_telephone, will be added as soon as the OK button is selected on the Create Attribute window.

FIGURE 21.23.

Creating an object type.

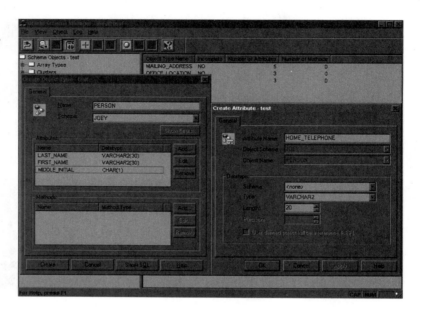

You can see in Figure 21.24 that I'm creating another object type, this time called customer. There are two other user-defined object types included in this definition: the person object type defined in the previous example and a mailing address object type. Notice the SQL used to create the object type is displayed at the bottom of the window.

Creating a VARRAY

A VARRAY contains multiple occurrences of the same item, such as a list of phone numbers or a list of item numbers on an order. When this list is defined, it can be used in an object table or as an attribute for another object type.

FIGURE 21.24.

*Object types
defined with other
object types.*

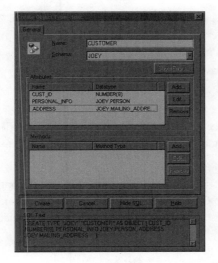

Figure 21.25 shows a VARRAY being created. This example is an array of up to 50 customers. A nested table could be used to accomplish the same thing. Using a VARRAY in this case makes sense only if there is a limit on the number of customers that should be grouped together and if the list will not be queried regularly. Because the VARRAY sets an upper limit on the number of entries, it can store the list more efficiently than a nested table. If the data in the list is to be queried, instead of being selected as a whole, it might be better to store the data in a nested table, because the VARRAY would have to be unloaded into a nested table anyway, in order to perform the query.

FIGURE 21.25.

*Creating a VARRAY
of customers.*

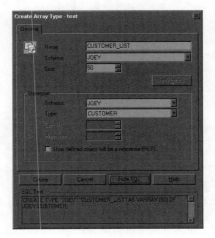

After you've created a VARRAY, it can be used in creating an object type. You could create an object type of sales_rep, for example, which uses the customer_list varray to track up to 50 customers for each sales rep.

Creating a Nested Table

As I mentioned in the previous section, a nested table can be used to store a list of related items instead of a VARRAY. If the items within the list need to be queried, or if there is no upper limit to the number of items in the list, it might make more sense to use a nested table instead of a VARRAY.

To create a nested table, right-click on Table Types on the Schema Manager window and then select the Create option. The Create Table Type window will appear, as shown in Figure 21.26. In the example, a list of items to be used on an order is placed in an order_line_items nested table.

FIGURE 21.26.

Creating a nested table.

As you can see in Figure 21.27, the nested table can now be used in defining additional object types.

Creating an Object Table

When I created user-defined datatypes in the previous examples, such as object types and VARRAYs, no storage was created, and no structure was created in which you could actually store data. In order to store one of these objects as a row of data, you must create an object table.

Administration Using Enterprise Manager

CHAPTER 21

509

21

ADMINISTRATION
USING ENTERPRISE
MANAGER

FIGURE 21.27.

Defining an object type with a nested table.

An object table is simply that: a table used to store data for an object type, with each row representing an occurrence of an object. Figure 21.28 shows the creation of an object table for the `sales_rep` object type defined earlier. You create an object table just like a normal table, except that you select the Object Table radio button on the General page of the Create Table window. This changes the General page and enables you to select the object type for which you wish to build a table.

FIGURE 21.28.

Creating an object table.

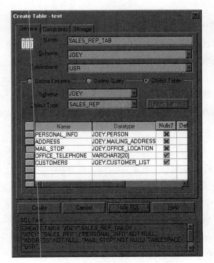

Managing Security

Oracle8 has introduced several long-awaited enhancements to Oracle's security, such as *password aging*. This section will discuss how these new features are incorporated into Oracle Security Manager.

Oracle passwords can now expire. If a password has expired, the user must change the password the next time he or she connects to the database. In fact, when you create an account, you can mark the password as expired, so that the user will have to reset the password upon the first logon.

You might also notice that you can give the user a status of locked or unlocked. When a user ID is locked, that ID cannot connect to the database. The user's profile will determine whether the account is unlocked after a period of time or whether it must be unlocked by an administrator.

Finally, you should notice that Security Manager grants the `Connect` role unless you select the Roles/Privileges tab and remove this granted role. Remember that `Connect` is a role that includes not only the `Create Session` privilege, but system privileges that allow the user to create a number of database objects. If the user is simply going to use an application and you don't want the user to create any database objects, you should have Security Manager grant `Create Session` instead of `Connect`.

If you are using Oracle Security Server, you can use global authentication to provide a single authentication point for all databases in your enterprise. This is a tremendous time saver for organizations with large numbers of users who need access to many databases. In Figure 21.29, you can see that global authentication requires you to enter additional information about the user's organization and location. See the *Oracle Security Server Guide* and the *Oracle Server Administrator's Guide* for detailed information on global authentication.

Password aging is implemented through the use of profiles. You can require passwords to expire in a certain number of days. You can also specify that an account with a expired password should be locked after a certain number of days because the account is no longer being used (see Figure 21.30). This makes it much easier to identify accounts that are no longer in use. There are also options for managing the complexity of passwords and for locking accounts after a number of failed logon attempts. Because all these options are set within profiles, you can create combinations of password aging and account locking that are appropriate for the various types of users in your database.

FIGURE 21.29.
Selecting global authentication.

FIGURE 21.30.
Password options for user profiles.

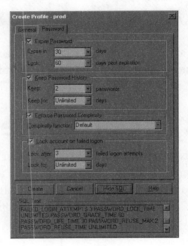

Managing Storage

Enterprise Manager includes a tool called Storage Manager that enables you to add datafiles, create rollback segments, put rollback segments online and take them offline, and analyze dependencies on your tablespaces. Many of these functions can be performed directly from the OEM console without starting Storage Manager.

The Tuning Pack includes a product called Tablespace Manager that enables you to coalesce free space in your tablespaces and deallocate unused space from objects, freeing the space for use once again.

It isn't necessary to deallocate all free space in a tablespace. You can choose to leave some of the unused space allocated to its current segment. You can then select an entire user or specific objects for deallocation, as show in Figure 21.31.

FIGURE 21.31.

Selecting users and objects for deallocation.

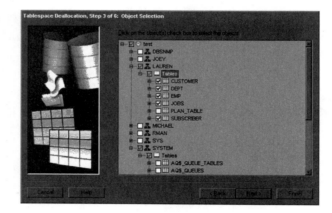

You are then given the option to override the default amount of free space to be left on an object-by-object basis. When you select Finish, a job will be submitted to perform the deallocation.

Diagnostic and Performance Tools

Most of the diagnostic and tuning tools provided by Enterprise Manager are, not surprisingly, located in the Diagnostic and Tuning Packs. Unfortunately, these are separately licensed products. If you were licensed for the Performance Pack you are in luck, for at the time of this writing, Performance Pack customers were given the opportunity to upgrade to the two new packs.

Oracle Performance Manager

Oracle Performance Manager is one of the tuning tools in the Tuning Pack. It provides a graphical representation of many of the hit ratios and statistics discussed in the performance tuning chapters later in this book. Figure 21.32 shows some of the memory-related graphs that can be displayed within Performance Manager. An example of the BUFFER CACHE HIT% graph is shown in Figure 21.33.

FIGURE 21.32.
Choosing a graph in Performance Manager.

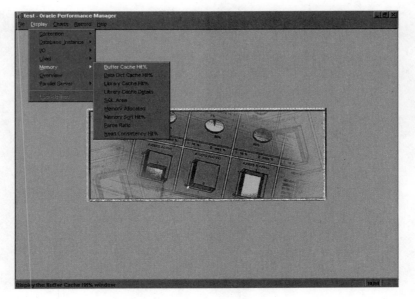

FIGURE 21.33.
Displaying the buffer cache hit percentage.

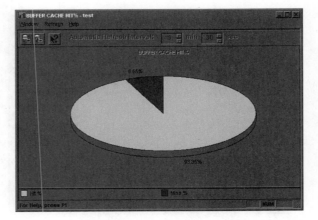

Performance Manager can be a good place to start if you have users complaining of slow response times or workstations that appear to be frozen. For example, imagine that users are calling you because it seems to be taking a long time to perform some transaction. You can look under the Contention section of the Display menu or you could look in the Database Instance section as in Figure 21.34. You can display the number of users waiting for some event and, more specifically, the number of users waiting for locks, as I did in Figure 21.35. You'll notice on the very large bar chart that two users appear to be waiting for locks.

FIGURE 21.34.

Preparing to display database instance information.

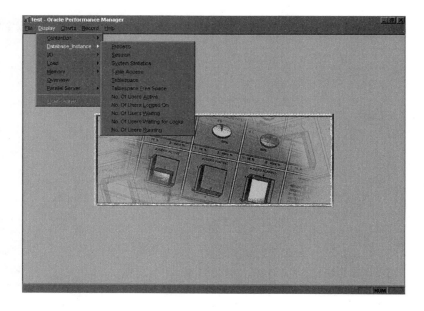

FIGURE 21.35.

Displaying the number of users waiting for locks.

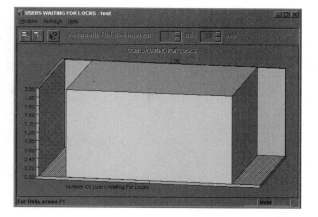

Oracle Lock Manager

Now that you've discovered a potential problem, you can use Oracle Lock Manager, another tool in the Diagnostics Pack, to resolve it. Lock Manager gives you a very nice representation of users holding locks and anyone who might be waiting as a result. In Figure 21.36, you can see that the user Michael has a lock on an object and two other users are waiting. Depending on what Michael might have been doing, and whether you

report to him or not, you might decide to kill his session and free up the other users. There is a kill session option under the Locks menu, or you can right-click on the session holding the lock, at which time you will be presented with the option of killing the session.

FIGURE 21.36.
Users waiting for locks.

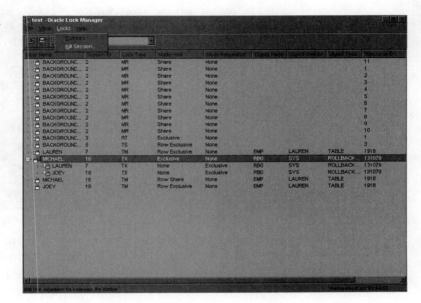

Oracle Expert and SQL Analyze

This section introduces two powerful tools provided with the Tuning Pack: Oracle Expert and SQL Analyze. Stepping through an entire tuning session and its output would be a lengthy process beyond the scope of this chapter, so this section focuses only on a summary of the tools and their benefits.

Oracle Expert (Figure 21.37) is a powerful tool provided with the Tuning Pack that offers tuning recommendations for new or existing databases based upon data gathered during tuning sessions. In the case of a new database, the recommendations are provided based upon information you provide about the database server, its average workload, and the expected database transactions.

FIGURE 21.37.

Oracle Expert.

You can decide between a general tuning session and a session focused on a particular problem area. This tuning session can capture data from a single point in time or over a specified period of time. Based upon the scope that you have set, Oracle Expert will provide recommendations for tuning the SGA and other instance-specific parameters, the reusability and access methods of your SQL, and the sizing and placement of database objects.

These recommendations are made on reports that you can generate at any time from the tuning session data. This data is stored in the Repository. As you run additional tuning sessions for a database, the reports will contain even better recommendations, because Oracle Expert will compare the instance data gathered over time during different levels of processing. The reports include instructional information explaining why certain recommendations were made. They also include warnings if there is a risk involved in making a tuning modification.

Although Oracle Expert will provide help with the reusability of your SQL and recommendations for adding or removing indexes, it does not provide any other guidance for making your SQL more efficient. SQL Analyze, a new product in the Tuning Pack, provides the tools to help you analyze and optimize your SQL.

SQL Analyze provides a tool called TopSQL, which identifies the SQL statements with the largest impact on your system. SQL Analyze will also step you through decisions you are making in writing a new SQL statement. You can save these tuning sessions in the Repository and continue working on them at a later time.

After you've identified a problem statement or entered a new SQL statement, you use SQL Analyze to perform an *explain plan* (see Figure 21.38). SQL Analyze will help you walk through the execution plan for your statement and examine any statistics available or the objects used in the plan. It will also help you analyze your join operations.

FIGURE 21.38.

Generate an explain plan with SQL Analyze.

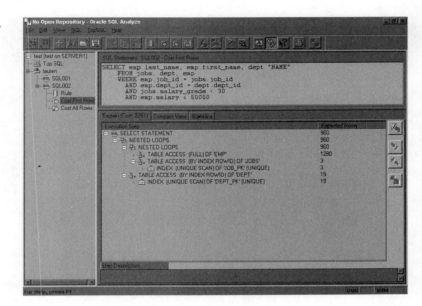

After you've examined the SQL statement, you can modify the structure of the statement or provide optimizer hints. You then compare the new statement by executing it and looking at statistics, or by generating another explain plan and comparing the two. A hint Wizard will even help make sure you use the correct syntax for your hints.

SQL Analyze will also let you know whether your statement is violating any SQL rules of thumb, such as operations that prevent the use of indexes.

Sample Net8 Configuration Files

Listings 21.2 through 21.6 show a set of configuration files from a UNIX database server. The tnsnames.ora and listener.ora files were used by the Intelligent Agent to generate the snmp_ro.ora and snmp_rw.ora files.

If you have just created your listener.ora and tnsnames.ora files, and you find an error in them after the Agent has generated the snmp files, you can stop the Agent, delete the snmp files, correct the error, and restart the Agent. The Agent will generate the snmp files any time it finds them missing.

Notice in Listing 21.6 I added a password so the `dbsnmp` database user ID does not sign on with a password of `dbsnmp`. If you've made any modifications to `snmp_rw.ora`, make note of these before you remove the file.

The last two Listings, 21.7 and 21.8, show the Net8 files from the console workstation.

LISTING 21.2. tnsnames FILE FROM DATABASE SERVER.

```
################
# Filename......: tnsnames.ora
# Name..........: LOCAL_REGION.world
# Date..........: 11-MAR-98 09:46:48
################
prod.world =
  (DESCRIPTION =
    (ADDRESS_LIST =
        (ADDRESS =
          (COMMUNITY = TCP.world)
          (PROTOCOL = TCP)
          (Host = server1)
          (Port = 1521)
        )
    )
    (CONNECT_DATA =
      (SID = prod)
        (GLOBAL_NAME = prod.world)
    )
  )
test.world =
  (DESCRIPTION =
    (ADDRESS_LIST =
        (ADDRESS =
          (COMMUNITY = TCP.world)
          (PROTOCOL = TCP)
          (Host = server1)
          (Port = 1521)
        )
    )
    (CONNECT_DATA =
      (SID = test)
        (GLOBAL_NAME = test.world)
    )
  )
```

LISTING 21.3. sqlnet.ora FILE FROM DATABASE SERVER.

```
################
# Filename......: sqlnet.ora
# Name..........: TCP.world
# Date..........: 11-MAR-98 09:46:48
################
```

Administration Using Enterprise Manager

CHAPTER 21

519

21

ADMINISTRATION
USING ENTERPRISE
MANAGER

```
AUTOMATIC_IPC = ON
TRACE_LEVEL_CLIENT = OFF
SQLNET.EXPIRE_TIME = 0
NAMES.DEFAULT_DOMAIN = world
NAME.DEFAULT_ZONE = world
SQLNET.CRYPTO_SEED = "-1241587199-1241552483"
```

LISTING 21.4. Listener.ora FILE FROM DATABASE SERVER.

```
#
# Listener.ora
# Version O96JUN23
# server1
#

SQLNET.AUTHENTICATION_SERVICES = (NONE)

USE_PLUG_AND_PLAY_LISTENER = OFF
USE_CKPFILE_LISTENER = OFF
LISTENER =
  (ADDRESS_LIST =
        (ADDRESS=
          (PROTOCOL=IPC)
          (KEY= prod.world)
        )
        (ADDRESS=
          (PROTOCOL=IPC)
          (KEY= prod)
        )
        (ADDRESS=
          (PROTOCOL=IPC)
          (KEY= test.world)
        )
        (ADDRESS=
          (PROTOCOL=IPC)
          (KEY= test)
        )
        (ADDRESS =
          (COMMUNITY = TCP.world)
          (PROTOCOL = TCP)
          (Host = server1)
          (Port = 1521)
        )
  )
STARTUP_WAIT_TIME_LISTENER = 0
CONNECT_TIMEOUT_LISTENER = 10
TRACE_LEVEL_LISTENER = OFF
SID_LIST_LISTENER=(SID_LIST=
  (SID_DESC=(SID_NAME=prod)
     (oracle_home=/u01/oracle/8.0.4))
  (SID_DESC=(SID_NAME=test)
     (oracle_home=/u01/oracle/8.0.4)))
```

LISTING 21.5. snmp_ro.ora FILE FROM DATABASE SERVER.

```
snmp.visibleservices = (LISTENER, prod.world, test.world)
snmp.shortname.LISTENER = LISTENER
snmp.longname.LISTENER = LISTENER_server1
snmp.configfile.LISTENER = /etc/listener.ora
snmp.SID.prod.world = prod
snmp.oraclehome.prod.world = /u01/oracle/8.0.4
snmp.address.prod.world = (DESCRIPTION =(ADDRESS_LIST =(ADDRESS =
➥(COMMUNITY = TCP.world)
                          (PROTOCOL = TCP)(Host = server1)(Port = 1521)))
                          (CONNECT_DATA =(SID = prod)(GLOBAL_NAME =
➥prod.world)))
snmp.SID.test.world = test
snmp.oraclehome.test.world = /u01/oracle/8.0.4
snmp.address.test.world = (DESCRIPTION =(ADDRESS_LIST =(ADDRESS =
➥(COMMUNITY = TCP.world)
                          (PROTOCOL = TCP)(Host = server1)(Port = 1521)))
                          (CONNECT_DATA =(SID = test)(GLOBAL_NAME =
➥test.world)))
ifile = /fin101201/oracle/7.3.4/network/admin/snmp_rw.ora
```

LISTING 21.6. snmp_rw FILE FROM DATABASE SERVER.

```
snmp.contact.LISTENER = ""
snmp.index.LISTENER = 1
snmp.contact.prod.world = ""
snmp.index.prod.world = 2
snmp.connect.prod.world.password = sams_oem
snmp.contact.test.world = ""
snmp.index.test.world = 3
snmp.connect.test.world.password = sams_oem
```

LISTING 21.7. tnsnames.ora FILE FROM CONSOLE WORKSTATION.

```
################
# Filename......: tnsnames.ora
# Name..........: LOCAL_REGION.world
# Date..........: 01-APR-1998 12.39.46 PM
# Generated by Enterprise Manager
################
prod.world=(DESCRIPTION=(ADDRESS_LIST =(ADDRESS = (COMMUNITY =
➥NMP.world)(PROTOCOL = NMP)
          (SERVER = SERVER1)(PIPE = ORAPIPE))(ADDRESS = (PROTOCOL =
➥TCP)(Host = SERVER1)
          (Port = 1521))(ADDRESS = (PROTOCOL = TCP)(Host = SERVER1)(Port
➥= 1526))
          (ADDRESS = (PROTOCOL = TCP)(Host = 127.0.0.1)(Port = 1521))
          (ADDRESS = (PROTOCOL = SPX)(Service = SERVER1_lsnr)))
          (CONNECT_DATA=(SID=PROD)(SERVER=DEDICATED)))
```

Administration Using Enterprise Manager

CHAPTER 21

521

21

ADMINISTRATION
USING ENTERPRISE
MANAGER

```
test.world=(DESCRIPTION=(ADDRESS_LIST =(ADDRESS = (COMMUNITY =
➥NMP.world)(PROTOCOL = NMP)
          (SERVER = SERVER1)(PIPE = ORAPIPE))(ADDRESS = (PROTOCOL =
➥TCP)(Host = SERVER1)
          (Port = 1521))(ADDRESS = (PROTOCOL = TCP)(Host = SERVER1)(Port
➥= 1526))
          (ADDRESS = (PROTOCOL = TCP)(Host = 127.0.0.1)(Port = 1521))
          (ADDRESS = (PROTOCOL = SPX)(Service = SERVER1_lsnr)))
          (CONNECT_DATA=(SID=TEST)(SERVER=DEDICATED)))

oemrep.world=(DESCRIPTION = (ADDRESS_LIST = (ADDRESS = (COMMUNITY =
➥tcp.world)
          (PROTOCOL = TCP) (Host = server2) (Port = 1521))
          (ADDRESS = (COMMUNITY = tcp.world) (PROTOCOL = TCP) (Host =
➥server2)
          (Port = 1526))) (CONNECT_DATA = (SID = oemrep)))
```

LISTING 21.8. sqlnet.ora FILE FROM CONSOLE WORKSTATION.

```
TRACE_LEVEL_CLIENT = OFF
names.directory_path = (TNSNAMES)
names.default_domain = world
name.default_zone = world
```

Summary

This chapter has provided installation and configuration instructions, as well as examples of working configuration files. It has also shown how Enterprise Manager has evolved to support Oracle8.

As you have seen, Oracle Enterprise Manager can offer great assistance in monitoring and administrating your organization's servers and databases. As you progress through the other chapters in this book, experiment with whichever Enterprise Manager tool is appropriate for that topic and compare the steps you would perform with this tool to any command-line processes shown in the examples. You will find that there are still some tasks that you will continue to perform from a command line or a script, but there are many others that are performed more quickly and easily with Enterprise Manager.

Oracle8 Tools

by Dan Hotka

IN THIS CHAPTER

Overview of Oracle8 Tools

The Oracle8 server comes with several tools that the Oracle Corporation has supplied with their products for years. Server Manager is the base administrative and monitoring tool for server-side tasks. Oracle has always supplied the Export and Import processes with the database as well as a Data Loader process. SQL*Plus is the main adhoc, character-mode interface to the Oracle environment.

Server Manager replaced SQL*DBA in the Oracle7.2 time frame. SQL*DBA had both a screen mode and a line mode and got its start in the Oracle6 days, taking on functionality from both SQL*Plus and IOR. SQL*Plus was used in Oracle4 and Oracle5 to do most administrative functions (as well as to provide a unique character-mode interface for SQL and reporting), adding space to the database, user and object administration, and so on. IOR was used in the Oracle4 and Oracle5 days to start and stop the Oracle environment. IOR stands for Initialize Oracle; it has 3 parameters: I for initialize, W for warm start, and S for shutdown. It was used to start and stop and for initial installs of the Oracle environment.

Export and Import have been a part of the Oracle product set since the Oracle4 days. They work together and provide functionality as their names imply. Export is used to put individual tables and user schemas or the entire database (all schemas and data) into an operating system file. This file is proprietary in nature and is only intended for processing by Import. Import reads this operating system file created by Export. These tools can be used to backup, recover, and move objects between Oracle instances or even between versions of Oracle.

SQL*Plus is the main adhoc, character-mode interface to the Oracle environment. SQL*Plus can also be used to create dynamic SQL*Plus scripts or even dynamic operating system-specific command language programs.

Besides Oracle's tools, there are several tools from other software vendors that effectively interface with the Oracle RDBMS.

Server Manager

Server Manager is a server-side tool for Oracle database administration. It has both a screen mode of operation and a line mode. The screen mode has a menu task bar, a view window, and an interactive window where commands can be entered. The line mode is much like SQL*Plus in that it is just a command prompt, can run SQL and PL/SQL interactively or from system files, but does not have any of the report formatting features of SQL*Plus. Server Manager is used primarily to start and stop the Oracle instances and to initiate backup and recovery. Server Manager is also a real-time monitor in that it formats and displays various performance and usage information, primarily from V$ tables.

Server Manager is started from a character mode environment. The interactive line mode is started by entering svrmgrl at the UNIX prompt.

> **TIP**
>
> Server Manager can process a file from the command prompt as well. svrmgrl @<*filename*> will start Server Manager and process the contents of <*filename*>.

Export/Import

Export and Import play two important roles in the Oracle environment: the unloading and loading of schemas and schema data and various backup and recovery functions.

Data Movement

Export can easily export the entire database, an entire user schema, or individual tables. The biggest issue with Export/Import is the data file created is proprietary to the Oracle environment. That is, Import cannot be used to populate any Oracle table except from a file created by Export. These routines easily handle most export and import situations within the Oracle environment.

> **NOTE**
>
> Oracle documentation recommends manually disabling referential-integrity constraints and importing the parent table, as some conflicts may cause errors during the load on some self-referencing table constraints.

Export has a direct path unload option; that is, it can access data directly from the Oracle data files and not use SELECT statements and the associated buffering overhead of the Oracle kernel. Export still can create only one file of output, which, depending on operating systems, may hit a file-size limit when exporting larger objects. Export and Import can handle all the new partitioning features, loading all partitions or single partitions, as desired. Import can also rename a schema owner. Both tools are accessed via command line. Both tools have a series of parameters that control the work to be done. Both tools have three modes of operations: an interactive mode, a command line mode (where the parameters are submitted via the command line), and a command line mode with a passed parameter file.

> **NOTE**
>
> With the direct path option set, Export cannot export rows that contain LOB, BFILE, REF, or object type columns, including VARRAY columns and nested tables.

Oracle's Export has been improved with Oracle8 in that it has direct-path access to the data; that is, it does not incur the overhead of the Oracle buffering in accessing the data to be exported. It goes directly to the underlying files and accesses the data directly.

> **NOTE**
>
> To utilize the direct path export option, you must specify it in a parameter file.

Listing 22.1 has the instructions to start Export, export the user Scott's schema (with the rows and the grants), and compress multiple table extents into one initial extent upon import.

LISTING 22.1. EXPORT COMMAND LINE EXAMPLE AND OUTPUT.

```
Unix->exp scott/tiger file=example.exp owner=scott grants=Y rows=Y
➥compress=y

Export: Release 8.0.3.0.0 - Production on Tue Feb 3 9:01:15 1998

(c) Copyright 1997 Oracle Corporation.  All rights reserved.

Connected to: Oracle8 Server Release 8.0.3.0.0 - Production
PL/SQL Release 8.0.3.0.0 - Production
Export done in US7ASCII character set
. exporting object type definitions for user SCOTT

About to export SCOTT's objects ...
. exporting database links
. exporting sequence numbers
. exporting cluster definitions
. about to export SCOTT's tables via Conventional Path ...
. . exporting table                        BONUS            0 rows exported
```

```
. . exporting table                         DEPT          4 rows exported
. . exporting table                          EMP         14 rows exported
. . exporting table                     SALGRADE          5 rows exported
. exporting synonyms
. exporting views
. exporting stored procedures
. exporting referential integrity constraints
. exporting triggers
. exporting posttables actions
. exporting snapshots
. exporting snapshot logs
. exporting job queues
. exporting refresh groups and children
Export terminated successfully without warnings.
```

The example in Listing 22.2 imports the file exported by Export. I told it to ignore any errors due to the object's existence.

LISTING 22.2. IMPORT COMMAND LINE EXAMPLE AND OUTPUT.

```
Unix-> imp scott/tiger  file=example.exp ignore=Y


Import: Release 8.0.3.0.0 - Production on Tue Feb 3 9:31:21 1998

(c) Copyright 1997 Oracle Corporation.  All rights reserved.

Connected to: Oracle8 Server Release 8.0.3.0.0 - Production
PL/SQL Release 8.0.3.0.0 - Production
Export file created by EXPORT:V08.00.03 via conventional path
. importing SCOTT's objects
. . importing table                         BONUS          0 rows imported
. . importing table                        "DEPT"          4 rows imported
. . importing table                         "EMP"         14 rows imported
. . importing table                    "SALGRADE"          5 rows imported

Import terminated successfully without warnings.
```

Incremental Backups

Oracle Export and Import also provide for object level backups. Export has a method of capturing the entire database of objects and two levels below that initial level of just exporting those objects that have changed since the prior incremental backup. This method of backup is known as Export Incremental Backups and is covered in depth in Chapter 23, "Backup and Recovery."

SQL*Loader

Oracle also comes with SQL*Loader, a table or multiple-table load facility. This tool is capable of reading a variety of formatted files from a variety of sources (disk files, tape, even named pipes), and with some logic, can populate multiple tables from one pass of the data file being loaded. SQL*Loader has a direct path load option, that is, a feature that allows SQL*Loader to ignore the Oracle kernel and directly load the data into Oracle blocks in the underlying files assigned to the tablespace.

> **NOTE**
>
> This is an unprotected write where there is no read consistency, undo ability, or archive logs of the event.

SQL*Loader can also save rejected records to a disk file.

The example in Listing 22.3 shows the SQL*Loader command line syntax and the associated control file that will load a single table with data from file EXAMPLE.DAT, and it contains some constant values that will populate the table as well.

LISTING 22.3. SQL*LOADER COMMAND LINE AND CONTROL FILE EXAMPLE.

```
Unix->sqlldr USERID=hotka/dan CONTROL=EXAMPLE.ctl, LOG=EXAMPLE.log,
BAD=EXAMPLE.bad


Unix->cat EXAMPLE.ctl
    load data
    infile 'EXAMPLE.DAT'
    append
    into table APPL_PROGRAM_TABLE
      (PROGRAM_NAME position(1:8) char,
    PROGRAM_SUFFIX constant 'COB',
    PROGRAM_SIZE position(15:22) integer external,
```

```
PROGRAM_PATH constant 'C:\COBOL',
ASSIGNED_ANALYST constant 'HOTKA')
```

SQL*Plus

SQL*Plus is the main adhoc, character-mode interface to the Oracle RDBMS. SQL*Plus can be used simply to process SQL statements one at a time, process SQL statements interactively with end users, utilize PL/SQL for procedural processing of SQL statements, list and print query results, format query results into reports, describe the contents of a given table, and copy data between databases. SQL*Plus can easily be used to produce a variety of types of character-mode reports. SQL*Plus can also be used to create dynamic SQL*Plus scripts or even dynamic operating system-specific command language programs. SQL*Plus can be used for some Oracle administration functions. SQL*Plus can be programmed to be interactive during a specific terminal session. SQL*Plus can process ANSI SQL as well as PL/SQL blocks.

> **NOTE**
>
> I highly recommend using svrmgr to create and maintain the individual Oracle databases. I would restrict SQL*Plus through the use of PRODUCT_USER_PROFILE table or PROFILES to prohibit end users from performing any administrative task.

This section will concentrate on utilizing SQL*Plus to format output into a variety of reports and will introduce methods of utilizing SQL*Plus to create dynamic data-driven SQL*Plus programs and operating system-dependent command language programs.

SQL*Plus has a variety of limitations, some being operating system specific. A complete list of limits or maximum values is found in *Oracle SQL*Plus User's Guide and Reference,* Appendix C.

SQL*Plus is typically available on any computer system that supports the Oracle RDBMS environment. In the client/server environment, SQL*Plus is available on all of the major graphical interfaces, including MS Windows and Motif.

There are 6 types of SQL*Plus commands:

- Initiating the SQL*Plus environment
- SQL*Plus execute commands
- SQL*Plus editing commands

22

ORACLE8 TOOLS

- SQL*Plus formatting commands
- Access commands for various databases
- Miscellaneous commands

SQL*Plus is an interactive adhoc environment that can also be pre-programmed with the use of SQL*Plus commands, SQL statements, and/or PL/SQL blocks submitted via a file. Upon successful login to SQL*Plus, the user, regardless of environment, will receive a SQL*Plus prompt, `SQL>`.

The basic SQL*Plus environment can be enhanced for each user or group of users by utilizing a file named `LOGIN.SQL`. This file should be located in the directory from which SQL*Plus is to be initiated (operating system dependent). Typical contents of this file are various `SET` commands that alter the SQL*Plus default settings for this particular user.

> **Tip**
>
> I have created these `LOGIN.SQL` files to contain column format commands for each column of the objects that the particular user or group of users has access to. This gives all adhoc queries a polished appearance.

The `PRODUCT_USER_PROFILE` table, owned by `SYSTEM`, is one way to provide product-level security that enhances the security provided by the `SQL GRANT` and `REVOKE` commands. This level of security is used to disable certain SQL and SQL*Plus commands for individual users.

There are various ways of initiating the SQL*Plus environment depending on the type of computer platform being utilized. To leave the SQL*Plus environment, simply type `EXIT` at the `SQL>` prompt and press Return or Enter.

The syntax in Listing 22.4 will initiate SQL*Plus and prompt the user for a valid username and password. Most UNIX environments implement the SQL*Plus command in lower case. Enter a valid password and press Enter or Return. SQL*Plus will then prompt for a password. The password will not appear on the screen.

Listing 22.4. SQL*Plus with logon prompt.

```
Unix> sqlplus

SQL*Plus Version 3.1.0 - Production on Tue Aug 1 14:30:20 1995
```

```
Copyright (c) Oracle Corporation 1979, 1991.  All rights reserved.

Enter user-name:
```

The following syntax will initiate SQL*Plus but not prompt for the user ID or password. If either user ID or password is not valid, SQL*Plus will give an error message and then prompt the user for a valid user ID and password as seen in Listing 22.4.

```
SQLPLUS userid/password.
```

The -S or -SILENT will not display the SQL*Plus version and copyright information in the following code line. This is handy when initiating reports written in SQL*Plus from a menu system where the appearance of a seamless application is desired.

```
SQLPLUS -S userid/password.
```

The following syntax will initiate the SQL*Plus environment and connect the user to the remote database identified by the *database* name. This database name can be a SQL*Net connect string, a SQL*Net alias name, or a SQL*Net database instance name.

```
SQLPLUS userid/password@database.
```

The following syntax will initiate the SQL*Plus environment and execute the SQL*Plus commands and the SQL (or PL/SQL blocks) contained within the file (SQL*Plus command file). The contents of this file are covered later in this chapter.

```
SQLPLUS userid/password @filename.
```

> **NOTE**
>
> Notice the difference between the last two examples, where `sqlplus userid/password@database` will access SQL*Net and `sqlplus userid/password @filename` will read a SQL*Plus command file. Notice the lack of a space in the first example after `password` and the space in the second example.

> **TIP**
>
> Always use the operating system dependent full path name with this filename.

The following syntax will initiate the SQL*Plus environment and expect the very first line of the file to contain a valid user ID/password, in this exact format. If the user ID and password are valid, SQL*Plus will process the SQL*Plus commands and the SQL (or PL/SQL blocks) contained within the file.

```
SQLPLUS @filename.
```

> **TIP**
>
> SQL*Net and a SQL*Plus command file can be used together in either of two ways: `sqlplus userid/password@database @filename` or the first line of the SQL*Plus command file contains a valid `userid/password@database`. To terminate a SQL*Plus command file, make `EXIT` the last line of the file.

The following syntax will initiate the SQL*Plus environment and execute the SQL*Plus commands and the SQL (or PL/SQL blocks) contained within the file. The command line parameters will be passed to variables inside the SQL*Plus command file and be identified inside this file by &1, &2, and so on. The usage of these parameters is covered later in this chapter.

```
SQLPLUS userid/password @filename param1 param2 ...
```

SQL*Plus Execute Commands

These commands are used to initiate the processing of SQL statements and PL/SQL blocks, measure the processing time of SQL or PL/SQL statements, execute non-Oracle programs, execute SQL*Forms programs, or attain additional help.

/ Execute the SQL statement or PL/SQL block currently in the SQL buffer. (This is probably the most used of the SQL*Plus commands.)

- `HELP topic`   Provides online assistance with SQL, PL/SQL, or SQL*Plus commands
- `HOST`   Executes non-Oracle commands (operating system-dependent) without leaving SQL*Plus
- `RUN`   Displays and executes the contents of the SQL buffer
- `RUNFORM`   Executes a SQL*Forms program without leaving SQL*Plus
- `TIMING`   Displays the system CPU time with the SQL prompt

SQL*Plus Editing Commands

The SQL buffer is a work area assigned to the SQL*Plus environment. This buffer only contains SQL or PL/SQL syntax. The contents of this buffer can be loaded, saved, and manipulated with the following commands.

- A or APPEND *new text*   Appends text to the end of the current line of the SQL buffer.
- C or CHANGE/target text/new text/   Changes the target text to the new text on the current line in the SQL buffer.
- DEL   Deletes the current line in the SQL buffer.
- EDIT *filename*   Utilizes an operating system-dependent text editor. To edit the SQL buffer with an operating system-dependent text editor, simply leave off the filename.
- GET *filename*   Reads an operating system-dependent file into the SQL buffer.
- I or INPUT *text*   Adds the text after the current line in the SQL buffer.
- L or LIST *number*   Displays the contents of the SQL buffer. When the *number* syntax is used, LIST will display the line number and make that line the current line in the SQL buffer.
- SAVE *filename*   Saves the contents of the SQL buffer to an operating system-dependent file.

TIP

An excellent method to utilize when creating SQL*Plus Command Files, utilizes these editing features to arrive at the query results desired: SAVE to the operating system, and then edit that file with EDIT to add the formatting and other desired features.

- START *filename param1 param2* ...   START will execute the contents of the SQL*Plus command file named in *filename* and pass any input parameters to the SQL*Plus command file.

> **TIP**
>
> I find it convenient to utilize this START feature when creating various database objects. It allows for complete control over the order in which the objects are created. I simply create a SQL*Plus command file named INSTALL.SQL, create each DDL statement in its own SQL*Plus command file, and add a START command in this INSTALL.SQL file for each of the DDL SQL*Plus command files.

SQL*Plus Formatting Commands

The SQL*Plus formatting commands are used to manipulate the result set from a SQL query.

- BREAK ON column_name options   This command controls the organization of rows returned by the query. BREAK can manipulate the appearance of the output by specifiying under what conditions a BREAK should occur and what actions should be taken at the BREAK. The output appearance can be controlled by skipping a line, skipping to top of next page, and providing totals when used in conjunction with COMPUTE. Any number of lines can be skipped at a BREAK point. BREAK points can be defined at the column level, for multiple columns, on a row, on a page, or on a report. See COMPUTE for BREAK examples. Entering BREAK by itself at the SQL prompt will display the current BREAK settings.

- BTITLE print_options and/or text or variable options   BTITLE is used to place text at the bottom of each page. There are various print options to position text at various locations. BTITLE will simply center the text if no print options are specified. PRINT OPTIONS include BOLD, CENTER, COL, FORMAT, LEFT, RIGHT, SKIP, and TAB. BTITLE spelled out by itself will display the current text setting. Other options that can be specified are ON and OFF. BTITLE is on by default.

- CLEAR options   Resets any of the SQL*Plus formatting commands, as well as clearing the screen.

- COLUMN column_name options   COLUMN is used to alter the default display attributes for a given column (column_name) of a SQL query. There are a variety of options but the more common ones are FORMAT, HEADING, JUSTIFY, NEWLINE, NEW_VALUE, and NOPRINT. The FORMAT option is useful in applying editing to numeric fields, date masks to date fields, and specific lengths to variable length character fields. The HEADING option overrides the SQL*Plus default heading for the particular column. The JUSTIFY option overrides the SQL*Plus column alignment to the heading default. The NEWLINE option will print the column on the beginning of the next line. NEW_VALUE assigns the contents of the column to a SQL*Plus variable (see

DEFINE). This value can then be used in conjunction with TTITLE or to store intermediate results for master/detail type reports and is useful to store and pass information between two or more separate SQL statements.

Examples:

```
COLUMN sal FORMAT $99,999.00 HEADING Salary

COLUMN home_dir NEW_VALUE home_path NOPRINT
```

The first SQL query would reference the *home_dir*; all other SQL queries would
then reference the *home_path* for the information returned by the first SQL query.

- COMPUTE function OF options ON BREAK options   COMPUTE calculates and prints
  totals for groupings of rows defined by the BREAK command. A variety of standard
  functions can be utilized. The most common option is the name of the column in
  the query that the total is to be calculated on. The BREAK option determines where
  the totals are to be printed and reset, as defined by the BREAK command.

Examples:

```
BREAK ON sales_rep SKIP 2

BREAK ON REPORT

COMPUTE SUM OF monthly_sales ON sales_rep

COMPUTE SUM OF commissions ON sales_rep

COMPUTE SUM OF monthly_sales ON REPORT

COMPUTE SUM OF commissions ON REPORT
```

This list will produce a report with totals of monthly_sales and commissions
when the sales_rep column value changes, and then skip two lines and produce
monthly_sales and commissions totals at the end of the report.

NOTE

The COMPUTE command resets the accumulator fields back to zero after printing.

- TTITLE print_options and/or *text* or *variable* options   TTITLE is used to place
  text at the top of each page. There are various print options to position text at various locations. TTITLE will center the text and add date and page numbers if no
  print options are specified. PRINT OPTIONS include BOLD, CENTER, COL, FORMAT,
  LEFT, RIGHT, SKIP, and TAB. TTITLE spelled out by itself will display the current
  text setting. Other options that can be specified are ON and OFF. TTITLE is on by
  default.

22

ORACLE8 TOOLS

Miscellaneous Commands

- ACCEPT *variable number* or char PROMPT *text* ACCEPT receives input from the terminal and places the contents in *variable*. This variable can already have been defined with the DEFINE command. If the PROMPT option is specified, the *text* will be displayed after skipping a line. The variable attributes of *number* or *char* can be defined at this time. The *variable* will be a char if not otherwise defined.

- DEFINE variable DEFINE creates a user-defined variable and assigns it to be of char (character) format. This variable can be assigned a default value at this time.

> **TIP**
>
> I find these DEFINE statements handy for assigning a variable_name to the input parameters coming into the SQL*Plus command file. Example: DEFINE SYSTEM_NAME = &1. This would create a character variable SYSTEM_NAME and assign it the text associated with the first input parameter. This makes SQL*Plus command file code easier to follow.

- DESC or DESCRIBE *database object* Displays the columns associated with a table, view, or synonym.

- PAUSE *text* PAUSE prints the contents of *text* after skipping a line, and then waits for the Return or Enter key to be pressed.

- PROMPT *text* PROMPT simply skips a line and prints the contents of *text*.

- REM or REMARK SQL*Plus will ignore the contents of this line when used in SQL*Plus command files. REMARK allows for documentation or other comments to be contained in these SQL*Plus command files.

- SET SQL*Plus System variable The SET command controls the default settings for the SQL*Plus environment. These settings can be altered automatically for each SQL*Plus session by including them in the LOGIN.SQL file, discussed earlier in this chapter. See Chapter 6 of Oracle's *SQL*Plus User's Guide and Reference* for a complete listing of the SET options.

  Some common SET options utilized for reporting are:

  SET LINESIZE 80 Controls the width of the output report line

  SET PAGESIZE 55 Controls the number of lines per page

  Some common SET options to suppress various SQL*Plus output are:

  SET FEEDBACK OFF Suppresses the number of rows returning messages

  SET VERIFY OFF Suppresses the substitution text when using &variables

SET TERMOUT OFF   Suppresses all terminal output, particularly useful in conjunction with the SPOOL command

SET ECHO OFF   Supresses the display of SQL*Plus commands

- SPOOL filename or options   Opens, closes, or prints an operating system-dependent file. Specifying SPOOL filename will create an operating system-dependent file where filename can contain the full path name of the file and extension. If no file extension is given, the contents of system variable SUFFIX will be appended (*filename*.SQL). Options include OFF or OUT. If OFF is specified, the operating system-dependent file is simply closed. If OUT is specified, the operating system- dependent file is closed and sent to the operating system-dependent printer assigned as the default printer to the user's operating system environment.

NOTE

If SPOOL *filename* is issued without issuing a SPOOL OFF or SPOOL OUT, the current operating system-dependent file is closed and the new one as specified by the SPOOL command is opened.

TIP

I prefer to write SQL*Plus-based reports utilizing the SET variables mentioned above in conjuction with the SPOOL command. I create the output report in the file specified by the SPOOL command and then control whether it is visually displayed to the terminal, optionally printed, or both by the use of operating system-dependent command language.

- UNDEFINE *variable*   UNDEFINE removes the previously DEFINEd *variable* from the SQL*Plus environment.

SQL*Plus Reporting Techniques

The remainder of this section will cover some common SQL*Plus report formatting features and SQL generation techniques.

This is a simple but common form of SQL*Plus formatting. The syntax in Listing 22.5 is in the form of a file that gets passed to SQL*Plus in the manner described previously, passing a command line parameter (&1 on line 1) and assigning it to the variable name ASSIGNED_ANALYST. The ASSIGNED_ANALYST variable is then used in the headings (see line 13) and again as part of the SQL query (see line 17). Lines 2, 3, 4, and 5 suspend all terminal output from the SQL*Plus environment. The && is utilized to denote substitution of an already defined variable. The report output (Listing 22.6) contains two breaks, one when the column APPLICATION_NAME changes (see line 9 of listing 22.5) and one at the end of the report (see line 10 of listing 22.5). Totals are also calculated for each of these breaks (see lines 11 and 12). The ¦ in the TTITLE command (see line 13) moves the following text onto its own line. Line 14 will open an operating system file named ANA-LYST.LIS in the current operating system directory. The .LIS suffix is a SQL*Plus system default. The order by clause of the query on line 18 insures that the breaks occur in an orderly manner.

LISTING 22.5. SIMPLE SQL*PLUS REPORT CODE.

```
 1:    define ASSIGNED_ANALYST = &1
 2:    set FEEDBACK OFF
 3:    set VERIFY OFF
 4:    set TERMOUT OFF
 5:    set ECHO OFF
 6:    column APPLICATION_NAME    format a12      heading 'Application'
 7:    column PROGRAM_NAME        format a12      heading 'Program'
 8:    column PROGRAM_SIZE        format 999999   heading 'Program¦Size'
 9:    break on APPLICATION_NAME skip 2
10:     break on report skip 2
11:     compute sum of PROGRAM_SIZE on APPLICATION_NAME
12:     compute sum of PROGRAM_SIZE on report
13:     ttitle 'Programs by Application ¦ Assigned to: &&ASSIGNED_ANALYST'
14:     spool ANALYST
15:     select APPLICATION_NAME,PROGRAM_NAME,nvl(PROGRAM_SIZE,0)
16:       from APPLICATION_PROGRAMS
17:      where ASSIGNED_NAME = '&&ASSIGNED_ANALYST'
18:      order by APPLICATION_NAME,PROGRAM_NAME
19:     /
20:    spool off
21:    exit
```

LISTING 22.6. OUTPUT OF SIMPLE SQL*PLUS REPORT.

```
Tue Feb 1
page    1
                              Programs by Application
                                 Assigned to: HOTKA


                Program
    Application Program          Size
    ----------- -----------      --------
    COBOL       CLAIMS           10156
                HOMEOWN          22124
```

```
               PREMIUMS              10345
                                  - - - - - - - - - -
     sum                             42625

  FORTRAN        ALGEBRA              6892
                 MATH1                7210
                 SCIENCE1            10240
                                  - - - - - - - - - -
     sum                             24342

     sum                             66967
```

Advanced Reporting Techniques

This section will cover more practical reporting uses for SQL*Plus.

Listing 22.7 is a cross tabular SQL*Plus command file. This report passes a command line parameter (&1 on line 1) and assigns it to the variable name RPT_DATE. The RPT_DATE variable is then used in the headings (see line 20) and again as part of the SQL query (see line 31). Lines 2, 3, 4, and 5 suspend all terminal output from the SQL*Plus environment. The report will be created in the operating system-dependent file SALES.OUT (see Listing 22.8). Column formatting commands control the appearance of the columns (lines 6 through 12). The combination of compute commands (lines 14 through 19), the sum statements in the query (lines 24 through 29), and the group by clause in the query (line 32) give the report output the appearance of a cross tabular report.

> **NOTE**
>
> I utilized a different TTITLE technique in Listing 22.7 (lines 20 and 21) from that of Listing 22.5 (line 13).

LISTING 22.7. CROSS TABULAR SQL*PLUS REPORT.

```
1:      define RPT_DATE = &1
2:      set FEEDBACK OFF
3:      set VERIFY OFF
4:      set TERMOUT OFF
5:      set ECHO OFF
6:      column SALES_REP          format a12 heading 'Sales¦Person'
7:      column NISSAN                   format 999999    heading
➡'Nissan'
```

continues

LISTING 22.7. CONTINUED

```
8:     column TOYOTA          format 999999   heading 'Toyota'
9:     column GM              format 999999   heading 'GM'
10:    column FORD            format 999999   heading 'Ford'
11:    column CRYSLER         format 999999   heading 'Crysler'
12:    column TOTALS                 format 999999   heading
➥'Totals'
13:    break on report skip 2
14:    compute sum of NISSAN on report
15:    compute sum of TOYOTA on report
16:    compute sum of GM on report
17:    compute sum of FORD on report
18:    compute sum of CRYSLER on report
19:    compute sum of TOTALS on report
20:    ttitle left '&&IN_DATE' center 'Auto Sales'  RIGHT 'Page: ' format
➥999 -
21:          SQL.PNO skip CENTER ' by Sales Person '
22:    spool SALES.OUT
23:    select SALES_REP,
24:        sum(decode(CAR_TYPE,'N',TOTAL_SALES,0)) NISSAN,
25:        sum(decode(CAR_TYPE,'T',TOTAL_SALES,0)) TOYOTA,
26:        sum(decode(CAR_TYPE,'G',TOTAL_SALES,0)) GM,
27:        sum(decode(CAR_TYPE,'F',TOTAL_SALES,0)) FORD,
28:        sum(decode(CAR_TYPE,'C',TOTAL_SALES,0)) CRYSLER ,
29:        sum(TOTAL_SALES) TOTALS
30:    from CAR_SALES
31:    where SALES_DATE <= to_date('&&RPT_DATE')
32:    group by SALES_REP
33:    /
34:    spool off
35:    exit
```

LISTING 22.8. CROSS TABULAR SQL*PLUS REPORT OUTPUT.

```
3-APR-98              Auto Sales
Page: 1
                  by Sales Person


Sales
Person          Nissan        Toyota          GM          Ford
Crysler         Totals
--------       --------      --------       --------    --------     --------     --
------
Elizabeth     5500            2500            0            0
4500    12500
Emily         4000            6000          4400          2000
0       16400
Thomas         2000          1000           6000          4000
```

```
1500        14500
  .........     .........     .........     .........     .........     ..
.......
            11500                    9500        10400           6000
6000
      43400
```

> **NOTE**
>
> I will now only include the specific SQL*Plus commands necessary to produce
> the desired output.

Listing 22.9 creates a Master/Detail SQL*Plus Report by utilizing the SQL UNION command. In this example, there are six separate types of lines to be printed: the Salesperson
(line 4), a line of dashes under the Salesperson (line 7), the detail line (line 10), a line of
dashes under the detail total (line 14), a total line (line 17), and a blank line (line 21).
There are six separate queries that have their output merged and sorted together by the
SQL JOIN statement (see lines 6, 9, 13, 16, 19, and 23). When using JOIN to merge the
output of two or more queries, the output result set *must* have the same number of
columns. The headings are turned off (line 2) because regular SQL*Plus column headings are not desired for this type of report. The first column of each query has an alias
column name of DUMMY. This DUMMY column is used to sort the order of the six types of
lines (denoted by each of the six queries). The DUMMY column's only role is to maintain
the order of the lines within the major sort field (SALES_REP_NO in this example), so the
NOPRINT option is specified in line 3. Listing 22.10 shows the output of the Master/Detail
SQL*Plus Report code.

LISTING 22.9. MASTER/DETAIL SQL*PLUS REPORT CODE.

```
1:     ttitle 'Sales Detail ¦ by Sales Rep'
2:     set HEADINGS OFF
3:     column DUMMY NOPRINT
4:     select 1 DUMMY, SALES_REP_NO,'Sales Person: ' ¦¦ SALES_REP
5:     from sales
6:     UNION
7:     select 2 DUMMY,SALES_REP_NO,'--------------------'
8:     from sales
9:     UNION
10:    select 3 DUMMY,SALES_REP_NO, rpad(CAR_MAKE,4) ¦¦ '     ' ¦¦
11:         to_char(SALE_AMT,'$999,999.99')
```

continues

LISTING 22.9. CONTINUED

```
12:    from sales_detail
13:    UNION
14:    select 4 DUMMY,SALES_REP_NO,'          ----------'
15:    from sales
16:    UNION
17:    select 5 DUMMY,SALES_REP_NO,'Total:  ' ||
18:          to_char(sum(TOTAL_SALES),'$999,999.99'))
19:    from sales
20:    UNION
21:    select 6 DUMMY,SALES_REP_NO,'          '
22:    from sales
23:    order by 2,1,3
24:    /
```

LISTING 22.10. OUTPUT OF MASTER/DETAIL SQL*PLUS REPORT CODE.

```
************************
      Thur Apr 2
      page    1
                                    Sales Detail
                                   by Sales Rep


Salesperson:  Elizabeth
- - - - - - - - - - - - - - - - - - - - - - - - - - -
Chrysler    $3,000
Chrysler    $1,500
Nissan      $2,000
Nissan      $2,000
Nissan      $1,500
Toyota      $2,500
- - - - - - - - - -
Total:      $12,500

Salesperson:  Emily
- - - - - - - - - - - - - - - - - - - - - - - - - - -
Ford        $1,000
Ford        $1,000
GM          $2,000
GM          $2,400
Nissan      $2,000
Nissan      $2,000
Toyota      $1,000
Toyota      $2,500
Toyota      $2,500
- - - - - - - - - -
Total:      $16,400
```

```
Salesperson:  Thomas
- - - - - - - - - - - - - - - - - - - - - - - - - - - -
Chrysler    $1,500
Ford        $1,000
Ford        $3,000
GM          $1,400
GM          $1,600
GM          $3,000
Nissan      $2,000
Toyota      $1,000
- - - - - - - - - - -
Total:      $16,400
```

Listing 22.11 creates a SQL*Plus Report utilizing different columns from different tables using the SQL UNION command. In this example, there are three different tables (see lines 8, 11, and 14) but there are only three columns of output. The first query contains the column names (see lines 6 and 7). This is due to the way the JOIN operator works. The queries after the first query must follow the number of columns and the type of column (text or numeric) based on the column definitions of the first query. The BREAK command (line 4) causes the OBJECT_NAME to print once and creates the blank line between the groupings of records. Listing 22.12 shows the output of Listing 22.11.

TIP

The next example uses the JOIN feature to display output from two or more tables within the same report.

LISTING 22.11. MULTI TABLE SQL*PLUS REPORT CODE.

```
1:    column OBJECT_TYPE       format a20        heading 'Object'
2:    column OBJECT_NAME       format a8         heading 'Name'
3:    column COMMENT    format a8        heading 'Comments'
4:    break on OBJECT_TYPE skip 1
5:    ttitle 'System Summary Report
6:    select 'Program' OBJECT_TYPE, program_name OBJECT_NAME,
7:         program_comments  COMMENT
8:       from program_table
9:    UNION
10:   select 'Command Language',cl_name, assoc_system
11:        from cl_table
12:   UNION
13:   select 'Files',file_name, 'File Size = ' ¦¦ file_size ¦¦  'Bytes'
14:      from file_table
15:   /
```

LISTING 22.12. OUTPUT OF MULTI TABLE SQL*PLUS REPORT CODE.

```
Thr Apr 2                                        page    1
                                    System Summary Report


Object                   Name              Comments
-------------------      ----------        ---------------------------------
Programs            AM1             Algebra Test 1
                    AM2             Algebra Test 2
                    AM3             Algebra Test 3

Command Language    CL1             AM1
                    CL2             AM2
                    CL3             AM3

Files               AM1.TST         File Size = 1200 Bytes
                    AM2.TST         File Size = 3000 Bytes
                    AM3.TST         File Size = 2200 Bytes
```

Listings 22.13 (method 1) and 22.14 (method 2) produce the exact same output as seen in Listing 22.15. Both of these methods will produce reports with information in fixed or predefined positions. Both of these methods could be utilized to print information on a pre-printed form. These particular examples were designed to be started from inside another process such as SQL*Forms because the only input parameter is an Oracle ROWID used to read and process a single row from the database (lines 1 and 26 in Listing 22.13, lines 1 and 42 in Listing 22.14).

These examples utilize the concatenation feature of SQL (¦¦) to blend text between database fields. Each column in the SQL statement represents an individual line in the report. Both examples have the standard column headings feature turned off (line 3 of Listing 22.13, line 4 of Listing 22.14). Both examples have a one-to-one relationship between a SQL column and a line of output. The methods differ in how the columns are formatted to create the individual lines.

The main difference in these two methods is the approach used in the individual line setup. Method 1 (Listing 22.13) uses the SQL command RPAD (see line 6) in combination with LINESIZE (line 2) to create an output line. The RPAD is a SQL function that is used to fill the line with blanks to position 80, and with LINESIZE set at 80 will cause the formatted line to appear on a line by itself. Method 2 (listing 22.14) uses the column command with the option NEWLINE specified in conjunction with a field alias name (see lines 6 and 22). The column command with the NEWLINE option will cause the formatted line to appear on a line by itself.

> **NOTE**
>
> Listing 22.13 uses lines 28 through 31 to skip to the top of a new page, where Listing 22.14 uses a break command to skip to a new page after each row of data from the database. The entire select command of each example formats one row of information from the database.

LISTING 22.13. METHOD 1: FIXED POSITION FORMATTING SQL*PLUS REPORT CODE.

```
1:      define  TICKET_ROWID = &1
2:      set LINESIZE 80
3:      set  HEADINGS OFF
4:      set FEEDBACK OFF
5:      spool TICKET
6:      select RPAD('---------------------------------------------------- -' ||
➡----------------
7:            null,80),
8:      RPAD('                            Customer Contact Survey' || null,80),
9:      RPAD('----------------------------------------------------------------
➡-
➡--------------' || null,80),
10:     RPAD(' Customer Name: '  || CUSTOMER_NAME || ' PHONE#: ' || PHONE ||
➡null,80),
11:     RPAD(' Customer Address:  ' || CUSTOMER_ADDRESS  || null,80),
12:     RPAD('                                     ' || CUSTOMER_CITY ||
➡CUSTOMER_STATE ||
13:            CUSTOMER_ZIP  || null,80),
14:     RPAD('----------------------------------------------------------------
➡-
➡--------------' || null,80),
15:     RPAD(' ' || TO_CHAR(CONTACT_DATE,'mm/dd/yy HH:MI || '  Caller: ' ||
➡CALLER ||
16:            null,80),
17:     RPAD('----------------------------------------------------------------
➡-
➡--------------' || null,80),
18:     RPAD('  Home Phone? ' ||  HPHONE_YN  || 'Best Time to call:  ' ||
➡CALL_TIME ||
19:     null,80),
20:     RPAD('   'Has Catalog? ' || CATALOG_YN || 'Desire Future Calls? ' ||
➡FUTURE_YN ||
21:     null,80),
22:     RPAD('----------------------------------------------------------------
➡--------------' || null,80),
23:     RPAD('PRINTED: ' || TO_CHAR(SYSDATE,'mm/dd/yy HH:MI || 'BY:  ' ||
24:
➡        OPERATOR || null,80)
```

continues

LISTING 22.13. CONTINUED

```
25:    from CUSTOMER_TABLE
26:    where ROWID = '&&TICKET_ROWID'
27:    /
28:    set PAGESIZE 1
29:    set  NEWPAGE 0
30:    select  null from dual;
31:    set PAGESIZE 0
32:    spool OUT
33:    exit
```

LISTING 22.14. METHOD 2: FIXED POSITION FORMATTING SQL*PLUS REPORT CODE.

```
1:    define TICKET_ROWID = &1
2:    set PAGESIZE 55
3:    set LINESIZE 80
4:    set HEADINGS OFF
5:    set FEEDBACK OFF
6:    column LINE1 JUSTIFY LEFT NEWLINE
7:    column LINE2 JUSTIFY LEFT NEWLINE
8:    column LINE3 JUSTIFY LEFT NEWLINE
9:    column LINE4 JUSTIFY LEFT NEWLINE
10:    column LINE5 JUSTIFY LEFT NEWLINE
11:    column LINE6 JUSTIFY LEFT NEWLINE
12:    column LINE7 JUSTIFY LEFT NEWLINE
13:    column LINE8 JUSTIFY LEFT NEWLINE
14:    column LINE9 JUSTIFY LEFT NEWLINE
15:    column LINE10 JUSTIFY LEFT NEWLINE
16:    column LINE11 JUSTIFY LEFT NEWLINE
17:    column LINE12 JUSTIFY LEFT NEWLINE
18:    column LINE13 JUSTIFY LEFT NEWLINE
19:    column LINE14 JUSTIFY LEFT NEWLINE
20:    break ON ROW SKIP PAGE
21:    SPOOL TICKET
22:    select '-------------------------------------------------------------
➡---------------' ¦¦ null LINE1,
23:    '                        Customer Contact Survey' ¦¦ null LINE2,
24:    '-------------------------------------------------------------------
➡---------' ¦¦ null LINE3,
25:    ' Customer Name:  '  ¦¦ CUSTOMER_NAME ¦¦ ' PHONE#:  ' ¦¦ PHONE ¦¦ null
➡LINE4,
26:    ' Customer Address:  ' ¦¦ CUSTOMER_ADDRESS  ¦¦ null LINE5,
27:    '                                  ' ¦¦ CUSTOMER_CITY ¦¦
➡CUSTOMER STATE ¦¦
28:            CUSTOMER_ZIP  ¦¦ null LINE6,
29:    '-------------------------------------------------------------------
➡---------' ¦¦ null LINE7,
```

```
30:      ' '  ¦¦ TO_CHAR(CONTACT_DATE,'mm/dd/yy HH:MI ¦¦ '  Caller: '  ¦¦
➥CALLER ¦¦ null
31:          LINE8,
32:      '-----------------------------------------------------------------
➥---------'  ¦¦ null LINE9,
33:      '  Home Phone? '  ¦¦   HPHONE_YN   ¦¦ 'Best Time to call:  '  ¦¦ CALL_
➥TIME ¦¦ null
34:          LINE10,
35:      '   'Has Catalog? '  ¦¦ CATALOG_YN ¦¦ 'Desire Future Calls? '  ¦¦
➥FUTURE_YN ¦¦ null
36:          LINE11,
37:      '-----------------------------------------------------------------
➥---------'  ¦¦ null LINE12,
38:      'PRINTED:  '  ¦¦ TO_CHAR(SYSDATE,'mm/dd/yy HH:MI ¦¦ 'BY:  '  ¦¦
➥OPERATOR ¦¦ null
39:          LINE13,
40:      '-----------------------------------------------------------------
➥---------'  ¦¦ null LINE14
41:      from CUSTOMER_TABLE
42:      where ROWID = '&&TICKET_ROWID'
43:      /
44:      spool OUT
45:      exit
```

LISTING 22.15. OUTPUT OF LISTING 22.13 AND 22.14: FIXED POSITION FORMATTING
SQL*PLUS REPORT.

```
        ----------------------------------------------------------------
-
--------
         Customer Contact Survey
        ----------------------------------------------------------------
-
--------
     Customer Name:  John Smith    PHONE#: 515 123-4567
     Customer Address:  123 Oak Street
                              Anytown  VA 12345
        ----------------------------------------------------------------
-
--------
     31-Aug-95 10:05  Caller:   DHotka
        ----------------------------------------------------------------
```

continues

LISTING 22.15. CONTINUED

```
-
- - - - - - - -
        Home Phone?     Y      Best Time to call:  8pm
        Has Catalog?    Y        Desire Future Calls?   N
        - - - - - - - - - - - - - - - - - - - - - - - - - - - - - - - - - - - - - - - - - - -
-
- - - - - - - -
     PRINTED: 3-Apr-98 8:25   BY:  DHotka
        - - - - - - - - - - - - - - - - - - - - - - - - - - - - - - - - - - - - - - - - - - -
-
- - - - - - - -
```

SQL*Plus Additional Functionality

The remainder of this chapter will discuss a variety of methods of formatting SQL*Plus output to create database-driven types of output (SQL code, operating system-dependent command language, script files for other Oracle products, and so on).

SQL Creating SQL

The classic example of using SQL*Plus formatting to create other SQL statements (hence the term "SQL creating SQL") is that of table cleanup after an employee leaves a company. The Oracle data dictionary table TAB is used in this example. The steps in Listing 22.16 can easily be entered at the SQL_Plus prompt (shown here as SQL>), or adapted to a SQL_Plus command file using features already learned.

LISTING 22.16. DROPPING ALL OF A USER'S TABLES EXAMPLE.

```
SQL>set headings off
SQL>set pagesize 0
SQL>set termout off
SQL>spool drop_tbl.sql
SQL>select 'DROP TABLE ' ¦¦ tname ¦¦ ';' from tab;
SQL>spool off
SQL>set termout on
SQL>start drop_tbl
```

This scenerio assumes that the login ID and the owner of the table objects to be dropped are one and the same. The first three commands are used to set up the SQL*Plus environment. The spool file drop_tbl.sql will capture the concatenated text and table names (tname) from the SQL query. The spool off closes the file and the start executes the drop table commands now inside the drop_tbl.sql file.

> **TIP**
>
> It is common practice to create versions of this and other SQL scripts that take command line parameters to do a variety of cleanup and monitoring tasks.

The creating database triggers code example in Listing 22.17 will add four auditing fields to the end of each table owned by the userid that runs this particular SQL*Plus command file. This script will also create a database trigger that will automatically maintain these four added fields.

Lines 1 through 7 (Listing 22.17) set up the SQL*Plus environment so that no extra messages appear in the cre_dbtrg.sql file (see line 8). Lines 9 through 14 create the SQL alter table statement that will add the audit fields to each table, and lines 15 through 33 will create the database triggers necessary to maintain these audit fields. Lines 35 through 38 reset the SQL*Plus environment so that all SQL commands and messages display. Line 40 then runs the SQL*Plus command file cre_dbtrg.sql (see Listing 22.18) that was just created.

LISTING 22.17. CREATING DATABASE TRIGGERS.

```
 1:    set ECHO OFF
 2:    set TERMOUT OFF
 3:    set FEEDBACK OFF
 4:    set VERIFY OFF
 5:    set PAGESIZE 0
 6:    set LINESIZE 80
 7:    set HEADING OFF
 8:    spool cre_dbtrg.sql
 9:    select    RPAD('alter table ' || TNAME || null,80),
10:        RPAD( '            add (inserted_by      varchar2(10), ' ||
➥null,80),
11:        RPAD( '                 inserted_date        date    , ' ||
➥null,80),
12:        RPAD( '                 updated_by       varchar2(10), ' ||
➥null,80),
13:        RPAD( '                 updated_date         date    ); ' ||
➥null,80)
14:    from TAB;
15:      select    RPAD(' create trigger trg_' || TNAME || null,80),
16:        RPAD(' before insert or update ' || null,80),
17:        RPAD('     on ' || TNAME || null,80),
18:        RPAD('    for each row ' || null,80),
19:         RPAD(' begin ' || null,80),
```

continues

LISTING 22.17. CONTINUED

```
20:            RPAD('   if :old.inserted_by is null then ' ¦¦ null,80),
21:            RPAD('     :new.inserted_by   := USER; ' ¦¦ null,80),
22:            RPAD('     :new.inserted_date := SYSDATE; ' ¦¦ null,80),
23:            RPAD('     :new.updated_by    := null; ' ¦¦ null,80),
24:            RPAD('     :new.updated_date  := null; ' ¦¦ null,80),
25:            RPAD('   else ' ¦¦ null,80),
26:            RPAD('     :new.inserted_by   := :old.inserted_by; ' ¦¦
➥null,80),
27:            RPAD('     :new.inserted_date := :old.inserted_date; ' ¦¦
➥null,80),
28:            RPAD('     :new.updated_by    := USER; ' ¦¦ null,80),
29:            RPAD('     :new.updated_date  := SYSDATE; ' ¦¦ null,80),
30:            RPAD('   end if; ' ¦¦ null,80),
31:            RPAD(' end; ' ¦¦ null,80),
32:            RPAD( '/' ¦¦ null,80)
33:      from TAB;
34:      spool off
35:      set FEEDBACK ON
36:      set TERMOUT ON
37:      set VERIFY ON
38:      set ECHO ON
39:      spool dbtrg.log
40:      start cre_dbtrg.sql
41:      spool off
42:      exit
```

LISTING 22.18. CREATING DATABASE TRIGGERS OUTPUT.

```
alter table EXAMPLE_TABLE
         add (inserted_by        varchar2(10),
              inserted_date      date    ,
              updated_by         varchar2(10),
              updated_date       date    );

create trigger trg_EXAMPLE_TABLE
 before insert or update
    on
    for each row
begin
 if :old.inserted_by is null then
     :new.inserted_by   := USER;
     :new.inserted_date := SYSDATE;
     :new.updated_by    := null;
     :new.updated_date  := null;
    else
    :new.inserted_by   := :old.inserted_by;
    :new.inserted_date := :old.inserted_date;
    :new.updated_by    := USER;
```

```
      :new.updated_date  := SYSDATE;
      end if;
  end;
  /
```

Third-Party Products

There are quite a number of tools available for the Oracle environment from companies other than Oracle Corporation. There are tools that assist the DBA with such tasks as tablespace reorganization, multiple types of database administration from one tool, schema management and movement, tuning, and backup and recovery. The Data Administrator uses modeling tools, SQL generators, and so on. Developers need code version control, coding environments, symbolic debuggers, and tuning aids. End users need OLAP tools.

Database Administration

Database administration is more than adding users and granting privileges. DBAs typically maintain a directory full of SQL scripts to perform various functions like adding users and privileges to various applications. If the requirements were to add a column in the middle of an object, it was quite a bit of work. Adding the column could be error-prone, and, if not done correctly, undoing the change could easily be more work than making the change in the first place.

Bradmark Technology, Inc.'s DB General Server Manager is an easy-to-use graphical interface that has quite a bit of Oracle administrative functionality. More information on this and other tools from Bradmark Technology is available from their Web site at www.Bradmark.com.

Embarcadero Technologies, Inc.'s product, DBArtisan is a multiple database (including Oracle RDBMS) administrative graphical tool. More information on this and other tools from Embarcadero Technology is available from their Web site at www.Embarcadero.com.

Platinum Technology, Inc.'s Enterprise DBA solves all of the issues of schema management, including schema and data movement, scheduling of tasks, recoverability and undo features and is an agent based/graphical user tool. More information on this and other products from Platinum Technology is available from their Web site at www.Platinum.com.

Data Movement

Data movement is a critical part of most any business today. Creating test environments and moving applications from a test to a production is a time-consuming and error-prone process. Once again, Platinum Technology's Enterprise DBA can help. It is an easy task for Enterprise DBA to replicate an entire schema, the entire database application, or any subset of it (useful in the creation of application test environments), including all of the data, some of the data, or none of the data.

Platinum Technology, Inc.'s Fast Unload for Oracle is a direct export data extract facility, reading the Oracle data directly from data files, eliminating the overhead of using the Oracle kernel and SELECT statements, while supporting a variety of output choices. Platinum Technology also bundles this tool with some of their others, such as TSReorg and Enterprise DBA, to enhance their performance.

```
-------------------------------------------------------------------
Fast Unload for Oracle: Release V1.4.3 - Thu Feb  5 17:02:52 1998
Copyright(c) 1996-1997 PLATINUM technology, inc. All rights reserved.
-------------------------------------------------------------------
Usage:
fastunload -b                                Write RAWs in binary mode
           -c                                Row byte count
           -C                                Column byte count
           -d                                SQL*Loader Delimited format
           -e                                ORACLE Direct Export Forma/
           -f { control filename }           Fast Unload control file
           -h                                Shows this information
           -i                                Informix dbload format
           -l { log_file }                   Fast Unload log filename
           -L { maxlongsize }                Max LONG/LONG RAW size
           -m [ n ]                          Odometer row count setting
           -n                                Shuts off data writing
           -o { filename [ filename ]...}    Output file pathname(s)
           -r [ n1 [ n2 ] ]                  Range of rows to unload
           -s                                Enable checksum
           -t { [owner.]TableName }          Table to unload
           -u { DBA username/password }      ORACLE DBA connect string
           -U { username/password }          ORACLE user connect string
           -v                                SQL*Loader VAR format
           -V                                SQL*Loader Fastload format
           -w [roundrobin¦sequential][row¦buffer]  Writing scheme
           -x [ n ]                          Fixed Format [VARCHAR size]
           -Z { CacheSize OufBuffSize }      Cache sizes in ORACLE Blocks
```

Tablespace Reorganization

Fragmentation with the Oracle RDBMS is a known issue. Managing and correcting fragmentation can be a difficult task with Oracle's referential integrity, object relationships all over the database, roles, permissions, packages, functions, triggers, and so on. Various tablespace fragmentation issues are covered in depth in Chapter 23. The market- place has several offerings in the tablespace reorganization arena.

ARIS Corporation's DFRAG is one such reorganization product. DFRAG has a long history with the Oracle environment and utilizes many features available within the Oracle RDBMS. DEFRAG has many features that would be attractive to DBAs. More information on this and other tools from ARIS Corporation is available from their Web site at www.Aris.com.

TSReorg is a premiere-quality tablespace/object reorganization agent-based product for Oracle and other SQL-based databases. It comes bundled with Platinum Technology's Fast Unload product and utilizes Oracle's own SQL*Loader with the direct path option, giving TSReorg superior speed. This tool handles all the complexities of today's SQL environment. More information on this and other products from Platinum Technology is available from their Web site at www.Platinum.com.

Quest Software ADHawk Spacer is a graphical client-side space management and table object reorganization tool. ADHawk Spacer supports Oracle RDBMS environments back to version six. It has a variety of analytical and reporting features. More information on this and other tools from Quest Software is available from their Web site at www.Quests.com.

Tuning Aids

Tuning is important to any computing environment, but actually tuning the individual SQL statements in a relational database (such as Oracle) can have a profound impact on application and overall system performance. Locating problem SQL, in itself, can be a challenge. Tuning the Oracle environment and tuning SQL statements is the topic of Chapter 24, "Oracle8 Database Tuning." There are many product offerings to aid the developer or DBA in finding and correcting problem SQL.

Bradmark Technology, Inc.'s SQL Performance Tuner has several features: to locate problem SQL, collect statistics by system, by user, or by object, and once identified, explain and tune the SQL statements. More information on this and other tools from Bradmark Technology is available from their Web site at www.Bradmark.com.

Platinum Technology, Inc.'s SQL*Station is actually a bundle of four tools: coder (PL/SQL development), debugger (symbolic PL/SQL debugger), code manager (version control and deployment), and Plan Analyzer. Plan Analyzer is a powerful Explain Plan tool capable of tuning and comparing both the rule-based and cost-based (first-row and all-rows) optimizer SQL execution plans, displaying valuable cost, and row and byte-count per-row in the explain plan. It has an interactive ability to add hints as well as many features to capture problem SQL, reports, and compares. More information on this and other tools from Platinum Technology is available from their Web site at `www.Platinum.com`.

Quest Software's SQLab is another offering in the SQL tuning arena. SQLab has features that discover and document problem SQL regardless of its originating application as well as tuning features. More information on this and other tools from Quest Software is available from their Web site at `www.Quests.com`.

Monitoring

Monitoring the Oracle environment is simply a necessity to many shops. As discussed in Chapter 19, "Oracle8 Administrative Requirements," there are three primary reasons for monitoring: proactive problem resolution, tuning issues, and trend analysis. Monitoring needs to happen all the time, not just when the response time is slow. Sometimes the Oracle environment is running just fine, from an Oracle point of view. Sometimes issues involving performance, such as memory swapping, cannot be monitored from an Oracle-based monitor.

Bradmark Technology, Inc.'s DB General Performance Monitoring monitors the Oracle RDBMS environment. Like most monitoring tools, DB General Performance Monitoring has a variety of scans and archives collected metrics and can notify the proper personnel in a variety of manners: email, pagers, SNMP messaging, and so on. The scans can be as broad as monitoring server metrics or as precise as individual SQL statements. This tool supports all three primary reasons for monitoring mentioned above. More information on this and other tools from Bradmark Technology is available from their Web site at `www.Bradmark.com`.

Platinum Technology's Enterprise Performance Management (EPM) monitors the server environment (UNIX, NT, OS/2), the Oracle environment, non-Oracle database environments, and the network environment, all from the background, for hundreds of servers, doing alarming, notification (paging, email, snmp, and so on), and corrective actions without having to have a console online. All monitoring is viewable from a single console, with no special languages to be learned to add functionality. EPM is powerful for all three needed monitoring: proactively monitors and alerts the right personnel (or corrects the problem), displays tuning metrics from the server, database, and network point of view, and stores historical information for trend analysis. All scans have extensive drill-down capabilities to view the detail level. Drill-downs include seeing who is causing a lock, the SQL statement level (with Explain Plan), physical disk I/O, what UNIX processes are being swapped, MTS, dispatcher load, to object management, and so on.

EPM has low system overhead, which makes it perfect for any computing environment. It even comes with a character-mode console for problem resolution remotely. EPM supports over 200 scan types for the Oracle8 RDBMS.

Quest Software AdHawk Monitor is a client-side Oracle monitoring product. AdHawk Monitor has a graphical console that utilizes SQL*Net for connectivity to the Oracle environment. This console gives AdHawk Monitor the ability to see system and user activity, drilling down to more detailed levels of information, including the actual SQL statements. AdHawk Monitor has the ability to make recommendations. More information on this and other tools from Quest Software is available from their Web site at www.Quests.com.

Summary

The objective of this chapter was to familiarize the reader with the many tools available to the Oracle8 server. I discussed all of the server-side tools including Server Manager, Export/Import, SQL*Loader, SQL*Plus, and several tools available from third-party software vendors.

Tools represented in this chapter appeared in alphabetical order. Additional information about each of the vendors listed in this chapter can be found at the following Internet Web sites:

www.Aris.com

www.Bradmark.com

www.Embarcadero.com

www.Platinum.com

www.Quests.com

My hope is that you can utilize the skills and the tools referenced here to make your administrative tasks simpler.

Backup and Recovery

by Dan Hotka

IN THIS CHAPTER

Any computing environment is subject to a variety of hardware or software failures and problems that can cause a loss of stored data. Natural disasters, power outages, computer program problems, and machine failures are hard to predict. Other considerations that need to be taken into account are accidental and intentional corruption or destruction of data.

Each application has specific data requirement needs. Some applications are data-entry-oriented (merchandise sales via a cash register or a terminal) where others are just information retrieval (typical data warehouse). In the event of software/hardware failure, for whatever reason, the ability to restore the data after the failure is corrected will be necessary. A backup in a computing environment entails making an electronic copy of data and/or programs on removable media. The frequency and extent of backups depend on the application and business needs. For example, a database that is loaded from flat files every evening may not require that any backups be performed at all, whereas OLTP applications may not have any acceptable data loss or downtime.

A system-level backup will copy all changes in the system configuration, programs, and data to a removable medium such as tape or a storage management device. An Oracle database backup is to recover from any type of error, with minimal data loss and a minimal amount of application unavailability. Oracle database backups have multiple options for the many business requirements for the applications and data. These various backup/business scenarios is the topic of this chapter.

These availability and backup needs can be met with both hardware and software solutions. Hardware solutions include RAID (with its disk mirroring options), uninterrupted power supply (enough power to bring the machine down gracefully or to maintain full hardware availability for hours or even days), and redundant standby systems. Software solutions include software mirroring of files (Oracle supports mirrored redo logs and control files), software to maintain the redundant standby system (Oracle's archive log mode and standby database options), and backup/recovery software (Oracle supplied, hardware vendor supplied, and third-party packaged software).

Overview of Oracle Data Availability Requirements

Applications address business needs. Availability, acceptable downtime, and acceptable data loss are all critical requirements when arriving at backup and recovery solutions.

Acceptable Data Loss

The data-accessibility requirements need to be completely understood prior to the production status of any application. The type of backup and recovery plan to implement depends on issues such as acceptable downtime, recovery time, intervals of backups, and acceptable data loss. Acceptable data loss and acceptable downtime will determine the type of backup strategy required for any application. The more critical the information and consistent availability, the more redundancy in both hardware and software will be required. Many hardware platforms support a great deal of fault tolerance, and some vendors specialize in fault tolerance. Oracle has several mirroring features that enhance the computer hardware fault tolerance and data recoverability.

24×7 Needs

Many business needs dictate minimal or absolutely no application downtime. Any data lost in a retail sales application would mean a loss of sales. Any loss of collected credit card charge data would be a loss in revenue. Any data lost in an emergency application could mean a loss of life.

Both hardware and software features need to be considered by the business need. Redundant and fault-tolerant hardware systems can provide fail-over systems, disk mirroring, and uninterrupted power. Oracle supports many features that aid in the protection of data. Oracle supports instance level recovery via the redo logs. In the event of media failure, Oracle's ARCHIVELOG mode can recover data to the last committed transaction. Oracle supports the software mirroring, or duplexing, of many critical files, such as the redo logs and control files. Oracle supports the concept of a "standby database," where two identical Oracle environments are maintained, one in active use and one in constant recovery mode. ARCHIVELOG mode is essential in this configuration because as the archive logs are created on the primary system, they are moved and applied to the standby system. In the event of machine failure, the standby database can be quickly brought online and is as current as the last applied archive log. The amount of acceptable data loss is in inverse proportion to the frequency these archive logs are created and applied to the standby database environment.

Data Warehouse Requirements

Oracle supports several features that can assist the recovery of a data warehouse. If the business requirements dictate that the data is for read-access only, Oracle's read-only tablespaces can be utilized. Oracle's read-only tablespaces eliminate the need for Oracle's read consistency and archive recovery features as the data is not allowed to change. The need to backup this tablespace, or to back it up more than once, is eliminated. These read-only tablespaces can reside on CD-ROM technology.

If the data warehouse is large, Oracle8's partitioning features may be of value for backup and recovery scenarios (as well as the obvious performance implications). Partitions can be individually backed up while online and available to applications. Partitions can be loaded independently of other partitions. If recovery is needed, recovery happens at the partition level, while the other partitions are still available to the application. This option alone can greatly enhance data availability to applications.

Scheduled Maintenance

Application-unavailable issues such as scheduled maintenance need to be considered as well. Periodic maintenance for backups and reorganizations is essential for a well-running database environment. Some applications have a batch mode, where all changes to the data is applied at one time, usually in the off hours. These applications lend themselves well for backup right after all of the updates. Data reorganization typically occurs on weekends, and can be a time-consuming process in Oracle's complex relationships with other objects (constraints, referential integrity, and so on).

The size of the data objects has a direct relationship to the time of backup, recovery, and database-maintenance tasks. The larger the database objects and the more critical the data availability requirements are, the more Oracle partitioning should be considered. Partitioning breaks larger objects into smaller, more manageable pieces.

Overview of Oracle Backup and Recovery Processes

There are many files that make up the Oracle8 database environment (see Figure 23.1). This section will give a brief description of each, their relative importance, and methods of backing up each.

The most important file is the control file. This file contains locations of all the other Oracle files, important recovery information, important startup and shutdown information, and, if Recovery Manager is implemented, the recovery files. Basically, if this file is lost or unrecoverable, the Oracle database cannot be started. Oracle allows for many control files to be maintained on disk as desired. These files are listed, with their operating-system full-path specifications, in the `INIT.ORA` parameter file. A control file can always be created with the following SQL statement `alter database backup controlfile to /tmp/<SID>.ctl`. The location and names of the currently maintained control files can be viewed with the following SQL statement `select name from v$controlfile`.

FIGURE 23.1.

Oracle database processes and related files.

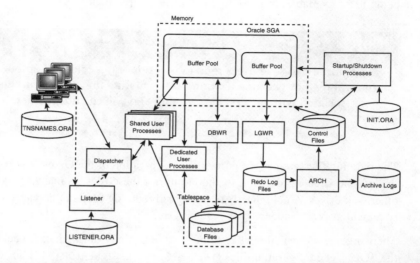

> **NOTE**
>
> When performing hot backups (backups with the database online and available), it is important to use this command to create a backup copy of the control file, *not* the control file that is currently on disk. The only time the real control files should be backed up is during a cold backup.

The database files are assigned to the Oracle tablespaces and contain the Oracle data dictionary and all application data. These are the main files to be backed up. Oracle supports two methods to back up these files, cold backups and hot backups. Both of these methods are discussed in detail later, but it suffices to say here that during a cold backup, it is important to copy all of these database files to a removable media, and during a hot backup it is important to copy all of the database files associated with the tablespace being backed up to a removable media. Database files can easily be viewed with the following SQL statement `select name from v$datafile`.

The redo log files are used to record all changes made to the database. These files are used during instance recovery to roll forward any committed changes to the data files and roll back any uncommitted changes to the data files. There are at least two of these redo logs online and available for the Oracle environment to record changes to data and schemas. If ARCHIVELOG mode is activated (complete discussion later in this chapter), the contents of these logs are saved to operating system files called Archive Logs before being made available for reuse by the Oracle environment.

> **NOTE**
>
> It is important to save these redo log files during a cold backup but absolutely not during a hot backup. Restoring these files at any other time than with all files associated with a cold backup could and will corrupt the database environment.

The redo log files are very important to the operation of the Oracle environment, and for this reason, Oracle provides a method to mirror these files, as many times as needed, to other disk drives. A complete list of assigned redo log files can be viewed with the SQL statement select member from v$logfile.

There are a few other files I like to back up, especially during a cold backup. They are the SQL*Net configuration files (TNSNAMES.ORA, LISTENER.ORA, and SQLNET.ORA). Another rather important file is the INIT.ORA file, the database startup parameter file.

ARCHIVELOG Mode

ARCHIVELOG mode, or archive redo log files, must be implemented if hot backups are to be performed, if "point-in-time" recovery is desired or if you need to recover database files after a disk crash or other media failure.

> **NOTE**
>
> The size of the archive redo log is determined by the size of the online redo log being archived.

> **TIP**
>
> There is no technical reason why the online redo logs have to be the same size, but I recommend that they be the same size to allow more control of the time needed to recover data in the event of media failure.

Automatic Archive redo log mode is easy to implement. The first step is to shut down the database and start up in `nomount` (exclusive) mode. In `svrmgrl`, enter the command `alter database archivelog`. Shut down the database. Edit the `INIT.ORA` file and uncomment two parameters that control this mode of operation. Uncomment the lines and set their values: `log_archive_start = true` and set `log_archive_dest = <oper-ating system full path name>`. The `log_archive_format` command is optional and is used to change the default naming convention of the archive log file itself (see the Oracle Database Administrator's guide for format options and advice). Start up the database using this `init.ora` file with these changes. The directory identified by `log_archive_dest` should now have an archive redo log file in it. They will be assigned sequential numbers and will only be used during a media-type recovery. The recovery process will prompt the computer operator for these log files by their names.

Mirroring these archive log files is also possible. To implement, simply set `log_archive_duplex_dest = <operating system full path name>` and restart the Oracle environment for this change to be active. The `log_archive_min_succeed_dest` parameter can be used to ensure that one or two archive files were successfully written to. The default for this parameter is 1, which means only one of the archive redo logs needs to be available for writing.

The frequency with which these archive log files are created can easily be controlled by the size of the online redo files or by entering the SQL command `alter database switch log file`. Checkpointing is a process where all database buffers are written to disk and a mark, a checkpoint, is recorded in the log as a quiet point in the database where all transactions are committed or rolled back. The frequency of the checkpoints has a dramatic effect on the speed of recovery. The checkpoint process is resource-intensive. Checkpointing can have a negative performance impact on an active Oracle environment with lots of active users with DML activity. Checkpoint frequency should be balanced against the amount of data in the logs being written. The `INIT.ORA` parameter `LOG_CHECKPOINT_INTERVAL = <integer>` controls the frequency of checkpoints. The integer is the number of megabytes written in the online redo logs between checkpoints. A checkpoint always occurs at a log switch, during the process of Oracle having filled one online redo log and beginning to use the next available online redo log. Archive log files are created as a part of the log switch process. The online redo logs need to be large enough to hold complete transactions but small enough to fit recovery time requirements.

23

BACKUP AND RECOVERY

> **TIP**
>
> On active systems, make the online redo logs hold enough data to fit the recovery-time window and set the LOG_CHECKPOINT_INTERVAL (number is in Oracle database blocks) to a size larger than the largest online redo log. This will ensure that checkpointing does not slow down the active system.

There are several SQL commands that will indirectly cause a checkpoint to occur. The obvious ones are any log file switch command, but other commands that will cause a checkpoint are alter tablespace begin backup, alter tablespace offline, and instance shutdown.

Cold and Hot Backups

Cold backups are done when the Oracle RDBMS is in a down state and all of the physical files and initialization files are backed up. This method can be supplemented with Oracle's Export and Import utilities to do incremental backups of changed objects, or better yet, supplement Oracle's ARCHIVELOG mode. If ARCHIVELOG mode is being utilized, all prior archive log files become irrelevant after a successful cold backup of all physical files is complete. This method is an "all-or-nothing" approach to recovery. If ARCHIVELOG mode is not utilized, and no other method is used to capture changes in the database, all changes are lost from the last cold backup.

Hot backups are done at the tablespace level, with the database up and available for reads and writes. Hot backups utilize the archive log files (ARCHIVELOG mode must be implemented) to store all writes while the physical tablespace files are being backed up. During recovery, all noncorrupted tablespaces are online and available. Oracle will prompt an operator for the needed archive logs to restore the tablespace.

> **NOTE**
>
> Cold backups should include the redo log files for any instance recovery required from the previous shutdown of the database. Hot backups should avoid the redo log files for this very reason. If the database is in an online status, the redo log files plays no role in any future media recovery scenario.

Incremental Backups

Oracle Export can be used to get individual data objects, functions, packages, user definitions, permissions, entire tablespaces, and even the entire database into operating-system files. Import can then import what was exported, to either the same Oracle instance or another Oracle instance. Export and Import tend to be rather slow, are sometimes limited by operating-system file limits, and are not well suited for very large databases (VLDB).

Oracle Export and Import also provide the method for incrementally backing up only those objects that have changed since the prior incremental backup. There are three levels of export for object backup and recovery: complete export, cumulative export, and incremental export. The level of the export is controlled by a parameter on the command line or in the Export parameter file. There are also three objects that track the time and type of Export backup: SYS.INCEXP, SYS.INCFIL, and SYS.INCVID, which are optionally created by the CATEXP.SQL file at database install time.

These three levels of export backup all build on one another. Incremental backups only have changes made to objects from the most recent incremental or cumulative export, in this order. Cumulative exports have all changes made to objects from the most recent cumulative or complete export backup. Complete export backups have all changes to objects from the next previous complete export. The three levels of export supersede each other, in that, when a complete export is done, all prior complete, cumulative, and incremental exports become obsolete. Similarly, when a cumulative export is done, all incremental exports to the next-most-recent cumulative export become obsolete. Incremental exports are the lowest level of export in this backup scenario.

The reason for all these levels is a factor of time. It takes longer to do the complete export than to do the cumulative and/or incremental export. This system was designed with the following model in mind. Do complete exports once a month. Do cumulative exports on each of the following weekends, and do incremental exports daily. Each cumulative export will contain all the changes to the database from either the previous cumulative or the complete export. The incremental exports will contain the tables (and all of their rows) with changes made on that particular day. This scenario is best used in a development or an environment with many end users doing their own object manipulation. This method of export/import gives the DBA great flexibility to restore single objects or data that was inadvertently dropped or deleted.

23

BACKUP AND RECOVERY

> **NOTE**
>
> Export with the Direct Path option is not available for complete, cumulative, or incremental exports.

The syntax for the Export process is the same as previously discussed with these additional options: FULL=Y and INCTYPE = COMPLETE (or CUMULATIVE or INCREMENTAL).

The Import process also has additional options: FULL=Y and INCTYPE = SYSTEM or RESTORE. The SYSTEM parameter will only restore changes owned by SYS. No user objects or data will be restored. Conversely, RESTORE will restore all other changes except for those owned by SYS.

When restoring a series of exported files, it is important to do the last export first with the INCTYPE=SYSTEM, and then do the necessary imports to restore the non-SYSTEM objects, in the correct chronological order, using the INCTYPE=RESTORE option.

> **NOTE**
>
> Import behaves differently in this mode in that it does not attempt to drop any tables first. It will be necessary to manually drop user objects to prevent duplicate rows in the object.

Figure 23.2 shows a typical incremental backup scenario utilizing the Export process. Point A on the time line is the complete backup. Point B is the first incremental backup and contains all of the changed objects from Point A to Point B. Point C is the first cumulative backup. At this point, the cumulative file contains all of the changed objects to the database from Point A, including those changed objects captured in the incremental backup of Point B. At Point C, the incremental backup from Point B is no longer of any value. The same is true of the relationship of Point C to Point F. Point F will contain all of the changed objects to the database from Point C, the last most-previous-incremental backup at the same level. Each level (complete, cumulative, or incremental) will contain the changed objects from the last incremental export of the same level.

To review a recovery scenario, say we have two weeks worth of incremental-type exports (Listing 23.1), beginning at the first of the month with a complete export, having cumulative exports on the weekend, and daily incremental exports. The filenames have the day of the week and the type of export: F being complete, C being cumulative, and I being incremental.

FIGURE 23.2.
A typical incremental Export scenario.

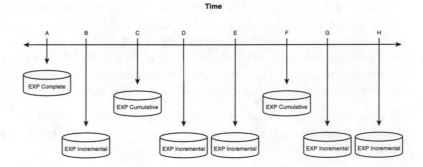

LISTING 23.1. INCREMENTAL EXPORT EXAMPLE.

```
 1: F1.exp
 2: I2.exp
 3: I3.exp
 4: I4.exp
 5: I5.exp
 6: I6.exp
 7: C7.exp
 8: I8.exp
 9: I9.exp
10: I10.exp
11: .
12: .
13: .
```

Now say some objects were corrupted on the 11th and were last updated on the 7th. A DBA could use the following scenario (Listing 23.2) to restore those objects. Remember, run the last export twice, once at the beginning with the SYSTEM parameter set and again last with the RESTORE parameter set.

LISTING 23.2. IMPORT RECOVERY SCENARIO.

```
1: IMP system/manager FULL=Y INCTYPE=SYSTEM FILE=I10.exp
2: IMP system/manager FULL=Y INCTYPE=RESTORE FILE=C7.exp
3: IMP system/manager FULL=Y INCTYPE=RESTORE FILE=I8.exp
4: IMP system/manager FULL=Y INCTYPE=RESTORE FILE=I9.exp
5: IMP system/manager FULL=Y INCTYPE=RESTORE FILE=I10.exp
```

High Availability Options

High availability is supported by many hardware features and by options in the Oracle software.

Hardware features include: UPS (uninterruptable power supply), multiple processors, and RAID technology disk drives. Some vendors, such as Tandem, specialize in redundant fault-tolerant systems that automatically switch all applications to a duplicate system where processing continues without interruption. RAID, or redundant array of inexpensive devices, has performance options (hardware data striping) and data-protection features (hardware disk mirroring with or without parity checking).

This section will concentrate on the features and benefits of RAID technology in an Oracle environment, and various Oracle options that increase availability and limit downtime.

RAID Drives

RAID is a bank of disk drives the computer will view as one physical drive. The Oracle environment will view a single RAID device as a single disk device as well.

There are five levels of RAID. RAID level 0 stripes data files across the available disk drives without any mirroring or parity checking. RAID level 1 identically mirrors disk drives. RAID levels 2, 3, and 4 are not used and do not apply to business systems. RAID level 5 is a combination of RAID level 0 and RAID level 1. RAID level 5 stripes data files, mirrors the striped disk segments across many available drives, and provides parity to ensure the accuracy of the reads and writes. Both RAID level 1 and RAID level 5 support a disk drive going bad with no impact on the application. Both RAID level 1 and RAID level 5 will support the bad disk drive being "hot swapped," that is, replaced with another physical drive, and the RAID environment will rebuild the information (striped data or a mirror) on the replacement drive.

> **TIP**
>
> RAID level 1 provides excellent fault tolerance for data availability.

> **NOTE**
>
> For performance reasons, RAID level 5 should *not* be used for Oracle structures that require performance such as the redo logs, TEMPORARY tablespaces, and ROLLBACK tablespaces.

Backups Versus RAID

RAID devices should not take the place of a regular backup schedule. Once again, business needs for data availability will dictate which scenario is best for the application. RAID technology brings a high degree of inexpensive fault tolerance to the computing environment. It certainly is NOT a replacement for system and/or database level backups.

> **NOTE**
>
> If the RAID controller or the RAID disk management software (anything other than the physical drives themselves) develops problems, the recoverability of information stored on the RAID device is unpredictable.

Standby Database

A standby database is a duplicate database environment, on duplicate equipment (with some exceptions), with identical levels of operating systems and identical levels of Oracle software. This standby database is in a constant state of recovery; as archive log files are closed on the primary database, they are transferred and applied to this standby database. This method incurs absolutely no overhead on the primary database and the only disadvantage is that the standby database is only as current as the last log file applied. A standby database is easy to use to replace the primary database so the amount of application downtime is minimal. These archive log files are easy to size and tune.

> **TIP**
>
> Mirror the archive log files to help prevent any data loss at all.

> **TIP**
>
> There is no limit to the number of standby database environments.

Standby databases are easy to create and maintain (see Figure 23.3). Standby databases require the exact same level of Oracle software and hardware operating system release levels as the database they back up. Standby databases also require the exact same computer processor type. It is recommended, but not required, that the same disk configuration exist. The Oracle database files are backed up utilizing either the cold or hot methods (as previously described) and moved to the standby system. This SQL statement will create the standby database's control file:

```
alter database create standby controlfile as <filename>
```

Move this file to the standby database. Use the following SQL statement to archive the current redo log and then manually copy this archive log file to the standby database: `alter system archive log current`.

> **TIP**
>
> I recommend a cold backup for the data file collection and transfer.

FIGURE 23.3.
Standby database configuration.

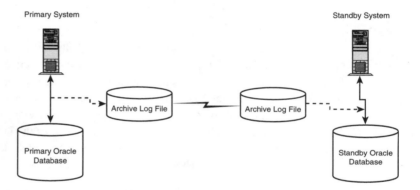

Maintenance of the standby database is quite easy. Start the standby database with the `startup nomount` option and issue the following command:

```
alter database mount standby database
```

The standby database is not open, so users cannot access this standby environment. As archive log files become available on the primary system, move them to the standby system and use the following command to apply the logged changes to the standby database: `alter database recover logfile <filename>`.

> **NOTE**
>
> There are options on some Oracle processes that do not create logged information, such as any "direct path load" or DDL with the UNRECOVERABLE option set. These operations will have to be applied to the standby environment as well.

If and when it is desirable to make the standby database the primary database, use the following SQL statement: `alter database activate standby database`. This will then allow access to the standby database as if it were the primary. I recommend that multiple names be specified in the SQL*Net `TNSNAMES.ORA` file to point to both the primary and this standby environment.

> **TIP**
>
> Do *not* activate the standby database until all of the log files have been applied.

It is my recommendation that complete duplicate hardware, including disk drives, be implemented with standby databases. When the standby database is activated, it simply becomes the primary. When the damaged environment is repaired, make it the standby environment, eliminating the need to quickly restore the original environment, and so on.

Backup Schemes

Backup schemes consist of a set of identified processes used to make copies of the targeted media, typically on some kind of removable media, to restore the environment to its original state prior to any hardware or software problem that made the original media inaccessible or unusable.

Oracle supports a variety of backup and recovery processes. These processes can be used in a standalone mode, or combined with other backup processes to provide a tailored, more comprehensive backup scenario for specific business needs.

Overview of Various Backup Schemes

Cold backup is the basis for several of the other backup options. Cold backups (as described earlier in this chapter) should be taken just after an Oracle installation, including the setup of all SQL*Net connectivity, with `ARCHIVELOG` mode turned on (if desired), online redo logs established and mirrored, and so on. This will give the DBA a solid basis for all the other types of recovery.

Cold backups are also useful in static systems that have a regular window for maintenance. For example, a good time to take a cold backup is right after a large load, possibly even an unprotected direct path load, of data. Incremental exports could be used to supplement object recovery between cold backups.

Hot backups allow for the backup of the physical database files while the database is open and in use. Shops with 24×7 requirement utilize hot backups for their tablespaces that are dynamic in nature. Database design, taking into account the backup and recovery needs, will have the greatest impact on recovery times. It is important that the dynamic objects be stored in separate tablespaces from those that are static in nature. This will allow cold backups to capture all the changes and hot backups to enhance the backup plan by only backing up those tablespaces with changes. As previously discussed in this chapter, the size of the redo logs, archive logs, and the checkpoint intervals has a direct impact on the amount of recovery time.

Figure 23.4 is a typical scenario utilizing ARCHIVELOG mode and a mix of cold and hot backup processes. Point A on the time line is the cold backup. The database is in a shut-down state and all of the files are backed up. Points B, C, and D are archive logs that were created as the online redo logs filled. Point E is a hot backup of the APPL table-space. If a media failure occurred between Point F and Point G to a file assigned to the APPL tablespace, the files associated with that tablespace would be restored and archive log file 4 would be prompted for and applied during the tablespace recovery process. If a media failure occurred once again between Point F and Point G to a tablespace data file other than the APPL tablespace, the database files from the cold backup at Point A would have to be restored, and each of the archive log files 1, 2, 3, and 4 would be prompted and applied.

FIGURE 23.4.

Typical
ARCHIVELOG mode
scenario.

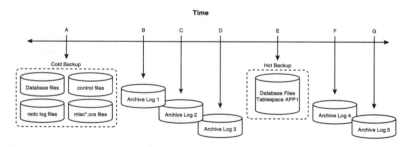

It is also important to back up tablespaces that have had direct path load or any unprotected DDL/DML commands applied to them. These commands gain their perfor-mance enhancements by *not* utilizing the normal read consistency and redo log recovery features.

Export and Import can play an important role in any development environment, adhoc end-user environment, and most backup scenarios that do not involve large volumes of data.

Standby databases require that the archive log files be applied as soon as they become available. I would recommend doing this task with a script that periodically viewed the DUMP_DEST directory for new archive log files, copied them to the standby system, and ran the command to apply the log to the standby environment. There are also third-party scheduling and monitoring tools that could perform this task automatically. A standby environment really does not need to be backed up itself because it is already a backup of another system. The primary system should have a backup plan in place and what is used for backup of the primary system could be used to re-set up the standby environment.

Deciding Which Scheme Is Best

Which backup scheme or plan is best is dictated by business needs. Backup plans should be tested to make sure that they are free of errors, are able to recover from various media or data loss scenarios, and meet the system availability time frames.

A backup set is the required files for a particular backup plan. Some backup sets build on other backup sets. For example, the archive log files would supplement the previous hot or cold backup sets. These archive log files become a backup set in themselves.

Backups should definitely be grandfathered; that is, several generations of backups need to be kept in existence for off-site storage and as a recovery mechanism in case the backup medium itself proves unusable during the recovery process. Depending on the nature of the information, some shops make copies of backup sets, keeping one on-site for a quick response to a recovery need and storing the second copy in a vault off-site.

The more critical the information, the more redundant the backup process should be.

23

BACKUP AND RECOVERY

> **TIP**
>
> It is not a bad idea to make duplicate copies of the archive log file backups and keep them for an extended period of time.

Automating Backup Schemes

I use SQL*Plus to do most of the work because it is an easy and flexible environment that can extract information stored in the database and format it properly for these scripts purposes. SQL*Plus scripts are easily understood and maintained.

Automating Cold Backups

See Listing 23.3 for a SQL*Plus script to determine the physical files and space required for backup. This information is useful for determining the amount of removable media to have available, particularly if the media needs to be formatted before it can be utilized. This script is executed through the SQL*Plus interface and utilizes information stored in the data dictionary table SYS.DBA_DATA_FILES. This is a simple SQL*Plus report that will identify the Oracle database files and their total size in bytes.

The Unix> line in Listing 23.3 is the syntax required to run the SQL*Plus script. Lines 5 through 8 turn off the SQL*Plus display output. Lines 9 through 14 apply simple SQL*Plus headings and column formatting. Line 15 opens an operating system file to store the results of the query. Lines 16 through 19 are the SQL query that retrieves the Tablespace information. Line 20 closes the operating system file.

LISTING 23.3. DETERMINING TABLESPACE SIZES SCRIPT.

```
 1: Unix>sqlplus system/<password>  @tablespace_size.sql
 2:
 3:
 4: rem File:  "tablespace_size.sql"
 5: rem
 6: rem Tablespace file and size report by Dan Hotka 2/15/1998
 7: rem
 8: set feedback off
 9: set verify off
10: set termout off
11: set echo off
12: ttitle 'Oracle Tablespace Physical Files'
13: column tablespace_name format a20 heading 'Tablespace'
14: column file_name format a40 heading 'File Name'
15: column bytes format 999,999,999 heading 'File Size'
16: compute sum of bytes on tablespace_name
17: compute sum of bytes on report
18: break on tablespace_name skip 2
19: break on report skip 2
20: spool tablespace.out
21: SELECT tablespace_name, file_name, bytes
22: FROM sys.dba_data_files
23: ORDER BY tablespace_name
24: /
25: spool off
26: exit
```

If the cold backup requires 12GB to be backed up to 8mm tape at 5GB per tape, three tapes are required to be formatted. With compression (hardware or software) the last tape might not be needed, but it's better to format extra than have to prepare more tapes with the database down.

Listing 23.4 shows how to create a list of files that the backup medium can act on. The `Unix>` line shows the syntax required to run the SQL*Plus script. Lines 5 through 9 turn off all SQL*Plus output formatting features. The output from this script will simply be a list of the Oracle database files currently being utilized by the Oracle RDBMS environment. Line 10 creates a file called `cold_back.lst`. Lines 11 through 20 is the SQL that retrieves the various data, control, and log filenames. Line 20 closes the `cold_back.lst` file.

LISTING 23.4. GATHERING OF DATA FILES.

```
 1: Unix>sqlplus system/<password>  @file_list.sql
 2:
 3: rem File "file_list.sql"
 4: rem
 5: rem Tablespace file listing script by Dan Hotka 2/15/1998
 6: rem
 7: set feedback off
 8: set verify off
 9: set termout off
10: set echo off
11: set head off
12: spool cold_back.lst
13: SELECT name
14: FROM v$datafile
15: UNION
16: SELECT name
17: FROM v$controlfile
18: UNION
19: SELECT member
20: FROM v$logfile
21: /
22: spool off
23: exit
```

The next script in Listing 23.5 is only necessary in Oracle8 environments that store binary objects (LOBS) outside the database environment.

Listing 23.5 demonstrates how versatile SQL*Plus can be in building and executing an operating system command file. This script formats the output necessary to locate and append the externally stored binary files to the file, `cold_back.lst`, created by Listing 23.4.

Once again, the `Unix>` line is the syntax required to run this SQL*Plus script. Lines 5 through 9 turn off all SQL*Plus output formatting features. Line 10 opens the file that

23

BACKUP AND RECOVERY

will contain the operating system command that will append the filenames to the output file created by Listing 23.4. Notice the UNIX-borne shell file suffix. Lines 11 through 14 select the external directory structure stored in the table SYS.DBA_DIRECTORIES, adding and appending the appropriate syntax for the UNIX operating system. Line 15 closes the newly created UNIX shell script. Line 16 then executes this command file, selecting all of the filenames from the appropriate directory structures and appending them to the filenames created by Listing 23.4. Line 17 cleans up the shell script after its use.

LISTING 23.5. ORACLE8 ONLY—ADDING EXTERNALLY STORED OBJECTS.

```
 1: Unix>sqlplus system/<password>  @bfile_list.sql
 2:
 3: rem File bfile_list.sql
 4: rem
 5: rem                 by Dan Hotka 2/15/1998
 6: rem
 7: set feedback off
 8: set verify off
 9: set termout off
10: set echo off
11: set head off
12: spool bfile.sh
13: SELECT 'ls ' || directory_path || '/' || directory_name || '/*.* >>
cold_back.lst '
14: FROM sys.dba_directories
15: /
16: spool off
17: host bfile.sh
18: host rm bfile.sh
19: exit
```

Listing 23.6 automates the cold backup procedure by utilizing techniques of extracting information from Oracle's data dictionary and not depending on an error-prone manually maintained list.

This code will need to be modified for the syntax of the particular backup medium and computing environment. Listing 23.6 uses standard UNIX commands to copy the previously prepared list of files required for a cold backup to a tape device.

LISTING 23.6. PROCESSING FILE LIST FOR COLD BACKUP.

```
1: Unix> filesystem_backup.sh <<EOF
2: #!/bin/sh
3:
4: tar -cvf <tape device> < cold_back.lst
5: EOF
```

```
6: Unix>
7: Unix>
```

> **NOTE**
>
> Replace the `tar` command for the syntax of the storage media being utilized.

This code can be used for UNIX raw partitions, putting one raw partition on a single tape.

```
Unix> rawpartition_backup.sh <<EOF
#!/bin/sh

tar for j in \`cat cold_back.lst\`
do
    echo "Put tape in tape device 0"
    pause "Hit Return to continue..."
    dd if=$j if=/dev/rmt0
done

EOF
Unix>
```

The following syntax (Listing 23.7) can be used to shut down and start up instances of Oracle. Cold backups *must* be done with the Oracle database in a "shutdown" status.

Make sure the environment variable `ORACLE_SID` is set to the instance of Oracle you want to shut down or start up.

LISTING 23.7. ORACLE SHUTDOWN/STARTUP SCRIPTS.

```
 1: Unix> svrmgrl <<EOF
 2: connect internal
 3: shutdown
 4: exit
 5: EOF
 6:
 7: Unix> svrmgrl <<EOF
 8: connect internal
 9: startup
10: exit
11: EOF
```

The steps required to do a cold backup from an Oracle RDBMS point of view are the following:

1. Determine the amount of backup media required by running Listing 23.3.

2. Create a list of Oracle datafiles to be backed up, utilizing Listing 23.4.

3. If this is an Oracle8 environment with externally stored binary files, utilize Listing 23.5 to supplement the list of data files requiring backup.

4. Add to that list all support files that make up the Oracle instance, including init[instance].ora files and control files. It wouldn't hurt to also include all the SQL*Net files. The following command could do all that:

```
ls    $ORACLE_HOME/dbs/init*.ora              \
      $ORACLE_BASE/admin/*/pfile/*.ora     \
         $ORACLE_HOME/network/admin/*.ora      \
      >> cold_back.lst
```

   You will want to modify this command for your environment.

5. Shut down the instance of Oracle to be backed up.

6. Run the shell script which processes the file listing appropriately (Listing 23.6).

7. Start up the instance of Oracle.

Automating Hot Backups

Hot backups differ from cold backups in that only one tablespace is backed up at a time, while the database is still online and available for use. IS departments that require true 24×7 availability of data will utilize this method of backup. VLDBs also utilize this method when a cold backup is not possible or feasible.

The ability to do hot backups relies on the Log Archive being turned on.

Recovery is accomplished by restoring the damaged files and initiating a recovery for that particular tablespace. During recovery, Oracle RDBMS will prompt the operator for the required archive log files.

Run the script in Listing 23.8 to create a list of files for each of the tablespaces to be backed up. For Oracle8 with externally stored binary objects, run Listing 23.9. After that, run the scripts in Listing 23.10 to create a list of the control files, initiate a log switch, and then create a backup list of all archive log files and SQL*Net files. Listings 23.11 and 23.12 show how to process this hot backup list of files, and Listing 23.13 ends the hot backup mode for the tablespace.

The Unix> line in Listing 23.8 is the command line used to put the tablespace in backup mode. The data is still available but all updates are written to the log files. When the end backup command is given (see Listing 23.12), these updates are then applied back to the tablespace. Line 5 of the script takes the input variable from the command line Unix> and assigns it a variable name. This makes the scripts more readable. Once again, lines 6 through 10 turn off all of the SQL*Plus formatting commands. Line 11 opens the output file `hot_back.lst`, a file that will contain names of all files to be backed up. Lines 12 through 15 is the actual SQL query that will extract the database filenames assigned to the tablespace being backed up.

LISTING 23.8. CREATING LIST OF TABLESPACE FILES FOR HOT BACKUP.

```
 1: Unix> svrmgrl <<EOF
 2: connect internal
 3: alter tablespace <TABLESPACE NAME> begin backup;
 4: exit
 5: EOF
 6:
 7: Unix>sqlplus system/<password> <TABLESPACE NAME> <<EOF
 8: rem
 9: rem Tablespace file cold backup script by Dan Hotka 2/15/1998
10: rem
11: define tname=&1
12: set feedback off
13: set verify off
14: set termout off
15: set echo off
16: set headings off
17: spool hot_back.lst
18: select  file_name
19: from sys.dba_data_files
20: where tablespace_name = &tname
21: /
22: spool off
23: exit
24: EOF
```

Listing 23.9 demonstrates how versatile SQL*Plus can be in building and executing an operating system command file. This script formats the output necessary to locate and append the externally stored binary files to the file, `hot_back.lst`, created by Listing 23.8.

LISTING 23.9. ADDING EXTERNALLY STORED OBJECTS.

```
1: Unix>sqlplus system/<password>  @bfile_list.sql
2:
3: rem File bfile_list.sql
4: rem
5: rem                 by Dan Hotka 2/15/98
6: rem
7: set feedback off
```

continues

LISTING 23.9. CONTINUED

```
 8: set verify off
 9: set termout off
10: set echo off
11: set head off
12: spool bfile.sh
13: SELECT 'ls ' ¦¦ directory_path ¦¦ '/' ¦¦ directory_name ¦¦ '/*.* >>
hot_back.lst '
14: FROM sys.dba_directories
15: /
16: spool off
17: host bfile.sh
18: host rm bfile.sh
19: exit
```

Once again, the Unix> line is the syntax required to run this SQL*Plus script. Lines 5 through 9 turn off all SQL*Plus output formatting features. Line 10 opens the file that will contain the operating-system command that will append the filenames to the output file created by Listing 23.8. Notice the UNIX-born shell file suffix. Lines 11 through 14 select the external directory structure stored in the table SYS.DBA_DIRECTORIES, adding and appending the appropriate syntax for the UNIX operating system. Line 15 closes the newly created UNIX shell script. Line 16 then executes this command file, selecting all of the filenames from the appropriate directory structures and appending them to the file-names created by Listing 23.8. Line 17 cleans up the shell script after its use.

The first Unix> script in Listing 23.10 creates a copy of the active control file in the UNIX directory tmp. The second Unix> command switches the log file to a new log file. This will enable the backup copy to have all changed data. The last Unix> command copies a few other important configuration files to the backup list, as well as the just-created control file in the tmp directory.

LISTING 23.10. ADD OTHER FILES TO HOT BACKUP FILE LIST.

```
 1: Unix> svrmgrl <<EOF
 2: connect internal
 3: alter database backup controlfile to /tmp/<oracle instance>.ctl;
 4: exit
 5: EOF
 6:
 7: Unix> svrmgrl <<EOF
 8: connect internal
 9: alter system switch logfile;
10: exit
11: EOF
12:
```

```
13: Unix>ls  /tmp/*.ctl
14: $ORACLE_HOME/rdbms/init*.ora
15: $ORACLE_HOME/admin/network/*.ora
16: <log_archive_dest>*.* >> hot_back.lst
```

The code in Listing 23.11 will need to be modified for the syntax of your particular backup medium and computing environment. This example uses standard UNIX commands to copy the required backup files to a tape device.

LISTING 23.11. PROCESSING FILE LIST FOR HOT BACKUP.

```
1: Unix> filesystem_backup.sh <<EOF
2: #!/bin/sh
3:
4: tar -cvf <tape device> < hot_back.lst
5: EOF
6: Unix>
7: Unix>
```

The code in Listing 23.12 can be used for UNIX raw partitions, putting 1 raw partition on a single tape. Consult your *Oracle System Administration Guide* for specifics on UNIX multi-volumn tape backup.

LISTING 23.12. PROCESSING FILE LIST FOR HOT BACKUP WITH UNIX RAW PARTITIONS.

```
1: Unix> rawpartition_backup.sh <<EOF
2: #!/bin/sh
3:
4: tar for j in \`cat hot_back.lst\`
5: do
6:     echo "Put tape in tape device 0"
7:     pause "Hit Return to continue..."
8:     dd if=$j if=/dev/rmt0
9: done
10:
11: EOF
12: Unix>
```

Listing 23.13 will end the hot tablespace backup, and Oracle will then apply any changes for the tablespace from the log files.

23

BACKUP AND
RECOVERY

LISTING 23.13 SCRIPT TO END THE TABLESPACE BACKUP MODE.

```
1: Unix> svrmgrl <<EOF
2: connect internal
3: alter tablespace <TABLESPACE NAME> end backup;
4: exit
5: EOF
```

Recovery Via Scripts

Cold backup recovery is accomplished by first taking the Oracle RDBMS completely down.

```
Unix> svrmgrl <<EOF
connect internal
shutdown abort
exit
EOF
```

After the system error/hardware failure is corrected, you can recover your Oracle database.

Load all the media from the backup. Restore all the physical tablespace files, control files, `init.ora` parameter files, and possibly the SQL*Net configuration files. Listing 23.14 shows how to restore all the files from a cold backup.

LISTING 23.14. RESTORING A COLD BACKUP.

```
1: Unix> cat >cold_rest.sh<<EOF_1
2: #!/bin/sh
3: tar xvf <tape device>
4: EOF
5:
6: Unix>
```

The following command can be used to start the database:

```
Unix> svrmgrl <<EOF
connect internal
startup
exit
EOF
```

Remember that all work since your last cold backup is lost unless some form of incremental backup has been done. Therefore, you would next have to recover your hot backups, or import any exports of changed objects.

Hot backup recovery is accomplished by recovering the damaged or lost tablespace files and applying the necessary archive log files. In Oracle7.3 and Oracle8, there are two dynamic tables, V$RECOVERY_STATUS and V$RECOVERY_FILE_STATUS, that can assist with determining the extent of recovery that is needed. If a restore of a tablespace is needed, it should be offline already; however, the following script will ensure that it is indeed offline.

```
Unix> svrmgrl <<EOF
connect internal
alter tablespace <TABLESPACE NAME> offline normal;
exit
EOF
```

Next, restore the last known hot backup. This will utilize techniques just like those in Listing 23.14.

Issue the following sequence of statements to initiate recovery:

```
Unix> svrmgrl <<EOF
connect internal
set autorecovery on;
alter database recover tablespace <TABLESPACE NAME>;
   *** dialog with operator prompting for required archive log files ***
alter tablespace <TABLESPACE NAME> online;
exit
EOF
```

The alter database recover tablespace <TABLESPACE NAME>; statement will begin a dialog with the operator, prompting the operator for the required archive log files. Consult your *Oracle Server Manual* for further details and recovery options.

23

BACKUP AND
RECOVERY

Summary

This chapter reviewed the many issues involved in protecting data from a variety of hardware and software problems that could render the data inaccessible or unusable. This chapter also reviewed various hardware and Oracle options required to create a complete backup and recovery plan. All backup scenarios are based on data-availability requirements dictated by the business needs of the data. Various methods of backup, the syntax, Oracle options, and methods of automating the backup process were all discussed.

Oracle8 Database Tuning

by Dan Hotka

IN THIS CHAPTER

Tuning Overview

This chapter will concentrate on a variety of Oracle tuning issues, beginning with some general issues surrounding tuning, such as responsibilities and timing. Oracle tuning will be covered in detail under these broad categories: operating system, Oracle RDBMS, database design, and SQL-level tuning. The chapter will conclude with a Tuning Checklist, an organized approach to Oracle tuning.

Who Is Responsible?

Several roles have responsibility for various tuning functions. All of these roles can be handled by a single person in smaller shops or by teams of people in larger shops. The system administrator needs to work closely with the database administrator to make sure the system environment is set correctly. The database administrator will handle the init.ora tuning parameters, monitoring, and I/O distribution. The DBA will work closely with the data administrator (or systems analyst) to determine object location needs. The DBA will monitor for resource-intensive SQL statements, but the developer will tune and re-implement offending SQL statements.

Proactive Tuning Versus Reactive Tuning

There are two basic modes for tuning, proactive and reactive, with corresponding rationales, planning, and responsibility. Proactive tuning involves capacity planning, including planning for the growth of objects, adequate data access response times, and financial benefits. Financial benefits can be achieved if the response times can be made adequate without having to purchase additional hardware. Reactive tuning simply addresses slow response times in response to user complaints.

Levels of Tuning

There are four distinct levels of tuning for any Oracle environment.

The first level of tuning, the operating system level, also includes the hardware platform. This level of tuning concentrates on the physical resources (CPU, memory, and disk), making sure the correct kernel parameters are set and that there is enough physical memory and disk to meet business applications needs and avoid unnecessary resource contention.

The Oracle RDBMS level of tuning consists of making sure that the available memory is being used in an efficient manner, that contention for various Oracle processes is minimal, that the database block size is correct for the efficient access of information, and that the Oracle disk-oriented resources are distributed properly.

Database design-level tuning has probably the biggest impact on how well applications will perform. Many factors have a direct impact on performance, including distributing related data objects in relation to available disk drives, controlling dynamic allocation, and avoiding fragmentation.

The final level of tuning is the SQL level. Finding and tuning a few frequently used, poorly performing or resource-intensive SQL statements can make a radical difference in performance gains to the application.

These levels are listed in the order of importance. It will be difficult to perform the next level of tuning if the prior level has not been considered and tuned. For example, you could tune SQL statements in level 4 and have performance enhancements, but if level 3 is tuned first, level 4 will have more options available and performance gains will be greater. In any tuning situation, it's best to consider each level of tuning, starting with level 1.

Operating System-Level Tuning

There are many application and Oracle sizing steps that should have been performed to ensure that the appropriate amount of hardware (CPU, memory, and disk) was purchased to support the business needs of the application. It is beyond the scope of this chapter to do this application sizing; for the examples here, we'll assume that an adequate amount of hardware was purchased. This chapter will focus on how to tune Oracle RDBMS to best take advantage of the available hardware.

The absolute very first step, even prior to installing the Oracle software, is to locate and read the *Oracle Installation Guide*. This document will discuss the latest changes in the Oracle software, options available during the installation process, and the *Oracle Optimal Flexible Architecture*. At Oracle installation time, there are many options to consider, such as database block size, the size of the original online redo log files, ARCHIVELOG mode, and so on. Considerable reactive tuning can be avoided by selecting options wisely.

24
ORACLE8
DATABASE TUNING

Memory Requirements

The *Oracle Installation Guide* will also list the correct UNIX kernel settings for several important memory parameters. Prior to installation, make sure SHMMAX (max size of a shared memory segment), SHMMHI (max number of shared memory segments), SEMMNI (minimum number of semaphores on the system), SEMMNS (max number of semaphores on the system), and SHMSEG (max number of segments per process) are all set to the recommended settings.

> **TIP**
>
> If Oracle is unable to allocate a semaphore, increase the SEMMNI and SEMMNS values. If Oracle is unable to attain shared memory, try increasing the SHMSEG value.

> **TIP**
>
> If available on your particular UNIX platform, pin or lock the SGA in physical memory to prevent it from being swapped or paged out of memory.

Use the UNIX program vmstat to monitor if the UNIX kernel is swapping processes out of memory. Swapping in an Oracle environment is not a good thing. It means some process was temporarily stored on disk to free memory for another, more urgent process to execute. If swapping is occurring, there are two options that can quickly remedy this situation. The first solution is to add more memory to the hardware platform. The second option involves the buffer-cache-hit ratio calculation (Listing 24.2) covered in depth in the next section. The size of the buffer cache can be reduced until the buffer-cache-hit ratio is adversely affected. Lowering the amount of db_block_buffers in the init.ora parameter will free physical memory. See the Oracle RDBMS level section on buffer cache tuning for a further discussion and a calculation for the buffer-cache-hit ratio.

> **TIP**
>
> Make sure there is enough memory so that there is no dynamic memory swapping occurring and the buffer-cache-hit ratio is not adversely affected.

Disk Requirements

This section will discuss disk drives (physical disk drives with UNIX file systems), raw partitions (no UNIX file system), and RAID drive technology (see Figure 24.1).

Disk drives with the UNIX file system are easy to monitor (with the sar command), easy to back up and restore, and in general, just plain easier to work with. The UNIX file system has a number of commands that allow easy access to disk drives. UNIX disk drives can be mounted most anywhere in the UNIX directory structure, adding a degree of logical application separation to multiple disk drives with the ease of access, backup and restore, and so on, all from a single UNIX directory.

FIGURE 24.1.
Raw versus file system disk access diagram.

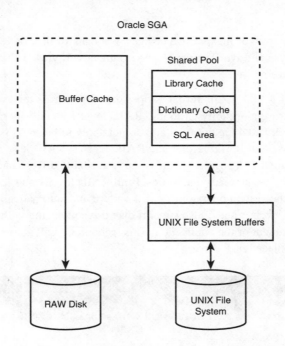

Raw partitions have no UNIX file system or the 15 percent performance overhead of UNIX file system drives. There is also about 10 percent additional disk space available without the UNIX file system overhead. Raw partitions are more difficult to administrate in general, and backup and recovery will be more complex.

> **NOTE**
>
> Raw partitions are 15 percent to 20 percent faster than file-system drives at the expense of being more difficult to administrate.

> **NOTE**
>
> Oracle Parallel Server requires the use of raw partitions for shared database files.

RAID, or redundant array of inexpensive devices, is a bank of disk drives the computer will view as one physical drive. The Oracle environment will view a single RAID device as a single disk device as well.

There are 5 levels of RAID. RAID level 0 stripes data files across the available disk drives without any mirroring or parity checking. RAID level 1 identically mirrors disk drives. RAID levels 2, 3, and 4 are not used and do not apply to business systems. RAID level 5 is a combination of RAID level 0 and RAID level 1. RAID level 5 stripes data files, mirrors the striped disk segments across many available drives, and provides parity to insure the accuracy of the reads and writes. Both RAID level 1 and RAID level 5 will automatically alert the system operator of a disk failure and automatically use the mirrored copy. RAID's levels 1 and 5 also support disk drive replacing without interruption to the UNIX environment or the application. This technology will automatically restore data to the newly replaced disk drive.

> **NOTE**
>
> RAID level 5 can have up to four physical writes for each disk write command issued.

There should be enough disk drives available on the hardware platform to separate the UNIX operating system, application software, and other UNIX processes. The Oracle software should be separated from the tablespace data files, and the SYSTEM, TEMPORARY, and ROLLBACK tablespace data files should be on separate drives as well. If the application has a lot of INSERT and UPDATE activity, the online redo logs should be on yet another separate disk drive. Depending on application needs, there should be enough disk drives to separate and load balance application I/O, enabling additional options in the database design level tuning. Each level of tuning aids the next level down. Application performance and fault-tolerant requirements will dictate the use of raw partitions and/or RAID drives. If RAID drives are utilized, RAID level 1 could have an Oracle mirrored set of redo logs (adding to the security of the data) as well as files associated with most any tablespace.

NOTE

It has been my experience that the best performance gains come from physically separating I/O traffic, something that is difficult to do with RAID level 0 and RAID level 5.

TIP

I would use RAID level 5 for mostly read applications that require a high degree of availability.

TIP

I would not use RAID technology for the SYSTEM, TEMPORARY, or ROLLBACK tablespaces unless the application demanded a fault-tolerant environment at the expense of performance.

Disk drive I/O can be monitored with the `sar -d` or `iostat -d` UNIX command. Either of these commands will report on read/write activity to all system disk drives. System administrators and/or database administrators should monitor system level disk drive I/O and make sure that it is spread as equally as possible across all available drives. Oracle database file I/O can be monitored with the Database I/O SQL statement (Listing 24.1). Review the statistics returned here with the statistics from the physical disk drives to see if object distribution within the Oracle environment is balanced and if the UNIX disk activity is balanced. If not, these statistics should help the DBA and the System Administrator determine the nature of the unbalanced disk activity.

LISTING 24.1. DATABASE I/O.

```
select b.name "File Name", a.phyrds "Physical Reads", a.phywrts "Physical
➥Writes"
from v$filestat a, v$datafile b
where a.file# = b.file#
```

24

ORACLE8 DATABASE TUNING

Oracle RDBMS-Level Tuning

Oracle RDBMS-level tuning concentrates on (1) monitoring and tuning the SGA, and (2) monitoring, tuning, and eliminating contention for various Oracle RDBMS common services such as rollback segments, online redo logs, and the TEMPORARY tablespace.

The System Global Area or SGA is comprised of several memory structures (see Figure 24.2). The SGA is comprised of the buffer cache, the log buffer, the sort area, and the shared pool, which consists of the library cache, the dictionary cache, and the SQL area.

FIGURE 24.2.

Oracle8 System Global Area.

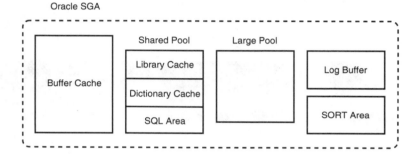

The buffer cache holds the database blocks read from disk. If other processes can use a data block already in the buffer cache to satisfy an I/O request, Oracle does not have to do a physical I/O, a time-consuming task. Oracle uses a least-recently-used (LRU) algorithm to keep the most active data blocks in the buffer cache. The size of the buffer cache is determined by the init.ora parameter DB_BLOCK_BUFFERS. The SQL statement in Listing 24.2 will calculate a buffer-cache-hit ratio. This ratio varies greatly depending on the type of application or applications utilizing the Oracle RDBMS.

TIP

Increase the DB_BLOCK_BUFFERS until the buffer-cache-hit ratio is unaffected by additional amounts of DB_BLOCK_BUFFERS. Then decrease the DB_BLOCK_BUFFERS until the buffer-cache-hit ratio begins to be adversely affected. This is the best way to determine the optimal size of the buffer cache.

LISTING 24.2. BUFFER-CACHE-HIT RATIO CALCULATION.

```
select round(((sum(decode(name,'db block gets',value))
        +   sum(decode(name,'consistent gets',value)))
        -   sum(decode(name,'physical reads',value))) /
```

```
            (sum(decode(name,'db block gets',value)) +
        +   sum(decode(name,'consistent gets',value))) * 100)
"Buffer Cache Hit Ratio"
from v$sysstat
```

The log buffer, or the redo log buffer, contains all the changed data blocks. These changed blocks are then written to the redo log files in a contiguous manner by the Oracle log-writer process. If the redo buffer waits, from the calculation in the following code, is greater than zero, processes are waiting for space to become available in the redo log buffer. Increase the init.ora parameter LOG_BUFFER and periodically check this calculation again.

```
select sum(value) "Redo Buffer Waits" from v$sysstat where name = 'redo
➡log space wait time'
```

The sort area is any SQL statement "order by" clause's work area. For peak performance, all sorts, or the majority of sorts, should be done in memory. The calculation in the following code will determine the number of disk sorts performed. Tune this area much like the buffer cache: increase the init.ora parameter SORT_AREA_SIZE until the result of the disk sorts calculation decrease's. Then reduce the SORT_AREA_SIZE init.ora parameter until the disk sorts increase. The point at which the disk sorts increase will be the optimal setting for this parameter.

```
select value "Disk Sorts" from v$sysstat where name = 'sorts (disk)'
```

The shared pool consists of the buffer areas library cache, dictionary cache, and the SQL area. The entire pool size is determined by the init.ora parameter SHARED_POOL_SIZE. The library cache keeps track of shared SQL and shared PL/SQL. Any SQL statement that matches the text of a SQL statement already in the SQL area has already been parsed. It is important that all SQL code follow coding standards so identical SQL statements in different applications even have the same upper/lowercase attributes. The library cache ratio (see the following code) should be below 1 percent. There are two solutions for an unacceptable ratio: increase the init.ora parameter SHARED_POOL_SIZE or make similar SQL statements identical.

```
Select (sum(reloads) / sum(pins))* 100 "Library Cache Ratio" from
➡v$librarycache
```

The other cache in the shared pool is the dictionary cache. The dictionary cache is similar in function to the library cache but is used for the Oracle dictionary SQL statements. If the dictionary-cache-hit ratio (see the following code) is greater than 10 percent, increase the SHARED_POOL_SIZE init.ora parameter.

```
select (sum(getmisses) / sum(gets) ) * 100 "Dictionary Cache Ratio" from
➡v$rowcache
```

If there is always free space in the shared pool, increasing the SHARED_POOL_SIZE will have no affect; the problem is dissimilar SQL statements. The following code (the shared-pool free memory SQL statement) monitors the size of the shared pool:

```
select bytes "Shared Pool Free Memory" from v$sgastat where name = `free
➥memory'
```

The large pool was introduced by Oracle8 to help alleviate contention in the shared pool. The large pool is defined by setting the LARGE_POOL_SIZE and LARGE_POOL_MIN_ALLOC parameters in the init.ora file. If defined, memory for session processes for the multi-threaded server and I/O buffer space for Oracle backup processes. The default behavior of these processes is to use the share pool.

Online redo logs, or redo logs, give the Oracle database the ability to recover from media failure. The backup/recovery options of this Oracle feature are covered in Chapter 23, "Backup and Recovery." The size and number of redo logs needed have a direct relationship to the frequency of hot backups, checkpointing, and the size of the redo logs. If the archive logs are being created frequently, depending on data availability needs, it may be desirable to make the redo logs larger and review the timings of hot backups and check-pointing. The redo log buffer can be monitored with the redo-log-waits SQL statement in the following code. If the log waits are greater than zero, processes are waiting for space in the redo log buffer. Increase the init.ora parameter LOG_BUFFER to correct this issue.

```
select value "Redo Log Waits" from v$sysstat where name = 'redo log space
➥requests'
```

Rollback segments give the Oracle RDBMS its read-consistency ability. These segments are stored in tablespace structures and are basically before-images of data blocks. They are similar to table and index objects in that they have similar storage parameters and grow by dynamically adding extents. They differ from other data objects in the fact that they have an "optimal size" feature that they will return to after dynamically extending. They are circular in nature, in that before-image data blocks are added in a sequential manner. When the end of the segment is reached, it wraps back to the beginning and continues writing. If the rollback segment is not large enough for the transaction that is using it, the error snapshot too old will be issued and the transaction will be rolled back. Single transactions cannot use more than one rollback segment at a time. Transactions can be pointed to particular rollback segments, particularly nice for known large transactions; they can be assigned to a large rollback segment. They need to be large enough to contain the largest update expected by a single transaction. The rollback segment space is made available again after a commit or rollback SQL statement marks the conclusion of the transaction. Rollback segments can be public (used by any data-base instance) or private (only used by the instance they are associated with). These rollback segments also play an important part of instance recovery. It is the job of these rollback segments to roll back any uncommitted transactions after an abnormal termination of the Oracle RDBMS or after a SHUTDOWN ABORT.

> **TIP**
>
> I recommend putting the rollback segments in their own tablespace for I/O distribution purposes.

The optimal-size option of rollback segments is nice for that occasional but not frequent large update. The rollback segment will dynamically grow while saving the before datablock images during the course of the update. After a commit or rollback, the rollback segment will release the extra extents and return to the optimal size.

> **TIP**
>
> Set the optimal size for the rollback segments for the typical transaction size expected. Assign large transactions to a large rollback segment.

If transactions have to wait for available rollback segments, there are not enough rollback segments. Use the following code (rollback segment waits SQL statement) to monitor for waits:

```
select waits "Rollback Segment Waits" from v$rollstat
```

The following code shows the syntax for implementing the rollback segment optimal size option. In this example, optimal size is set to 150KB, so once the rollback segment added 3 extents (the storage clause of this example has the extents at 50KB each), the Oracle RDBMS will maintain the size of this rollback segment from this time on at 3 extents. The optimal size option is a nice automatic rollback segment resizing feature but at considerable overhead for the Oracle RDBMS.

```
CREATE public rollback segment rb_1
tablespace <tablespace name>
storage (initial 50K next 50K OPTIMAL 150K maxextents 10)
```

If rollback segment shrinks (see the following code) or continually grows, the DBA should research the application that is consistently having large update transactions and assign the transaction to its own rollback segment, or make the default size of the rollback segments larger.

```
Select shrinks "Rollback Segment Shrinks" from v$rollstat
```

24

ORACLE8 DATABASE TUNING

init.ora Parameters

The init<Oracle SID>.ora file is the startup parameter file that Oracle uses to size the SGA, determine ARCHIVELOG mode, and so on. The rest of this section is a list of the more important init.ora parameters and a brief description of what each affects and how it should be set. Listing 24.3 is an example init.ora file from an Oracle 8.0.3.

LISTING 24.3. EXAMPLE INIT.ORA PARAMETER FILE.

```
db_name = oracle
db_files = 20
control_files = (/ora8/v8.0.3/dbs/initORA8.ora,
/disk2/ora8_control_file/initORA8.ora)

db_file_multiblock_read_count =  8

db_block_buffers =  200

shared_pool_size =  50000

log_checkpoint_interval = 10000

processes =  150

dml_locks =  200

log_buffer =  8192

sequence_cache_entries =  10

sequence_cache_hash_buckets =  10

# audit_trail = true t
# timed_statistics = true

# log_archive_start = true

background_dump_dest=/ora8/v8.0.3/trace
user_dump_dest=/ora8/v8.0.3/trace

db_block_size = 2048
```

BACKGROUND_DUMP_DEST is the directory location where the alert.log and any trace files will be created.

CHECKPOINT_PROCESS is set to true or false depending on whether checkpointing is desired. Checkpointing creates a quiet point in the database when all buffered information is written to disk. A mark is placed in the archive log files that indicates a checkpoint happened. Checkpointing happens at archive log file switches or when the number of blocks defined in `log_checkpoint_interval` is reached.

`CONTROL_FILES` lists the Oracle-maintained control files. I highly recommend listing at least three, each on separate disk drives. To create additional control files, simply copy the original to the new locations with the Oracle database in a shutdown state. List all control files with their full path and they will be automatically maintained by the Oracle RDBMS.

`DB_BLOCK_BUFFERS` is the size of the buffer cache in the SGA.

`DB_BLOCK_SIZE` is the size of the database blocks. It is used in the `CREATE DATABASE` SQL statement and appears here basically for reference.

`DB_FILES` determines how many operating-system files Oracle can have access to at any one time. The online redo logs are part of this number as well. This parameter does cause SGA space to be used.

`DB_FILE_MULTI_BLOCK_READ_COUNT` is how many blocks will be read with each read request. This value×`DB_BLOCK_SIZE` should equal 64KB.

`HASH_JOIN_ENABLE` defaults to `true`, enabling memory hash joins (discussed in the "SQL-Level Tuning" section later in this chapter).

`HASH_AREA_SIZE` defaults to twice the `SORT_AREA_SIZE`.

`HASH_MULTI_BLOCK_IO_COUNT` defaults to `DB_FILE_MULTI_BLOCK_READ_COUNT`.

`LARGE_POOL_SIZE` defaults to 0 and can be specified in KB or MB.

`LARGE_POOL_MIN_ALLOC` is the minimum size of the large pool.

`LOG_ARCHIVE_BUFFERS` and `LOG_ARCHIVE_BUFFER_SIZE` deal with the writing of the online redo logs to the archive logs. These parameters may need to be increased only if archiving directly to tape devices and the redo log buffers are waiting on archive log buffers to become available.

`LOG_ARCHIVE_DEST` is where the archive logs are created if log archive mode is enabled.

`LOG_ARCHIVE_FORMAT` determines the naming convention used for the archive logs created.

`LOG_ARCHIVE_START` enables or disables the log archive mode.

`LOG_BUFFER` determines the size of the redo log buffer in the SGA.

`LOG_CHECKPOINT_INTERVAL` is used to determine the frequency of checkpointing. This number is set to the number of redo buffer blocks processed before taking a checkpoint.

24

ORACLE8 DATABASE TUNING

MAX_ROLLBACK_SEGMENTS identifies the maximum number of rollback segments that can be kept available for user processes.

OPTIMIZER_GOAL is used by the cost-based optimizer and can globally force an applications default behavior by specifying FIRST_ROWS or ALL_ROWS.

OPTIMIZER_MODE defaults to COST and will use the cost-based optimizer if there are collected statistics. Changing this parameter to RULE will use the rule based optimizer unless SQL hints are specified. If CHOOSE is specified and any of the objects involved have statistics, Oracle will use the cost-based optimizer.

ROLLBACK_SEGMENTS identifies rollback segments by name, assigning them to this Oracle environment.

SHARED_POOL_SIZE is the size of the shared pool in the SGA.

SHARED_POOL_RESERVED_SIZE is used for packages.

SHARED_POOL_RESERVED_MIN_ALLOC is the minimum memory allotment.

SORT_AREA_SIZE is the size of the sort area in the SGA.

SQL_TRACE is used to collect tuning statistics from the Oracle environment. It is set to false by default.

TIMED_STATISTICS is used by some v$ table statistics that are relative to clock time. It is set to false by default.

Database Design-Level Tuning

Database design-level tuning builds on the disk I/O distribution concept discussed in the O/S Level tuning section. It is important for this level of tuning to have multiple disk drives available. The DBA and System Admininstrator may need to monitor and redistribute disk I/O while tuning in this manner. It is important to locate related objects on different disk drives, preferably on different disk controllers as well. Physical location of related objects (including those involved with referential integrity) will have a direct effect on performance. The better the I/O distribution on the available disk drives, the better overall performance will be.

An extent is a unit of storage, a contiguous group of data blocks, that is used by data-oriented objects such as tables and indexes. The storage clause either is the default storage clause of the tablespace or is defined at CREATE <object type> SQL statement. When objects use up all the data blocks in the initial extent, Oracle creates the next extent, based again on parameters from the storage clause, and the object then begins storing data in this next extent. The adding of additional extents is known as *dynamic allocation* and is an expensive and time-consuming process for Oracle. Size INITIAL EXTENT and NEXT EXTENT accurately to limit the amount of dynamic allocation that occurs. Row chaining and row migrations are also expensive processes for Oracle. How these occur is discussed in depth in the following section on fragmentation. It suffices to say that a significant amount of row chaining and row migration will have a negative impact on performance and is easy to avoid.

Table/Index Relationships and Tablespaces

The more evenly I/O is spread across many data-related devices, the better performance is going to be. There are many techniques for striping or placing parts of objects (both table and index) across many available disk drives. RAID technology can stripe data from a hardware point of view, spreading small but even-sized increments of data files across many disk drives. Oracle8 supports partitioning that easily puts portions of tables and indexes in many tablespaces.

> **TIP**
>
> Treat RAID partitions as separate disk drives. It will defeat the purpose of distributing the I/O if related objects all use the same RAID devices.

Review the FROM and WHERE clauses of frequently used or large result set SELECT statements. Try to keep the indexes on separate disk drives from the tables. Referential integrity can make this selection distribution easy. Always put the parent table, child tables, and the primary/foreign key indexes all on separate disk drives if possible.

The SQL statement in Listing 24.4 can be used to monitor both growth and the number of extents, as well as the maximum number of extents assigned.

24

ORACLE8
DATABASE TUNING

LISTING 24.4. SEGMENT GROWTH AND EXTENT ASSIGNMENT.

```
SELECT   tablespace_name "TABLESPACE",
         segment_name "SEMENT",
         extents "EXTENTS",
         max_extents "MAX EXTENTS",
         bytes "SIZE",
         owner "OWNER"
  FROM   dba_segments
 WHERE   owner not in ('SYS','SYSTEM','SCOTT','NET_CONF')
   and   extents > 1
ORDER BY tablespace_name,owner,segment_name;
```

Partitioning

Oracle8 partitioning takes advantage of all the benefits of tablespaces discussed so far. Oracle8 can partition or distribute table data and index leaves across many tablespaces based on key fields. Figure 24.3 shows what the famous DEPT table might look like after being partitioned on the field DEPT_NO. The DEPT table contains 4 rows with DEPT_NO equal to 10, 20, 30, and 40.

FIGURE 24.3.

DEPT *table parti-tioned.*

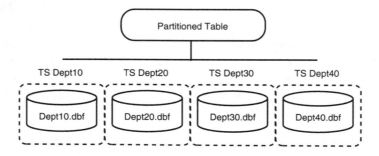

Partitioned tables/indexes are nothing more than a logical collection of tablespaces. The partition levels can be accessed individually, or the entire structure can be accessed as traditional or nonpartitioned tables are today. This flexibility can greatly enhance an application's performance and availability.

Partitioning greatly enhances database performance. I/O activity can be easily distributed because existing partitions are easy to split. The Oracle optimizer recognizes partitions and can select only from partitions that contain the data being selected. The Oracle Parallel Server utilizes the number of partitions to determine how to divide the query work.

With partitioning, availability is higher, backups are easier, recovery is shorter. Partitions can be backed up online, taking advantage of the hot backup benefits tablespaces already have. This makes the backup/recovery process much quicker. If media recovery is needed on a particular tablespace that belongs to a partitioned object, the unaffected parts of the object (the other partitions) are accessible.

Partitions must contain fields only from the object and may contain one or more fields. More than one field would be a multicolumn partition key. Partitions can share tablespaces or have one partition per tablespace. Tablespaces still have the same space attributes, backup/recovery, and so on, as nonpartitioned tablespaces. It is a good idea to use the MAXVALUE on the final partition to eliminate the chance of getting a 1440: Inserted partition key is beyond highest legal partition key.

Partition tables may *not* contain LONG, LONG RAW, or LARGE OBJECTS (LOB).

The example in Listing 24.5 of the familiar EMP table has a partition key on DEPTNO, putting DEPTNO values greater than 30 in partition P40. Note the naming conventions. Partitions must have a name but, like the tablespace names, they do not have to follow any particular pattern. The names here give some meaning to what data is actually being stored in the partition. This will be helpful for end users and/or developers accessing data by partition only.

LISTING 24.5. PARTITION TABLE EMP EXAMPLE.

```
create table EMP (
  EMPNO               NUMBER(4) NOT NULL,
  ENAME               VARCHAR2(10),
  JOB                  VARCHAR2(9),
  MGR                 NUMBER(4),
  HIREDATE        DATE,
  SAL                   NUMBER(7,2),
  COMM              NUMBER(7,2),
  DEPTNO           NUMBER(2) NOT NULL)
partition by range(DEPTNO)
(partition P10 values less than(11) tablespace TS_EMP_10,
 partition P20 values less than(21) tablespace TS_EMP_20,
 partition P30 values less than(31) tablespace TS_EMP_30,
 partition P40 values less than (MAXVALUE) tablespace TS_EMP40);
```

The following code (query and DML examples) demonstrates how individual partitions can easily be accessed.

```
select ENAME,SAL from EMP partition (P30);

update EMP partition (P20)
   set SAL = SAL * 10;
```

This next example, Listing 24.6, utilizes a multicolumn partition key. The value here is that once the data in a certain partition is no longer needed, the whole partition can simply be dropped.

LISTING 24.6. MULTICOLUMN PARTITION KEY EXAMPLE.

```
create table  ORDERS  (
  ORDID               NUMBER (4) NOT NULL,
  ORDERDATE          DATE,
  COMMPLAN           VARCHAR2 (1),
  CUSTID             NUMBER (6) NOT NULL,
  SHIPDATE_MM        NUMBER (2) NOT NULL,
  SHIPDATE_YY        NUMBER (2) NOT NULL,
```

24

ORACLE8
DATABASE TUNING

continues

LISTING 24.6. CONTINUED

```
TOTAL                NUMBER (8,2)
partition by range (SHIPDATE_YY,SHIPDATE_MM)
partition Q197 values less than(97,04) tablespace TS_Q197,
partition Q297 values less than(97,07) tablespace TS_Q297,
     .
     .
     .
```

Partitions are easy to administrate. Partitions can be moved between tablespaces, they can be divided into additional partitions, they can be truncated, added, or dropped, and they can be individually queried, updated, inserted, and deleted from. Listing 24.7 displays some new SQL syntax that perform's these basic administrative functions.

LISTING 24.7. PARTITIONING SQL ADMINISTRATIVE EXAMPLES.

```
ALTER TABLE ADD PARTITION
ALTER TABLE DROP PARTITION
ALTER TABLE MOVE PARTITION
ALTER TABLE SPLIT PARTITION
ALTER TABLE TRUNCATE PARITITION
ALTER TABLE EXCHANGE PARITITION
```

Indexes don't necessarily have to be partitioned. DBAs and developers have a range of options based on their availability, performance, and/or management needs.

Indexes can be equi-partitioned; that is, they can be partitioned with the same number of partitions as the underlying table. These indexes are well suited for primary key/foreign key indexes. There are four other types of indexes: prefixed, nonprefixed, local, and global.

Listing 24.8 would create an equi-partitioned index for the EMP table created previously.

LISTING 24.8. EQUI-PARTITIONED INDEX.

```
create index IDX_EMP on EMP (DEPTNO)
local
partition by range(DEPTNO)
(partition Pi10 values less than(11) tablespace TS_INX_EMP_10,
 partition Pi20 values less than(21) tablespace TS_INX_EMP_20,
 partition Pi30 values less than(31) tablespace TS_INX_EMP_30,
partition Pi40 values less than (MAXVALUE) tablespace TS_INX_EMP_40);
```

Prefixed indexes are those where the indexed columns are the exact same key as the table partition key. Nonprefixed indexes are *not* based on the table partition key. Local indexes are equi-partitioned indexes, that is, they have the same number of partitions and key divisions as the table. Global indexes are not equi-partitioned; they can have a different number of partitions from that of the table and contain different key data.

Listing 24.9 is an example of a local prefixed index from the EMP table. Notice the index column is the same as that of the EMP partition key (prefixed) and there are the same number of partitions (local).

LISTING 24.9. LOCAL PREFIXED PARTITIONED INDEX.

```
create index IDX_EMP on EMP (DEPTNO)
local
partition by range(DEPTNO)
(partition Pi10 values less than(11) tablespace TS_INX_EMP_10,
 partition Pi20 values less than(21) tablespace TS_INX_EMP_20,
 partition Pi30 values less than(31) tablespace TS_INX_EMP_30,
partition Pi40 values less than (MAXVALUE) tablespace
TS_INX_EMP_40);
```

Listing 24.10 is an example of a nonprefixed local index. Notice the index column and partition key are different from the previous EMP table.

LISTING 24.10. LOCAL NONPREFIXED PARTITIONED INDEX.

```
create index IDX2_EMP on EMP (EMPNO)
local
partition by range(EMPNO)
(partition P1 values less than(11) tablespace TS2_INX_EMP_10,
 partition P2 values less than(MAXVALUE) tablespace TS2_INX_EMP_20);
```

The flowchart, shown in Figure 24.4, should help you decide which partition index combination is best for particular application needs.

Controlling Fragmentation

Fragmentation is best described as a grouping of noncontiguous database objects. Fragmentation usually means extra resources are consumed (disk I/O, rotational delay of the disk drives, dynamic extensions, chained blocks, and so on) to perform the requested database function. Not all fragmentation is bad. Consider disk striping. Striping is spreading fragments out over multiple disks to aid in distributing I/O.

Most fragmentation in the Oracle environment is not the good kind, though. Tablespace fragmentation doesn't necessarily affect performance, but a significant amount of disk space can be wasted. Deletes can leave unused space behind in data blocks and leave smaller disk segments unused in the tablespace, wasting tablespace space. The Oracle process PMON periodically coalesces contiguous unused smaller extents into single larger available extents but does not reshuffle used extents so that all free space in the tablespace is together. The only way to fix wasted space in blocks is to export the data, drop the object, and then import the data back. The only way to fix unused tablespace due to fragmentation is to reorganize the whole tablespace.

FIGURE 24.4.

Partitioning Index Decision Tree.

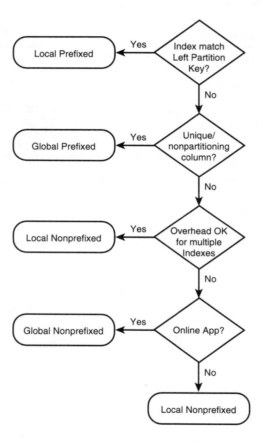

Extent interleaving occurs when two or more data objects in the same tablespace are dynamically growing in such a way that extents are no longer contiguous with the other extents of the object. Oracle performs best with a minimal number of extents, and when extents are next to each other. The fewer extents, the fewer trips Oracle has to make to the data dictionary to find out where the next extent is. Having extents sprinkled all over the tablespace also causes excessive disk head movement (*disk thrashing*), a time-consuming I/O bottleneck. Objects that are involved in this interleaving should be exported, dropped, and re-created. Extent interleaving can be completely eliminated by simply putting tables with static or very little growth together in a tablespace and putting each dynamically growing object in a tablespace by itself. This increases tablespace maintenance but eliminates this type of fragmentation.

There are two events that will cause an extra read/write process for Oracle per row being accessed. These events are row chaining and row migration. They differ in what actually happens, but the end result is the same: extra I/O to read or write the desired information.

Row chaining is caused when a row being inserted is larger than the Oracle block size. Oracle will *chain*, or link by block number, an additional block (or blocks) to hold the remaining data from the row. This chained block is not indexed and cannot be referenced without first referencing the original block. This greatly slows the data access as Oracle has to wait for an additional I/O to retrieve the chained block. If there is significant chaining, performance can be seriously affected. The only way to correct chaining is to export the whole database, initialize the database with a larger block size, and then import the whole database, or locate the object and its data into an Oracle database that already has a larger block size.

Row migration is caused by an update that grows the row past available space in its current block. Oracle will relocate the updated row to a different block where it will completely fit, leaving a ROWID pointer in the original block that references the new row location in another block. Like row chaining, there is no other way to access this row in the new location except by accessing the original location first. Once again, Oracle will have to wait while an additional disk I/O is performed to retrieve the new row. It can also be a time-consuming process for Oracle to locate a new data block with enough free space to hold the new row. Row migration can be limited by making adjustments to the PCTFREE parameters in the storage clause. PCTFREE is the amount of space left in each Oracle block after insertions for the purpose of accommodating future updates. Altering the PCTFREE clause will not have any affect on any existing migrated rows. The table will have to be exported, dropped, and then imported.

SQL-Level Tuning

SQL-level tuning is the final area of tuning. The 80/20 rule applies very well here. Twenty percent of the SQL statements will utilize over 80 percent of the resources. It is this 20 percent that needs to be well tuned.

There are various monitoring tools available, discussed in detail in Chapter 22, "Oracle8 Tools," that can identify resource-intensive and/or long-running SQL statements. Tuning these will have the biggest impact on application performance. There are also a variety of explain-plan tools available from Oracle Corporation and other vendors. Oracle Enterprise Manager has a SQL-monitor tool available. Oracle has always provided a variety of ways of capturing performance information in the form of trace files. These trace files are interpreted by TKPROF, a tool not for the novice. The remainder of this chapter will discuss various features of tuning at the SQL level, the two optimizer choices, indexing features, and the SQL statements themselves.

Application Code

There are some features that aid in

- The run-time performance of applications, namely procedures, functions, and triggers
- Better design of SQL statements
- The use of unrecoverable transactions
- Pinning application code in the shared pool
- External procedures

Oracle8 implemented a new ROWID format. It uses 64-bit encoding. For sizing purposes, ROWID takes 10 positions in the row. The ROWID contains an object number (6 positions), file number (3 positions), block number (6 positions), and slot number (3 positions). Oracle8 refers to the old ROWID format as *restricted* ROWID).

Oracle supports the compilation of functions, procedures, and triggers (procedural objects). The resulting p-code is stored in the data dictionary, along with the procedural object. The p-code is then used when the objects are referenced, saving considerable run-time time by not having to create the p-code on demand. The compiler is automatically invoked when the procedural object is created or altered. Changes to the table structures can invalidate procedural objects, requiring them to be compiled again at run time. The following code shows the SQL syntax for invoking the compiler.

```
alter procedure <PROCEDURE NAME> compile
alter function <FUNCTION NAME> compile
alter trigger <TRIGGER NAME> compile
```

If the procedure or function is part of a package, the whole package can be compiled or just the body.

```
alter package <PACKAGE NAME> compile package
alter package <PACKAGE NAME> compile body
```

Some SQL statements with nested subqueries can create an enormous amount of I/O traffic. Let's consider the examples in Listings 24.11 and 24.12. Listing 24.11 is a correlated subquery where the inner query is executed one time for each row returned by the outer query. Listing 24.12 produces the same result but with less I/O as it queries the look up table (the subquery of Listing 24.11) once, not once per each row.

LISTING 24.11. CORRELATED SQL STATEMENT.

```
update EMP
set sal = sal * 10
where exists
    (select 'x' from DEPT
      where DEPT.deptno = EMP.deptno)
```

LISTING 24.12. PL/SQL LOOP EXAMPLE.

```
DECLARE
cursor c1 is select deptno from dept;
work_deptno  number;
BEGIN
open c1;
loop
    fetch c1 into work_deptno;
    EXIT when c1%NOTFOUND
update emp
    set sal = sal * 10
    where deptno = work_deptno;
end loop;
END;
```

Unrecoverable transactions are simply transactions that are not recoverable via the Oracle recovery processes. They do not use the rollback segments, the online redo, or, if implemented, the archive log processes. The UNRECOVERABLE clause can be used with create table <TABLE NAME> as select …, create index <INDEX NAME>, and alter table <TABLE NAME> add constraint …. SQL*Loader with the direct path option does not use any of Oracle's transaction-consistency or recovery features either. If any of these processes fails, the creator may need to manually drop the objects being loaded or created and re-execute the process.

The dbms_shared_pool package can be used to lock packages, procedures, and functions in the shared pool. Likewise, when these packages, procedures, and functions are no longer required, the dbms_shared_pool package can also remove these locked packages from the shared pool (see the following example syntax).

```
dbms_shared_pool.keep('<PROCEDURE NAME>')
dbms_shared_pool.unkeep('<PROCEDURE NAME>')
```

24

ORACLE8 DATABASE TUNING

External procedures were introduced with Oracle8. They allow additional functionality between the database and other external systems. These external procedures can be referenced in PL/SQL, which utilizes the Net8 listener process to call the external routine (C program today, futures include C++, Java, and CORBA). The Net8 listener calls `extproc`, which in turn executes the external routine. The `extproc` will also pass any returned values back to the originating PL/SQL routine via the listener. Figure 24.5 illustrates a simple call from a PL/SQL routine on one machine, utilizing the listener, accessing a "c" program that sends a fax.

FIGURE 24.5.

External procedure call.

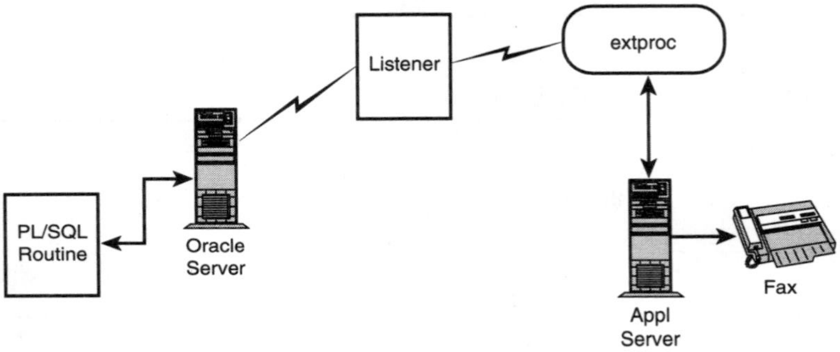

Indexing

Oracle7 introduced several new indexing options that improve on the traditional B*tree indexes. Oracle7 introduced star queries, histograms, and hash joins. Oracle8 introduced bitmap indexes, index-only tables, and reverse key indexes.

Bitmap indexes are for those columns in larger tables that have just a few possible values such as sex fields, color fields, and so on. A bitmap index is really just a two dimensional array of bits with one axis containing the index values and the other axis containing a bit position for each row in the table. Oracle can quickly find rows in the index by simply searching for nonzero values. Figure 24.6 pictures how the famous EMP table might look in a bitmap index.

FIGURE 24.6.

EMP bitmap index.

	Rows													
	1	2	3	4	5	6	7	8	9	.	.	.		
10	1	0	0	1	0	1	0	0	0	1	1	0	0	0
20	0	0	1	0	0	0	1	0	0	0	0	0	1	0
30	0	1	0	0	1	0	0	1	0	0	0	0	0	1
40	0	0	0	0	0	0	0	0	1	0	0	1	0	0

Low-cardinality indexes are easily identified for possible bitmap indexes. The SQL statement in the following code will return a list of existing indexes with just a few distinct values.

```
select owner "Owner", index_name "Index Name", distinct_keys "Distinct
➥Keys"
from DBA_INDEXES
where distinct_keys < 15
```

A star query involves one larger table being joined with several smaller tables, where the larger table has a concatenated index key and each of the smaller tables is referenced by part of that concatenated key. The Oracle cost-based optimizer (cost-based optimizer details later in this chapter) recognizes this arrangement and builds a memory-based temporary table very similar to a cluster of all of the smaller tables.

A histogram might be useful when some column values occur more often than others so that there is not an even distribution of values throughout the object. Prior to histograms, the cost-based optimizer assumed even distribution of values throughout the object. Think of histograms as a series of buckets making up a percentage of the size of an object (see Figure 24.7). Histograms come in two flavors: width-balanced and height-balanced. Width-balance is where the values are divided into an even number of buckets and the optimizer can easily determine which buckets have a higher count. In height-balanced histograms, each bucket has the same number of column values, but a column value may span more than one bucket. Figure 24.7 illustrates what the EMP table might look like in both kinds of histograms.

FIGURE 24.7.

EMP *histogram.*

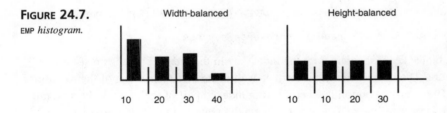

Histograms are implemented via the analyze SQL statement by specifying column parameter. Histograms defaults to 75 buckets; a maximum of 255 buckets can be defined. Histograms can be created for indexes, tables, or clusters.

> **NOTE**
>
> Histogram information can be viewed by accessing USER_HISTOGRAMS, ALL_HIS-
> TOGRAMS, or DBA_HISTOGRAMS. The number of buckets in a column's histogram
> can be viewed by accessing USER_TAB_COLUMNS, ALL_TAB_COLUMNS, or
> DBA_TAB_COLUMNS.

Hash joins greatly enhance the performance of two joined tables, where one table is significantly larger than the other. Hash joins replace the "sort-merge" join algorithm and is only supported by the cost-based optimizer. The hash join works by splitting two tables into partitions. A partition is read into memory and a hash table is created. This hash table is then used to map join columns from the other table, eliminating the sometimes resource-expensive sort-merge. In the hash join method, both tables are scanned only once. In sort-merge, the smaller table can actually be read many times. The sort-merge works by sorting the two result sets being joined over the join columns and then merging the results via the join columns. Hash joins are only supported by the cost-based optimizer and are implemented by the init.ora parameters HASH_JOIN_ENABLED, HASH_MULTI-BLOCK_IO_COUNT, and HASH_AREA_SIZE.

The reverse-key index reverses the order of the bytes of the key but keeps the order of the keys in a concatenated key. Reverse-key indexes are really useful in keeping the index balanced with sequence-number type keys. Regular indexes can be made reverse key, and reverse-key indexes can be made regular (see the following syntax examples).

```
create index <INDEX NAME> on <TABLE NAME> (<COLUMN NAME(S)>) reverse

alter index <INDEX NAME> rebuild noreverse/reverse
```

Index-only tables keeps the data with the index key in the index. There is no separate table structure. The index will not perform as well if the data takes most of the room in the block. The overflow option is where the nonindexed part of the row will be stored if the row size is over the percentage given. This will create a similar effect to that of row chaining. Index-only tables may not be replicated, they have additional indexes, and partitioning will be supported in Oracle8.1. Listing 24.13 is a syntax example for index-only tables.

> **TIP**
>
> The smaller tables associated with a star query are an excellent use for index-
> only tables.

LISTING 24.13. INDEX-ONLY TABLE SYNTAX.

```
create table <TABLE NAME>
    (field descriptions
    .
    .
    <FIELD NAME>
    primary key (<KEY FIELDS>))
organization index tablespace <TABLESPACE NAME>
pctthreshold 20
overflow tablespace <TABLESPACE NAME>
```

Parsing

When Oracle receives a SQL statement for processing, it parses it, checking it for proper syntax, and develops an execution plan for that particular query. This execution plan can be visualized with the explain-plan feature described in detail later in this chapter. Oracle7 introduced the shared SQL area, where identical (and I do mean identical) SQL statements need not be reparsed but can be stored in memory for possible reuse. The SQL area, combined with the library and dictionary cache, comprises the shared pool, and allows identical, frequently used SQL statements to be parsed only once. Tuning this area is discussed in the "Oracle RDBMS-Level Tuning" section earlier in this chapter.

Optimizers

Oracle8 supports two optimizers, the rule-based optimizer and the cost-based optimizer. The optimizers tell Oracle the best execution path for a particular SQL statement. The rule-based optimizer is the original Oracle optimizer. The cost-based optimizer was introduced with Oracle6.

The rule-based optimizer uses a series of 19 rules to decide this path (see Table 24.1). The lower the rank, the more performance benefit from the rule. Tuning is accomplished by making the rule-based optimizer make different selections. For example, adding an index would alter the rule selection, as would adding a function to an indexed field in a WHERE clause of a SQL statement (used to disable the use of an index), and most important, the way the SQL statement is coded has a great effect on which rules are selected. There is the concept of a driving table, or the table that will be compared to the others in a join SQL statement (multiple tables listed in the FROM clause). Since Oracle parses SQL statements from end to front, the driving table in a rule-based optimized SQL statement will be the last one listed in the SQL statement. There are a few other dependencies that can affect this decision, but for the most part, sometimes performance gains can be substantial just by changing the order of the tables in the FROM clause.

> **NOTE**
>
> There is no guarantee between releases of Oracle that the rank and order processing of these rules remains constant. It is important to test applications when moving to newer versions of Oracle software.

TABLE 24.1. RULES FOR RULE-BASED OPTIMIZER.

Rank	Where clause predicates
1	ROWID = constant
2	unique indexed column = constant
3	entire unique concatenated index = constant
4	entire cluster key = cluster key of object in same cluster
5	entire cluster key = constant
6	entire nonunique concatenated index = constant
7	nonunique index = constant
8	entire noncompressed concatenated index >= constant
9	entire compressed concatenated index >= constant
10	partial but leading columns of noncompressed concatenated index
11	partial but leading columns of compressed concatenated index
12	unique indexed column using the SQL statement BETWEEN or LIKE options
13	nonunique indexed column using the SQL statement BETWEEN or LIKE options
14	unique indexed column < or > constant
15	nonunique indexed column < or > constant
16	sort/merge
17	MAX or MIN SQL statement functions on indexed column
18	ORDER BY entire index
19	full table scans

The cost-based optimizer makes its decisions based on a cost factor, derived from precollected statistics for the objects in the SQL statement. The ANALYZE SQL statement is used to collect these statistics. Since larger objects take longer to collect the statistics, Oracle offers an ESTIMATE option on the ANALYZE command so that only a percentage of rows are used to gather the statistics. Since the cost-based optimizer bases its execution-path decisions strictly on these collected statistics, it is important to keep the statistics current with dynamically changing objects.

> **NOTE**
>
> The rule-based optimizer does *not* support partitioned tables, index-only tables, reverse indexes, histograms, hash joins, bitmap indexes, parallel query, star joins, or basically any new indexing/performance feature since Oracle7.3.

Enabling the cost-based optimizer is accomplished by running the ANALYZE command to collect statistics. The init.ora parameter, OPTIMIZER_MODE, must be set to CHOOSE or COST, or can be set at the user session level with the ALTER SESSION command. Disabling the cost-based optimizer is easily done by either resetting the init.ora parameter OPTIMIZER_MODE or simply deleting the statistics. If there are current SQL statements in the shared pool that have execution plans based on newer statistics, Oracle will invalidate the SQL in the shared pool, forcing it to be reparsed, using the new statistics the next time the SQL statement is accessed.

The ANALYZE command does use sorts and can be a time-consuming, resource-intensive process for larger objects. The ESTIMATE option of the ANALYZE command gathers a sampling of information from the object to base its statistics on. The following is a sample ANALYZE command:

```
analyze table <TABLE NAME> estimate
```

> **TIP**
>
> If data is skewed or is not evenly balanced throughout an object, histogram statistics should be created. The more statistics gathered, the better decisions the cost-based optimizer will make. The following is an example of creating a histogram with 10 buckets. Additional information on histograms can be referenced in the *Oracle 8.0 Tuning Guide*, Chapter 8.
>
> ```
> analyze table <TABLE NAME> compute statistics for columns
> ➥<COLUMN NAME> size 10
> ```

24

ORACLE8 DATABASE TUNING

Hints are used to influence the cost-based optimizer. Hints can be used to control the optimizer's goal, access methods, join conditions, parallel, and partitioning options. Hints are specified in the SQL statement syntax. The following shows an ALL_ROWS hint in the EMP table.

```
select /*+ ALL_ROWS */ ename, sal from EMP where SAL > 1000
```

The optimizer goal hint controls one of three modes: RULE will force the rule-based optimizer, FIRST_ROWS (best response), and ALL_ROWS (best throughput) will use the cost-based optimizer and force the optimizer to the desired goal. Most of the access-method-controlling hints are listed in Table 24.2.

TABLE 24.2. ACCESS METHOD HINTS.

Hint	Description

AND_EQUAL	Use the AND_EQUAL hint when more than one equality criterion exists on a single table.
	
	```select/*+ AND_EQUAL(emp,PK_EMP,EMP_NAME) */ ename,dname```
	```from emp, dept```
	```where emp.deptno = dept.deptno```
	```and ename = 'SMITH'```

CACHE	Use the CACHE hint to place the entire table in the buffer cache. The table is placed at the most recently used end of the buffer cache. This hint is good for small tables that are accessed often.
	
	```select/*+ CACHE(emp) */ ename,dname```
	```from emp, dept```
	```where emp.deptno = dept.deptno```

CLUSTER	Use the CLUSTER hint to access a table in a cluster without the use of an index.
	
	```select/*+ CLUSTER(emp) */ ename,dname```
	```from emp, dept```
	```where emp.deptno = dept.deptno```

FULL	Use the FULL hint to perform a full table scan on a table.
	
	```select/*+ FULL(emp) */ ename,dname```
	```from emp, dept```
	```where emp.deptno = dept.deptno```

HASH	Use the HASH hint to access a table in a hashed cluster without the use of an index.
	
	```select/*+ HASH */ ename,dname```
	```from emp, dept```
	```where emp.deptno = dept.deptno```

INDEX	Use an INDEX hint to instruct Oracle to use one of the indexes specified as a parameter.
	
	```select/*+ INDEX(emp,PK_EMP) */ ename,dname```
	```from emp, dept```
	```where emp.deptno = dept.deptno```

INDEX_COMBINE	The INDEX_COMBINE forces the use of bitmap indexes.
	
	```select/*+ INDEX_COMBINE(emp,ENAME) */ ename,dname```
	```from emp, dept```
	```where emp.deptno = dept.deptno```

Hint	Description

NOCACHE	Use the NOCACHE hint to place the blocks of the table at the beginning of the buffer cache so as not to age any blocks out.
	
	`select/*+ NOCACHE(emp) */ ename,dname`
	`from emp, dept`
	`where emp.deptno = dept.deptno`

NOPARALLEL	Use the NOPARALLEL hint to not use multiple-server processes to service the operations on the specified table.
	
	`select/*+ NOPARALLEL(emp) */ ename,dname`
	`from emp, dept`
	`where emp.deptno = dept.deptno`

ORDERED	Use the ORDERED hint to access the tables in the FROM clause in the order that they appear.
	
	`select/*+ ORDERED(emp,dept) */ ename,dname`
	`from emp, dept`
	`where emp.deptno = dept.deptno`

PARALLEL	Use the PARALLEL hint to request multiple server processes to simultaneously service the operations on the specified table.
	
	`select/*+ PARALLEL(emp) */ ename,dname`
	`from emp, dept`
	`where emp.deptno = dept.deptno`

PUSH_SUBQ	The PUSH_SUBQ evaluates subqueries earlier, rather than as a filter operation.
	
	`select/*+ PUSH_SUBQ */ ename,dname`
	`from emp, dept`
	`where emp.deptno in`
	`    (`
	`  select deptno from dept)`

ROWID	Use the ROWID hint to access the table by ROWID.
	
	`select/*+ ROWID(emp) */ ename,dname`
	`from emp, dept`
	`where emp.deptno = dept.deptno`

STAR	STAR hint invokes the STAR query feature.
	
	`select/*+ STAR */ ename,dname`
	`from emp, dept`
	`where emp.deptno = dept.deptno`

USE_CONCAT	USE_CONCAT is used when a SQL statement has multiple criteria ORed together.
	
	`select/*+ USE_CONCAT */ ename,dname`
	`from emp, dept`
	`where emp.deptno = dept.deptno`

24

ORACLE8 DATABASE TUNING

continues

TABLE 24.2. CONTINUED

Hint	Description

USE_HASH	Use the USE_HASH hint to perform a hash join rather than a merge join or a nested loop join.
	
	`select/*+ USE_HASH */ ename,dname`
	`from emp, dept`
	`where emp.deptno = dept.deptno`

USE_MERGE	Use the USE_MERGE hint to perform a merge join rather than a nested loop join or a hash join.
	
	`select/*+ USE_MERGE */ ename,dname`
	`from emp, dept`
	`where emp.deptno = dept.deptno`

SQL Tuning

SQL tuning involves the use of the explain-plan table, or the use of Oracle or third-party tools that display the contents of the explain-plan table. Oracle tools include Oracle Enterprise Manager Top Session, TKPROF (examines trace files), and the EXPLAIN command combined with a SQL statement to display the results. This section will discuss how to interpret explain plan results and list coding techniques that will help avoid problems when coding SQL statements.

The explain plan is a necessity for tuning SQL statements for both the rule-based and cost-based optimizers. Listing 24.14 shows how to load the plan table and query the results. This plan table can be set up for any user by running the $ORACLE_HOME/rdbms/admin/utlxplan.sql script from SQL*Plus. Some tools display important cost-based optimizer statistics (such as Platinum Technology SQL Station, Figure 24.8) that greatly aid in the tuning process of SQL statements. Please note that the plan table results of Listing 24.14 to that of Platinum Technology's SQL Station in Figure 24.8 are from the same SQL statement. The largest performance gains will be had by tuning the top four or five steps of the explain plan. It would be difficult at best to determine the order of processing of any of the steps in Listing 24.14. Also note the numbers in parentheses just to the right of each explain step in Figure 24.8. These figures are the cost-based cost, the number of rows affected, and the number of bytes affected by this step. Step 1 in Figure 24.8, Table Access [FULL], should usually be avoided; reviewing the row count and bytes affected, it would cause a performance degradation to resolve this full table access.

FIGURE 24.8.

*SQL station
explain plan
display.*

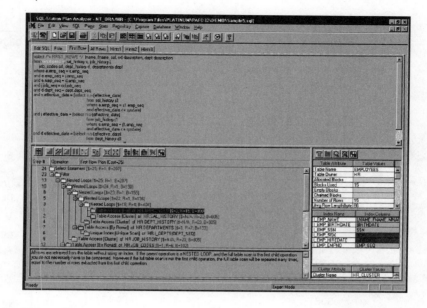

LISTING 24.14. EXPLAIN PLAN TABLE AND RESULTS.

```
EXPLAIN PLAN INTO PLAN _TABLE FOR
select lname, fname, sal, cd.description, dept.description
from employees e, sal_history s, job_history j,
     job_codes cd, dept_history d, departments dept
where e.emp_seq = s.emp_seq
and e.emp_seq = j.emp_seq
and e.emp_seq = d.emp_seq
and j.job_seq = cd.job_seq
and d.dept_seq = dept.dept_seq
and s.effective_date = (select max(effective_date)
                        from sal_history s1
                        where e.emp_seq = s1.emp_seq
                        and effective_date <= sysdate)
and j.effective_date = (select max(effective_date)
                        from job_history j1
                        where e.emp_seq = j1.emp_seq
                        and effective_date <= sysdate)
and d.effective_date = (select max(effective_date)
                        from dept_history d1
                        where e.emp_seq = d1.emp_seq
                        and effective_date <= sysdate);

select COST, OPERATION, OPTIONS, OBJECT_NAME
from PLAN_TABLE;
```

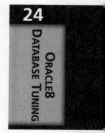

24

ORACLE8
DATABASE TUNING

continues

LISTING 24.14. CONTINUED

```
COST       OPERATION                         OPTIONS          OBJECT_NAME
.........  .............................     ............     ...........
    26 SELECT STATEMENT
       FILTER
    26 NESTED LOOPS
    25 NESTED LOOPS
    24 NESTED LOOPS
    22 NESTED LOOPS
    18 NESTED LOOPS
     3 TABLE ACCESS                          FULL             EMPLOYEES
       TABLE ACCESS                          CLUSTER          SAL_HISTORY
       TABLE ACCESS                          CLUSTER          JOB_HISTORY
       TABLE ACCESS                          CLUSTER          DEPT_HISTORY
     1 TABLE ACCESS                          BY ROWID         JOB_CODES
       INDEX                                 UNIQUE SCAN      I_JOBS
       TABLE ACCESS                          BY ROWID         DEPARTMENTS
       INDEX                                 UNIQUE SCAN      I_DEPTS
       SORT                                  AGGREGATE
     1 TABLE ACCESS                          CLUSTER          DEPT_HISTORY
       INDEX                                 UNIQUE SCAN      I_EMP_EMPNO
       SORT                                  AGGREGATE
     1 TABLE ACCESS                          CLUSTER          JOB_HISTORY
       INDEX                                 UNIQUE SCAN      I_EMP_EMPNO
       SORT                                  AGGREGATE
     1 TABLE ACCESS                          CLUSTER          SAL_HISTORY
       INDEX                                 UNIQUE SCAN      I_EMP_EMPNO
```

24 rows selected.

> **NOTE**
>
> Oracle's TKPROF process is the only process I am aware of from Oracle
> Corporation that displays the cost, row, and byte information per explain step.

Explain plans can be difficult to interpret. Indenting the explain steps greatly aids in the understanding of the order of the explain steps. The more common explain steps are discussed in Table 24.3.

TABLE 24.3. EXPLAIN PLAN STEPS.

Access Rule	Description
AND-EQUAL	Index values will be used to join rows.
CONCATENATION	SQL statement UNION command.

Access Rule	Description
FILTER	FILTERs apply "other criteria" in the query to further qualify the matching rows. The "other criteria" include correlated subqueries, and HAVING clause.
FIRST ROW	SQL statement will be processed via a cursor.
FOR UPDATE	SQL statement clause "for update of" placed row level locks on affected rows.
INDEX (UNIQUE)	SQL statement utilized a unique index to search for a specific value.
INDEX (RANGE SCAN)	SQL statement contains a nonequality or BETWEEN condition.
HASH JOIN	SQL statement initiated a hash-join operation.
MERGE JOIN	SQL statement references two or more tables, sorting the two result sets being joined over the join columns and then merging the results via the join columns.
NESTED LOOPS	This operation is one form of joining tables, as opposed to a merge join. One row is retrieved from the row source identified by the first child operation, and then joined to all matching rows in the other table, identified in the second child operation.
NONUNIQUE INDEX (RANGE SCAN)	The RANGE SCAN option indicates that Oracle expects to return multiple matches (ROWIDs) from the index search.
PARTITION (CONCATENATED)	SQL statement will access a partitioned object and merge the retrieved rows from the accessed partitions.
PARTITION (SINGLE)	SQL statement will access a single partition.
PARTITION (EMPTY)	The SQL statement makes reference to an empty partition.
SORT (ORDER BY)	SQL statement contains an ORDER BY SQL command.
SORT (AGGREGATE)	SQL statement initiated a sort to resolve a MIN or MAX type function.

continues

24

ORACLE8 DATABASE TUNING

TABLE 24.3. CONTINUED

Access Rule	Description
SORT (GROUP BY)	SQL statement contains a GROUP BY SQL command.
TABLE ACCESS (FULL)	All rows are retrieved from the table without using an index.
TABLE ACCESS (BY ROWID)	A row was retrieved from a table based on the ROWID of the row.
TABLE ACCESS (CLUSTER)	A row is retrieved from a table that is part of an indexed cluster.
UNION	SQL statement contains a DISTINCT SQL command.

Oracle8 has introduced three new columns: partition_start, partition_stop, and partition_id. These three new fields will aid in the tuning of SQL statements that access partitioned objects. partition_start and partition_stop show the range of partitions affected by this explain step. The partition_id is the identification number for that particular explain step.

Finally, there are both good and poor ways to code SQL statements. Here are some guidelines for SQL statement coding that will help both the rule-based and the cost-based optimizers.

DON'T use calculations in the WHERE clause on indexed columns. Unless the intended behavior is to disable the index use, any function on indexed columns will ignore the index.

DO use the IN operator instead of NOT. Try to avoid using the NOT command by using >=, <=, and so on.

DON'T use an index if more than 20 percent of the rows will be returned by the query.

DO use array processing whenever possible (Export and Pro*C applications).

DON'T use subqueries if other solutions exist (PL/SQL loop, for example).

DO use hints to ensure the desired execution-plan results.

DON'T write applications that use SQL execution-plan defaults. The Oracle Corporation makes no guarantees that default behavior will be maintained in future releases, or even between different hardware platforms.

Tuning Checklist

1. Read the *Oracle Installation Guide* that comes with the distribution software.
2. Make sure SHMMAX, SHMMHI, SEMMNI, SEMMNS, and SHMSEG are all set properly.
3. Ensure that there is enough memory to avoid swapping but ensure maximum Oracle performance.
4. The UNIX software, application software, and Oracle software should all be on separate disk drives.
5. Make sure system level I/O is evenly distributed across all available disk drives.
6. Tune the System Global Area (including the buffer cache, shared pool, log buffer, and sort area).
7. Monitor and alleviate redo log and rollback segment contention.
8. Distribute related objects (including referential integrity related objects) on different disk drives.
9. Partition tables and indexes when possible.
10. Monitor for extent interleaving, perform tablespace reorganizations as needed.
11. Monitor and alleviate excessive row chaining and row migration.
12. Recompile procedures, functions, packages, and triggers when they become invalidated.
13. Utilize better SQL coding techniques.
14. Use unrecoverable transactions for large "create table as" and data loads.
15. Pin frequently used application code into the shared pool.
16. Utilize bitmap indexes, star queries, histograms, hash joins, index-only tables, and reverse key indexes.
17. Tune frequently used and resource-intensive SQL statements.

Summary

This chapter supplies the reader with an in-depth study of the four tuning levels associated with any Oracle environment: operating system tuning, Oracle RDBMS tuning, database design tuning, and SQL statement tuning. Each level depends on the other levels. Each level of tuning should be evaluated per application needs in the order listed in this chapter. There is no single magical solution to any performance issue, but Oracle provides a rich environment of options so that most any Oracle application can access data in the most optimal manner.

Oracle8
Application Tuning

"It's not my job." Perhaps tuning applications is not your problem. Perhaps you already have more than enough problems to deal with and do not want to get into any more. However, you still should have a basic understanding of application and query tuning. Why? Because odds are, if you have a performance problem with the system as a whole, the first words out of people's mouths are going to be about the need for database tuning—they will tell you about how messed up your system is. You should, of course, perform the database tuning steps listed in the previous chapters to ensure that you know what you are talking about before you open *your* mouth. However, once you prove that the database is performing within normal limits, you may want to be able to track down the real cause to make your case more convincing. That is where a little knowledge about application tuning can make you dangerous.

The majority of application tuning work I have run across involves optimization of queries against the database. Although you may think up situations where you might want to tune transactions, most of these situations lead to splitting input/output loads between disks and other such things that are grouped within the realm of database tuning. However, generally speaking, the process of updating rows, deleting rows, and inserting new rows is relatively well-defined and follows a single course. The most you can do is make sure you have indexes that match the typical update/deletion criteria used and let Oracle do its work.

Queries, however, are another matter. The real value of database management systems to most organizations is not the capability of storing data (flat files did that successfully). The real value of a DBMS is the capability of rapidly and accurately recalling data from the database. This is where man-years of labor were spent in older systems as each developer had to build smarter query algorithms to find data in a reasonable time frame. Not every query is the same, though. Some may require you to scan the entire table (that is, you use almost every column in the table as part of your where clause). Others may look only at a single, indexed column in a single table. Still others may link a half-dozen tables using complex join criteria.

It seems pretty obvious that a search method that works well for one of these types of queries is probably not the best method for the others. In fact, Oracle and most other databases have a number of search algorithms in their systems that are designed to handle different needs. This is what enables them to work in such a large number of environments and applications. When an application is performing slowly on a well-tuned database, the first thing you should check is how the query is being processed to ensure that it is as efficient as it can be.

This chapter explains what you can do to make a query run more efficiently in an Oracle system, starting with a discussion of the factors that you can control when issuing a query. Then you learn about the two optimizers that Oracle provides. These are the components within the system that determine the search algorithm, or execution plan, that will be used to process the query. Then you explore steps you can take to optimize the query. Finally, being trained as a scientist, I go over a brief discussion on the value of experimenting with different factors to optimize the query. Unless you devote a percentage of your time to this discipline, you will probably not be able to look at a query, make two changes, and then watch as it flies.

Factors Designers Can Control

The process begins with a request for information. In an Oracle database system, this usually starts with a SQL query. Some development tools give you a graphical interface to enable you to tell it what you want, but these are merely convenience tools that eventually generate the SQL query and pass it to Oracle. Once the query is formed, Oracle goes through a number of steps to get the answer to the user. The steps related to the choice of an execution plan and execution of the query are shown in Figure 25.1.

FIGURE 25.1.
Query execution steps.

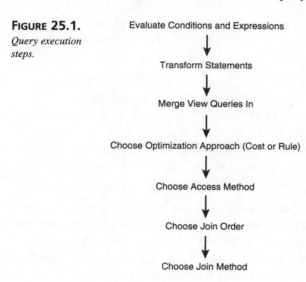

Evaluate Conditions and Expressions

↓

Transform Statements

↓

Merge View Queries In

↓

Choose Optimization Approach (Cost or Rule)

↓

Choose Access Method

↓

Choose Join Order

↓

Choose Join Method

The first step in figuring out ways to make queries perform better is to understand the factors that you can control. Perhaps one of the most frustrating things about query optimization is that the basics of SQL do not provide you with much in the way of direct controls over the query execution process. Of course, this lack of control is one of the things people like most about a database management system—it handles all the details. In most cases, the DBMS will choose a plan that is far better than most programmers can implement. However, especially in large databases with large tables, you may need a little bit better control in those cases where Oracle chooses a plan that does not work out well.

The first item you need to control in Oracle version 7.1 and later is which type of query optimization Oracle performs. There are two optimizers available. The first is the latest version of the optimizer that Oracle has used for some time—the *rule-based optimizer*. It gets its name from the fact that Oracle has programmed in a series of rules about how to read the SQL statement in order to determine the execution plan. You can write some really poor queries if you are not careful with this optimizer. The other optimizer is referred to as the *cost-based optimizer*. It looks beyond the pure format of the SQL you write to determine the sizes of the tables and indexes involved with the query to determine the best execution plan.

Once you choose your optimization method, you have to work with your queries to help ensure that the optimizer chooses the best method for your needs. If you are using the cost-based optimizer, you need to ensure that you routinely take statistics on your database objects. This ensures that Oracle has the information it needs to make wise decisions. This optimizer ignores the order in which you list items in your SQL statements; therefore, your only choice is to override the optimizer (as described later in this chapter).

The Oracle optimizers are a nice idea overall. You get to access your data without concerning yourself with search algorithms or physical storage parameters. You don't even have to decide when to use an index or which index to use. This all works well in the vast majority of queries I have run across. Every now and then, however, you will run across a query that joins a lot of big tables and takes forever to execute. This is the time for manual intervention into the execution plan process. Intervention is needed usually only in very large instances (that is, greater than 25GB in size).

The forms of intervention in the execution plan process can be separated into three general areas (see Figure 25.2). The first form of intervention is the *hint*. You can add a hint to any of your SQL query statements. You can literally tell it the execution plan it should be using. You can also tell it the order in which you want the tables to be processed. This can be pretty powerful, but you should avoid using it unless you have queries that have problems. Later versions of Oracle may have even better execution plans available to them. If you code in a lot of hints, you'll miss out on the opportunity to use these new execution plans. (Most places do not have the kind of time to go through a large application and clean out all the hints and then retest it for speed.)

The second form of intervention is *goals*. This construct enables you to tell Oracle whether you want to choose an execution plan that gets the entire query completed quickly or returns the first few rows of data quickly. For large reports that are not printed until you have completed them, you are typically concerned about getting all rows returned as quickly as possible. However, if you are displaying a list of values on the screen for the users, you may want to get them a few rows to read while the rest of the query is being completed. This enables them to read and analyze data and avoid screen dead time that leads to user complaints. These goal options use cost-based optimization whether there are statistics present or not. (With no statistics, the chance of making poor decisions is higher.)

FIGURE 25.2.

Intervention with Oracle execution plans.

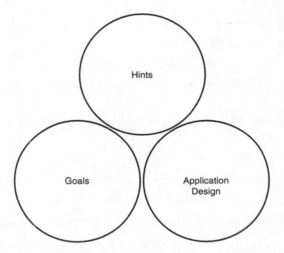

The final form of intervention is the application design itself. You can often improve performance by using SQL over PL/SQL constructs. You also can eliminate unnecessary information from the query that can cause additional work for Oracle. Finally, you can try various combinations of query constructs, such as UNION and UNION ALL to try to improve performance. There are certain constructs that force certain execution plans (such as the dreaded merge-join) which are less efficient. I usually wind up doing a little experimentation with these options to find the construct that works best for a given query.

The Rule-Based Optimizer

The concept behind the rule-based optimizer is simple. It looks at the SQL statement to determine all the possible ways it can execute the query. Then it selects the one on its list of queries it thinks will be most effective. The key here is that it has a simple list of possible ways to approach the problem that is fixed for all types and sizes of tables. The following is the basic order in which the execution plans are selected by the rule-based optimizer.

1. Access a single row by using its internal row ID.

2. Access a single row by a join formed out of a cluster of tables.

3. Access a single row by combining a hash cluster key with a unique or primary key from a table not in the cluster.

4. Access a single row by a unique or primary key.

5. Access by joining rows in a cluster together.

6. Access by hash cluster keys.

7. Access by using a cluster index key.

8. Access by using a composite index.

9. Access by using a single-column index.

10. Access by using a bounded range search on indexed columns (for example, >25 but <50).

11. Access by using an unbounded range search on indexed columns (for example, >5).

12. Access by joining tables using a sort-then-merge algorithm.

13. Access by finding the maximum or minimum of an indexed column.

14. Access by using the ORDER BY clause on indexed columns.

15. Access by performing a full table scan (read every row in the table).

As you can see, unless you use clusters, you have a very simple list of ways to attack the problem. The rule-based optimizer also does not have a clue as to which table to access (that is, which will return the fewest number of rows) first, based on this data. Another point to note is that you wind up doing a full table scan if you do not have a where clause to specify rules for joining tables or selecting rows from the tables. The rule-based optimizer is relatively simple in the way it approaches things and can be easily fooled.

There is a little more to the evaluation process than has been described so far. The rule-based optimizer will catch a few other ways to make the statement more efficient than you coded it, but not many. Here is the list of steps that the optimizers go through.

1. Evaluates your SQL to determine the expressions and conditions.

2. Modifies the statements into an equivalent join statement that may be more efficient.

3. Merges the queries used for any views that are accessed by the query into the query.

4. Chooses whether to use the rule-based or cost-based approach. The overall database can be set to use either cost-based or rule-based optimizers based on the `OPTIMIZER_MODE` parameter which defaults to cost but can be set to rule. You can also use the alter session command to change the optimizer mode for a particular job you are running.

5. Chooses access paths for each of the tables accessed in the query.

6. If two or more tables are joined, chooses the order in which the tables are joined.

7. If tables are joined, chooses the method of joining.

With all of that said, I tend to use the rule-based optimizer unless I have a reason not to use it. First, some of my feelings come from the fact that the cost-based optimizer did not work very well until recent releases of the Oracle product (which is probably an unfair bias). The rule-based optimizer also has the beauty of being simpler to maintain. I do not have to gather statistics and keep them current. The rule-based optimizer is good enough for the vast majority of databases with which I have worked. There are however, a growing number of large databases where efficiency is essential (you can be inefficient on a 50-row table, but not on a 5-million-row table). These are the cases in which the cost-based optimizer can help you out. There is no harm in trying out the cost-based optimizer in your test environment to see whether it can benefit your applications. Your situation might benefit enormously from this tool. One note is that Oracle has put a lot of effort into improving the cost-based optimizer (for example, the new algorithms for star schemas that came with Oracle8) and will probably shift to the cost-based optimizer as the only algorithm some day.

The Cost-Based Optimizer

Imagine having to design an execution plan manually. All you know is the SQL for an application's queries. You have no way to guess which is the smaller, look-up table and which is the monstrous main data table. You have no idea whether you are dealing with a huge or small query, whether you can perform your sorts in memory, or whether you will have to use disk sorting. How can you be expected to come up with a good execution plan?

These are the problems faced by the rule-based optimizer. It gets only the syntax and a list of objects that it does not understand. It does its best, but it winds up making assumptions that cause it to pick the best plan for the majority of queries of this type. The cost-based optimizer takes a little extra information that you have been kind enough to gather for it and uses this information to make better guesses at the optimal query path (see Figure 25.3). This can prevent, for example, scanning through a huge table to find rows to join to a little look-up table (it is much faster the other way around).

25

**ORACLE8
APPLICATION
TUNING**

FIGURE 25.3.

*Cost-based opti-
mization.*

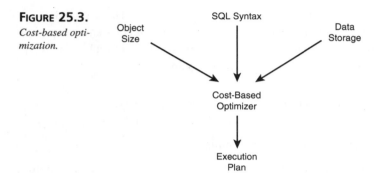

The statistics you gather cover several different topics that can be used to determine the most efficient query. The cost-based optimizer looks at the number of rows and how the objects are stored. Next, it performs some calculations for the impacts on the three major system resources—CPU, memory, and input/output. It then is run through an algorithm (which factors in the goals you have set up) to determine which query will give you the best performance. I get a headache just thinking about all the calculations I would have to go through to determine which approach is best for a complex query joining multiple tables. However, that is what the software gets paid to do.

An important topic when discussing the cost-based optimizer is statistic collection. The following are a few thoughts of mine on this subject.

- You need to gather statistics every time you make a significant change to the number of rows stored in the database.

- You need to gather statistics every time you make a change to the database schema (adding a table or index, for example).

- If you have a large number of rows in the table and most of the rows are similar to one another in terms of size and complexity, you can use estimation to reduce the time you need to gather statistics. This allows you to gather statistics more often which can be helpful.

- Statistic gathering is a prime candidate for a scheduled job. Gather your statistics at night when the system is relatively idle because the statistics gathering process can be somewhat statistic demanding.

There is probably an entire series of papers written on the internal functioning of the cost-based optimizer. It is important that you understand the basics of what this optimizer does and what it can do for you. You should seriously consider using it in very large instances, where there's a mixture of small look-up tables and huge data tables. It could be a useful option in any instance where queries are taking longer than desired under the rule-based optimizer. Of course, you always want to ensure that you are properly tuned before you tell the developers to rewrite their applications, or before you change optimizers.

Execution Plans

Let's start with the brute force approach to finding information—the full table scan. This basic approach dates back to the days of flat files. The mind-set is that if you read every row in the table, you will find your answer (see Figure 25.4). Although it may not be the most brilliant plan possible, it has its uses. For example, if you have a specific query that is looking for a specific combination of a large number of columns, or you want to produce a detailed report showing all data stored in the database, this is exactly what you want. However, if you're looking up a single row of information using a common key value, you'll waste a lot of time with this access method.

FIGURE 25.4.
The full table scan.

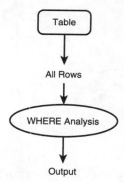

The next simplest method is using an index to access only the rows of data you need. This typically cuts down on a lot of input/output to the table and also speeds access due to the more efficient storage algorithms used for indexes. Figure 25.5 illustrates the basic concepts of this approach. Obviously, if a table is really small or you are using all the columns of the table in your where clause, it's not worth the effort of using an index (because you will read in all the columns of the table when reading the index and then read the table for any remaining columns).

The first two methods deal with access to a single table. These basic table search methods are often combined to obtain data from multiple tables and join it. There are two common algorithms for merging this data—merge-join and nested loop. Let's start with the merge-join algorithm (see Figure 25.6).

FIGURE 25.5.
Indexed searches.

FIGURE 25.6.
The merge-join approach.

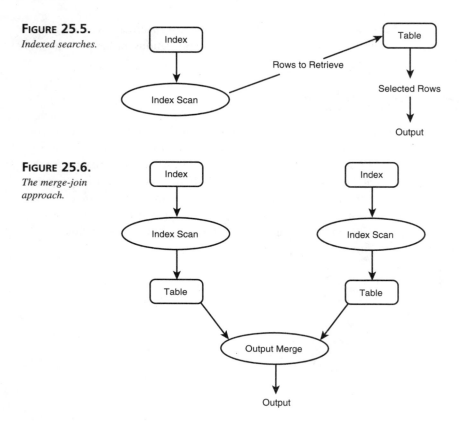

The main alternative to the merge-join is the nested loop. In the large, multi-table queries you often see with a large data warehouse, you almost always want to see nested loop joins being performed rather than the merge-joins. I mentioned earlier in this chapter about some 30-minute queries that turned into 30-second queries. These were queries that initially used the merge-join algorithm and were converted to use the nested loop approach. The basic improvement comes from using the results of the first query to narrow the search of the second, as opposed to performing two independent queries and then trying to mesh the results together. Figure 25.7 shows the nested loop approach.

There are a number of other algorithms that could be called into play when using compound queries (UNION, UNION ALL, and INTERSECT). Depending on the details of your individual query, some of these can improve your performance. You may have to adjust the SQL in your query to get Oracle to use these statements, but I have seen examples where it is definitely worth it. Figure 25.8 illustrates the concepts behind these algorithms.

FIGURE 25.7.
The nested loop approach.

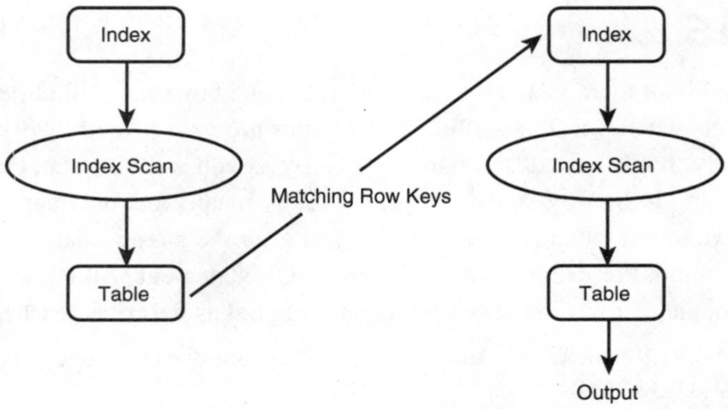

FIGURE 25.8.
Compound query approaches.

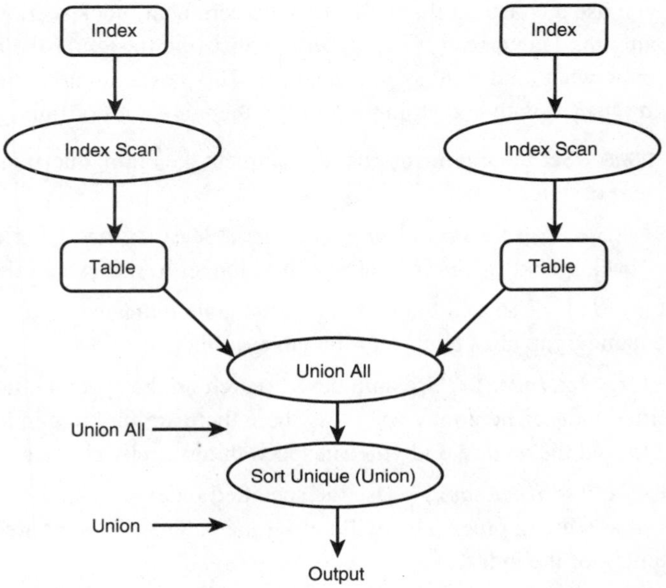

There's a lot more to the process of optimizing queries than can be covered in these pages, and there are many books on the subject. Some good information can be gathered from your server concepts manual and the applications developers guide that normally comes with the complete Oracle documentation set. This is a complex topic with which at least some of your more senior developers should be familiar. Perhaps you may want to loan them copies of these books if you are still having performance problems after you finish tuning your instance (it could save you some time).

25

ORACLE8 APPLICATION TUNING

Hints

Some people out there just can't take a hint. Oracle, however, will almost always listen to your hints whenever it can follow them. Hints are your primary weapon when you have a query that is basically sound and exactly as you want it to be, but Oracle still is not processing it the way you want. (This usually means that the query is too slow.) You merely have to put the correct hint syntax just after the `select` statement to get Oracle to change its mind. For example, the following SQL statement will be optimized to obtain the first couple of rows in the fastest manner (a goal as described earlier).

```
select /*+ FIRST_ROWS */ last_name,first_name,golf_score
    from golf_scores
    where last_name='GREENE';
```

Basically, you use a construct that looks like the comment block sections in many common programming languages (`/*...*/`) with a plus sign to signify the hint (+). The key here is to know what kind of hints you can give. The most common hints are shown in the following list (as with everything in Oracle, there are a lot of lightly used options):

- `ALL_ROWS`   Set the optimizer goal to complete the entire query in the most rapid manner possible.

- `FIRST_ROWS`   Set the optimizer goal to get at least the first couple of rows of the query back quickly, even if it takes a little longer to retrieve all the rows.

- `FULL(table)`   Use a full table scan on the table indicated. You can use either the table name or an alias to specify the table of interest.

- `INDEX(table index)`   Use an indexed search on the specified table using the specified index. There may be cases where there are multiple indexes that could be used to find the values, and you can speed things up by choosing the right one.

- `INDEX_ASC(table index)`   Use the specified index to scan the specified table, but do it in ascending order. This will help if the values you want are likely to be at the beginning of the index.

- `INDEX_DESC(table index)`   Use the specified index to scan the specified table, but do it in descending order. This will help if the values you want are likely to be at the end of the index.

- `AND_EQUAL (table index ...)`   Merge the results from the specified single column indexes to determine which rows of the table are needed.

- `ORDERED`   Join the tables in the order in which they appear in the FROM clause.

- `USE_NL (table table ...)`   Use the nested loop algorithm to join tables together, with the first table specified being the inner table on the join.

- USE_MERGE (table table ...)   Use the merge-join algorithm to join the tables together.

Here are a few more examples of queries that use hints:

```
select /*+ ALL_ROWS */ analysis,date_run,result
   from lab_tests
   where analysis_type = 'CHEMICAL';

select /*+ USE_NL(a) */ analysis,result,action_to_take
   from lab_tests a,test_actions b
   where a.result = b.result and
      a.analysis_type = 'CHEMICAL';

select /*+ INDEX(lab_tests lab_tests_types) analysis,date_run,result
   from lab_tests
   where analysis_type = 'CHEMICAL';
```

The application developers guide in your Oracle documentation set contains a pretty good discussion of the options available to you with hints. You can do a lot with hints to make Oracle do what you want it to do, rather than what it thinks it should be doing. The nice thing about tuning queries is that you can isolate the SQL and run multiple timing tests using a variety of hints until you find the one that works best. You do not have to worry about damaging the data because you would be testing update, insert, or delete statements. You may want to be considerate about the impact your testing might have on user response time if you are issuing some really nasty test queries.

Index Design

Indexes are the easiest and often best techniques to consider when you want to improve the performance of a query. Most access speed problems in new applications are due to a lack of an appropriate index. Once again, it can make a night-and-day difference in your performance. The best thing is that it's relatively simple to determine which indexes you need. You merely look at the SQL statements you issue and see what you are using in the where clause.

You do have to be judicious regarding what you build the indexes on—indexes consume disk space that might be tight. You do not get much benefit from indexes that are almost as large as the tables themselves. Finally, indexes do have an impact on the performance of updates, insertions, and deletions from the table. With these points aside, an index can be the simplest and best way to improve query performance when you have a few key fields on which you're always searching.

General Guidelines

So far, you have learned that there are various execution plans and that some are better than others. You also know that you may need to try several alternatives before you find the one that works best for you. However, you do not know yet how to figure out which execution plan Oracle is using. This was intentional, because the output has little meaning until you have the basic concepts of query execution under your belt. Now you're ready to jump into the subject of analyzing how your queries are being processed.

The basic procedure is relatively simple, but there is no single good source that explains it from end-to-end. It begins when you run the query you're curious about with the `trace` utility turned on. All this `trace` utility does is make an output file in the `udump` directory for the Oracle instance that contains data on how the query was attacked. (It usually is a sequentially numbered file with a `.trc` extension.) I like to extract the SQL in question and put it in a separate SQL file with the command to start the `trace` utility right before it. In that way, I can run the script from SQL*Plus. The command to turn on the `trace` utility is

```
alter session set sql_trace = true;
```

You also need to make sure that the `TIMED_STATISTICS` parameter in the initialization file is set to `TRUE`. Once this trace file is produced (that is, you run the query), you must find out where Oracle put the trace results. You have to look through the `udump` directory to find the file that was made at the time you created and ran the query (I use the `ls -lt` command in UNIX). It's not convenient, but you have to find the filename before you can decode the output file to produce a report. This file is not very readable. You need to use the `tkprof` utility to turn this data into something designed for human beings. Here is the format of the command that will give you this report:

```
tkprof trace_dir/filename.trc outfile.prf explain=user sys=no
```

This takes the `filename.trc` file in the `trace_dir` directory and runs it through `tkprof`. It stores the output of this process in the `outfile.prf` directory. The `user` parameter is used to connect to Oracle as a user to get some additional information. This is not the most convenient utility, but it does provide some useful outputs. The report has some general information at the top about the number of fetches performed and the time to perform the operation. It then goes into a series of execution plan results from which you can test and plan your strategies, similar to the following:

```
SELECT STATEMENT
  MERGE JOIN
    SORT                JOIN
      TABLE ACCESS      FULL            GOLF_SCORES
```

```
SORT            JOIN
   TABLE ACCESS    FULL           GOLFERS
```

In this example, I show the results of a join between two tables based on some common key (golfer ID). This query selects all applicable rows from the first table and then all applicable rows from the second table. It then joins them together in memory to form the resulting output. Depending on the number of rows to be retrieved and the overall size of the table, this type of query can be quite time consuming when using the merge-join execution plan.

There is a UNIX shell script called "bench" included on the disk that executes a SQL script. It has the command to set tracing on and to run it through all the steps in the process. Very few people actually type all these commands at the command line.

Now let's look at some general guidelines on the optimization process. It is really tough to come up with general guidelines for the process of query execution. However, the following steps show how I normally approach it. This should work for most cases.

1. First, make sure your instance is properly tuned.

2. Run the query with trace mode on and run it through `tkprof` to determine how the query is being approached by Oracle. You can use the explain plan command in SQL*Plus, but the output is much more difficult to read than if you use `tkprof` (even though it contains the same basic information on the execution plan).

3. If the query returns a few rows that are selected based on columns commonly used as criteria but are not in an existing index, consider building an index of these columns to solve this problem. If there is an index that it should be using, try giving it a hint to use that index.

4. If tables are joined via merge-join, try to get Oracle to use nested loops to meld the data.

5. For nested loops, try to ensure that it does the search against the smaller table first (it will be listed last in `tkprof` output).

6. When all else fails, experiment with some of the alternatives to see whether you can improve performance.

The Value of Experimentation

By now you may be a little overwhelmed with all the options available to you in the query optimization world. How do you know which one will work best in your particular circumstance? There are a few people who have worked with this so much that they know right away which is the best method, and whether you need to use a hint to get

Oracle to follow this execution plan. I am not one of these folks, and very few of the DBAs I have met can do this off the top of their heads.

How should you figure out which is the best solution? I am trained as a physicist. Some of my fellow students sat at their desks and tried to figure out the elegant theories that explained everything. I liked to go into the laboratory and see what the reality of the situation was. Most scientists believe that theories are only as good as they match up with reality (while philosophers sit around and debate what reality is). Therefore, my favorite solution to the problem of tuning a query is to experiment with it. I build my SQL script that turns tracing on and then run it though the process described previously to see what it's doing and how long it takes to do it. I then vary the format of the SQL (add UNIONs and so forth) and give it a variety of hints. After it's all over, I look at the `tkprof` outputs to see which of the various alternatives provides me with the response time I want.

Summary

This chapter has covered the basics of application tuning within an Oracle database. Obviously, there are entire books devoted to the subject of optimal database object design. The Oracle8 Server has improved optimization routines, especially for such common database constructs as the star schema. Because the database is getting better at choosing execution plans, it's easier for developers to form queries that will be executed efficiently. However, you still need to make judicious use of indexes and configure your database correctly to get the best performance possible.

Oracle8 and the Web

IN THIS PART

ODBC/JDBC

by Scott Wheeler

IN THIS CHAPTER

CHAPTER 26

Overview of ODBC

JDBC and ODBC are similar in their purpose and structure in that they exist to allow easy access of data from programs via a common programming interface. In the following chapter you explore the pros, cons, capabilities, and limitations of both ODBC and JDBC when accessing Oracle8.

To effectively use any software product, it is important to understand the general structure and purpose of its creation. The following section will introduce the purpose of ODBC and offer a brief synopsis of its evolution.

ODBC's Purpose

Open Database Connectivity (ODBC) is the industry-accepted standard Application Programming Interface (API) that enables programs to access data in many different formats and locations, which includes most database management systems as well as some of the most popular file formats such as Microsoft Excel. ODBC uses Structured Query Language (SQL) to access the data, regardless of what format the data is in or where the data is located. The ability to use one standard, SQL, to access many different sources of data gives a developer a great degree of database independence and code independence.

ODBC's Evolution

The first ODBC version 1.0 desktop database drivers were released in August 1993 due to a need for a common data access method to use with Microsoft Windows–based applications, which were gaining tremendous popularity at the time. The drivers enabled Microsoft Windows developers to provide database access to their programs, through a relatively simple, standard interface. ODBC was a significant factor in the revolutionary effect client/server computing had on corporate culture in the '90s in addition to helping establish Microsoft Windows as the operating system of choice for client/server computing.

Due to the popularity of ODBC versions 1.0, version 2.0, 3.0, and 3.5 were released in December 1994, October 1995, and October 1996, respectively. In each release, enhancements were focused around speed, new operating system compatibility (Windows 95 and NT), and providing access to functionality present in some of the more advanced database systems ODBC accessed (for example, cursor management, double-byte character sets, and so on).

RDO, DAO, OLE DB, ADO, and Other Acronyms

RDO, OLE DB, and ADO are an evolution by Microsoft to address the current issues and anticipated future needs of developers. The following excerpts describe each of the components and their relevance to data access, ODBC, and Microsoft's strategy going forward.

RDO (Remote Data Objects) was important in that it allowed Microsoft's Visual Basic 4 and 5 to access ODBC-enabled data sources without going through the "jet engine" that existed in most Microsoft development tools at that time. The result was much better performance for Visual Basic application that used RDO rather than the traditional ODBC approach.

In contrast, DAO (Data Access Objects) utilizes OLE DB to access the data via ODBC and the Microsoft jet engine. Additionally, OLE DB is a C++ API that represents the fundamental component for data access in Microsoft's current Component Object Model (COM) strategy. It is meant to be more robust and handle "future" data sources, including, not replacing, ODBC. Currently, OLE DB does not fundamentally change the use of ODBC driver in access Oracle (or other) data sources.

ADO (ActiveX Data Objects) is Microsoft's current target object model. It is different than DAO and RDO in that you no longer have to navigate through the complexities of Microsoft's object hierarchy, but it does utilize OLE DB as its data access method. Microsoft has also stated that all its products will standardize on ADO as the common object model for development.

Oracle's ODBC Evolution

Although ODBC drivers for Oracle were available from various companies as early as 1994, Oracle made ODBC drivers widely available to its customers in early 1995. Additionally, Oracle enabled its development tools to use ODBC to access data sources other than Oracle during 1995. Starting in 1996, Oracle made all of its ODBC drivers available for download from the Web at no cost and continues to do so.

To get the most recent version of Oracle's ODBC drivers, Oracle's Web site continues to be the best source of free ODBC drivers, although there are a few vendors (Simba, Intersolve, and so on) who still make high quality ODBC drivers for Oracle.

ODBC Architecture

Although there a several components involved in connecting to a data source via ODBC, ODBC itself is made up of two major components: the ODBC application (Driver

Manager) and the database driver. Both of these components are written to a common application and data driver ODBC API specification. The ODBC API specification identifies the functions that should be supported in the specific ODBC version. The current ODBC version is version 3, and within this version the functions are broken into the following categories: Core, Level1, and Level2. The Oracle ODBC drivers currently support all but a few functions defined in the version 3.0 specification. (The exceptions are identified later in this document in the Oracle8 optimization section.)

A visual representation of the components involved in the submission of a SQL request through ODBC can be found in Figure 26.1.

FIGURE 26.1.

SQL request through ODBC.

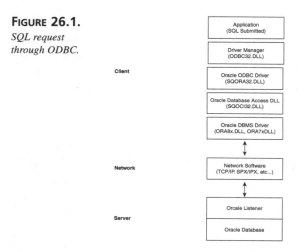

> **NOTE**
>
> ODBC and Net8 (formerly SQL*Net) are both required on every client that uses ODBC to access Oracle data. Additionally, the Net8 drivers (Oracle DBMS Driver) for each version of the Oracle database you plan to connect to must exist on each client machine that accesses data through ODBC, although the backward compatibility of the database drivers may allow you to access most of Oracle's functionality. The Net8 drivers are referred to as Required Support Files in the Oracle Installer program. The installation and configuration of the ODBC drivers will be explained in the following section.

ODBC Setup, Usage, and Limitations

First-time users will find the following section on setup and usage useful in getting ODBC configured to access Oracle8.

Oracle8 ODBC Setup

There are two basic steps in installing a working ODBC driver for Oracle8. The first is the installation and configuration of Oracle's Net8, which is covered in Chapter 3, "Oracle8 Network Computing," and the second is the installation and configuration of the ODBC software for Oracle8.

Installing Oracle8 ODBC Drivers

As mentioned previously, ODBC drivers for Oracle can be downloaded from the Oracle Web site for free. After downloading the file, double-click on the file to unZip it and read the readme.txt file located in the directory you have unzipped the file in. It will guide you through installing the software via Oracle's Installer.

Configuring Oracle8 ODBC Drivers

The following are the steps for configuring Oracle8 ODBC drivers:

1. In Windows NT or 95, double-click the 32-bit Administrator icon from the Control Panel or in the Oracle for Windows NT/95 folder, as shown in Figure 26.2.

FIGURE 26.2.

Accessing the ODBC Administrator.

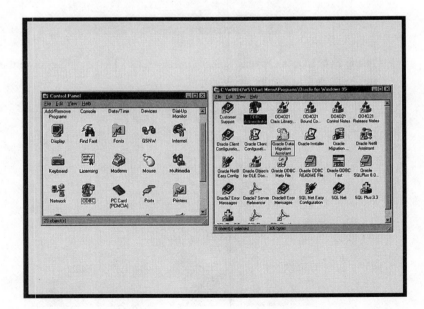

2. In the User DSN (Data Source Name) or the System DSN, choose the Add button, as shown in Figure 26.3.

> **NOTE**
>
> Use the System DSN tab if you are the sole user of your machine (that is, no one else has a separate Windows login name and password) or you want everyone who uses your machine to have access to these ODBC configurations. Otherwise, specify the ODBC data source in the User DSN tab.

FIGURE 26.3.

Adding the ODBC Data Source Name.

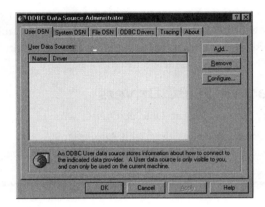

3. In the list of Data Drivers, select Oracle ODBC Driver and choose the Finish button as shown in Figure 26.4.

FIGURE 26.4.

Create a new ODBC Data Source.

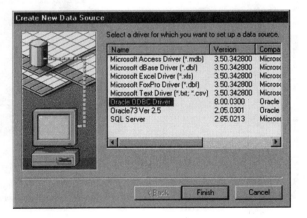

4. The Oracle8 ODBC Driver Setup dialog box is displayed as illustrated in Figure 26.5. In the Oracle8 ODBC Setup dialog box, enter the following:

- **Data Source Name:** The name that will be displayed to anyone who wants to use this ODBC configuration to connect to the data source you are setting up.

- **Description:** A full description of the data source you are connecting to. This description will be displayed when selecting this data source in the future.

- **Service Name:** For Oracle, this is usually referred to as the *Host String* or *Connect String*. It is the name for the Oracle database found in the TNSNAMES.ORA file or on the Oracle Names server, which is used by Net8 to find the correct Oracle database. You can set up this name in the Oracle Net8 Assistant.

- **UserID:** (Optional) You can specify the user ID of the Oracle database user here. If not specified, you will be prompted for the username when you connect through this ODBC connection.

- **Connect to Database in Read-only Mode:** If selected, data can only be read via this ODBC connection.

- **Prefetch Count:** This defines how many records will be read from the database at a time. The performance implications of this option are discussed in the ODBC Optimization section later in this chapter.

- **Option:** Not supported as of Oracle V8.0.3.

- **Library:** Not supported as of Oracle V8.0.3.

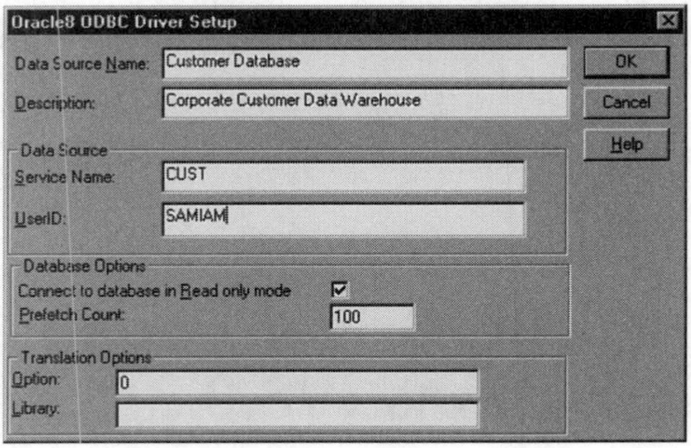

FIGURE 26.5.
ODBC Driver Setup.

5. At this point your ODBC connection is configured. Click the OK button and the data source should appear in the Data Source Administrator main window, as depicted in Figure 26.6.

FIGURE 26.6.

Data Source
Administrator
window.

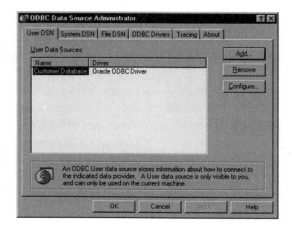

Connecting to Oracle8

The following is a code segment from a Visual Basic program that connects to a database as user Scott with password Tiger and the ODBC data source Customer Database (as specified in Figure 26.5). It then issues a query through ODBC to get all the usernames from the database we have specified previously and display them (one at a time) in a message box.

```
Dim oraDb As Database
Dim oraRset As Recordset
Set oraDb = OpenDatabase(ODBC, False, False, _"ODBC;DSN=Customer Database;
UID=SCOTT;PWD=TIGER")
Set oraRset = oraDb.OpenRecordset("select username from all_users",
➥dbOpenDynaset)
While Not oraRset.EOF
    MsgBox oraRset(1)
    oraRset.MoveNext
Wend
```

Oracle ODBC Driver Capabilities and Limitations (V8.0.3)

Although most capabilities of ODBC and Oracle8 are mutually supported, there are some limitations, as outlined in the next sections.

ODBC Functions Not Supported

- `SQLExtendedFetch`   Only `FETCH_NEXT` is available.

- `SQLMoreResults`   The Oracle database does not support multiple result sets, therefore more results are not available. `SQL_NO_DATA_FOUND` will always be returned by this function.

- `SQLBrowseConnect`   Not currently supported.

- `SQLSetPos`   Usage support can be achieved through the Microsoft ODBC cursor library.

SQL Syntax Not Supported

- `WHERE CURRENT OF CURSOR-NAME`   Not supported for a positioned `DELETE` or `UPDATE` statement.

- `DROP TABLE`, `DROP VIEW`, and `REVOKE`   These statements cannot specify the `CASCADE` and `RESTRICT` clauses.

NOTE

`DATE` Datatype   Because the ODBC driver maps the `DATE` datatype to the `SQL_TIMESTAMP` datatype, it always returns both the date and time parts of a `DATE` column.

Oracle8 ODBC Optimization and Troubleshooting

Due to the subjective nature of performance tuning, information in the following sections has been grouped based on the type of operations being performed.

Performance, General

- `SQLExecDirect`—Using `SQLPrepare` and `SQLExecute` to prepare the SQL statement may not get significantly better performance if the SQL being executed is performed against the system with any frequency, which is the case in many moderate-to-heavily used online applications. This is due to Oracle's caching of SQL and reuse of the prepared SQL statement.

- Set the `SQL_ATTR_NOSCAN` attribute of the ODBC `SQLSetConnectAttr` function or the ODBC `SQLSetStmtAttr` function to `TRUE` if you are not using ODBC escape clauses.
- Use the ODBC `SQLBindCol` function, instead of the ODBC `SQLGetData` function, to retrieve values from `SELECT` statements. Although both will retrieve data into variables, the `SQLBindCol` binds your variable directly to the values returned from the `SELECT` statement, whereas the `SQLGetData` function grabs the values from a temporary result set after the query returns the values. `SQLGetData` will be slower due to the extra function call and the dynamic nature of its data retrieval.

Update Performance

- Set the `SQL_ATTR_AUTOCOMMIT` attribute of the ODBC `SQLSetConnectAttr` function to `OFF`, and perform manual `COMMIT` or `ROLLBACK` operations using the ODBC `SQLEndTran` function.
- Although `SELECT` statements are never blocked by `UPDATE` statements, the Oracle server will wait indefinitely for lock conflicts between two update transactions. You can limit the amount of time that the Oracle server will wait for locks to be resolved by calling the ODBC `SQLSetConnectAttr` function before connecting to the data source. Specify a nonzero value for the `SQL_ATTR_QUERY_TIMEOUT` attribute in the ODBC `SQLSetStmtAttr` function.

OR

- You can set the Oracle8 ODBC Driver's `LockTimeOut` entry in the `oraodbc.ini` file. The value you enter for the `LockTimeOut` parameter is the number of seconds after which an Oracle server will time out if it cannot obtain the requested locks. In the following example, the Oracle server will time out after 60 seconds:

```
[Oracle ODBC Driver Common]
Driver Logging=0
RemoveControlChars=NO
LockTimeOut=60
```

Select Performance

- If you are only reading data (only `SELECT` statements), you can specify Connect to Database in Read-Only Mode when you are setting up the ODBC data source in the ODBC Administrator, or set the `SQL_ATTR_ACCESS_MODE` attribute of the ODBC `SQLSetConnectAttr` function to `SQL_MODE_READ_ONLY`.

- For large result sets, use the ODBC SQLFetchScroll function instead of the ODBC SQLFetch function due to SQLFetchScroll's capability to view the result set before it has been completely retrieved from the database.

- Set the Prefetch Count for Database Options in the Oracle8 ODBC Setup dialog box to a value greater than 1. Usually 25 to 100 is a good range for applications displaying a list of rows from the database on a screen. Increasing this value instructs the server to return multiple rows in a single fetch operation to the client's cache, thus improving performance for applications designed to return groups of adjacent rows to users. Choose a value that works best for your application.

Troubleshooting via Logging

You can enable Oracle8 ODBC driver to identify problems with applications via its logging function. When logging is enabled, log files are written to the current working directory. It should be noted that log files can become quite large and slow down performance. Therefore, enable logging only when necessary, and disable it when it is no longer needed.

Installing the Oracle8 ODBC driver creates the following section in the oraodbc.ini file:

```
[Oracle ODBC Driver Common]
Driver Logging=0
RemoveControlChars=NO
LockTimeOut=0
Proxy Access=0
```

A value of 0 for logging indicates that Oracle8 ODBC driver logging is turned off.

To enable Oracle8 ODBC Driver logging, you need to insert a valid Oracle8 ODBC driver logging value plus 1 for the Driver Logging entry:

```
[Oracle ODBC Driver Common]
Driver Logging=7
```

Valid Oracle8 ODBC driver logging values are shown in Table 26.1. To enable more than one type of logging, add the logging values and then add 1, as shown in the table. For example, to log ODBC entry points (a value of 2) and ODBC main functions (a value of 4), insert a value of 7 (2 + 4 + 1) after the equal sign.

The driver log, oraodbc.log, is written to the application program's current working directory.

TABLE 26.1. DRIVER LOGGING VALUES.

Value	Value + 1	Description
0	–	Disable logging
2	3	Log ODBC entry points
4	5	Log main functions
6	7	Log ODBC entry points and main functions
8	9	Log ODBC utility functions
10	11	Log ODBC entry points and utility functions
12	13	Log ODBC main functions and utility functions
14	15	Log ODBC entry points, main functions, and utility functions
16	17	Log only SQL statements and errors

Start with a value of 17. It is usually the best Oracle8 ODBC driver logging value to start with for problem solving, because it logs only the SQL statements sent to the server and any errors that are returned from the server.

Last Words on ODBC

Regardless of the architecture and functionality changes to both client programs and database servers, ODBC continues to be one of the primary means of getting data to and from client programs in a client/server environment. The benefit is that security comes with ODBC's popularity, because any data access method replacing ODBC will need to fully address the migration path off ODBC, or suffer failure and nonacceptance. It is also true that new functionality delivered by database vendors, such as the new functionality in Oracle8, will be—and is—accessible through ODBC. Although ODBC has some minor limitations, its greatest weaknesses are attributable to client/server development in general. The greatest of these is the support and configuration of individual PCs. All in all, ODBC is the primary data access method of the semitechnical user and will probably continue to be so for some time.

Overview of JDBC

In effectively using JDBC, its purpose and architecture need to be examined. The following section introduces the purpose of JDBC and offers a brief synopsis of its architecture and evolution.

JDBC's Purpose

Java Database Connectivity (JDBC) is the industry-accepted standard Application Programming Interface (API) that enables developers using the Java development language to access data in many different formats and locations. As its name implies, Java Database Connectivity (JDBC) is similar to ODBC, because its design goals and general architecture are the same. They both access data, regardless of format or location, through a single interface. Although most access through JDBC is via SQL, there is nothing that limits JDBC from using query languages other than SQL to access data sources, as long as the data resulting from the query is returned in a format that complies with the JDBC specification.

JDBC's Evolution

In the summer of 1996, shortly after the Java Development Kit V1.0 specification came out, the JDBC kit was also produced by Sun. As of JDK 1.1, JDBC was a part of the specification and JDBC drivers were available for most major databases. This gave Java a true universality, because it could run on any platform, and with JDBC, could access most data sources through a non–vendor-specific interface. Currently, there are more than 30 companies making JDBC drivers to access most data sources that are available in the market today, including drivers to access ODBC data sources through JDBC. To get more information on JDBC drivers, visit `www.javasoft.com`.

Oracle's JDBC Evolution

Shortly after JDK 1.0.2 was released, Oracle made the JDBC drivers for Oracle7 available free of charge. In addition to the initial JDBC drivers, Oracle also produced two related products that greatly enhanced JDBC options for use in Internet/intranet applications: JDBC Thin and SQLJ. All the Oracle JDBC-related products currently support JDK 1.0.2 and JDK 1.1+. In addition, both Oracle7 and Oracle8 databases are supported, except the JDBC Thin driver, which supports only Oracle 7.2 or later (including Oracle8).

Although the Oracle JDBC drivers are what you would expect (JDBC functionality plus support for Oracle-specific functionality), the SQLJ and JDBC Thin products are different enough to warrant additional discussion.

JDBC Thin

JDBC Thin is one of the most exciting products for enabling "Thin Client" computing to come along to date, due to its ability to connect Java client programs to Oracle databases without having Net8 installed on the client. To achieve this, the JDBC Thin driver is written completely in Java and establishes a direct connection to the Oracle database server via a lightweight, Java sockets implementation of Oracle's Net8 protocol. The only requirement is that the client machine support TCP/IP, which any machine that is Internet/intranet-enabled does by default.

SQLJ

SQLJ is another addition to the Oracle precompilers such as Pro*C for C, Pro*COBOL for COBOL, and Pro*Fortran for FORTRAN. Perhaps a better name for SQLJ might have been Pro*Java. As in other Oracle precompilers, SQLJ enables a developer to embed SQLJ statements directly into the Java code without having to know JDBC. The SQLJ program is run against the Java code and translates the SQLJ clauses into Java classes, which make the database requests via JDBC. The Java type system then assures that the SQLJ-generated classes are called with correct numbers and types of arguments. At this point, the Java code is ready to be complied with the Java compiler and run as a Java program or applet. The benefits to using SQLJ are that it performs data type checking by making the Java program call the generated classes.

Oracle precompilers are tremendously helpful in languages where the alternative to the precompiler is coding to the OCI (Oracle Call Interface—Oracle's database API). SQLJ also has the benefit of checking the SQL at compile time, which eliminates finding any SQL errors when the Java code is run.

In defense of JDBC (which is the alternative to SQLJ in Java), the coding of SQL is not any more complicated than SQLJ, and no generated code needs to be examined when debugging code. (SQLJ generates separate Java classes to handle the SQL calls.) Additionally, in environments where multiple database vendors are used, it is probably more cost effective to have developers using a common interface such as JDBC as their data access language.

JDBC Architecture

There are two major components in JDBC. The first is the JDBC API, which defined the API for Java programmers accessing the database. The second was the JDBC driver API, which defined the common interface that database vendors needed to write device drivers for so that Java could access their databases.

JDBC Setup, Usage, and Limitations

The following section will enable developers to understand the JDBC setup and configuration process.

Oracle8 JDBC Setup

For JDBC and SQLJ, there are two basic steps for installing JDBC for Oracle8; for JDBC Thin, only the second step is necessary.

1. Install and configure Oracle's Net8. This is covered in Chapter 3 of this book.
2. Install and configure the JDBC software for Oracle8.

Installing Oracle8 JDBC Drivers

The JDBC drivers for Oracle can be downloaded from the Oracle Web site free. After downloading the file, double-click on the file to unZip it and read the readme.txt file located in the directory in which you have unZipped the file. It will guide you through installing the software via Oracle's Installer.

Configuring Oracle8 JDBC Drivers

The configuration of the JDBC drivers is covered in the installation, but is so simple it can be summed up in two steps:

1. Set the PATH to [ORACLE_HOME/BIN], where ORACLE_HOME = your machine's Oracle home directory (for example, c:\ORANT, C:\ORAWIN95, and so forth).
2. Set the CLASSPATH to [ORACLE_HOME/JDBC/LIB/classes102.zip or classes111.zip]. The Zip files depend on whether you are using the JDK (Java Development Kit) v1.0.2 or 1.1+.

Testing Connectivity

Here are the three steps for using JDBC/OCI8:

1. You may specify the JDBC drivers you want to use at a machine level via the parameter jdbc.drivers=my.substitute.Driver in your Java code to make sure the appropriate driver is loaded (refer to #1 in Listing 26.1). Alternatively, you may place the same statement in the ~/.hotjava/properties file on your local machine, which is not recommended for most situations.

2. Connect to the database by including the statement at #2 in Listing 26.1. Although the example shows one method to connect, there are four alternatives that may be used:

```
1. Connection conn = DriverManager.getConnection
("jdbc;oracle;scott/tiger");
```

```
2. Connection conn = DriverManager.getConnection
("jdbc;oracle:","scott","tiger");
```

```
3. Connection conn = DriverManager.getConnection
("jdbc;oracle:@database","scott","tiger");
```

```
4. java.util.Properties info = new java.util.Properties();
  info.addProperty ("user", "scott");
  info.addProperty ("password","tiger");
  Connection conn = DriverManager.getConnection
("jdbc;oracle:",info);
```

3. Issue queries and receive results using standard JDBC syntax, as demonstrated in #3 and 4 in Listing 26.1.

LISTING 26.1. (NUMBERING IS FOR REFERENCE ONLY)

```java
import java.sql.*;

class Employee
{
  public static void main (String args [])
       throws SQLException, ClassNotFoundException
  {
// #1
    // Load the Oracle JDBC driver
    Class.forName ("oracle.jdbc.driver.OracleDriver");

    // Connect to the database
    // You can put a database name after the @ sign in the connection
       URL
    // we have used "local" as our database name.  Scott and tiger
       are the user
    // name and password
// #2
    Connection conn = DriverManager.getConnection
    ("jdbc;oracle;oci8:@local", "scott", "tiger");
    Statement stmt = conn.createStatement ();
// #3
    ResultSet rset = stmt.executeQuery ("select username from
    all_users");
// #4
    while (rset.next () )
        System.out.println (rset.getString (1));
    stmt.close ();

  }

}
```

Capabilities and Limitations

Although JDBC is a universal data access method for Java, there are several capabilities and limitations that are worth mentioning.

Capabilities

Firewalls: Currently, Net8 (including JDBC Thin drivers) has the capability to connect through much of the most popular firewall software (Checkpoint, SunSoft, CISCO Systems, Milkyway Networks, Trusted Information Systems, Raptor, Secure Computing Corporation, and Global Internet). If you require the capability of connecting through a firewall, you should contact the firewall vendor to see what configuration is needed.

Considerations

- **SQLJ & JDBC drivers**   Make sure all machines are configured with Net8 and the TNSNAMES.ORA or Names Server configuration to connect to the appropriate databases and database versions.
- **JDBC Thin drivers**   Make sure that any changes to Oracle database listeners, IP addresses, or DNS names are reflected in your Java code. This is due to the static coding of connection properties when using JDBC Thin drivers.

JDBC, General

- Errors: JDBC errors will be formatted as if they are from an Oracle7 database, even if you are connecting to an Oracle8 database.
- CursorName: Oracle JDBC drivers do not support the getCursorName and setCursorName calls.
- Catalog Arguments to DatabaseMetaData Calls: There is no Oracle equivalent of the JDBC catalog arguments to DatabaseMetaData calls. Oracle JDBC drivers ignore catalog arguments.
- SQL92 Outer Join Escapes: Use the (+) Oracle syntax for outer joins.
- PL/SQL BOOLEAN and RECORD types: These are not supported in the Oracle JDBC drivers.
- IEEE 754 Floating-Point Compliance: There can be small differences between the results of computations performed by Oracle and Java.

JDBC Thin

Database Version Support   The Thin JDBC driver supports only Oracle7.2 database versions and later; it can also access Oracle8 databases.

Oracle-Specific Functions

Although JDBC covers most functionality needed to access Oracle8, there are some Oracle-specific capabilities built into Oracle's JDBC drivers.

REFCURSORs as ResultSets

You can convert a REFCURSOR value returned by a PL/SQL block into a ResultSet. JDBC enables you to call a stored procedure that executes a query and returns a ResultSet. The following example demonstrates the use of REFCURSORs. Make sure to add import oracle.jdbc.driver.*; to the beginning section of your Java code so that the Oracle JDBC driver classes are imported for use in your code.

```
CallableStatement callStmt;
ResultSet resultCursor;

// Use a PL/SQL block to open the cursor
callStmt = conn.prepareCall("begin open ? for select cust_name from
➥customer; end;");

callStmt.registerOutParameter (1, OracleTypes.CURSOR);
callStmt.execute ();
resultCursor = ((OracleCallableStatement)callStmt).getCursor (1);

// Use the cursor like a ResultSet
while (resultCursor.next ())
  {System.out.println (resultCursor.getString (1));}
```

Execution Batching

The JDBC drivers allow a user to batch INSERTs and UPDATEs to the server, which reduces round trips to the server. OraclePreparedStatement.setExecuteBatch is used to set a prepared statement object's batch size:

```
import java.sql.*;
import oracle.jdbc.driver.*;
import java.io.*;
import java.util.*;

Connection conn =  DriverManager.getConnection
("jdbc;oracle;oci8:@local","scott","tiger");
```

```
// this statement opens a file and converts it to an data input stream in
order to read it
// line by line
DataInputStream inputStream = new DataInputStream(new
FileInputStream("inputfile.csv"));

PreparedStatement prepStatement = conn.prepareStatement ("insert into
customer values (?, ?, ?)");

//Change batch size for this statement to 10
((OraclePreparedStatement)ps).setExecuteBatch (10);

String inputLine;

while ((inputLine = inputStream.readLine()) != null)
   {
     // the following line calls a method that takes a
     // line read from the file and parses it into multiple
     // fields -
     Vector rowValue = parseRow(inputLine);

     // The following 3 statements insert the file fields in the Vector
     // created before into a row in the table Customer
     prepStatement.setInt (1, rowValue.elementAt(0).toString());
     prepStatement.setInt (2, rowValue.elementAt(1).toString());
     prepStatement.setInt (3, rowValue.elementAt(2).toString());

    //The following statement queues this for later execution
    // on every 10th statement, the inserts will be posted to the
    // database.
    prepStatement.executeUpdate ();

}      // End of While Loop

// This statement sends any remaining inserts to the database
((OraclePreparedStatement) prepStatement).sendBatch ();

prepStatement.close();

}
```

PL/SQL Stored Procedures

Oracle JDBC drivers support execution of PL/SQL stored procedures and anonymous blocks. The following example shows a Java class callPLSQL calling an Oracle stored procedure and a function:

```
/*
 * This example show how to call Oracle store procedures
 * or functions from java via JDBC
 */
import java.sql.*;
```

```
class callPLSQL
{
  public static void main (String args [])
      throws SQLException, ClassNotFoundException
  {
    // Load the driver
    Class.forName ("oracle.jdbc.driver.OracleDriver");

    // Connect to the database with the user "scott", the
    // password "tiger" and the TNS connect string "LOCAL"
    Connection conn =
      DriverManager.getConnection ("jdbc;oracle;oci8:@LOCAL", "scott",
      "tiger");


// Call a procedure with an IN/OUT prameter
// The procedure name is oracle_in_out_proc
    {
      CallableStatement inoutProc = conn.prepareCall ("begin
oracle_in_out_proc (?); end;");

//  The following line registers the out parameter as being
//  of type Char in position 1 of the stored procedure
      inoutProc.registerOutParameter (1, Types.CHAR);
//  The following line assigns the literal "testing" to the
//  first input variable of the proc (it is now being used
//  for input and output
      inoutProc.setString (1, "testing");
//  The next line executes the proc
      inoutProc.execute ();

      System.out.println ("Out argument is: " + inoutProc.getString (1));
    }
// Call to a function with an OUT parameter and a return code
//  This is similiar  to the call above, but the first "?" is
// assigned to the return value from the function.
    {
      CallableStatement funcout = conn.prepareCall ("begin ? := funcout
      (?); end;");
      funcout.registerOutParameter (1, Types.CHAR);
      funcout.registerOutParameter (2, Types.CHAR);
      funcout.execute ();
      System.out.println ("Return value is: " + funcout.getString (1));
      System.out.println ("Out argument is: " + funcout.getString (2));
    }
  }
}
```

Database Metadata

The Oracle JDBC drivers support all database metadata entry points. A full description of the Metadata class can be found in the Java.Sql specification in JDK 1.1+.

Streaming Data

The JDBC support of streaming, either from database to client or client to database (for all stream conversions—binary, ASCII, and Unicode), allows an efficient means to BLOB.

```java
/*
 * This example shows how to stream data from the database
 */
import java.sql.*;
import java.io.*;

class streamExample
{
  public static void main (String args [])
      throws SQLException, ClassNotFoundException, IOException
  {
    // Load the driver
    Class.forName ("oracle.jdbc.driver.OracleDriver");
    // Connect to the database
    // You can put a database name after the @ sign in the connection URL.
    Connection conn =
      DriverManager.getConnection ("jdbc;oracle;oci8:@", "scott",
      "tiger");

    // It's faster when you don't commit automatically
    conn.setAutoCommit (false);

    // Create a Statement
    Statement stmt = conn.createStatement ();

    //
    // You can insert the data in Example.txt into the database.
    File inFile = new File ("Example.txt");
    InputStream inputStr = new FileInputStream ("Example.txt");
    PreparedStatement prepStmt =
      conn.prepareStatement ("insert into example (the_key, long_value)
values (?, ?)");
    // Insert the key into the first column and the contents of
    // the file into the second column.  The last attribute
    // gives the AsciiStream the length of the file
    prepStmt.setAsciiStream (2, inputStr, (int)inFile.length ());
    prepStmt.setString (1, "FirstExample");
    prepStmt.execute ();

  }
}
```

prefetch

One of the best features of an Oracle database is its ability to fetch more than one row at a time. This greatly increases performance by reducing the number of trips between the client program (Java) and the Oracle database. The following example shows a Java program that connects to an Oracle database and sets the prefetch to 100 for the connection. This results in the program requesting 100 rows at a time for any query using this connection in the program.

```
/*
 * This example show how to call Oracle via JDBC
 * and use Oracle's prefetch functionality
 */
import java.sql.*;
// You need to import oracle.jdbc.driver.*  for the
// Oracle specific extentions
import oracle.jdbc.driver.*;


class oraPrefetch
{
  public static void main (String args [])
       throws SQLException, ClassNotFoundException
  {

    // Load the Oracle JDBC driver
    Class.forName ("oracle.jdbc.driver.OracleDriver");
  // Connection to retrieve the tables to be extracted
    Connection Con = DriverManager.getConnection
("jdbc;oracle;oci8:@LOCAL", "scott", "tiger");
    Statement tableStmt = Con.createStatement ();
  // ** Oracle specific extention to prefetch 100 rows at a time
    ((OracleConnection)Con).setDefaultRowPrefetch (100);
  // ** Get all tables in the database
      ResultSet rset = tableStmt.executeQuery ("select table_name from
      all_tables");
  }
}
```

Define Query Columns

Defining columns allows a programmer to define the types of columns in a query, which saves a round trip to the database to get the column types. The following example demonstrates setting the columns of a query to String types:

```
/*
 * This sample shows how to use the "define columns"
 * extensions in Oracle.
 */
```

```
import java.sql.*;

// You need to import oracle.jdbc.driver.* in order to use the
// API extensions.
import oracle.jdbc.driver.*;

class defineColType
{
  public static void main (String args [])
      throws SQLException, ClassNotFoundException
  {
    // Load the JDBC driver
    Class.forName ("oracle.jdbc.driver.OracleDriver");

    // Connect to the "LOCAL" database as "scott" and password
    // "tiger"
    Connection conn =
      DriverManager.getConnection ("jdbc;oracle;oci8:@LOCAL", "scott",
      "tiger");

    Statement stmt = conn.createStatement ();

    // Call DefineColumnType to specify that the column will be
    // retrieved as a String to avoid NUMBER to String conversion
    // A round-trip to the database to get the column type is
    // also avoided.  The (OracleStatment)stmt portion of the following
    // statement is Oracle specific and is needed to allow us to
    // call the defineColumnType method.

    ((OracleStatement)stmt).defineColumnType (1, Types.VARCHAR, 2);

ResultSet rSet = stmt.executeQuery ("select empno from emp");
    while (rSet.next ())
    {
      System.out.println (rSet.getString (1));
    }
    stmt.close ();
  }
}
```

Last Words on JDBC

Although JDBC is limited to Java, it is of primary importance to the next generation of
applications, because it builds on Java's strengths. JDBC (specifically Oracle's JDBC
Thin) enables a developer to create applications with the functionality of a Windows-
based client/server application, while not having to deal with the configuration and support of the application user's PC. It is also encouraging to see JDBC develop very robust
capabilities and support over a very short period of time, as compared to ODBC or other

data access methods. As in ODBC's involvement with the success of client/server applications, JDBC will play a major role in the success of Thin Client/Internet-based applications being developed now and in the future.

Summary

Both ODBC and JDBC have their separate and distinct roles in facilitating the access of data from Oracle8. ODBC, after several years of enhancements and underlying architecture changes from Microsoft, remains the primary method of accessing Oracle data from the Microsoft Windows environments. JDBC, in contrast, has been created solely for use by programs written in Java and exists on almost every hardware and operating system combination in existence. In their respective areas, both ODBC and JDBC will be the primary means of accessing Oracle data for some time to come.

Oracle Web
Application Server

by Stephen L. O'Hearn

In This Chapter

Oracle's Web Application Server 3.0 is one of the most important products Oracle has ever released. The WAS 3.0 is much more than a way to send Oracle database information across the Web to your browser: WAS promises to reinvent application development and deployment as we have known it. It is the only open, standards-based, fully scalable platform for delivering applications from virtually any source, across any Web-based network, to virtually any platform, in a manner that is less expensive and faster to deploy than other methods. Its flexible development options, highly distributed architecture, solid reliability, robustness, and fault tolerance, make it the leading tool for the development and deploying of mission critical enterprise applications. There really is no other product that competes with it.

The WAS is an application server that works with virtually any Web server, such as Netscape, Spyglass (which comes bundled with the WAS), Apache, or Microsoft. It has the ability to work with different, and even incompatible, Web servers to process incoming requests through multiple ports.

The cartridge architecture of the WAS allows developers to deploy applications written in PL/SQL, Java, Perl, C, and virtually any other language. Developers can manage cartridges independently, taking cartridges up and down as needed without affecting the others, and even incorporate third-party server extensions. Load balancing and application partitioning are all accomplished easily.

The WAS is at the heart of Oracle's Network Computing Architecture (NCA). It is based on the CORBA (Common Object Request Brokerage Architecture) model, an industry standard for empowering distributed objects across a network to achieve cross-platform interoperability. In other words, the WAS lets you use multiple programs, files, and other resources, including legacy code and the latest Java applet, and regardless of any language or operating system, integrate everything into one robust application, delivered to any user anywhere.

Background: The Internet, the WWW, and Intranets

Unless you're that guy on a Pacific Island in that one episode of Gilligan's Island who thought that World War II was still in progress, chances are you know about the Internet. But just in case you're that guy, here's a brief review.

Review for That Guy

In 1969, an agency of the United States Department of Defense known as the Defense Advanced Research Projects Agency (DARPA) recognized that the United States was building a very valuable resource: several computer centers, located at various universities and government agencies around the country, containing a growing amount of electronic documents with scientific and other data, each with their own local user community of people who were exchanging email messages and computer files about their research. DARPA decided to connect these electronic communities of people to each other, encouraging America's leading research centers to increase their exchange of information, and building a redundant network that could stay operational even if part of the network were damaged, such as in a war or natural disaster.

The network was built on the TCP/IP suite of protocols, and built on a backbone of high-speed data communications lines connecting the major computer systems. It was designed to support electronic mail and the transfer of files back and forth between the various online members of the electronic community—in other words, to increase information exchange among the scientific research community.

Over time, other existing networks were connected, new organizations got connected, one thing led to another, and the International Network of computers, or Internet, began to grow.

In 1989, Tim Berners-Lee created a communications protocol intended to support the widespread distribution of files, including text and images, to the various computers on the Internet, regardless of what brand of hardware or what sort of operating system was involved. Within a few short years, the World Wide Web grew astronomically, as "Web sites" mushroomed everywhere, publishing everything from "Joan's Recipes" to the *New York Times*, and empowering anyone with a computer to publish information to the masses more quickly and less expensively than any other media ever known.

Today, the Internet supports a number of services, such as File Transfer Protocol (FTP), electronic mail, Usenet news (the electronic bulletin board system, also known as Newsgroups), Gopher, Internet Relay Chat (IRC), Telnet, and the World Wide Web (WWW), as well as others. Nobody really knows how many people are connected worldwide, but the estimates are far into the many millions.

The Web is the reason this chapter is in this book. While it is an outstanding file delivery mechanism, its potential as an application deployment tool is only beginning to be fully realized—led by Oracle's Web Application Server.

Web Architecture

In order to understand the Oracle Web Application Server product, you must first have some understanding of the Web itself.

The term "Web" is used to refer to the World Wide Web, but sometimes it's used to refer to an intranet. The World Wide Web is a subset of the Internet. An intranet is a closed network, not connected to the Internet, but that uses the same communication protocols, Web servers, and browsers, that are used on the World Wide Web. It is estimated that there are more Web servers supporting corporate and other intranets throughout the world than there are Web servers on the actual World Wide Web.

The Web is made up of a network of computers running Web server software, available to receive and process requests from any client software. For example, when you log in to the Internet and start up your browser software, such as Netscape Navigator or Internet Explorer, you can enter a Web address in the Location field, such as:

```
http://www.corbinian.com
```

then press your Enter key. This causes your browser (client) to attempt to establish a connection with the Web server located at the Web address you gave. Once the connection is established, the browser makes a request of the server. Generally the request is for a file, such as a text file or image file, located on the server. Sometimes the request is for a program that resides on the server. The server receives the request and processes it: if the request was for a program, it executes the program through a special gateway, and gets the result; if the request was for some sort of file, it locates the file. The server then either sends the requested information back to the client (the program output or the file), or it sends back a message explaining why it cannot fulfill the request. Finally, the server terminates the connection.

The last step—termination of the connection—is why HTTP is described as "stateless," and it's an important point to consider when designing Web-enabled applications.

Hypertext Transport Protocol (HTTP)

The Hypertext Transport Protocol is the communication protocol used by Web servers and Web clients to talk with each other. The protocol is relatively simple, with all transactions following the same basic pattern. Each request—either from client to server, or server to client—consists of three parts:

- The request or response line
- A header section
- The entity body

Here's an example of a request line from a client to a server:

```
GET /home.html HTTP/1.0
```

This is a request to use the GET method, one of two methods by which a client is allowed to ask for a document (the other is POST). The client is requesting the document home.html and is telling the server that it can use HTTP version 1.0.

The client may follow with a header section that contains more text instructions to the server, informing the server of the type of browser it's using, and what kind of files it is able to accept, such as GIFs (a kind of image file), text, and so on. One blank line marks the end of the header.

Next, if the request were for some sort of program, the client might send some additional information, such as the parameters required for the program. The manner in which it supplies the parameters is dependent upon whether the client is making a GET request or a POST request.

Once the server receives the client's request, it processes the request, determines if the request is valid, and if it is able to serve the request. Depending on what the server does, it might send back the requested file. If the request were to run a program, the server will send back the program's output. If the server was unable to serve the request for any reason, it will send back one of several HTTP response codes, such as 500 Internal Server Error, or 503 Service Unavailable.

Uniform Resource Locator (URL)

Uniform Resource Locators, or URLs, are character strings that are used to specify the address of a resource (file, program, and so on) on the Internet. For example:

```
http://www.corbinian.com/macmillan/article.htm
```

URLs have a specific syntax. In the above example, the first part, http://, is telling the browser to employ HTTP as the communications protocol, as opposed to gopher, ftp, or some of the other options available. The www is a machine name for the host, and the corbinian.com is the address of the host. This host name points the browser to the computer housing the Web server software that the client wants to communicate with. Once connected, the rest of the URL maps to different resources available to that Web server, and the mapping is dependent on that Web server's configuration. Generally speaking, most URLs are pointing to some directory or subdirectory on a hard drive (like /macmillan) connected to the host machine, with the final part of the URL, which in this example is article.htm, pointing to some particular file in that subdirectory.

> **NOTE**
>
> Contrary to popular belief, the part of the URL in the example that indicates this is the World Wide Web is not the www, but the `http://`. The www is a machine, and many (but not all) administrators just tend to pick the www name to identify the machine running the Web server. The `http`, on the other hand, is distinctly a Web protocol, and is the giveaway that this is a Web address.

(The WAS has some powerful features for redirecting incoming URL requests in some unique ways. But more on that later.)

By embedding URLs in Web pages in a *hyperlink*, users are able to click a hyperlink, which tells the Web server to go get the resource identified by that URL, and to replace the existing display in the client with the new resource. This is how documents on the Web are connected and is the essence of the "webbiness" of the Web.

The Common Gateway Interface (CGI)

HTTP is intended to serve up static files—that is, unchanging stored text or image files. The CGI was created to add the ability to execute programs. If a Web server is configured to support CGI, then an incoming request can ask for a program to be executed, as opposed to asking for a static file. The request for a program is coded into the URL, by asking for a program by name, and including its subdirectory. If the request Web server is properly configured, it will recognize the subdirectory as a CGI subdirectory, and route the request through the CGI to have the program executed. The program's output is then sent back to the Web server, which serves the output to the client.

Since the request to run a program is coded into the URL, the hyperlinks that are embedded in Web documents can be used to not only request new text and images to be displayed, but to execute programs, regardless of where the program resides on the network.

Multipurpose Internet Mail Extensions (MIME)

MIME is part of HTTP, and is a standard that allows various forms of data, such as video, sound, executables and other binary files, to be sent across the network as they are, without having to perform any file conversion. Internet servers and email clients use MIME to attach various file types to email messages. HTML can use MIME to embed multimedia in files that are requested by clients.

Some file types require special software to be properly incorporated in the client browser. These "plug-ins" can be added to the client's browser on an as-needed basis to run streaming video, play sound files, or read complex document formats. Using MIME, Web servers can communicate with clients to recognize if a plug-in is present or not, download files as appropriate, or inform a user that a plug-in needs to be downloaded.

Software developers can use MIME to incorporate multimedia or various file formats in their Web applications.

Cookies

HTTP is inherently stateless. In other words, as each request is made and answered, the client and server terminate their mutual connection. There is not a persistent recognition that spans multiple requests. While this is not a problem for simple file delivery, which is what HTTP was originally intended to support, it is a big problem for applications running through the gateway that need to maintain some sort of continuity among several transactions. For example, you cannot have a client log in and be validated for a series of transactions unless you can recognize that client's individual transactions among all the various incoming requests coming from across the network.

Cookies were created to address this problem. A cookie is a tiny file, often just a long number but sometimes with some brief keywords or other text strings, that the server temporarily stores on the client through the browser. The server often makes a note somewhere of who it gave the cookie to and why. Then later, when the next request comes in from that client, the server can see the cookie, compare the cookie number or codes with its internal notes, and confirm that yes, this is the user who already logged on and is validated.

Cookies are used when you shop on the Net and put things in your "shopping cart" before going to the "check out" stand. And they're used by applications where a client needs to go through a series of transactions before deciding to either save their work or abandon what they've done.

Cookies can be given time limits, so that they expire at a certain time. They can also be associated with the server that sent them, so that a client that gets cookies from a second server doesn't mix up its cookies from the first server.

Hypertext Markup Language (HTML)

HTML is the language of Web browsers. In order to understand how to deploy applications across the Web, you must understand HTML. Fortunately, it's relatively easy to get productive with HTML.

HTML is a subset of the Standard Generalized Markup Language (SGML), a standard for providing a generic structure documents so they can be displayed in a reasonably similar manner on any platform. HTML consists primarily of language *tags*, brief commands that tell a Web browser (such as Netscape Navigator) how to format text, graphics, and other information. The tags themselves do not appear in the final display, but their results do.

For example, the following text tells a browser to display one word in a sentence in bold print:

```
Print one of the words in this sentence in <B>bold</B> print.
```

This sentence, when included in an HTML file, would display in a browser like this:

> Print one of the words in this sentence in **bold** print.

Table 27.1 shows a few examples of HTML tags.

TABLE 27.1. HTML TAG EXAMPLES.

This Text with Embedded HTML Tags	*Results in This Output: Explanation*
Original HTML:	`Hello!  I'm Dr. Van Nostrand.`
Browser Display:	`Hello!`
	`I'm Dr. Van Nostrand.`
Explanation:	` ` is the single tag for a carriage return. Browsers ignore actual carriage returns; you must use tags. A period is automatically followed by two spaces, even if it's after `Dr.`
Original HTML:	`<I>Oracle8 Unleashed</I>`
Browser Display:	*`Oracle8 Unleashed`*
Explanation:	`<I>` is a tag pair. All text between the `<I>` and the `</I>` is in italics.
Original HTML:	`<B><I>Oracle8 Unleashed</B>,`
	`edited by Rosemarie Graham</I>`
Browser Display:	**`Oracle8 Unleashed`**`, edited by Rosemarie Graham`
Explanation:	Tags can overlap and be combined.

The point of HTML is to allow files to be delivered to any platform without requiring that platform to have any special software other than the Web browser. For example, consider Figure 27.1, which is the text of a newspaper article.

FIGURE 27.1.

An example news-paper article.

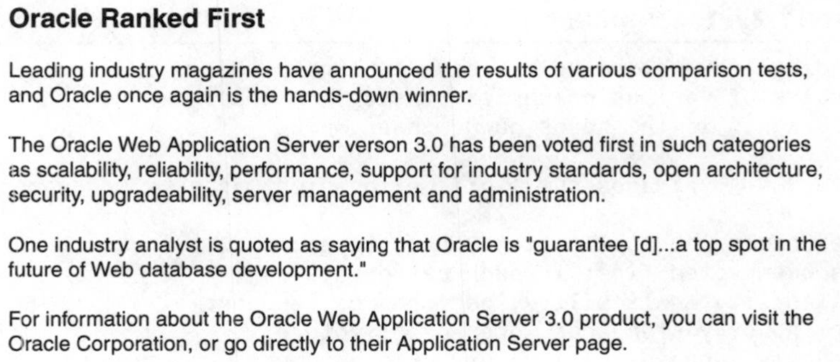

Oracle Ranked First

Leading industry magazines have announced the results of various comparison tests, and Oracle once again is the hands-down winner.

The Oracle Web Application Server verson 3.0 has been voted first in such categories as scalablility, reliability, performance, support for industry standards, open architecture, security, upgradeability, server management and administration.

One industry analyst is quoted as saying that Oracle is "guarantee [d]...a top spot in the future of Web database development."

For information about the Oracle Web Application Server 3.0 product, you can visit the Oracle Corporation, or go directly to their Application Server page.

The article starts with a headline, which should be printed larger than the main body of the text, centered at the top of the application display window.

Non-Web applications, such as a traditional client/server GUI application, would contain instructions to tell the client to display the headline in, for example, Times New Roman, 24 point font, starting at some particular X and Y coordinate point on the screen. If the client doesn't have the right font, you could be in trouble. And if the client monitor doesn't have enough room to handle the display, the headline won't necessarily appear centered, and might even run off the side of the screen. In other words, detailed knowledge of the client's capabilities and limitations must be taken into consideration by the application developer, and must be considered for every environment from which a client might attempt to access the application—or you must restrict your client's environment options.

To deliver this article across the Web to a browser, you would first convert it to an HTML file, as shown in Listing 27.1.

LISTING 27.1. NEWSPAPER ARTICLE WITH EMBEDDED HTML TAGS.

```
<HTML>

<HEAD>
<TITLE>Demo Web Page:  Newspaper Article</TITLE>
</HEAD>

<BODY BGCOLOR="#FFFFFF">

<H1 ALIGN=CENTER>Oracle Ranked First</H1>

<HR>
```

continues

LISTING 27.1. CONTINUED

```
Leading industry magazines have announced the
results of various comparison tests, and Oracle
once again is the hands-down winner.<P>

<IMG SRC="../images/num_1.gif" align=right vspace=10 hspace=20>

The Oracle Web Application Server version 3.0
has been voted first in such categories as
scalability, reliability, performance, support
for industry standards, open architecture,
security, upgradeability, server management
and administration.<P>

One industry analyst is quoted as saying that
Oracle is "guarantee[d] ... a top spot in the
future of Web database development."<P>

For information about the Oracle Web Application
Server 3.0 product, you can visit the Oracle
Corporation
<a href="http://www.oracle.com">home page</a>,
or go directly to their
<a href="http://www.olab.com/">
Application Server page</a>.

</BODY>
</HTML>
```

In Listing 27.1, HTML tags are embedded in the text to instruct the Web browser how to format the output.

The HTML file in Listing 27.1, when displayed in a Web browser, looks like Figure 27.2.

With HTML, the developer and end user are both freed from platform-specific considerations. Instead, the developer embeds tags into the text of the newspaper article that instruct the browser to print the headline, as in the example, a first-order heading, using whatever default font is available to the browser. The browser does the work of selecting the font at the time it displays the article. The client's operating system is irrelevant, its specific fonts are not an issue, and the browser is given the freedom to approximate the GUI management on the client, including centering, paragraph wrapping, and incorporation of any image files, all within the general guidelines defined by the HTML file.

FIGURE 27.2.
Browser display-ing newspaper article.

The result is that different browsers don't necessarily display a page in exactly the same way on every client. But the display is consistent enough and, with proper use of HTML table tags, developers get enough control to give their applications a professional appear-ance, yet still take advantage of the generic HTML display tags.

Graphic images, stored in separate files, can also be incorporated into the HTML file by reference, and delivered easily by the server to the client at the time of the request.

TIP

If you have a browser, you can experiment with HTML by simply creating a reg-ular ASCII text file that contains HTML tags, storing the file on your hard drive, and opening that file with your Web browser (generally by selecting FILE-OPEN FILE from the browser's pull-down menu). To incorporate graphic images, just put the image files on your hard drive, and reference them with the IMG tag, using the proper directory reference relative to the original HTML file. You can even incorporate images from across the Web, but be careful—don't violate any copyright laws or use another Web server's processing resources inappropriately.

Java

Java had a relatively quiet introduction in 1991 as *Oak*, a language intended to support the creation of device drivers, primarily for the purpose of networking household appliances. But in 1995 it rocketed to the forefront of the Internet stage, when the industry realized that it has the ability to deliver object-oriented, cross-platform, mission-critical applications. Today, many analysts believe Java will become "the COBOL of the '90s."

The power and uniqueness of Java comes from the fact that it runs in what is called a Virtual Machine (VM). A VM is a software layer between the Java application and the hardware it runs on, creating an environment within which the application can expect the same behavior regardless of what hardware it is actually running on. Developers are able to program without concern for the specifics of the user's platform. The final program, once written, can run on any machine.

In addition, a layer of security exists that prevents Java from doing anything destructive to the local environment, such as secretly deleting files, affording protection to the end user from viruses or errant applications running amok.

What HTML has meant for file serving on the Web, Java promises to be for application distribution. It's capable of delivering high-quality, robust applications with the look and feel of sophisticated GUI tools, such as Oracle's Forms product.

JavaScript

JavaScript is an object-based (but not truly object-oriented) scripting language created by Netscape and Sun. It is interpreted, rather than compiled. JavaScripts can run on the client in most browsers, and can also run on the server with Netscape's LiveWire environment. It is platform-independent, and, although it's not as powerful as Java, it's easier to program scripts more quickly, especially for novices.

Network Computing Architecture

The Network Computing Architecture (NCA) builds on existing Web technology, incorporates various standards, and provides the first framework within which serious, mission-critical application development and deployment in a networked environment are possible. Also known as Oracle's Open Network Computing Architecture, the NCA realizes the potential of Web technology for cost-effective cross-platform application deployment by integrating the strengths of traditional client/server programming with distributed objects. In a word, the NCA is revolutionary.

The core of the Network Computing Architecture is based on the CORBA distributed object model.

CORBA, the Common Object Request Broker Architecture, is an Object Request Broker (ORB). It was established by the Object Management Group (OMG), a consortium of over 700 companies representing the entire computer industry. (The only exception: Microsoft is promoting their own ORB standard called DCOM.)

A CORBA ORB is interoperable, meaning that objects (such as a COBOL program, or a set of C++ classes) do not need to know the language-specific issues required to invoke another object, but instead can abide by published interface requirements, and invoke any other object regardless of its specific implementation. Using CORBA'S Interface Definition Language (IDL), existing applications (for example, COBOL, CICS, IMS, and so on) can be "wrapped" and made to look like an object on the ORB. Using CORBA 2.0's Internet Inter-ORB Protocol (IIOP) services (say *that* three times fast), any ORB can connect to any other ORB on the network.

In March of 1996, Marc Andreesen of Netscape said "The next shift catalyzed by the Web will be the adoption of enterprise systems based on distributed objects and IIOP (Internet Inter-ORB Protocol). IIOP will manage the communication between the object components that power the system. Users will be pointing and clicking at objects available on IIOP-enabled servers."

CORBA advances the ability of distributed objects to communicate across the network. The NCA takes this further, to build a foundation on which diverse applications can be implemented and communicate within the same architecture.

The NCA consists of three platforms: (1) the universal data server, (2) the application server, and (3) the universal client.

The Universal Data Server. This could be the Oracle8 RDBMS, but the WAS will work well with non-Oracle data servers as well.

The Universal Application Server. This is the WAS 3.0, including the listener, Web request broker, and cartridges (applications).

The Universal Client. This could be a PC with browser software, such as Oracle's Power Browser, Netscape Navigator, or the Internet Explorer. It could also be a computer known as a *thin client*, an inexpensive stripped down PC with few of the peripherals that most PCs today come with. All that is required is a monitor, keyboard, modem or network card, browser software, and either a local hard drive or some other mechanism to cache Web pages. Oracle's vision for the thin client is the Network Computer, or NC, from the Oracle subsidiary Network Computer Inc. (NCI).

These three platforms, and the entire NCA, are depicted in Figure 27.3.

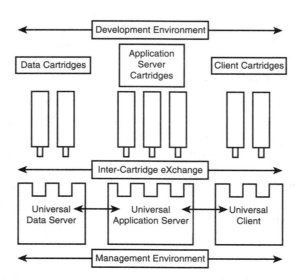

FIGURE 27.3.
The Network Computing Architecture (NCA).

To understand the primary goal and benefits of the NCA, it's helpful to understand some things about the history of network architecture.

Background

Most corporations and organizations set up their own private networks long before the advent of the Internet, and even while the Internet was quietly growing. Most organizations still prefer and require some sort of closed private network. This section describes the evolution of these networks, and how the Web is impacting them today.

Before client/server networks, the *host-based* model was widely used. Host-based networks consisted of a series of "dumb" terminals connected to one or more large mainframe computers. The dumb terminals didn't run any software other than the bare necessities to connect to the mainframe. All application software and data was resident on the mainframe, and dumb terminals were essentially a viewport into the mainframe. Users worked on dumb terminals to run software on the mainframe. Among the advantages of a host-based system: centralized maintenance, such as backups and upgrades. There were many disadvantages, though. Mainframes tended to be closed systems—software that ran on one brand of mainframe wouldn't run on another. Operating systems were very different. The cost of switching from one vendor's system to another was often prohibitively high. Furthermore, since the mainframe was extremely expensive to begin with (many cost millions of dollars), the system wasn't horizontally scalable. Once the user capacity of one mainframe reached its maximum, to add just one more user meant adding another mainframe—a major investment in hardware. Nor was it vertically scalable—if the application required just a little more CPU or storage, and the mainframe was maxed out, the investment required could be significant.

Finally, graphical user interfaces (GUI), which are intuitive and require little training or lead time to get users operational, were not practical in a host-based system. (Contrary to popular belief, GUIs were created in the 1960s by Xerox, not by Apple or Microsoft). A graphical user interface manages communication with the user by a complex set of graphic images, icons, buttons, check boxes, and detailed reaction to mouse movements. Since all applications ran on the host, and since the programs that manage GUI displays are, by nature, communications-intense, GUI displays tended to clog up the network. The network was (and is) the weak link in the chain, and couldn't handle the extra load while still supporting all of its other responsibilities. So while GUIs were technically possible, they were definitely impractical.

All of this changed with the *client/server* model, which consists of a series of personal computers (PCs) linked together in a Local Area Network (LAN), all connected to a single inexpensive central file server or some other dedicated PC set aside to be the network's server. Files common to everyone are stored on the server; files that the client uniquely requires are stored on the client. The entire network cost could be counted in the thousands of dollars, rather than in the millions. By incorporating PCs instead of dumb terminals, the responsibility of executing applications can be shared by the client, offloading most of the work from the server, and allowing a less powerful server to handle more clients more effectively.

The client/server model offers many advantages. It can support different hardware and software from different vendors. It's possible to link PCs and Macintosh computers by using all sorts of network and application software, yet have everything connected in one LAN. Also, client/server networks scale easily. To add another user usually means just adding another PC. If the server reaches its capacity of how many PCs it can support, the cost of another server is incidental compared to the host-based mainframe. The same is true for applications and data—the cost is relatively low to accommodate software growth. And since each user is running a PC on their desktop, GUI management can be handled on the client, instead of at the server, which eliminates the network bottleneck for GUIs that existed in the host-based model, making advanced GUI displays very practical.

But client/server systems are not centralized. The maintenance costs of a client/server system can be deceptively high. If something goes wrong, the responsibility of maintenance can be difficult to assign—is the problem in the PC? The Macintosh? The network itself? The server? Different operating systems, applications, and diverse resources combined in one network, which was first presented as a great advantage, have the potential for creating a maintenance nightmare if the hardware and software diversity gets out of hand. A troubleshooter must have familiarity with the entire system, and MIS departments find it difficult to identify personnel that individually possess a working knowledge of all the components. Furthermore, software and hardware upgrades, application deployment, and maintenance work on the network requires either the MIS department to travel from PC to PC, or requires each user to bear some of the burden.

Enter Tim Berners-Lee, the father of the World Wide Web (mentioned earlier). While working at the European Laboratory for Particle Physics (CERN), in 1989, Berners-Lee's vision was to support the widespread distribution of files, including text and images, that combined the best elements of both the host-based and client/server models. He moved all of the files off of the client and back to the server. The Web browsers he created are really a generic application to handle the complex GUI management on the client, instead of the server, making GUI systems across the network practical for the first time. For more information, see the previous discussion about Web Architecture.

Interestingly, the Web really represents something of a combination of host-based networks and client/server networks. But it's designed for serving files and, even with the addition of CGI (described earlier), the Web cannot handle complex applications.

Oracle's Network Computing Architecture builds on Web technology to make complex applications possible. The NCA represents the best of the host-based model with the best of the client/server. In the NCA, as Sun Microsystems puts it, the "network is the computer." As in the Web, the NCA moves all applications and data back to the server, and leaves a Web browser, the generic GUI management tool, on the client. In NCA terminology, the client is often called a *thin client*, something between a PC and a dumb terminal. It doesn't have the peripherals (CD-ROM, floppy drive, and so on), except for possibly a relatively small hard drive or some other feature to cache pages from the browser. Instead, all maintenance, backups, upgrades, and so on are done on the network, which can be an intranet or the Internet, and programs are downloaded across the network on an as-needed basis.

The NCA is fully scalable, allowing any combination of hardware to serve client requests. It is easy to maintain—in fact, users don't have to maintain anything. Instead, the network can be managed effectively by a professional team, doing backups and upgrades, and freeing the user from having to address those issues. If the system has a problem, the network team addresses it, and the users are not bothered with it. In many ways, it's a return to the original host-based computing platform, when users worked on dumb terminals and ran software that was stored only on the host.

In a number of live presentations on the NCA concept, Larry Ellison, the founder and CEO of the Oracle Corporation, has frequently mused at what life would be like if common household appliances had the same complexity of maintenance as a PC. For example, you never hear someone say something like "Sorry, I can't go out tonight, I'm staying home so I can upgrade my TV to version 7.0." Nobody has to go to training class to learn how to use their washing machine. Nobody has to get a refrigerator adapter when they find out their latest leftovers aren't compatible with their existing refrigerator. Yet computer users deal with these issues all the time. Software that runs on a Macintosh won't run on a PC. Upgrading from one version of Windows to another is a significant effort. Ellison's argument is that this is unacceptable, and, in order for computer technology to reach the masses, the PC must become as easy to use as any common household appliance.

In a recent presentation to a Japanese IT convention, Ellison was asked by a member of the audience if the network will be stable enough—won't it crash from time to time? Isn't it risky to place so much dependence on the network? Ellison's response was to ask the audience member another question: what is the last thing that crashed on you: your telephone, or Windows 95? The audience roared with laughter, making the answer obvious. Yes, a network can experience problems once in a rare while, but when a network is maintained by a professional technical staff on a full-time basis, the burden of the rote, technical system maintenance is lifted off of the consumer, who can spend her time focusing on her actual work. We can just dial a phone number and start talking, not worrying about whether our phone has the same bit-switch error-checking parity as the phone of the person we're calling.

The number of networks we already depend on is impressive: plumbing, electricity, highways, television, radio—all networks professionally run by others, that consumers use frequently, yet do not worry about personally maintaining, upgrading, or troubleshooting. Why should a computer user experience anything different?

Furthermore, in the NCA world, software is modularized so you only download those parts of the software that you need. If you just want to type a memo, no need to fire up the Granddaddy Power Word Processor 2200. You get the resources you need when you need them, regardless of their location on the network. The magic that makes this happen is the Oracle Web Application Server.

Oracle Web Application Server Architecture

The Oracle WAS 3.0 is the Universal Application Server platform for the Network Computing Architecture model. It consists of one or more Web Listeners, Dispatchers, a Web Request Broker, and cartridges, or server-side applications.

Web Listener

The Web Listener, also known as the HTTP Daemon, or HTTP server, listens for requests from clients. When a client sends a request to the WAS across a network, using HTTP, the Listener receives it and determines what sort of request the client is making. If the request is for a static file or CGI script, it handles the request directly: it finds the appropriate static file, or executes the requested CGI script, and sends back the file or script output to the client. If the request is for an application, however, it forwards the request to the Dispatcher component.

The Listener can accept incoming requests from multiple IP address/port combinations.

Oracle's WAS comes bundled with the Spyglass Web Listener, an independent product that is used as a Web server on its own. The bundled version is configured for use with the Oracle WAS. Other popular Web servers can be used instead, such as Netscape, Apache and Microsoft's Webserver software, so if you're already using one of those Webservers, you don't have to change to integrate the WAS. The Installation Guide that comes with WAS contains instructions on how to configure those Web servers to work with WAS. Oracle has plans to integrate with other Web server software in the future.

Dispatchers

The Dispatcher tracks server-side applications, and sends incoming requests to them, as they are received from the Web Listener.

The Listener and Dispatcher run together as one process, yet are distinct components. Multiple Listener/Dispatcher combinations can be run on the same machine or on different machines, allowing the WAS to handle multiple requests simultaneously, from different connections on different sets of ports. This can help to improve performance rather significantly, depending on your application performance requirements.

Even though they run as one process, the Dispatcher can work with any Listener, so if you choose not to use the bundled Spyglass listener, but instead configure a different Listener for use with the WAS, the Dispatcher will still function.

Web Request Broker (WRB)

The Web Request Broker (WRB) is the core of the WAS. It is a CORBA compliant Object Request Broker (ORB) (see the earlier discussion on CORBA). It receives and processes incoming requests, analyzes them to determine which application is being requested, and regardless of where they are on the network, invokes the relevant cartridges as necessary. It also provides various services to these cartridges as required. The WRB performs load-balancing, address translation, security functions, and manages and monitors the execution of applications throughout the entire system.

The WRB consists of several processes, listed in Table 27.2. The processes include such things as the Virtual Path Manager, which helps to route the incoming request to the appropriate cartridge by analyzing the virtual path—a portion of the URL—and determining the cartridge that is being asked for. The Logger service keeps track of requests and messages in a file or in the database for later review. It provides a generic interface to all cartridges, so that any cartridge can write log data.

TABLE 27.2. WEB REQUEST BROKER PROCESSES.

Process	Description
mnorbsrv	Object Request Broker (ORB) service
mnaddsrv	ORB address server
mnrpcmnsrv	Remote Procedure Call (RPC) name server
wrbcfg	Web Request Broker (WRB) Configuration Provider
wrblog	WRB Logger service
wrbasrv, wrbahsrv	WRB Authentication service
wrbroker	WRB
wrbvpm	Virtual Path Manager
wrbfac	Cartridge Factory—one per cartridge instance

For more information about the Authentication service, see Web Security.

If your configuration of the WRB includes distribution of processes across multiple nodes, most of the WRB processes will stay on the primary node. The cartridges and the cartridge factory processes (wrbfac's) run on the remote nodes. The Authentication service may also be configured to run on remote nodes as well.

Transaction Management

This option, which is only available in the WAS 3.0 Advanced Version, is used by applications that must lock records in one Web display, and takes the user through a series of hyperlinks before deciding to either COMMIT the set of changes or ROLLBACK the entire set of changes.

To appreciate the significance of this service, we must first understand what Oracle does in a multi-user environment. When a user logs in to a system and accesses a record in a table, Oracle locks that record in that table for that user, allowing that user the time to decide to either COMMIT his changes, or ROLLBACK the data to its original state. While the user is online, and before deciding to either COMMIT or ROLLBACK, other users may log in and query the same record. But Oracle's built-in, row-level locking mechanism prevents that second person from doing work that will conflict with the first user—for example, changing data in another part of the same record. The first user can complete his or her work, possibly performing multiple INSERT, UPDATE, and DELETEs, until finally deciding to either COMMIT or ROLLBACK all of his work. For mission critical multi-user RDBMSs, this is a required capability.

Unfortunately, it's not easily accomplished on the Web. The Web uses HTTP, which is a stateless protocol. In other words, users don't really "log in" to a session, but instead they "connect" for a single request. When that request has been answered, the connection is terminated. There is no login session in which the database can easily maintain "state", over which a lock can persist.

If a transaction can be accomplished within one HTTP request, there is no problem. But some transactions requires multiple requests—for example, letting the user click through multiple hyperlinks, displaying different pages, entering or modifying data in various fields, and then finally reaching a Web screen in which the user decides to COMMIT or ROLLBACK his or her work. Each click is an HTTP request, and every Web screen that follows is a response. And each response results in a terminated connection.

One way to create a persistent session is through the use of cookies. This method is manageable for such things as user authentication (when combined with other features), but transaction management is potentially more complex when juggled across multiple incoming requests. The developer can create an internal session table of some sort, and write logic into each application that locks records according to a particular user request. The application can issue cookies, to keep track of who implicitly requested which lock, and associate timeouts with each lock in case someone who requests a lock just turns off their machine and walks away without performing either a COMMIT or a ROLLBACK. After all, there is no logoff process for users other than the end of a single request and, if you choose to ignore that for maintaining state, there's no dependable logoff process at all.

Custom application tracking of login sessions is doable, but requires a significant amount of programming effort. To provide assistance to this very commonly required scenario, the WRB provides Transaction Services. For example, in PL/SQL, developers can create a set of stored procedures, and associate them together as one transaction. One procedure is defined as the BEGIN procedure of the transaction, another as the COMMIT, and still another as the ROLLBACK. A set of procedures is defined as the boundaries of the transaction—in other words, the procedures whose work will be accepted as affecting the locked records. When the BEGIN procedure is invoked for any reason, Oracle issues a series of cookies and performs the necessary locks to create a persistent session. The locks stay until either the COMMIT or ROLLBACK procedure is invoked, or until the developer-specified timeout occurs.

The C cartridge also has transaction service support. The Java cartridge is not yet currently supported, but will be soon.

As stated earlier, the developer can create the code necessary to support persistent transactions without the Transaction Service, which theoretically makes it possible to do in any cartridge. But the Transaction Service saves a lot of development and testing effort.

Invoking a Cartridge from a Client—An Example

To appreciate how clients, the WRB, and cartridges work, it's helpful to understand how the WAS looks at incoming Web addresses. Consider the following URL:

```
http://www.corbinian.com/demo/plsql/bookstore$.order_form?customer_id=1234
&first_order=T
```

This particular URL contains the following parts:

URL portion	Description
http://	This is the type of protocol being requested. Most Web browsers will also allow non-Web protocols, such as FTP (File Transfer Protocol) and others.
www	This is the machine for the host.
corbinian.com	This portion is the host name. Host names are often shown as the domain name, which is a text variable representing an IP address. An IP address is a series of 4 numbers, separated by periods, each of which ranges from 0 to 255. Each location on the network has a unique IP address. Domain names are essentially variables that are used to represent the IP address, and a master lookup table of domain names and IP addresses is distributed around the network so all systems know which physical address to connect to for any valid domain name. If the information located at one physical address needs to move to another, the master table that translates IP addresses is changed and all programmed calls to the domain name will now point to the new address—in other words, existing code that references the URL needs no modification.
	If WAS is running at a particular Web site, this is enough of a URL to reach it. In other words, the rest of the URL is processed by the WAS.

`demo`	Once the URL reaches this point, the WAS has received it, and refers to its internal configuration to determine what to do next. If, for example, WAS was configured to have a PL/SQL Cartridge Agent called `demo`, this portion of the URL would inform WAS to route this incoming request to the PL/SQL Cartridge.
`bookstore$`	By now the WAS has identified this request as a request for a PL/SQL stored procedure. `bookstore$` is the name of a stored package in the database. The particular database that this package is stored in is defined in the Database Access Descriptor (DAD), an ASCII file created by the Webserver Administrator as part of the initial configuration of the PL/SQL Cartridge. Once the WAS determined that this request was for a PL/SQL cartridge, it looked to the DAD to identify which database the request is for. Then it confirms that the package `bookstore$` is a valid package in that database.
`order_form`	This is the name of the procedure in the stored package `bookstore$`.
`?customer_id`	This is the first parameter being passed to the procedure. The stored packaged procedure parameter is `customer_id`. The first parameter in any URL is preceded by a question mark. The stored packaged procedure `BOOKSTORE$.ORDER_FORM` must have a corresponding `CUSTOMER_ID` parameter.
`=1234`	The value being passed to the `customer_id` parameter (1234).
`&first_order`	The second parameter, `first_order`. Note that all parameters following the first are preceded by an ampersand. Again, the procedure must have this parameter.
`=T`	The value being passed to the second parameter (`T`). Note that numbers and characters can be treated the same—no quotes. In spite of this, the stored packaged procedure parameter declaration can be specific—`NUMBER`, `DATE`, and so on. As long as the incoming data is consistent, there will be no problem.

Cartridges

Cartridges are applications that run on the server. The WRB invokes them on an as-requested basis. Each cartridge is a separate process that can be started and stopped independently as required. Furthermore, each cartridge process, called an instance, is usually run in multiples—you can have 20 PL/SQL cartridge instances running on different machines within the network, and ten instances of another cartridge, all managed by the WRB.

There are many advantages to this division of cartridge processes. The architecture lends itself well to load balancing and application partitioning. Most importantly, if one cartridge fails, the other cartridges are not affected. A cartridge, running as a separate instance, could experience complete failure, infinite loops, and so on, and not cause a problem to the other cartridges, even other instances of the same cartridge. This robustness of performance is a great feature.

The WAS comes bundled with several cartridges, including the following:

- PL/SQL
- Java
- C
- LiveHTML
- Oracle Worlds (VRML)
- Perl
- ODBC

Some of the most commonly used cartridge options are described in the following sections.

PL/SQL

If you're an Oracle developer, I know what you're thinking: "Enough with all this architecture nonsense—how do I get the data out of the database, and into a browser?" This is your section.

Oracle provides a number of stored procedures and functions to be used with PL/SQL when building Web applications.

Consider the PL/SQL procedure in Listing 27.2.

LISTING 27.2. PL/SQL TO CREATE STORED PROCEDURE MY_FIRST_PAGE.

```
CREATE OR REPLACE PROCEDURE my_first_page
IS
BEGIN
  htp.htmlOpen;
  htp.headOpen;
  htp.title('My First Page');
  htp.headClose;
  htp.bodyHead;
  htp.header('1','Welcome to my first page.');
  htp.line;
  htp.p('This is the first page ' ||
        'I ever created using PL/SQL.');
  htp.bodyClose;
  htp.htmlClose;
END;
/
```

> **NOTE**
>
> This procedure contains a number of calls to procedures in the Oracle provided package HTP, designed to support the creation of HTML files. This package comes with WAS, and is not a standard PL/SQL package.

If you execute this code in SQL*Plus, it will create a stored procedure called `my_first_page`. Next, you could start your Web browser, and, depending upon how the WAS is configured at your installation, you could enter a URL in the location such as the following:

```
http://www.corbinian.com/demo/owa/my_first_page
```

This would instruct the Web server to execute the `my_first_page` procedure that will write this file, which isn't stored anywhere, but is instead sent across the network to the browser, as shown in Listing 27.3.

LISTING 27.3. MY_FIRST_PAGE OUTPUT (HTML FILE).

```
<HTML>
<HEAD>
<TITLE>My First Page</TITLE>
</HEAD>
<BODY>
<H1>Welcome to my first page.</H1>
<HR>
```

```
This is the first page I ever created using PL/SQL.
</BODY>
</HTML>
```

This HTML will appear in the browser as shown in Figure 27.4.

FIGURE 27.4.

my_first_page, displayed in a browser.

As you can see, an understanding of HTML is required, since all output written to the file and sent to the client to be displayed in the browser must be an HTML file.

Oracle provides a set of packages that contains procedures and functions for use with the WAS. The packages used the most often are the HTP and HTF packages. The HTP package consists of procedures to print various HTML tags. The HTF package contains the same set of instructions, but as functions instead of procedures; the two exist so you can embed functions from HTF in the procedure calls to HTP. For example, consider this code:

```
htp.tableData('This cell in the table is not in bold print!');
```

This uses the `tableData` procedure to print a cell in a table. But what if you wanted to wrap the text in the HTML bold tag? You could do this:

```
htp.tableData(htf.bold('This cell in the table is in bold print!'));
```

Of course, you could also have done this:

```
htp.tableData('<B>This cell in the table is in bold print!</B>');
```

This code contains the actual HTML bold tag pair in the character string (`'<B>'`), and it has the same effect as using the HTF packaged function call. For that matter, you could also just use the `htp` print procedure to do everything:

```
htp.p('<TD><B>This cell in the table is in bold print!</B></TD>');
```

This example also prints the cell and makes the text bold, using a simple print procedure and the HTML tags spelled out. However, it can be difficult to read, especially when combined with several other print statements. On the other hand, some of the HTP procedures that have several parameters can be difficult to read, too, more so than the original HTML. I find that I use HTP procedures to write most of the code, with a few actual HTML tags once in a while as required.

Table 27.3 shows some of the more commonly used features of HTP and HTF. If you don't already know something about HTML, this table won't mean anything to you—see the section on HTML first. Note that while case sensitivity is not an issue in HTML, the Oracle documentation tends to display HTP and HTF procedures in the case shown—that is, in lower case letters, but capitalizing any second word in the concatenated string (with no use of underscores), for example, `centerOpen`, or `tableData`. This is just a formatting issue and obviously (well, obviously to PL/SQL programmers) has no bearing on functionality.

TABLE 27.3. COMMONLY USED HTP PROCEDURES (AND HTF FUNCTIONS) AND THEIR OUTPUT.

Procedure Name and Parameters	*Output Format*
`anchor2(curl, ctext, cname,` `ctarget, cattributes)`	`<A HREF="curl" NAME="cname"` `cattributes>ctext</A>TARGET="ctarget"`
`bodyOpen(cbackground, cattributes)`	`<BODY background="cbackground" cattributes>`
`bodyClose`	`</BODY>`
`bold(ctext, cattributes)`	`<B cattributes>ctext</B>`
`center(ctext)`	`<CENTER>ctext</CENTER>`
`centerOpen`	`<CENTER>`
`centerClose`	`</CENTER>`

`formOpen(curl, cmethod, ctarget,`
`cenctype, cattributes)`
`METHOD="cmethod"`
`TARGET="ctarget"`
`ENCTYPE="cenctype"`
`cattributes>`
	`<FORM ACTION="curl"`

`formClose`	`</FORM>`
`formCheckbox(cname, cvalue,` `cchecked, cattributes)`	`<INPUT TYPE="checkbox" NAME="cname"` `VALUE="cvalue"CHECKED="cattributes">`
`formRadio(cname, cvalue,` `cattributes)`	`<INPUT TYPE="radio" NAME="cname" cchecked,` `VALUE="cvalue" CHECKED cattribute>`

Procedure Name and Parameters	Output Format
formReset(cvalue, cattributes)	`<INPUT TYPE="reset" VALUE="cvalue" cattributes>`
formSubmit(cname, cvalue, cattributes)	`<INPUT TYPE="submit" NAME="cname" VALUE="cvalue" cattributes>`
formText(cname, csize, cmaxlength, cattributes)	`<INPUT TYPE="text" NAME="cname" cvalue, SIZE="csize" MAXLENGTH="cmaxlength" VALUE="cvalue" cattributes>`
headOpen	`<HEAD>`
headClose	`</HEAD>`
header(nsize, cheader, calign, cnowrap, cclear, cattributes)	`<Hnsize ALIGN="calign" NOWRAP CLEAR="cclear" cattributes>cheader</Hnsize>`
hr(cclear, csrc, cattributes)	`<HR CLEAR="cclear" SRC="csrc" cattributes>`
htmlOpen	`<HTML>`
htmlClose	`</HTML>`
img(curl, calign, calt, cismap, cattributes)	`<IMG SRC="curl" ALIGN="calign" ALT="calt" ISMAP cattributes>`
italic(ctext, cattributes)	`<I cattributes>ctext</I>`
line	(See HR)
mailto(caddress, ctext, cname, cattributes)	`<A HREF="mailto;caddress" cattributes>ctext</A>`
nl	` `
para	`<P>`
paragraph(calign, cnowrap, cclear, cattributes)	`<P ALIGN="calign" NOWRAP CLEAR="cclear" cattributes>`
tableOpen(cborder, calign, cnowrap, cclear, cattributes)	`<TABLE "cborder" NOWRAP ALIGN="calign" CLEAR="cclear" cattributes>`
tableClose	`</TABLE>`
tableRowOpen(calign, cvalign, cdp, cnowrap, cattributes)	`<TR ALIGN="calign" VALIGN="cvalign" DP="cdp" NOWRAP cattributes>`
tableRowClose	`</TR>`
tableData(cvalue, calign, cdp, cnowrap, crowspan, ccolspan, cattributes)	`<TD ALIGN="calign" DP="cdp" ROWSPAN="crowspan" COLSPAN="ccolspan" NOWRAP cattributes>`

27

ORACLE WEB
APPLICATION
SERVER

> **NOTE**
>
> The presence of anything for cchecked results in CHECKED.
>
> The presence of the cnowrap parameter causes NOWRAP to appear. If cnowrap is NULL, NOWRAP will not appear.
>
> The presence of cismap causes ISMAP to appear.

Once a PL/SQL developer understands how to display data in HTML, it is a relatively simple thing to integrate information from the database into a display. Listing 27.4 is an example of a PL/SQL procedure that queries the database and displays the results in an HTML file.

LISTING 27.4. PL/SQL PROCEDURE WITH HTML AND DATABASE DATA MERGED.

```
CREATE OR REPLACE PROCEDURE list_donors
(region_code_in VARCHAR2)
IS
  CURSOR c1 IS
    SELECT do.donor_id donor_id
         , do.lastname || ', ' || do.firstname full_name
         , do.state state
         , TO_CHAR(do.amount,'$999,999,999.99') amount
      FROM donors do
     WHERE do.region_code = region_code_in;
  c1_var c1%ROWTYPE;
  --
  cookie_id_var INTEGER;
  --
BEGIN
  --
  -- Most of my applications start with a call
  -- to a routine that checks the user's cookie.
  -- This is a call to the check_cookie procedure
  -- in a package I created called util$.
  --
  util$.check_cookie(cookie_id_var);
  --
  -- If the cookie has a problem, it will be
  -- dealt with in the check_cookie procedure.
  -- If control reaches this point, then the
  -- user has been authenticated.  In addition,
  -- if I need to know the user's identity
  -- for this procedure, the cookie can help
  -- identify her.
  --
```

```
htp.htmlOpen;
htp.headOpen;
htp.title('DEMO:  Show a list of all donors');
htp.headClose;
htp.bodyOpen;
htp.header('1','List of All Donors','center');
htp.line;
--
htp.centerOpen;
htp.tableOpen;
--
htp.tableRowOpen;
htp.tableData('Donor Name');
htp.tableData('State');
htp.tableData('Amount','right');
htp.tableRowClose;
--
OPEN c1;
LOOP
   FETCH c1 INTO c1_var;
   EXIT WHEN c1%NOTFOUND;
   --
   htp.tableRowOpen;
   htp.tableData(htf.anchor2(detail_donor?donor_id_in=' ||
                             TO_CHAR(c1_var.donor_id),
                         c1_var.full_name));
   htp.tableData(c1_var.state);
   htp.tableData(c1_var.amount,'right');
   htp.tableRowClose;
   --
END LOOP;
CLOSE c1;
--
htp.tableClose;
htp.centerClose;
--
htp.bodyClose;
htp.htmlClose;
--
EXCEPTION
  WHEN OTHERS THEN
     --
     -- It's a good idea to at least have a "WHEN OTHERS"
     -- exception handler.  Otherwise, if something goes
     -- wrong, you'll just get a general HTTP header
     -- response from the server, instead of the Oracle error
     -- message.  To see the Oracle error message, you either
     -- have to look through the web servers logs, or
     -- create a procedure (ours is "show_error") that
```

continues

LISTING 27.4. CONTINUED

```
    -- captures the error message and code, and displays
    -- them on a web screen, in much the same fashion
    -- that this procedure writes to a web screen.
    --
    util$.show_error('list_donors',SQLERRM,SQLCODE);
END;
/
```

Listing 27.4, when executed, will create a stored procedure called list_donors. This procedure, when stored in our database and accessed via a browser, displays as Figure 27.5.

FIGURE 27.5.

list_donors *output browser.*

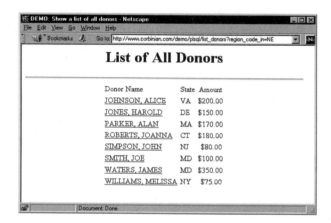

By clicking View -> Page Source in the browser's pull-down menu, we can display the HTML shown in Listing 27.5.

LISTING 27.5. list_donors HTML SOURCE.

```
<HTML>
<HEAD>
<TITLE>DEMO:  Show a list of all donors</TITLE>
</HEAD>
<BODY>
<H1 ALIGN="center">List of All Donors</H1>
<HR>
<CENTER>
<TABLE >
<TR>
<TD>Donor Name</TD>
<TD>State</TD>
```

```
<TD ALIGN="right">Amount</TD>
</TR>
<TR>
<TD><A HREF="detail_donor?donor_id_in=2">JOHNSON, ALICE</A></TD>
<TD>VA</TD>
<TD ALIGN="right">             $200.00</TD>
</TR>
<TR>
<TD><A HREF="detail_donor?donor_id_in=4">JONES, HAROLD</A></TD>
<TD>DE</TD>
<TD ALIGN="right">             $150.00</TD>
</TR>
<TR>
<TD><A HREF="detail_donor?donor_id_in=8">PARKER, ALAN</A></TD>
<TD>MA</TD>
<TD ALIGN="right">             $170.00</TD>
</TR>
<TR>
<TD><A HREF="detail_donor?donor_id_in=7">ROBERTS, JOANNA</A></TD>
<TD>CT</TD>
<TD ALIGN="right">             $180.00</TD>
</TR>
<TR>
<TD><A HREF="detail_donor?donor_id_in=6">SIMPSON, JOHN</A></TD>
<TD>NJ</TD>
<TD ALIGN="right">             $80.00</TD>
</TR>
<TR>
<TD><A HREF="detail_donor?donor_id_in=1">SMITH, JOE</A></TD>
<TD>MD</TD>
<TD ALIGN="right">             $100.00</TD>
</TR>
<TR>
<TD><A HREF="detail_donor?donor_id_in=3">WATERS, JAMES</A></TD>
<TD>MD</TD>
<TD ALIGN="right">             $350.00</TD>
</TR>
<TR>
<TD><A HREF="detail_donor?donor_id_in=5">WILLIAMS, MELISSA</A></TD>
<TD>NY</TD>
<TD ALIGN="right">             $75.00</TD>
</TR>
</TABLE>
</CENTER>
</BODY>
</HTML>
```

27

ORACLE WEB
APPLICATION
SERVER

Notice how we were able to create this page: by issuing fixed HTML print commands, using a loop to display the the rows of database data, and merging a portion of the

HTML print commands with the FETCH to populate the variables that display in the HTML table.

A few other points to notice:

- For numeric data, you need to specify right justification in the tableData tags, something that SQL*Plus and Reports normally do automatically.

- Arguments for tableData and other HTP procedures are generally VARCHAR2 datatypes. In this case, DONOR_ID and AMOUNT are stored in the database as numeric values. For AMOUNT, this listing did the TO_CHAR conversion in the SELECT statement itself, formatting the data as it extracted it. You could SELECT it as numeric, but you would have to do a TO_CHAR conversion to get the HTP procedure, which in this case is tableData, to accept it.

- Each record for FULL_NAME is hyperlinked to another stored procedure, called DETAIL_DONORS. DETAIL_DONORS takes a single parameter, DONOR_ID. This parameter is embedded in the hyperlink, with each record's appropriate DONOR_ID. This way, when the output displays in the client browser, the user can click the name of a particular donor. The hyperlink will pass the appropriate DONOR_ID to the procedure as a parameter and display details on only that donor.

TIP

If you want to incorporate client-side JavaScript in your application, you have two choices. You can embed the actual JavaScript in the PL/SQL procedures to write the HTML output—in other words, write JavaScript code into the HTML file. Or you can store the JavaScript code in separate files on the server, and use HTML tags to reference the files. This second method is actually easier if you want to debug and modify the JavaScript without having to recompile your packages and procedures.

Oracle provides a series of other packages to deal with the special Web-related issues of a PL/SQL Web application. Several are described in Table 27.4.

TABLE 27.4. OTHER ORACLE-PROVIDED PL/SQL PACKAGES FOR USE WITH WAS.

Package	Description
OWA_COOKIE	For sending, receiving, and managing cookies.
OWA_ICX	Procedures for the Inter-Cartridge Exchange.
OWA_IMAGE	Image map handling.
OWA_OPT_LOCK	Locking records, obtaining ROWIDs, and so forth to implement an optimistic locking model.
OWA_PATTERN	Provides some Perl-like text pattern matching features to support the conversion of Perl scripts into PL/SQL stored procedures.
OWA_SEC	Procedures to deal with security features.
OWA_UTIL	Very useful package that includes various utilities, including those that get CGI environment variables, generate MIME type responses, redirect URLs, print preformatted tables of data, and so forth. Lets you deal directly with HTTP.

Stored Procedures and Cookies

Since users who log in to the Web are not necessarily using Oracle schema names (see the discussion on Security), you cannot use the USER pseudo-column to identify your users. Furthermore, HTTP is stateless; login "sessions" do not exist on the Web as they do on a client-server system (see the earlier discussion on Cookies). So how can you identify who a user is when a procedure is invoked?

One approach is to build some extra functionality into the login process. When users log in, create a cookie—some lengthy number you create internally will work (you could use a SEQUENCE). Using the OWA_COOKIE package, you download this number to the user's client, the number is stored on their machine and you keep a copy of it in an internally stored Web session table. You can also use the OWA_SEC and OWA_UTIL packages to confirm the user's physical IP address at the time of log in, and store that in the Web session table with the cookie number, along with any user specific runtime options relevant to the application.

After that, any procedure that the client requests could include a cookie check (using OWA_COOKIE) to do the following:

- Get the client's cookie.
- Compare the cookie with the internal Web session table.
- Identify any relevant runtime options or other variables concerning the user's transaction.

A check to a procedure like this should occur at the beginning of every single stored procedure that needs to know who the user is.

In this fashion, cookies can be used to maintain a record of a user's transactions across several procedure calls, as in the "shopping cart" application used by many Web stores.

Java

The Java cartridge is intended to run Java classes on the server. These Java classes can return HTML to the browser with embedded Java applets to run on the client.

The primary purpose of the Java cartridge is to maintain a Java Virtual Machine instance, receive incoming requests for Java classes, and identify, validate, load, and invoke the `main()` method of whatever Java class is requested. Just as PL/SQL procedures can create HTML dynamically, so too can Java server-side components create HTML files with the results of queries to the database merged in with the HTML formatting tags. The WAS sends these HTML files back to the browser, resulting in the display of information from the database in the browser.

Oracle provides a number of Java classes to support development with the Java cartridge.

The `oracle.html` package of classes is shown in Table 27.5. It's similar to the PL/SQL HTP and HTF packages described earlier—the `oracle.html` package is used to generated HTML tags. If you have any familiarity with HTML, you can get an idea of what many of them probably do just from their names.

TABLE 27.5. JAVA CLASSES FROM THE `oracle.html` PACKAGE.

Anchor	Applet	BlockQuote
CheckBox	Color	Comment
CompoundItem	Container	DefinitionList
DirectoryList	DynamicTable	Embed
Form	Frame	Frameset
Hidden	HtmlBody	HtmlException
HtmlFile	HtmlHead	HtmlPage
HtmlRuntimeException	HtmlStream	IHAlign
IHtmlItem	IHtmlItemImpl	ITableFrame
ITableRules	ITarget	IValign
Image	ImageMap	ImageMapArea
Item	Link	List
MenuList	MetaInfo	Option

OrderedList	PasswordField	Preformat
Radio	Reset	Select
SimpleItem	Submit	Table
TableCell	TableDataCell	TableHeaderCell
TableRow	TableRowCell	TextArea
TextField	unOrderedList	XObject

Oracle provides other Java classes in addition to the `oracle.html` to help Web-enable Java applications. These are listed in Table 27.6.

TABLE 27.6. OTHER ORACLE-PROVIDED JAVA PACKAGES FOR USER WITH WAS.

Package	Explanation
oracle.lang	Functions to map Unicode and NLS character sets
oracle.owas.wrb	Access to various WRB services
oracle.owas.wrb.nls	Allows converting between NLS, Unicode, ISO, or IANA standard names and encodings
oracle.owas.wrb.services.http	Access to HTTP
oracle.owas.wrb.services.logger	Access to the WRB logging service
oracle.plsql	Classes that deal with PL/SQL datatype issues
oracle.rdbms	Implements a session to an Oracle database

At the time of this writing, Oracle Corporation has announced some major initiatives to increase its support of Java. Watch for the use of Java, in both WAS and throughout the Oracle product, to become as significant as the use of PL/SQL, if not more so.

ODBC

The ODBC cartridge allows applications to access data from other data sources using the Open Database Connect (ODBC) standard. Currently, Oracle supports access to Sybase, Informix, and Microsoft SQL Server, in addition to the Oracle RDBMS through the ODBC cartridge. As part of the configuration of the cartridge, you must specify which databases you want to access, and include some specific instructions to inform the cartridge how to access the particular database you want to include. These instructions are stored in the initialization file (`.odbc.ini`), which the cartridge refers to when it is invoked.

When invoking the cartridge, you have three "request modes" to choose from: Execute, Tableprint, and Stringprint. The differences have to do with how data is returned to the browser:

- **Execute mode:** This mode is good for INSERTs, UPDATEs, and DELETEs. It returns a success or failure message, but no data.

- **Tableprint mode:** This mode is good for SELECT statements whose output is rather standard. It returns the results of the SELECT statement in the form of an HTML table.

- **Stringprint mode:** This mode is good for SELECT statements whose output requires special formatting. It enables you to integrate the output of the SELECT statement with fixed text, including hyperlinks and other HTML tags.

Each mode is chosen at invocation. For example, consider the following URL:

```
http://www.corbinian.com:87/odbc/stringprint?database=ORACLE7&dsn=
demo&username=scott&password=tiger&sql='SELECT+name,state+FROM+contacts&
outputstring=%1+lives+in+%2.<br>
```

When the WRB receives this incoming request via the Web Listener, it sees the odbc string that follows the corbinian.com host name and 87 port and compares its mapping to see how to route this request. Assuming odbc is mapped to the ODBC cartridge in the WRB configuration, it determines that this is intended for the ODBC cartridge, and routes the request to the cartridge.

When the ODBC cartridge receives the request, it sees that the request is for stringprint mode, for the database that its configuration file maps to the ORACLE7 parameter, the demo instance, and logging in as username scott, password tiger. The SQL statement to execute is:

```
SELECT name, state
FROM    customers;
```

Finally, the output is returned as follows:

```
JOE SMITH lives in VIRGINIA.<br>
ALICE JOHNSON lives in MINNESOTA.<br>
HOWARD JONES lives in FLORIDA.<br>
(...etc...)
```

(Note: <br> is the HTML tag for a carriage return.)

To combine the flexibility of the stringprint mode with tables (which are built in to tableprint), you must invoke the ODBC cartridge from within another cartridge, and use the other cartridge to do the more specific custom formatting, HTML tags, and so on. This is, in fact, the real intent behind the ODBC cartridge: not to be used on its own, but rather to be incorporated into calls from other cartridges.

There are some security considerations with the ODBC cartridge. Since calls to the cartridge include the `sql` parameter, which allows any valid DML statement to be used, then a user could theoretically build his or her own URL to invoke the cartridge, with a SQL parameter such as `DELETE contacts`. There are some steps you can take to prevent this, such as only allowing certain IP addresses to access the system, or turning on password security for the ODBC cartridge. If password security is used, application developers must embed the password in their URL's that call the ODBC cartridge. Therefore, developers must take extra steps to ensure that their applications' calls to the ODBC cartridge do not include the password in any HTML that is written to the browser. Instead, any embedded hyperlinks to executables must first refer to a procedure that, in turn, redirects the call to the ODBC cartridge. Otherwiser, a savvy user can click the View -> View Source menu option in his or her browser, and in a couple of minutes identify the password to the ODBC cartridge from the HTML code.

The cartridge can use the WRB's Inter-Cartridge Exchange features, or the browser can access the cartridge directly.

(Note: The ODBC cartridge is only available with the advanced version of WAS 3.0.)

OCI

The Oracle Call Interface (OCI) Cartridge employs the OCI that has already been used primarily for accessing Oracle databases from applications written in C. It offers some significant improvements in performance over ODBC. From the developer's point of view, it behaves the same as the ODBC cartridge. It uses the same execute, tableprint, and stringprint modes, but it performs much faster than the ODBC.

Other Oracle-Provided Cartridges

Oracle is committed to creating and distributing additional cartridges for the WAS. Some examples are

- C cartridge
- Live HTML cartridge
- Perl cartridge

In addition to these, you can create your own custom cartridges.

Custom Cartridges

You can also create your own custom cartridges, using the WRB's Application Programming Interface (API). Currently, custom cartridges are written in C; Oracle is expected to support other languages for cartridge creation in future releases of the WAS.

Creating a custom cartridge requires a healthy understanding of cartridge architecture, more than is described here. It involves coding the cartridge, defining the various functions that WRB expects of a cartridge, and configuring the WRB to use your cartridge. While it involves some work, it's not terribly difficult. And it enables you to customize the WAS rather extensively.

Web Request Broker's InterCartridge Exchange (ICX)

The InterCartridge Exchange is a service of the Web Request Broker that allows one cartridge to call on services in another cartridge. In other words, an application written in one language can, through the ICX, use the services of another cartridge without any knowledge of that called cartridge's language.

For example, say you've written an application in PL/SQL that needs to access another database via ODBC. Your PL/SQL code can contain a call to the ODBC service, using the Oracle provided packaged procedures called `utl_http.request` and `utl_http.request_pieces` for use with the PL/SQL cartridge. These procedures let your application send a request to an ODBC service, and get responses back.

The ICX is modeled after HTTP. Requests via the ICX act like HTTP, and appear the same as an incoming HTTP request to the called cartridge, regardless of whether the calling cartridge is on the same node as the called cartridge, or across the network in a distributed configuration. And ICX allows any cartridge to make calls to any other cartridge, regardless of the languages involved.

Accessing Non-Oracle Databases

The first tier in the Network Computing Architecture model is the universal data server, which does not necessarily mean an Oracle database. The WAS has several mechanisms by which you can access data sources other than Oracle:

- ODBC and OCI cartridges, described in the previous section "Cartridges," include two methods by which any cartridge can access non-Oracle data sources.

- Java developers can use Java's JDBC classes. Java Database Connectivity (JDBC) is a Java API to SQL databases. It consists of a set of Java classes that can access any SQL database. Applications written in the WAS Java cartridge can use JDBC as an alternative to the ODBC cartridge for accessing a non-Oracle database.

- Oracle offers a feature known as Transparent Gateways (TG), which can integrate WAS with a large number of common database sources, such as Sybase, Informix, and other products. Through TG, any SQL*Net-compatible tool can access these other RDBMSs, even allowing for queries that join Oracle tables with non-Oracle tables. Oracle also offers Procedural Gateways that enable you to use non-Oracle transaction procedures as though they were stored procedures in the Oracle database. Finally, the Gateway Toolkit empowers developers to create their own gateways for all Windows NT ODBC-compliant RDBMSs. Note that the Oracle Gateways are a separate Oracle product and are not bundled with the WAS.

Web Security

Security is one of the most important issues with any Web application, more so than with traditional client-server systems. Since anything on a network is inherently more accessible, the probability of attempted hacks to a system is higher. But more significantly, the stateless nature of Web sessions, while providing significant benefits, also introduces some security questions that must be addressed before any serious application deployment can take place.

WAS provides a number of features to assist with the prevention of unauthorized access to your application.

User Authentication

The WAS offers several options for user authentication. One approach is to create user names and passwords that reside in the WAS, in other words, that you create through the WAS Administrator, and that are stored in files with the Web server. The passwords are encrypted in a similar manner as the Oracle database passwords, but the user names are not in the database.

When setting up these user names and passwords, you must choose between two options: Basic authentication, or Digest authentication. From the user's point of view, there's no difference between the two. The difference is in how the passwords are transmitted from client to server. When the user enters a password using Basic Authentication, the password is encoded in Base64 format, and transmitted to the server. Under Digest authentication, the password itself is not sent, but an MD5 checksum is sent instead. The advantage: it's impossible to decipher the MD5 checksum. When the server receives the checksum, it can tell that the client must know the password without receiving the actual password.

Instead of configuring usernames and passwords through the WAS, another approach is to use Oracle schema names (user names). This is a new feature with WAS 3.0, believe it or not, and to appreciate why, it's important to understand how the WAS is configured. When a new cartridge is set up in the WAS, a Database Access Descriptor (DAD) must be created. This is a set of instructions telling the cartridge how to access its data source.

For example, when setting up a PL/SQL cartridge, you must define that cartridge's database access. The DAD is given one associated user name in the database—that's one—to service all incoming client requests. In previous versions of the WAS, this meant that the entire collection of users accessing that cartridge was seen as one (probably really busy) user to the database. To provide any sort of database user names and passwords meant that the application developer had to develop and manage user names and passwords themselves. Oracle user names (schemas) could not be used.

This changed with WAS 3.0, which allows for either option. When creating a DAD in WAS 3.0, if you just leave the user name and password blank during the configuration process, users who log in to the application will be prompted by the listener to enter an Oracle user name and password. Also, any roles you may have set up for that user account will function for the user's login session.

The WAS also provides methods that allow you to work with the physical IP address from which a user is accessing the system. Every user on the network is associated with a physical address. By telling the WAS to, for example, only accept incoming requests from a given IP address, you effectively prevent any unauthorized access from anywhere else. You could also work the other way—allow access from anywhere except for one particularly troublesome IP address, one from which you know you've had attempted hacks in the past. This is possible, but not very effective, since a hacker can just try from somewhere else. But both options exist, and the first is very effective if your application's user requirements will allow for it.

Persistent User Verification

In a traditional client-server environment, users log in to a system by entering a user name and password. This causes the client to issue a request to establish a connection to the server. The server receives the request, validates the user, and established a connection. Then, as long as the user stays connected to the system, the server can confidently recognize each new user request as coming from the validated user.

In HTTP, it is not possible to stay "connected." Each request sent from a client to a server is an independent, autonomous request. The server can receive the client's first request to log in, validate the request, and send back a confirmation. But the client and server cannot connect, meaning that each new request from the client requires some sort of validation.

It's something like the difference between making a phone call and writing an email letter. When you telephone someone, a connection is established. Once you identify the person on the other end, you can confidently assume the rest of the conversation is, indeed, with the person you identified at the beginning of the phone call.

But when you exchange letters with someone, you need to identify that each new letter is, indeed, from the person with whom you are intending to correspond.

In Web-enabled applications, the burden of confirming the identity of each new client request (not just each login session, but each individual request, for example, to display one new page) is generally on the application. For one example of how to implement this, see the section about the PL/SQL cartridge and Cookies.

> **TIP**
>
> WAS 3.0 offers a new feature in the PL/SQL cartridge to help control user access: the Package/Procedure Protection feature. When a stored package or procedure is protected, no one is able to access the URL directly—you can't just type the URL for that procedure in your browser and get access, only another stored procedure can get access. In other words, if you build your application so that the initial login procedures are unprotected, and then protect all other packages and procedures, the user will always have to enter via the login procedures. This is a great security feature. But it may cause a problem if a user wants to use any third party tools, such as Microsoft Excel and its Web Query feature (available in Excel 97 with the Web Authoring Option), which downloads Web information directly from a given URL into an Excel spreadsheet (complete with formatting). If you find that you must leave some procedures unprotected, you can user a cookie check and IP address confirmation to lock out any invalid users, by having each unprotected procedure perform these checks up front, and raising an exception for any users without the right cookie number and IP address combination.

Secure Sockets Layer (SSL)

The WAS supports Secure Sockets Layer, which is a standard for both encryption of transmitted information, as well as for confirmation of the identity of either the client or server to each other. The SSL works as a layer in the TCP/IP stack (beneath the Application Layer).

SSL not only encrypts communication between the client and server, but it also incorporates digital certificates to confirm the identity of either the client, server, or both. A digital certificate is an encoded digitized alphanumeric code that uniquely identifies the server to a third party, usually Verisign, an independent organization. It is a time-consuming thing to obtain a digital certificate. It usually requires the corporation, organization, or whoever is operating the server, to provide documentation to confirm their identity, such as their Articles of Incorporation. A Dun and Bradstreet number is required under certain circumstances, as well as other information confirming the requesting party's identity, address, type of business, and so on. The process can take as much as several weeks to get approval. But once the identity is established, the digital certificate is provided to the server, and the administrator must configure the server software to incorporate the certificate. Then, when any client attempts to connect to the server using SSL, the server provides the certificate as confirmation of the server's identity. The user is then usually notified, through his browser, that an SSL request has been made, and he is given a choice to accept or deny. The user is also often given the option of viewing the digital certificate's associated text information—in other words, the server owner's name (the corporation, organization, and so on), address, and so on. Once the user accepts the request, SSL transmission begins. The browser usually displays some graphic, such as a key, or lock, or something, to indicate that the browser is operating in SSL.

All of this is to help guarantee to the client that the server is, indeed, who it claims to be. But what if the server requires confirmation of who the client is? Client-side digital certificates are also possible, but require a similar effort to obtain. Obviously, this is not a simple effort. For those regular users who will be accessing your system from the same location every time, client-side digital certificates are possible, but not always practical. Each situation has its own demands, and the choice is up to you.

Once SSL has been set up on your server, it's relatively easy to implement in an application: one slight change in the URL for any given resource is all that is required. For example, this is a URL for a non-SSL hyperlink:

```
http://www.corbinian.com/macmillan/article.htm
```

And this is a URL that incorporates SSL:

```
https://www.corbinian.com/macmillan/article.htm
```

In other words, to have your users log in with SSL transmission, just publish a slightly different URL and your client's first connection will incorporate SSL. On the other hand, you can have a client connect to your application as usual, and then within your application incorporate a hyperlink to a portion in which you choose to incorporate SSL by just modifying the hyperlink.

As long as your application's internal hyperlinks use relative addressing, the application will not require modification to incorporate SSL.

General Guidelines

There are many other security issues to consider. Here are some general suggestions to follow:

- When someone knows the URL for an application, he or she can just enter it into his or her browser. Make sure your application's modules, individual procedures, and so forth are protected, or put something in the beginning of each module to check for user authentication (see the discussion about PL/SQL cartridges and cookies for an example).

- The WAS Adminstrative Listener, by default, is available on the network along with the application. Watch this carefully. Don't let it be too available to the general community. Change its default settings. Change its port. Change its access from username access to IP-restricted access. And don't let it run when you don't need it. You can shut it down and start it back up later (make sure you know how to restart before you shut it down).

- I can't tell you how many contracts I've worked on when I've tried to log in to the Oracle account SYSTEM with the default password MANAGER, and got right into this crucial DBA account, even on installations that have been in business for years. Change your default passwords!

- Don't make operational data immediately accessible through the Web. In other words, don't let your cartridges have access to your only live copy of a database. Instead, store your original data source in a different user account; then create a second account that uses snapshots to copy data, and have your Web applications access the snapshots. Better still, for read-only Web applications, such as a data warehouse, put the original data on a different physical machine and use a periodic manual procedure to move data from the source to the Web database. This will guarantee that no hacker could possibly attack your source data through the Web applications.

Remember, while the WAS offers good security features, there is never any guaranteed protection. You can never eliminate the possibility of a successful attack, not with any system. You can only minimize it.

One final important note regarding security: Most successful hacks into an application do not come from computer wizardry but from classic con games. Someone calling your central operations center pretending to be working late on a project on a Sunday night and who demands to know the password to the SYSTEM account or his entire project will fail—this scenario is more likely to be a successful hack than someone sitting in his home office trying every password he can think of to get into your system. All the software security features in the world will not help you at all if your office procedures are not tight. Keep that in mind when establishing a security program for your application.

Developer/2000 and the Oracle WAS

The latest version of Developer/2000, version 2.0, includes some truly amazing features when combined with Developer/2000 Server (separately, Forms Server and Reports Server) and the WAS. These features allow developers to create applications as usual, but deploy them across the Web.

Forms

When forms runs on the Web, the form application itself is stored on the server. When a user requests a form, the Developer/2000 Java applet is downloaded to their browser and the Java applet communicates with the form application, which executes on the server, to exchange information with the application regarding display, user input, and so on. The Java applet is able to recreate the form in the user's browser in a rather striking manner, looking virtually identical to the original application. This truly is an amazing benefit to developers, allowing cost-effective and rapid application deployment, which now consists of storing the application on the server and publishing its URL to your users.

Forms can be delivered across the Web because of the way that Oracle happened to originally build the Forms product. The logic that controls the display is loosely integrated with the logic of the application and its integration with the database. As a result, Oracle is able to separate these two components, sending the display management to the Developer/2000 Java applet that downloads to the user's browser, and retaining the application's executable on the server. As the application (the FMX) executes on the server, it sends "bundles" of interface commands from the Forms Server to the Forms Client for managing and directing the client's form display. All triggers are processed on the server, and all user interface processing occurs on the Forms Client.

Since the Forms Client is a generic Java applet, you don't need to download separate applets for each application or each form. The Forms Client is smart enough to download only those Java class files that it needs. As the Forms Client makes additional requests during the user session, additional class files are downloaded on an as-needed basis. This keeps the Forms Client thin and efficient.

To deploy a form on the Web, you need to generate the form for the operating system that the application server is running on, either UNIX or Windows NT. If your form has already been running on a client of UNIX or NT server, don't make the mistake of thinking that this is good enough—you must generate the form on the server operating system. You don't need to do anything to the FMB file, you just need to move the FMB to the environment that is being used on your server, and generate the FMX file there.

For your users to access your form, you must create a static HTML file with hyperlinks to click to start your application. These hyperlinks should point to your FMX files, including any relative addressing required, just like any other hyperlink URL for a local file or application. Note that for these links to function you need to make sure FORMS45_PATH and TK23_ICON (or FORMS50_PATH and TK30_ICON) contain the directory where your FMX files are stored, or the hyperlinks won't find your application.

You also have to move any associated image files to the same directory that your installation of the WAS keeps static HTML files.

Keep in mind that you don't have to use the Oracle webserver software for this to work, but it helps. You do need the Developer/2000 and Developer/2000 Server software.

27
ORACLE WEB APPLICATION SERVER

NOTE

The Developer/2000 Java applet requires version 1.1.2 of Java, which most browsers available at the time of this writing don't support. To address this, Oracle ships an Applet Viewer that supports Java 1.3, and that works with the Developer/2000 Java applet.

CAUTION

When designing Forms that will be used on the Web, keep the following in mind:

- Timers (created with the CREATE_TIMER built-in procedure) are not allowed; the WHEN-TIMER-EXPIRED trigger will not work.
- Any graphic objects that are referenced by the form, such as icons in a toolbar, for example, must conform to Web standards. In other words, you can use GIF images and JPG images, but not ICO files. Any image files that are used must be stored in the server in the same directory as the static HTML files.
- You can't use ActiveX, OLE, or VBX.
- The mouse event triggers WHEN-MOUSE-MOVE, WHEN-MOUSE-LEAVE, and WHEN-MOUSE-ENTER don't work.
- The Autoskip item property doesn't work.

continues

- The built-in procedure Set_Window_Property cannot minimize or maximize windows. And there is no MDI support in Web-world.
- The built-in procedure Get_Item_Property cannot get object handles.
- Because the form is actually executing on the server, the Host command, ORA_FFI, and user exit output display on the server, not the client—in other words, not in the browser.
- Java doesn't support combo boxes, so it shows them as pop lists instead.

Reports

Reports Builder 3.0 (known as Reports Designer in version 2.5), will deploy reports in either HTML or Adobe Acrobat PDF across the Web. You can schedule jobs to run at predetermined specific times, creating output files that remain on the Web server waiting to be downloaded. You can also set up the Reports Server, together with either the Reports Web Cartridge or the Web CGI, and allow users to execute reports on demand, dynamically creating output in either HTML or Adobe Acrobat PDF file format and sending output to the invoking client browser.

This is yet another truly amazing technology. Existing reports, written in Reports Designer 2.5, can be compiled in Reports Builder 3.0 and be immediately Web-enabled.

The Reports Server does not require the WAS. It can be run through a Web server CGI. But the Reports Server runs significantly faster when combined with the WAS and the Reports Web Cartridge, which provides native integration. Once up and running, the Reports Web Cartridge is always available, while the CGI interface starts and stops the executable with every invocation.

> **NOTE**
>
> The Portable Document File (PDF) format, from Adobe Corporation, has become the de facto standard for distributing publication quality document files across the Internet to any platform. Anyone who downloads a PDF document must use the Adobe Acrobat Reader in order to read the document. The Reader is a free Web browser plug-in, is widely available, and runs on most platforms. Some browsers are starting to bundle it with their product.
>
> The reason PDF is so popular: It allows you to create the sort of complex documents that are normally published at great expense. They can be distributed

easily as email attachments or in whatever manner possible, since they are platform-independent. PDF files can include hyperlinks, security options, and other features. The Adobe Corporation estimates that over a quarter of a million Web sites are already using PDF in one form or another. The IRS distributes their tax forms in PDF format. Many companies distribute their corporate annual reports in PDF format. Oracle distributes some of its online documentation in PDF.

The Reports Builder, when publishing in PDF format, can incorporate graphic images, including photographs, specific fonts and detailed formatting instructions. The output will appear and print exactly, not approximately, as I've described the HTML approach to file distribution, but precisely as originally created.

Graphics

The combination of the Graphics Server and any Web browser (the "Graphics Client") empowers developers to create graphic images that are driven by data from the database, and are deployed across the Web. These graphics can be integrated with Forms and Reports as desired.

Requests to the Graphics Server begin when the client is presented with an HTML file that contains hyperlinks that they can use to make a request for a graphic image. When the client makes the request, it is sent through the WAS, which forwards it to the Graphics Server. The Graphics Server generates the image and stores it in a file on the server. It also creates an HTML file that contains a tag to display the image file, and the Graphics Server sends the HTML file as output back to the client. The client (Web browser) receives the HTML file, displays it, and, according to the tag, incorporates the server-stored image file in the browser display.

This allows the Graphics Server to dynamically generate graphic images and deliver them to a standard Web browser.

Designer/2000 and the Oracle WAS

Oracle's Designer/2000 includes a Web server Generator that will take basic modules defined in the Designer/2000 repository and generate Web-enabled applications. The output is in the form of PL/SQL packages, intended for use with the PL/SQL Cartridge, described earlier. Each package contains a set of PL/SQL procedures that will, when invoked, present a series of Web pages for users to query data, display the results, and view details of their query. Designer/2000's module preferences influence the way Designer generates the code, controlling the formatting and performance of the finished module.

If you already have an existing application in one of the many languages supported by Designer/2000, you can reverse engineer (in versions prior to 2.0), or "recover" (in version 2.0), the application into Designer's repository, and then generate that application via Web server Generator to create a Web-enabled application.

WAS Product Purchase

WAS is available for Windows NT and HP-UX. You are required to purchase Oracle Application Developer Kit licenses with a purchase of WAS, and the price for the WAS includes the ADK.

The price for each operating system and version includes licensing for eight concurrent devices per processor configuration; to get more devices, you must purchase additional kits.

The WAS comes in a Standard Version and an Advanced Version, described in the following sections.

Standard Version

The Standard Version is the basic product, and contains all WAS 3.0 features, except for those included in the Advanced Version.

Advanced Version

The Advanced Version includes all of the Standard Version features, plus the following:

- **The Transaction Service:** This is a service of the WRB that is modeled on the XA interface defined by the X/Open. It is used by applications that require transactions that span multiple HTTP requests. In other words, if your Web screens need to lock records on one page and take the user through a series of hyperlinks before being ready to commit or rollback changes, you would benefit from this option.

- **The Content Service:** This enables you to save arbitrary documents or data objects in repositories.

- **The ODBC Cartridge:** See the earlier discussion about this.

- **Distributed Cartridges:** You need this feature if you intend to run any cartridges on remote nodes. Without it, you can still run cartridges, but they will all be on the same node.

Web Developer Suite

One way to obtain the WAS and all related Oracle development tools in one cost-effective package is to get the Oracle Web Developer Suite. Version 1.6 of the Oracle WDS includes full development licenses for the these products:

- Designer/2000
- Developer/2000 and Developer/2000 Server
- Oracle Web Application Server 3.0, Advanced Edition
- Oracle Data Server, Enterprise Edition
- Oracle Web Development Kit (which includes the last prerelease of Oracle AppBuilder for Java)
- Open Tools Initiative CD-ROM
- 1-Year Oracle Technology Network membership

The Suite includes everything required to create applications, including the Oracle RDBMS, at a lower price than if you purchased each product separately. It's available for Windows NT and UNIX platforms, including Sun Solaris, IBM AIX, HP-UX, and DEC Alpha UNIX.

The Future of Oracle Web Application Server

Most applications are going to the Web, meaning either the World Wide Web, corporate intranets, or extranets. The WAS is the most powerful, flexible tool a developer can have to meet any challenge in the new environments. Armed with the WAS, developers can develop in any language, access any database, and deploy to any platform. No better option exists now, nor is there one anticipated, that can empower developers to face any Web-related programming challenge like the WAS.

The follow-on product to Oracle's Web Application Server 3.0 is called Oracle Application Server 4.0. OAS 4.0 will come in two editions: the Application Server 4.0 and the Application Server 4.0 Enterprise Edition.

The scheduled release date for Application Server 4.0 is the end of the fourth quarter, fiscal year 1998. The Enterprise Edition is due to come out in the first quarter of fiscal year 1999.

27

ORACLE WEB APPLICATION SERVER

Summary

The Oracle Web Application Server is truly a revolutionary product. It provides the most robust, reliable, and secure method to deliver virtually any program written in any language to any user on any platform. It gives the developer full flexibility to incorporate various resources into one application, to access data from any source, and to do so in a way that is as accessible and user friendly as possible. It is fully distributed, supports industry standards, and is fully scalable and less expensive to maintain than previous methods, such as client/server. As part of the Network Computing Architecture, the WAS provides the opportunity to achieve a great goal: the establishment of the computer as a ubiquitous state-of-the-art tool for everyone, with the power of a network behind it, that is as easy to use as a common household appliance.

Implementation of Oracle8

PART
VI

Oracle8 Cartridges

by Meghraj Thakkar

Overview of Oracle8 Cartridges

Oracle8 is an object-relational database management system. In addition to supporting relational data, it allows you to have object types.

Oracle's Network Computing Architecture (NCA) is a very appropriate environment for distributed computing. NCA is a three-tier approach consisting of the following components:

- Clients
- Application servers
- Database servers
- Interconnection between the different tiers

There are several benefits of using the NCA approach:

- Robust client/server model
- Easy deployment on the Web
- Extensible and plugable components—cartridges
- Use of object-oriented paradigms

NCA Cartridges

The Network Computing Architecture makes use of three categories of cartridges:

- Client cartridges
- Application cartridges
- Data cartridges

Client Cartridge

In a client/server model, operations on server data are typically executed on the server, but applications can be executed either on the client or the server. This results in thick clients. The client cartridges, on the other hand, are used to support thin clients. It is important to carefully define and distinguish what constitutes direct and necessary GUI support and what constitutes application functions. NCA's CORBA/IIOP communication mechanisms are used for inter-cartridge communication.

Application Cartridge

In the NCA, the application cartridge contains all the substantial application logic. The application server provides a mechanism for enabling applications, programs, and objects to communicate with each other. The Oracle Web Application Server uses and extends the HTTP-based communication mechanism. It also supports

CORBA/IIOP-based communication methods. The applications, programs, and objects should have the following features:

- They should "register" with the application server and provide certain hooks.
- They should follow the underlying communication protocols. On the Oracle Web Application Server, the objects are identified by URLs and request services from other objects through HTTP requests and getting responses in the same manner. Process states are preserved across HTTP requests.

An application cartridge is an object that uses the services of an application server and/or other cartridges to do the following:

- Enhance the functionality of the application server (PL/SQL cartridge, PERL cartridge, and so on)
- Be part of a bigger computation task

> **TIP**
>
> Even though application cartridges are managed by the application server, they can communicate with each other without the help of the application server (through the use of Java RMI, for example). When the cartridges communicate with each other without the help of the application server, they will not be able to take advantage of features such as load balancing.

28

ORACLE8 CARTRIDGES

In a complete solution, the application cartridge typically makes use of another stand-alone application, such as a browser, to handle the user interface and database servers to provide data storage and transaction control functions.

Application cartridges can add to the services provided by the application server. Other application cartridges, with or without involving the application server, can use these services. For example:

- The PERL application cartridge allows the Web application server to execute PERL scripts.
- By using the PL/SQL cartridge, the application server allows clients to connect to the Oracle database and execute PL/SQL scripts.

It should be noted that application cartridges can be anything, but they should be managed by the application server and make use of the underlying communication-related services. Unlike database servers, which have the notion of datatypes, the application server has no notion of datatypes. Application servers do not impose any programming methodology. Application cartridges should use HTTP-based or CORBA-based methods to communicate with other cartridges and applications.

Data Cartridges

A data cartridge is a software component that consists of datatypes, methods, and interfaces for a domain. These data cartridges extend the object type support provided by Oracle8 within the framework of Oracle's Network Computing Architecture.

Table 28.1 shows examples of some cartridges provided by Oracle8.0.4.

TABLE 28.1. CARTRIDGES PROVIDED BY ORACLE.

Data Cartridge	Database Model	Supported Behavior
Time Series	Ordered List of Tuples	Rolling averages, period comparisons, calendars
Text	Tokenized serial byte stream	Display, compress, reformat, and index
Video	Structured large object of serial image data	Play, compress, rewind, pause, and skip
Network	Object types of nodes, connections, and routes	Configuration of the network topology
Spatial	Geometric objects such as points, lines, polygons, and so on	Intersect, contain, and so on
Image	Structured large object	Crop, rotate, reformat, and so on

Example: A Hypothetical Network Cartridge

This data cartridge would define the following object types:

- Nodes—It represents any addressable element in the network.
- Connection—It represents a link between the node. It contains information about the distance between nodes.
- Route—It represents a path in the network and contains a collection of connections.

The cartridge uses PL/SQL or external 3GL procedures to implement the following methods:

- `FindShortestRoute (Node1, Node2)`   This method can be used to find the shortest route between any two specified nodes.
- `FindAllNodesReachableFrom (Node)`   This method can be used to find all the nodes that can be reached from a specified node.
- `FindMinimumHopRoute (Node1, Node2)`   This method can be used to find the path from Node1 to Node2 with the least number of nodes in between.

You can index the different object types mentioned earlier to make the processing of these methods more efficient.

This data cartridge can now be customized by different industries to suit their environments. For example, in the telecommunication industry, the datatypes can be used to model telephone networks. In the transportation industry, the datatypes can be used to model freight transport, and so on.

Sample Data Cartridges Provided by Oracle8

There are several cartridges provided by Oracle8. The next sections look at some of them.

Context Cartridge

The Context cartridge provides a GUI administration tool to configure Oracle8 in order to allow the following:

- Full-text retrieval and advanced linguistic services
- Automatic identification and delivery of key themes and theme summaries
- Use text from a variety of formats such as HTML, ASCII, PDF, PowerPoint, Excel, and so on, and original formats defined externally

For single-byte languages supported by Oracle8, there are several features provided by context that can be used:

- Exact word or phrase searching
- Boolean operations such as `and`, `or`, `not`, and so on
- Fuzzy matching
- Wild-card searches
- Proximity searches
- Multilingual stemming
- Thesaurus framework

Image Cartridge

The Image cartridge provides native image datatype support for two-dimensional images. It allows the following:

- Format transcoding, compression, and specialized image processing
- Queries based on intrinsic image attributes such as color, structure, and texture
- Images stored as inline binary large objects (`BLOB`s), external flat files as `BFILE`s, or even on CD-ROMs
- Support for image interchange formats such as BMP, CALS, GIF, PCX, JFIF, Pict, SUN Raster, TIFF, and others

28

ORACLE8
CARTRIDGES

- Support for popular compression schemes such as CCITT G3/ G4, RLE, LZW, and JPEG

Time Series Cartridge

The Time Series cartridge provides the ability to manipulate time-dependent data. Some of its key features include the following:

- Built-in calendar support; also allows user-defined calendars
- Time series functions to allow analysis of time-series data
- Time scaling functions to allow transformation from one time scale to another

Video Cartridge

The Video cartridge delivers audio and video using standard network technology. Some of the features of this cartridge are the following:

- CD-quality audio
- Intuitive controls such as PLAY, SEEK, PAUSE, and STOP
- Multiple clients can receive full-screen, full video at the same time
- Use of Oracle VideoMarker for video annotation and indexed playback
- Macromedia Director and Authorware support
- SNMP support
- Oracle Video Client to embed OLE Custom Extension (OCX)
- Plug-ins delivered via the Web
- A variety of query functions such as extraction/trim, arithmetic, aggregate, boolean, dominate, and so on

Spatial Data Cartridge

This cartridge allows the efficient storage and manipulation of spatial data. Some of the features of this cartridge include the following:

- Two-tier queries using primary and secondary filters, resulting in fast access
- Use of "tiles" to provide spatial indexing
- Support for domain comparison operators such as touch, overlap, inside, and disjoint
- Support for basic geometric forms such as point and point clusters, and line and line strings

Virage Data Cartridge

This cartridge incorporates Virage's Media Management System, which is used to manage digital media assets and their associated metadata, via the following two components:

- *Video Cataloger.* Watches, listens to, and reads a video. Uses extracted information such as keyframes, audio profiles, and so on to build a storyboard index.

- *Media Manager and Browser.* Searches the content from the storyboard. Manages permissions to access the asset. Version control via checkin and checkout.

Cartridge Architecture

Figure 28.1 shows the data cartridge architecture and how a data cartridge fits with the rest of the Oracle8 environment.

FIGURE 28.1.
The NCA architecture and how cartridges fit into it.

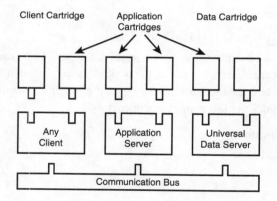

28

ORACLE8
CARTRIDGES

As seen from above, the end user communicates with the Oracle8 server via a GUI interface on the client side. The client and server communicate using the Oracle Net3 protocol. One of the processes on the server side will run the 3GL data cartridge-specific code. The server and the 3GL library code use Oracle Call Interface (OCI).

Application Designing Using NCA Cartridges

There are several design considerations when building business solutions based on the Network Computing Architecture.

- *Client cartridge and application cartridge.* The client cartridge should package all the operations and functions that directly control the user interface. The rest of the operations and functions should be divided between the application and the data cartridge. In NCA, the clients will be thin, so the application designers of the NCA solution should pay careful attention to the distribution of the functionality between the various cartridges.

- *Application cartridge and data cartridge.* The data cartridge should package all the operations and functions that extend the Oracle8 database with new types or new behavior. The fact that a function performs SQL-based data access is not sufficient to package the function as a data cartridge; it should really be packaged as an application cartridge. Server-based extensions, which are integrated with the server and packaged as a single unit, qualify as data cartridges.

> **NOTE**
>
> Application cartridges can execute on either the application server or on the data server, but a data cartridge can execute only on the data server.

Data Cartridge Components

A data cartridge typically contains one or more object datatypes. While defining an object datatype, a data cartridge makes use of the built-in datatypes, such as `integer` and `varchar`. It may even reference another datatype defined in other data cartridges. A data cartridge generally includes the following components:

- Object type specification
- Object type method code
- External library calls
- External library

Advantages of Data Cartridges

Data cartridges have a lot of advantages because the objects that are defined in the cartridge allow you to centralize the definitions and rules, which can then be used in different types of applications. There are several advantages to this approach.

- Packaging of domain-specific expertise allows the cartridge to access the corporate information repository and add more meaning to the data and its use.
- The cartridge can be used across different sections of the industry, making it versatile.
- It can open up new business opportunities.

Data Cartridge Extensions

You can create a new data cartridge, or you can extend the functionality of an existing data cartridge. The data cartridge to extend could be Oracle-supplied or custom-built, if you have a data-cartridge "people." Different companies can add new data elements as well as new methods to this cartridge to represent their employees and their own special policies.

Difference Between Data Cartridge and Application Cartridge

Within the Network Computing Architecture, the data cartridges are a means to extend the functionality of Oracle Server to new domains. Data cartridges can have a variety of uses, from the broad horizontal spectrum such as Spatial, Image, Time Series, and Context, to a narrow and focused vertical set such as Portfolio, Telecom, Video, and Audio.

Data cartridges have the following features:

- Data cartridges are server-based. The cartridge components reside on the server or are accessed from the server (in the case of external procedures and error messages). On the other hand, application cartridges reside at the application server, get data from the data server, and process it locally at the client.

- They typically define and implement domain-specific object datatypes. Users of data cartridges can use the new types in their application in the same manner that they use the built-in types. For example, after the Image cartridge has been loaded, the user can easily define a table called `Employee` that has a column called `Photo` of the type `image`.

- The server can be extended by defining new row-sources or extensible data sources. In this case the data is actually outside the database, but it can be logically integrated into the database by means of abstract tables.

- The components of the data cartridge are packaged together as one unit. In other words, the types, packages, external procedures, users, and so on that comprise the cartridge can be installed and uninstalled as a single unit.

- They can be integrated with the server engine such that the server can take special action when dealing with the domain. For example, the queries can be optimized by having a more meaningful interpretation of the domain.

> **NOTE**
>
> In Oracle8.1, the data cartridge will be able to more closely integrate with the server engine by means of *interfaces*. For example, an interface with the indexing engine will make it possible to create a more meaningful domain-specific indexing scheme.

Developing Cartridges

Before you begin the actual development of a cartridge, you have to be clear about the purpose of the cartridge. You have to decide what functionality the cartridge will provide to developers and users. The following steps need to be performed after the functional definition has been dealt with:

- *Decide the objects that will be exposed and that will provide the cartridge functionality*. It is very important to choose the objects and name them such that they represent the domain they are extending. Also, use similar names for the objects.

- *Using object-oriented methodologies to define all the object attributes and their methods*. It will help to use an object-oriented paradigm when developing a data cartridge.

- *Interfaces between object methods and existing 3GL code*. Keep the interface between the SQL method of the objects and the existing 3GL code as simple as possible. Minimize the number of calls to library routines, and also try to do as much work as possible in each call.

- *Package existing 3GL code*. The existing 3GL code should be packaged in a DLL. Create new entry points that will be used by the SQL code of the object's methods.

- *Define and write the object's type specification and the PL/SQL code*. The object methods can be written entirely in PL/SQL, or they may even call the external library. If the external library is called, the definitions for the library and the arguments that are passed must be defined accurately.

- *Sample debugging program*. A sample program can be created by using the externally visible definitions. This will serve as a debugging tool during the development phase.

Designing a Data Cartridge

There are several things to keep in mind while designing a data cartridge. Object data types (ODT)

- Should not keep global data.
- Should not attempt to keep state information across transactions.
- Do not support inheritance.
- Do not have private or protected elements.
- Do not have private or protected methods.
- Must not have name space collisions.

In order for multiple cartridges to operate, make sure that the following schema objects are unique:

- Directory names
- Library names
- Package names
- Type names
- Table names

A well-defined naming scheme must be used to achieve such uniqueness. I suggest the following naming scheme.

```
"OOOOCCCSSSSSSSSSSSSSSSSSS"
```

Where

> OOOO represents the organization name up to 4 characters
>
> CCC represents the cartridge type and tag up to 3 characters
>
> SSS... represents the Schema Object name.

Oracle8's Extensibility Feature

The developer can use Oracle8's extensibility features to declare new datatypes, make use of different programming languages, and leverage new constructs to model and store data in the Oracle8 database. The following constructs are the building blocks for developing data cartridges:

- Object types
- Collections
- Large object types

Object Types

Oracle8 allows developers to add new datatypes by making use of *object types*. Object types are similar to classes in Java or C++. They bundle a data structure and the functions and procedures associated with that structure. An object type must be associated with a column of a table before it can store any data. Each row object in an object type column has a unique identifier known as an Object ID (OID).

Object types consist of attributes and variables that define the data structure they represent, and methods, functions, and procedures that manipulate the underlying data structure. An object type consists of two parts.

- *Specification*. This defines the attributes and the publicly accessible methods.
- *Body*. This implements the publicly and privately declared methods.

The following example shows how to create a simple object type:

```
create type complex as object (
    real_part real,
    im_part real,
    member function addcomplex (x complex) return complex
    );
create type body complex as
    member function addcomplex (x complex) return complex is
    begin
    return complex (real_part + x.real_part, im_part+ x.im_part);
    end addcomplex;
end;
```

> **TIP**
>
> Methods can be implemented in PL/SQL, C, or in later releases using Java. For an example of implementing methods in C, please refer to the section on external procedures later in this chapter.

> **TIP**
>
> The attributes of object types can be other object types, collections, or large objects.

Collections

A collection is an ordered group of elements of the same datatype. The position of an element in the collection is determined by a unique subscript. Collections behave like arrays, except that collections can only have one dimension and must be integer-indexed. Collections can be attributes of an object type. Oracle8 provides two types of collections:

- Nested tables
- Variable-size arrays

Nested Tables

Nested tables are like one-dimensional arrays, with the following exceptions:

- They are unbounded and therefore can grow dynamically.
- They do not retain ordering; in other words, the order of insertion is not necessarily the order of retrieval.
- When declaring a nested table, use the keyword TABLE in conjunction with the CREATE TYPE statement.

The following example shows how to declare a nested table collection type:

```
create type projects as table of varchar2(25)
create type employee as object (
    emp_id      integer(4),
    emp_name    varchar2(25),
    emp_addr    varchar2(40),
    emp_proj    projects)
```

Variable-Size Arrays

VARRAYs have the following features:

- They have a fixed lower bound of 1 and a user-defined upper bound.
- They are like one-dimensional arrays and do not grow dynamically.
- They preserve the ordering of elements.

The following example shows how to create a VARRAY:

```
create type projectIDs as varray(20) of number(2)
create type department as object (
    dept_id     number(2),
    dept_name   varchar2(20),
    dept_projid   projectIDs)
```

Large Object Types

Large objects are used for storing raw, unstructured data such as text, images, audio, or video. LOBs are divided into two parts.

- LOB *index*. The LOB data is broken into chunks of the underlying data stream. The LOB index maintains a b-tree index of these chunks.

- LOB *storage*. It is the tablespace of the file that stores the raw information.

Access to the LOB data is provided through PL/SQL packages and OCI APIs.

Oracle8 supports two types of LOB data: internal and external.

Internal LOBs

Internal LOBs are stored in tablespaces and participate in the transactional model. They can be committed or rolled back just like any other Oracle8 data type. Oracle8 introduces the following three LOB types to replace the Oracle7 datatypes LONG and LONG RAW:

- BLOBs (Binary Large Objects)—Used to store unstructured data.
- CLOBs (Character Large Objects)—Use to store single byte-width character data.
- NCLOBs (National Character Large Objects)—Used to store fixed-width, multi-byte character data.

The LOB data types have the following advantages over LONG and LONG RAW:

- Multiple LOB columns can exist in the same table.
- LOBs can be stored out-of-line in a particular tablespace.
- LOBs can be up to 4GB.
- LOBs can be used as attributes of object types.

External LOBs

External LOBs are stored as files outside the database and do not participate in the transactional model. External LOBs are stored as BFILE datatype, which is actually a pointer to a file.

External Procedures

Oracle8 supports the calling of DLL functions and procedures from PL/SQL code. As a result, you can have data cartridges whose methods are external C routines. By using external C routines, developers can take advantage of the efficiency of a 3GL, and can use the flexibility of calling Win32 APIs and manipulating COM objects.

There are two steps before a developer can call an external procedure from PL/SQL:

1. Register the DLL's location with Oracle8's data dictionary:

   ```
   Create or replace library external_lib as
   'e:/datacartridge/debug/cartridge.dll';
   ```

2. Declare the prototype of the C routine in the Oracle8 data dictionary.

The following example shows how to implement an object type that uses an external procedure as a method:

```
Create or replace package data_package as
    function ext_func (data CLOB) return binary_integer;
end;
create or replace package body data_package as
    function ext_func (data CLOB) return binary_integer is external
name "c_func"
        library external_lib
        language C
        with context
        parameters (
            context,
            data OCILOBLOCATOR
        );
end;
create or replace type ext_objtype as object (
    data          CLOB,
    member function    ext_objtype_func return binary_integer
);
Create or replace type body ext_objtype is
    member function ext_objtype_func return binary_integer is
    begin
        return data_package.ext_func(data);
    end;
end;
```

The following C code shows the function prototype of the external function:

```
#Include <oci.h>
#define DLLEXPORT __declspec(dllexport) __cdecl
int DLLEXPORT c_func (OCIExtProcContext *ctx, OCILobLocator *lobl);
int c_func (OCIExtProcContext *ctx, OCILobLocator *lobl)
{
    /*Place function code here */
    return 0;
}
```

The following code shows the testing of the external callout using PL/SQL:

```
Declare
    i binary_integer;
    x ext_objtype;
```

```
begin
    x := ext_objtype(EMPTY_CLOB());
    I := x.ext_objtype_func();
    DBMS_OUTPUT.PUT_LINE('ext_objtype_func() returned ' ¦¦ I);
end;
```

OCI Callbacks

In Release 8.0.3, Oracle introduced four new OCI APIs, which can be used for external procedure callbacks. External routines can call back the Oracle8 Server using the OCI interface:

- `OCIExtProcAllocCallMemory()`   Allocates *n* bytes of memory for the duration of the external procedure.

- `OCIExtProcRaiseExcp()`   Raises an Oracle error number.

- `OCIProcRaiseExcpWithMsg()`   Raises a user-defined exception.

- `OCIExtProcGetEnv()`   Retrieves a set of OCI handles that should only be used for callbacks.

An external procedure can perform the following functions using these OCI APIs:

- Manipulate LOB data

- Fetch and update data

- Execute SQL and PL/SQL

Debugging External Procedures

Traditionally, a developer could use Visual C++'s symbolic debugger to set break points in a DLL loaded by a process without symbolic debugging information. External procedures cannot be debugged in this manner because debugging must be spawned on demand by the listener process. Embedding the DebugBreak() Win32 API call at the beginning of an external procedure will allow developers to debug these procedures.

Example: Step by Step Data Cartridge Development

The following details the development of a data cartridge "Data Store." This cartridge can be used to store a set of data in an Oracle8 character LOB (CLOB). The stored data can be processed for statistical analysis such as minimum and maximum values, averages, regression, and so on.

1. Create an object type containing attributes and methods that would define the "Data Store" and its functionality.

The methods are declared as external because the kind of processing that would be supported by this cartridge would be most efficiently performed in PL/SQL, and therefore the methods should be coded in a 3GL like C or C++ and dispatched from the server. C is more efficient for external procedures.

```
Create or replace type DataStore as object (
          pid integer,
          name varchar2(20),
          date_created date,
          value   clob,
          member function DataMinimum return integer,
          member function DataMaximum return integer,
        pragma  restrict_references(DataMinimum, WNDS, WNPS),
          pragma  restrict_references(DataMaximum, WNDS, WNPS));
```

2. Declare a package to hold all the external procedures.

```
Create or replace package DataStore_package as
          function datastore_findmin (data clob) return integer;
          function datastore_findmax (data clob) return integer;
          pragma restrict_references (datastore_findmin, WNDS,
WNPS);
          pragma restrict_references (datastore_findmin, WNDS,
WNPS);
        end;
```

3. Implement the body of object type `DataStore`.

```
Create or replace type body DataStore is
        member function DataMinimum return integer is
          x integer := DataStore_package.datastore_findmin(data);
          begin return x ; end;
        member function DataMaximum return integer is
          y integer := DataStore_package.datastore_findmax(data);
          begin return y ; end;
end;
```

4. Create a PL/SQL name for the library in which the implementation of the external procedure will be found.

```
Create or replace library datastore_lib as '<directory_of_library> /
libdatastore.so'
```

5. Declare the package body and tie the package functions to 3GL functions of the library.

```
Create or replace package body DataStore_package as
          function datastore_findmin(data clob) return integer is
external
          name "c_minimum" library datastore_lib language c with
context;
          function datastore_findmax(data clob) return integer is
external
          name "c_maximum" library datastore_lib language c with
context;
        end;
```

6. Implement the necessary 3GL routines.

The CLOB passed as argument to the external procedure is used by the routine as a pointer to the LOB locator. It calls the database and reads the CLOB incrementally.

```
#Include <oci.h>
int c_minimum (OCIExtProcContext *ctx,  OCILobLocator  *lobl)   {
        ub1 bufp[MAXBUFLEN];
        sword  retval;
        init_handles (ctx);
        retval = OCILobRead(...., lobl, bufp, ....);
        return (process_min(bufp));
}

#Include <oci.h>
int c_maximum (OCIExtProcContext *ctx,  OCILobLocator  *lobl)   {
        ub1 bufp[MAXBUFLEN];
        sword  retval;
        init_handles (ctx);
        retval = OCILobRead(...., lobl, bufp, ....);
        return (process_max(bufp));
}
```

Testing the Developed Data Cartridge

1. Create a database table that will hold instances of the DataStore type.

```
Create table DataStore_table of DataStore;
```

2. Insert a row into the DataStore table.

```
Insert into DataStore_table values (1, 'test1', to_date
('03-28-1998', 'MM-DD-YYYY'),
EMPTY_CLOB() );

commit;
```

3. Populate the LOB using an OCI program that uses the OCI routine OCILobWrite() to read data from a file and copy it into the clob attribute of the DataStore.

4. Compile the c_miminum and c_maximum routines and put them into the library.

5. Using PL/SQL, invoke the data cartridge methods.

```
Select d.DataMimimum(), d.DataMaximum() from DataStore_table d;
```

Deploying Cartridges

There are several tasks that need to performed before you can start using the cartridges. In this section we will take a look at several of these tasks.

Data Cartridge Installation and Operation

Installation involves the following steps:

1. Putting the data cartridge at the correct place.

   This involves placing the dynamic link libraries, help documentation, and other supporting files at a particular location.

2. Making the Oracle server aware of the object data type definitions.

   You can make the server aware of the ODT definitions by running a SQL script logged in with a privileged account.

3. Granting users the rights to use the data cartridge.

The entire process of packaging and installing of cartridges can be divided into four phases:

1. Java developers define the libraries of actions, dialogs, and queries. These libraries are used as input to the component definition tool and the installer runtime.

2. Developers specify the files that form a component, the dependencies between the components, and the flow during the installation process.

3. Defining the component and session variables settings creates customized drivers.

4. The software is installed, and the users can provide input to the dialogs or the dialog inputs are provided via drivers.

Definition of Libraries

Libraries are collections of related Java classes that are used for implementing specific functionality during an installation. The Cartridge Packager uses libraries to make actions, dialogs, or queries available to the installation developer. Libraries can be uniquely defined by specifying the following:

- Library name
- Library version
- All the actions, dialogs, and queries in the library
- Names of classes that implement an action
- Exceptions that occur during an action

There are three types of libraries:

- Action libraries
- Dialog libraries
- Query libraries

Action Library

Action libraries are collections of actions that can be added by the developers to the action flow. Actions are only available in the state change phase. The Cartridge Packager provides default action libraries, and it also allows the developers to import additional custom-developed libraries.

The default action library provided with the cartridge packager includes the following:

- Add item to registry
- Append file
- Copy files
- Create user
- Create group
- Change password
- Create icon/Program group (Windows only)
- Rename file
- Relink
- Set environment variable

Actions may be platform-specific–applicable and implemented for certain platforms only—or they may be polymorphic. Depending on the platform, they can implement different logic to perform the same action.

Actions are defined using the following two steps:

1. Select a set of action objects and the associated variables.
2. Define the logical flow and associations between the action objects.

> **NOTE**
>
> Associated with each action object is an Undo function that is used during the uninstall procedure to reverse the effect of that action object.

Dialog Libraries

Dialogs are used by the end users during the installation process to set variables. The installer first runs through its standard set of dialogs, and then it runs through the dialogs of each component that has been selected during the installation process. The Cartridge Packager provides default dialog libraries, and it also allows the developers to import additional custom-developed libraries.

The default dialog library provided with the Cartridge Packager includes the following:

- Directory dialog
- Password dialog
- Single selection
- Single text field
- Multiple selection

Dialogs are defined using the following two steps:

1. Select a set of dialog objects and the associated variables.
2. Define the logical flow and associations between the dialog objects.

Queries Library

During the installation process, queries can be used to obtain information about the target machine. The information that results from the query can be used to influence the flow of the rest of the install process.

> **NOTE**
>
> Actions can change the state of the target machine, while queries only retrieve information about the target machine.

Installation Flow

There are several things that must be considered during the definition of the installation flow:

- Specify the variables and their associations with dialogs and actions
- Specify the dialogs, which control the customization and also influence the flow of the installation
- Specify actions using variables, expressions, and decision controls

Summary

Cartridges provide a powerful and flexible mechanism for the customization and extension of the Oracle8 engine. They are a very important component of the Network Computing Architecture and allow the overall functionality of the system to be distributed into either the client, application, or data cartridges. As server-based components, data cartridges allow the storage, management, manipulation, and retrieval of complex data just like traditional data, thereby supporting the business model in a better way.

Oracle is committed to further extend this technology in the future. There are two initiatives underway at Oracle to enhance the usage of the cartridges.

- Support of Java as a native language in the Oracle8 kernel.
- Improved extensibility by supporting inheritance of object types, methods, and data.

Using Oracle8 Objects in PL/SQL and SQL

by Advanced Information Systems, Inc.

IN THIS CHAPTER

The Advantages of Using PL/SQL Within Java

There is nothing fundamentally different about embedding PL/SQL in a traditional language than doing it in Java. The only difference is that Java addresses the new development standards for the Internet and the World Wide Web. Java is the code that allows you to write applications using the HTTP protocol that will run on any machine with a *Java Virtual Machine (JVM)*.

For instance, this would allow the ability to write an *applet* over the Web that sold airplane tickets. Users on Apple Macs, PCs, UNIX Machines, and DEC VMS software could all run browsers, surf the Web, and buy airplane tickets from your company.

With many typical approaches, the logic for searching through the database, booking an airline flight, and handling credit card payments would exist in the Java applet. This would create a larger amount of Java code, in the form of compiled .CLASS files. A longer download time would be necessary because the user's browser would need to download your applet before running it.

Instead you might consider moving a great deal of the applet logic into our business database. This database is already storing transactions made over the Web, storing customer information, and querying flight schedules. The business database will still need to be accessed regardless of where your business and process logic is placed. By storing much of the logic in your database, you reduce the size of the applet and speed up your Web application by reducing network traffic, as shown in Figure 29.1.

In Oracle, the ideal way to store application logic is by using PL/SQL. Because PL/SQL is a rich, quasi-object-oriented and highly structured language, complex logical algorithms can be written using it. Furthermore, much of what we call application logic is simply different SQL calls that represent different views or operations on data. By storing this logic using PL/SQL, you have a seamless SQL interface and thus save processing speed and simplify the maintenance of source code.

With these advantages, most Java/Oracle application efforts would benefit from database logic stored separately from the Java Applet and instead *packaged* in PL/SQL.

FIGURE 29.1.

Database logic inside a Java applet creates a network bottleneck, whereas Java with remote calls to PL/SQL results in a thinner applet.

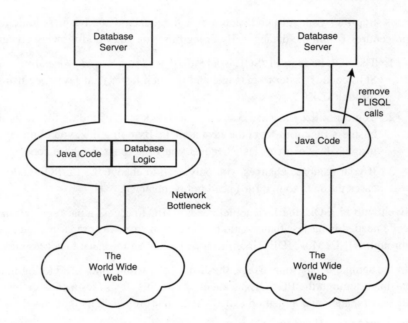

Consider the following small package skeleton of PL/SQL logic:

```
package sell_airline_tickets
is

function get_next_flight_no(departure_date in date, origin in varchar2,
destination varchar2)
return varchar2;

function book_flight(flight_no in number, passenger_name in varchar2)
return varchar2;

function get_price(flight_no in number, class_of_travel in varchar2)
return
number;

procedure update_frequent_flier_miles(card_id in number, flight_no in
number);

end;
```

Here you see three activities that might contain a great deal of code; activities that find airline flights, book them, and get their price. Instead of placing all of the conditional logic, looping, and database logic in a Java application, you can code these modules in PL/SQL and then simply access them in the Java code.

This simplifies your Java code and moves the database and business logic into stored procedures within the database. By doing this, you gain the following advantages:

1. The SQL code in PL/SQL is already parsed in a *stored procedure*. This type of SQL code is easier to manage, and is much faster than Java code using SQL run through JDBC.

2. You centralize database code in your database, thus hiding the methods of these business functions from the Java applets. By doing this, you eliminate sifting through Java source files whenever you want to fix database code.

3. If your database changes, you only need to change the PL/SQL code. In many cases the Java source files need not be changed.

Even with PL/SQL, the Java applet needs JDBC to access a package, but the amount of code needed is far less than would be the case if Java was preparing and issuing SQL through JDBC. Most JDBC interfaces will allow an interface to access Oracle.

In the sample database interface, the Java applet would only need to log in to use the business logic in the PL/SQL packages. To do this, Java uses a class called DriverManager and a method called getConnection. The method has three forms:

```
getConnection(String url);
getConnection(String url, Properties props);
getConnection(Sring url, String userid, String password);
```

Let's populate the second form and the all-important Properties class. Using an Oracle driver, you would write Java code like this:

```
java.util.Properties props = new java.util.Properties();

props.put("host", "ORACL");
props.put("user", "airline");
props.put("password", "echo");   /* our password is echo */
java.sql Connection DbConn = DriverManager.getConnection("jdbc.Oracle8,
props);
```

To call procedures or functions from Oracle does not require some of the complex JDBC commands needed just to execute one SQL statement. A Java applet can execute hundreds of SQL statements within a PL/SQL package using only the simple *call* method.

The method has this general form:

```
call procedure_name(arg1, arg2...argn);
```

Or to return a value from a function:

```
var = call function_name(arg1, arg2...argn);
```

This Java class allows us to use the PL/SQL function
➥'update_frequent_flier_miles' even within HTML text once we have defined
➥its existence using the above methods of the DriverManager. For
➥instance, to display the number of frequent flier miles that a customer
➥has on an HTML page we would make the following call:

```
<FONT  COLOR="#000000" SIZE=3>String SQL = "{call
update_frequent_flier_miles( "+ card_id + "," + flight_no + ")}";
```

After this step, you prepare your new buffer using JDBC:

```
java.sql.CallableStatement my_statement = DbConn.prepareCall(SQL);
```

If you want, you can specify the name of the procedure more directly. Instead of calling
update_frequent_flier_miles, you could use the schema and/or package name, like
this:

```
call airline_db.sell_airline_tickets.update_frequent_flier_miles,
```

This enables Java code to access logic from many different schemas and packages, not
just ones that the developer wrote.

Different Ways That Java Can Package PL/SQL

Not only is it advantageous on the Java end of things to move SQL to the server, but it
can be advantageous for the database logic to be packaged in specific Java structures that
will allow it to be used as an object-oriented building block that many different developers can use. The two major methods for doing this are by using Interface Definition
Language (IDL) or RMI.

The Language of Cartridges

IDL is based on the CORBA standard that Oracle embraces. The end product of an IDL
is an Object Request Broker (ORB). Because ORBs are designed with this common standard, using them allows people to access your database logic embedded in your Java
code in a standard way.

A typical IDL statement would first consist of the creation of a distributed object. For
your airline application, it might look something like this:

```
module AirlineTicketSales
{
    interface flight_data
    {
```

```
        attribute    string flight_no,
        attribute string flight_date,
        attribute string origination,
        attribute string destination,
        attribute long frequent_flier_no,
        attribute string class_of_travel;

        void get_travel_info;
        void sell_ticket;
        void update_customer_info;
    };
};
```

By storing this file as `airline.idl` and then running `idltojava -fclient -fserver airline.idl`, source code for this template is generated. This includes stubs, classes, and helper and holder classes. These `.java` files then, of course, need to be compiled to `.class` files before the final implementation code is written so that testing can occur.

RMI—Distributed Computing Tool

RMI existed before the IDL interface and the CORBA standard. Because of this, RMI is more stable and has been used in older versions of Java. Using your airline database access methods, RMI splits your classes for information needed on both the client (the machine running the applet) and the server (the machine where our database is), as shown in Figure 29.2.

FIGURE 29.2.

RMI generates client and server Java code from your original Java file.

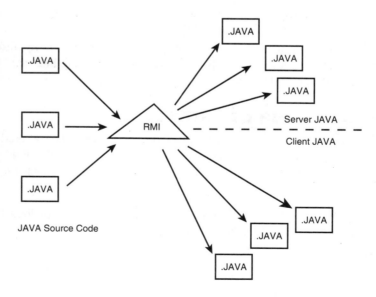

Roughly speaking, this is how RMI would treat a Java class describing airline travel:

1. Split the class into two parts—one to hold data, and the other to implement the methods on the server.
2. Define how remote access will occur. This will extend the `java.rmi` class.
3. Develop an Airline Control RMI component for the server. This will extend the `java.rmi.server` class.
4. Compile these classes, create stubs for coding, and create wrappers for remote methods.

Essentially, RMI breaks up your business Java class into a portion of information needed on the server and another portion needed on the client, and creates an interface between them.

The Future—J/SQL

Oracle and other vendors are working to build compilers that will recognize SQL directly within Java code without using the complicated methods in this chapter, which need to be reworked for each class that uses a database! Using PL/SQL Packages within Java cuts down on the amount of code you need to write, considering you only need to concern yourself with the input and output of these packages. Yet with J/SQL, much of this tedious JDBC will be eliminated. Hopefully, the major vendors will agree on a standard that is portable between database platforms and won't frustrate us, as is the case with the current precompiler differences between vendors. With J/SQL, the database will become more object-oriented and the Java language will become more relational, thus evolving both technologies.

Summary

Because Microsoft appears to be in complete dominance of the computer world today, it might be tempting to snuggle up by a fireplace and just code database/Internet applications in ActiveX. Yet we must look back to the days when IBM was king and remember that on some days every emperor is wearing no clothes.

With this in mind, we should instead turn to the Java language which will survive the political upheavals of the computer world due to its flexibility. Yet, we cannot become enamored with Java alone; instead we must realize that Java, just like any programming language, needs to communicate with Relational Databases. With this in mind, we will find that Oracle offers many very powerful methods to give the Java language quick access to the Oracle8 Server. With these tools, we can transform the client/server paradigm so that our "client" can be anyone in the world that has access to the Internet, thus making Oracle8 the truly "universal server."

Data Warehouses

by Matt Larson

IN THIS CHAPTER

Introduction

Businesses have often understood how important operational data is to the survival of the company. They spend millions collecting data during the course of business. Unfortunately, most businesses fail to properly utilize the data. Once the operational benefits have been gained, the data is forgotten. Due to the increasingly competitive marketplace, businesses are looking to their data to gain an edge over the competition.

What Is a Data Warehouse?

A data warehouse is a central repository of data used for analysis by decision makers. The data is pulled from the operational data stores into the warehouse where it is massaged into a format that is easy to utilize. The decision makers receive a simplified business view of the company data that can easily be used for analysis.

Why Would a Company Need a Data Warehouse?

Established 20 years ago, the fictitious Acme company has grown into a worldwide corporation that sells office supplies to over 30,000 businesses on four continents. Acme has always understood that current technology is a vital tool. In the last 10 years, Acme has amassed a computer network that consists of over 700 servers. Some of these servers are mainframes running on MVS, some are mid-range systems running on VMS and UNIX, and the newest servers are running on Windows NT. This open environment has been beneficial at the business unit level. Each business unit was allowed to purchase the best possible solution to its problem. However, it has become increasingly difficult to answer critical business questions that span more than one business unit.

The CEO recently contemplated expanding the sales force by 10%. In order to make an informed decision, the CEO asked about the relationship between the number of salespeople and profitability. There are several pieces of information needed to answer this question.

- Sales data
- Accounting data
- Employment data
- Market and economic trends

Data analysts ran into several problems while attempting to answer this simple question (see Figure 30.1).

1. Data cannot be found. Often the data needed to answer a business question is available within the corporate data stores. Unfortunately, this data may reside on any server within the enterprise. Without a central data catalog, finding the data is so difficult that the question often remains unanswered.

2. Data is duplicated. Throughout the typical organization, many processes are duplicated. In Acme, the company records orders into a database as the orders are taken. The shipping department also has a separate database that records the orders actually shipped. Some business processes alter the order database, some alter the shipping database, and some affect both databases. The data analysts are forced to choose between two databases, which may both be partially incomplete.

3. Data is in unusable form. Unusable data is data recorded or stored in a format that cannot easily be utilized. An example is data stored on tape. Although the data does exist, it cannot be accessed if it's sitting on a closet shelf. Another example is data collected in a custom program format. This data cannot be retrieved without the original program that created it.

FIGURE 30.1.

Operational data.

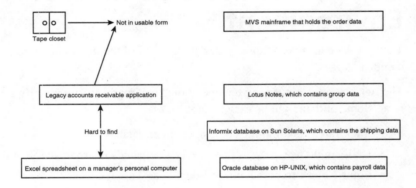

Eventually the data analysts gather the data they need. They compile a report and present it to the CEO. The report says that salespeople added to the sales force in the past year have not contributed to a higher profit. Instead, they appear to be taking sales away from existing salespeople. The CEO takes one look at it the report and asks about the profit potential of additional advertising. The data analysts, having spent two weeks on the sales force report, look at each other in amazement. There has to be a better way.

There is—data warehousing.

The Six Steps to Creating a Data Warehouse

There are six steps involved in creating a data warehouse. The steps are usually performed in sequential order, although some may be performed together.

1. Document the operational environment.
2. Choose the data warehousing technologies.
3. Design the data warehouse model.
4. Develop the extraction and scrubbing routines.
5. Build the metadata repository.
6. Create the multidimensional reports and cubes.

Document the Operational Environment

The data warehouse is going to pull data from all of the important systems in the company.

The first step in documenting the operational environment is to identify all of the systems. Some of them will be easy to spot.

- Mainframes that run the company's order database.
- UNIX midrange systems that run the company's internal payroll system.
- Lotus Notes server that holds group data.

Some of the systems will be harder to identify.

- Excel spreadsheets kept by managers to track projects.
- Old systems that are no longer used but contain needed historical data.
- Systems that are referenced only through another system. This step seems relatively easy, yet it is not uncommon for a system to go unnoticed. This type of mistake can be costly to fix.

The second step in documenting the operational environment is to determine what data is stored in each system. This must be done at the column level. In other words, the columns for every important table must be clearly understood. Depending on the environment, this step may take months to finish. For example, Oracle Applications 10.7

contains thousand of tables with valuable data. All of these tables must be fully understood and documented. This will become even more difficult with older systems. It may be difficult to find an analyst who understands how to interpret the table structures.

Choosing the Data Warehousing Technologies

After documenting the current systems, it is time to choose the technologies that will be used to implement the data warehouse. Several types of software must be chosen:

- Operating system of the data warehouse
- Database for the data warehouse
- Data warehouse modeling tools
- Data warehouse development tools
- Data warehouse monitoring tools
- Extraction and scrubbing tools
- Reporting tools
- OLAP server (optional)
- Data mining tools (optional)

TIP

This is a list of suggestions to keep in mind when choosing a vendor.

- Choosing the "best" product is not always the proper solution. Instead, choose a quality product that has a good chance of becoming an industry standard. Often this is more dependent on the company marketing the product than on the product itself. A company such as Microsoft or Oracle will have the marketing forces to drive a smaller competitor out of the market.
- Use a smaller vendor for custom needs (this is often the case for the extraction/scrubbing process). A small, startup company is more likely to give the needed attention than a large corporation with an immense number of clients.
- Choose a product that follows industry standards closely. This will allow the data warehouse team to easily change vendors in the future if deemed appropriate.

30

DATA WAREHOUSES

There are a large number of vendors supplying this software. It can be difficult to evaluate and choose the best product. The technology has the potential of making or breaking the data warehouse project. Therefore, it is imperative to spend time evaluating various software packages from several vendors.

Designing the Data Warehouse Model

The data model is a blueprint of how the data will look when it resides inside the data warehouse. It is quite different from the data models in operational environments. Typically, operational data models include the following:

- Relational model
- Hierarchical model
- Network model
- Flat files model
- Object-oriented model

The relational model is currently the most popular. It is capable of allowing a large number of small transactions. These transactions are typically used to support the organization. One example is the work of the data entry clerk. The data entry clerk enters one record at a time into the database. There may be thousands of clerks performing this function at the same time. This results in several thousand small requests to the database. The data warehouse, on the other hand, usually services a small number of large requests used for decision making. This special type of system requires a completely different model. The most popular data warehouse model is the star schema.

The Star Schema

The star schema is designed for slicing and dicing data into a format that is easy for executives to understand. The star schema is made up of two types of tables.

- Fact tables
- Dimension tables

Fact Tables

The fact table contains two types of columns. The first type of column contains the information that is likely to be calculated.

- Sale amount
- Percentage of margin
- Sales commission
- Discount
- Cost to make product

These items are usually numbers, but can be text. These facts make up the grain of the table. The other type of column in the fact table is the reference column to the dimension tables. These columns store the primary key values of the dimension tables.

The fact tables are usually the largest tables in the database. The data warehouse design team must work to find a balance between the size of the table and the usability of its data.

Dimension Tables

The dimension tables contain data that will be used to selectively include or exclude data that will be returned from the fact table. The data stored in the dimension table is usually text, but sometimes it will be a number. An example of this is a zip code. Although the zip code is a number, it will not be used in mathematical functions such as the average, sum, or standard deviation. Instead, it will be used to determine the data from the fact table that will be returned. An executive might ask for the total sales from the 90210 zip code. This will use the zip code dimension field to select only the sales in the fact table that occurred in that zip code. An executive is unlikely to ask the data warehouse to determine the average zip code. The dimension tables will usually be much smaller than the fact table.

Figure 30.2 shows five tables. The fact table is the Sales table. This company sells service contracts for software support. The first four columns of this fact table are keys used to join with the four dimension tables.

- service_id
- time_id
- sales_person_id
- customer_id

The other columns in the Sales table make up the grain of the table.

- amount_of_sale
- number_of_months
- cost_to_provide_service
- sales_commission

FIGURE 30.2.

A star schema.

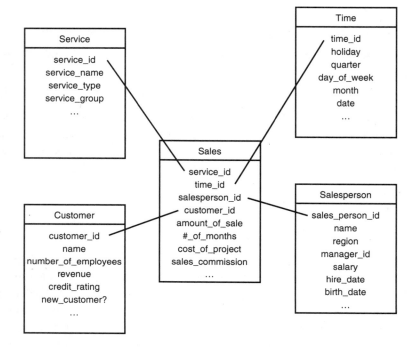

Time Dimension

The first dimension table is the time dimension. Many people question the need for the time dimension. They often wonder why a simple date column would not be sufficient. In the OLTP environment they would be correct. However, in a data warehouse, the data is being used for decision making and needs to be tied into the business environment. The time dimension can recognize business events that will be important to the users, such as the following:

- Fiscal year
- Fiscal quarter
- Day of the week
- Holiday
- Special event

The company may notice a jump in sales on Wednesday, February 14. This may seem abnormal except that February 13 is a special event. February 13 is the date of a new bonus structure for the sales team. Most salespeople wanted to close sales after the new structure was in place. The company may have lost sales as a result of procrastination by the sales force. Management may use this information to adjust the way bonus structures are implemented.

The following are some questions that may be answered with the time dimension:

- What was the average sale during the fourth quarter?
- What was the total sales commissions paid for sales made on Fridays during the last three months?
- How many sales are usually made on a holiday?
- When are we most likely to make a sale: at the beginning, middle, or end of the quarter?

Service Dimension

The service dimension describes the services being sold. This table will have a relatively small number of rows, since fewer than 1,000 services are provided. It will usually be a table with a large number of columns. These columns detail everything that can be known about the service, such as the following:

- Service type
- Service name
- Location of service (onsite or offsite support)
- Internal group
- Date the service was first offered

Here are some questions that may be answered with the service dimension:

- What is the average sale in software support? In hardware support?
- What is the sales total for Oracle RDBMS support during the last quarter?
- Which service is the most profitable?

Salesperson Dimension

The salesperson dimension records information about the salesperson who achieved the sale. This dimension will often be used for spatial analysis. The columns in this dimension contain information about the salesperson that is easy to group, as shown in the following list. Notice that the name and address information of the salesperson is not recorded. That information is not relevant for high-level decisions.

- sales_person_id
- sales_manager_id

- salary
- birthday
- region
- number of years at the company

The following questions are the type that may be answered with the salesperson dimension.

- What is the sales total per month for salespeople who are making over $35,000 per year?
- What is the average age of our sales force? (This one doesn't actually use the fact table.)
- Which region has the highest total sales?

Customer Dimension

The customer dimension is often the most valuable dimension in this particular type of star schema. It can record information about the customer that will allow management to better understand the customer base. Some of the data included would be the following:

- Customer name
- Zip code
- City
- State
- Number of employees
- Revenue
- Credit rating
- Repeat customer or new customer

Some of the questions the customer dimension might answer are the following:

- What is the average sales commission to companies with over 500 employees?
- What is the average length of a sales contract for companies in New York or New Jersey?
- What is the number of sales over two million dollars made to companies with a poor credit rating?

Using All the Dimensions

The true benefit of dimensions is that they can all be used together. The data from the fact table can be filtered using any of the dimension tables.

The following are examples of the kinds of questions that may be answered with multiple dimensions:

- What was the most profitable service in region 5 during the first quarter? (Time, Service, and Salesperson)

- Who was our largest customer (in sales) in the software support area? (Customer, Service)

- Which region has paid the most in sales commissions during December? (Salesperson, Time)

- What is the average length of sales contracts for companies with revenues of over 500 million dollars that purchased Oracle RDBMS onsite service contracts during the last fiscal year? (Time, Service, Customer)

The star schema is a data warehousing model that provides a flexible, simple architecture for decision support systems. It is the most proven and accepted model in this area.

Designing the Data Refresh Process

The data warehouse is typically designed to be updated on a periodic basis. The data warehouse design team must determine the periodic refresh interval for each group of data. Some tables will need to be updated nightly. The Sales table is a good candidate for a nightly refresh because it is constantly changing. Other tables, such as lookup tables, change much less frequently.

An example of this is the Shipping table. The Shipping table contains the shipper_id, name, address, phone number, and shipping code. The Shipping table has three rows (see Table 30.1).

TABLE 30.1. SHIPPING TABLE

ID	Name	Address	Phone	Shipping Code
1	Federal Express	101 Lincoln Ave.	303-555-1112	A788D6
2	United Parcel Service	121 10th St.	303-555-4444	11118786657
3	U.S. Post Office	6556 Main Rd.	303-555-8878	U454IUYO

Because the company rarely adds or changes shipping companies, this table can be updated much less frequently inside the data warehouse.

Some data brought into the data warehouse is refreshed based on a schedule outside of the data warehouse design team's control. Data derived from accounting cycles will be

30

DATA
WAREHOUSES

updated inside the data warehouse according to the accounting cycle dates. A company that completes all of its accounting for each month on the 15th of the following month will refresh the data on the 16th of the month. Other data will not be periodic in nature. Press releases are often random in nature and will need to be added as quickly as possible.

It's important for the data warehouse design team to remember that not all the data is current at a single point in time.

Scalability

The data warehouse design team must ensure that the data warehouse is scalable. It is easy for programmers to forget scalability issues and create a process that is destined to be rewritten. The programmers and designers must test all processes at the highest possible load level that can be expected in the data warehouse. Scalability of the data warehouse is not difficult to achieve if it is remembered. The data warehouse must be scalable in many ways.

1. *Extraction and scrubbing process.* The designers need to ensure that the functions being performed on the data can be expanded easily without recoding the process. For example, if the current extraction process is pulling data from an Oracle database, it may not need to use the parallel query option. However, as the data grows in size, the parallel query option may be needed. If the extraction programmer allows a parallel clause to be determined at run time, the process may begin using the parallel query option if it is needed.

2. *Table structures.* The data warehouse design team may decide to perform a join between two tables as they would in an operating environment. A more scalable solution may be to combine the tables into one nonrelational table. In other situations it may be more scalable to use object tables.

3. *Client processes.* The client processes must be programmed to allow the data warehouse to scale to a large number of clients. If the client causes a large burden on the data warehouse by issuing unneeded or incorrect queries, the data warehouse will be limited to a small number of users.

Utilizing Oracle8 Features in the Data Warehouse

The data warehouse design team should be aware of the features of the database that contains the data warehouse. It is often appropriate to bring in a database guru on that particular database. Oracle8 has several features that will enhance the data warehouse environment. The three new Oracle features that I have found to be most helpful are partitioning, indexing, and hints.

Partitioning

Partitioning allows a table or index to be split into several physical structures while maintaining a single logical structure. Partitioning is often used in data warehousing to split a table into sections based on a time series. Figure 30.3 shows a Sales table partitioned by year. The 1994 and 1995 partitions currently reside in tablespaces that are offline. This typically means that they are stored on tape and are not accessible without the data being reloaded. The 1996 and 1997 partitions of the Sales table reside in read-only tablespaces. These partitions cannot be updated without the intervention of the database administrator. The 1998 partition is in a normal read/write tablespace. The users of this partition are only granted select (read-only) access. However, the extraction and scrubbing processes still have the ability to add data to those tables.

FIGURE 30.3.
*A partitioned
Sales table.*

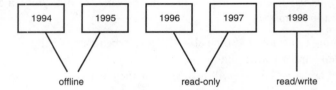

Indexing

Oracle8 has five types of indexes:

- B-tree (most common type of index)
- B-tree cluster (used for clusters)
- Hash clusters (uses a mathematical function to determine matching rows)
- Reverse key (distributes I/O access to the index)
- Bitmap indexes (used for low cardinality columns)

Each indexing scheme is valuable in certain situations and most data warehouses use all of them.

> **TIP**
>
> Bitmap indexes were designed by Oracle Corporation for data warehouse applications. They have proven to be a gold mine for the data warehouse designers who use them.

30

**DATA
WAREHOUSES**

Hints

Oracle has provided some hints that cannot be passed up. The most important hint to the data warehouse is the star hint. The star hint tells the database to join the large fact table after joining all of the smaller dimension tables.

Monitoring Tools

Monitoring tools are used to oversee several aspects of the data warehouse. They monitor the speed of the extraction and scrubbing processes, as well as the queries being issued by the users. As they collect information, the data warehouse team can adjust the structure of the data warehouse to improve performance for the users. They may also detect resource that are being wasted by some users. For example, a manager in a small department may ask for the total breakdown of all sales for every product the company sells. This query may take two days to run and use 10% of the data warehouse resources. The data warehouse team may inquire into the relevance of this query and may ask that manager to stop running it.

The monitoring tool should also be able to detect when data is being queried unnecessarily. This often happens when the metadata is incorrect. The metadata may point the user to the incorrect data. The user will realize he or she has received the incorrect data and continue on to find the correct data. The data warehouse team may incorrectly optimize access to the bad table when they should be fixing the metadata that is pointing users to the wrong data. Monitoring tools can provide the ability to notice trends that may point to incorrect or misleading metadata.

The monitoring tools also record the length of time it takes to complete a query. If the query runs for an extended period of time, the monitoring tool should alert the design team that something may be wrong. The design team can then decide the proper course of action.

Develop the Extraction and Scrubbing Routines

The extraction and scrubbing processes can be one of the most time-consuming efforts of the data warehouse project. Often this step will take up the largest portion of resources allocated to the data warehouse project.

The first step in the extraction and scrubbing processes is to determine which data from the operating environment has changed since the last time the data warehouse was refreshed. This step is difficult because it may pull data from hundreds of different sources. It will be easy to determine the changed data for some sources. Others will require much more effort.

There are three basic ways to determine what data has changed.

- Auditing logs
- Full refreshes with data selection performed inside the data warehouse
- Code changes in the existing applications

Auditing Logs

The easiest sources to extract data from will have an auditing function built into them. The data warehouse extraction team needs to understand and develop applications to work with these auditing processes. Data warehouses that work with Oracle databases often pull the changed data from the redo logs. The redo logs are a convenient place to find data that has changed. It also avoids changing the application code or interfering with the performance of the operational database. In essence, a data warehouse that is pulling information from an Oracle operational database can do so without the database or application being affected in any way. Most modern databases contain these types of logs. The logs enable the database to recover if an error occurs in its processing. One of the tricks of using this extraction tool is determining the format of the log files. The log files are usually stored in an internal binary format. Software packages designed to extract data from logs may already exist for some databases. Platinum and BMC have developed packages that can read Oracle redo logs, as well as Microsoft SQL Server transactions logs and IBM DB2 logs. Older or unpopular technologies may not have commercial software available that can read their logs. If this is the case, the extraction team must either develop a custom utility or find another method for refreshing the data warehouse.

Full Refreshes with Data Selection Performed Inside the Data Warehouse

Another way to refresh the data warehouse is to pull all of the data from the operating environment to the data warehouse on a nightly basis. When the data warehouse receives the data, it must determine which data to keep. This solution has many problems.

First, the amount of data transferred to the data warehouse can be enormous. For example, a company may have one terabyte of important data in its operational systems. Every night, one terabyte of data must be pulled from the operating databases, across the network, and into the data warehouse. After the data warehouse receives the terabyte, it

30

DATA WAREHOUSES

must perform heavy processing that will discard approximately 95% of the data. This process could take days to complete. Since most data warehouses have an 8-hour refresh window, this simply is not possible. That much data cannot be moved through the entire process in such a short amount of time.

A second problem with pulling all of the data from the operating database is that the operating database will slow down considerably during the refresh process. The users of the operational database will notice an enormous degradation of query response time. A data warehouse team that imposes these types of problems on the operational team will not be very popular.

Code Changes in the Existing Applications

The third way to refresh the data warehouse is to code changes in the operational applications to report the data that has been inserted, updated, or deleted. This may also be done at the database level through triggers, snapshots, and possibly advanced replication. This is usually the worst solution. The data warehouse team must write code for the data warehouse, as well as rewrite and debug code that may have existed for years.

Determining the changed data can be quite a bit of work. After the data has been identified, the team must determine what must be done to the data to prepare it for the data warehouse tables. There are several types of scrubbing actions the data warehouse team must identify.

The first action is to change the operational data to adhere to standards determined in the design phase. These standards must be applied to all operational data sources. For example, one application may store the date as mm/dd/yy in a character field. The Oracle database stores the date as a 7-byte date code that records the date down to the second. An application that stores the date in the mm/dd/yy format may require extra logic structures in the extraction process. In a human resources application it is important to understand that the century has not been recorded. A year of 40 may indicate 1940 when an employee was born, or it may indicate 2040 when the employee may begin withdrawing from his or her 401k retirement account.

A second example of standards is how sex is recorded. One application may record sex as male and female. Another application may record sex as "m" and "f." This type of conversion is simple to code, but difficult due to the large number of fields in different applications that must be converted.

A second action the extraction scrubbing team must address is data merging. Data merging occurs when information that needs to be stored in a single table or column in the data warehouse is actually pulled from several tables or columns in the operational environment. For example, a company with an order database on a UNIX machine and a shipping database on an NT platform may find the need to pull information from both databases to create a complete record of sales. The extraction process must pull data from each environment and determine how the data will be merged through a series of complex rules.

The extraction team is also responsible for populating summary tables. These summary tables are stored inside the data warehouse and are based on other data inside the warehouse (see Figure 30.4). The data warehouse team may decide to populate summary tables at a different time than the extraction. However, this solution will result in a large increase in disk I/O. A better solution is to have the extraction processes build the summary tables as they are building the base tables.

FIGURE 30.4.
Extraction process that populates summary tables.

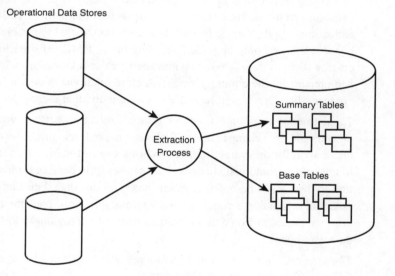

The extraction team must also update metadata in the following areas:

- Descriptions about the data
- Refresh schedule
- Size of the data
- Groups permitted to use this table
- Original location of the data

The maintenance of the metadata should be an automatic process that is performed by the extraction process.

The extraction team must keep several things in mind while developing extraction and cleansing processes.

- *The processes must be fast.* The team must determine the amount of data that could potentially be processed by these routines in the future. The code must be fast enough to accomplish its work within the 8-hour refresh period.

- *The operational technologies will continue to change.* An example of this is the upgrade of an operational environment from Oracle7 to Oracle8. In the upgrade, Oracle Corporation has changed the format of the redo logs. An extraction process based on the Oracle7 redo logs may have to be re-written. It is also important that the data extraction team understands the future intentions of the operating environments. It may be beneficial to choose an extraction tool that will keep up with the underlying technology. For example, a data warehouse pulling data from an Oracle database can use software from a vendor such as Platinum or BMC for the data extractions. As the Oracle format changes from Oracle7 to Oracle8, the data warehouse team need only upgrade their Platinum or BMC software to continue processing the new data. These vendors keep a close relationship with Oracle to track and prepare for the coming changes. A close relationship with a large software company like Oracle will be difficult for an individual data warehouse team.

- *The extraction team must keep in constant contact with the operational teams.* Operational data changes often. Tables are moved, renamed, and deleted. It is not uncommon for the extraction team to bring over erroneous or incomplete data due to unknown operational changes. This can result in passing on inaccurate information to the users who make decisions based on this data. False information has the potential of sending a company in the wrong direction. Thus the relationship between the extraction and operational teams is paramount to the validity of the data warehouse.

- *The extraction processes should be robust.* They must be able to recover from a failure without starting over. The data set can be so large that it may not be possible to kick off the entire process again.

The extraction processes must also verify the data before it is released to the users. This verification process performs several basic functions. One of these functions can use statistical formulas to determine the probability of data validity.

For example, a company may have always had between one and two million dollars in sales per day. If new data from the operational environments shows sales of only one hundred thousand dollars per day, the data must be verified by a data analyst before it is released to the user community. This type of verification performs three functions.

First, it checks the validity of the data warehousing extraction processes. In this case, the extraction process may have performed an improper math function as it pulled the data into the warehouse.

Second, it checks the validity of the operational processes. For this anomaly, the operational processes may have lost the records of some sales.

Third, the verification process may alert management to business problems. If the total sales has actually fallen by 90 percent, management will want to get this information as quickly as possible.

The verification process can be worth its weight in gold. Because almost all operational systems will tie into the data warehouse, the verification process can act as a company-wide alarm system.

> **NOTE**
>
> A Fortune 500 company had a problem in their accounts receivable system. It had underbilled customers for a total loss of over 30 million dollars. The data warehouse verification process detected the error and reported it to a data warehouse analyst. The money that was recovered was enough to pay for the entire data warehouse.

What About Data Marts?

Data marts are defined in several ways throughout the industry. Unfortunately, the term has never settled into one definition. This would explain the confusion that takes place when the data mart topic is brought up.

Most of the definitions can be classified into two major categories (see Figure 30.5).

- The first definition defines the data mart as a piece of the data warehouse. It is used to build the data warehouse in small steps. After all data marts have been created, they will be merged into one data warehouse. Data marts will pull data directly from the operational environments.

- The second definition defines the data mart as a subset of data that is pulled from the data warehouse. The data is pulled from the operational environments into the data warehouse. The data marts can choose what data they would like to see from the data warehouse. The data is pulled into the data marts and massaged into a more usable format.

FIGURE 30.5.

Two definitions of data marts.

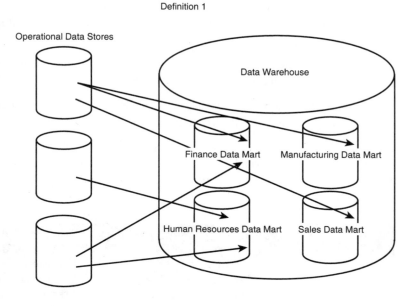

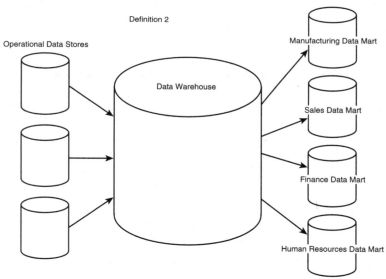

Data marts are a fairly recent addition to the data warehousing movement. They have become increasingly useful for several reasons.

First, they can be developed in a short period of time (usually 3 to 6 months per data mart). Due to the rapid development pace, they may begin paying for themselves sooner than a data warehouse.

Second, the designers will learn to build better data marts as they receive feedback from existing data marts. Usually the team has become much more sophisticated in data mart design after building its first data mart.

Another reason for the popularity of data marts is the ability to pick a small set of data for the first iteration of the data mart process. Several factors are considered.

- What data is the easiest to extract from the operating environments?
- What data will be the most utilized by management?
- What data mart best resembles the rest of the data warehouse project?

After management has seen the benefits of a data mart, it is easier to receive funding for additional data marts or an entire data warehouse.

Another benefit of data marts is cost. A data mart usually costs several hundred thousand dollars to implement. This relatively small amount of money is easier for management to approve than a multi-million-dollar data warehouse. Due to the fact that financing is often done at the departmental level, it's often easier to gain approval for a data mart because the department understands how the data mart will be used. It is much harder to find financing at the corporate-wide level.

Although data marts have many benefits, they are not without problems. A data mart has the potential of becoming yet another isolated system. Companies sometimes allow the development of data marts without the proper coordination between them. This coordination is not easy to achieve. Data marts are designed in parallel, with each team making decisions that will later affect the data warehouse. For example, one team may decide on the date format yyyy/mm/dd. This data mart may standardize on that format to the detriment of the data warehouse project as a whole.

Before any data mart development begins, a base data warehouse design should be in place. This design does not need to delve into the details of code for extraction, but it needs to document the current systems. It must do this to establish the standards necessary for the data warehouse project to be successful. Once a data mart team understands the overall guidelines, they can design a data mart that can be easily tied into the data warehouse at a later date.

The data mart team must also decide on the type of data mart. If it is a data mart that will eventually merge directly into the data warehouse (Definition 1), it must use the

30

DATA WAREHOUSES

same technology as the future data warehouse. If this is the case, the data mart team will design extraction processes to work directly with the data mart.

If the data mart will eventually pull data from the data warehouse (Definition 2), the data mart team must design extraction processes to extract the operational data to the data warehouse. Next, the data mart will pull the data from the data warehouse. This will allow the data warehouse to incorporate the data used in the data mart without rewriting extraction processes. This also gives the data mart designer the ability to choose the technology of the data mart, which may differ from the data warehouse technology. This type of data mart requires that a corporate-wide data warehouse team establish data standards and technologies before the data mart project can begin. The data warehouse team will also need to present a complete data model for all data that the data marts will be using.

Metadata

Metadata is data about data. It is all the information a user or administrator needs to fully utilize the data. The metadata will reveal such things as where to find the data, what data exists on a certain topic, who created the data, where it came from, and who has permission to use it.

Metadata is one of the most neglected parts of the data warehouse. It is similar to documentation in that almost everyone realizes its value, but few actually find time to develop it. Without proper metadata, it can be difficult for users to work with the data warehouse. The three types of metadata in a data warehouse are system, management, and business metadata.

System Metadata

System metadata is data that will not be changed by the data warehouse team. The system data is maintained by the technologies used by the data warehouse. Inside the Oracle database there are virtual system tables such as dba_tables, dba_indexes, and dba_users. These tables describe what type of data is inside the database. This type of metadata is almost always used exclusively by system or database administrators. It is typically too raw to give directly to the users.

Management Metadata

Management metadata explains all the details of data management. The following are some examples of management metadata:

- Source of the data
- Schedule of when the data is updated
- Calculations that occurred on the data
- Splitting or merging of tables
- Process to determine missing values through defaults or data derived from data mining
- Technologies used in this process
- Knowledge learned by the data warehouse team

One example of management metadata is recording the process of reading the redo logs for the data extraction process. If the team has chosen a vendor to perform the retrieval of data from the redo logs, they should document the functions of the tool that is being used. This will allow the data warehouse team to understand the impact of a new software release by the redo log vendor. If the team has chosen to design its own tool to extract information from the redo logs, it is important to document the format of the redo logs as well as the API of the custom tool.

A second example of management metadata is user activity. This includes recording the CPU and disk I/O of queries issued by the users. This form of metadata allows the data warehouse team to properly bill each department for its usage of the system. It also allows the team to better understand what types of queries are being issued. This will reveal the following:

- Tuning needs
- The need for additional data
- Data that is not being used

The data warehouse team must decide if data is not being used because of a lack of interest or a lack of metadata that prevents users from finding or understanding the data. If the users are not interested, this data may be moved to a less expensive media or deleted.

Business Metadata

Business metadata is directly pointed to the business users. It allows users to find and understand the data in the data warehouse. Typical business metadata models will contain a search engine. The search engine allows users to look up data sources based on key words. This search engine will return the hits on the specific key word as well as suggest similar terms that may be more appropriate. If the user determines that the key word he chose was incorrect, he can choose one of the words the metadata dictionary has suggested. The user is also given a detailed description of the true meaning of the data and how it should be interpreted.

The business metadata also contains a subset of the information found in the data warehouse management metadata.

- Source system of the data
- Schedule of when the data is updated
- Calculations that occurred on the data

Other business metadata includes connections to other data sources such as online documentation, Web sites, and reports on industry and economic trends.

Although metadata is easy to explain, it can be difficult to implement. One reason is a lack of metadata standards. A group called the Metadata Coalition is attempting to standardize this field. They are a group of vendors trying to enhance the sale of all of their products by bringing metadata into the mainstream. The Coalition is developing a metadata standard, but it is still in its infancy.

Executive Information Systems

The executive information system (EIS) is a module of the data warehouse that is specifically designed for high-level executives. The EIS must meet the following requirements:

1. Easy to use
2. Easy to access
3. Fast

Easy to Use

Executives do not have the time or patience to learn a difficult product. They must be able to intuitively learn the functions of the EIS as they need them. This piece will determine the success or failure of the EIS. It is wise to consider a Web-based EIS system. This provides several benefits. First, the Web is traditionally a simple tool to use. Most executives feel more comfortable using a Web page than a separate application. A Web-based EIS also allows the executive to bypass the often problematic installation procedure of an EIS client-based application.

Easy to Access

The executive must be able to access the EIS from offices, board rooms, and even airplanes. A Web-based solution could be deployed on the Internet to allow the executive to use the EIS from any personal computer with an Internet connection.

> **CAUTION**
>
> Be aware of the security problems that an Internet-based EIS can bring. Consult a security expert BEFORE putting the EIS in place.

Fast

Executives will not wait three days for a query to be returned. To avoid this problem, the executive information system must be proactive in the way queries are executed. One of the best ways to decrease query response time is to create summary tables.

Summary tables allow the executives to issue high-level queries without reading all of the low-level data.

Figure 30.6 shows how an executive could issue several different queries that will all be returned quickly. If the executive were to pose the query "What is the total sales for our company?," this would be easily answered by a summary table that contains the total sales for each region. Notice that the summary table that contains the total sales for the whole company is not used. Although a table of that size would be very small, it would be useless for any other query. Instead, summary tables are made at levels of summarization that can be used by as many queries as possible. The region sales summary table is a good candidate to satisfy this query due to its small size. This table will be scanned into the database in a single disk I/O. The Oracle database reads blocks in increments of the `db_file_multiblock_ read_ count` parameter. On HP UNIX, the maximum I/O allowed by the operating system is 64KB. Because most Oracle data warehouse applications will use an 8KB block size, the `db_file_multiblock_ read_ count` parameter should be set to 8. Oracle will read 64KB at a time during full table scans.

```
db_block_size X db_file_multiblock_ read_ count = the amount Oracle will
read for each I/O during a full table scan
8K * 8K = 64K
```

Because the total size of both the region and national Sales tables is less than 64KB, they will both be read in one operating system I/O. Because the same amount of I/O will be used, it is best to keep the data summarized at the lower level.

30

DATA WAREHOUSES

FIGURE 30.6.

Summary tables.

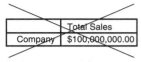

	Total Sales
Company	$100,000,000.00

Summarized by company (1 row)

Region	Total Sales
1	$20,000,000.00
2	$25,000,000.00
3	$30,000,000.00
4	$10,000,000.00
5	$15,000,000.00

Summarized by region (5 rows)

Store	Region	Total Sales
1001	1	$ 100,000.00
1002	1	$ 200,000.00
1003	2	$ 50,000.00
1004	2	$ 85,000.00
1005	5	$ 70,000.00
...	...	...

Summarized by store (100 rows)

Sales Detail Table				
Store	Region	Product	Sale Price	Tax
1001	1	Boots	$ 20.00	$ 1.20
1001	1	Socks	$ 6.00	$ 0.36
1001	1	Jacket	$ 80.00	$ 4.80
1001	1	Jeans	$ 32.00	$ 1.92
1001	1	Purse	$ 40.00	$ 2.40
1001	1	Shoes	$70	$ 4.20
1001	1	Watch	$120	$ 7.20
...	...	...	...	...

Detail records for each sale
(100,000,000 rows)

What happens when the executive asks for the total sales for each store? The Region table will not be able to handle this query. This query can do one of two things:

- It can read the base order table's 100 million rows and calculate the total sales per store.

- It can read from another summary table that is one level down from the Region table. This summary table will have the total sales for each store. The query will read 1000 rows instead of 100,000,000. This option will run approximately 100,000 times faster than the first solution.

These examples show how summary tables are important to the speed of the EIS. However, it is not easy to implement summary tables. A traditional query using ANSI SQL does not have the ability to choose different tables based on the existence of summary tables. The EIS must be intelligent enough to perform this function for the database. This will be performed using metadata that tells the report engine how to construct the SQL statement.

A second way the EIS can speed up queries is by denormalizing tables. Relational databases are normalized to prevent redundancy. The lack of redundancy provides faster operation as well as cleaner data. In the data warehouse, redundancy can be used as a tool to speed up queries. An example is the Sales table (see Figure 30.7).

FIGURE 30.7.

Denormalizing tables for fast access.

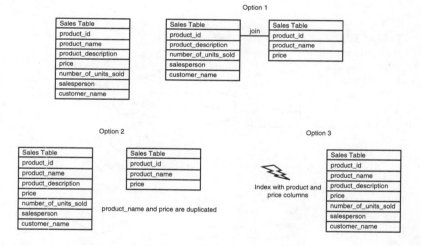

The EIS system designer has noticed that the most used fields in this table are `product_id`, `product_name`, and `price`. The designer also notices that these fields are almost always used together. In order to speed up the queries that use these fields, the analyst moves those fields into a separate table. The queries will run faster because they do not have to read the additional fields. When the data is stored with the other fields, the database will retrieve the data in all of the fields including the unneeded ones. Initially one might pull those fields from the original table and join the two tables with a one-to-one relationship. This would prevent redundant data and help minimize the size of the EIS. However, queries that are pulling data from both tables would be much slower. A good solution is to keep the data for the important fields in both places.

An even better solution would be to place an index on both of those columns. Some databases have the ability to read only the indexes if the needed data resides in the index. In other words, all requests that are only asking for those columns could be satisfied simply by looking at the index and never actually hitting the table. Unfortunately, Oracle doesn't currently support index-only reads.

Client- or Server-Based

The EIS design team must determine whether the EIS is client based or server based (see Figure 30.8). A client-based system will pull all data directly from the data warehouse and manipulate the data into usable form. The EIS would need to build the summary tables and store them inside the data warehouse or on the client itself. Queries issued by several clients will not cooperate and share resources in a client-based scenario.

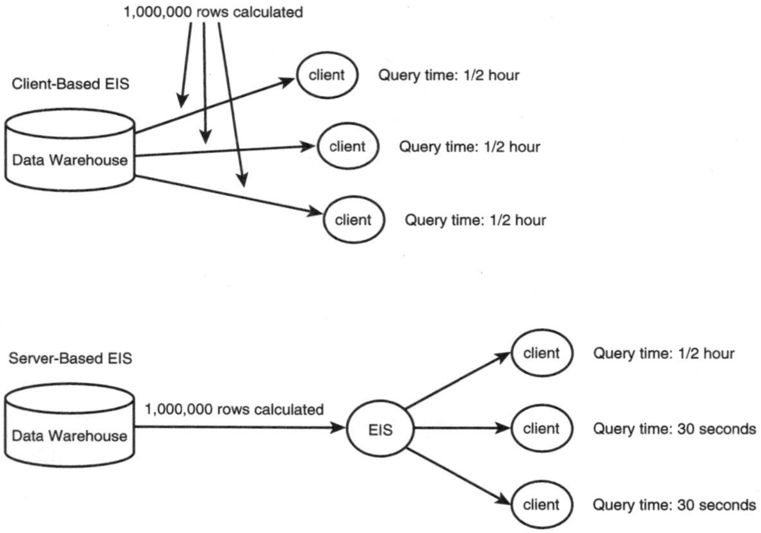

FIGURE 30.8.

Client- versus server-based executive information systems.

For example, three clients may ask for the total sales in region 1. Each query performs the entire task of calculating the total sales at the detail level.

A better solution is to use a server-based EIS. The server-based EIS will be able to analyze the queries of all users and optimize those most frequently used. It will also be able to create summary tables, redundant tables, and other forms of denormalization at the server level. The EIS will be a completely different system than the data warehouse. This gives the EIS much more flexibility in restructuring data for speed and ease of use. The server-side EIS will cache query results from users. If one user requests the sales of toothbrushes in region 1, the EIS will calculate that result. If any other user requests the same data, the EIS will return the results quickly. This is especially useful when several departments are using the EIS. At various times in the fiscal year, multiple users issue the exact same query within days of each other. A query that may take several hours to run will only take that long for the first user who executes it. Subsequent users will receive results in seconds.

External Data

External data is pulled from various sources outside of the organization, which allows the users to see the overall business environment. For example, a graph that shows the sale of a particular product may have several confusing dips. However, when the external data is shown, it may be revealed that a competing product was heavily advertised during the periods of slower sales. Other external data includes the following:

- Economic trends
- Industry data purchased from information companies such as A.C. Nielson
- Articles about the company or product
- Competitor advertising
- Competitor job advertisements

Data Mining (Panning for Gold)

Organizations have an enormous amount of data collected in the operational systems as well as in the data warehouse. Once the data is properly contained inside the data warehouse, it becomes easy for executives to ask data-related questions. However, executives do not know what questions they need to ask. Data mining searches though the data and finds relationships between different sets of data. If the relationships are considered valid, the tool alerts the executive team of its importance. Data mining is done by using complex statistical methods to determine relationships between the data. The relationships may be intra-table or inter-table. An easy relationship to see is the intra-table relationship between the city and the state inside the Customer table (see Figure 30.9).

The data mining tool will show a high confidence factor between the relationship of a city equal to New York City and a state equal to New York. Since the confidence level is 100%, the user can assume that a relationship does exist. Unfortunately, the user has not learned much from this discovery. This relationship is well known and irrelevant to normal business.

FIGURE 30.9.

An intra-table relationship.

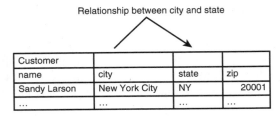

IF city=New York City
THEN state=New York
Confidence = 99.7%

The other type of data mining is inter-table. An example is the relationship between salespeople earning over $30,000 per year and the sale of product X. This type of data mining uses the join between the Salesperson table and the Sales table to determine a relationship (see Figure 30.10).

FIGURE 30.10.

An inter-table relationship.

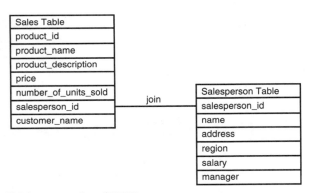

IF Salesperson salary >$30,000
THEN 10% more likely to sell product X
Confidence = 78%

Data Mining Models

The data mining tool will typically develop a model that can be applied to determine relationships.

The first model is the `if/then` model.

```
Example:
IF     a customer requests an address change
THEN   the customer is likely to purchase household goods
```

With this model, a mail-order company would send a household goods catalog to all customers who change their address.

A second model is classification. The analyst will determine groups and use the data mining tool to place items into each group. For example, a business may have four classifications of their credit rating system.

- Great credit
- Average credit
- Bad credit
- Not enough information

The data mining tool will use these parameters to classify customers into one of the categories.

A third model is clusters. Clusters are similar to the classification model, except that the data mining tool determines the groups instead of the analyst. Using this same example of customer credit ratings, the data mining tool may cluster groups of people into five categories.

- Customer can be trusted with up to $5,000,000.
- Customer can be trusted with up to $2,000,000.
- Customer can be trusted with up to $500,000.
- Customer can be trusted with up to $100,000.
- Customer can be trusted with up to $100.

The data analyst must decide how to use the clusters the data mining tool has developed. In this case, the analyst may decide that all customers who are in the last category (trusted with only $100) should not be visited by any more salespeople.

The next model is sequences. Sequences show a pattern of events over time that are likely to recur. A car dealership may use sequences to sell accessories on new cars.

1. Client purchases vehicle.
2. Client uses dealership for oil changes.
3. Client purchases highly profitable accessories for vehicle.
4. Client purchases another car within three years from same dealer.

This sequence may lead the car dealer to provide oil changes for a low fee to all customers who purchases vehicles. The sequence may indicate that oil changes performed at the dealership will lead to additional profits in accessories and vehicle sales.

Another data mining model is market basket analysis. Market basket analysis looks at the relationship between products and determines which products are likely to be bought together. For example, a data mining tool may determine that bread and milk are likely to be bought together. Based on this information, a grocery store may place milk and bread in the same area of the store. The store hopes that a customer who comes in to buy milk will see the bread and purchase it.

The data mining tool uses several mathematical techniques to perform this analysis. The following is just a small list of the current techniques:

- Neural networks
- Decision trees
- Standard statistics
- Memory-based reasoning
- Genetic algorithms
- Link analysis

These techniques all can lead to the discovery of important data relationships. Each performs different functions and discovers different pieces of information. Thus it is important not to choose a single tool that utilizes only one or two of these techniques. Instead, it is beneficial to use several tools that use the entire spectrum of techniques for a complete data mining tool set.

These data mining techniques typically need three sets of data to develop a model. The first set of data is the training set. This set is used to develop the initial models. The second set of data is the test data. The test data is used to test the models that were created using the training set. If the models prove to be accurate in the test set, the model can be assumed to be correct for use with real data. The third set of data is called the application data. This is the data the model will actually be used against. As time passes, the model will receive feedback on its accuracy. Each time feedback is received, the model will determine if it needs to be changed.

After the models have been developed and tested, they can be presented to the executive community to use for decision making.

Before the relationships can be presented to executives, the data analyst must perform several functions:

1. *Eliminate erroneous relationships.*
   ```
   IF    Salesperson last name is greater than 10 characters
   THEN    Salesperson will sell 5% more than a salesperson with
   less than 10 characters in their last name
   ```

This relationship although statistically possible is clearly unreasonable and, thus, should not be presented to an executive.

2. *Eliminate unimportant relationships.* An unimportant relationship is one that may provide insight into the business of the company but is of little significance. This type of relationship is not worth taking to the executive level.

```
IF    paper clips are purchased in bulk
THEN    10% of the purchase cost will be saved
```

Although this relationship is valid, it is not important enough to present to an executive.

3. *Eliminate most relationships with low confidence levels.* Only relationships that are highly correlated should be reported to executives.

```
IF    advertise in DBMS magazine
THEN    sales improve .2%
confidence factor 10%
```

This relationship shows that 10% of the time a company has advertised in *DBMS* magazine, sales have increased .2%. Unfortunately, this confidence factor is not high enough to establish a true relationship.

4. *Propose specific recommendations based on the relationships.* For example, if the data shows a clear relationship between advertising in *The Wall Street Journal* and increasing sales, the data analyst should attempt to determine the proper increase in advertising in *The Wall Street Journal* for maximum profitability. The data analyst should present the relationship as well as the potential solution to the executive. Executives appreciate the extra step and often act on the proposal quickly.

There are several ways of communicating this data to executives.

- Email
- GroupWare
- Web page
- Meetings
- Published reports

Summary

This chapter provides a brief introduction into the world of data warehousing. It details the six steps to creating a data warehouse. These steps include documenting the existing environment, choosing the proper data warehousing technologies, designing the data warehouse model, developing the extraction and scrubbing routines, building the metadata repository, and creating multidimensional cubes.

30

DATA WAREHOUSES

The chapter also explains data marts, executive information systems, and data mining. Understanding how all the pieces fit together hopefully will help you create rock-solid data warehouses. Be sure to read Chapter 33, "Working with Very Large Databases," for additional information on Oracle features that can be used in a data warehouse.

Large Online Transaction Processing Systems

by Derek C. Ashmore

IN THIS CHAPTER

CHAPTER 31

Online Transaction Processing (OLTP) Overview

Online Transaction Processing (OLTP) applications are applications that record information about a specific business unit function. For example, most banks have OLTP applications in which bank officers can enter information about new customers or accounts for those customers. OLTP applications, by definition, obtain most input manually from an end user.

This chapter provides recommendations on how to effectively design, code, and administrate OLTP applications that use Oracle as an underlying database. Typically, OLTP applications have extensive availability requirements. For example, one of my clients administrates credit card accounts. If this system isn't available, customers cannot use their credit cards for purchases. This can mean lost revenue and ill will from customers.

Another of my clients uses an OLTP application to record treatments for patients in a hospital. This information is used to inform nurses which patients get which treatments. Application outages cost the hospital in many ways, including vulnerability to lawsuits when prescribed treatments are missed, the ill will of patients who suffer lack of treatment, and so on. Frequently, large OLTP applications also have high availability requirements.

Typically, non-MVS platforms provide high availability capabilities via clustering technology. Clustering technologies allow UNIX, and more recently Windows NT servers, to be tightly coupled enough to share memory and disk. In other words, each node or machine in the cluster can access the same set of disks. Furthermore, machines, which are clustered, often can share memory.

Oracle supports clustering technologies with an add-on called the *Oracle Parallel Server (OPS)*. This add-on allows you to have multiple instances (one on each node) providing access to the same database (the same set of data files). This means that each instance has access to the same set of tables, indexes, sequences, and so on. OPS is often used with OLTP applications because of the high availability requirements, so this chapter will provide an overview of clustering technologies and OPS.

Typically, OLTP applications have large numbers of users (over 1,000), mainly small targeted transactions that involve small result sets for most queries (keyed updates, deletes, and selects), and a large proportion of writes. Depending upon the application, this chapter will provide recommendations on how to effectively design and configure databases for this type of load. Furthermore, we will provide recommendations on how to effectively structure database access within applications to make them more efficient and less resource intensive.

OLTP applications typically have large numbers of users, so most are hosted on RISC platforms running some variety of UNIX. At the time of this writing, Windows NT is simply not scalable enough to handle these types of applications. This chapter will give you recommendations on how to configure UNIX servers to support OLTP applications. Discussion of performance tuning Windows NT is purposely omitted from this chapter because Windows NT cannot yet effectively support OLTP applications with thousands of users.

OLTP Database Design

This section will provide an overview of OLTP database design and configuration issues, including the use of OPS to meet typical high availability requirements of OLTP applications. We will also discuss database design and configuration issues for non-OPS applications, as well as UNIX configuration considerations.

Parallel Server Architecture Review

The objectives of OPS are to provide high availability by supporting clustering technologies, and to provide scalability by increasing the amount of CPU and RAM allocated to a database. As you'll see later in the chapter, because of the operating system level locking introduced by clustering technologies, scalability is only achieved with OPS if you observe a design restriction called *application partitioning*.

Clustering technologies allow two or more machines, often called *nodes*, to be tightly connected so that they can share access to the same disks and, on some platforms, common memory. Although each node in the cluster shares resources with another machine(s), it retains the ability to operate separately. That is, each node has an IP address and runs processes independently.

Clustering technologies use statistics to our advantage in the same way that many types of RAID do. Both clustering and RAID technologies provide hardware redundancy to reduce the probability of an outage. For example, consider a data file that is mirrored (RAID-1). In this example, two copies of a data file exist at all times. The probability that both copies will be lost at the same time due to a disk crash is less than the probability that one copy will be lost.

Although disk crashes are the most common form of hardware failure, other components of a server can fail as well. For example, I've seen many controllers and network cards fail. Memory can fail. The RISC chip can fail. All of these failures can cause a server crash, or at least make it unavailable to applications. By providing redundancy for all parts of a server (not just the disk, as RAID does), you lower the probability that an outage will occur. It's less likely that both nodes in a two-node cluster will crash simultaneously than that a standalone server will crash.

Clustering technologies also provide automatic failover at the operating system level. That is, if one node in the cluster crashes, another node will automatically assume its network transmissions and even assume its IP address in addition to its own. All network transactions in progress when the node dies will encounter errors, but all new work for the failed node will be assumed by one of the other nodes in the cluster. All batch processes running on the failed node will die with the node. We will discuss this later in the chapter.

As we've alluded, clusters can contain more than two nodes. I've seen applications running OPS hosted on three or four nodes. Due to cost considerations, clusters containing three nodes or more are done primarily on business-critical applications. For example, one of my clients used a three-node cluster to service an OLTP application that approves credit card transactions. My client determined that at some points in the year (such as Christmas Eve), they can easily lose in excess of one million dollars an hour through loss of service. In cases like this, three or four node clusters are used to further decrease the probability of an outage.

Most clustering technologies provide operating system-level locking for disk space. In a cluster, it is possible that multiple nodes are writing to the same data file at the same time. In fact, using OPS, all instances can update the same tables and indexes, which in turn means that at an operating system level they are writing to the same data files. In a cluster, the operating system will ensure that no two nodes are attempting to write the same blocks on the same disk at any given time.

On most platforms, the service that manages operating system-level locking in a cluster is called the *Distributed Lock Manager (DLM)*. Most DLMs operate on an operating system block level, which is not to be confused with an Oracle block. We will see later in the chapter that DLM behavior dictates much about how we design OPS databases and applications. DLM behavior can effectively dictate whether or not an OPS application scales.

Because DLMs between platforms differ, Oracle8 Server introduces the *Integrated Distributed Lock Manager (IDLM)*. The IDLM provides a locking mechanism between platforms so that OPS locking will be much more consistent between platforms.

Using OPS, a separate instance is started on each node in the cluster. Each instance has a separate name and SGA. Furthermore, each instance has the same capabilities as non-OPS instances.

Although instances in OPS share data and control files, they do not share redo log files. Each instance in OPS is assigned a redo log thread that has redo log groups and members associated with it. The CREATE/ALTER DATABASE commands are used to create and manage these multiple threads. There should be one thread for each instance of a database.

Although each instance has its own initialization parameter file, several parameters must be set identically between instances. The following initialization parameters must be identical between instances of the same database:

CACHE_SIZE_THRESHOLD	CONTROL_FILES
CPU_COUNT	DB_BLOCK_SIZE
DB_FILES	DB_NAME
DML_LOCKS	GC_FILES_TO_LOCKS
GC_LCK_PROCS	GC_ROLLBACK_LOCKS
LOG_FILES	MAX_COMMIT_PROPAGATION_DELAY
PARALLEL_DEFAULT_MAX_SCANS	PARALLEL_DEFAULT_MAX_INSTANCES
ROLLBACK_SEGMENTS	ROW_LOCKING

> **NOTE**
>
> DML_LOCKS must be identical only if set to zero. Oracle recommends (in its documentation for 8.0.4) that LM_LOCKS, LM_PROCS, and LM_RESS should be set to the same value for all instances in the cluster.

OPS Locking Considerations

Database-level locking within an Oracle database using OPS is identical to locking in a non-OPS environment. In addition to database-level locking, we now have to consider locking caused at an operating system level, which is now initiated by the IDLM (or DLM in Oracle 7.x).

Before I discuss instance locking in detail and present an example, let's talk about why we should care. Instance locks take much longer and require considerably more system resources than the database locks you are familiar with in the non-OPS world. Internal database locks require latches and enqueues. On most platforms, it can take as long as 1/10 of a second to acquire an instance lock. This is about 1,000 times as long as it takes to acquire both latches and enqueues, which are required for an internal database lock. Furthermore, instance locks are required in addition to internal database locks. It is because of the inordinate amount of time it takes to acquire instance locks that we need to examine instance locking in some detail.

TABLE 31.1. RELATIVE LOCK ACQUISITION TIMES.

Class of Lock	Actual Time Required	Relative Time Required
Latches	1 microsecond	1x
Enqueues	1 millisecond	1000x
Instance Locks	1/10 second	100,000x

IDLM/DLM locks are often referred to as *instance locks* because they are assigned to the instance, not an individual user. The significance of this is that if two users within the same instance update rows that are next to each other on the same block, only one instance lock is necessary to perform the operations.

Instance locks are often created at instance startup. Each lock has three possible states: null, shared, and exclusive. A null lock has been created but is currently unassigned. Null locks exist because of the overhead needed to create and terminate them. A shared lock allows all nodes in the cluster to read data within the lock, but no nodes can write data within the lock. You should note that this differs considerably from the way reads (or selects) are handled internally within the Oracle instance. In the non-OPS world, reads do not initiate locks and do not block writers. Hence, in the OPS world, readers can effectively prohibit or block writers.

Instance locks in exclusive mode can write data contained within the lock. Instance locks are assigned to an entire instance, so multiple users within the instance can update, insert, or delete data within the lock, but users within other nodes cannot.

There are two classes of instance locks: Parallel Cache Management (PCM) locks and Non-PCM locks. PCM locks are instance locks associated with tables, indexes, and clusters. Essentially, they are instance locks on data files. Non-PCM locks are locks used on dictionary cache and control files.

When one instance attempts to read or write data, that instance requests the appropriate PCM lock from the IDLM. If the requested lock conflicts with an existing PCM lock already held by another instance, the IDLM notifies the instance holding the existing PCM lock while the instance requesting the lock waits. This method of inter-instance communication to resolve lock conflicts through the IDLM is called *pinging*. When the instance holding the PCM lock acknowledges the ping and releases the requested block, the requesting instance is granted a PCM lock.

IDLM locks also differ by when they are unassigned (become null locks). Using *hash locking*, an IDLM lock isn't actually unassigned until another node requests it to be unassigned. With *fine-grain locking*, an instance lock is unassigned after the unit of work is completed. Fine-grain locking will hurt read-only scans of tables with large result sets, but will reduce pinging. Hash-locking will potentially increase pinging activity, but will help in systems with little instance contention.

Let's walk through the preceding example and count the locking operations that happen in an OPS and non-OPS world. To simplify the example greatly, we will ignore usage of rollback segment space and temporary tablespace for the moment. We will also assume that the table being modified has no indexes or referential integrity constraints. After we walk through the simplified example, we will discuss the effect these things would have on the results. The reader should also note that the example assumes hash locking.

1. Instance Clerks becomes the owner of the PCM lock covering data block 12345, containing row 1 of table `purchase_order`, and updates the row.

   To update a row, the data block 12345 must first be read. Depending upon what happened before this call, Instance Clerks may have had to issue a ping to acquire the PCM lock. Instance Clerks may have had to perform a physical I/O as well.

2. Instance Supervisors requests the block to update row 4.

   At this point, the IDLM issues a ping to Instance Clerks, because it presently holds a PCM lock from step 1. Until a PCM lock is granted, the end user issuing the update for row 4 waits.

3. Instance Clerks writes the data block to disk and releases the PCM lock (but still has a row-level RX lock on row 1).

   Instance Clerks incurs a physical I/O to write the data block to disk. Note that even though the PCM lock is being released, Instance Clerks still has a row-level exclusive lock on row 1.

4. Instance Supervisors becomes the owner of the block and the PCM lock and then updates row 4. (Note: Instance Supervisors must reread the block to get the current copy.)

   Instance Clerks obtains the PCM lock and also issues a row-level exclusive lock for row 4. Note that Instance Supervisors must reread the block to get a current copy of the block, because it has changed since it was last used by this instance. Depending upon operating system-level buffering, this may or may not result in a physical I/O.

5. Instance Clerks requests the block to update row 7.

   At this point, the IDLM issues a ping to Instance Clerks, because it presently holds a PCM lock from step 1. Until a PCM lock is granted, the end user issuing the update for row 7 waits.

6. Instance Supervisors writes the data block to disk and releases the block and the PCM lock (but still has a row-level RX lock on row 4).

Instance Clerks incurs a physical I/O to write the data block to disk. Note that even though the PCM lock is being released, Instance Supervisors still has a row-level exclusive lock on row 4.

7. Instance Clerks becomes the owner of the block and PCM lock and updates row 7. (Note: Instance Clerks must reread the block to get the current copy.)

   Instance Clerks obtains the PCM lock and also issues a row-level exclusive lock for row 7. Note that Instance Supervisors must reread the block to get a current copy of it, because it has changed since it was last used by this instance. Depending upon the operating system-level buffering, this may or may not result in a physical I/O.

8. Instance Clerks commits its transaction, and still owns the PCM lock and the master copy of the block until another instance requests the block. (All row-level locks for rows 1 and 7 are released—Instance Supervisors still has an RX lock on row 4 with the transaction in progress.)

   As a result of the commit, row-level locks for rows 1 and 7 are released. Note that even though Instance Supervisors does not have a PCM lock on block 12345, it has a row-level lock on row 4 with a unit of work in progress.

Let's summarize locking activity for the preceding example and examine it in relation to the relative times to acquire locks presented earlier. In the example, locks were allocated in steps 1, 4 and 7. Both latches and enqueues are required for the row-level exclusive (type RX) locks on rows 1, 4, and 7. We count latches and enqueues separately because they have different relative weights. Remember that it takes 1,000 times as long to acquire an enqueue as it does a latch. Furthermore, remember that it takes 100,000 times as long to acquire a PCM lock as it does a latch, and 100 times as long as it takes to acquire an enqueue.

In Table 31.2, I display the number of latch, enqueue, and PCM-lock acquisitions made for steps 1, 4, and 7. When you multiply the lock acquisitions by the appropriate relative weights and add them up, you find that it takes considerably longer to acquire the resources involved in an OPS world than it would in a non-OPS world. In other words, you would expect both transactions to take 100 times as long in an OPS world as they would in a non-OPS world in this example.

Large Online Transaction Processing Systems

CHAPTER 31

789

31

LARGE ONLINE
TRANSACTION
PROCESSING

TABLE 31.2. EXAMPLE LOCAL AND PCM LOCK COUNT.

Step	Latch count (1x)	Enqueue count (1,000x)	PCM-lock count (100,000x)	OPS weighted total	Non-OPS weighted total
1	1	1	1	101,001	1,001
4	1	1	1	101,001	1,001
7	1	1	1	101,001	1,001
Total	3	3	3	303,003	3,003

You may recall that when I described the example, I unrealistically assumed away the effects of indexes, rollback segments, temporary tablespace, and referential integrity issues on locking. In reality, PCM locks are required to read and write blocks belonging to indexes, rollback segments, and temporary tablespaces as well. In addition, referential integrity rules cause reads, and in some cases writes (in the case of DELETE CASCADE rules for foreign keys) on other tables or indexes. Reads and writes caused by referential integrity are no different than any other application reads and writes.

If the column(s) in the where clause of the update statement in steps 1, 4, and 7 was indexed, reads on those index blocks would increase the number of PCM locks needed for each of the updates. Furthermore, if the columns changed by the update statement were foreign keys, PCM locks on the relevant table and index blocks of the parent tables would also be required. Either one of these situations would drastically increase the number of PCM locks required and would drastically increase the relative time required for the operation.

To illustrate, consider the following example of an update statement:

```
update purchase_order_line set po_nbr = 666 where po_nbr = 555 and
po_line_nbr = 2
```

Assume that there is an index on po_nbr and po_line_nbr. Also assume that po_nbr is a foreign key to the table purchase_order, and purchase_order has an index on po_nbr. As a result of the update statement, PCM locks to consult the index on purchase_order_line to obtain the RID of the row to be updated. Furthermore, both table purchase_order and its index are read to validate the new value for po_nbr. PCM locks are necessary to accomplish this.

Although this example does not use temporary tablespace, PCM locks apply to temp space just like any other kind of space. You can minimize contention by assigning different temporary tablespaces to users of different instances. Because rollback segments can be assigned to one instance, PCM locking problems associated with RBS space can be minimized relatively easily.

This example illustrates why PCM locking considerations deserve the attention we're giving them in this chapter and why OPS applications do not necessarily scale, even though they have more hardware resources. In fact, you may be wondering why you even should consider using OPS at this point.

Later in the chapter, we will discuss a design technique called *application partitioning* that can drastically reduce the number of PCM locks acquired, as well as some physical I/O and pinging that are required. We will revisit this example later in the chapter as an illustration of the effects of application partitioning.

Parallel Server Design Practices

Despite the preceding locking example, which might make you apprehensive about using OPS, there are ways to design OPS applications in ways that minimize locking issues. Furthermore, for OLTP applications with high availability requirements and a high cost to downtime, OPS is a necessity. The single most effective design technique for making OPS applications scalable is *application partitioning*.

Application Partitioning

Application partitioning works by having all users writing to a given set of tables connect to the same instance. To use the preceding example, if clerks and supervisors who were connected issued updates from the same instance, only one PCM lock for block 12345 would be needed. This is because PCM locks are assigned at an instance level, not a user level. When we look at the relative cost of locking, as we did when we walked through the example, we would only have one PCM lock instead of three. In other words, our relative cost for locking would have been 103,003 instead of 303,003, an improvement of approximately 67%.

Effectively partitioning requires more in-depth knowledge of your end users' requirements than is necessary in a non-OPS world. The first step in partitioning is to estimate the number of select, update, insert, and delete operations per table. An example of this type of research is provided in Table 31.3.

TABLE 31.3. EXAMPLE TABLE ANALYSIS FOR APPLICATION PARTITIONING.

Table	selects	updates	inserts	deletes
CUSTOMER	250,000	2,000	30	20
ACCOUNT	1,000,000	300,000	45	30

After identifying the most heavily hit tables, do some analysis to determine which types of users are causing the load. Make sure that those users log in through the same instance. An example of this type of analysis is presented in Table 31.4.

Large Online Transaction Processing Systems
CHAPTER 31

791

31

LARGE ONLINE
TRANSACTION
PROCESSING

TABLE 31.4. EXAMPLE END USER ANALYSIS FOR TABLE ACCOUNT.

User group	selects	updates	inserts	deletes
TELLERS	10,000	4,000	45	30
MANAGERS	500	100	0	0
ATMs	989,500	285,900	0	0

Given the information in Table 31.4, we would place all ATM transactions in one instance and all tellers and managers in another. In this way, we minimize PCM locking issues.

Parallel Server Initialization Parameters

All initialization parameters prefixed by GC_ are OPS related. Please refer to the *Parallel Server Concepts and Administration Guide* for a complete list of initialization parameters and how to use them. The most important parameters are presented in Table 31.5.

TABLE 31.5. IMPORTANT PARALLEL SERVER INITIALIZATION PARAMETERS.

Parameter	Definition
GC_FILES_TO_LOCKS	Specifies number and size of PCM locks
GC_ROLLBACK_LOCKS	Limit of DLM locks per public RBS
GC_RELEASABLE_LOCKS	Limit of DLM locks per session
GC_DB_LOCKS	Database limit of DLM locks
GC_LOCK_PROCS	Lock processes per instance

GC_FILES_TO_LOCKS allows us to predefine PCM locks, specify whether or not they are hash or fine-grained, and which data datafiles they will be used for.

The value of GC_FILES_TO_LOCKS is quite sophisticated in its format. One of its simpler formats is <file#1>=<Nbr Locks>:<file#2>=<Nbr Locks>: ... Consider the following example of a GC_FILES_TO_LOCKS setting:

```
GC_FILES_TO_LOCKS = "1=500:2=100:3=200:4=500:5=50"
```

This setting defines 500 PCM locks (hash by default) for use with data file 1 (the system tablespace). It also defines various numbers of locks to be used with other data files, which presumably contain application tables, indexes, temporary tablespace, or rollback segments.

Each PCM lock protects one database block by default. If we want locks to protect more blocks, we append an !x to the locks specification, where x is the number of blocks assigned to each lock. Let's revisit a slightly modified version of our example:

```
GC_FILES_TO_LOCKS = "1=500!50:2=100!25:3=200:4=500:5=50"
```

In our modified version, each of the 500 locks for the system tablespace protect 50 database blocks. If our block size was 2KB, each PCM lock used for the system tablespace would be 100KB.

Because PCM locking greatly affects the performance of OLTP applications running OPS, you'll spend a great deal of time tuning these parameters to be sure that transactions aren't waiting for locks to become available. GC_DB_LOCKS and GC_RELEASABLE_LOCKS effectively dictate how many PCM locks are available database-wide. Not all locks provided by GC_DB_LOCKS and GC_RELEASABLE_LOCKS need to be statically assigned to individual data files. We can leave some free for Oracle to use as needed.

Database Configuration Issues

This section addresses database configuration considerations for large OLTP applications. To a large extent, configuration issues are similar between large OLTP applications and other types of databases. However, there are significant database configuration differences for large OLTP applications. Several differences we will talk about involve rollback segment definitions, as well as setting the transaction attributes on indexes and tables.

I/O Considerations and File/Disk Placement

As with all databases, large OLTP databases should have tables and indexes placed on separate devices. Often I will also place temporary tablespace and rollback segment space on devices separate from tables and indexes. Although we would like to separate temporary tablespace from rollback segment space, putting both on the same device is an acceptable concession because very few operations use them both. Chapter 24, "Oracle8 Database Tuning," has more details on the placement of data files.

If you're using OPS, consider placing all read-only tables, indexes, and clusters in a read-only tablespace. This will reduce PCM-locking activity for these tables. The disadvantage is that changing tables in a read-only tablespace requires an ALTER TABLESPACE command to change tablespace before and after the change. Typically, ALTER TABLESPACE is not a privilege given to application users or developers.

You're more likely to have more concurrent transactions updating the same block due to a large number of users, so consider increasing the INITRANS and MAXTRANS for both indexes and tables. The maximum number of transactions that can simultaneously hold row-level locks on the same table or index block is set by MAXTRANS. If MAXTRANS isn't set high enough, users will experience periodic hanging.

OLTP applications' SQL operations typically affect small result sets. Furthermore, there are typically very few sequential read operations. With this type of load, large block sizes are relatively inefficient. For example, reading or writing in 16KB blocks is inefficient when you are typically using only a few hundred bytes within that block. I recommend 2KB or 4KB block sizes for OLTP applications as a general rule of thumb.

If you are using clusters, make sure that the database block size is larger than the estimated amount of space required by each cluster key and its associated rows. Clusters physically force the order in which rows are stored in one or more tables, and typically are used to reduce the overhead associated with joins. For example, if the estimated space occupied by a key value and its associated rows is 6KB, we would define the database with an 8KB block size even though it breaks our rule of thumb. Clusters become very inefficient if keys and the associated rows span blocks. Elsewhere in this chapter we will discuss clusters in more detail.

Asynchronous I/O

Asynchronous I/O is available on most UNIX platforms for both reads and writes. Asynchronous I/O specifies that Oracle does not have to wait for read and write instructions to be completed by the operating system, but can do other work in the meantime. The use of asynchronous I/O for both reads and writes is highly recommended. Unfortunately, the mechanics of implementing asynchronous I/O differs between platforms. When using asynchronous I/O, set DB_WRITERS = 1. There is no danger of creating a performance bottleneck by having only one DBWR process, because all I/O instructions are non-blocking.

Checkpoints

I normally recommend setting the CHECKPOINT_PROCESS parameter to True so that the log writer process doesn't have to handle checkpoints. Setting the CHECKPOINT_PROCESS parameter to True means that checkpoints are handled by the CKPT (or checkpoint) process instead of a DBWR (or database writer) process. I usually recommend setting the CHECKPOINT_PROCESS to True for all applications.

Rollback Segments

Because most OLTP applications have large numbers of small transactions, most rollback segments should be defined with a relatively small initial and extents size (such as 20KB). Each extent should be sized so that on average each transaction requires only one extent. With large numbers of users, we should have large numbers of rollback segments to avoid contention. Please refer to Chapter 24 for ways to detect rollback segment contention.

I usually preallocate one rollback segment with large initial and next extents (1MB) for long-running transactions. For example, batch processing typically issues longer transactions and requires more rollback segment space than OLTP transactions. Long-running transactions can specify that Oracle is to use the large rollback segment. To specify a specific rollback segment, issue a SET TRANSACTION instruction as the first SQL statement of the transaction.

For example, to specify that rollback segment RBS_BIG is to be used for a long-running transaction, issue the following statement:

```
Set transaction use rollback segment rbs_big
```

This statement must be the first SQL statement in the transaction, so it must be reissued immediately after any rollback or commit.

If the application is OPS, each instance in the database should have a large number of private rollback segments. That is, each instance should have a set of rollback segments that is not used by any of the other instances. Furthermore, to alleviate PCM locking concerns (yes, PCM locking occurs when rollback segments are allocated as well), each set of private rollback segments should have a separate tablespace.

Memory Allocation Issues

The memory allocation issues for OLTP applications are no different than for other types of databases. Be sure to pay close attention to buffer cache, shared pool, and sort area memory allocation, as described in Chapter 24. Because sort_area_size specifies the amount of memory used for sorting per user (as a result of order by or group by clauses in SQL statements), tuning sort_area_size can have a great effect on machine memory allocation.

Clusters

Clusters are a way to physically control the ordering of rows according to a common key value. Multiple tables can reside in a cluster, but all tables must contain the common key columns. Clusters are frequently used to reduce the I/O associated with joins.

Large Online Transaction Processing Systems

CHAPTER 31

795

31

LARGE ONLINE
TRANSACTION
PROCESSING

Furthermore, a *cluster index* (an index that is placed on a cluster instead of an individual table) is required. Cluster indexes are used in much the same way that regular indexes are.

OLTP applications have I/O loads that are largely random, not sequential. Clusters make random reads more efficient, impair writes, and impair sequential reads. One must be very careful in using hash clusters. Hence, clusters are effective constructs to use on sets of tables in which most operations are random reads. Furthermore, all tables in this set have to share a common column or set of columns that can be used as a key.

Hash clusters are similar to ordinary clusters, except that lookups occur based on a hashed value of the key. This can shorten query time for random selects but is harder to tune. Hash clusters also bypass the need for a clustered index, so the number of physical I/Os needed for each select is less than in a regular cluster.

Please refer to the *Oracle SQL Reference* for a complete syntax. Overall, the syntax of the `CREATE CLUSTER` command is similar to the creation of tables in that it provides for tablespace and storage clauses. The cluster key is contained within parentheses immediately after the cluster name. The size clause refers to the amount of space in bytes to reserve for each cluster key and its associated rows. If the size estimate is too low, retrieval from the cluster becomes resource intensive.

Here's an example of a cluster:

```
create cluster customer_data (customer_nbr number)
pctfree 5
size 2000
tablespace user_data
storage (initial 120M);
```

Only use clusters or hash clusters on sets of tables that are frequently joined and where random reads are the majority of the application load. I only consider using clusters in situations where random reads are over 75% of the load, but this is an arbitrary percentage on my part.

Do not use clusters for tables that are dynamic (that dramatically grow and shrink during processing). Also, do not use clusters in situations where any of the columns within the common key are updated, because Oracle may have to relocate the row. Depending on the growth rate of tables within the cluster, you may have to drop, re-create, and reload tables within the cluster periodically.

Index-Only Tables

Index-only tables (IOTs), introduced in Oracle8, are indexes in which non-indexed columns are stored adjacent to the index key value. As of Oracle8, IOTs cannot be partitioned. They must specify a primary key.

IOTs were created to reduce I/O associated with keyed lookups. In situations where the index and table are separated, I/O occurs for the index pages as well as the data pages, whereas with IOTs, I/O only occurs for the index pages. Like clusters, IOTs greatly benefit random access and hurt sequential access.

Only use IOTs in situations where random operations (reads or writes) are the majority of the load. I tend to use IOTs instead of clusters in situations where tables are only joined some of the time. As with clusters, I don't use IOTs in situations where tables grow or shrink rapidly during processing. Depending on the growth rate of the IOT, you may have to drop, re-create, and reload it periodically.

Objects and Embedded Objects

If you use objects instead of tables for large OLTP applications, do not incorporate methods within the objects. As we'll discuss later in the chapter, PL/SQL is discouraged for large OLTP applications. With the effort that Oracle Corporation is putting into object orientation, I have no doubt that object-oriented features of Oracle will have a place in large OLTP applications at some point in the future.

Use of Transaction Processing Monitor Software

Transaction Process (TP) monitor software provides a communication wrapper around TCP/IP networks. Applications using TP monitors write service requests that reside on the server and obtain data through input from the client. Usually these service requests are written in a 3rd-generation language, such as C or C++. The TP monitor manages client/server communications, not SQLNet.

On the server, TP monitors consolidate service requests into *request routers* or *brokers*. Each request router handles transactions from many clients. The number of request routers or brokers is configurable. In this way, TP monitors are similar to SQLNet's MultiThreaded Server, which uses one process to service multiple clients. Although there is overhead involved in running the request brokers, it reduces the number of processes on the server (which is desirable in a large OLTP application).

TP monitoring packages (such as BEA's Tuxedo) improve performance for large OLTP applications in several ways. First, due to their architecture, they limit the number of processes on the server so that MTS does not have to be used. Second, they force the use of 3GL code for access, which is more efficient than other types of access. It should be noted that Oracle8 makes several improvements in XA, which can be used to improve performance when using TP monitors such as Tuxedo.

XA is Oracle's support for the X/Open-compliant applications. It's an application programming interface (API) standard that governs complex interplatform transactions and is supported by many TP monitors including Tuxedo. By providing XA, Oracle-based transactions can be part of a multiplatform transaction.

For example, in an X/Open transaction, I can update customer information located within DB2/MVS as well as an Oracle database implemented on a UNIX platform as a single unit of work. The X/Open API provides a way to roll back or commit the transaction transparently on both platforms. This is often referred to as a *two-phased commit*. Furthermore, the X/Open API permits me to rehost any part of the transaction without having to change client code.

The additional advantages and disadvantages of using the X/Open API, as well as details on how to use it, are beyond the scope of this chapter. You can find more information about BEA's Tuxedo and its support for X/Open transactions from BEA's Web site at www.beasys.com.

Oracle8 makes several improvements over V7.3 in XA. The two most important improvements are that it now supports OPS and no longer uses *cached sessions*. Cached sessions were supposed to improve the performance of XA applications by retaining memory allocated by an XA transaction. Memory retention would enhance performance in subsequent executions of the same transaction. As those of you who have worked with XA in applications with large amounts of transactions know, the increased number of sessions and the characteristics of these cached sessions cause enough problems to out-weigh the benefits.

UNIX Configuration Issues

In OLTP applications with large numbers of users, UNIX configuration decisions and tuning at an operating system level are more important than they are in smaller systems. In this section, we discuss some of those issues and highlight important considerations for OLTP systems.

Raw Volumes Versus File System

A frequent debate among database designers and administrators is whether data files should reside on raw volumes or file systems. The debate is complicated by the fact that there are so many different UNIX platforms with so many different volume managers, and technological advances are continuously being made on all of them. As with any decision, there are advantages and disadvantages to both raw volumes and file systems.

The most frequently cited advantage to using file systems is ease of administration. It is far easier to back up, recover, and manipulate file system file scripts than to manipulate raw devices. Furthermore, in most shops, no involvement from UNIX system administra-tors is required to create data files when file systems are being used. Most shops do not permit DBAs to create and administrate raw volumes, so space management requires coordination between people and groups that often leads to bureaucracy and red tape.

Over the past few years, improvements have been made in file systems that provide buffering and caching at an operating system level that is not available on raw devices. On most systems, the performance difference between having data files on raw volumes and on file systems is imperceptible. However, even with buffering improvements, raw devices are still more efficient than file systems. In OLTP applications where server performance easily can be a bottleneck, I recommend that all data files be defined as raw devices. Although I usually use file systems in most kinds of systems, I insist on raw devices for large OLTP and VLDB databases.

UNIX Utilities for Performance Tuning

UNIX performance-tuning utilities differ widely per platform. However, quite a lot of information can be obtained from the `iostat` and `vmstat` utilities that are available on all UNIX platforms I'm acquainted with. In this section we will discuss these utilities, things to watch for with large OLTP applications, and how to alleviate resource bottlenecks.

Performance tuning at the UNIX and database levels basically consists of identifying bottlenecks and removing them to increase system throughput. With `iostat` and `vmstat`, we can detect resource bottlenecks at a UNIX level. Some administrators prefer using `sar` instead of `vmstat`. As a consultant who works in many different shops, I prefer `vmstat` because many shops don't provide DBAs the necessary privileges to run `sar`.

iostat

The `iostat` utility provides information about disk utilization. It can be used to detect I/O bottlenecks or *hot disks*. Hot disks are those that have no surplus capacity, which often limits system throughput (the number of transactions processed per hour) because transactions cannot obtain data on the hot disk as fast as requested.

Once hot disks are identified, there are primarily two ways to correct the problem. One way is to move some of the data files on the hot disks to separate disks. In other words, we spread the work around to the point where no disk is considered hot. The other way is to tune SQL within the application to eliminate or reduce some of the application I/O (see Chapters 24 and 25, "Oracle8 Application Tuning," on how to tune SQL).

Although `iostat` is universally available on different UNIX platforms, the output and options differ per platform. We will talk about chief differences between the top three major platforms: AIX, Solaris, and HP-UX. (Before I'm lynched in some circles, these "top" platforms are determined strictly by market share. This does not imply any judgments about the technical capabilities of any UNIX operating system or platform.)

Large Online Transaction Processing Systems

CHAPTER 31

799

31

LARGE ONLINE
TRANSACTION
PROCESSING

`isotat` can be executed from the command line as follows:

Format:	`iostat [interval] [count]`
Parameters:	`interval` — Length of time in seconds between observations
	`count` — Number of observations to take (default is indefinite)
Examples:	`iostat 5 5`
	`iostat 5`
	`iostat`
	`Iostat -xtc 5 5` (on Solaris only)
Notes:	`-xtc` is preferred for Solaris and unavailable in HP-UX and AIX.
	Always ignore first observation with all three platforms.

The first observation from `iostat` should be ignored. AIX and Solaris have similar output for `iostat`. Statistics are given for each physical device. (Note: hardware RAID devices often display as one physical device.) The most important column is percent busy (`%b`). Disks over 85% busy are hot disks. The optimal state is to have a roughly even distribution for I/O workload among all disks.

Output 31.1 shows the Solaris `iostat` output produced by using `iostat -xtc 5 5`.

OUTPUT 31.1. SOLARIS IOSTAT OUTPUT.

extended	disk	statistics			tty		cpu								
disk	r/s	w/s	Kr/s	Kw/s	wait	actv	svc_t	%w	%b	tin	tout	us	sy	wt	id
sd15	0.1	0.7	0.8	5.4	0.0	0.0	64.9	0	1	0	13	13	2	6	79
sd16	0.7	1.6	12.7	17.8	0.0	0.0	13.6	0	2						
sd17	0.7	1.6	12.7	18.4	0.0	0.0	13.9	0	2						
sd18	0.1	0.7	0.7	5.5	0.0	0.0	61.1	0	1						
sd24	2.5	1.0	40.4	7.4	0.0	0.0	8.7	0	2						
sd25	2.1	0.9	35.5	7.2	0.0	0.0	9.1	0	2						
sd26	2.5	1.0	40.5	7.4	0.0	0.0	8.5	0	2						
sd27	2.5	1.0	40.5	7.4	0.0	0.0	8.2	0	2						
sd28	2.1	0.9	35.6	7.3	0.0	0.0	8.8	0	2						
sd29	2.5	0.9	40.6	7.4	0.0	0.0	8.2	0	2						

Unfortunately, `iostat` output for HP-UX is considerably less useful. Although you get raw data about the amount of data read or written along with the number of operations, no information about disk capacity is presented. Hence, there is no way to deduce the percentage busy and no way to determine which disks are hot disks. HP provides a motif utility called `glance` that provides some of this information.

Output 31.2 shows the HP-UX `iostat` output produced with `iostat 5 5`.

OUTPUT 31.2. HP-UX IOSTAT OUTPUT.

```
device    bps    sps    msps

  c0t6d0    0    0.0    1.0
  c0t4d0    0    0.0    1.0
  c0t5d0    0    0.0    1.0

bps == Kilobytes transferred per second
sps == Number of seeks per second
msps == Milliseconds per average seek
```

vmstat

The `vmstat` utility provides information about CPU and memory utilization. By using `vmstat`, we can determine if there are CPU bottlenecks or memory allocation problems. CPU bottlenecks, like disk bottlenecks, are important because they limit transaction throughput. Memory allocation problems are important because if memory is overallocated, the server dedicates CPU and disk resources to swapping memory. In other words, memory problems will contribute to CPU and disk utilization problems.

> **TIP**
>
> Solve memory allocation problems before addressing disk and CPU bottlenecks.

CPU bottlenecks can be alleviated by tuning the application and reducing its CPU requirements, or by adding more CPU chips to the server (if possible). Tuning application SQL can help reduce an application's CPU requirements. Even though databases are thought to have more to do with I/O than CPU
utilization, SQL instructions applications issue spend CPU cycles as well as I/O cycles. Memory allocation problems are alleviated by reducing memory allocated to the database or adding memory to the server. Memory allocation problems can cause problems with disk or CPU utilization, so I normally fix them before other types of problems.

Format:	`vmstat [interval] [count]`
Examples:	`vmstat 5 5`
	`vmstat 5`
	`vmstat`
Notes:	Always ignore first observation.

Fortunately, `vmstat` output for AIX, HP-UX, and Solaris is similar. I've presented output from `vmstat` on a Solaris system in Output 31.3.

OUTPUT 31.3. SOLARIS VMSTAT OUTPUT.

```
procs     memory            page              disk          faults      cpu
 r b w   swap  free  re  mf  pi  po  fr de sr s1 s1 s1 s1  in   sy   cs us sy id
 0 0 0   720   344   5   6  33  62  71  0  2  1  2  2  1 236  291  225 13  2 85
 0 0 0 991976 8048  11   0  27  88 124  0  7  1  3  2  1 308 2416  434 49  5 46
 0 0 0 991976 8056  17   0 188 176 339  0 35  0  7  5  0 315 2492  456 47  4 50
 0 0 0 991976 8104  10   0  48  99  99  0  0  0  4  3  0 254 1874  323 47  4 49
 0 0 0 991976 8032   9   0 958  32 438  0 101 0 17 17  0 347 2787  395 57  6 37
 0 0 0 991976 8016   7   0 1771 99 801  0 218 4 32 32  4 474 2741  448 55  9 36
```

The columns I pay attention to the most are the following:

Section	Column	Description
procs	r	Number of processes being run during the interval
	b	Number of processes waiting for I/O
	w	Number of processes that have been swapped out
page	pi	Number of memory pages paged in during the interval
	po	Number of memory pages paged out during the interval
cpu	us	Percent of time CPU is used for user processes
	sy	Percent of time CPU is used for system processes
	id	Percent of time CPU is idle

If paging (both `pi` and `po`) is greater than zero for most intervals, you have overallocated memory. In Output 31.3, notice that because `pi` and `po` are always greater than zero, the server in the example has memory allocation problems. If there is a severe shortage of memory, you will see processes being swapped out (`w` column greater than zero).

If the `id` column is zero for most intervals, chances are that you have a CPU bottleneck. Often, if the CPU bottleneck is severe, the Run queue (column `r`) will be high as well.

A significant number of processes waiting for I/O can indicate a disk utilization problem. The `iostat` utility should be used to confirm that one or more hot disks exist and to determine which disks are at issue.

Data File/Volume Size

Many UNIX systems will serialize writes to individual files or raw volumes to ensure data consistency. In other words, if 100 users issue `update`, `insert`, or `delete` statements that affect the same data file at roughly the same time, the underlying operating system will serialize those writes and perform only one write at a time. This means that if both the data files and the write transaction volume are large, we may have a locking bottleneck on these data files at an operating system level.

If we make all data files no larger than 400MB to 500MB in size, we reduce the possibility of write bottlenecks at an operating system level. This recommendation holds regardless if data files are created as raw volumes or within file systems.

> **TIP**
>
> Performance for OLTP databases can be increased by keeping all data files under 500MB in size.

Use of RAID and Mirroring

Data redundancy of any type will necessitate unwanted workload on the server. However, with most OLTP applications, some form of data redundancy is required to ensure high availability and point-in-time requirements. As you're no doubt aware, there are many forms of disk redundancy (RAID-1 (mirroring), RAID-5 (parity), RAID-6 (double parity), and others). Most types of disk redundancy are available via a logical volume manager, such as Veritas, or at a hardware level in some type of disk subsystem. Chapter 24 has a more detailed description of RAID options.

Hardware RAID has superior performance to software RAID. In OLTP databases with high transaction volume, consider using hardware RAID if possible. Benchmarks I've conducted in the past suggest that the performance of read operations is identical between mirroring and RAID-5. These benchmarks also revealed a 10% performance degradation for write operations on RAID-5 volumes when compared to mirrored volumes. Because of these benchmarks, I tend to recommend mirroring as opposed to RAID-5.

Database Schema Design Practices

OLTP applications with large numbers of users present design considerations other than that of OPS. This section will describe some of these considerations and provide recommendations on OLTP design.

With every type of application, designers must decide which processing should occur on the server and which should occur on the client. In recent years, we have seen the development of *multitier* architectures in which application processing occurs on a server separate from the server that supports the database. In OLTP applications that support high transaction volumes with large numbers of servers, our main application design goal is to offload work from the server. Depending on your application architecture, this may or may not be the same server that's supporting application batch processing. The reason that offloading work from the database server is paramount for high-transaction OLTP applications is that database server capacity is more likely to be the source of performance bottlenecks than any other portion of the system.

OLTP Application Development

Large OLTP applications have special development considerations. In this section, we will detail those considerations and present a number of development tips. We will also discuss application security for OLTP applications.

Application Design and Coding Practices

This section will detail a series of development tips for large OLTP applications.

> **TIP**
>
> Avoid using PL/SQL, including triggers, stored procedures, functions, and packages, for large OLTP applications.

Even though Oracle8 makes several performance improvements in PL/SQL, it is still too slow for large numbers of transactions. Given that in large OLTP applications you want to conserve your CPU cycles, avoid PL/SQL as much as possible with this type of application. This means that you will not want to use database triggers either. Have this work performed by the application(s) directly. PL/SQL has very legitimate uses in many types of applications, but not for large OLTP applications.

> **TIP**
>
> Avoid using external procedures for large OLTP applications.

When Oracle8 came out, I was excited about trying out external procedures as a possible performance improvement over PL/SQL. It turns out that even though compiled C code is more efficient than PL/SQL, the overhead involved in calling external procedures often makes them slower to execute than PL/SQL. Furthermore, a process (called extproc) is run for each user calling an external procedure, which effectively means that they aren't usable for OLTP applications with large numbers of users. Please refer to Chapter 15, "Object-Oriented Extensions in Oracle8," for a detailed discussion about external procedures.

> **TIP**
>
> Avoid using column functions for large OLTP applications.

Although column functions are programmatically convenient, they are resource intensive. Instead of using column functions such as `substr`, do it in the application. I've experienced a 50% performance improvement by doing an equivalent of `substr` in C, as opposed to a column function. There are exceptions, of course. The following functions are often necessary for datatype conversions or selects with GROUP BY clauses: `count`, `sum`, `min`, `max`, `to_date`, and `to_char`. It is often more efficient to group results (use `count`, `sum`, `min`, `max` in a SELECT statement with a GROUP BY clause) with SQL than within the application.

> **TIP**
>
> Qualify searches by `rowid` whenever possible.

Frequently in OLTP applications, developers "select for update" to place a row lock on a row to ensure that it doesn't change between selected transactions. In the `select`, also pick up `rowid` and use it in the `update` statement. By using `rowid`, you bypass the index and do at most one physical I/O to update or delete the row.

Here's an example `update` statement that uses the `rowid` effectively:

```
Update account set balance=:new_balance where rowid = :host_rowid
```

> **TIP**
>
> Use host variables instead of literals in WHERE clauses whenever possible.

When SQL statements are submitted to Oracle, they are parsed (access path is determined) and placed into the shared pool. If like SQL statements are submitted, there is no need to reparse the statement. Using literals instead of host variables makes SQL statements that would otherwise be identical look different. Thus, by using literals, Oracle is forced to parse more SQL statements than it otherwise would.

For example, Listing 31.1 contains C code with two like `update` statements. These `update` statements would otherwise be identical except for the literals in the `set` and `where` clauses. These literals will cause Oracle to parse these `update` statements twice.

LISTING 31.1. BADLY WRITTEN C CODE.

```
char      sqlstmt[1024];
EXEC SQL connect scott/tiger;
if SQLCODE == 0) {
EXEC SQL
        Update account set balance=10000 where cust_nbr = '111-11-1111';
EXEC SQL
        Update account set balance=20000 where cust_nbr = '222-22-2222';
    EXEC SQL commit;
    }
    ........
```

Listing 31.2 contains C code that's functionally identical to Listing 31.1, but that illustrates host variable usage. In Listing 31.2, Oracle will only have to parse the statement once. Although the example illustrates the savings of one reparse, potential savings from host variable usage is substantially greater.

LISTING 31.2. EXAMPLE C CODE ILLUSTRATING HOST VARIABLE USAGE.

```
EXEC SQL BEGIN DECLARE SECTION;
VARCHAR     h_cust_nbr[12];
Int         h_balance;
EXEC SQL END DECLARE SECTION;

EXEC SQL connect scott/tiger;
if SQLCODE == 0) {
    h_balance = 10000;
    h_cust_nbr.len = 11;
    sprintf(h_cust_nbr.arr, "111-11-1111");
EXEC SQL
        Update account set balance=:h_balance where cust_nbr =
    ➥:h_cust_nbr;
    h_balance = 20000;
    sprintf(h_cust_nbr.arr, "222-22-2222");
EXEC SQL
```

continues

LISTING 31.2. CONTINUED

```
        Update account set balance=:h_balance where cust_nbr =
        ➥:h_cust_nbr;
EXEC SQL commit;
}
......
```

Let's broaden our example to say that the update of balances is a transaction executed 10 million times a day by 3,000 users for many different balances and customers in a large OLTP application. If all of these update statements were submitted with literals as illustrated in Listing 31.1, Oracle would have to parse 10 million update statements. However, if these updates were submitted using host variables as illustrated in Listing 31.2, and the same code was used in all transactions so that the statement did not differ in any way, Oracle would parse the statement once and reuse it from the shared pool from then on.

> **TIP**
>
> Avoid using ODBC for client connectivity for large OLTP applications.

You may not realize it, but ODBC can be resource intensive on both the server and the client. For large OLTP applications, I am more concerned about resources consumed on the server. If you choose to ignore this tip, use either the SQLPassThru option or RDO. These options will reduce server overhead but in many cases will not allow array processing, which is highly desirable.

> **TIP**
>
> If you haven't already done so, migrate from rule-based optimization to cost-based optimization.

Unlike the other tips and recommendations in this section, I now recommend cost-based optimization for all types of applications, not just large OLTP applications. My reasons for this recommendation are the following:

- Rule-based optimization hasn't been enhanced to accommodate new Oracle8 features.
- Cost-based optimization can adjust for changes in your database.
- Cost-based optimization often has a lower learning curve for application developers.

As much as many database administrators still love rule-based optimization, cost-based optimization is Oracle's stated direction. Oracle will most likely continue to provide existing rule-based optimization features for backward compatibility, but no enhancements are being made in the rule-based optimizer to include new Oracle8 features, such as partitioned tables, index-only tables, and object types.

With rule-based optimization, we explicitly control the access path all of the time. This is not necessarily a good thing. Database objects often change in ways that weren't accurately estimated beforehand. Furthermore, the pace of most projects precludes the possibility of performing a thorough SQL review. Cost-based optimization (assuming frequent gathering of statistics) can alter the access paths of your SQL statements when the database changes, as well as compensate for poorly written SQL to some extent.

Rule-based optimization requires a detailed knowledge of the optimizer and how the syntax of the SQL statement affects Oracle's access path. Most junior application developers do not have a detailed knowledge of the rule-based optimizer and how it works. The access path provided by the cost-based optimizer is often better than a poorly written SQL statement under the rule-based optimizer.

Please refer to Chapter 24 for more detailed information about the differences between cost- and rule-based optimization, as well as information about hint usage.

Application Security

Application security is an important issue for most OLTP applications, but it is rarely addressed in books of this kind. OLTP applications are most commonly coded with one of the three security models. The first model involves coding the application to circumvent database-level security and to manage security internally within the application. The second model is where the application merely relays the user ID and password to the database, which either accepts or rejects the database connection. The third is a hybrid of the first two that relies on both application-enforced and DBMS-enforced security.

Application-Enforced

When security is enforced by the application, a generic user ID/password is used for the database. Often, this generic ID is known to all developers. Once database connectivity is established, the application then handles security (if security is provided at all) in a custom-coded way. Sometimes the application doesn't require a user ID or password at all. I'm constantly surprised at the number of OLTP applications that use a generic user ID and password that don't provide any means of user verification at all.

Generally, generic user IDs and passwords present a security risk because they often cannot easily be changed without adversely affecting other users and batch processes. Hence, people may have access when they should not (people who quit, transfer departments, or are terminated).

Developers who choose this method often don't provide any sort of user authentication, and do so for programming simplicity. Unfortunately, this simplicity is provided at the expense of any real security. Very few developers take the trouble to custom-develop security code.

DBMS-Enforced

When security is enforced by the Oracle database, the application will often provide a screen on which a user enters a user ID and password. These are then used to format a connect statement to establish database connectivity. With this kind of enforcement, the connect will receive an error if the user can't be properly authenticated.

When security is DBMS enforced, often we create public synonyms for application schema tables, views, procedures, and so on and grant the appropriate access to users via a role. Please refer to Chapters 13, "Oracle System and Object Privileges," and 14, "Roles and Grants," for a detailed discussion of security privileges, roles, and grants. Because of public synonyms and potential naming conflicts, a database that uses DBMS-enforced security often services one and only one schema. However, this is usually the case with large OLTP applications anyway.

DBMS-enforced security does have a price. The need to add, drop, and modify users creates a maintenance headache. However, maintenance can be made manageable. I usually write stored procedures that can add users, drop users, and change user passwords. I create these procedures under an account that has been granted the DBA role and grant execute privileges to selected end users who act as application administrators. In this way, I place the burden of security maintenance on the end users.

Hybrid Approach

Some applications, such as those marketed by Peoplesoft, use a hybrid of the previous two approaches. They store the password to a generic application ID in an encrypted application table. End user IDs are used only to connect and have read access only to the table with the encrypted password. The application then decrypts the password and uses the generic ID to service the application.

The advantage to this method is that it is harder for end users to directly manipulate application tables through SQL*Plus or other tools. For most users, it means that application data must be manipulated through the application. It also places faith in the encryption mechanism used by the application because the password is essentially being stored somewhere.

I usually recommend using either DBMS-enforced security or a hybrid approach. Application-enforced security is usually too lax for comfort.

Oracle8 Auditing Features

For sensitive OLTP applications, end users may have auditing requirements. Oracle provides some auditing features, but often Oracle's audit trail does not contain what end users want it to contain. Using Oracle's auditing features, we can track which SQL statements end users issue and which type of operation was attempted (insert, update, and so on). However, Oracle auditing does not record which rows were affected.

If there is a question about somebody's actions, often there are questions about which rows and tables were affected. Oracle8 auditing features cannot provide this level of detail. Most developers will custom-write auditing capabilities for OLTP applications for this reason.

If you do use Oracle's auditing capabilities, target the auditing to selected operations and tables. Also remember to purge audit data after a while.

OLTP Administration and Maintenance Considerations

This section will address various administration and maintenance considerations for large OLTP applications, such as backup and recovery, batch processing, and performance problems to expect over time.

Backups and Recovery Considerations

Take hot backups when batch processing isn't running. For many OLTP systems, this means taking the hot backup during the day. The primary reason is that updates, inserts, and deletes are logged. Frequently, the number of writes, and thus the number of redos, is higher during batch processing than at any other time. During hot backups, Oracle logs the entire block before each change is made, and the number of archive files is greatly inflated. So you should look for a time during the day where writes are minimized.

I always recommend that recoveries be periodically tested. Data loss for large OLTP applications tends to be expensive to replace manually due to labor costs. In fact, if recoveries are periodically tested, you can provide effective time estimates in the event that a recovery of the production environment is needed. If the database is large, you may need to tune the backup and recovery process as well as the application.

Even though cold backups are not theoretically necessary, I usually recommend doing one every week. The database can be opened and used without any archive files if need be. In applications with high availability requirements, however, it may be difficult to find time to do a cold backup.

Batch Data Loading

If possible, remove indexes before performing loads on tables. It is more efficient to load a table without indexes and then build that table afterwards than it is to load tables with indexes in place. Also, use SQL*Loader whenever possible. SQL*Loader's ability to bypass the database engine makes it faster than conventional path loads. If for some reason you must use a custom-written `insert` program, use array processing with a 3rd-generation language like C or COBOL.

Object Fragmentation

You may recall that objects (tables, indexes, and clusters) have `INITIAL` and `NEXT` extent specifications in their `storage` clause. Objects that have many extents (or are fragmented) are less efficient than objects that are contained within contiguous space because there's more head contention. Furthermore, when managing fragmented objects, Oracle often has to issue its own SQL statements (also known as *recursive calls*) against system tables to keep track of where all the fragments are. Recursive calls of this sort contribute to CPU overhead, which we don't want in large OLTP applications.

Fragmentation Detection

Objects that are fragmented can be listed by issuing the following SQL statement:

```
Select owner, segment_name, segment_type, extents
From SYS.DBA_SEGMENTS
Where owner not in ('SYS','SYSTEM') and extents >= 2
Order by 4 desc;
```

The only way to correct fragmentation is to drop and re-create the fragmented objects with more space allocated in their first extents.

Periodic Maintenance

If you are using cost-based optimization, you must gather statistics periodically by using the `ANALYZE` command. `ANALYZE` should be run periodically for all tables and indexes not owned by `SYS` and `SYSTEM`. An example of gathering statistics for a table and index is presented in Listing 31.3.

LISTING 31.3. ILLUSTRATION OF THE ANALYZE COMMAND.

```
Analyze table fred estimate statistics;
Analyze index fred_pk estimate statistics;
```

With ANALYZE, you have a choice of estimating statistics or computing them. Estimating statistics means projecting them using a sample of pages from the object being analyzed. Computing statistics means literally calculating them with information obtained from every block in the object. On large objects, this will take a long time and a lot of temporary tablespace. Usually, estimating statistics is good enough.

Because inserts and deletes often degrade performance of indexes over time, I periodically rebuild all indexes. Oracle7.3 and later make rebuilding indexes very easy with the alter index rebuild syntax. Listing 31.4 illustrates the rebuilding of an index with the rebuild syntax. It is interesting to note that with this syntax, you don't need to be concerned about referential integrity issues. It used to be that if an index was used for a primary key, you had to disable the primary key and all related foreign keys to rebuild the index. The rebuild syntax doesn't require this.

LISTING 31.4. ILLUSTRATION OF THE ALTER INDEX REBUILD COMMAND.

```
Alter index fred_pk rebuild;
```

OLTP Implementation Issues

Large OLTP applications have a variety of implementation issues that are not like implementation issues associated with other types of applications.

Stress Testing

Performance tuning for OLTP applications with large numbers of users is often time consuming, but is no different for large OLTP applications than for other types of applications. Please refer to Chapters 24 and 25 of this book for additional help with performance tuning.

There is no effective substitute for stress testing. Database administrators can use experience and general design principles when designing and implementing databases, but there is no effective way to predict system performance without subjecting the server and database to real application load. For an effective stress test, try to have at least 5% of the load. The smaller the stress test's user base, the less accurate the stress testing will be. I'm amazed at the number of clients I have that do not make time for any kind of stress test before production.

Project Management and Planning Issues

OLTP applications with large numbers of users have project management and planning issues as well as technical issues. Extra time and resources need to be set aside for several activities within the project. First of all, stress testing and tuning activities will take application developer resources as well as database administrator resources. Keep in mind that tuning is an iterative cycle that usually results in database configuration and even coding changes between iterations. If effective stress testing is not possible within the project, try using a phased implementation. That is, add end users in waves so that performance bottlenecks can be identified before they hinder the end users.

Second, if the application uses OPS, allocate extra time in the physical database design phase for database administrators so that they can effectively partition data access between instances. Furthermore, hardware and software costs often escalate when OPS is used.

Summary

Oracle OLTP applications with large numbers of users have many special considerations in terms of database design, analysis, application development, and maintenance. Large OLTP applications often have high availability requirements requiring clustering technologies. Clustering technologies allow you to tightly couple machines so that they can share memory and disk. Oracle supports clustering technologies and high availability requirements with Oracle Parallel Server (OPS).

OPS does provide high availability, but due to operating system locking considerations inherent in clustering technologies, OPS applications are not necessarily scalable. Clustering technologies require Oracle to acquire instance locks in order to read or manipulate data. Instance locking can be minimized by ensuring that users who write to tables log in to the same instance. Instance locking for temporary tablespace and rollback segments can also be minimized by separating rollback segments and temporary tablespace assignments for users logged into different instances.

OLTP applications with large numbers of users have operating system-level considerations as well. We discussed how `vmstat` can be used to detect memory allocation or CPU bottleneck problems frequently found in large OLTP applications. We also discussed how `iostat` can help detect disk bottlenecks, and that you should correct memory allocation problems first because they can cause CPU bottlenecks or even I/O bottlenecks on the disk that contains paging space.

Large OLTP requirements may dictate the use of clusters or, more recently, index-only tables. Clusters and IOTs can only be used in cases where the load is predominantly reads and the object size doesn't vary considerably over time. We also discussed the possibility of using TP Monitor products to reduce overhead on the database server.

During the course of the chapter, we discussed many development and coding tips that should be given consideration for large OLTP applications. We also discussed differing administrative differences between large OLTP applications and others.

Media and Complex Data Servers

by Advanced Information Systems, Inc.

IN THIS CHAPTER

What Is a Media Server?

The Oracle Media Server is an inevitable response to the growing demand for video and sound commodities by both consumers and business. When we refer to video and sound commodities, we refer to either those commodities explicitly video and sound, such as a movie VHS tape, or to those commodities, like an engineering database, that simply use video and sound implicitly as part of their presentation.

If we look at relational theory, there is nothing inherent to it that prevented any RDBMS vendor from supplying a rich, endless object library of media objects since the theory took form in 1971. Media data has always been just a type of data. Just as written text is a type of data which we call character data; media data is just another type of data. Therefore, media data can exist as an atomic element in a relational database.

Media data is simply a type of data because it is characterized as a series of bit patterns just as character data is formed from bit patterns. Like character data, these patterns need a translation process to retrieve and display them. In the case of character data, displaying this data is done through standard console interfaces. Displaying media data is more difficult, requiring applications to read in the media data format and display the results to the user in real-time.

From a practical perspective, just as storing characters in a formal database is valuable, so is the storing of media objects. With a database you can manage, back up, and retrieve data within a uniform organized structure. Both simple and complex data can be organized within a database to facilitate user requests (see Figure 32.1).

FIGURE 32.1.

An RDBMS manages data requests; this data can include media objects.

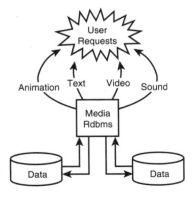

Traditional multimedia has not been characterized as users requesting data from a database. Multimedia has been characterized as the broadcasting of media data—media data that is determined to be popular by the broadcasting agent.

In the traditional case of radio and television, different organizations have simply chosen one piece of media data, a movie for instance, and have broadcast their media "product" at a particular time. The only choice the consumer has in the market is which of the many broadcasts presented to choose.

Moving further in the direction of choice for the consumer regarding media objects would be the video store or the record store. Here consumers physically pick and choose the product they want to purchase or rent from a huge assortment of media objects.

In this second case, many of the tasks of a database are being performed by people running around. The video store can be seen as the storage of all the media data available. The shopper is the user who is requesting this stored information. The problem with this method is it reminds us of a day before databases, where data physically resided as organized and filed documents that needed to be manually retrieved. The user needs to go to the video store or someone has to go from the store to the user to complete the transaction of a video rental.

Databases originally became popular because they eliminated the need to keep huge amounts of physical documentation at the fingertips of users who needed the data. Users did not have to physically move to the place where the data resided. Instead, data could be stored and quickly accessed by users who had a computer. The disk space to store the data and sort it was far smaller than the filing cabinets needed to hold the data.

Just as traditional data is more efficiently stored on disk drives and organized by a database, you can see that media data could also benefit from the same revolution. In the video store, the shoppers are actually getting in their car, driving to a location, and browsing a large number of physical objects, VHS tapes. In a sense these people are performing database access methods. If you view the local video store database, the people who work and shop there are performing tasks that could be performed by a DBMS system (see Figure 32.2).

FIGURE 32.2.

All of the actions in the store are slow, time-intensive tasks that could be better completed by a computer.

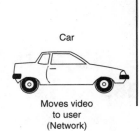

Car

Moves video to user (Network)

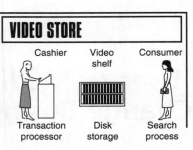

VIDEO STORE

| Cashier | Video shelf | Consumer |
| Transaction processor | Disk storage | Search process |

This analogy argues for Video on Demand (VOD), a concept that Oracle has heavily pushed for. With Video on Demand, a consumer treats video rental in the same way a database user regards traditional data. With VOD, the consumer logs into a database, browses data (videos), and chooses which video he or she wants to rent for his or her media entertainment.

This concept can also be applied to our most primitive media example of pure broadcasting. A broadcasting company, such as a movie channel, can take real-time requests from users who want a myriad of different media products. This allows the broadcast to offer more than one product per time-slot for the many media consumers who want different things (see Figure 32.3).

FIGURE 32.3.

A network using a video server can maximize everyone's media preference.

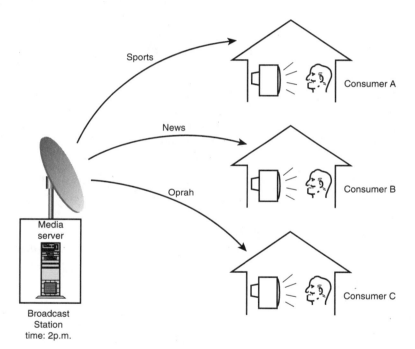

New Uses of Media Objects That Will Change Business

In today's world there are many products and services for which video is used, but is either stored in a filing cabinet or broadcast at certain times for certain people. Here are some area's of both business and home consumption where video databases will be playing a larger role.

Presentations

Many of today's presentations are very dry and make use of a person speaking directly to an audience, which might involve a great deal of travel time. They also use 2D visual aids, such as slide-shows, graphics, or charts.

If presentations can be encapsulated into media objects, a great deal of time and money invested in human resources to deliver the presentation can be saved. By turning a presentation into video, a client can view it at his or her convenience. The viewer also sees a polished version of the presentation from the best seat in the house.

In the future, by storing presentation video as data, you will be able to "mix" different media objects and tailor them for a particular client. You can also stage presentations interactively, giving the audience the ability to ask a certain set of questions.

Online Training

Traditional computer training or related training that can be presented through video has been done by physically having a "teacher" and a set of "students" gather together. By storing training video, sound, and text as a media object, you allow students to go through the material at a time that is most convenient without the need for the physical presence of a teacher. With media-based training, students can learn at their own pace, not bound by the artificial pace of a classroom setting and schedule.

Help Desk Support

Media is simply more natural for us than written text. With media as data, if a user needed to learn how to write a macro for his or her word processor, he or she could simply access online media that visually presents the steps required to accomplish the task. This method would be far easier for the user than learning through help files or listening to a voice on the telephone. Since the world is full of sights and sounds, it is a more intuitive way for us to learn.

Kiosks

Kiosks now take the form of video units consumers can use at a store to get special discounts and to receive online coupons. With media, these things become easier to use and online commercials and messages can be sold to the suppliers of retail stores to showcase their products.

Video on Demand (VOD)

This is an area that could easily earn a huge chunk of traditional media revenues. If a service can offer VOD, allowing the user to choose from thousands of video products, it will have a distinct advantage over traditional broadcast media. The broadcast competitor can only offer one choice in a given time-slot that will have to be superior to or cheaper than all of the products a VOD provider can offer.

Home Shopping

The Internet has already given the ability to do some shopping using traditional screens with fixed text. In the future, people will be more willing to shop when they can browse a store in 3D and view selections as they would if they were actually shopping there. A media presentation of shopping is more intuitive than a series of traditional text-based screens.

Electronic Banking

The Internet has popularized electronic banking, yet this medium is also characterized by simple graphics and screens. With media data, users will have a more intuitive view of their portfolios and new ways of easily navigating to other financial instruments that can be bought and sold.

Personalized News Service

Today many companies that supply pagers are now downloading simple text information on news events a customer wants to see. For instance, if a user wants sports scores, that information will be downloaded. If another individual wants only local news, bullets of news will be downloaded.

With the use of media, you can download more complex objects for people who want customized news. The sports fan can download video images of all the important events, and the person who wants local news can, instead, receive this news in visual form.

Games

Traditionally, video games existed in an arcade where consumers would purchase time to play. After the revolution of the home PC, users would purchase games for use on their personal computer. Sophisticated gaming computers also existed for use on TV sets. But the user still had to purchase a physical game cartridge to use the game.

Today, with the World Wide Web, there has emerged the concept of *virtual arcades*, which are online gaming centers where users can browse and play entertaining or educational games for a price. In this market you have the scenario of many users pulling up many different media objects. Because the number of users is quite large and media objects are very large in terms of storage space, media-databases will be needed to store the vast amount of media data that comprises online games.

Reference

HTML, the foundation of the World Wide Web, was designed for research to be done on documents without needing to know where those documents were located. By simply extending this definition, to allow for media objects and simple documents, computing can provide the ability to research subjects that not only contain text but more complex graphics. Users can bring up this visual information in the same way they would bring up a document. There would be no need to know the actual physical location of where the media was stored. This will speed up research efforts and make it more enjoyable for the young.

Oracle's Answer to Media Data

Since we have demonstrated natural and profitable ways in which media information can be treated as data to be accessed by different users with different needs, it is clear that a database that can handle media objects is a valuable tool for this upcoming media revolution.

Oracle has clearly seen the value of a media database and the future revenues that different media ventures could earn. Oracle has created a series of different tools to facilitate media within the framework of relational databases.

Oracle offers a number of products that allow database users to store and display this new and valuable form of data. These major offerings are: Oracle Media Server, Oracle Media Net, and Oracle Media Objects. You will see how they fit together to create a multimedia database solution.

The Oracle Media Server

This product is the center of what Oracle offers. It provides the ability to store media objects, such as video or sound, and to organize them in a database structure. The Oracle Media Server is just a database server with the special function of handling media objects instead of simple character and numeric data.

Oracle has renamed many of its traditional database structures so the components of the video server are full of completely different names. But the components of the media server are only a special case of the components of a traditional RDBMS. Look at the different components of the video server and their functions:

- *Media Data Store.* The Media Data Store (MDS) is simply a set of files on a file system that store multi-media data and can deliver this data real-time according to the specifications of the application. The MDS is really only a glorified tablespace for media data.

  Although this object is like a tablespace, the MDS is far more sophisticated when it comes to sizing estimates. You are dealing with huge amounts of media data where a change in time for the presentation could dramatically increase disk size. For instance, at a 1.2 MPS playback rate, a minute of video data will only need 72MB, while an hour of video will obviously need 72×60, or 4,320MB.

  When creating the MDS, you can also set bandwidth parameters, which determine how wide you will need your bandwidth to be. This parameter is a function of megabytes-per-second multiplied by the number of concurrent users.

  The Media Data Store (MDS) comes with a series of low-level utilities that help assist the Video Database Administrator (VDBA) to manage and manipulate the files of the MDS. Here are a few of the utilities that the MDS provides:

  - `mdschecksum`   This is a simple utility used to make sure video data is not corrupted over time. When new video data is registered in the MDS, a `checksum` can be run to generate a unique number for that data. If you run the `mdschecksum` on this same file a month later and the number is different, you have a problem. This is a very important tool for video storage because the volume and the interdependence of the data is usually more emphasized than in a traditional database.

  - `mdsconcat`   This low-level function is more like an editing tool. Just like the strcat function in the C language, `mdsconcat` concatenates two video files together. This is helpful if you are presenting media as a series of shorter video clips in a given sequence.

    Many times you might be given 100 video files that you need to place in a certain sequence. This function will concatenate these 100 files into one file that is in the correct order. This function thus helps to make the media creation environment easier to manage.

  - `mdscopy`   This is a very valuable function that I wish were available with a traditional relational database. It allows the user to move or copy MDS files to another MDS volume or to a directory on the Media Server. The MDS counterpart in the RDBMS is the tablespace, and to move a tablespace is a much more complicated effort than one straightforward command like this.

- `mdscreate` This is similar to the create tablespace command in that it creates a file in a specified MDS volume. This file can now be used to store video data. One note of caution though: This utility simple allocates space for the file on disk, and does not wipe out any old data; therefore don't assume your old data is destroyed if you run an `mdscreate` on the same data volume.

- `mdsdelete` Again, this would be similar to a drop tablespace command. This command simply removes a file or files from an MDS volume.

- `mdsdir` This command is simply used to list file information and general information regarding an MDS volume.

- `mdsdiskmode` This allows the user to place a disk in rebuild mode if there is ever a need to rebuild an MDS volume.

- `mdsdump` This low-level function is probably the last thing you want to use; it dumps a file in an MDS volume into hexadecimal data. It really is designed for only low-level debugging of bad MDS files.

- `mdslock` This is an important utility that locks a file in an MDS volume for read-only activity. This comes in handy if you have just spent 3 days working on a media file and don't want anyone else to change it. With the lock on, any number of users can still read the file and enjoy the video output.

- `mdsrebuild` This command rebuilds MDS data on a disk after a disk failure. Be advised to consult the latest Oracle documentation before using this function and to have a failure strategy in place. This command currently works only with RAID storage because RAID gives Oracle potential copies of the same data.

- `mdsrename` This command allows you to rename a file on an MDS volume.

32

MEDIA AND COMPLEX DATA SERVERS

- `mdstar`   This command allows you to perform backups from an MDS volume to tape or from tape to an MDS volume.

- `mdstruncate`   Use this command to truncate an existing file in an MDS volume; many files fill up with useless space and this is a good way to reclaim the space.

- `mdsundelete`   This command will allow you to "undelete" a file removed using the `mdsdelete` function.

- `mdsunlock`   This command will unlock a file put in read-only mode in an MDS volume.

- `mdsvolinit`   This command is crucial. Once you have defined your data storage for MDS volumes using the voltab file, you need to run this command to actually create the definition of the MDS volume to each of the volume's disks.

- `mdsvstat`   This is a primitive monitoring and administration tool that gives you information on an MDS volume and general statistics.

- *The Video Pump*. The video pump reads in information from the Media Data Store, which is like a tablespace and stores data. The pump is simply the process to read in this information. Unlike the Oracle read process, video must run in real time, so the pump is more sophisticated in that it allows users to control parameters such as the maximum data transmission rates, the number of packets sent at a time, and even memory settings for internal buffers.

  Also, unlike the Oracle kernel that handles reads without as much direct control from the user, the video pump can be started and stopped separately from the database. To start your own video pump called `mypump`, the command is

  `svcstart mypump`

- *The Voltab File*. This file is similar to the traditional Oracle control files; it is in the voltab file that the user defines the disk space needed for the Media Data Store. This file is also much more complex because you are dealing with media objects, other parameters such as the parity, transfer rates, and the RAID specification for the disks your Media Data Store will be sitting atop.

  The Media Data Store (MDS) is created when you create a voltab file. Unlike a control file, you need to manually create this file. In some respects it is similar to an `init.ora` file, yet it holds much of the disk information for the disk space needed by the MDS.

  Figure 32.4 shows a typical media server and its Data Store.

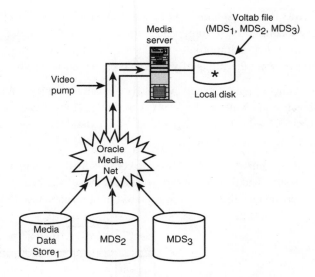

FIGURE 32.4.
Oracle has re-designed its RDBMS components for media.

Oracle Media Net

This product is the link between the Media Server and the outside world. It allows for the quick transmission of media images over a network. Because media images are much larger than textual or numeric data, the networking tasks and optimizations take on a greater importance. To have successful media online, one must have the ability to move this huge amount of information quickly across a network.

The Media Net really consists of three processes:

- The OMN Address Server (`mnaddrsrv`)
- The OMN Name Server (`mnrpcnmsrv`)
- The OMN Process Server (`mnprocsrv`)

These three processes create a layer over the inherent network in the same way as SQL*Net. This shelters people using media data from network specifics. With the OMN Name Server, Oracle's Media Applications know exactly which servers are available to "pump" media data from.

Oracle Media Objects

Oracle Media Objects (OMO) is the tool that allows for the joining together of media objects into a real-time stream of entertaining or informative media. The main class that this package revolves around is the media object.

Oracle Media Objects is a *media authoring tool* because it allows you to build complex media objects (like a commercial) from basic media data such as sound, static bitmaps, and digital video streams. It is important to understand that the authoring tool, to a great degree, will determine what the limits of your video presentation will be.

When speaking of Oracle Media Objects, we of course ask ourselves, "What about the methods?" All objects come with *methods*, ways of doing things. Oracle uses a scripting language called Oracle Media Talk, which allows us to extend the basic authoring capabilities and create custom video methods.

Creating a multimedia commodity such as a movie consists first of locating digital sources, such as picture and sound, and then editing those sources into a "final cut." After this is finished, a new object emerges that is not always the sum of its parts (see Figure 32.5).

FIGURE 32.5.

The final media product is a set of Oracle media objects edited for consumption.

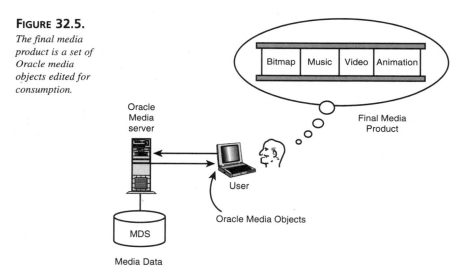

Because of this creative process, the authoring tool must offer as much flexibility as possible. The tool must also provide organization to help media authors organize the sometimes chaotic and large sets of data objects with which they work. Oracle Media Objects needs to be a virtual production studio and editing room used for the creation of media presentations.

The Components of Oracle's Media Objects

Oracle Media Objects comes with the basic building blocks for defining most media presentations. Here are some of the major objects and their uses for the aspiring media author.

- *Bitmap*. This object allows for the manipulation of bitmap images in the video presentation. You could be creating an interactive history lesson on multimedia and be using this object to import scanned photographs of the Civil War. The interesting thing about bitmaps is that they are very large objects compared to a text string or a number. Yet these objects are important in multimedia backgrounds.

- *Movie*. This is probably the most complex object within Oracle's Media Objects. A movie is a set of video images that are played in a certain sequence at a certain speed. Oracle's movie object allows the user to receive either real-time video or video from a huge file of bit images. With the authoring tool, users can edit video in the same way one would edit movie video in a traditional studio.

- *Sound*. This object allows for a mixing studio of digital sounds. Sounds can be imported from outside sources or played from sound files on disk. This object gives the user control over sound modification, fading, and echo, and allows the user to specify small sections of a sound to be spliced with other sections. This object and its methods create a virtual mixing studio for the media author.

- *Pallette*. Many times video images are first changed in terms of their color scheme. Oracle offers the Palette object to allow the media author the ability to change the color and tones of any visual object.

- *Path*. The path object allows the video author to take images and animate them. This is helpful for traditional animations like games, or for new forms of media advertising. For instance, you can have a bitmap object of an airplane and set it in motion along a path. To do this you specify a series of points the object can travel against. Moving images like these make for more intuitive media presentations (see Figure 32.6).

- *Button*. This object allows the media author to accept user control in the navigation through a media presentation. It might be used as a list of choices regarding an online training program (see Figure 32.7).

FIGURE 32.6.

By setting up an animated path for animation you can present a travel itinerary easier.

FIGURE 32.7.

Buttons can be used to allow users to choose video from smaller preview windows.

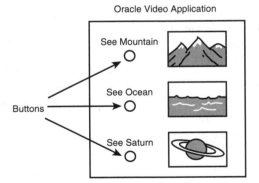

- *Field.* This might be a simple text field to allow a customer to search for a movie name and then simply rent the video for display in their own home (see Figure 32.8).
- *Shape.* To give many media applications structure and form, geometric shapes, such as an ellipse, can create custom boundaries and methods for displaying video. Oracle has incorporated shape objects to allow for this type of media authoring (see Figure 32.9).

FIGURE 32.8.

A simple field to search for video can add a great deal of power to a video library or Video on Demand (VOD).

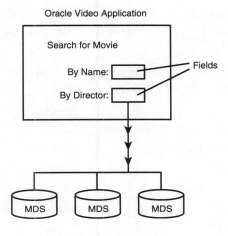

FIGURE 32.9.

By inserting video into small frames, you can use multiple presentations to teach.

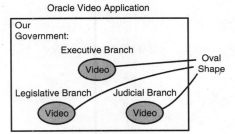

Additional objects we haven't mentioned, like pick-lists, data grids, and group radio buttons, provide more traditional ways to allow users to interactively design and build a video presentation. This enables you to create applications that have both video and many non-video components, such as data-entry screens and traditional menus.

You must remember that, along with these objects, you have the Oracle Media authoring environment, which is a graphical front-end combined with a powerful scripting language. Media objects can be dragged on to a canvas with many layers. Painting tools allow the author touch-up capability with his or her media editing. Along with the graphical tools, this front end allows the user to enter the scripting language of Oracle Media Talk.

Oracle Video Custom Control

Don't throw away your Visual Basic. Because the Oracle Corporation realized that many users would want to build applications with video without using Oracle's front-end tools, Oracle has invested a great deal of money to make the Oracle Video Server an open serv-

server. It is realized that many video applications, even if they utilize the Oracle Video Server, will utilize different tools like Visual Basic in the building of the client front end.

Since the client front-end might be written in Visual Basic, Oracle has come up with a series of Objects called Custom Controls that can be used by Visual Basic or even the virtually non-existent Oracle Power Objects package.

Here are some of the properties and methods you can use with the Oracle Video Custom Control. Remember that this offering can be plugged into Visual Basic just like other third-party tools that enhance the functionality of VB to perform special tasks.

- `BorderStyle`   This property can be set to `0` (No Border) or `1` (Border) to define the video screen within the application.

- `ClipboardFrameFormat`   This specifies the file format used when copying a frame, it is a Boolean value or either `0` or `1`:

  `1`   BMP file

  `0`   Device Independent Bitmap

- `HasVideo`   This attribute is used to see if the Oracle Video Custom Control has a video prepared or not.

  `0`   No video prepared

  `Non-zero`   Video is prepared

  Here would be a sample piece of code using this control:

```
Private Sub GetReadyToPlay()
    myvideo.ImportStreamAs

    If myvideo.HasVideo = true then
rem we have video
    Else
rem we don't have video
    End If
End Sub
```

  Notice that `true`/`false` behave in a similar way to the C language in that `true` is any non-zero number and `false` must be zero.

- `ImportFileSpec`   This attribute is set with the proper filename and path to either the Oracle Media Data Store or a valid operating system-dependent filename. This attribute must be used before `Prepare` or `Play` to open the video file for usage.

- `LengthFrames`   This is an important attribute because it gives the length in frames of a piece of video. If it returns a zero, it means that no video is prepared.

- `LengthTime`   This attribute gives the length of a video stream in milliseconds. It, too, must be called after the video is prepared or it will return a zero.

- `PlayVolume` This attribute allows you to set the volume between 0 and 9, where 0 is no sound and 9 is the loudest. The attribute is read/write because the media author may need to adjust this during a presentation.

- `CopyFrame` This method only works with certain drivers because it is designed to copy a frame of video to the Microsoft Clipboard. Here is a sample call using this function:

```
Private Sub UserClick()
    myvideo.CopyFrame
    MyPicture.Picture = Clipboard.GetData()
End Sub
```

  `ImportFileAs`

- `ImportFileSpec` This is a very important property that will display for the user a list of videos from which he or she can choose. `ImportFileAs` sets the `ImportFileSpec` of the user's choice and performs a `Prepare`, which links the client to video file.

  Here is a code stub using this powerful property:

```
Private Sub UserClick()
    myvideo.ImportFileAs
    myvideo.play
End Sub
```

  With these two lines of code a user can both pick an available video from a list and then watch it begin to play.

- `ImportSreamAs` If you are indeed using the Oracle Media Server and not just a set of files to store your video data, call this function. It also sets the `ImportFileSpec` and performs a `Prepare`. You use this method when receiving data from the Oracle Media Server. The `ImportFileSpec` is used to retrieve a native video file outside of Oracle, like an MPEG file.

- `Pause` This is a simple method to use when you need to, or the user wants to, pause a video clip. It is also tricky because while the video is paused you can alter `PositionFrames` and/or `PositionTime`, which will change the place were the video will start up again after it has been paused. One simple call of the `Pause` method will pause your video:

```
Private Sub UserPauseClick()
    myvideo.Pause()
End Sub
```

- `Play` This method simply plays video starting from the current position. If you do not issue a `Prepare` before calling `Play`, `Play` will do an implicit `Prepare`, but it will cause the video stream to be slower.

Here is a code snippet where you give the user a choice of video and then play it for him or her:

```
Private Sub UserClicksOnSuperBowl()
    myvideo.ImportFileSpec = superbowl.mpi
    myvideo.Prepare
    myvideo.Play
End Sub
```

- `PositionFrames`   This attribute displays the current position of the playing frames. The answer is given in frames.

- `PositionTime`   This attribute can be used to display the current position in a video file. By resetting the `PositionTime`, you can jump forward and backward in your video presentations.

- `ShowControls`   This is a Boolean that sets the other controls as either visible or not visible.

- `ShowPosition`   This determines if the position of a video's progress is displayed onscreen or not.

- `ShowVideoInfo`   This determines if video information, like the format, time, and frame, need to be displayed to the user.

- `ShowVolume`   This determines if the volume control is hidden from the user or not; it is also a Boolean value of `true` or `false`.

- `Video Format`   This displays the current format of the Prepared video. For instance if the video was in MPEG format this attribute would display `MPG`.

- `Prepare`   This method needs to be called to set up a new link between a video file or MDS area and the client machine. In the earlier example, you call `Prepare` before you call `Play` because `Prepare` sets up a link so you can play video.

- `Release`   This method is called when your application is finished with the video link between the client machine and either a file or the Oracle MDS. It frees up the resources used in the `Prepare` statement.

- `Stop`   This is called to stop the current stream of video. Here is a code sample that uses `Stop` and `Release` when a user presses an exit key:

```
Private Sub UserClicksOnExit()
    myvideo.Stop
    myvideo.Release
End Sub
```

Oracle's Media Cartridge

Oracle has encapsulated its media object around the CORBA standard cartridge. This will allow for seamless integration of media applications across multiple operating systems. This is because the CORBA standard is based on Java, which can run off of multiple operating systems that have a JVM (Java Virtual Machine).

With Oracle's Media Cartridge you could have a media *applet* that you could run over the World Wide Web and run on any piece of hardware/software that supported a standard browser. Oracle's media cartridge is simply another packaging of the media product functionality for Web-based applets or intranets (see Figure 32.10).

FIGURE 32.10.

The video cartridge is only a standard way Oracle hopes to allow video applications to be built over the Web.

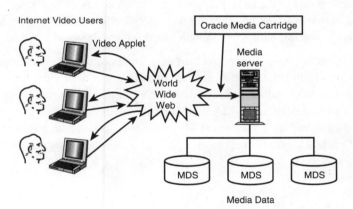

A multimedia applet running over the Web revolutionizes Web page design and the whole concept of a passive Web page. By renting, selling, and advertising over the Web using video, we are moving to a much more dynamic set of Web page standards that move in real-time to the motions and whims of the user.

Because Oracle is trying to push this new CORBA standard, they are compelled, almost politically, to offer media support for development of CORBA-compliant multimedia applications. Although this is one path, one could also use a Microsoft environment of Visual Basic and Windows NT; yet this approach creates a limitation, because to build these applications over the Web, one must employ ActiveX, which limits you to a Microsoft-friendly audience.

Summary

Oracle has not dropped the ball regarding media data at all. In fact, Oracle has created a complex and sophisticated product that it hopes will grab the market. Oracle has already worked on some large deals involving huge telecommunications interests wanting to broadcast a media application to millions of users.

Part of this battle between media giants, such as cable companies versus phone companies, will go into the courts and governments of the world. Regardless, Video on Demand (VOD) applications are coveted by both telephone and cable companies that simply want to be able to offer more people more choices, and thus gain greater revenues. Oracle is one of the large players in this arena and is in for a long battle with video, just as it is in for an uphill battle with its NC offering. This is why Oracle today offers a very powerful, industrial-strength video server—because it has to.

Because of Oracle's commitment to video data, and because video data can be easily organized in a relational database, smaller companies that need video stream applications should consider this product. Simply creating an online training center can save a large company a great deal of money. More importantly, with the ability to use video over the Web, a company will gain a technical advantage over its competitors. Media is perception, and Oracle's Media Server can completely change the perception of the company that chooses to use it.

Working with Very Large Databases

by Meghraj Thakkar

CHAPTER 33

Very large databases (VLDBs) are in the range of terabytes and before long will become petabytes. The task of managing and maintaining databases increases at least proportionally, if not exponentially, with their size. With the increase in the data, the tasks such as backups, recovery, data loads, purging, and data reorganization become more and more complex and time consuming. Most of the customers who have large databases installed usually have additional requirements such as high availability, high response time, and high scalability.

Introduction

There are several design issues that need to be considered when creating very large databases in order to take full advantage of the features provided by Oracle8. This will also have a major impact on the management and performance of VLDBs.

This chapter addresses the various issues related to designing and managing VLDBs under Oracle8 or migrating them from Oracle7. We will also discuss the different features provided by Oracle8 from a VLDB perspective. Some of these features are

- Table partitioning
- Index partitioning
- Parallel DML (PDML)
- Bitmap indexes
- Backup and recovery using Recovery Manager (RMAN)
- Object technology
- Data cartridges

Oracle8 and High-End Database Systems

You should be very careful when dealing with high-end applications. These applications tend to test the database limits, and one has to be very creative to make these applications run optimally. High-end applications have one or more of the following characteristics:

- A very large database ranging in size from several gigabytes to terabytes.
- An extremely high number of concurrent users in the tens of thousands.
- A database system that should provide high availability (24×7×52)

- A highly heterogeneous environment that uses a number of components to make the system work
- Systems with heavy transactional loads

Most of the high-end database environments are implemented by using mainframes and non-relational databases, because even though relational database systems are easy to use and manage, they are not able to handle the types of load imposed by high-end systems.

Oracle8 provides several features that allow it to work in an acceptable manner in such high-end environments. These features are discussed in the following sections.

Partitioned Tables and Indexes

Oracle8's data partitioning features can simplify the demanding tasks involved when dealing with large amounts of data. Table 33.1 shows some problems faced in VLDB systems and how Oracle8 attempts to resolve those problems.

TABLE 33.1. PROBLEMS IN VLDB SYSTEMS AND ORACLE8'S SOLUTIONS TO THEM.

Problem	Oracle8's Solution
Performing full table scans on a large table can degrade performance.	Oracle8 provides the ability to perform parallel DMLs and query individual partitions. The optimizer is "partition aware" and eliminates searches from partitions that do not apply to a particular SQL query.
High availability is required in a system. Mission-critical applications depend on a table that is not available due to media failure.	Oracle8 allows you to recover at the partition-level and minimizes the downtime.
VLDBs are difficult to manage.	Oracle8's partition-level management simplifies a lot of administrative tasks.

Managing a Large Number of Users

Oracle8 and Net8 provide four possible solutions to achieve more concurrent connections per Oracle8 instance:

- **MultiThreaded Server (MTS)**—MTS pools connections and does not allocate a single thread per connection. As a result, it avoids stack overflow and memory allocation errors that would occur from a dedicated connection per thread. The multithreaded server configuration allows many user threads to share very few server threads. The user threads connect to a dispatcher process that routes client requests to the next available server thread, thereby supporting more users.

- **Connection Manager**—Concentrates multiple clients into a single multiplexed data connection, even if the clients use different protocols. It is ideal for those users who need to use the applications continuously.

- **Connection pooling**—Places idle users in a suspended mode and reassigns their physical connections until they become active again. It is ideal for users who need to be logged on all the time, but don't need to really use the application.

- **Orastack**—Allows customers to change the amount of the default reserved stack space used by each Oracle thread. Use this utility with caution.

Deferred Transaction Support

In VLDB systems, there are usually several tasks and applications that can benefit from deferring the execution of low-priority transactions. Third-party solutions like Transaction Processing Monitor (TP Monitor) or Message-Oriented Middleware (MOM) have problems because they are not able to protect the deferred transactions against system failure, and there is additional overhead associated with them. Oracle8 provides a new feature—advanced queuing—which is a database-centric solution that protects deferred transactions.

Parallel Query Enhancements

Oracle8 provides several enhancements to parallel query:

- Parallel DML (insert, update, and delete).
- All queries can be run in parallel, including those based on index scans.
- Partition-aware optimizer.
- Intra-partition parallelism.
- Inter-partition parallelism.

Parallel Server Enhancements

Oracle8 provides several enhancements to Parallel Server:

- Improved distributed lock manager.
- Reverse-key indexes for minimizing data block contention.
- Improved application failover provides high availability by transparently migrating connections from a failed node to a working node.

Oracle8 Features for Large Databases

Oracle8 has a lot of features that can be used to support the tremendous demands placed by high-end applications, and it provides a viable alternative to the mainframes and non-relational databases that are difficult to manage.

Table Partitioning

Very large databases usually contain several huge tables and indexes rather than a large number of small objects. Partitioning, a very important Oracle8 feature, allows developers and DBAs to break these huge tables into smaller, more manageable pieces. By using partitioning, you can create a single large table or index across several tablespaces and, at the same time, control space allocation for each piece of the object. Another advantage of partitioning is the ability to perform maintenance on a part of the table or index without affecting the rest of the table or index. As a result, the overall management and maintenance of data becomes more flexible because it is at the partition level—a much finer-grained level—while queries can still be performed at the table level.

Oracle7 allows a type of table partitioning by creating a set of tables and placing them on different disks or different tablespaces and having different storage clauses. A UNION ALL operation can be performed to obtain a larger table. The problem with this approach is that the application needs to be aware of the underlying structure. The application has to know which underlying table to modify. Any addition or deletion of tables affects the overall view, and it is not possible to work with just part of the view if all the underlying tables are not available. Earlier versions of Oracle prevented the insertions, updates, and deletions through views, which makes this approach not very useful.

Using Oracle8, partitioned tables can be created dynamically. Oracle8 can determine the underlying partition, which needs to be modified when a table is modified. It should be understood that applications do not need to be modified in order to run against the newly partitioned tables. In most cases you can perform partition-level operations in parallel with the same operations on other partitions of the same table, thereby improving the overall performance.

DBAs face a lot of challenges on a daily basis, such as the following:

- Defining and creating large tablespaces
- Balancing I/O to minimize disk contention
- Pinging (in Oracle Parallel Server environments)

Use of Oracle8 partitioning can help in all these areas by providing the capabilities discussed in the following sections.

High Availability

Oracle8 provides high availability by allowing partitions to be independent entities—partition autonomy. This reduces the amount and duration of scheduled downtime by allowing the downtime operations to be performed while the database is open and in use. Part of the table can be taken offline and the rest of the table can be accessed.

Improved Performance

Partitioning improves performance by using a divide-and-conquer paradigm and parallelism. Most operations performed in Oracle7 at the table level can now be performed in Oracle8 at the partition level. It is important to understand that the level of parallelism and the resulting performance gains are strongly affected by the database design.

> **NOTE**
>
> The partitioning strategy used in Oracle7 may not be sufficient to make optimal use of Oracle8 features.

Easy Management of Data

Data management involves backup, recovery, moving data in and out of the database, and data reorganization in order to take care of fragmentation and performance problems. In Oracle7 the unit of data management was the table, while in Oracle8 the unit of data management is a partition. As the table grows in size, the partition does not necessarily grow in size; instead, the number of partitions increases. Parallel data loads can be performed resulting in faster data loads. Partitions also allow a part of the table to be relocated to another drive.

> **NOTE**
>
> You can have up to 64,000 partitions per table.

The following guidelines can be used for determining when partitioning of tables should be done:

- Tables used to perform parallel data manipulation (PDML) should be partitioned.
- Tables that need to be accessed using parallel index should be partitioned.

- Tables containing historical data should be partitioned because you may need to take part of these tables offline.

- If you are migrating from Oracle7 and then identifying views, which are obtained from UNIONs, these are great candidates for partitioned tables.

- Large tables greater than 2GB should be partitioned.

- A table should be partitioned if certain portions of the table are modified and the rest are read only.

- Tables in a parallel server that are modified by multiple instances should be partitioned to minimize pinging, resulting in improved performance.

The following tables cannot be partitioned:

- Tables that are part of a cluster

- Tables containing LOBs, LONG, LONG RAW, or object types

- Index-organized tables

There are several challenges associated with using partitioned tables:

- The required tablespaces should be created before creating the partitioned tables.

- It is very important to determine a backup strategy that will have minimum impact on active applications because, if a partition is taken offline and you have queries that try to access data in that partition, the queries will fail.

- The size of tablespaces should be determined to support the size and growth of the partition that will be using the tablespace.

- The layout of partitioned tables and tablespaces should be done with the space and performance impact on the overall system in mind.

The following example shows the usage and creation of a partitioned table.

I would like to create a Sales table that would store sales data. This table should be partitioned with the presumption that the months of December, January, and February have the most sales. The storage of this partition should be larger compared to the other partitions. The syntax for such a table can be seen in Listing 33.1.

LISTING 33.1. CREATING A Sales TABLE.

```
Create table sales
(sales_id    varchar(12),
day          number(2),
month        number(2),
year         number(4),
store_id     number(4))
partition by range(month)
```

continues

33

WORKING WITH
VERY LARGE
DATABASES

LISTING 33.1. CONTINUED

```
(partition P1 values less than (4)
tablespace sales1 storage
(initial 10M next 10M pctincrease 0),
partition P2 values less than (7)
tablespace sales2 storage
(initial 4M next 4M pctincrease 0),
partition P3 values less than 13
tablespace sales3 storage
(initial 4M next 4M pctincrease 0));
```

In this listing, the tablespaces are sized based on the data expected to be supported by them.

> **NOTE**
>
> Partitioning can be done based on numbers as well as character data.

> **NOTE**
>
> You can have multicolumn partition keys.

Partitioned Indexes

There are many different types of indexing options provided by Oracle8.

> **NOTE**
>
> A bitmap index on a nonpartitioned table cannot be partitioned.

> **NOTE**
>
> A bitmap index on a partitioned table must be a local index.

Table 33.2 summarizes the types of indexes that can be created on partitioned and non-partitioned tables.

TABLE 33.2. INDEX TYPES AND PARTITIONING IN ORACLE8.

Index type	Partitioned table	Nonpartitioned table
Partitioned Index	Yes	Yes
Nonpartitioned Index	Yes	Yes
Bitmap Index	Local	Not Partitioned

The following sections discuss several types of indexes possible in an Oracle8 system.

Local and Global Indexes

In a local index, all keys in the index partition have a corresponding row in the table partition, and the keys do not overlap with keys in other partitions. Partition maintenance is independent because whenever an underlying table partition is modified, only one index needs to be modified. As a result, the different partitions can be worked on independently; for example, users can access one partition through a SQL query while another partition is offline for maintenance.

> **NOTE**
>
> Local indexes are equi-partitioned with the partitions of the underlying table, while global indexes are normally not equi-partitioned with the partitions of the underlying table.

> **NOTE**
>
> Even if for some reason the global index is equi-partitioned with the partitions of the underlying table, the optimizer is not aware of it and therefore partitions are not eliminated from the query plan.

> **NOTE**
>
> Oracle8 does not support global nonprefixed indexes.

Local Prefixed

An index is prefixed if the leftmost columns of the index exactly match the same columns of the partition key—in the same order with the same number of columns. This index can be unique or nonunique. Unique indexes guarantee that to get to the data you will have to access only one index partition, while nonunique indexes guarantee that to get to the data you will have to access only one index partition if the full partition key is provided as part of the WHERE clause.

Local Nonprefixed

An index is nonprefixed if it is not partitioned on a left prefix of the index columns.

Global Prefixed

A global index is one in which the index range may include more than one partition. Global indexes are harder to manage than local indexes, and they do not provide partition independence. As a result, it is not possible to take part of the global index offline and continue work on the rest of the index.

An index can be range partitioned with the following restrictions:

- Cannot be a cluster index.
- Cannot be an index for a cluster table.
- A bitmap index on a partitioned table must be a local index.

NOTE

Each partitioned index is built as a separate B-tree structure.

There are several things to consider when using partitioned indexes:

- Whether an index will be local or global.

  The only usage of a global index I have seen is to get uniqueness in nonpartition key columns. You may be able to find other uses of the global index.

- Whether an index will be prefixed or nonprefixed.
- If the overhead of scanning multiple partitions is acceptable from a performance standpoint.
- An understanding of when partition independence is needed.

> **NOTE**
>
> It is more expensive to scan a nonprefixed index than a prefixed index.

> **NOTE**
>
> For Online Transaction Processing (OLTP) systems, global indexes may provide improved performance by minimizing the number of index probes.
>
> Historical tables should have local indexes.
>
> Local, nonprefixed indexes may improve performance through parallel DML for Decision Support Systems (DSSs).

A partitioned index may be marked as index unusable (IU) in the following circumstances. When this happens, the index should be rebuilt.

- Direct-path SQL load will mark affected local or global indexes as IU if the load is not successful.

- If the local index maintenance is bypassed while an `IMPORT PARTITION` of conventional path SQL load is being performed.

- Statements such as `alter table move partition`, which change the ROWIDs of local or global indexes.

- Global indexes are marked as IU if operations like `alter table truncate partition`, which remove rows, are performed.

- Operations like `alter table split partition`, which modify the local index definition but do not cause index rebuild.

Index-Only Tables

The following operations are allowed on index-only tables:

- `Select`, `Insert`, `Update`, and `Delete`.
- `Drop/Truncate table`.
- `Export/Import/SQL*Loader`.
- `Analyze`.
- `Explain Plan`.
- Constraints are fully supported.

Index-only tables have the following restrictions:

- Primary key is required.
- Cannot create any other type of index on index-only tables.
- Cannot be part of a cluster.
- Does not support LOBs datatype.
- Does not support replication.
- Cannot be partitioned.
- No CTAS (Create Table As Select) operations.

Parallel DML (PDML)

Very large databases are benefited tremendously by the ability of Oracle8 to allow data manipulation operations in parallel. Oracle8 allows you to perform parallel inserts, updates, and deletes on partitioned tables. In VLDB systems it can be very difficult to insert, update, and delete a large number of rows because of the time constraints involved in running application programs in such systems.

Parallel Insert

Parallel insert allows the insertion of rows into partitioned and nonpartitioned tables with multiple write streams.

Parallel insert can be of two types: direct path and parallel direct path.

Insert with Direct Path

This method works similar to the direct path option of SQL*Loader. Rows are inserted above the high-water mark of the table and, on successful insertion, the high-water mark is updated to the new values.

Insert with Parallel Direct Path

This method works similarly to the parallel direct path option of SQL*Loader. Rows are inserted into the temporary extents of the table's tablespace and are then merged with the existing extents.

Parallel insert implies two types of parallelization:

- Parallel write streams into a single nonpartitioned table.
- Multiple inserts simultaneously into separate partitions.

The type of insert used depends on the type of table you are inserting into and the hints provided in the insert statement.

Parallel Update and Delete

Prior to Oracle8, very large databases were constantly faced with the problem of updating and deleting large amounts of data in a short period of time, for example:

- Data archiving
- Data loads
- Routine deletions of data from DSS systems
- Batch update/delete jobs in OLTP systems
- Backup/recovery

Parallel updates and deletes make use of parallel processes or slaves that perform the actual work. These operations are similar to parallel query, and the number of slaves depends on several factors such as the optimizer, system resources, and hints used.

> **NOTE**
>
> There is no parallelization with nonpartitioned tables.

> **NOTE**
>
> There is no parallelization within a single partition of a partitioned table.

It should be clear from this discussion that partitions are very important in the usage of parallel DML, and this fact should be considered during database design. Factors to consider include the following:

- The number of partitioned tables.
- The number of partitions within the partitioned tables.
- Partition sizes.
- Type of indexes.
- Enough rollback segments—(n+1) rollback segments for an n-way parallel DML.

Bitmap Indexes

Oracle8 provides five types of indexing schemes:

- B*-tree indexes
- B*-tree cluster indexes

- Hash cluster indexes
- Reverse key indexes
- Bitmap indexes

Indexes provide pointers to the rows in a table that contain a particular key value. Regular indexes store a list of ROWIDs for each key corresponding to the rows with that key value. Bitmap indexes use a bitmap for each key value. Each bit in the bitmap corresponds to a possible ROWID, and a set bit means that the corresponding ROWID contains the key value for which you are looking. Internally, even though a bitmap uses a different representation, it provides the same functionality as a regular index because a mapping function converts the bit position to an actual ROWID.

Use of bitmap indexes provides the following advantages in a Data Warehousing application:

- A significant reduction in space usage compared to regular indexes (for low cardinality columns only)
- Efficient Parallel DMLs
- Improved response time for ad hoc queries

The following new initialization parameters can be used with bitmap indexes:

- CREATE_BITMAP_AREA_SIZE   Default 8MB. This parameter determines the amount of memory allocated for creating bitmap indexes. This parameter cannot be dynamically altered at the session level. The higher the cardinality, the more memory needed for improving performance.
- BITMAP_MERGE_AREA_SIZE   Default is 1MB. This parameter determines the amount of memory used to merge bitmaps retrieved from index range scans. This parameter cannot be dynamically altered at the session level. Large values for this parameter can improve performance because bitmap indexes must be sorted before being merged together.

Bitmap indexes have the following restrictions:

- Rule-based optimizer does not consider them.
- They cannot be used for checking referential integrity.
- SORTED_INDEX flag does not apply for bitmap indexes with direct load.
- Subqueries that have a predicate of the form col=(subquery) cannot be used as keys for a bitmap index.
- The ALTER TABLE command, which adds a column to a bitmap index or modifies a bitmap-indexed column, causes the index to be invalidated.

Bitmap indexes can significantly improve the performance of queries with the following characteristics:

- Tables being queried contain many rows.
- Low cardinality columns.
- The individual predicates on the bitmapped columns (low-cardinality) should select a large number of rows.
- The WHERE clause of the select statement contains multiple predicates on low-cardinality columns.

Index Fast Full Scans

Oracle8 introduces an alternative to full table scans called the index fast full scan (FFS). An FFS is performed on a table when the index contains all the columns requested in the query. The index scan is fast because the entire index is read using multiblock reads, which is much faster than full table scans. An index fast full scan is specified by means of the INDEX_FFS hint in the query, and it should be used when the size or number of columns in the index is significantly less than the size or number of columns in the table being accessed. For example

```
SELECT /*+ INDEX_FFS(department, dept_idx) */  dept_id, dept_loc_city,
dept_loc_state FROM department;
```

Reverse Key Indexes

When a very large database system uses OLTP applications, there is a very common contention problem associated with tables that use sequences or other such structures to generate primary keys. The problem is that everyone is inserting an index at the end of the index, resulting in contention for the last free leaf block. Oracle8 provides a feature called *reverse order indexes* that attempts to solve this problem by storing the index in reverse key order. For example, a column with a key value of MEGH would be stored as HGEM. As a result of this reverse key storage, the contention for the last free leaf block should be resolved, resulting in a more random distribution of values.

It should be noted that such reverse key indexes are useful for equality lookups only because the reversal of value results in a loss of relationship needed during range scans. For example, suppose you have an index on the last_name and the values are Smith, Robinson, King, Trent, and Simpson. If a regular B*-Tree is created on this column and you execute a query to find all the people whose last names start with S, you can easily find Smith and Simpson. However, in a reverse key index, the values would be stored as htims, nosnibor, gnik, tnert, and nospmis. Therefore, the range scan is not efficient.

Tuning for Very Large Databases

Tuning a VLDB system involves tuning the database environment and then tuning the queries and transactions that are most demanding on the system resources.

The following tips can be used to improve the performance in a VLDB:

- Make the System Global Area (SGA) as large as possible. Recommended size is 2 percent of the database size. Check your operating system manuals for the largest supported size.

- Set the DB_BLOCK_SIZE to be the highest value supported by Oracle on your platform.

- Use the partitioning techniques described earlier in the chapter and create partitioned tables and indexes to distribute the I/O load among the components of the partitioned table.

- Use local indexes where possible because they are efficient and easy to manage.

- VLDB systems would have very large sorts and transactions, and you can improve the performance by using the enhanced parallel query options discussed earlier in the chapter.

- Make use of fully indexed tables.

- Create and use bitmap indexes.

- Use indexes with care, because in VLDB systems, indexes, if not used properly, can degrade performance. Check the hit ratio to see if the blocks in the SGA are being reused. If the hit ratio is less than 90 percent, it indicates that the indexes are not used properly. VLDB has large tables and the associated indexes are also very large. As a result, the SGA may not be able to hold the index blocks.

- Size the SGA properly and minimize the amount of physical disk access that the queries may be performing.

- Properly plan the physical layout of the files on disk with the intention of minimizing I/O contention. Consider using RAID systems and disk mirroring.

> **TIP**
>
> The SGA keeps track of the blocks accessed. Blocks accessed by means of an index access or via a table access with ROWID are held the longest, while blocks accessed via a table scan are removed earlier.

- Data proximity is very important in dealing with VLDB systems. Maximize data proximity by inserting records into a table sequentially and order them by columns frequently used in range scans. This will increase the reusability of data blocks in the SGA because now the index and table blocks that would be loaded are reduced.

> **TIP**
>
> Range scan of indexes followed by table access via ROWID *does not* perform well in VLDB systems.

- Consider using table scans when reading a large quantity of rows. This is more important in VLDB than in smaller systems. This is due to the manner in which the SGA deals with data blocks. Index scans would cause the blocks read in to the SGA to stay in the SGA for a long time and may remove other blocks from the SGA, while table scanned blocks would be flushed out quickly.

Transaction Management in VLDB Systems

Most of the transactions in a VLDB system are batch data loads. This is true in about 99 percent of such systems because it is much faster to populate the large database by using techniques such as Direct Path SQL*Loader instead of an operator keying in the information. These batch loads may account for about 80–85 percent of the transactions in such systems, so you should try and focus all your energies on optimizing their performance.

> **TIP**
>
> Perform your batch jobs when online transactions are not occurring in the system—this will minimize rollback segment-related problems in VLDB systems.

Rollback Segment Considerations

As mentioned earlier, VLDBs are characterized by batch jobs. It is very beneficial to create a few large rollback segments instead of a lot of small rollback segments.

> **TIP**
>
> Use the following to force a transaction to use a particular rollback segment.
>
> ```
> Set transaction use rollback segment RB1;
> ```

TIP

Use good naming conventions in order to easily identify rollback segments you will use for your batch operations.

Archiving Considerations

Archiving allows you to recover your database in case of a media failure and should be used as a general good practice. However, when performing a batch data load, you have to realize that the operations involved are a large amount of INSERTs, which you can easily regenerate by re-executing the data load. It will definitely help to disable archiving for the duration of the database load.

CAUTION

If there are other transactions going on concurrently with your batch job and a media failure occurs during the load, you may not be able to recover the other transactions.

TIP

Use the following to put the database in ARCHIVELOG mode:

```
On UNIX,
C: > svrmgrl
SVRMGR> connect internal
SVRMGR> shutdown
SVRMGR> startup mount
SVRMGR> alter database archivelog
SVRMGR> alter database open;
```

TIP

Use the following to put the database in NOARCHIVELOG mode:

```
On UNIX,
C: > svrmgrl
SVRMGR> connect internal
SVRMGR> shutdown
SVRMGR> startup mount
SVRMGR> alter database noarchivelog
SVRMGR> alter database open;
```

- Disable the logging of large tables by using `nologging`. When `nologging` is set for a table, none of its transactions will be logged, which results in improved performance. This option gives you the flexibility of placing your database in the archive mode while leaving the large tables in the `nologging` mode.

> **TIP**
>
> If a table uses the `BLOB` and the `CLOB` datatypes, you can set the `LOB` portions of the table to be in `nologging`.

- Keep your indexes up to date by rebuilding them after major changes such as bulk inserts, updates, and deletes. Inefficient indexes will be directly reflected in the overall system performance.

Use the following tips to enhance the performance of data loads:

- Disable table constraints.
- Disable triggers on the table. (Tables that are bulk loaded should not have triggers to begin with.)
- Drop indexes prior to data load, and then re-create the indexes.
- Use Direct-Path SQL*Load for data load. This will improve performance because data will be loaded above the high-water mark.

   Full table scans would read the blocks up to the high-water mark, and this can result in performance degradation if you have deleted a lot of rows.

> **TIP**
>
> There are two ways you can change the high-water mark: drop and re-create the table, or truncate the table.

- Use the `APPEND` hint for the creation of aggregate tables. Aggregate tables are usually created by using information from another table. The `APPEND` hint allows insertion after the high-water mark and can be a significant performance improvement.
- Wherever possible use the `TRUNCATE` command to delete large amounts of data. Combining this with the partitioning feature, the parallel becomes possible.
- The optimizer is partition aware, but if you know the partition that needs to be considered, you can query the partition by specifying it in the `FROM` clause. For example:

33

WORKING WITH
VERY LARGE
DATABASES

```
Select *
From sales (part4)
Where month between 10 and 12;
```

> **CAUTION**
>
> The suggestion in the previous example should be used carefully, because if for some reason you change the information stored in a partition or rearrange the partitions such that part4 is no longer the partition, the previous query will not work.

Consider rearranging the partition structure of a partitioned table after periodic use.

> **TIP**
>
> Use the Alter table command to add, drop, exchange, move, modify, rename, split, and truncate partitions.

Operation of a Large Database

The definition of a very large database keeps changing because operating systems and hardware enhancements continue at a rapid pace, and the database size is not a factor anymore for defining the database as being "large." It is more realistic to look at the recovery time of the database and define a database to be "large" if it cannot be recovered in 24 hours. VLDB systems need special considerations as compared to smaller systems, and some of the suggestions in dealing with them might even be opposite of what a DBA would have done for smaller databases.

A VLDB typically consists of:

- A small number of large tables that account for about 90 percent of the data. These tables change dramatically in size with the passage of time.

- A lot of small code tables that are generally static and do not change much in size as time goes by. You should be able to size these tables properly. Try to use storage parameters so a code table can fit in one extent. These tables should generally be free from fragmentation.

- A lot of aggregate tables that are derived from the large tables. These may or may not change in time, depending on your application. The purpose of these tables is to improve performance.

- Frequently needed data.
- Queries that are complex but perform the same data massaging and aggregation.
- Several temporary tables. These tables are used during data loads.

TIP

Codes tables with more or less the same size should be placed in a tablespace whose default storage parameters are appropriate for all of them. This will improve the reusability of extents.

TIP

Codes tables are static in nature and therefore it would be beneficial to use a low pctfree setting.

TIP

If large transaction tables are truncated and then reloaded with information, set pctfree to a low value; otherwise set pctfree to a high value.

TIP

If a large transaction table grows at a constant rate, set pctincrease to 0. Otherwise, set it to an appropriate non-zero value.

Rollback Segments Design

A VLDB usually has three different types of transactions. Table 33.3 shows the rollback segments that should be used for these types of transactions.

TABLE 33.3. ROLLBACK SEGMENTS TO USE BASED ON TRANSACTION TYPES.

Transaction Type	Rollback Segment
Batch loads	Large, dedicated rollback segments
Batch aggregates	Medium-sized rollback segments
Small and short user transactions	A lot of small rollback segments

Backup and Recovery Using Recovery Manager (RMAN)

A database backup represents your data, and it can be used to reconstruct lost information. Backup includes important database components such as control file, datafiles, and archive logs. In case of a media failure, the database backup can be a life saver. Oracle8 enhances the support of backup and recovery operations by kernel integration of the backup and recovery operations, and also through the introduction of a tool—Recovery Manager.

Recovery Manager provides an interactive interface to backup and recovery operations by means of a character or GUI front-end with its own command language. Recovery Manager can be used for creating, managing, and restoring the backups of a database, while maintaining superior performance and high availability of the database.

Recovery Manager has several features:

- Allowing backup of the entire database or a subset of the database in one operation
- Avoiding operator errors and also checking for database corruption
- Automatic parallelization of backup and recovery
- Minimizing redo generation
- Allowing hot and cold backups
- Supporting tape backups in conjunction with vendor-supplied tape management software like Legato or Epoch

> **NOTE**
>
> In Oracle8.0.4, Legato is provided as the default media manager.

When using the Recovery Manager in Oracle8, the recovery process for the entire database or part of it is very straightforward, because the RMAN can restore the appropriate backups and archive logs as needed.

Information about the backups and the archived logs is placed in a recovery catalog. The recovery catalog is a set of database objects that stores information related to the entire backup and recovery activities performed against the database(s).

The following things should be considered when using a recovery catalog:

- Reports can be printed using the recovery catalog to get information on all the backup and recovery activities.

- One recovery catalog can be used to keep information on multiple Oracle8 databases.

- In order to avoid a single point of failure, the recovery catalog of one database should be placed in another database, while the recovery catalog of a second should be placed in the first.

- Larger sites with multiple databases may use one recovery catalog for all of them, thereby simplifying the administration of the catalog.

> **NOTE**
>
> For smaller databases, there is a RMAN mode that allows the recovery catalog to be optional and gets all the needed information from the control file. When in this mode the following operations are not possible:
>
> - Point-in-time recovery
> - Automatic recovery when the control file is not current

> **NOTE**
>
> The Enterprise backup utility is not supported in Oracle8.

> **NOTE**
>
> See Oracle Bulletin 108898.604, titled "Automating Cold Backups on Windows NT," for examples of a script-based approach.

Oracle8 provides three ways of taking database backups:

- *Export.* This method does not allow a way to perform fast backup and also requires the database to be shut down; it is, therefore, not very useful for backing up VLDB.

- *O/S level backup.* This method requires a lot of manual procedures and should be used carefully because errors during database backup and/or restore can result in a corrupt database.

- *Recovery Manager.* This method uses the information of the database to automatically locate, backup, restore, and recover datafiles, control files, and archived logs. It allows very fast backups by backing up only the changed blocks.

Recovery Manager allows commands to perform the following:

- Backup, restore, copy, and recover
- Maintenance of the recovery catalog
- Maintenance of the stored scripts
- Reporting

Using Recovery Manager—Examples

Before using RMAN with the recovery catalog and a particular target database, you need to perform the following tasks:

- Create a user called `rman`.
- Connect as `rman` and run a script called `catrman.sql`, located in the `$ORACLE_HOME/rdbms/admin` directory.
- Register the target database with the recovery catalog.

> **NOTE**
>
> The target database should at least be mounted. In addition, a unique number that is generated internally, called `db identifier`, is used to identify the database.

Before issuing a backup, restore, copy, or recovery command, a channel must be allocated that sets up a connection from RMAN to a target database instance by starting a server process on a target database. The type of I/O device that will be used is also specified during channel allocation. It is important to note that each allocate channel command uses a separate connection to the target database, and multiple backup sets or file copies can be read or written in parallel.

Examples of Backup and Restore Using RMAN

The following is an example of database backup (except offline tablespaces):

```
run{
allocate channel dev1 type 'sbt_tape';
backup skip offline (database format '%d_%u');
}
```

The following is an example of backing up a tablespace:

```
run{
allocate channel dev1 type disk;
backup
(tablespace system, tablespace1, tablespace2
format '/oracle/backups/%d_%u');
}
```

The following is an example of backing up a datafile:

```
run{
allocate channel dev1 type disk;
backup
(datafile '$ORACLE_HOME/dbs/user1.dbf'
format '%d_%u');
}
```

The following is an example of restoring a datafile:

```
run{
allocate channel dev1 type 'sbt_tape';
sql "alter tablespace tablespace1 offline immediate";
restore tablespace tablespace1;
recover tablespace tablespace1;
sql "alter tablespace tablespace1 online";
release channel dev1;
}
```

If a datafile cannot be accessed due to a disk failure, it must be restored to a new location or switched to an existing datafile copy. The following is an example that opens two channels—one to disk and the other to tape. It also moves the datafile to a new location and performs a restore of the datafile.

```
run{
allocate channel dev1 type disk;
allocate channel dev2 type 'sbt_tape';
sql "alter tablespace tablespace1 offline immediate";
set newname for datafile '/uo1/oracle/datafiles/data1.dbf' to
'/uo2/oracle/datafiles/data1.dbf';
restore (tablespace tablespace1);
switch datafile all;
recover tablespace tablespace1;
sql "alter tablespace tablespace1 online";
release channel dev1;
release channel dev2;
}
```

In a VLDB, the backup and recover strategy is extremely important due to the requirements for high availability. It is important to consider the frequency and the type of backups you will be performing.

Table 33.4 describes the types of failure that can occur.

TABLE 33.4. FAILURE TYPES.

Failure Type	Description
Statement failure	This is a logical failure in the processing of the statement, such as an incorrect syntax usage. Oracle usually returns an error message indicating the cause of such failure.
Process failure	This is usually a failure in a user process, such as an abnormal disconnection or termination of the process. Usually an error is returned and Oracle and other processes continue to work.
User or application error	Based on the type of error, you may need to perform point-in-time recovery. For example, a user accidentally deletes some data that is not supposed to be deleted.
Instance failure	This error represents a situation that prevents the instance (system global area and the background processes) from continuing to work. It can be due to a hardware or software problem.
Media failure	This represents a problem with the disk containing the data. A common situation is a disk head crash that prevents physical reading or writing of the files on disk.

types Within types

Oracle8 provides the ability to create types that can be used to simplify data representation. For example, name and address can be created as types that can be used in several table definitions.

```
Create type name_type(
first_name     varchar(25),
middle_name     char(1),
last_name     varchar(25));

Create type address_type(
street          varchar(30),
city          varchar(25),
state          varchar(2),
zip_code     number(5));

create table employee(
name          name_type,
hire_date      date,
address        address_type,
number procedure     give_tenure,
number function      give_salary number);
```

```
create table managers(
name           name_type,
department     varchar(10),
number function    give_number_of _team_members number);
```

As seen from this example, you can standardize and reuse type definitions, which results in simplifying data management.

Object Views

Object views allow you to create virtual object tables from data of either built-in or user-defined types stored in relational or object tables in the VLDB. Object views can be used as a powerful security mechanism because they allow you to provide a version of an underlying table that does not contain certain data—sensitive data—and also it may restrict the type of operations that can be performed against it.

Using object views you can

- Perform object-oriented operations without modifying the relational structure of the database
- Use legacy data with object-oriented applications
- Transparently and gradually migrate from relational tables to object-oriented objects

Object views provide the following advantages:

- Relational data makes up a row of an object view and can traverse the network as a unit, resulting in improved performance.
- Relational data can be fetched into the client-side object cache and mapped to C or C++ structures. As a result of this, 3GL applications can manipulate the data easily.
- Provide flexibility by allowing different in-memory representations of the same relational data.
- Allow for the co-existence of relational and object data in the same database.

Table 33.5 shows the various datatypes supported by Oracle8.

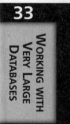

33

WORKING WITH
VERY LARGE
DATABASES

TABLE 33.5. ORACLE8 DATATYPES.

Data format	Supports
Datatype	Scalar, Video, Spatial, Image, User-Defined
Data model	Relational, Multidimensional, Object-oriented
Application	DSS, OLTP

VARRAY

This is a new datatype supported in Oracle8. Like a regular array, it is an ordered list of elements. But, unlike an array, it is of variable size. You need to specify the maximum size when creating a VARRAY.

```
create type price as varray(1000) of number;
create type products (product_name varchar(20), product_value price);
```

Summary

Operating systems and hardware and software enhancements are making it feasible for companies to use very large databases. Oracle8 has taken on the challenging task of realistically supporting such VLDB systems by providing several key features discussed in this chapter.

When you are dealing with a VLDB, you have to consider a lot of things that normally would not be considered in smaller databases, such as physical and logical design aspects that are more critical for VLDBs. Tuning of VLDBs takes on a new meaning, due especially to a more focused approach needed for system global area (SGA) usage.

Several administrative tasks, such as backup and recovery, become more challenging due to the high demands placed by VLDBs. This chapter discusses Oracle8 as a viable solution for such tasks.

INDEX